T0189244

Lecture Notes in Computer Science

Lecture Notes in Artificial Intelligence 14391

The series Lecture Notes in Artificial Intelligence (LNAI) was established in 1988 as a topical subseries of LNCS devoted to artificial intelligence.

The series publishes state-of-the-art research results at a high level. As with the LNCS mother series, the mission of the series is to serve the international R & D community by providing an invaluable service, mainly focused on the publication of conference and workshop proceedings and postproceedings.

Hiram Calvo · Lourdes Martínez-Villaseñor ·
Hiram Ponce
Editors

Advances in Computational Intelligence

22nd Mexican International Conference on Artificial Intelligence, MICAI 2023
Yucatán, Mexico, November 13–18, 2023
Proceedings, Part I

Editors
Hiram Calvo
Center for Computing Research
Instituto Politécnico Nacional
Ciudad de México, Distrito Federal, Mexico

Lourdes Martínez-Villaseñor
Facultad de Ingeniería
Universidad Panamericana
Ciudad de México, Mexico

Hiram Ponce
Facultad de Ingeniería
Universidad Panamericana
Ciudad de México, Mexico

ISSN 0302-9743 ISSN 1611-3349 (electronic)
Lecture Notes in Artificial Intelligence
ISBN 978-3-031-47764-5 ISBN 978-3-031-47765-2 (eBook)
https://doi.org/10.1007/978-3-031-47765-2

LNCS Sublibrary: SL7 – Artificial Intelligence

This Springer imprint is published by the registered company Springer Nature Switzerland AG
The registered company address is: Gewerbestrasse 11, 6330 Cham, Switzerland

Preface

The Mexican International Conference on Artificial Intelligence (MICAI) is a yearly international conference series that has been organized by the Mexican Society for Artificial Intelligence (SMIA) since 2000. MICAI is a major international artificial intelligence (AI) forum and the main event in the academic life of the country's growing AI community.

This year, MICAI 2023 was graciously hosted by the Instituto de Investigaciones en Matemáticas Aplicadas y en Sistemas (IIMAS) and the Universidad Autónoma del Estado de Yucatán (UAEY). The conference presented a cornucopia of scientific endeavors. From incisive keynote lectures and detailed paper presentations to hands-on tutorials, thought-provoking panels, and niche workshops, the spectrum of activities aimed to cater to a wide audience. Moreover, we continued the legacy of announcing the José Negrete Award, the SMIA Best Thesis in Artificial Intelligence Contest's results. This year, the historic and culturally rich city of Mérida, Yucatán was our chosen rendezvous.

MICAI conferences publish high-quality papers in all areas of AI and its applications. The proceedings of the previous MICAI events have been published by Springer in its Lecture Notes in Artificial Intelligence (LNAI) series (volumes: 1793, 2313, 2972, 3789, 4293, 4827, 5317, 5845, 6437, 6438, 7094, 7095, 7629, 7630, 8265, 8266, 8856, 8857, 9413, 9414, 10061, 10062, 10632, 10633, 11288, 11289, 11835, 12468, 12469, 13067, 13068, 13612, and 13613). Since its foundation in 2000, the conference has grown in popularity and improved in quality.

The proceedings of MICAI 2023 are published in two volumes. The first volume, *Advances in Computational Intelligence*, contains 24 papers structured into three sections:

- Machine Learning
- Computer Vision and Image Processing
- Intelligent Systems

The second volume, *Advances in Soft Computing*, contains 25 papers structured into three sections:

- Natural Language Processing
- Bioinformatics and Medical Applications
- Robotics and Applications

The two-volume set will be of interest for researchers in all fields of artificial intelligence, students specializing in related topics, and the general public interested in recent developments in AI.

The conference received for evaluation 115 submissions from 17 countries: Bolivia, Brazil, Colombia, Cuba, Denmark, Ecuador, Spain, USA, France, The Netherlands, Italy, Kazakhstan, Mexico, Peru, UK, Russia, and Sweden. Gender representation also echoed with 90 male authors and 21 female authors adding their voice. From these submissions, 49 papers were selected for publication in these two volumes after 3 reviews per submission in a double-blind peer-reviewing process carried out by the international Program Committee. The acceptance rate was 43%.

The international Program Committee consisted of 80 experts from 10 countries: Australia, Brazil, France, Germany, Japan, Kazakhstan, Mexico, Russia, Spain, and UK.

Three workshops were held jointly with the conference:

- WILE 2023: 16th Workshop on Intelligent Learning Environments
- HIS 2023: 16th Workshop of Hybrid Intelligent Systems
- CIAPP 2023: 5th Workshop on New Trends in Computational Intelligence and Applications

We want to thank all the people involved in the organization of this conference: the authors of the papers published in these two volumes –it is their research work that gives value to the proceedings– and the organizers for their work. We thank the reviewers for their great effort spent on reviewing the submissions and the Program and Organizing Committee members.

A special acknowledgment goes to the local committee led by Antonio Neme, whose meticulous coordination has been instrumental in realizing MICAI 2023 in Mérida, Yucatán, Mexico. Our thanks extend to IIMAS's director, Ramsés Mena, and its academic secretary, Katya Rodríguez. We are also indebted to Anabel Martín from the Faculty of Mathematics at the UADY for her invaluable assistance in securing the university facilities.

The entire submission, reviewing, and selection process, as well as preparation of the proceedings, was supported by Microsoft's Conference Management Toolkit (https://cmt3.research.microsoft.com/). Last but not least, we are grateful to Springer for their patience and help in the preparation of these volumes.

In conclusion, MICAI 2023 is more than just a conference. It is a confluence of minds, a testament to the indefatigable spirit of the AI community, and a beacon for the future of Artificial Intelligence. As you navigate through these proceedings, may you find inspiration, knowledge, and connections that propel you forward in your journey.

The MICAI series website is www.MICAI.org. The website of the Mexican Society for Artificial Intelligence, SMIA, is www.SMIA.mx. Contact options and additional information can be found on these websites.

November 2023

Hiram Calvo
Lourdes Martínez-Villaseñor
Hiram Ponce

Organization

Conference Committee

General Chair

Hiram Calvo	Instituto Politécnico Nacional, Mexico

Program Chairs

Hiram Calvo	Instituto Politécnico Nacional, Mexico
Lourdes Martínez-Villaseñor	Universidad Panamericana, Mexico
Hiram Ponce	Universidad Panamericana, Mexico

Workshop Chair

Hiram Ponce	Universidad Panamericana, Mexico

Tutorials Chair

Roberto Antonio Vázquez Espinoza de los Monteros	Universidad La Salle, Mexico

Doctoral Consortium Chairs

Miguel González Mendoza	Tecnológico de Monterrey, Mexico
Juan Martínez Miranda	Centro de Investigación Científica y de Educación Superior de Ensenada, Mexico

Keynote Talks Chairs

Gilberto Ochoa Ruiz	Tecnológico de Monterrey, Mexico
Iris Méndez	Universidad Autónoma de Ciudad Juárez, Mexico

Publication Chair

Hiram Ponce	Universidad Panamericana, Mexico

Financial Chairs

Hiram Calvo — Instituto Politécnico Nacional, Mexico
Lourdes Martínez-Villaseñor — Universidad Panamericana, Mexico

Grant Chair

Leobardo Morales — IBM, Mexico

Local Organizing Committee

Abigail Uribe Martínez — Universidad Autónoma del Estado de Yucatán, Mexico
Abraham Mandariaga Mazón — Universidad Autónoma del Estado de Yucatán, Mexico
Ali Bassam — Universidad Autónoma del Estado de Yucatán, Mexico
Anabel Martin — Universidad Autónoma del Estado de Yucatán, Mexico
Antonio Aguileta — Universidad Autónoma del Estado de Yucatán, Mexico
Antonio Neme — Universidad Autónoma del Estado de Yucatán, Mexico
Blanca Vázquez — Universidad Autónoma del Estado de Yucatán, Mexico
Joel Antonio Trejo Sánchez — Universidad Autónoma del Estado de Yucatán, Mexico
Jorge Perez-Gonzalez — Universidad Autónoma del Estado de Yucatán, Mexico
Julián Bravo Castillero — Universidad Autónoma del Estado de Yucatán, Mexico
Karina Martínez — Universidad Autónoma del Estado de Yucatán, Mexico
Mauricio Orozco del Castillo — Universidad Autónoma del Estado de Yucatán, Mexico
Nidiyare Hevia Montiel — Universidad Autónoma del Estado de Yucatán, Mexico
Nora Cuevas Cuevas — Universidad Autónoma del Estado de Yucatán, Mexico
Nora Pérez Quezadas — Universidad Autónoma del Estado de Yucatán, Mexico

Program Committee

Ari Barrera Animas	Universidad Panamericana, Mexico
Asdrúbal López Chau	Universidad Autónoma del Estado de México, Mexico
Belém Priego Sánchez	Universidad Autónoma Metropolitana Unidad Azcapotzalco, Mexico
Bella Martinez Seis	Instituto Politécnico Nacional, Mexico
Betania Hernandez-Ocaña	Universidad Juárez Autónoma de Tabasco, Mexico
Claudia Gómez	Instituto Tecnológico de Ciudad Madero, Mexico
Daniela Alejandra Ochoa	CentroGEO-CONACyT, Mexico
Dante Mújica-Vargas	CENIDET, Mexico
Diego Uribe	Tecnológico Nacional de México - ITL, Mexico
Eddy Sánchez-DelaCruz	Tecnológico Nacional de México - Campus Misantla, Mexico
Eduardo Valdez	Instituto Politécnico Nacional, Mexico
Efrén Mezura-Montes	Universidad Veracruzana, Mexico
Eloísa García-Canseco	Universidad Autónoma de Baja California, Mexico
Elva Lilia Reynoso Jardon	Universidad Autónoma de Ciudad Juárez, Mexico
Eric Tellez	CICESE-INFOTEC-CONACyT, Mexico
Ernesto Moya-Albor	Universidad Panamericana, Mexico
Félix Castro Espinoza	Universidad Autónoma del Estado de Hidalgo, Mexico
Fernando Gudino	UNAM, Mexico
Garibaldi Pineda Garcia	Applied AGI, UK
Genoveva Vargas-Solar	University Grenoble Alpes, CNRS, France
Gilberto Ochoa-Ruiz	Tecnológico de Monterrey, Mexico
Giner Alor-Hernandez	Tecnológico Nacional de México - ITO, Mexico
Guillermo Santamaría-Bonfil	BBVA México, Mexico
Gustavo Arroyo	Instituto Nacional de Electricidad y Energías Limpias, Mexico
Helena Gómez Adorno	IIMAS-UNAM, Mexico
Hiram Ponce	Universidad Panamericana, Mexico
Hiram Calvo	Instituto Politécnico Nacional, Mexico
Hugo Jair Escalante	INAOE, Mexico
Humberto Sossa	Instituto Politécnico Nacional, Mexico
Iris Iddaly Méndez-Gurrola	Universidad Autónoma de Ciudad Juárez, Mexico
Iskander Akhmetov	Institute of Information and Computational Technologies, Kazakhstan
Ismael Osuna-Galán	Universidad de Quintana Roo, Mexico
Israel Tabarez	Universidad Autónoma del Estado de México, Mexico

Jaime Cerda	Universidad Michoacana de San Nicolás de Hidalgo, Mexico
Jerusa Marchi	Federal University of Santa Catarina, Brazil
Joanna Alvarado Uribe	Tecnológico de Monterrey, Mexico
Jorge Perez Gonzalez	UNAM, Mexico
José Alanis	Universidad Tecnológica de Puebla, Mexico
José Martínez-Carranza	INAOE, Mexico
Jose Alberto Hernandez-Aguilar	Universidad Autónoma del Estado de Morelos, Mexico
José Carlos Ortiz-Bayliss	Tecnológico de Monterrey, Mexico
Juan Villegas-Cortez	UAM - Azcapotzalco, Mexico
Juan Carlos Olivares Rojas	Tecnológico Nacional de México - ITM, Mexico
Karina Perez-Daniel	Universidad Panamericana, Mexico
Karina Figueroa Mora	Universidad Michoacana de San Nicolás de Hidalgo, Mexico
Leticia Flores Pulido	Universidad Autónoma de Tlaxcala, Mexico
Lourdes Martinez-Villaseñor	Universidad Panamericana, Mexico
Luis Torres-Treviño	Universidad Autónoma de Nuevo León, Mexico
Luis Luevano	Institut National de Recherche en Informatique et en Automatique, France
Mansoor Ali Teevno	Tecnológico de Monterrey, Mexico
Masaki Murata	Tottori University, Japan
Miguel Gonzalez-Mendoza	Tecnológico de Monterrey, Mexico
Miguel Mora-Gonzalez	Universidad de Guadalajara, Mexico
Mukesh Prasad	University of Technology Sydney, Australia
Omar López-Ortega	Universidad Autónoma del Estado de Hidalgo, Mexico
Rafael Guzman-Cabrera	Universidad de Guanajuato, Mexico
Rafael Batres	Tecnológico de Monterrey, Mexico
Ramon Brena	Instituto Tecnológico de Sonora, Mexico
Ramón Zatarain Cabada	Tec Culiacán, Mexico
Ramón Iván Barraza-Castillo	Universidad Autónoma de Ciudad Juárez, Mexico
Roberto Antonio Vasquez	Universidad La Salle, Mexico
Rocio Ochoa-Montiel	Universidad Autónoma de Tlaxcala, Mexico
Ruben Carino-Escobar	Instituto Nacional de Rehabilitación - Luis Guillermo Ibarra Ibarra, Mexico
Sabino Miranda	INFOTEC-CONACyT, Mexico
Saturnino Job Morales	Universidad Autónoma del Estado de México, Mexico
Segun Aroyehun	University of Konstanz, Germany
Sofía Galicia Haro	Sistema Nacional de Investigadoras e Investigadores, Mexico
Tania Ramirez-delReal	CentroGEO-CONACyT, Mexico

Vadim Borisov	Branch of National Research University "Moscow Power Engineering Institute" in Smolensk, Russia
Valery Solovyev	Kazan Federal University, Russia
Vicenc Puig	Universitat Politècnica de Catalunya, Spain
Vicente Garcia Jimenez	Universidad Autónoma de Ciudad Juárez, Mexico
Victor Lomas-Barrie	IIMAS-UNAM, Mexico

Contents – Part I

Machine Learning

Contents – Part II

Robotics and Applications

Machine Learning

Stock Market Performance Analytics Using XGBoost

Nisar Hussain[1(✉)], Amna Qasim[1], Zia-ud-din Akhtar[2], Ayesha Qasim[3], Gull Mehak[1], Luciana del Socorro Espindola Ulibarri[1], Olga Kolesnikova[1], and Alexander Gelbukh[1,2,3]

[1] Institute of Polytechnic Nacional, Mexico City, Mexico
nisar.hussain8400@gmail.com, lespindolau1500@alumno.ipn.mx, {kolesnikova,gelbukh}@cic.ipn.mx

[2] Punjab University Lahore, Lahore, Pakistan

[3] Comsats University Islamabad, Lahore Campus, Islamabad, Pakistan

Abstract. A stock market is a collection of buyers and sellers of equity that are ownership statements for firms that have publicly listed stocks on a stock exchange. In the past few years, we have seen huge losses caused by the destruction of lives and hence there is a requirement for a life cycle prediction strategy that can be reliable and precise. Forecasting market trends, which are crucial for creditors, asset retailers, and critical researchers, are an important part of financial time series projections. Investors must correctly predict equities to make large gains. However, due to market volatility, this form of prediction is highly challenging. We suggest that an investor might utilize deep learning to make decisions. The main goal is to create a model utilizing deep learning techniques. In this regard, we have put forth a concept. In this regard, a component of our work focuses on integrating suitable techniques to combine financial data from multiple sources. Here, we proposed a concept by integrating deep learning with technological research. Technical analysis examines historical market trends using stock charts to forecast potential future market directions for that industry. In other words, the technical analysis uses OHLC (close, open, low, high) prices in conjunction with historical experience to produce a market map that predicts an asset's direction. Data from the KSE Stock Exchange is used to evaluate the analysis's success. There are other unconventional learning techniques, but XGBoost is one of the most popular. The Term XGBoost refers to the engineering objective of increasing the computational capital limitations for expanded tree algorithms. In this research, we use XGBoost to forecast valuations. We have obtained a historical data frame of more than 16 years of daily collected data for our selected stock which we will investigate.

Keywords: Stock Market · XGBoost · Simple Moving Averages (SMA) · Recurrent Neural Network (RNN) · Karachi Stock Exchange

Supported by organization x.

H. Calvo et al. (Eds.): MICAI 2023, LNAI 14391, pp. 3–16, 2024.
https://doi.org/10.1007/978-3-031-47765-2_1

1 Introduction

There is such a vast amount of constantly changing data in this pervasive environment, it is quite difficult to foresee the future and react to a particular forecast. It is the biggest difficulty in time series estimation. The main goal is to evaluate and implement deep reinforcement learning techniques for stock behavior.

Over the years, a group of clearly defined data points in the financial domain is evaluated. Time-series analysis comprises tests, the identification of key characteristics and statistics, and a review using time-series data calculation techniques. There are two distinct kinds of time-series data: one is single variate, while the other is multivariate. Most of the data in time - series are categorical forms. On such a dataset, the prediction is inaccurate. The open, close, date, volume, low, and high indexes for the share market are the financial data that we will employ to assess the company's market performance.

To assess the market performance, the accuracy of predicting business failures is a major challenge. Therefore, various neural network models have been designed to predict business crises and financial difficulties. Additionally, neural networks are used to analyze changes in stock market data and detect suspicious behavior in stock price manipulation [1]. Recent processes for inventory marketplace forecasts rely upon essential evaluation techniques. Using headlines connection with forecast S & P 500 index adjustments by using the neural model network and event illustration vectors for display, for example, Comparison tries to forecast consumer behavior by using past demand evidence on LSTM networks. This research is better than traditional deep mastering algorithms and gives attention to improving a prediction model using numerical or textual knowledge.

The following are some of the main issues that we address in this research:

- How to efficiently predict stock share price using single variable value?
- How to accurately forecast market exchange prices using several variable values?
- What is the accuracy of the forecast of results?
- How is the company stock data used for the correlation between the two sectors of companies?

2 Related Work

Innovative approaches for stock exchange prediction are utilizing web news. The existing models use single-user data, or the data is not correlated if it is obtained from multiple sources. This paper proposes an approach of correlated information of indicators obtained from different data sources like web news, and socialmedia.

That will provide a collective impact on the market as different markets are affected by the rising and falling of each other [2].

A hybrid model is developed to forecast the stock market behavior by integrating ICA (Independent Component Analysis) and the kernel methods. To select important indicators input, they used ICA and then kernel estimation methods for the S & P500 and Dow-Jones, Nasdaq indices. Kernel methods produce satisfactory prediction accuracy and gain rates for given indices [3].

The analyst used the ELM to render portfolio forecasts dependent on detailed stock price knowledge and industry data for stock market patterns [4]. The authors of [2] have predicted stocks employing the LSTM algorithm and transforming data into a 30-day span with a 3-day earning rate and ten learning features. The prediction accuracy is improved from 14.3 27.2 % from traditional techniques [5].

For adversarial training, the researchers propose a framework of LSTM with RNN to forecast the high-frequency stock market. Authors are using real traders to evaluate the effect of the model on prediction enhancement with rolling partition info [6].

Companies in the increasingly dynamic retail apparel sector are continually introducing approaches to change product characteristics in order to satisfy consumer expectations and desires closely. Although the lifecycles of mod goods are quite small, vast volumes of past facts that are gathered and stored in corporate repositories will help the concept of inventory and buying strategies. This study examines the use of a deep learning approach in forecasting the sales of new products in the fashion industry in future seasons. This study seeks to encourage a fashion retailer in its purchases and therefore the analyzed data set is a real data set provided by this company [7].

A data-based Deep Learning methodology for the estimation of time series related to financial time series will be implemented in this book. The period patterns for inventories and ETFs in NYSE or NASDAQ are forecast by a deep learning system. Our approach builds on a neural network (NN), which is used to predict stock and ETF temporal trends in crude financial data. The analyst creates an investment strategy that takes advantage of NN's probabilistic performance and maximizes the average return to manage commission-driven trading. The suggested program has demonstrated statistically important effective forecasts of developments in the capital markets and this test has proven that the investment approach is competitive. The result is good for two years of back-testing for contemporary criteria [8].

Time Series Predicting is a very powerful computational tool that can predict the future results of a system based on how the system has behaved in the past. A number of specific occurrences, normal as well as man-made, can be predicted via neural networks and machine learning. Predictions based on previous program responses are especially valuable for problem-solving when program input variables cannot be specified clearly. Yet neural network modeling has its own challenges: it is challenging to choose a neural network design for a certain problem because a very simple model will not function and an overly complex model may contribute to overfitting and data storage. A comparative analysis of multiple neural networking systems and diverse learning strategies is performed in this paper to get a better understanding of how the consistency of the predictions varies in different approaches to solving a particular issue [9].

The paper explores how machine learning turns unstructured data into word vectors to forecast the market trajectory of stocks. First of all, the computer understands and translates terms from financial news into vectors. Such contextual vectors are used to forecast the potential prices of main Thai stocks in the Stock Exchange of Thailand using the TensorFlow deep learning framework. The findings show that a trader will always gain an extraordinary income from trading within 5 min of the press release [10].

Thus, all these works inspire us to find and apply models to identify techniques with remarkable performance in this genre for Karachi Stock Exchange (KSE).

3 Methodology and Development

In this research, we describe various approaches, techniques, and the working principles of the classification problem. Through previous studies, multiple investigators have established market price dynamics or variations of supply movements utilizing various approaches. We also introduced many changes and enhancements and bring adjustments to the work that we have done, to make a meaningful difference. The analyses were carried out on market data from Pakistan. In the sense of Pakistan stock market data, particularly data from the Karachi Stock exchange. The proposed method is divided into distinct phases: data gathering from KSW, Merging of the Dataset, processing, Implementation of Algorithms, results, Visualization, and Comparison as shown in Fig. 1.

3.1 Dataset Description

The data from the stock market have been subject to specified technical metrics. The first conclusion was made, based on the near variations in rates on consecutive days. The feature variables contained the functional predictor values and the original stock column values. We collect stock data from 800 different companies, our data series spans the period from 01/01/2003 - 30/08/2019. To construct our model, we use different methods and strategies. Our model uses 80 training data and the remaining 20% for test data.

3.2 Data Preparation

We calculate several variables in the dataset such as symbol, date, high, low, open, close, and volume.

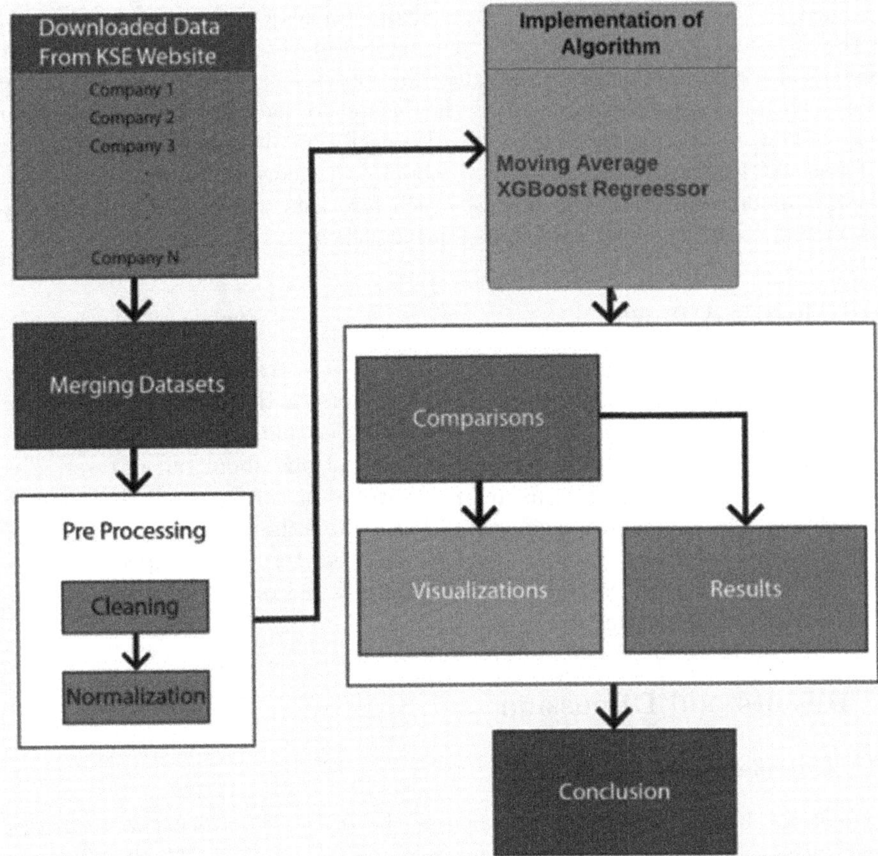

Fig. 1. The flow chart of the Stock Market Performance Analytics using Deep Learning Approach

- The Open and Close columns show the start and end of the stock on a specific day.
- The Low and High Columns show the lowest and highest stock price on a specific day of trading.
- The Volume Column indicates the number of shares sold or bought on a specific day

3.3 Using XGBoost for Stock Trend and Prices Prediction

XGBoost stands for eXtreme Gradient Boosting. XGBoost is the leading model for working with standard tabular data (in contrast to more exotic data types, such as videos and images, the data type that we store in Pandas Dataframes). To achieve maximum precision, XGBoost models require more knowledge and tuning than Random Forest techniques.

The Gradient Boosted Decision Trees algorithm is an extension for XGBoost. In the Gradient Boosted Decision Trees algorithm we go through cycles that create and merge new models in an ensemble process repeatedly. We begin the process with the error measurement in the dataset for each observation. We then create a new model that we can forecast. We apply predictions to the "collection of forecasts" from this error prediction model. We incorporate predictions from all prior models to produce a forecast. Such forecasts will be used to quantify new errors, create the next prototype, and attach it to the ensemble.

3.4 Moving Average

'Average' is one of the most common items in our everyday lives. The measurement of average marks to assess overall results or the discovery of average temperatures in recent days are both daily activities that we frequently do. This is also a strong starting point for making assumptions about our dataset. The average value of a previously measured range would be the expected closing price for each day. The rolling average method that utilizes the current value range for each sample is used, not the static average. In other terms, the expected values are considered for each corresponding step while the oldest observed value is taken out of the collection.

4 Results and Discussion

4.1 Correlation of Stock

Correlation ship is a figure that measures the extent to which two securities move with each other in the finance and investments industries. Correlations are used as the correlation coefficient for advanced portfolio management, which is between $+1.0$ and -1.0.

Correlation Test. In this method, we analyze the correlation of share price changes in one period with the previous period. Perhaps, we can choose any period but usually, economists prefer daily weekly, and monthly periods. Random walk theory states that this correlation is equal to zero meaning the expected profit for the speculator.

The daily return percentage of the two stocks can be compared now to verify how correlated. Let's first see a stock in Fig. 2 as compared to themselves.

We just compared the daily percentage change of UBL with itself. So, the correlation is $P = 1$ as expected. Now we are going to compare UBL with MCB correlation in Fig. 3.

In the above Fig. 3 We just compared the daily percentage change of UBL with MCB. Thus, the coefficient of correlation between UBL and MCB stock returns is 0.72.

The coefficient of correlation can be interpreted as a measure of two things. The first aspect is that the two variables involved usually shift in the same

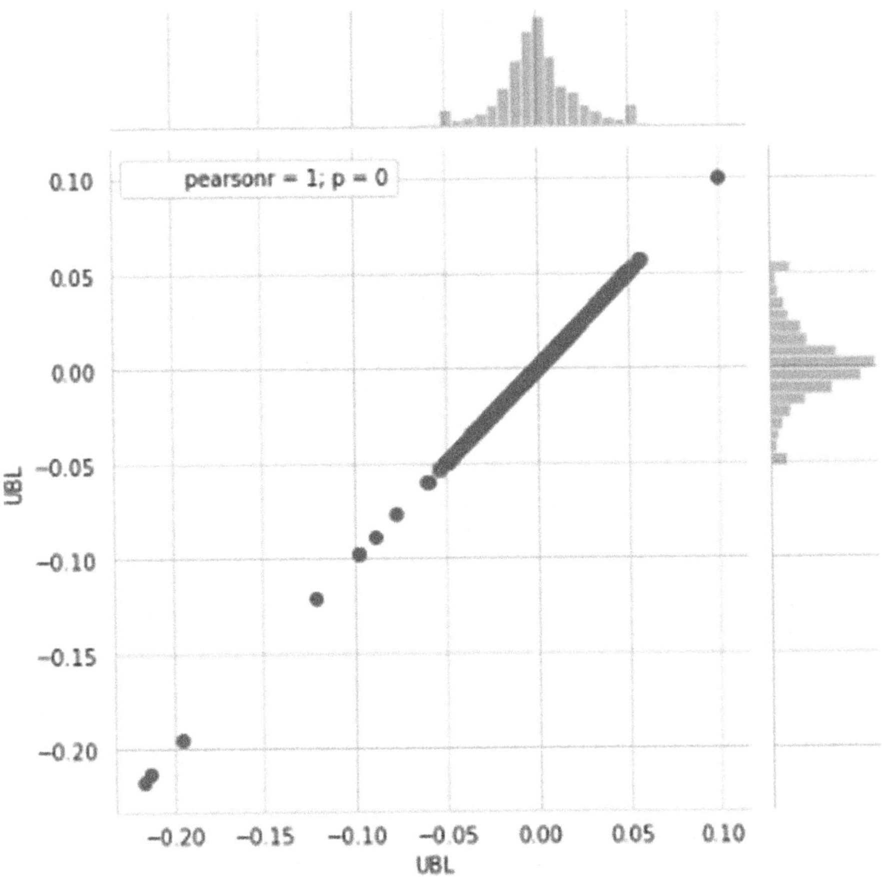

Fig. 2. UBL with itself correlation

direction. When they are, the coefficient of association is optimistic. Otherwise, it will be negative. The second aspect that will tell us is how close these movements are. A 1 or −1 correlation coefficient represents an entirely negative correlation or a perfect positive correlation.

- The coefficients of correlation always vary from −1 to 1. A result of 0 shows that no correlation is found.
- Therefore, with the result of P = 0.72 from the other part of this article, stocks UBL and stock MCB are extremely correlated. Both stocks have stock changes in the same direction and normally approximately the same magnitude.

So, we see a linear relationship between it's daily return values should arise when two stocks are perfect (and positively) correlated.

This comparative study can be replicated conveniently with Seaborn and pandas with any imaginable stock combination in our ticker list. This plot can be generated with sns.pairplot().

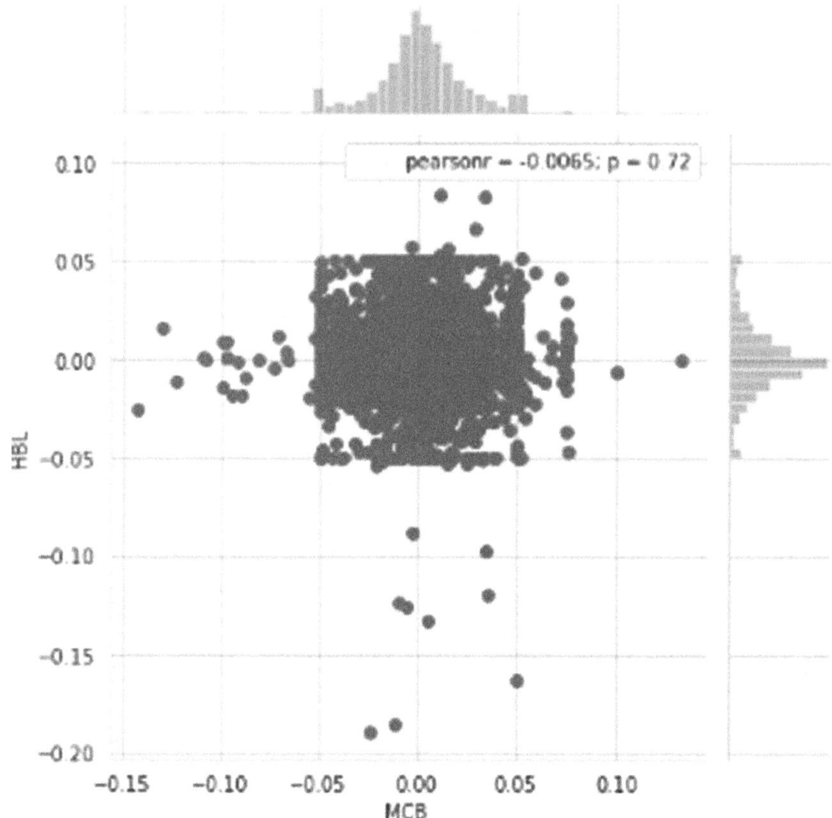

Fig. 3. UBL with MCB correlation

Calculating Correlation Between Stocks. A pair plot shows a relationship in a dataset on a pair basis. The pair plot method generates an axis grid such that any data vector is spread over one row on the y-axis and across one column on the x-axis. The pair plot is shown in Fig. 4

We can see above all the relationships between all the stocks on daily returns. A fast look reveals a significant association of daily returns between MCB and BOP. This individual comparison could be interesting to study. Although calling sns.pairplot() is fantastic, sns.PairGrid() can be used for full monitoring of the graph, including the kind of plots that suit the median, the upper, and the lower. This is an example of how Seaborn utilizes the maximum force to achieve this result.

4.2 XGBoost Regressor

XGBoost is a Machine Learning algorithm based on decision trees that employ a method of gradient boosting. Artificial neural networks tend to circumvent all

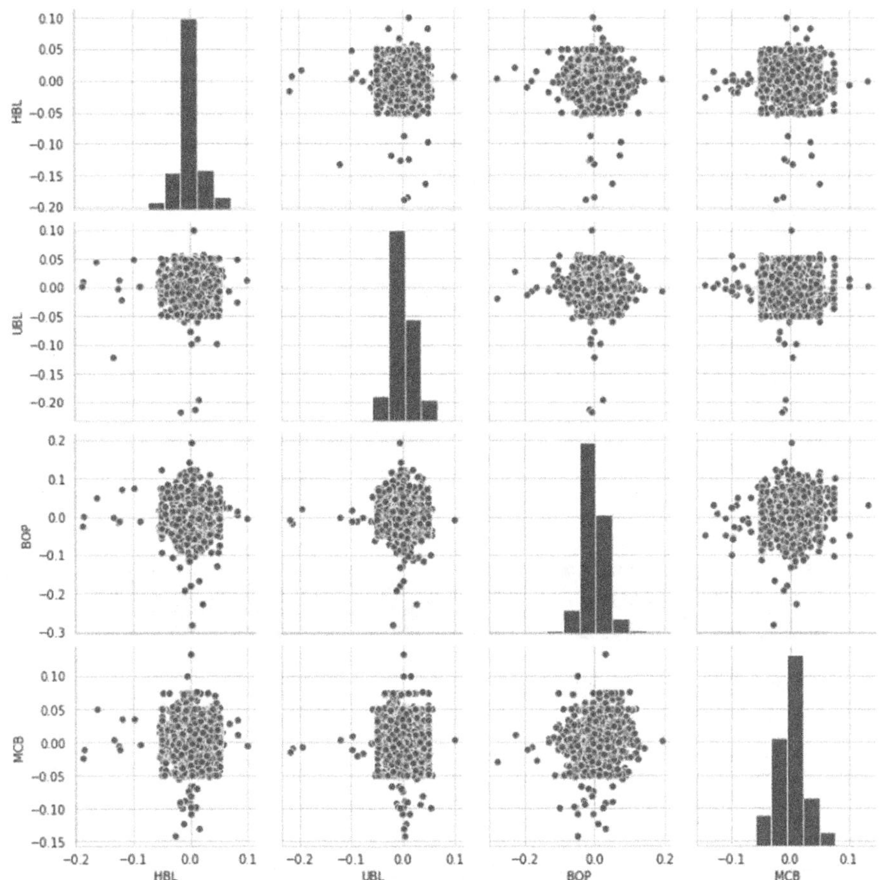

Fig. 4. Pairplot relationships on daily returns

other architectures or structures in prediction problems concerning unstructured data (images, language, etc.). But in relation to structured/tabular small to medium, tree-based decision algorithms are currently considered to be the best. We get the best performance results with an accuracy of 94/

In Fig. 11 we calculate the few moving averages to be used as features SMA5, SMA10, SMA15, SMA30, and EMA9.

4.3 MACD

Moving Average Convergence Divergence (MACD) is an indicator that shows the relationship between the two moving averages of the price of a product as depicted in Figs. 5 and 6 which shows the implementation of fine-tune XGBoost Regressor code and XGBoost Regressor Model code.

```
%%time

parameters = {
    'n_estimators': [100, 200, 300, 400],
    'learning_rate': [0.001, 0.005, 0.01, 0.05],
    'max_depth': [8, 10, 12, 15],
    'gamma': [0.001, 0.005, 0.01, 0.02],
    'random_state': [42]
}

eval_set = [(X_train, y_train), (X_valid, y_valid)]
model = xgb.XGBRegressor(eval_set=eval_set, objective='reg:squarederror', verbose=False)
clf = GridSearchCV(model, parameters)

clf.fit(X_train, y_train)

print(f'Best params: {clf.best_params_}')
print(f'Best validation score = {clf.best_score_}')
```

```
Best params: {'gamma': 0.01, 'learning_rate': 0.05, 'max_depth': 8, 'n_estimators': 200, 'random_state': 42}
Best validation score = 0.8562882629520983
CPU times: user 42min 49s, sys: 22.1 s, total: 43min 11s
Wall time: 11min 10s
```

Fig. 5. Implementation of Fine-tune XGBoost Regressor Code.

```
%%time

model = xgb.XGBRegressor(**clf.best_params_, objective='reg:squarederror')
model.fit(X_train, y_train, eval_set=eval_set, verbose=False)
```

```
CPU times: user 2.47 s, sys: 19 ms, total: 2.49 s
Wall time: 634 ms
```

```
XGBRegressor(base_score=0.5, booster=None, colsample_bylevel=1,
             colsample_bynode=1, colsample_bytree=1, gamma=0.01, gpu_id=-1,
             importance_type='gain', interaction_constraints=None,
             learning_rate=0.05, max_delta_step=0, max_depth=8,
             min_child_weight=1, missing=nan, monotone_constraints=None,
             n_estimators=200, n_jobs=0, num_parallel_tree=1,
             objective='reg:squarederror', random_state=42, reg_alpha=0,
             reg_lambda=1, scale_pos_weight=1, subsample=1, tree_method=None,
             validate_parameters=False, verbosity=None)
```

Fig. 6. XGB Regressor Model Code

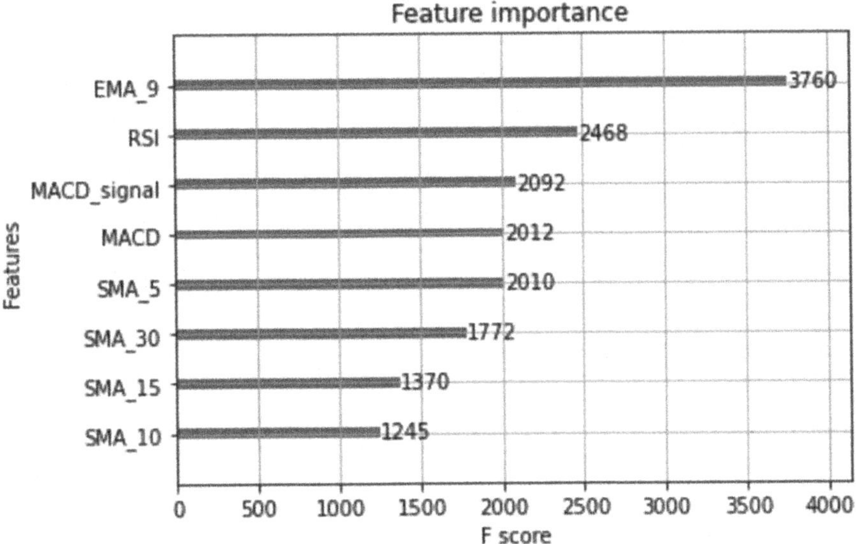

Fig. 7. Feature Importance of the Stock

Calculate and visualize predictions

```
y_pred = model.predict(X_test)
print(f'y_true = {np.array(y_test)[:5]}')
print(f'y_pred = {y_pred[:5]}')
```

```
y_true = [107.43 105.62 105.71 105.31 105.43]
y_pred = [108.988754 108.12867  107.73953  106.88535  106.79385 ]
```

```
print(f'mean_squared_error = {mean_squared_error(y_test, y_pred)}')
```

```
mean_squared_error = 9.499237151213544
```

Fig. 8. Calculate and visualize predictions

```
predicted_prices = df.loc[test_split_idx+1:].copy()
predicted_prices['Close'] = y_pred

fig = make_subplots(rows=2, cols=1)
fig.add_trace(go.Scatter(x=df.Date, y=df.Close,
                         name='Truth',
                         marker_color='LightSkyBlue'), row=1, col=1)

fig.add_trace(go.Scatter(x=predicted_prices.Date,
                         y=predicted_prices.Close,
                         name='Prediction',
                         marker_color='MediumPurple'), row=1, col=1)

fig.add_trace(go.Scatter(x=predicted_prices.Date,
                         y=y_test,
                         name='Truth',
                         marker_color='LightSkyBlue',
                         showlegend=False), row=2, col=1)

fig.add_trace(go.Scatter(x=predicted_prices.Date,
                         y=y_pred,
                         name='Prediction',
                         marker_color='MediumPurple',
                         showlegend=False), row=2, col=1)

fig.show()
```

Fig. 9. Calculate and visualize predictions Model

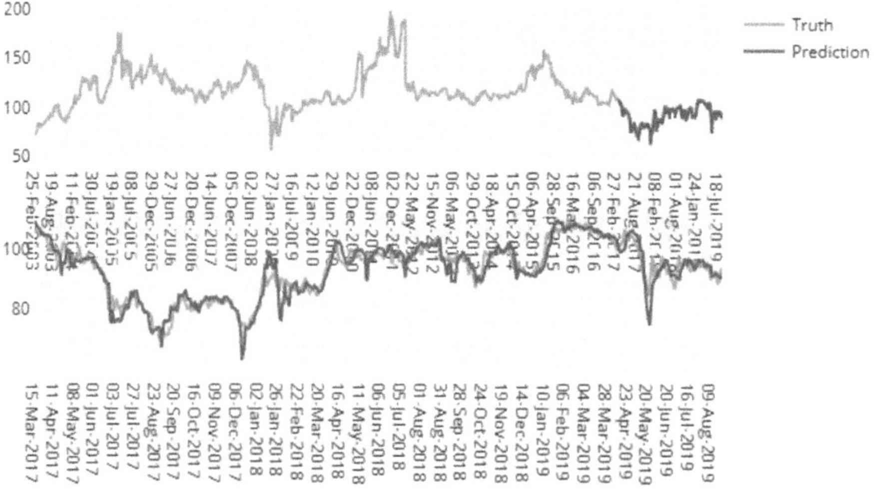

Fig. 10. Calculate and visualize predictions of the stock

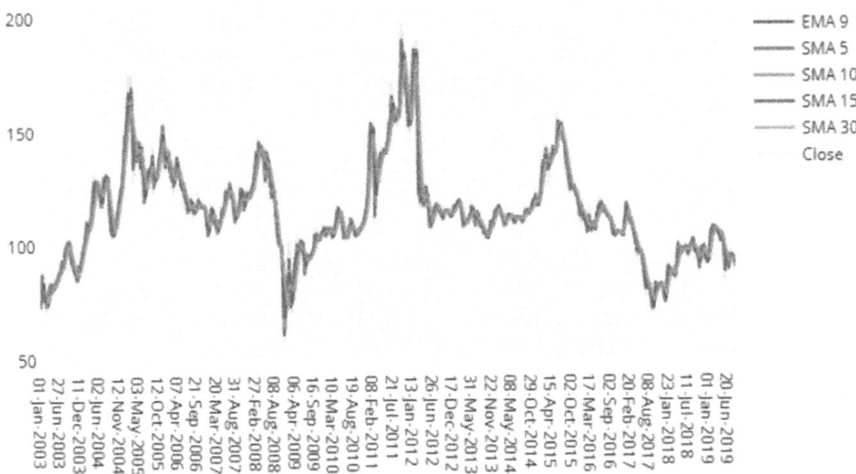

Fig. 11. Moving averages to be used as features: SMA5, SMA10, SMA15, SMA30, and EMA9.

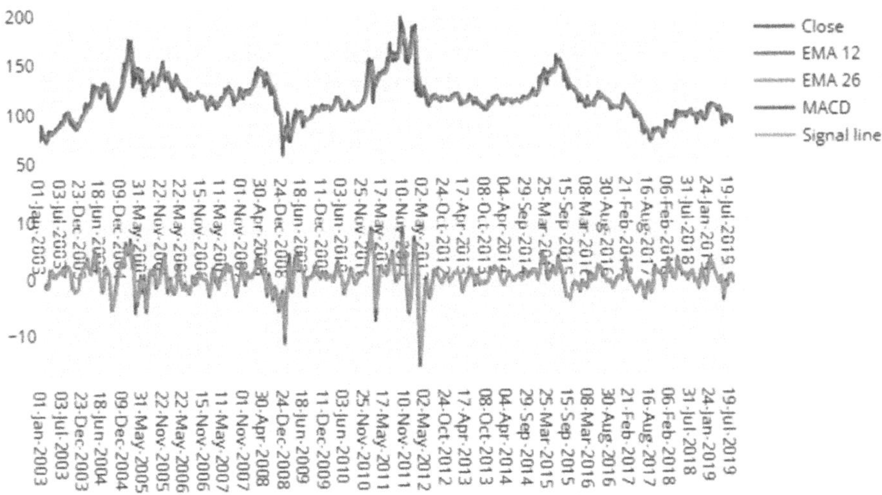

Fig. 12. Moving Average Convergence Divergence of FFC stock

5 Conclusion

We used XGBoost for the estimation of the market price of KSE in this research. Here we have equipped the Moving Average and XGBoost Regressor with a stock price of KSE. Figure 7 shows the important features of the stock data for which XGBoost model is used. The obtained model is used to forecast stock prices of the KSE stock market banking and fertilizer industry and to predict stock prices for different KSE companies. It is obvious from the results depicted in

Fig. 8, 9, 10, 11 and 12 that the patterns in the stock market can be identified by the models. Moving Average has proven greater results in the proposed study because it is able to detect accelerated process changes when a certain window is used to forecast the next moment.

References

1. Rasel, R.I., Sultana, N., Hasan, N.: Financial instability analysis using ANN and feature selection technique: application to stock market price prediction. In: 2016 International Conference on Innovations in Science, Engineering and Technology (ICISET), pp. 1–4: IEEE (2016)
2. Chen, K., Zhou, Y., Dai, F.: A LSTM-based method for stock returns prediction: a case study of China stock market. In: 2015 IEEE International Conference on Big Data (Big Data), pp. 2823–2824: IEEE (2015)
3. Ince, H., Trafalis, T.B.J.E.C., E.C. Studies, and Research, A hybrid forecasting model for stock market prediction, vol. 51, no. 3 (2017)
4. Kim, Y., Jeong, S.R., I. J. I. J. A. S. C. A. Ghani, "Text opinion mining to analyze news for stock market prediction," vol. 6, no. 1, pp. 2074–8523 (2014)
5. Li, X., et al.: Empirical analysis: stock market prediction via extreme learning machine, vol. 27, no. 1, pp. 67–78 (2016)
6. Zhang, X., Zhang, Y., Wang, S., Yao, Y., Fang, B., Philip, S. Y. J. K.- B. S.: Improving stock market prediction via heterogeneous information fusion, vol. 143, pp. 236–247 (2018)
7. Loureiro, A.L., Migueis, V.L., da Silva, L.F.: Exploring the use of deep neural networks for sales forecasting in fashion retail. Decis. Support Syst. **114**, 81–93 (2018)
8. Navon, A., Keller, Y.: Financial time series prediction using deep learning, arXiv preprint arXiv:1711.04174 (2017)
9. Ertuna, L.: Stock Market Prediction Using Neural Network Time Series Forecasting, ed: May, 2016
10. S. Selvin, R. Vinayakumar, E. Gopalakrishnan, V. K. Menon, and K. Soman, "Stock price prediction using LSTM, RNN and CNNsliding window model," in 2017 international conference on advances in computing, communications and informatics (icacci), 2017, pp. 1643–1647: IEEE

1D Quantum Convolutional Neural Network for Time Series Forecasting and Classification

Mayra Alejandra Rivera-Ruiz[1(✉)], Sandra Leticia Juárez-Osorio[1], Andres Mendez-Vazquez[1], José Mauricio López-Romero[2], and Eduardo Rodriguez-Tello[3]

[1] CINVESTAV Unidad Guadalajara, Av. del Bosque 1145, colonia el Bajío, C.P. 45019 Zapopan, Jalisco, Mexico
{mayra.rivera,sandra.juarez,andres.mendez}@cinvestav.mx
[2] CINVESTAV Unidad Querétaro, Libramiento Norponiente 2000, Fracc. Real de Juriquilla, C.P. 76230 Santiago de Querétaro, Querétaro, Mexico
jm.lopez@cinvestav.mx
[3] CINVESTAV Unidad Tamaulipas, Km. 5.5 Carretera Victoria - Soto La Marina, C.P. 87130 Victoria, Tamaulipas, Mexico
ertello@cinvestav.mx

Abstract. The 1D Convolutional Neural Network (1D CNN) is a kind of Artificial Neural Network (ANN) that has been shown to obtain state-of-the-art performance levels on several applications with minimal computational complexity and whose advantages are well established. In this article, we propose a 1D quantum convolution, which extracts local features by means of a quantum circuit in a way similar to the classical convolution. In this work, we test the performance of the proposed 1D quantum convolutional layer building a 1D Quantum Convolutional Neural Network (1D QCNN) that consists of the 1D quantum convolution followed by classical layers. The proposed model is compared with classical models for both time series forecasting and classification tasks including benchmark and real-world datasets. The obtained results show that the 1D QCNN can successfully extract features from temporal data, and in certain cases outperform classical models in terms of accuracy and convergence.

Keywords: Quantum Neural Netwoks · Time Series

1 Introduction

Machine Learning refers to the use of statistics, mathematics, and computer science to allow computers to learn from data. Those algorithms have been successfully used in tasks such as classification, regression, image classification, and forecasting, among others. On the other hand, Quantum Computing is the processing of information in devices based on the laws of quantum theory and it is a research field that in the last decades has had a rapid growth. It is a new

H. Calvo et al. (Eds.): MICAI 2023, LNAI 14391, pp. 17–35, 2024.
https://doi.org/10.1007/978-3-031-47765-2_2

paradigm that comprises aspects of computer science and quantum mechanics, it emerges as a solution to problems that classical computers struggle to solve efficiently [17,25].

Recently both disciplines have been combined into hybrid algorithms of Quantum Machine Learning (QML) with the objective of looking for advantages such as a speed-up in the convergence of algorithms, recognizing new patterns unable to appear in classical algorithms, obtaining better results in the usual metrics, or dealing better with high levels of noise [11,20,25].

Different approaches exist on how to combine both disciplines according to the type of data (classical or quantum data) and the information processing device (classical or quantum) [25]. For the case of supervised learning problems with classical data and a quantum device, many approaches are explored in literature [11,20,26]. Quantum versions of classical algorithms such as support vector machine [21], nearest neighbor [13], and decision tree [14] have been implemented, exhibiting quadratic or even exponential speedups. Neural Networks are a classical successful algorithm and, inspired in those architectures and inheriting some of its features [27], the Variational Quantum Circuits (VQC) have been widely developed in recent years [4]. These VQC have also been used to build the quantum version of Classical Convolutional Neural Networks (CNN) [7,10,12]. Further explanation of VQC will be provided in Sect. 2.2.

In literature, many examples can be found in which the QML algorithms outperformed or at least matched the results provided by their classical counterparts, both in toy datasets [15,18,24] and in real applications such as classification of medical images [9,22,29], detection of defects in materials [32] and time series forecasting [2]. In particular, Quantum Convolutional Neural Networks (QCNNs) have been applied in toy datasets such as MNIST and Fashion MNIST [7,10] but also in real applications, for example, the detection of protein distance prediction [8] and the recognition of patients infected by COVID-19 [9]. This work presents a 1D Quantum Convolutional Neural Network (1D QCNN).

Our contributions lie in designing and implementing the following novel approaches:

- We propose a 1D quantum convolutional layer that fully resembles its classical counterpart where a quantum circuit acts as a feature detector along the input vector.
- We propose a hybrid Quantum-Classical model: 1D Quantum Convolutional Neural Network (1D QCNN). This model incorporates the 1D Quantum Convolutional layer followed by classical layers.
- We conducted a series of time series forecasting and classification experiments to compare the performance of the proposed model with classical models.

The rest of the paper is organized as follows. Section 2 gives a background in quantum computing. In Sect. 3, the quantum convolution and the proposed architectures are presented. The experimental setups and results are presented in Sect. 4. Finally, the conclusions are presented in Sect. 5.

2 Preliminaries

In this section, we discuss the necessary background on the basic concepts of quantum computing.

2.1 Quantum Computation

The concept of quantum computers was proposed by Feynman in 1982 to simulate quantum systems, especially many body systems, which would be hard to simulate in classical computers [5]. He claimed that nature is not classical and that if a simulation is to be done, it was necessary to develop a computer based on quantum mechanics rules and challenged computer scientists to study this new model. 40 years after Feynman's idea, quantum hardware has progressed, but the accuracy of quantum processors is still limited [19]. Even with those limitations, quantum algorithms demonstrate supremacy in certain problems, such as Shor's algorithm for factoring with polynomial complexity or Grover's search algorithm with quadratic speed up with respect to its classical counterpart [17].

Quantum vs. Classical. Macroscopical systems are well defined by the laws of classical physics but a microscopic system isolated from its surroundings exhibits non-classical features such as [17,19]:

- Uncertainty: There is a fundamental limit in the precision with which certain pair of complementary observables can be simultaneously known due to the Heisenberg's uncertainty principle.
- Collapse: In quantum mechanics, a system is described by a wave function, which exists in a superposition of multiple possible states and when a measurement is performed, the system collapses to one of them.
- Entanglement: Two or more quantum systems can be correlated in a such a way that the state of one system cannot be described independently of the state of the other system, regardless of the spatial separation between them.

Qubits. Analogously to the bit in classical computing, the quantum bit or qubit is the basic unit of information processing used in quantum computing. The qubit is a two-level quantum system hence it can be in a superposition of the two independent states $|0\rangle$ and $|1\rangle$ until it is observed. In other words, the state of the qubit is a combination of being $|0\rangle$ and $|1\rangle$ at the same time [17].

The basis states $\{|0\rangle, |1\rangle\}$ are given by

$$|0\rangle = \begin{pmatrix} 1 \\ 0 \end{pmatrix} \quad \text{and} \quad |1\rangle = \begin{pmatrix} 0 \\ 1 \end{pmatrix}. \tag{1}$$

Using Dirac's Bra-Ket notation the state of the qubit $|\Psi\rangle$ can be written as:

$$|\Psi\rangle = \alpha|0\rangle + \beta|1\rangle \qquad \alpha, \beta \in \mathbb{C}, \tag{2}$$

When a qubit is measured, the state $|0\rangle$ is obtained with probability $|\alpha|^2$, or the state $|1\rangle$ is obtained with probability $|\beta|^2$. For example, for a qubit in the state $|\phi\rangle = \frac{1}{\sqrt{2}}|0\rangle + \frac{1}{\sqrt{2}}|1\rangle$, when measured, gives $|0\rangle$ fifty percent of the times and $|1\rangle$ fifty percent of the times. Because the sum of probabilities must be one α and β satisfies the normalization condition: $|\alpha|^2 + |\beta|^2 = 1$, which means geometrically that the qubit's state is normalized to length 1 [17].

In quantum mechanics, the interactions and dynamics of particles are mathematically represented within the framework of the Hilbert space. The space of n qubits is given by the tensor product space of the qubits:

$$|\Psi\rangle = \sum_{(q_1, q_2, \dots, q_n) \in \{0,1\}} C_{q_1, q_2, \dots, q_n} |q_1\rangle \otimes |q_2\rangle \otimes \dots \otimes |q_n\rangle. \tag{3}$$

With:

$$\sum_{(q_1, q_2, \dots, q_n) \in \{0,1\}} \|C_{q_1, q_2, \dots, q_n}\|^2 = 1, \quad C_{q_1, q_2, \dots, q_n} \in \mathbb{C}. \tag{4}$$

Hereafter, n denotes the number of qubits.

2.2 Quantum Circuits

Quantum gates are unitary operators (they meet the property $U^\dagger U = 1$) that perform a linear transformation in qubits. This unitarity allows operations to be reversible [17]. Those quantum operations can be applied in sequence to a certain number of qubits, generally initialized in the state $|0\rangle$. This sequence is known as a quantum circuit and the state after passing the initialized state through it is given by:

$$|\Psi\rangle = \prod_{i=1}^{k} U_i |0\rangle^{\otimes n}, \tag{5}$$

where n is the number of qubits.

The Bloch sphere is a spherical representation of the possible states of a qubit, showing pure states at the poles and superposition states on the equator, allowing for a visual understanding of qubit behavior. Some of the most common gates in Quantum Computing are Pauli's matrices σ_x, which flip quantum bits from $|0\rangle$ to $|1\rangle$ and vice-versa, σ_y which makes a π rotation around the y axis and σ_z which makes also a π rotation around the z axis. By using those Pauli matrices, a rotation of the qubit in the Bloch sphere can be performed by the Pauli rotations: $R_x = e^{-i\frac{\theta}{2}\sigma_x}$, $R_y = e^{-i\frac{\theta}{2}\sigma_y}$ and $R_z = e^{-i\frac{\theta}{2}\sigma_z}$. Another common gate is the Hadamard gate, which creates a superposition state between two qubits $\{\frac{|0\rangle+|1\rangle}{\sqrt{2}}, \frac{|0\rangle-|1\rangle}{\sqrt{2}}\}$. Also, other gates are capable of performing a transformation in two or more qubits. For example, a common gate is the CNOT, which performs the NOT operation on the target qubit only when the control qubit is $|1\rangle$ and otherwise leaves it unchanged [17].

As in the classical case, quantum circuits can be represented graphically, where two gates in parallel indicate their tensor product, and two gates in series are equal to their matrix product, where the order of appearance in the circuit is opposite to that of multiplication.

2.3 Variational Quantum Circuits

Variational Quantum Circuits (VQC) are trainable quantum circuits that are widely used as quantum neural networks for different tasks. VQC are quantum algorithms that capture correlations in data using entangling properties [24]. In today's noisy intermediate-scale quantum computers (NISQ), which suffer from noise and qubit limitations, the VQC is the leading strategy due to their shallow depth [4].

In Fig. 1 the general schema of a VQA is shown. The first step is to encode the N-dimensional classical input $\mathbf{x} = (x_1, ..., x_N)$ into a vector in the Hilbert space. This is accomplished by applying a unitary transformation $U_{\text{in}}(\mathbf{x})$ to the initial state, which is generally chosen as $|0\rangle^{\otimes n}$ [4]. The method for doing this encoding is still an open question but some of the strategies to perform this step are:

- Amplitude Encoding: The classical N features are associated with the probability amplitudes of quantum states of $log_2 N$ qubits [25]:

$$U_{\text{in}}(\mathbf{x}) : \mathbf{x} \in \mathbb{R}^N \longrightarrow |\Psi_{\text{in}}(\mathbf{x})\rangle = \frac{1}{\|x\|} \sum_{i=1}^{N} x_i |0\rangle. \tag{6}$$

- Rotation Encoding: Embeds the classical vector x of N features into N qubits in the following way:

$$U_{\text{in}}(\mathbf{x}) : \mathbf{x} \in \mathbb{R}^N \longrightarrow |\Psi_{\text{in}}(\mathbf{x})\rangle = \bigotimes_{i=1}^{N} \left(\cos\left(\frac{x_i}{2}\right) |0\rangle + \sin\left(\frac{x_i}{2}\right) |1\rangle \right), \tag{7}$$

  where $\bigotimes$ indicates the tensor product.

After encoding the classical input, the state vector is passed through a set of quantum operations depending on an optimizable parameter $\boldsymbol{\theta}$ [4]. Now, the encoded vector $|\Psi_{\text{in}}(\mathbf{x})\rangle$ is mapped to $|\Psi\rangle = U(\boldsymbol{\theta})|\Psi_{\text{in}}(\mathbf{x})\rangle$, and $U(\boldsymbol{\theta})$ can be decomposed as L layers:

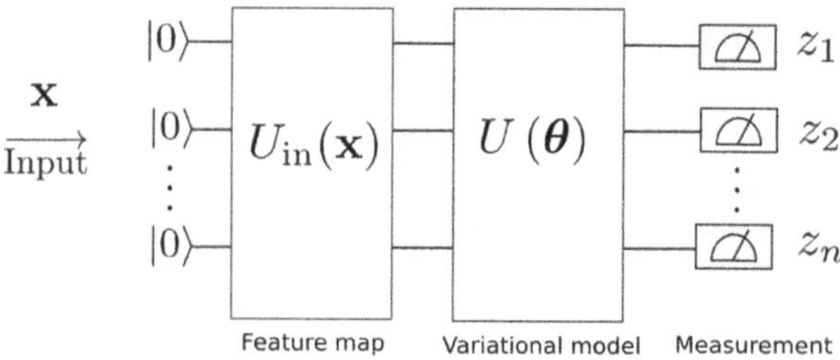

Fig. 1. Illustration of a Variational Quantum Circuit (VQC). The classical input $\mathbf{x}$ is encoded into a quantum state $|\Psi_{\text{in}}(\mathbf{x})\rangle$ by applying a unitary transformation $U_{\text{in}}(\boldsymbol{\theta})$ to the initial quantum state $|0\rangle^{\otimes n}$. Then, a unitary transformation $U(\boldsymbol{\theta})$ with trainable parameters is applied. Finally, a measurement is made on the qubits.

$$U = U_L ... U_l ... U_1, \tag{8}$$

with each layer U_l is a combination of either a single qubit rotations and multiple qubit gate to entangle two or more qubits [24].

When the state has passed through the circuit, an observable (a physical quantity) M is measured. This measurement is given by the expectation value, which is given by:

$$\langle M \rangle = \langle \Psi | M | \Psi \rangle, \tag{9}$$

which means that the operator M is applied to the output state $|\Psi\rangle$ that comes out of the VQC and the result of that is multiplied with $\langle \Psi |$. The usual choice for this observable is the Pauli Z operator. The circuit is calculated a number of times S and the expectation value is obtained by averaging over the measurements of each run. One way to map this result to a label is for example to assign the probability of obtaining a state of the computational basis to one of the labels. With the prediction and the actual label is possible to calculate the cost function to perform the optimization of the trainable parameters [3]. After that, the derivative of the expectation value is calculated with respect to the trainable parameters in order to minimize the cost function and optimize the parameters [3,4,23].

Although the capacity of Quantum Neural Networks (QNNs) needs to be further explored, there are several studies that show that in certain cases they offer advantages in terms of the number of parameters and trainability [1,16,24].

Amira Abbas et al., demonstrate that QNNs have a higher effective dimension than classical neural networks [1].

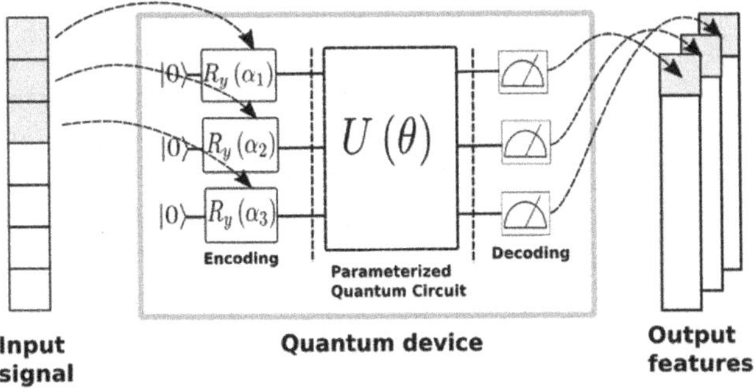

Fig. 2. Illustration of the 1D quantum convolution. A VQC is used to extract features from the data. A VQC of n qubits slides over input tensor subsections and outputs n features maps.

3 1D Quantum Convolution

In order to propose an extension of the classical 1D CNN, we design a 1D quantum convolution. The state $|\Psi\rangle$ of n qubits can be represented as a unit vector in a Hilbert space $\mathcal{H}$ of dimension 2^n (see Eq. 3), which is high dimensional and difficult to simulate by a classical computer. We hypothesize that the large dimensionality of the quantum Hilbert space can benefit the extraction of meaningful features from data. Moreover, quantum circuits perform well even in the presence of noise [6]. The proposed 1D Quantum Convolution is shown in Fig. 2.

The 1D quantum convolution works in a similar way to the 1D classical convolution. The main difference lies in the way in which the 1D quantum convolution performs the operations. Instead of using element-wise matrix multiplication operations, the 1D quantum convolution takes as input subsections of one-dimensional signals and utilizes a VQC to create a feature map. The VQC slides over subsections of the input tensor extracting the features. First, the considered part is encoded into an initialized quantum state and then a parameterized quantum circuit is applied. The parameterized quantum circuit involves a unitary transformation $U(\boldsymbol{\theta})$ given by Eq. 8. The optimizable parameter $\boldsymbol{\theta}$ is determined during the training. Finally, the information is decoded making measurements on all qubits. The measurements are real numbers given by Eq. 9. Then, by performing quantum measurements on each qubit we get each output channel. The number of output feature maps is equal to the number of qubits. Since the outputs of the 1D quantum convolution are vectors with real components, we can stack the proposed quantum layer with other quantum or classical layers.

In order to evaluate the 1D quantum convolution, we propose a hybrid Quantum-Classical model, called 1D Quantum Convolutional Neural Network (1D QCNN) which consists of one 1D quantum convolutional layer followed by classical layers. The 1D QCNN is applied to two tasks: time series forecasting and time series classification. The forecasting and classification performance of the proposed 1D QCNN is compared with two classical models: 1D CNN and Multilayer Perceptron (MLP). The overall architecture for each time series problem is as follows:

- Forecasting: 1D QUANV-CONV1-ReLU-POOL1-FC1-ReLU-FC2
- Classification: 1D QUANV-ReLU-POOL1-CONV1-ReLU-POOL2-CONV2-ReLU-POOL3-FC1-ReLU-FC2

The details of each model depend on each dataset and are described in the next section.

In both cases, for the 1D quantum convolution, a kernel of size 3 is chosen, so 3 values have to be encoded into the quantum circuit. The data encodings for forecasting and classification task are respectively:

$$|\Psi_{\text{in}}(x_1, x_2, x_3)\rangle = \bigotimes_{i=0}^{n-1} R_z(x_1) R_y(x_2) R_z(x_3) |0\rangle^{\otimes n}, \tag{10}$$

and

$$|\Psi_{\text{in}}(x_1, x_2, x_3)\rangle = \bigotimes_{i=0}^{n-1} R_x(x_i) |0\rangle^{\otimes n}, \tag{11}$$

with $n = 8$ and $n = 3$.

In the case of the forecasting task, Eq. 10 can be seen as the repetition of the encoding in parallel that in [28] is shown to increase the expressivity of the model. In [28] it is shown that a quantum circuit of this kind can be written as a partial Fourier series and then repeating the encoding would extend the frequency spectrum. The fact that the quantum circuit can be seen as Fourier series suggests that this approach is suitable for problems related to time series forecasting.

Once the encoding has been done, the state vector is passed through the variational circuit, which in this case was chosen as in Fig. 3a for the forecasting problem and Fig. 3b for the classification problem. The configurations were chosen in this way following the intuition explained in [24] which indicates that using rotations of trainable angles does not require extra conditions for the model parameters and that the use of entangling gates improves the expressivity of the model. Then, the expectation value of the variable σ_z is measured in each qubit.

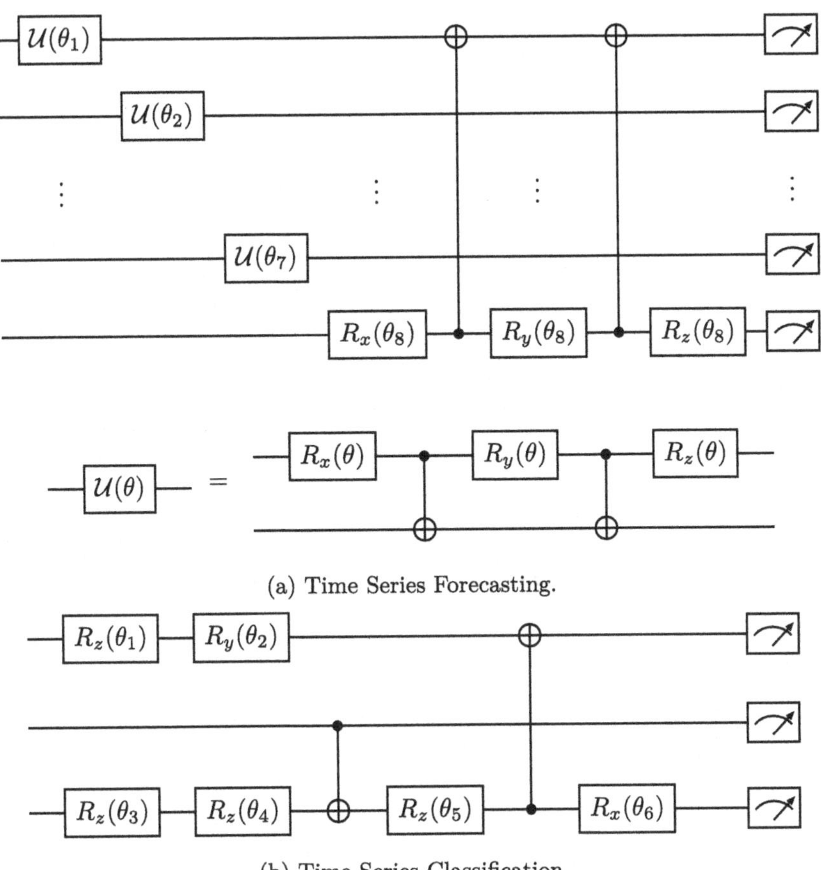

(a) Time Series Forecasting.

(b) Time Series Classification.

Fig. 3. Parameterized Quantum Circuits ($U(\boldsymbol{\theta})$) used for time series forecasting and classification. $U(\boldsymbol{\theta})$ is made up of Pauli rotations with trainable angles and CNOT gates.

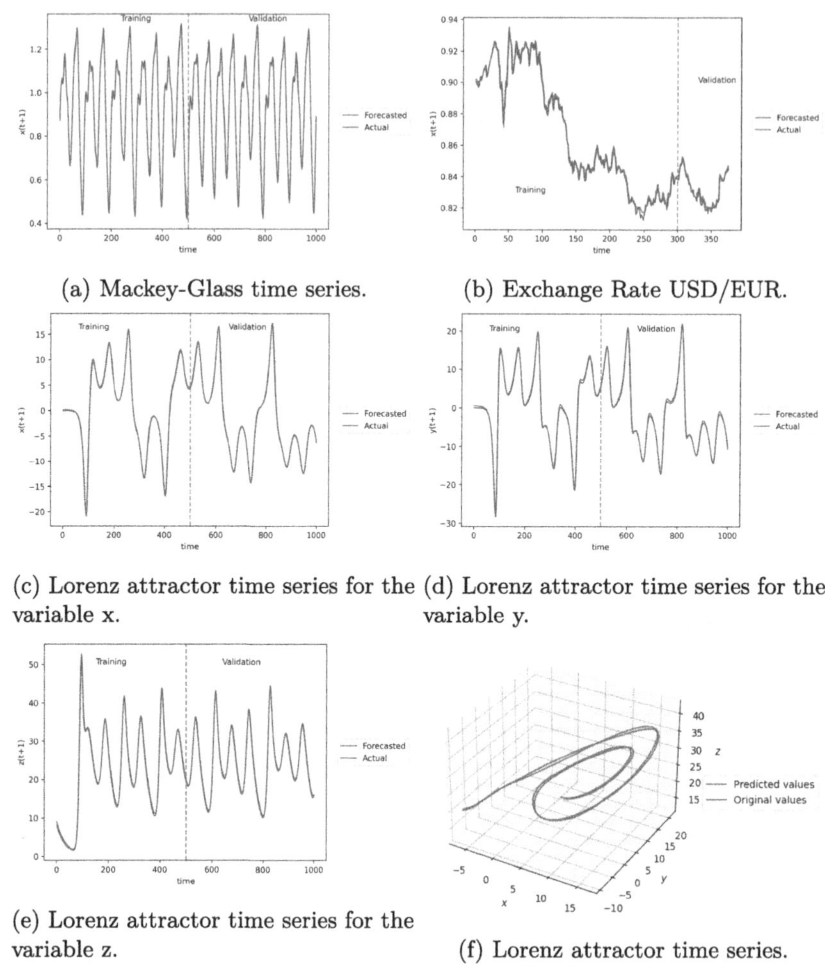

(a) Mackey-Glass time series.

(b) Exchange Rate USD/EUR.

(c) Lorenz attractor time series for the variable x.

(d) Lorenz attractor time series for the variable y.

(e) Lorenz attractor time series for the variable z.

(f) Lorenz attractor time series.

Fig. 4. Actual and forecasted outputs using the 1D QCNN.

4 Results and Discussion

4.1 Time Series Forecasting

In this section, the effectiveness of the proposed quantum machine learning architectures is assessed by employing them in three standard time series datasets: Mackey-Glass time series, Lorenz attractor, and USD-to-euro currency exchange rate forecasting. The experiments conducted for this research utilize the built-in Pennylane simulator *lighting.qubit* and PyTorch.

To ensure a fair comparison, the same optimizers, learning rates, and the number of epochs (50 for all cases) are applied to the MLP, CNN, and the proposed models. Additionally, the time series data is scaled using the min-max normalization formula, which confines it within the range of $[0, 1]$. The Adam optimizer is utilized with a learning rate of $5e - 4$. The evaluated metrics are Root Mean Squared Error (RMSE), Mean Absolute Error (MAE), and Mean Absolute Percentage Error (MAPE).

Mackey-Glass Time Series. The Mackey-Glass time series data is generated from a differential equation with the form:

$$\dot{x} = \alpha x(t - \tau)\,(1 + x^{\gamma}(t - \tau)) - \beta x(t) \quad (19), \tag{12}$$

where the parameter τ represents the time delay. To obtain a numerical solution, the Runge-Kutta method was employed, starting with an initial condition $x(0) = 1.2$ and using an integration step of 0.1. The values of α, β, and γ are set to 0.2, 0.1, and 10, respectively.

For building our model, we use 1000 simulation data points defined as:

$$[x(t - 18), x(t - 12), x(t - 6), x(t); x(t + 6)] \quad (20) \tag{13}$$

Here, t ranges from 19 to 1018. The first 500 points are designated as training data, while the remaining points are reserved for testing. In the model, we consider the vector x with components $x(t-18)$, $x(t-12)$, $x(t-6)$, and $x(t)$ as the input, and the last component $x(t+6)$ as the output variable.

The model is the 1D quantum convolutional layer described in Sect. 3 followed by a classical convolutional layer with 8 input channels, 8 output channels, a kernel size of 3, a stride of 1, and padding. The ReLU activation function is applied after the convolutional layer. A max pooling operation with a kernel size of 4 is performed. The features are then flattened and passed through a fully connected layer with 8 input neurons and 16 output neurons. The ReLU activation is applied after this layer, followed by a final fully connected layer with 16 input neurons and 1 output neuron.

The model was tested against an MLP with input dimension 4, followed by two hidden layers with sizes 8 and 16 respectively. The output layer consists of a single neuron with ReLU activation. The model was also tested for a CNN in which the quantum convolutional layer was substituted for a first layer with 1 input channel, 8 output channels, a kernel size of 3, a stride of 1, and padding to maintain the input size.

Table 1 displays a comparison of the three models in terms of RMSE, MAE, and MAPE. It is evident that all three models exhibit similar metrics, yet the 1D QCNN model outperforms the classical models. The 1D QCNN model improved the results of MLP, which was the best of the two tested classical models, by 66% in RMSE. Also a 57% improvement with respect to MLP was obtained in MAE and MAPE.

Figure 4a provides a visual comparison of the actual and forecasted values for both the training and testing phases. Additionally, Fig. 5a depicts the convergence of the three models. It is noteworthy that the 1D QCNN exhibits faster convergence compared to the classical convolutional model.

Exchange Rate USD/EURO. The data regarding the exchange rate between USD and EUR is obtained from [31]. The data is collected for the period from January 1, 2020, until July 8, 2021, with a daily time step. We utilize 376 simulation data points to construct the model, defined as:

$$[x(t-4), x(t-3), x(t-2), x(t-1), x(t); x(t+1)] \quad (25) \tag{14}$$

where t ranges from 5 to 380. The initial 300 data points are employed for the training phase, while the remaining data points are used for testing.

The model consists of the custom 1D quantum convolutional layer described in Sect. 3 followed by a classical convolutional layer with 8 input channels, 8 output channels, a kernel size of 3, a stride of 1, and padding. ReLU activation is applied after the convolutional layer. A max pooling operation with a kernel size of 5 is performed. The features are then flattened and passed through a fully connected layer with 8 input neurons and 16 output neurons. ReLU activation is applied after this layer, followed by a final fully connected layer with 16 input neurons and 1 output neuron.

Table 1. Comparison results among the proposed 1D QCNN, 1D CNN, and MLP for the Mackey Glass, Exchange Rate USD/EURO, and Lorenz attractor.

Data	Network	Parameters	RMSE	MAE	MAPE
Mackey Glass	1D QCNN	385	0.0091	0.0073	0.0080
	MLP	473	0.022	0.017	0.019
	1D CNN	393	0.027	0.023	0.026
Exchange Rate	1D QCNN	385	0.0028	0.0020	0.0025
	MLP	385	0.0032	0.0025	0.0030
	1D CNN	393	0.0031	0.0024	0.0030
Lorenz attractor	1D QCNN	419	0.4935	0.3440	0.1122
			0.6996	0.5398	0.1929
			0.7941	0.7063	0.0300
	MLP	464	0.4902	0.3744	0.1435
			0.7219	0.5719	0.1508
			0.8666	0.7523	0.0325
	1D CNN	427	0.4590	0.3651	0.1179
			0.6288	0.4704	0.1980
			0.8694	0.8041	0.0282

The proposed model was tested against a 3-layer MLP with input dimension 5, two hidden layers of size 16 each, and a single output neuron. The ReLU activation function was used for all layers. The model is also compared with 1D CNN, which consists of substituting the quantum convolutional layer for a first layer with 1 input channel, 8 output channels, a kernel size of 3, a stride of 1, and padding to maintain the input size.

In Table 1 a comparison between the models is presented for RMSE, MAE, and MAPE. As can be observed, the three models present comparable metrics but the classical models are outperformed by the 1D QCNN. Compared with the best result of the classical models, in this case, 1D CNN, the 1D QCNN model showed an improvement of 9.6% in RMSE and a 16% improvement in both MAE and MAPE.

In Fig. 4b the comparison between the actual and forecasted values can be observed for both training and testing. Also, in Fig. 5b the convergence of the three models is presented and it can be observed that both 1D QCNN and MLP converge faster than the classical convolution.

Lorenz Time Series. The Lorenz equations are given by

$$\begin{aligned}\dot{x} &= \sigma(y - x),\\ \dot{y} &= -y - zx + \rho x,\\ \dot{z} &= -\beta z + xy.\end{aligned}$$

The numerical solution is obtained with the Euler method taking parameter settings $\sigma = 10$, $\rho = 28$ and $\beta = 8/3$, and using the initial conditions: $x(0) = 0$, $y(0) = -0.01$ and $z(0) = 9$.

The 1D quantum convolutional layer described in Sect. 3 was utilized, followed by a classical convolutional layer with 8 input channels, 8 output channels, a kernel size of 3, a stride of 1, and padding. ReLU activation is applied after the convolutional layer. A max pooling operation with a kernel size of 3 is performed. The features are then flattened and passed through a fully connected layer with 8 input neurons and 16 output neurons. ReLU activation is applied after this layer, followed by a final fully connected layer with 16 input neurons and 3 output neurons.

This model was compared with an MLP consisting of an input dimension of 3, followed by two hidden layers with sizes 21 and 11 respectively. The output layer consists of 3 neurons with ReLU activation. Also, a comparison was made with a CNN consisting of replacing the quantum convolutional layer for a layer with 1 input channel, 8 output channels, a kernel size of 3, a stride of 1, and padding.

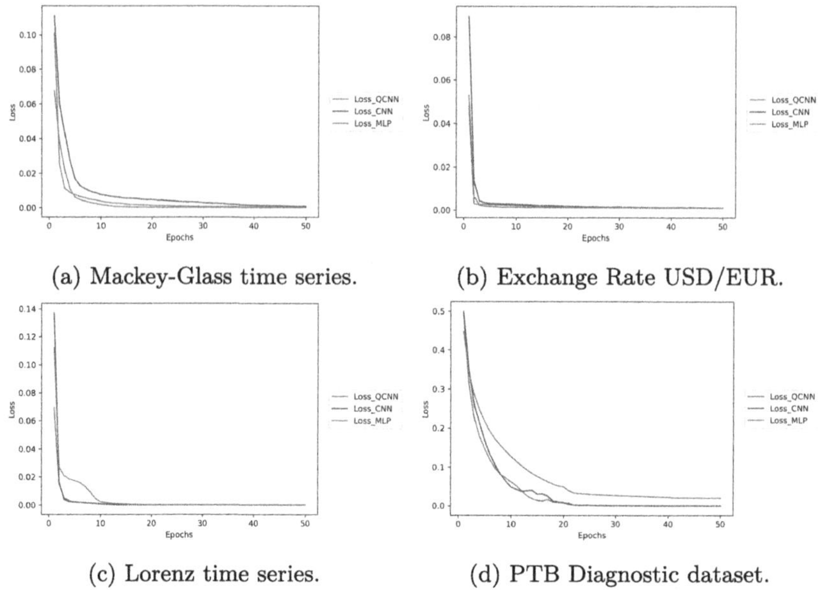

(a) Mackey-Glass time series.

(b) Exchange Rate USD/EUR.

(c) Lorenz time series.

(d) PTB Diagnostic dataset.

Fig. 5. MSE loss curves of the 1D QCNN, 1D CNN and MLP.

Table 2. Comparison results among the proposed 1D QCNN, 1D CNN, and MLP for the PTB Diagnostic dataset.

Network	Parameters	Accuracy (%)
1D QCNN	1534216	98.125
1D CNN	1534222	98.062
MLP	97282	96.250

Table 3. Classification report from the confusion matrix.

Network		Precision	Recall	F1-Score	Support
1D QCNN	N	0.9765	0.9862	0.9813	800
	A	0.9861	0.9762	0.9812	800
	Average	0.9813	0.9812	0.9812	1600
1D CNN	N	0.9788	0.9825	0.9807	800
	A	0.9824	0.9788	0.9806	800
	Average	0.9806	0.9806	0.9806	1600
MLP	N	0.9512	0.9750	0.9630	800
	A	0.9744	0.9500	0.9620	800
	Average	0.9628	0.9625	0.9625	1600

In Table 1, we present a comparison of the three models for time series forecasting of the Lorenz attractor in the dimension x, y, z. The 1D QCNN model demonstrates superior performance compared to the classical models in certain metrics. Specifically, the 1D QCNN model achieves lower RMSE and MAE values in some cases, indicating its effectiveness in capturing the dynamics of the Lorenz attractor. However, all models still exhibit comparable overall performance. Compared with 1D CNN, which presented the best result of the two classical models, the 1D QCNN model improved by 5.7% in MAE for the x direction and in 12% for the z direction. In MAPE, 1D QCNN outperformed 1D CNN by 4.8% and 2.5% in the directions x and y, but 1D CNN improved by 6% in z. In RMSE, the 1D CNN presented a better performance of 6.8% in the x direction, 10% in y, and 8.6% in z.

In Figs. 4c–4e the actual points are compared with the forecasted outputs obtained using the 1D QCNN model in the training and validation phases for the dimension x, y, and z respectively. In Fig. 4f the actual and forecasted values for the validation phase are compared in a three-dimensional plot. Finally, in Fig. 5c the loss curves are presented for the three models and it can be observed that the quantum model exhibits a faster convergence.

4.2 Time Series Classification Using PTB Dataset

In this paper, we use the PTB Diagnostic dataset that consists of Electrocardiogram (ECG) records. The PTB diagnostic database obtained from [30], contains 14552 samples belonging to two classes: 4046 normal and 10506 myocardial infarction (abnormal) ECG beats. Hereafter, "A" and "N" denote normal and abnormal classes respectively. The sampling frequency of this database is equal to 125 Hz. Additionally, the ECG signals are zero-padded to the fixed size 187. Representative samples of normal and abnormal ECG beats are shown in Fig. 6. In our experiments, we used 4000 samples of each class and a random 80:20 train-test split.

The QCNN architecture includes the 1D quantum convolutional layer described in Sect. 3 followed by ReLU activation and max pooling operation with a kernel size of 2. Then, 2 classical convolutional layers with 64 and 128 output channels, respectively are applied. Both convolutional layers have a kernel size of 3, a stride of 1, and padding. Additionally, the ReLU activation function is applied to both convolutional layers and each one is followed by a max pooling layer. The last part of the architecture consists of a fully connected layer with 512 neurons with ReLU activation function followed by a fully connected layer for classification.

The model is compared with MLP and 1D CNN. All models were trained using the Adam optimizer with Cross-Entropy Loss, 50 epochs, and an initial learning rate of $1e-3$. During training, we reduce the learning rate by using the StepLR scheduler with step size and learning rate decay equal to 20 and 0.1, respectively.

From Fig. 5d we can observe that the 1D QCNN and 1D CNN are comparable in terms of convergence speed whereas the MLP converges slower. As we can see in Table 2 1D QCNN outperforms classical models in terms of accuracy, overcoming the 1D CNN and MLP by 0.063% and 1.875% respectively.

The confusion matrices shown in Fig. 7 give us an overview of the correctly and incorrectly classified samples during the testing phase. We can observe that the majority of predictions correspond to diagonal elements, which is a good indicator since a perfect classifier would imply off-diagonal elements equal to zero.

From Tables 2 and 3 we can observe that the 1D QCNN outperforms the other models in terms of accuracy as well as average precision, recall and F1-score. Regarding specific classes, the 1D QCNN has the highest precision for class "A", the highest recall for class "N" and the highest F1-score for both classes when compared to the other models. Thus, the 1D QCNN is superior to the classical models 1D CNN and MLP, except that the precision metric for class "N" and the recall metric for class "A" are slightly lower when compared to the 1D CNN.

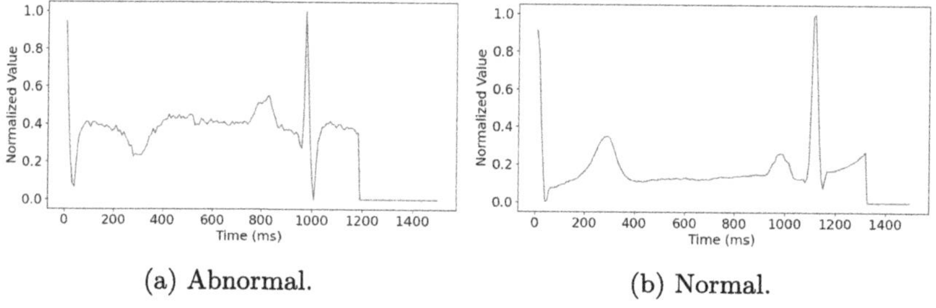

Fig. 6. Sample plots of heartbeats of two classes for the PTB dataset.

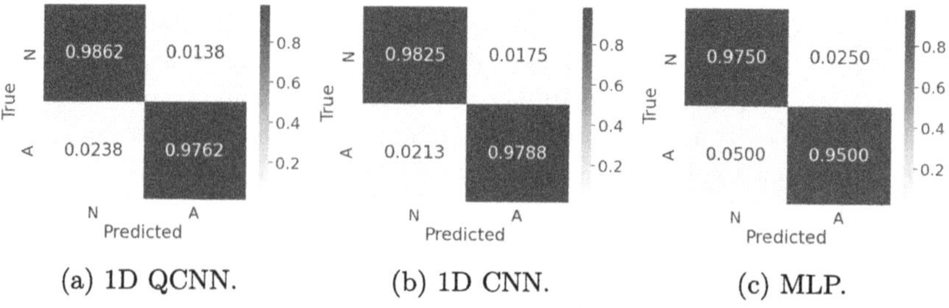

Fig. 7. Normalized Confusion Matrices of the 1D QCNN, 1D CNN and MLP.

5 Conclusions

In this paper, we present a 1D quantum convolution that uses a quantum circuit to extract features from input data. In order to evaluate its ability as a feature detector we propose a Quantum Convolutional Neural Network for time series forecasting and classification.

In this work, we conducted a series of experiments with the benchmark datasets Mackey Glass and Lorenz attractor that correspond to univariate and multivariate time series, respectively. Additionally, two real-world univariate time series, USD-EURO exchange rates, and PTB database were utilized. The former dataset was used for time series forecasting and the latter for time series classification. In all scenarios, the proposed 1D QCNN shows a competitive performance when compared to its classical competitors, the 1D CNN and the MLP. Therefore, the proposed 1D quantum convolution is capable of effectively extracting local features from the input vector.

In an upcoming study, a comprehensive evaluation of the proposed 1D QCNN architecture will be conducted, encompassing comparisons with alternative encoding methods and exploration of different variational layers. Furthermore, a deeper analysis of the theoretical justification behind the variational layers depicted in Figs. 3a and 3b will be undertaken.

References

1. Abbas, A., Sutter, D., Zoufal, C., Lucchi, A., Figalli, A., Woerner, S.: The power of quantum neural networks. Nat. Comput. Sci. **1**(6), 403–409 (2021)
2. Alejandra, R.R.M., Andres, M.V., Mauricio, L.R.J.: Time series forecasting with quantum machine learning architectures. In: Pichardo Lagunas, O., Martínez-Miranda, J., Martínez Seis, B. (eds.) Advances in Computational Intelligence, MICAI 2022, vol. 13612, pp. 66–82. Springer, Cham (2022). https://doi.org/10.1007/978-3-031-19493-1_6
3. Bergholm, V., Izaac, J., Schuld, M., Gogolin, C.: PennyLane: automatic differentiation of hybrid quantum-classical computations (2022)
4. Cerezo, M., et al.: Variational quantum algorithms. Nat. Rev. Phys. **3**(9), 625–644 (2021)
5. Feynman, R.P.: Simulating physics with computers. In: Feynman and Computation, pp. 133–153. CRC Press (2018)
6. Havlíček, V., et al.: Supervised learning with quantum-enhanced feature spaces. Nature **567**(7747), 209–212 (2019)
7. Henderson, M., Shakya, S., Pradhan, S., Cook, T.: Quanvolutional neural networks: powering image recognition with quantum circuits. Quantum Mach. Intell. **2**(1), 2 (2020)
8. Hong, Z., Wang, J., Qu, X., Zhu, X., Liu, J., Xiao, J.: Quantum convolutional neural network on protein distance prediction. In: 2021 International Joint Conference on Neural Networks (IJCNN), pp. 1–8. IEEE (2021)
9. Houssein, E.H., Abohashima, Z., Elhoseny, M., Mohamed, W.M.: Hybrid quantum-classical convolutional neural network model for COVID-19 prediction using chest X-ray images. J. Comput. Des. Eng. **9**(2), 343–363 (2022). https://doi.org/10.1093/jcde/qwac003

10. Hur, T., Kim, L., Park, D.K.: Quantum convolutional neural network for classical data classification. Quantum Mach. Intell. **4**(1), 3 (2022). https://doi.org/10.1007/s42484-021-00061-x
11. Li, W., Deng, D.L.: Recent advances for quantum classifiers. Sci. China Phys. Mech. Astron. **65**(2), 220301 (2021). https://doi.org/10.1007/s11433-021-1793-6
12. Liu, J., Lim, K.H., Wood, K.L., Huang, W., Guo, C., Huang, H.L.: Hybrid quantum-classical convolutional neural networks. Sci. China Phys. Mech. Astron. **64**(9), 290311 (2021)
13. Lloyd, S., Mohseni, M., Rebentrost, P.: Quantum algorithms for supervised and unsupervised machine learning (2013)
14. Lu, S., Braunstein, S.: Quantum decision tree classifier. Quantum Inf. Process. **13**, 757–770 (2014). https://doi.org/10.1007/s11128-013-0687-5
15. Mari, A., Bromley, T.R., Izaac, J., Schuld, M., Killoran, N.: Transfer learning in hybrid classical-quantum neural networks. Quantum **4**, 340 (2020). https://doi.org/10.22331/q-2020-10-09-340
16. Mitarai, K., Negoro, M., Kitagawa, M., Fujii, K.: Quantum circuit learning. Phys. Rev. A **98**, 032309 (2018). https://doi.org/10.1103/PhysRevA.98.032309, https://link.aps.org/doi/10.1103/PhysRevA.98.032309
17. Nielsen, M.A., Chuang, I.L.: Quantum Computation and Quantum Information. Cambridge University Press, Cambridge (2000)
18. Park, G., Huh, J., Park, D.K.: Variational quantum one-class classifier. Mach. Learn. Sci. Technol. **4**(1), 015006 (2023). https://doi.org/10.1088/2632-2153/acafd5
19. Preskill, J.: Quantum computing 40 years later. Nat. Rev. Phys. **4**(1) (2023). https://doi.org/10.1038/s42254-021-00410-6
20. Ramezani, S.B., Sommers, A., Manchukonda, H.K., Rahimi, S., Amirlatifi, A.: Machine learning algorithms in quantum computing: a survey. In: 2020 International Joint Conference on Neural Networks (IJCNN), pp. 1–8 (2020). https://doi.org/10.1109/IJCNN48605.2020.9207714
21. Rebentrost, P., Mohseni, M., Lloyd, S.: Quantum support vector machine for big data classification. Phys. Rev. Lett. **113**(13), 130503 (2014). https://doi.org/10.1103/physrevlett.113.130503
22. Sameer, M., Gupta, B.: A novel hybrid classical-quantum network to detect epileptic seizures. medRxiv, pp. 2022-05 (2022)
23. Schuld, M., Bergholm, V., Gogolin, C., Izaac, J., Killoran, N.: Evaluating analytic gradients on quantum hardware. Phys. Rev. A **99**(3), 032331 (2019). https://doi.org/10.1103/physreva.99.032331
24. Schuld, M., Bocharov, A., Svore, K.M., Wiebe, N.: Circuit-centric quantum classifiers. Phys. Rev. A **101**, 032308 (2020). https://doi.org/10.1103/PhysRevA.101.032308, https://link.aps.org/doi/10.1103/PhysRevA.101.032308
25. Schuld, M., Petruccione, F.: Supervised Learning with Quantum Computers. Springer, Cham (2018). https://doi.org/10.1007/978-3-319-96424-9
26. Schuld, M., Sinayskiy, I., Petruccione, F.: An introduction to quantum machine learning. Contemp. Phys. **56**(2), 172–185 (2014). https://doi.org/10.1080/00107514.2014.964942
27. Schuld, M., Sinayskiy, I., Petruccione, F.: Simulating a perceptron on a quantum computer. Phys. Lett. A **379**(7), 660–663 (2015). https://doi.org/10.1016/j.physleta.2014.11.061
28. Schuld, M., Sweke, R., Meyer, J.J.: Effect of data encoding on the expressive power of variational quantum-machine-learning models. Phys. Rev. A **103**(3), 032430 (2021). https://doi.org/10.1103/physreva.103.032430

29. Shahwar, T., et al.: Automated detection of Alzheimer's via hybrid classical quantum neural networks. Electronics **11**, 721 (2022). https://doi.org/10.3390/electronics11050721
30. Fazeli, S.: ECG heartbeat categorization dataset (2018). https://www.kaggle.com/datasets/shayanfazeli/heartbeat. Accessed 28 Feb 2023
31. Antweiler, W.: Pacific exchange rate service (2023). http://fx.sauder.ubc.ca/data.html. Accessed 20 Jan 2023
32. Yang, Y.F., Sun, M.: Semiconductor defect detection by hybrid classical-quantum deep learning. In: 2022 IEEE/CVF Conference on Computer Vision and Pattern Recognition (CVPR). IEEE, June 2022. https://doi.org/10.1109/cvpr52688.2022.00236

Hand Gesture Recognition Applied to the Interaction with Video Games

Lorena Isabel Barona López(✉), César Israel León Cifuentes, José Miguel Muñoz Oña, Angel Leonardo Valdivieso Caraguay, and Marco E. Benalcázar

Artificial Intelligence and Computer Vision Research Lab, Departamento de Informática Y Ciencias de la Computación (DICC), Escuela Politécnica Nacional, Quito 170517, Ecuador

lorena.barona@epn.edu.ec

Abstract. In this work, a hand gesture recognition system was created for 11 different gestures. The system employed CNN-LSTM artificial neural networks and followed the CRISP-ML(Q) process model. The aim was to incorporate software engineering practices into machine learning projects. The system uses Electromyography (EMG) and Inertial Measurement Unit (IMU) signals as input to compute a gesture label and the time of occurrence in the signal. The system is integrated with a video game that utilizes hand gestures as input. A system usability scale (SUS) survey was done by ten final users in order to measure the interaction with the video game using gestures as the main way of interaction. The complete application evaluation obtained a SUS score of 75, or a B grade.

Keywords: Artificial Neural Networks · Electromyography · Hand Gesture Recognition · Inertial Measurement Unit · Quaternion · Real Time

1 Introduction

Hand gesture recognition (HGR) is a research field where the primary goal is to detect specific human gestures and use them to convey information or for command and control purposes. The hand gesture recognition problem consists of identifying the class (from a predefined set of classes) and the instant of occurrence of a given movement of the hand [1]. With this information, hand gestures can provide a natural means of interaction and can help to reduce the dependency on peripheral devices such as mice, keyboards, controllers, and touchscreens. Some areas of application of hand gesture recognition are sign language, robotic control, virtual environments, and PC applications [2]. Hand gestures can be represented in many ways, using sensors such as gloves [3], web cameras [4], infrared cameras [5,6], inertial measurement units (IMU) [7], and electromyography (EMG) [8]. On one hand, superficial electromyography (sEMG) records the muscle's electrical activity from the surface of the skin, reflecting the generation and propagation of motor unit action potential. Muscle-computer interfaces that

H. Calvo et al. (Eds.): MICAI 2023, LNAI 14391, pp. 36–52, 2024.
https://doi.org/10.1007/978-3-031-47765-2_3

use this signal demonstrated good recognition accuracy on static gestures, which involve different muscle activations [8]. On the other hand, IMUs can register directional changes such as rotation and translation, achieving better results at discriminating dynamic gestures [7,9]. In particular, the combination of inertial measurement units with electromyography can improve the classification accuracy of a hand gesture recognition system that uses both dynamic and static gestures. Furthermore, there is evidence in the literature of the performance of such systems, even using different models and gesture sets. The results found in the literature are shown in Table 1.

Table 1. Classification accuracy of models using EMG and IMU in the literature.

Model	Classification accuracy	Number of users
Linear Discriminant Analysis (LDA) [9]	95,97%	4
Hidden Markov Models (HMM) [10]	74,3%	5
Linear Bayesian Classifier [11]	94,32%	5
Support Vector Machines (SVM) [12]	99%	3

As it was presented, most of hand gesture recognition systems in the literature were developed using machine learning. Nevertheless, according to a status report on enterprise machine learning [13], one of the biggest challenges in these types of projects is to meet objectives that deliver value to stakeholders. This is caused by the partial or total absence of scalability, version control, model reproducibility, technical debt, and a long time until deployment [14]. Then, it is crucial that machine learning practitioners find a method to resolve or at least minimize these issues in order to achieve stakeholder's alignment. This paper proposes a system for static and dynamic hand gesture recognition that uses deep learning (Convolutional Neural Network CNN - Long short-term memory LSTM models), EMG, and IMUs used in a video game. The main contributions of this article are the following: i) The development of a hand gesture recognition system for eleven hand gestures, static and dynamic. This HGR uses a process model that supports stakeholder's alignment and project success criteria and ii) The development, integration, and usability evaluation of the HGR system by means of a video game.

The rest of this paper is structured as follows. In Sect. 2, the process model and activities are presented. The accuracy evaluation of the HGR system and usability test are shown in Sect. 3. Some conclusions of this research are drawn in Sect. 4, as well as a description of the future work related to this paper.

2 Methodology

In this section, the complete application architecture proposed is illustrated in Fig. 1. This architecture has two principal components: an HGR system and a video game application (dancing video game), which use sockets as a communication interface between them. Using this architecture will support the application's maintainability since the components can be replaced without introducing any defect in the other component.

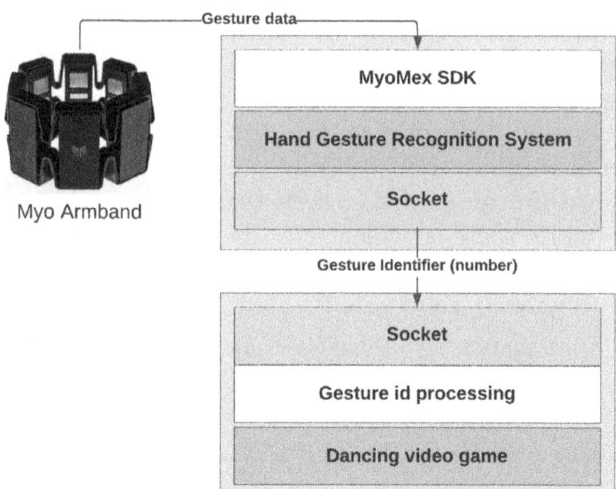

Fig. 1. Application architecture

2.1 Hand Gesture Recognition

In order to build the HGR, this work used Cross Industry Standard Process for Machine Learning with Quality Assurance (CRISP-ML(Q)) [15] as a process model focused on value delivery and reduction of technical debt. This process model is suitable for scenarios where a machine learning model is deployed and maintained as part of a product or service, which in fact is the scenario for this HGR system. In this section, it will be described how the activities proposed in CRISP-ML(Q) guided the development of the machine learning application. A summary of the phases proposed by this process model is proposed below:

Business and Data Understanding. This activity focuses on the definition of scope, project success criteria, and project feasibility. The scope definition encompasses the development of a hand gesture recognition system for eleven hand gestures, with special attention on response time measured from the input of signals, to the label generation. The HGR system will use convolutional and LSTM neural networks, and it will recognize the gestures shown in Fig. 2.

The next pair of tasks defined in this phase are data collection and verification. The first task was not performed in this work since the data were already collected. The acquisition process is described in [16]. For data verification, a data description was done as follows. Sensors Myo Armand and GForce Pro return a normalized discrete vector $E(n, w) \in [-1, 1]^8$ for each $n, w \in \mathbb{Z}^+ \times \mathbb{Z}^+$, where n is an instant of time, w a sample number and each component $E_i(n, w) \in [-1, 1]$ has data from channel i recorded by the sensor, with $i = \{1, 2, \ldots, 8\}$ [17]. Additionally, the sensors return a rotation vector (IMU) $\theta(n) \in \mathbb{R}^4$ that represents each quaternion component w, x, y, z, such that $\|\theta(n)\| = 1$ [18]. Because of the

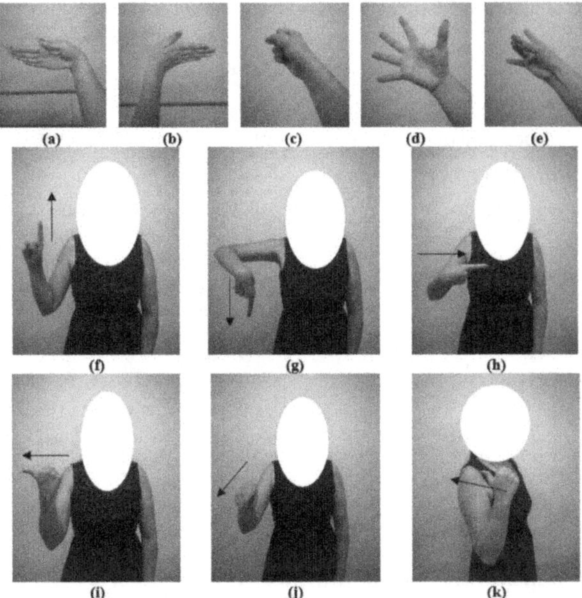

Fig. 2. Defined gestures to recognize using HGR system. (a) wave in, (b) wave out, (c) fist, (d) open, (e) pinch, (f) up, (g) down, (h) left, (i) right, (j) forward, (k) backward.

record time interval of these sensors, two signals are recollected: $\underline{S} \in [-1, 1]^{I \times 8}$ for sEMGs and $\underline{Q} \in \mathbb{R}^{J \times 4}$ for quaternions, with $I, J \in \mathbb{Z}^+$.

After the data description, which encompasses data from 100 users [19], a sheet of data requirements was elaborated. These data requirements can help to determine if new user's samples are correct and can be used. The required properties for each sample set are shown in Table 2.

Data Preparation. This activity produces a dataset that is ready to be used as an input to the modeling phase. Then, data selection, cleaning, construction, and standardization tasks are carried out.

Prior to data selection, a feature selection was done using two signal representations proposed in [17]. The sEMG signal is defined as the sum of all the filtered channels centered on zero, using a low-pass Butterworth filter for each channel. The quaternion signal is defined by $\theta'(t) = \sum_{i \in \{w,x,y,z\}} |\theta_i(t) - \bar{\theta}_i(t)|$, where $\theta_i(t)$ represents the quaternion component vector w, x, y, z and $\bar{\theta}_i(t)$ is the mean of each quaternion component. After feature selection, the data selection was done in a 2-step fashion. The first step was a manual segmentation, that consist on recording timestamps (Ground Truth) of the signals. Each muscular activation or rotation delta is bounded by a time interval. The second step was the automatic identification of signal windows with enough gesture information. For this purpose, the Ground Truth was used to verify if a window had at least

Table 2. Required properties and values on a user's sample set.

Property	Value
Number of samples per user	360
Number of samples per gesture	30
Time interval required to record a sample	5 s
sEMG's sampling frequency	200 Hz (Myo Armband) or 500 Hz (GForce Pro)
Quaternion's sampling frequency	50 Hz
sEMG's channel number	8
Quaternion's representation structure	Quaternion coefficient vector
Gesture label data type	Categorical, chosen from the class set: backward, forward, up, down, left, right, fist, pinch, waveln, waveOut, relax
Max number of samples with missing values	4

75 % of its points inside the timestamps, or whether at least 50% of the Ground Truth was in the window. Additionally, an energy vector was computed using the function represented by $E = \sum_{i=2}^{L} |x_i \cdot |x_i| - x_{i-1} \cdot |x_{i-1}||$, where x_i is a sEMG or quaternion signal sample, and L is the signal length [20].

Data cleaning was done after data selection. In data cleaning, a noise reduction was applied to sEMG signals and a normalization function was applied to quaternions. The data construction task used the cleaned data and derived new features in the time-frequency domain using spectrograms for each of the sEMG signal channels [21] and quaternion vector component. Since the sEMG signals were recorded using different sampling rates, the values used for spectrogram computation such as overlapping, stride, and internal sliding window were represented using units of time, instead of a number of points. A brief description of the data selection, cleaning, and construction is presented in Fig. 3. Subsequently, the constructed data was saved in a structure that contains the Ground Truth and the sequence data (such as sEMG and quaternion spectrograms with an optional gesture label if it was present on the original dataset).

Modeling. This activity focuses on model selection and training. Model selection was defined after doing literature research where it was found that CNN-LSTM models can learn to recognize gestures of different complexity and duration [22]. In this work, two CNN-LSTM models were developed using almost the same architecture. The CNN architecture helps the model extract implicit features and can learn to represent images throughout domains [22]. The proposed structure for the CNN is based on GoogLeNet's [23], which introduces sparse layers inside convolutional layers in order to reduce overfitting and the usage of computational resources. The convolutional layer used is proposed in [24]. The feature extraction layer was built using six sparse layers and two additive resid-

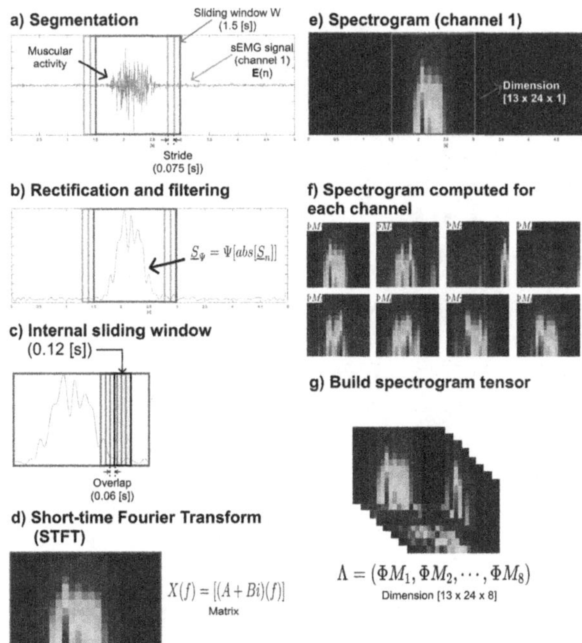

Fig. 3. Data selection, cleaning, and construction for a sEMG signal.

ual blocks [24]. The complete structure of the feature extraction layer is shown in Fig. 4.

The remaining parts of the model architecture consist of a LSTM layer, a fully connected layer, an activation function, and an output layer. The LSTM layer can learn dependencies over a large range of sequential data. A dropout layer was added in the dynamic gesture model to reduce overfitting. The complete architecture for each model is depicted in Fig. 5. The fixed hyperparameters used to train each model are shown in Table 3.

In addition to the CNN-LSTM models, a linear logistic classifier (LLC) was developed using energy vectors as inputs. This classifier will help the hand gesture recognition system to determine if a gesture is static or dynamic and use one of the CNN-LSTM models.

Evaluation. This activity was carried out using two approaches: Individual model evaluation and HGR system evaluation. Firstly, the confusion matrix for each of the CNN-LSTM models was computed. Then, in order to compute evaluation and recognition accuracy, a recognition pipeline was proposed. The systems start with sEMG and quaternion signals, a 12-feature vector is calculated using the energy function, the linear logistic classifier is used to determine if the gesture is static or dynamic, then the gesture is preprocessed and classified

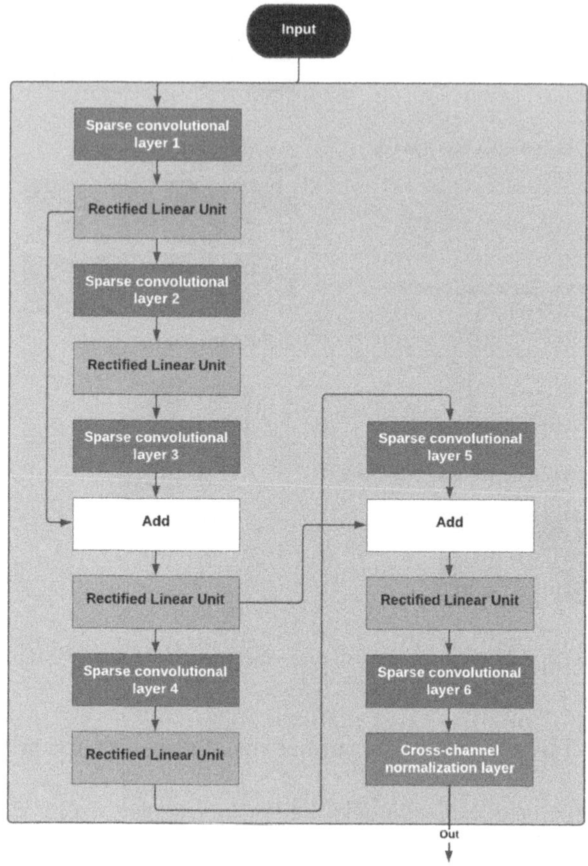

Fig. 4. Convolutional feature extraction layer.

Table 3. Hyperparameter configuration for static and dynamic gesture models.

Hyperparameter	Static gesture model	Dynamic gesture model
Epochs	10	30
Learning rate	0.001	0.04
Learning rate decay	0.2	0.2
Learning rate drop period	8	8
Mini-batch size	64	64
Sequence length	Shortest	Shortest
LSTM layer output mode	Sequence	Sequence

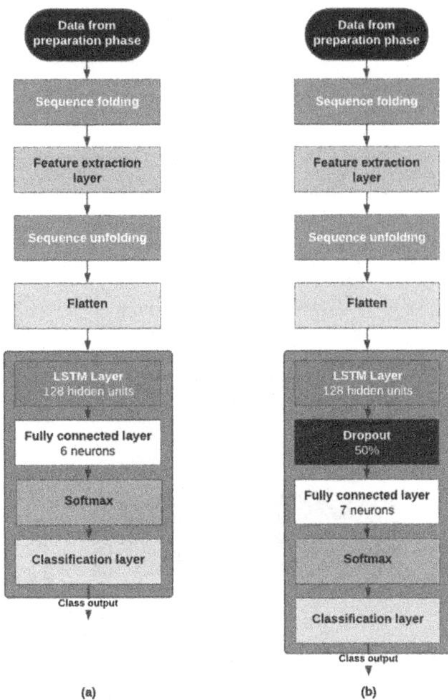

Fig. 5. CNN-LSTM architecture for a) static gestures and b) dynamic gestures.

using one of the CNN-LSTM models. As a result, a timestamp vector and a label sequence are obtained. Using a postprocessing algorithm [24], a uniform label sequence is returned and saved in a file that is sent into an evaluation program. Then, classification and recognition accuracy, as well as the confusion matrix of the whole system are computed. An outline of the proposed pipeline is presented in Fig. 6.

Deployment. In order to use the developed machine learning application, it's necessary to define the communication interface between the armband and the video game. The communication between the sensor and the HGR system was handled using MyoMex SDK for Myo Armband [25]. The operation behavior of the system is depicted in Fig. 6. Finally, the communication between the HGR system and the video game was established using sockets, since both applications work in the same device. With this communication, the HGR system sends a number that represents one of the eleven gestures to the video game.

2.2 Video Game Application

Several methodologies have been proposed for the creation of video games, but very few are suitable for the development of a music video game. Therefore, the SUM methodology has phases that promote the development of a quality video game. In addition, this methodology considers various elements that a video

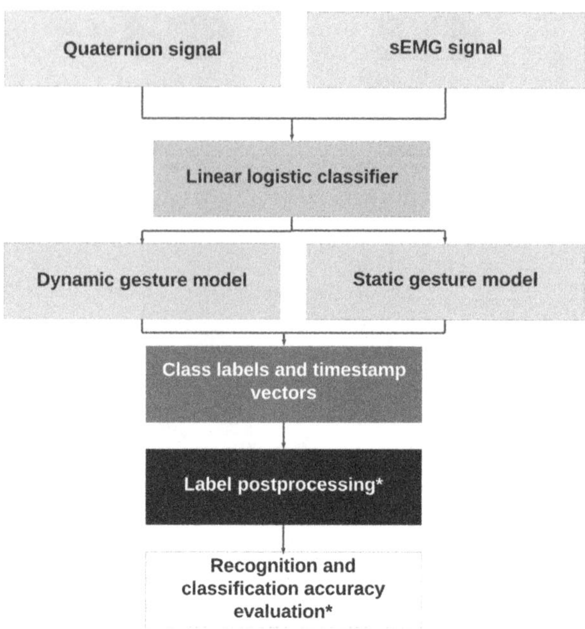

Fig. 6. Proposed pipeline for testing and operation of the HGR system. Steps marked with * are exclusive for evaluation.

game must have as well as the context of the video game. This methodology aims to develop high-quality video games in terms of time and cost, taking into account continuous improvement. This constitutes an efficient administration of the resources assigned for the development and the risks of the project. In addition, SUM suits multidisciplinary development teams involving participants with diverse skills in different fields [26,27]. It is important to mention that this methodology is suitable for short-term projects(less than one year) [28,29].

SUM has five phases in its life cycle. In the "Concept" phase we define key aspects of the video game such as the story, the characters, the target audience, and other important aspects. During the "Planning" phase, the schedule is drawn up, the development team is formed, and the functional and non-functional characteristics of the video game are defined. In the "Elaboration" phase, the video game is developed taking into account technical aspects and the characteristics of the video game defined in the two previous phases. Later, in the "Beta" phase, errors are corrected and features that the user wants are added. Finally, in the "Closing" phase, the finished video game is delivered, and an evaluation of the project is carried out for future improvements to the methodology used in the development [26–28].

Throughout the application of SUM methodology for the development of the video game, several artifacts were generated, enabling the reduction of uncertainty of the characteristics of the video game. The first artifact is the conceptualization of the video game. Table 4 summarizes the artifact of this phase and the important aspects that were obtained.

Table 4. Conceptualization of the video game

Feature	Description
Video game genre	Music video game
Graphics	3D environment (dance stage and Dancer Animated Model)
Gameplay and interaction	Use of the bracelet to manipulate the video game
Sound	Dance and menu songs
Roles	3D model of a dancer performing dance steps as required
History	None
Environment	Dance floor with various colored lights
Target audiences	Man or woman over 18 years old who has a bracelet to control devices and programs through hand gestures (the sensor controls some computer program that serves as entertainment). In addition, the user must have the full motor capacity of his right arm to perform the gestures

In addition, the relationship between the gestures that the recognition model will recognize to manipulate the video game in a natural and intuitive way is defined. Following the methodology, the development of the video game is planned, in terms of time, cost, and development team. Moreover, a formal definition of the characteristics of the video game was made using user stories. User stories are useful for the implementation of functional and non-functional features, as well as their validation and verification in the development phase. Table 5 shows a summary of the user stories that were planned for the development of the video game. Additionally, this table includes their priority for implementation and the estimated effort required to complete each story.

Table 5. User stories

ID	Name	Priority	Estimation
H07	Dance in the video game	1	5
H06	View the songs	2	3
H01	Display main menu	3	1
H05	Display instructions	4	1
H04	View scores	5	1
H03	Set the game volume	6	1
H02	Exit the game	7	1

In the elaboration phase, the implementation of the functions described in the previous phase was carried out, taking into account the information embodied in the generated artifacts. Moreover, customer feedback was taken into account to modify both the technical and visual aspects of the video game. The navigation diagram of the application is shown in Fig. 7.

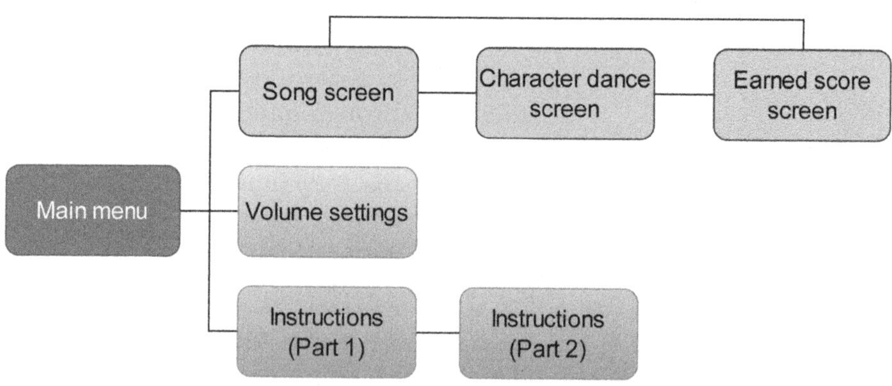

Fig. 7. Video game navigation diagram

To conclude the development of the video game, the closing phase was carried out. During this phase, the developed video game was delivered with all the changes and modifications requested by the client, including the integration between the gesture recognition model and the application. This was done through sockets, where a number sent from the recognition model was mapped in the application with the name of the gesture. Table 6 shows how the number that is sent from the model when recognizing a gesture (translation of the name of the gesture in the application).

Table 6. Relationship of gesture between the model and the application

Gesture number	0	1	2	3
Gesture name	NoGesture	WaveIn	WaveOut	Fist
Gesture number	4	5	6	7
Gesture name	Open	Pinch	Up	Down
Gesture number	8	9	10	11
Gesture name	Left	Right	Forward	Backward

3 Results

This section shows the confusion matrices for each CNN-LSTM model, as well as the classification and recognition accuracy for the HGR system. Moreover, a usability evaluation of the game using hand gestures was performed.

Individually, each deep learning model was evaluated using the validation samples in the dataset. Figure 8 shows the evaluation results for each of the static gestures, with a classification accuracy of 84.49%. Likewise, Fig. 9 shows evaluation results for the dynamic gesture model, with a classification accuracy of 80.77%.

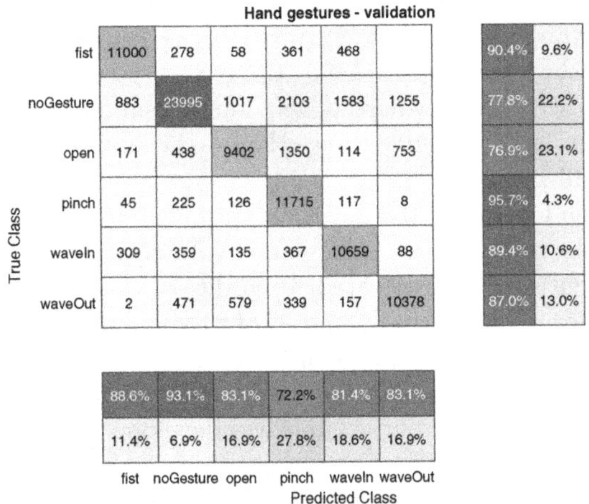

Fig. 8. Confusion matrix for static gesture model over validation samples

On the other hand, training an evaluation of the linear logistic classifier was performed by selecting a user set, then half of the data was used for training, and the other half for evaluation. The evaluation results of the linear logistic classifier show a classification accuracy of 93.02%.

HGR system evaluation was done using a portion of the dataset that doesn't have Ground Truth information or labels. With this data, the output values of

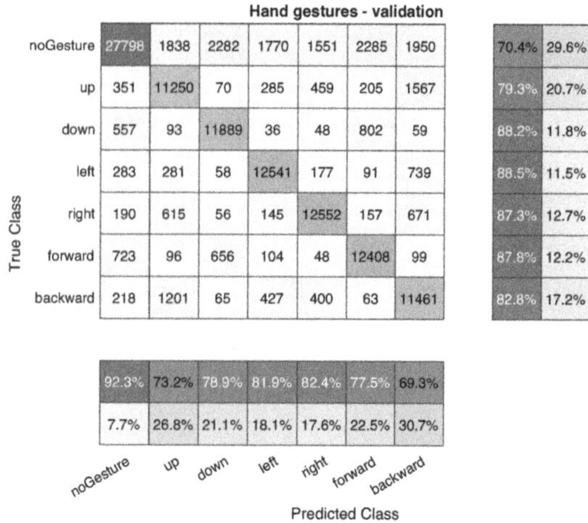

Fig. 9. Confusion matrix for dynamic gesture model over validation samples

the system were sent to an evaluation program unavailable to the developers of the model in order to compute classification and recognition accuracy.

Furthermore, due to the use case for the HGR system, it was necessary to verify the response time of the system. Response time was measured during the classification of input data, which starts with the feature vector computation and finishes with the label sequence and timestamp vector. Figure 10 shows the processing time distribution, where it was found that the mean response time of the HGR system is $29.26 \pm 10.82[ms]$. Hence, the success criterion defined for this system is fulfilled.

On the other hand, during the development of the music video game, a main screen, instructions for using the video game, volume adjustments, and a screen to select the desired song were created. In addition, an environment was developed where the player can see the 3D model of a dancer dancing when the gesture requested by the video game is performed at that moment. Figure 7 shows the navigation diagram resulting from the entire development.

In addition, the visual part of the game was developed mainly with 3D models and objects (dance floor). It should be noted that the menus and texts on each screen are 2D objects that in turn complement the appearance of the video game and provide functionality and feedback when the user performs an action. In Fig. 11 you can see a screenshot of the video game where the 3D model of the dancer is located. The dancer is located on a dance floor and information appears about the song that she/he is going to dance to, the score, and the gesture that is required for the dancer to perform a dance step.

Once the success criteria of both components have been verified, the value proposition was assessed using System Usability Scale (SUS) [30], since the results of this survey can differentiate between usable and unusable systems effectively. It consists of a 10-item questionnaire with five response options between

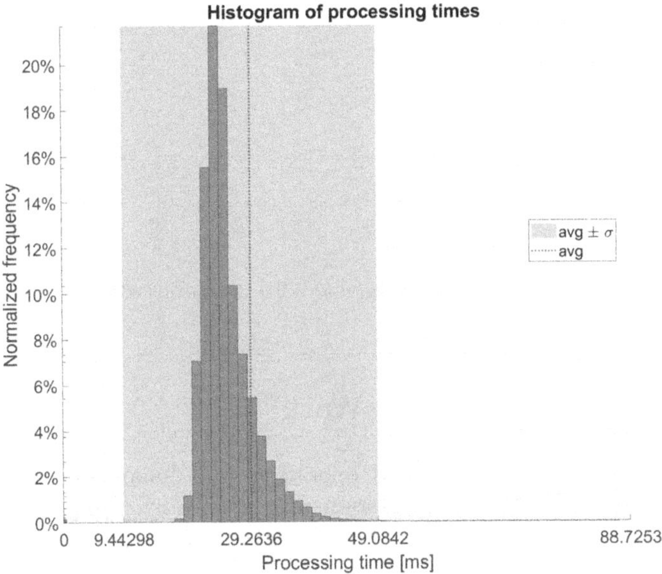

Fig. 10. Histogram of signal processing times of the developed HGR system

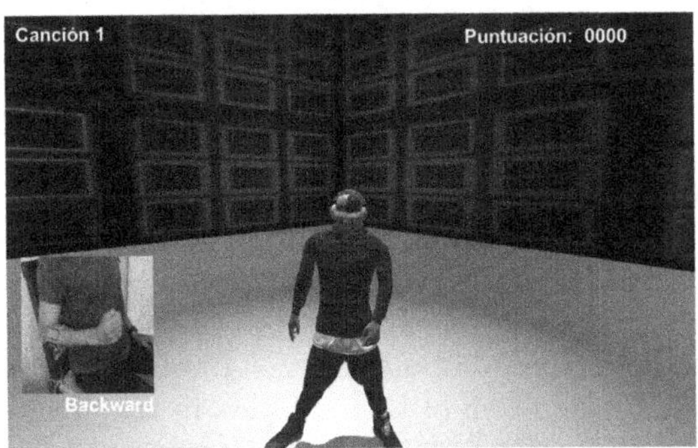

Fig. 11. Video game screen

strongly agree to strongly disagree. The questionnaire was applied to 5 men and 5 women after using the video game for 2 and a half minutes. Then, the SUS score was computed and interpreted for each respondent using grade scales proposed in [31]. The adjective and grade scales are shown in Fig. 12.

The results show that 6 of 10 participants gave a grade greater than or equal to B. In addition, the application obtained a grade of B with 75 points out of 100. These results show that although for most people the application has a high degree of usability, it is necessary to improve the interaction.

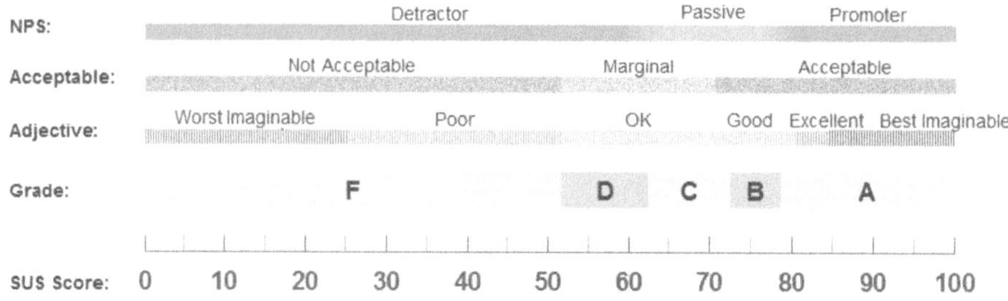

Fig. 12. Grades, adjectives, acceptability, and NPS categories associated with raw SUS scores [31]

4 Conclusions and Future Work

In this paper, the development and operation of a hand gesture recognition system was presented. The HGR system uses electromyography, inertial measurement units, and CNN-LSTM models to classify gestures. The output of this system was used on a video game that uses hand gestures as the main way of interaction.

Different types of evaluation were performed in the HGR system: confusion matrices and classification accuracy. It was proved that the selected architecture for CNN-LSTM allows the system to work in real-time.

The video game was suitable to be used through The hand gesture model. The use of gestures allows the user a more fluid, dynamic, and unconventional interaction with the video game.

It was demonstrated that user experience using the video game was not affected by the response times of the recognition system. Nevertheless, the user experience was affected by HGR classification accuracy. The HGR system evaluation showed that dynamic gestures were misclassified among them. It could be the cause of the SUS score (75 points out of 100) provided by final users.

For future work, the addition of LSTM layers in the architecture should be evaluated to improve the performance of the HGR system. Additionally, a single-model pipeline will be evaluated. It will require changes in the data preparation activities. For the improvement of the video game, the functionality of adding or removing songs, choosing different 3D models of the dancer, and settings such as resolution could be included. In this way, the video game will be better adapted to the different needs of users.

Acknowledgment. The authors gratefully acknowledge the financial support provided by the Escuela Politécnica Nacional (EPN) for the development of the research project "PIGR-22-09 Avances para el desarrollo de un prototipo de prótesis mioeléctrica de mano y control avanzado de su operación usando Inteligencia Artificial".

References

1. Benalcazar, M.E., Motoche, C., Perez, M.: Real-time hand gesture recognition using the Myo armband and muscle activity detection, pp. 1–6, IEEE (2017)
2. Oudah, M., Al-Naji, A., Chahl, J.: Imaging hand gesture recognition based on computer vision: a review of techniques. J. Imaging **6**(8), 73 (2020)
3. Jiménez, L.A.E., Benalcázar, M.E.: Gesture recognition and machine learning applied to sign language. IFMBE Proceedings **60**, 233–236 (2017)
4. Lamberti, L., Camastra, F.: Handy: a real-time three color glove-based gesture recognizer with learning vector quantization. Expert Syst. Appl. **39**, 10489–10494 (2012)
5. Mantecón, T., del-Blanco, C.R., Jaureguizar, F., García, N.: Hand gesture recognition using infrared imagery provided by leap motion controller. In: Blanc-Talon, J., Distante, C., Philips, W., Popescu, D., Scheunders, P. (eds.) ACIVS 2016. LNCS, vol. 10016, pp. 47–57. Springer, Cham (2016). https://doi.org/10.1007/978-3-319-48680-2_5
6. Lu, W. Tong, Z., Chu, J.: Dynamic hand gesture recognition with leap motion controller. IEEE Signal Process. Lett. **23**, 1188–1192 (2016)
7. Moschetti, A., Fiorini, L., Esposito, D., Dario, P., Cavallo, F.: Recognition of daily gestures with wearable inertial rings and bracelets. Sensors (Basel, Switzerland), **16**, 8 (2016)
8. Geng, W., Du, Y., Jin, W., Wei, W., Hu, Y., Li, J.: Gesture recognition by instantaneous surface EMG images open. Sci. Rep. **6**, 36571, (2016). https://doi.org/10.1038/srep36571
9. Huang, Y., et al.: Preliminary testing of a hand gesture recognition wristband based on EMG and inertial sensor fusion. In: Liu, H., Kubota, N., Zhu, X., Dillmann, R., Zhou, D. (eds.) ICIRA 2015. LNCS (LNAI), vol. 9244, pp. 359–367. Springer, Cham (2015). https://doi.org/10.1007/978-3-319-22879-2_33
10. Georgi, M., Amma, C., Schultz, T.: Recognizing hand and finger gestures with IMU based motion and EMG based muscle activity sensing (2015)
11. Chen, X., Zhang, X., Zhao, Z.Y., Yang, J.H., Lantz, V., Wang, K.Q.: Hand gesture recognition research based on surface EMG sensors and 2D-accelerometers. In: Proceedings - International Symposium on Wearable Computers, pp. 11–14 (2007)
12. Wolf, M., et al.: Decoding static and dynamic arm and hand gestures from the JPL BioSleeve. In: IEEE Aerospace Conference Proceedings (2013)
13. Algorithmia: 2020 state of enterprise machine learning
14. Sculley, D., et al.: Hidden technical debt in machine learning systems (2015)
15. Studer, S., et al.: Towards CRISP-ML(Q): a machine learning process model with quality assurance methodology (2020)
16. Zea, J., Benalcázar, M.E., López, L.I.B.: An open-source data acquisition and manual segmentation system for hand gesture recognition based on EMG. In: ETCM 2021–5th Ecuador Technical Chapters Meeting (2021)
17. Benalcázar, M.E., Jaramillo, A.G., Zea, J.A., Paéz, A., Andaluz, V.: Hand gesture recognition using machine learning and the Myo armband. In: 25th European Signal Processing Conference, EUSIPCO, pp. 1040–1044 (2017)
18. Bernhardt, P.: How i learned to stop worrying and love quaternions (2015)
19. Artificial Intelligence and Computer Vision Research Lab: EMG-IMU-EPN-100+. https://laboratorio-ia.epn.edu.ec/en/resources/dataset/emg-imu-epn-100. Accessed 01 Sept 2023

20. López, L.I.B., Caraguay, A.L.V., Vóscornez, J.P., Benalcázar, M.E.: An energy-based method for orientation correction of EMG bracelet sensors in hand gesture recognition systems. Sensors **20**, 6327 (2020)
21. Reaz, M., Mohd-Yasin, F.: Techniques of EMG signal analysis: detection, processing, classification and applications. Biol. Proced. **8**, 11 (2006)
22. Sironi, E., Wermter, S.: An analysis of convolutional long short-term memory recurrent neural networks. Neurocomputing **268**, 76–86 (2017)
23. Szegedy, C., et al.: Going deeper with convolutions. In: Proceedings of the IEEE Conference on Computer Vision and Pattern Recognition (CVPR), pp. 1–9 (2015)
24. Ripalda, F.M.F.: Desarrollo de un modelo de reconocimiento de gestos de la mano utilizando señales EMG y Deep Learning (2021)
25. Tomaszewski, M.: Myo SDK MATLAB MEX wrapper (2022)
26. Nuñez, H.G.R.: Videojuego educativo en 3d para dispositivos móviles android, enfocado al aprendizaje de la lógica de programación para usuarios entre los 5 a 18 años de eda (2017)
27. Rojas, H.D.L.: Implementación de un juego serio multiplataforma para el desarrollo de la orientación espacial en niños de 6 a 8 añ0 (2017)
28. N. Acerenza, et al.: Una metodología para desarrollo de videojuegos: versión extendida (2009)
29. Pabon, F.M.P.: Diseño y desarrollo de un video juego educativo con agentes inteligentes aplicando la metodología sum. caso de estudio: TIC-TAC-TOE (2015)
30. Brooke, J.: Sus: a quick and dirty usability scale. Usability Eval. Ind. **189**, 11 (1995)
31. Sauro, J.: 5 ways to interpret a Sus score - measuringu (2018)

Multiresolution Controller Based on Window Function Networks for a Quanser Helicopter

Oscar Federico Garcia-Castro[1(✉)], Luis Enrique Ramos-Velasco[1], Rodolfo Garcia-Rodriguez[1], Mario A. Vega-Navarrete[1], and Enrique Escamilla-Hernández[2]

[1] Postgraduate Program of Aerospace Engineering, Metropolitan Polytechnic University of Hidalgo, Tolcayuca, Mexico
{213220003,lramos,rogarcia,mvega}@upmh.edu.mx

[2] ESIME Culhuacan, National Polytechnic Institute, Mexico City, Mexico
eescamillah@ipn.mx

Abstract. To improve neural network (NN) performance, new activation functions, such as ReLU, GELU, and SELU, to name a few, have been proposed. Windows-based functions, such as flat-top or atomic functions, used in processing signals have begun to be used in NNs for dynamical systems. Although wavelet functions are the most popular, some additional functions with similar properties must be evaluated. This paper presents a window function neural network (WFNN) for identification tasks. Using the identification by WFNN, the self-tuning gains of the proportional multi-resolution (PMR) controller are carried out. To show the performance of the proposed approach for different window functions, numerical simulations of the Quanser helicopter of 2 degrees of freedom are presented.

Keywords: Multiresolution analysis · Intelligent control · Window function · Quanser helicopter · Neural network

1 Introduction

The activation functions for artificial neural networks (ANNs) are relevant because they add non-linearity to the output ANN, which helps to learn powerful operations. The new activation functions, such as rectified linear unit (ReLU) and scaled exponential linear unit (SELU), have been used recently in convolutional ANNs to solve some drawbacks in deep learning, e.g., the vanishing gradient or velocity to traditional activation functions. However, activation functions applied in intelligent control to dynamical systems remain using traditional sigmoid or hyperbolic tangent [2,4].

An ANN used in the approximation of a dynamical system is the radial basis function (RBF) network, where the typical activation function is the Gaussian

H. Calvo et al. (Eds.): MICAI 2023, LNAI 14391, pp. 53–64, 2024.
https://doi.org/10.1007/978-3-031-47765-2_4

function; however, as an alternative, the called wavelets have been used, well-known as WaveNets [19]. In recent years, new functions used in digital signal processing have been used as activation functions, for example, atomic functions [6]. But many others with similar properties need study and evaluation performance in dynamical systems, such as window functions (WFs). WFs are characterized by having a main lobe on either side of the origin and side lobes on either side. Additionally, WFs allow for the transformation from the time domain to the frequency domain.

In this paper, it proposes to use WFs as activation functions of the RBF-ANN. This paper proposes the use of WFs as activation functions of the RBF-ANN. In particular, it used cosine sum windows (CSWs) as an activation function, characterized by good frequency resolution, low peak sidelobe ratio, and excellent sidelobe decay. CSWs comprise a constant term and a cosine function [17]. Among the most popular functions are Hamming, Hann, Kaiser, Gaussian, and Chebyshev. This paper applies an ANN using CSWs for identification tasks. Also, a multiresolution analysis (MRA) based on wavelet theory is proposed to control a dynamical system. MRA decomposes and represents a signal at its different frequency levels [16]. Although some approaches using MRA have been reported in automatic control [1,9,11,18] and robotics field [3,10]; few of them use CSWs. To design the controller, the MRA decomposes the tracking error signal, and its respective gain scales the generated components, which are then added together to generate the control signal. Therefore, the MRA provides a much higher resolution than a traditional proportional-integral-derivative (PID) controller [12]. This controller is called a proportional multiresolution (PMR).

Thus, in this paper, an intelligent controller is based on two principal components: *a)* an identification scheme based on WFNN adding a layer of infinite impulse response (IIR) filters and *b)* a PMR controller using self-tuning of the feedback gains. Under several conditions, simulation results are presented of the proposed approach on a Quanser helicopter of two degrees of freedom. To the authors' knowledge, this is the first time CSWs have been used as an activation function of the RBF-ANN for identification tasks. The remainder of the paper is organized as follows. Section 2 presents the PMR controller scheme, including WFNN-IIR, and the simulation results are provided in Sect. 3. Finally, Sect. 4 makes concluding remarks.

2 Application of the Control Scheme to the Helicopter Model

Let the continuous state-space form of the non-linear model of the 2-Degrees of Freedom, DoF, Quanser helicopter model given by, [5,15]

$$\dot{\mathbf{x}}(t) = \mathbf{f}(\mathbf{x}(t)) + \mathbf{g}(\mathbf{x}(t))\mathbf{u}(t), \quad \mathbf{y}(t) = \mathbf{C}\mathbf{x}(t) \tag{1}$$

where $\mathbf{x}(t) := \begin{bmatrix} x_1 \; x_2 \; x_3 \; x_4 \end{bmatrix}^\top \equiv \begin{bmatrix} \theta(t) \; \phi(t) \; \dot{\theta}(t) \; \dot{\phi}(t) \end{bmatrix}^\top$ is the vector state with θ and ϕ the pitch and yaw angular positions, respectively, $\mathbf{u}(t) = \begin{bmatrix} u_1(t) \; u_2(t) \end{bmatrix}^\top$

the vector control, and $\mathbf{y}(t) = \left[x_1(t)\ x_2(t)\right]^\top$ the output system. Finally, the vector field $\mathbf{f}(\mathbf{x}(t))$, and the matrices $\boldsymbol{g}(\mathbf{x}(t))$ and $\boldsymbol{C}$ are given as [7]:

$$\mathbf{f}(\mathbf{x}(t)) = \begin{bmatrix} x_3 \\ x_4 \\ -29.2988\cos x_1 - 9.2602x_3 - 0.5555x_3^2 \sin x_1 \cos x_1 \\ \dfrac{-0.318x_4 + 0.0960x_3x_4 \sin x_1 \cos x_1}{0.0432 + 0.0480\cos x_1} \end{bmatrix}$$
$$\boldsymbol{g}(\mathbf{x}(t)) = \begin{bmatrix} 0 & 0 \\ 0 & 0 \\ 2.3613 & 0.8334 \\ \dfrac{0.0086}{0.0432 + 0.048\cos x_1} & \dfrac{0.0068}{0.0432 + 0.048\cos x_1} \end{bmatrix}, \quad \boldsymbol{C} = \begin{bmatrix} 1\,0\,0\,0 \\ 0\,1\,0\,0 \end{bmatrix}. \tag{2}$$

Now, assuming measurements at a constant sampling period $T = 5$ ms, a discrete state-space form of the nonlinear model can be obtained. That is, based on the method of first-order Euler approximation where $\dot{\mathbf{x}} \approx (\mathbf{x}(t+T) - \mathbf{x}(t))/T$ and evaluating at time $t = kT$, (1) is rewritten as

$$\mathbf{x}((k+1)T) = \mathbf{x}(kT) + T\Big(\mathbf{f}\big(\mathbf{x}(kT)\big) + \mathbf{g}\big(\mathbf{x}(kT)\big)\mathbf{u}(kT)\Big), \quad \mathbf{y}((k+1)T) = \mathbf{C}\mathbf{x}((k+1)T) \tag{3}$$

while the input-output representation with $k \equiv kT \Rightarrow k+1 = T(k+1)$ is given as

$$\mathbf{y}(k+1) = \underbrace{\mathbf{C}\Big(\mathbf{x}(k) + T\mathbf{f}\big(\mathbf{x}(k)\big)\Big)}_{\Upsilon(k)} + \underbrace{\mathbf{C}T\mathbf{g}\big(\mathbf{x}(k)\big)}_{\Gamma(k)}\mathbf{u}(k) \tag{4}$$

where $k \geq 0 \in \mathbb{Z}$. Notice that (4) is used only for analysis and numerical simulation purposes because it is assumed that $\Upsilon(k)$ and $\Gamma(k)$ are unknown, and a WFNN-IIR approximates these. Additionally, the controller design is based on MRA. The idea behind MRA is to adapt a signal to the needs of a particular application [16]. For this, a successive approximation to the signal is made by decomposing it into $N+1$ signals by wavelet transforms and immediately rebuilding it where N represents the resolution level; see Fig. 1.

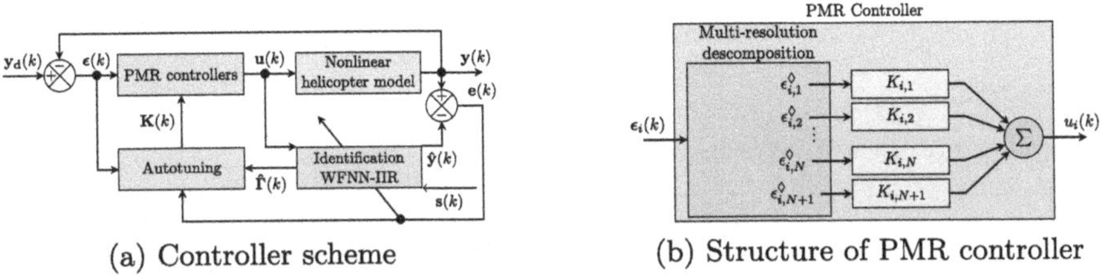

(a) Controller scheme

(b) Structure of PMR controller

Fig. 1. Block diagram of the multi-resolution control scheme and the structure of PMR controller used for the helicopter model.

2.1 Dynamic Identification

The helicopter input-output dynamics (4) is approximated by WFNN-IIR, as seen in Fig. 2 where the NN has two inputs and two outputs with $J \in \mathbb{R}^+$ neurons. A WFNN has the same topology as an RBF-NN. Thus, a WFNN-IIR consists of four layers: input, hidden, output, and filtered.

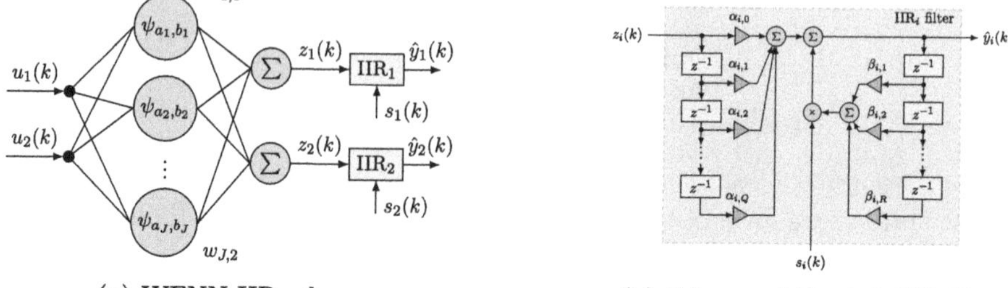

(a) WFNN-IIR scheme

(b) Scheme of the i-th IIR filter

Fig. 2. Schemes of the WFNN-IIR and the IIR filter.

Table 1. Coefficients of the window functions [14].

WF	η_0	η_1	η_2	η_3	η_4	η_5	H
EFT1	0.13996936	0.27964655	0.26715302	0.20212094	0.09288944	0.01824432	6
EFT2	0.18810150	0.36923120	0.28701879	0.13076879	0.02487969	0	5
EFT3	0.20142488	0.39291808	0.28504554	0.10708192	0.01352957	0	5
EFT4	0.20978545	0.40753007	0.28117922	0.09247573	0.00904112	0	5
EFT5	0.21375736	0.41424355	0.27860627	0.08592806	0.00746476	0	6
Blackman	0.42	0.5	0.08	0	0	0	3
Blackman-Harris	0.35875	0.48829	0.14128	0.01168	0	0	4
Hanning	0.5	0.5	0	0	0	0	2
Hamming	0.54	0.46	0	0	0	0	2

Furthermore, the CSWs have the form [13, ch. 3]

$$C_{\mathrm{sw}}[\lambda] := \sum_{h=0}^{H}(-1)^h \eta_h \cos\left(\frac{2\pi h\lambda}{\Lambda}\right), \quad 0 \le \lambda \le \Lambda \tag{5}$$

where $\Lambda \in \mathbb{Z}^+$ represents the window length, H indicates the number of coefficient and η is the signal amplitude. In Table 1 the coefficients of the windows functions used in this paper are shown, where the coefficients should be normalized, that is, $\sum_{h=0}^{H} \eta_h = 1$ as in [14].

To use a WF in the proposed identification scheme, (5) is rewritten for the j-th neuron as

$$\psi_j := \psi_{a_j,b_j}(k) = \sum_{h=0}^{H} \eta_h \cos\big(Gj\tau^*(k,\tilde{u},a_j,b_j)\big) \tag{6}$$

where $\{a_j \neq 0,\ b_j\} \in \mathbb{R}$ are the scaling and shifting parameters, while $\tilde{u}(k) = u_1(k) + u_2(k)$ is a scalar, $\tau^*(k,\tilde{u},a_j,b_j) := \big\|\tilde{u} - b_j\big\| \cdot (1/a_j)$ and G is a constant equals to 3/16, [14]. In this way, the output $\mathbf{z}(k)$ of WFNN is calculated as follows:

$$\mathbf{z}(k) = \begin{bmatrix} z_1(k) \\ z_2(k) \end{bmatrix} \equiv \sum_{j=1}^{J} \psi_{a_j,b_j}(k) \cdot w_{i,j}(k): \quad i = \{1,2\} \tag{7}$$

where $w_{i,j}(k) \in \mathbb{R}$ represents the synaptic weight. Finally, the output $\hat{\mathbf{y}}(k)$ of IIR filters is evaluated,

$$\hat{\mathbf{y}}(k) = \begin{bmatrix} \hat{y}_1(k) \\ \hat{y}_2(k) \end{bmatrix} \equiv \underbrace{\sum_{q=0}^{Q} \alpha_{i,q}(k) \cdot z_i(k-q)}_{\hat{\Upsilon}_i(k)} + s_i(k) \underbrace{\sum_{r=1}^{R} \beta_{i,r}(k) \cdot \hat{y}_i(k-r)}_{\hat{\Gamma}_i(k)}; \quad i = \{1,2\} \tag{8}$$

where $s_i \in \mathbb{R}$ is the persistent signal, the feedback and feed-forward coefficients of the IIR filter are given by $\{\alpha_{i,q},\ \beta_{i,r}\} \in \mathbb{R}$, and $\{Q \geq 0,\ R > 0\} \in \mathbb{Z}$ indicate the number of coefficients used.

To train the WFNN-IIR is used the back-propagation algorithm where the identification error is defined as

$$\mathbf{e}(k) = \big[e_1(k)\ e_2(k)\big]^\top \equiv \mathbf{y}(k) - \hat{\mathbf{y}}(k). \tag{9}$$

To generate the adaptation laws of the WFNN-IIR, a method of the descent of gradient is used, $\nabla C_\gamma(k)$, where γ refers to the parameters of the WFNN-IIR and $C(k)$ the cost function defined as

$$C(k) := \frac{1}{2}\sum_{i=1}^{2} e_i^2(k) \tag{10}$$

Thus, the adaptation law for each parameter is defined as, [8]

$$\gamma(k+1) = \gamma(k) + \mu_\gamma \nabla C_\gamma(k) \tag{11}$$

where

$$\nabla C_{w_{i,j}}(k) = -\tilde{u}(k)\bar{e}(k) \sum_{q=0}^{Q} \alpha_{i,q}(k) \cdot \psi_j(k-q) \tag{12}$$

$$\nabla C_{b_j}(k) = -\tilde{u}(k)\bar{e}(k) \sum_{r=1}^{R} \beta_{i,r}(k) \cdot \frac{\partial \psi_j(k-r)}{\partial b_j} \tag{13}$$

$$\nabla C_{a_j}(k) = \nabla C_{b_j}(k) \cdot \tau^*(k,\tilde{u},a_j,b_j) \tag{14}$$

$$\nabla C_{\alpha_{i,q}}(k) = -\tilde{u}(k)\bar{e}(k) \cdot z_i(k-q) \tag{15}$$

$$\nabla C_{\beta_{i,r}}(k) = -\tilde{u}(k)\bar{e}(k) \cdot \hat{y}_i(k-r) \tag{16}$$

with $\bar{e}(k) = e_1(k) + e_2(k)$ and $\mu_\gamma \geq 0 \in \mathbb{R}$ the learning rate for the parameter γ.

2.2 Proportional Multi-resolution Controller

MRA is characterized because it gives a high scale–low frequency, a low scale–high frequency, and $N-1$ medium scale elements–medium frequency, [12]. Thus, to implement a PMR controller, it is necessary first to define the i-th tracking error $\epsilon_i(k)$ given by

$$\epsilon_i(k) := y_{d_i}(k) - y_i(k) \tag{17}$$

where $y_{d_i}(k)$ and $y_i(k)$ is the desired and real positions of the helicopter model, and the tracking error $\epsilon_i(k)$ has been stored in a tracking vector $\boldsymbol{\epsilon}_i(k)$. Thus, the PMR controller uses the MRA through wavelet theory to obtain the representation of $\boldsymbol{\epsilon}_i(k)$ as [12]

$$\boldsymbol{\epsilon}_i(k) = \underbrace{\sum_{\ell=-\infty}^{\infty} c_{N,\ell} \cdot \varphi_{N,\ell}(k)}_{\substack{\text{high scale–low frecuency}\\ \text{term}\\ \epsilon^{\diamond}_{i,1}(k)}} + \underbrace{\sum_{\imath=1}^{N-1} \sum_{\ell=-\infty}^{\infty} d_{\imath,\ell} \cdot \psi_{\imath,\ell}(k)}_{\substack{\text{medium scale–medium frequency}\\ \text{terms}\\ \epsilon^{\diamond}_{i,2}(k),\ \dots,\ \epsilon^{\diamond}_{i,N}(k)}} + \underbrace{\sum_{\ell=-\infty}^{\infty} d_{N,\ell} \cdot \varphi_{N,\ell}(k)}_{\substack{\text{low scale–high frequency}\\ \text{term}\\ \epsilon^{\diamond}_{i,N+1}(k)}} \tag{18}$$

where $\psi(k)$ and $\varphi(k)$ are the wavelet function and its scaling function, respectively; with c and d the approximation and detail coefficients, computed as [12]

$$c_{\imath,\ell} = \sum_{\ell=-\infty}^{\infty} \boldsymbol{\epsilon}_i(k)\overline{\varphi_{\imath,\ell}(k)} \quad \text{and} \quad d_{\imath,\ell} = \sum_{\ell=-\infty}^{\infty} \boldsymbol{\epsilon}_i(k)\overline{\psi_{\imath,\ell}(k)} \tag{19}$$

being $\overline{\varphi_{\imath,\ell}(k)}$ and $\overline{\psi_{\imath,\ell}(k)}$ the conjugate functions corresponding to $\varphi(k)$ and $\psi(k)$, respectively. See Fig. 1b.

Thus, the elements of the signal $\boldsymbol{\epsilon}_i(k)$ are weighted by a proportional gain $K_{i,n}(k)$ and added to obtain the i-th control signal,

$$\mathbf{u}(k) = \begin{bmatrix} u_1(k) \\ u_2(k) \end{bmatrix} \equiv \sum_{n=1}^{N+1} K_{i,n}(k) \cdot \epsilon^{\diamond}_{i,n}(k) : \quad i = \{1, 2\} \tag{20}$$

and the gains of the controller PMR are given by

$$\mathbf{K} = \begin{bmatrix} \mathbf{K}_1(k) \\ \mathbf{K}_2(k) \end{bmatrix} = \begin{bmatrix} K_{1,1}\ K_{1,2} \dots K_{1,N}\ K_{1,N+1} \\ K_{2,1}\ K_{2,2} \dots K_{2,N}\ K_{2,N+1} \end{bmatrix}. \tag{21}$$

2.3 Autotune of the Gains

To autotune the feedback gains, the parameter $\hat{\Gamma}_i(k)$ of the WFNN-IIR is used, representing the signal that gives information about the identification process together $e(k)$. Thus, the update control signals are defined as [15]:

$$K_{i,n}(k+1) = K_{i,n}(k) - \mu_{K_{i,n}} \hat{\Gamma}_i(k) \left(\epsilon^{\diamond}_{i,N+1}(k) - \epsilon^{\diamond}_{i,N}(k) \right) \tag{22}$$

where $\mu_{K_{i,n}} \in \mathbb{R}$ is the update rate.

3 Results

The PMR controller with a WFNN-IIR was developed using MATLAB R2021a, and the goal of simulations is that the angular positions of helicopter follows the desired trajectories. Initially, there are two sets of simulations in the open loop:

(a) The first uses a third-order polynomial function to define the desired trajectories, which helps adjust the WFNN-IIR initial values.
(b) The second applied a step function for the desired trajectories and is used to demand WFNN-IIR in the identification process.

The closed-loop tests are also performed to set up the initial conditions of the PMR controller and thus check its robustness.

3.1 Open-Loop Simulation Results: Identification Process

Using a pre-training of the WFNN-IIR, not only the parameter values were found as $J = 6$, $P = 2$, $Q = 4$, and $R = 2$ but also its initial values, see Table 2. From these values of WFNN-IIR and from both polynomial and step functions, each function from the Table 1 was tested by evaluating its accuracy by the determination coefficient[1] R^2 and the results obtained are shown in Fig. 3. Similarly, the root mean square error (RMSE) is obtained on each axis and the average is calculated. The results are given in Table 3. Finally, Fig. 4 indicates the identification errors for each case.

Table 2. Initial values of the WFNN-IIR parameters.

Parameter	Symbol	Initial value	Learning rate
Scaling	$\mathbf{a}$	$\{a_j = 1 : 1 \leq j \leq J\}$	10^{-5}
Shifting	$\mathbf{b}$	$\{b_j = j : 1 \leq j \leq J\}$	10^{-10}
Synaptic weights	$\mathbf{W}$	$\mathrm{random}(\pm 0.001, P, J)$	5×10^{-7}
Feedback coefficients	$\boldsymbol{\alpha}$	$\mathrm{random}(\pm 0.5, P, Q+1)$	5×10^{-1}
Feedforward coefficients	$\boldsymbol{\beta}$	$\mathrm{random}(\pm 0.5, P, R)$	5×10^{-3}
Persistent signal	s	100	–

(a) Polynomial Signals. As seen in Fig. 3a, all the WF had a "very high" correlation level (between 0.9 and 0.99), especially for the yaw axis. Additionally, the Hamming WF has the best performance according to RMSE. Figure 4a shows that each identification error $\mathbf{e}(k)$ converges to zero.

[1] Determination coefficient is defined as $R^2 = 1 - \mathrm{RSS}/\mathrm{TSS}$ where the $\mathrm{RSS} = \sum(y_{d_i} - \hat{y}_i)^2$ is the residual sum of squares, the $\mathrm{TSS} = \sum(y_{d_i} - \bar{y}_i)^2$ is the total sum of squares, and $\bar{y}_i$ is the average of desired positions for each axis [8].

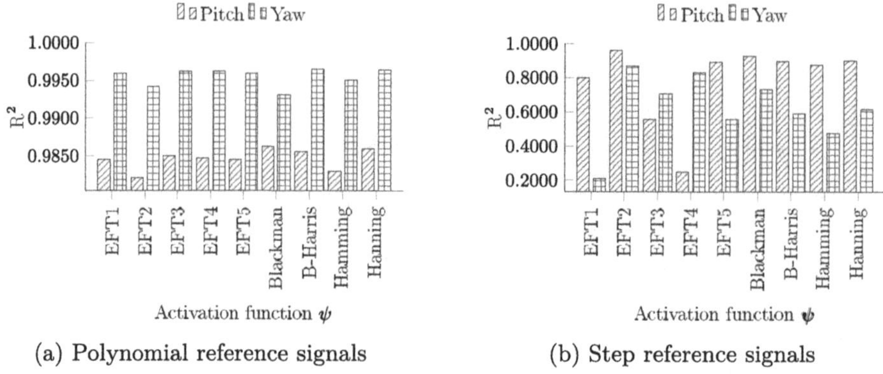

(a) Polynomial reference signals

(b) Step reference signals

Fig. 3. R^2 for the identification error of the dynamic model.

Table 3. RMSE for the identification of plant dynamics.

Polynomial reference signals

Function	$RMSE_1$	$RMSE_2$	$RMSE_{avg}$
Blackman	2.6406	1.3437	1.9922
Blackman-Harris	2.7081	0.9470	1.8275
EFT1	2.8094	1.0242	1.9168
EFT2	3.0156	1.2291	2.1223
EFT3	2.7583	0.9920	1.8751
EFT4	2.7893	0.9896	1.8894
EFT5	2.8080	1.0309	1.9195
Hamming	2.9463	1.1334	2.0398
Hanning	2.6737	0.9697	1.8217

Step reference signals

Function	$RMSE_1$	$RMSE_2$	$RMSE_{avg}$
Blackman	1.4577	1.3319	1.3948
Blackman-Harris	1.7383	1.6549	1.6966
EFT1	2.4387	2.2920	2.3653
EFT2	1.0501	0.9413	0.9957
EFT3	3.6461	1.3989	2.5225
EFT4	4.7451	1.0674	2.9063
EFT5	1.7941	1.7168	1.7554
Hanning	1.7132	1.5998	1.6565
Hamming	1.9295	1.8725	1.9010

(a) Polynomial reference signals using Hanning function

(b) Step reference signals using EFT2 function

Fig. 4. Identification errors of the dynamics in open-loop.

(b) Step Signals. Similarly, Fig. 3b shows that some WFs have a "high" correlation level (greater than 0.7), although, in others, the level is "low" (less than

0.2). According to the RMSE obtained, the function with the best performance was EFT2. Also, in Fig. 4b, the identification errors $\mathbf{e}(k)$ converge to zero and present peaks for the discontinuities in the reference signals.

In the following subsection, the functions Hamming and EFT2 will be used as activation functions in the control scheme.

3.2 Closed-Loop Simulation Results

A decomposition level is given as $N = 5$ and the wavelet function $\psi(k)$ for simulations. In this case, the wavelet function used was the Daubechies 2 tap (bd2). The initial gain values used were $\mathbf{K}_1(0) = \left[100\ 100\ 75\ 0\ 0\ 0\right]^\top$ and $\mathbf{K}_2(0) = \left[300\ 100\ 75\ 0\ 0\ 0\right]^\top$ for each axis with an update rate $\mu_{K_{i,n}}$ equal to 10^{-3}.

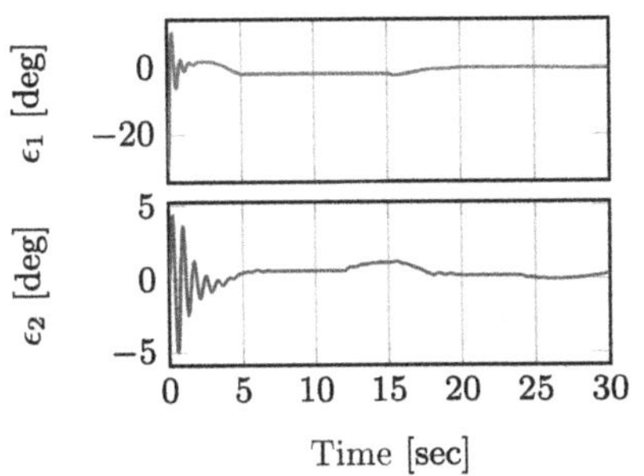

(a) Polynomial reference signals, using Hanning function

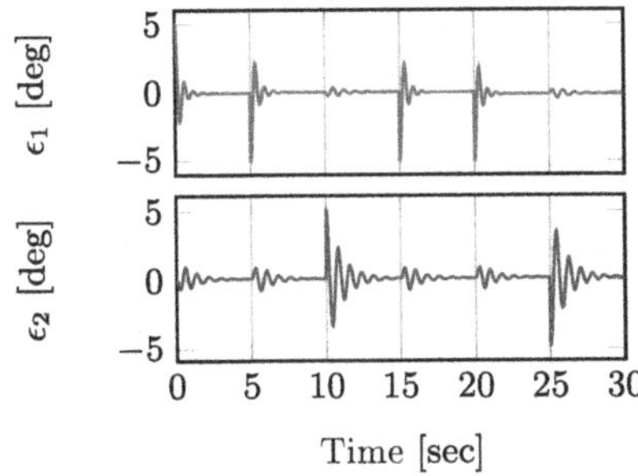

(b) Step reference signals, using EFT2 function

Fig. 5. Tracking errors in closed-loop.

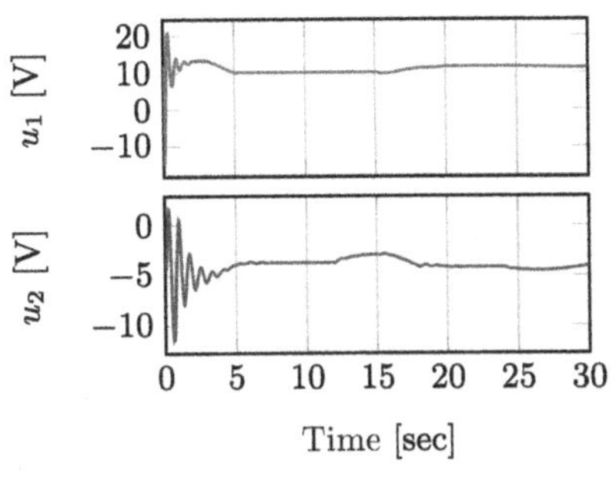

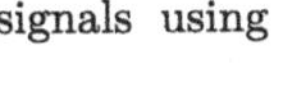

(a) Polynomial reference signals using Hanning function

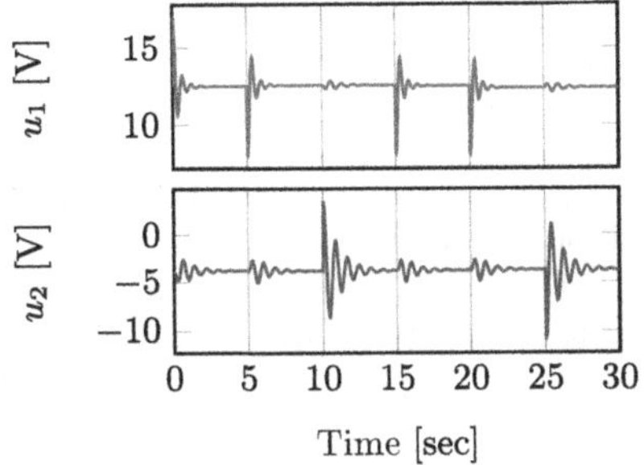

(b) Step reference signals using EFT2 function

Fig. 6. Control signals in closed-loop.

(a) Polynomial Reference Signals. As seen in Fig. 5a, the tracking error converges to zero in the two helicopter axes. Furthermore, the control signal is shown in Fig. 6a. It has a soft behavior, in addition to keeping within the physical parameters of each engine [7]: ±24 V for the pitch motor and ±15 V for the yaw motor.

(b) Step Reference Signals. Similarly, the tracking error converges quickly to zero in the two axes as shown in Fig. 5b, but they have peaks for the discontinuation of the reference signal. Furthermore, the control signal in Fig. 6b has a constant signal, which changes for such discontinuities but maintains the voltages accepted by the engines.

3.3 Comparative Between PMR and PID Controllers

Now is presented a comparative tracking performance between an adaptive PID controller, [5], and the proposed PMR controller.

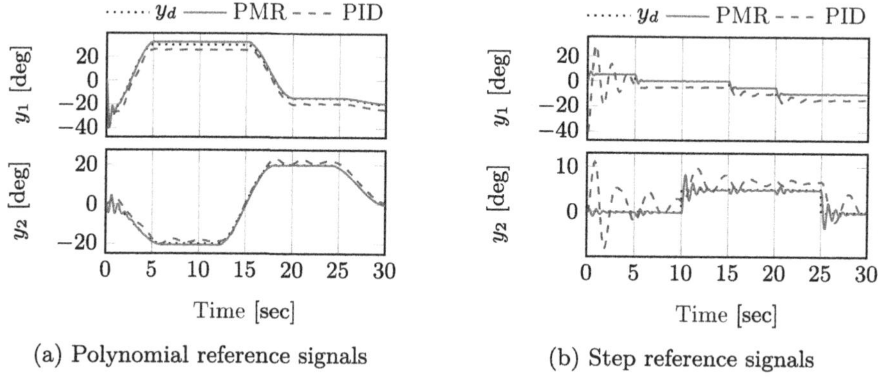

(a) Polynomial reference signals

(b) Step reference signals

Fig. 7. System response with PID and PMR controllers.

(a) Polynomial Reference Signals. Figure 7a shows how the adaptive PID controller does not converge to the desired position on both axes of movement, while the PMR does. Although Fig. 8a shows that the PID and PMR control signals have similar behavior. However, the PMR signal shows a swing in the first five seconds of operation.

(b) Step Reference Signals. The Figs. 7b and 8b indicate that the adaptive PID controller cannot reach the desired position and the control signal it generates exceeds the engine voltages, to compensate for the discontinuity of the reference signal. On the other hand, the PMR controller performs the task satisfactorily.

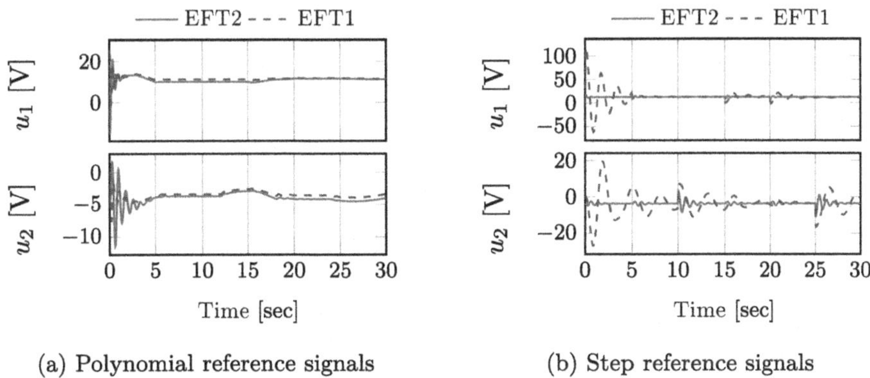

(a) Polynomial reference signals

(b) Step reference signals

Fig. 8. Comparision of control signals between an adaptive PID and the PMR control schemes.

4 Conclusions and Future Work

According to the results obtained, the performance of the identification algorithm depends on the reference signal used in the simulation cases. Due to the compact support of the WFs, the Hanning WF showed the best results for polynomial reference signals, while for step reference signals, the EFT2 was the best option. Besides, the relationship between the WFNN-IIR and the kind of controllers, just like its self-tuning rule, determines the performance of the control scheme.

Therefore, it is concluded that adaptive PMR controllers improved their performance compared to adaptive PID controllers because the PMR controller can use two or more gains. In comparison, the PID scheme can only use three gains. Additionally, the MRA allows for studying system signals at various frequency levels and reducing a specific frequency that instability the system.

Finally, the adaptable PMR controller will be implemented for future work to validate the simulation results obtained.

Acknowledgments. This work was partially supported by the Consejo Nacional de Humanidades Ciencia y Tecnología (CONAHCYT) under reference number 1148156.

References

1. Bernard, C.P., Slotine, J.E.: Adaptive control with multiresolution bases. In: Proceedings of the 36th IEEE Conference on Decision and Control, San Diego, CA, USA, 1997, vol. 4, pp. 3884–3889 (1997). https://doi.org/10.1109/CDC.1997.652468
2. Chen, S., Billings, S.A.: Neural networks for nonlinear dynamic system modelling and identification. Int. J. Control **56**(2), 319–346 (1992). https://doi.org/10.1080/00207179208934317

3. Díaz López, F.A., Ramos Velasco, L.E., Domínguez Ramírez, O.A., Parra Vega, V.: Multiresolution wavenet PID control for global regulation of robots. In: 9th Asian Control Conference (ASCC 2013), 23–26 June 2013, Istanbul, Turkey, pp. 1–6. IEEE (2013). https://doi.org/10.1109/ASCC.2013.6606328
4. Feng, J., Lu, S.: Performance analysis of various activation functions in artificial neural networks. J. Phys. Conf. Ser. **1237**(2), 022030 (2019). https://doi.org/10.1088/1742-6596/1237/2/022030
5. Garcia-Castro, O.F., et al.: RBF neural network based on FT-windows for autotunning PID controller. In: Advances in Computational Intelligence, pp. 138–149. Springer Nature, Switzerland (2022). https://doi.org/10.1007/978-3-031-19493-1_11
6. Hernandez-Matamoros, A., Hujita, H., Escamilla-Hernandez, E., Perez-Meana, H., Nakano-Miyatake, M.: Recognition of ECG signals using wavelet based on atomic functions. Elsevier BV **40**(2), 803–814 (2020). https://doi.org/10.1016/j.bbe.2020.02.007
7. Inc., Q.: User manual 2 DOF helicopter experiment, set up and configuration. Markham, Ontario (2012)
8. James, G., Witten, D., Hastie, T., Tibshirani, R.: An Introduction to Statistical Learning. STS, vol. 103. Springer, New York (2013). https://doi.org/10.1007/978-1-4614-7138-7
9. Jeevan, L.G., Malik, V.: A wavelet based multiresolution controller. J. Emerg. Trends Comput. Inf. Sci. **2**(Special Issue), 17–21 (2010)
10. Lindemann, S.R., LaValle, S.M.: Multiresolution approach for motion planning under differential constraints. In: Proceedings 2006 IEEE International Conference on Robotics and Automation, 2006. ICRA 2006, Orlando, FL, USA, pp. 139–144 (2006). https://doi.org/10.1109/ROBOT.2006.1641174
11. Nejadpak, A., Mohamed, A., Mohammed, O.A.: A wavelet based multi-resolution controller for sensorless position control of PM synchronous motors at low speed. In: 2011 IEEE International Electric Machines & Drives Conference (IEMDC). IEEE (2011). https://doi.org/10.1109/iemdc.2011.5994913
12. Parvez, S., Gao, Z.: A wavelet-based multiresolution PID controller. IEEE Trans. Ind. Appl. **41**(2), 537–543 (2005). https://doi.org/10.1109/TIA.2005.844378
13. Prabhu, K.M.M.: Window Functions and Their Applications in Signal Processing. Taylor & Francis Group (2018). https://doi.org/10.1201/9781315216386
14. Reljin, I.S., Reljin, B.D., Papic, V.: Extremely flat-top windows for harmonic analysis. IEEE Trans. Instrum. Meas. **56**(3), 1025–1041 (2007)
15. Vega-Navarrete, M.A., et. al.: Output feedback self-tuning wavenet control for underactuated euler-lagrange systems. IFAC-PapersOnLine **51**(13), 633–638 (2018). https://doi.org/10.1016/j.ifacol.2018.07.351
16. Vetterli, M., Kovačević, J.: Wavelets and Subband Coding. Prentice-hall (1995)
17. Yamaoka, T., Kageme, S.: New class of cosine-sum windows. IEEE Access **11**, 5296–5305 (2023). https://doi.org/10.1109/ACCESS.2023.3236606
18. Zhang, P., Daraz, A., Malik, S.A., Sun, C., Basit, A., Zhang, G.: Multi-resolution based PID controller for frequency regulation of a hybrid power system with multiple interconnected systems. Front. Energy Res. **10** (2023). https://doi.org/10.3389/fenrg.2022.1109063
19. Zhang, Q., Benveniste, A.: Wavelet networks. IEEE Trans. Neural Networks **3**(6), 889–898 (1992). https://doi.org/10.1109/72.165591

Semi-supervised Learning of Non-stationary Acoustic Signals Using Time-Frequency Energy Maps

Esteban Guerra-Bravo[1], Arturo Baltazar[1](✉), and Antonio Balvantín[2]

[1] Robotics and Advanced Manufacturing Program, Cinvestav-Saltillo, Av. Industria Metalurgia #1062, Ramos Arizpe 2500, Coah. Mexico, Mexico
arturo.baltazar@cinvestav.edu.mx

[2] Department of Mechanical Engineering, Universidad de Guanajuato, Salamanca-Valle de Santiago km. 3.5, Salamanca 36886, Gto. Mexico, Mexico

Abstract. Non-stationary signals are time-varying signals that represent various real-world phenomena, such as biomedical signals, vibrating machinery, and acoustic signals, among others. Their accurate classifying is crucial to enhance diagnostic capabilities and predict critical events. A widely used method of characterization is based on time-frequency mapping techniques, which capture both temporal and frequency information. However, this approach introduces redundant information and difficult the extraction of relevant features for accurate classification. This paper presents a robust classification method for non-stationary signals using time-frequency maps focusing on relevant information while minimizing redundancy. The proposed methodology extracts non-stationary features from STFT maps using a background subtraction technique based on singular value decomposition (SVD). Then, principal component analysis (PCA) is implemented for dimensionality reduction, clustering, and classification using vectorized foreground maps. The method was tested using non-stationary ultrasonic signals. The results demonstrate the effectiveness of the proposed method in extracting features from the STFT maps, resulting in a significant separation between clusters of classes. The experimental results highlight the robustness and effectiveness of the method.

Keywords: Non-stationary signals · Unsupervised classification · Short-Time Fourier Transform · Background subtraction · Principal Component Analysis

1 Introduction

Non-stationary signals are time-varying signals commonly encountered in physics, engineering, and nature. Examples include sound signals, vibrating machinery, earthquakes, guided waves, and certain electroencephalogram (EEG) states, among others. Characterization and correlation of the signals with the

H. Calvo et al. (Eds.): MICAI 2023, LNAI 14391, pp. 65–76, 2024.
https://doi.org/10.1007/978-3-031-47765-2_5

propagation properties of the environment become a complex problem for a human operator. The analysis of transient dispersive signals has been proposed using a time-frequency representation. This is especially relevant for application in dispersive signals with multi-vibrational modes. Our focused application in this work is with ultrasonic signals traveling in mechanical guides such as plates and cylinders which can produce highly dispersive transient signals. Signal characterization and classification for these types of signals is not an easy problem to solve. For example, using short-time Fourier transform (STFT) has been of particular interest in the detection of relevant features, carrying out the measurements of closely spaced vibration modes, or increasing time-frequency resolution in dispersive signals [1]. Even though a time-frequency map has advantages, the amount of information in the matrix of the time-frequency map is several times the size of the initial time data vector, making it computationally expensive to monitor changes, especially when these are small and localized in data space. Model-based damage prediction methods, using numerical, analytical, or semi-analytical approaches, encounter difficulties when dealing with dispersive signals. Furthermore, signal-based methods have been parallelly developed with an emphasis on time-domain signal analysis using thresholding or signal subtraction [2]. Most recently, the development of artificial intelligence has allowed the implementation of different techniques such as pattern recognition, and neural networks, just to mention a few ([3–5]). One challenge these methods face is dimensionality reduction. For multidimensional data, methods based on probabilistic models, such as principal component analysis (PCA) obtained using single-value decomposition (SVD) have been proposed to reduce data complexity by identifying the direction of maximum variance. Research on SVD applications for image processing and classification has been intensively studied in recent years. In facial recognition, PCA has been used for feature extraction and classification, in conjunction with machine learning algorithms [6,7]. The aim of this work is to develop a method for the classification of non-stationary signals. The proposed method incorporates time-frequency energy maps representation of signals, background subtraction, and PCA dimensional reduction, this allows reliability and accuracy of classification. This research uses a database obtained from non-stationary dispersive ultrasonic signals. The specific objectives are: first, to develop a set of test non-stationary acoustic signals formed by three classes with only small differences between them. Second, to develop an algorithm for signal classification of STFT energy maps using PCA dimensionality reduction and background removal. And third, to evaluate the effectiveness of the proposed method using the experimental signal database. The paper is structured as follows. The first section provides the fundamentals of STFT maps for nonstationary signals. It is followed by a description of the PCA dimensionality reduction. Next, the background subtraction method is discussed as a method for filtering out irrelevant information. Then, the proposed method is described. Finally, the proposed method is tested using the experimental database, and an analysis of the results is provided.

2 Methods

2.1 STFT Maps

The short-time Fourier transform (STFT) gives a representation of a time-domain signal as a time-frequency distribution. The algorithm of the discrete STFT divides the signals into overlapping frames to reduce artifacts at their frame boundary. Each of the frames is a discrete fast Fourier transform (FFT) which is appended to create a matrix of the magnitude and phase of the signal. The tuning parameters of STFT of an input real-valued signal $x(n)$ of length L are: 1) the sampled window function h of length N that is related to the length in time of a section of $x(n)$ and 2) the overlap size R that determines the step size the window is shifted across the signal. Thus, the discrete STFT is given by

$$s(m, \beta)^T = \sum_{n=0}^{N-1} x(n + Rm)h(n)e^{-2\pi j\beta n/N}, \tag{1}$$

where $m \in [0 : w]$ and $\beta \in [0 : v]$, $w = \frac{L-N}{R}$ is the largest frame index such that the windows are fully contained in the time range of the signal, and $v = \frac{N}{2}$ is the frequency index. The energy of the STFT yields the spectrogram representation $s(m, \beta) =| s(m, \beta) |^2$. The horizontal axis of an STFT plot represents time and the vertical axis represents frequency. In the discrete case, the time axis is indexed by the frame indices m, and the frequency axis by the frequency indices β, forming a matrix $S\ [v \times w]$ of complex values. Thus, the resulting spectrogram will be several times the size of the time signal depending on the resolution, a schematic representation of the STFT method applied to an ultrasonic signal is shown in Fig. 1.

2.2 Dimensionality Reduction Using PCA

Principal component analysis (PCA) is a statistical technique for dimensionality reduction. The approach proposed in this work is inspired by applications in artificial image classification [8]. PCA exploits the property that any matrix $A\,[m \times n]$ can be decomposed using single-value decomposition (SVD). In the case of a real STFT matrix S, SVD of the matrix $S\ [v \times w]$, v can be seen as the number of samples (frequency bins) and w the number of variables (time bins) with the mean of each column w assumed zero. The singular value decomposition of S can be expressed as

$$S = U\Sigma V^T, \tag{2}$$

with dimensions $S^{[v\times w]}$, $U^{[v\times v]}$, $\Sigma^{[v\times w]}$ and $V^{[w\times w]}$; Σ is the diagonal matrix of singular values (σ_i) of non-increasing magnitude $(\sigma_1 \leq \sigma_2 \leq \cdots \leq \sigma_w \leq 0)$. If the covariance matrix of S is given by $C = S^T S/(n-1)$, we can show that

$$C = \frac{V\Sigma U^T U\Sigma V^T}{(v-1)} = V\frac{\Sigma^2}{v-1}V^T, \tag{3}$$

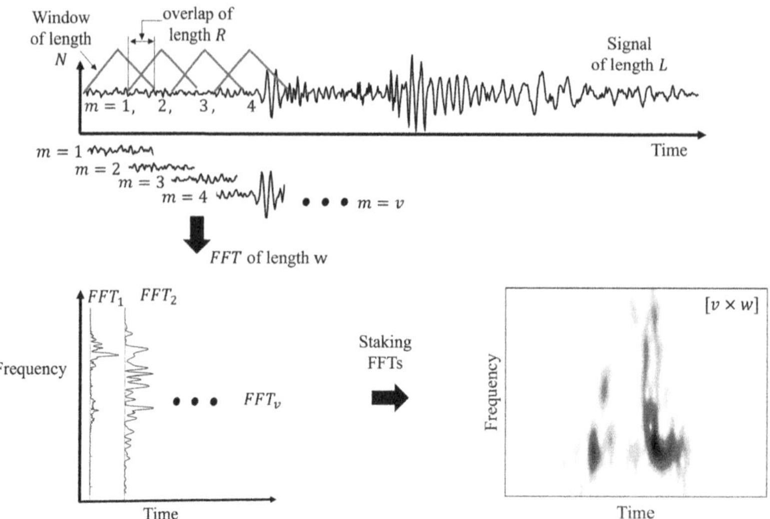

Fig. 1. Overview Short-time Fourier transform (STFT) method.

where V is a matrix with the principal directions and the singular values are related to the eigenvalues of covariance with $\sigma_i = \frac{\Sigma^2}{v-1}$. Thus, PCA of S matrix using the covariance $C = S^T S$ gives the correlation of the columns, with the principal components giving the directions of maximum variance in the column space. On the other hand, S^T provides the correlation between rows given by the matrix $C^T = SS^T$, and, the principal components now represent the directions of maximum variance in the row space. It is often not a common practice to construct the matrix SS^T because of its large size since it is normally expected that number of rows (samples) to be higher than the number of columns (features) causing higher computational cost [9,10]. For C the principal components are given by

$$PC = V\Sigma^2 V^T V = V\Sigma^2. \tag{4}$$

The principal components are the matrix product $V\Sigma^2$, and the variance of the ith component is equal to σ_i^2. The first principal components are the most informative components having the relevant information of the covariance matrix. So, when only the largest values of $\hat{\Sigma}$ are sufficient to represent S, it implies dimensionality reduction with lower computational storage requirements than the original matrix. This property is explored in this work.

An example of the classification problem of STFT maps taken from non-stationary acoustic signals with different types of perturbation is given in Fig. 2. It shows the STFT maps for three different signal conditions, namely Class 1 (undisturbed), Class 2 (perturbation #1), and Class 3 (perturbation #2) (see description of signals below). Despite the disturbances applied, the STFT maps exhibit similar patterns, making it challenging to classify the signals. Figure 2d is a scatter plot of the two first principal components obtained directly from the

STFT data. The plot does not allow class discrimination of the three classes. To overcome this problem a technique based on background subtraction is implemented as part of the proposed method.

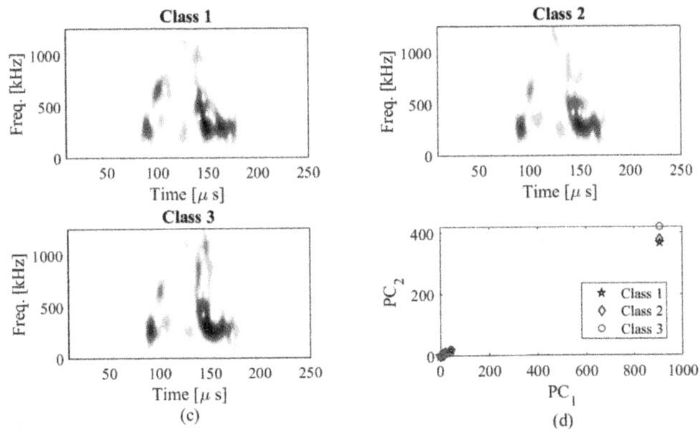

Fig. 2. STFT maps for a) Class 1 (undisturbed), b) Class 2 (perturbation #1), and c) Class 3 (perturbation #2), d) and their corresponding first and second principal components.

2.3 Background Subtraction

Background subtraction is a widely used technique to detect moving objects in a sequence of frames from static cameras [11]. The task is to detect a moving object from the difference between a current image and a reference one, called a background image. Our hypothesis is that by implementing background subtraction, the STFT maps can be classified. In background operation, a subspace U_l corresponding to the associated column eigenvector of the largest eigenvalues (l) of A is built using the invariant information of the set of vectorized maps. In our case, the matrix A is given by vectorization of the STFT maps (S_i), that is

$$\mathbf{A} = [S_1, S_2, ..., S_n], \tag{5}$$

where S_i is a $(m \times 1)$ vector with m = number of elements of STFT matrix, thus $\mathbf{S}$ is a $(m \times n)$ matrix with n = number of STFT maps used to perform SVD. The background B for a new map J can be found by projecting it into the subspace U_l ,

$$B = U_l(U_l^T J). \tag{6}$$

The foreground F of the map J is then obtained through a simple subtraction [12]

$$F = J - B. \tag{7}$$

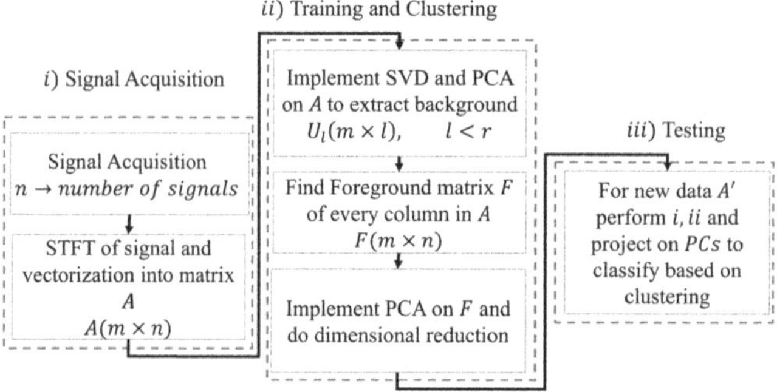

Fig. 3. Diagram illustrating the steps of the proposed method.

3 Description of Proposed Method

The diagram in Fig. 3 illustrates the methodology of the proposed classifier, consisting of three main stages: i) signal acquisition, ii) training and classification, and iii) testing. In the signal acquisition stage i), n signals are acquired and represented in the time domain. The signals are subjected to a transformation using STFT to derive their corresponding time-frequency domain representations. The resulting time-frequency maps are then vectorized and organized into a data matrix A. The training and classification stage ii)

yields the foreground matrix F. Next, PCA is utilized to reduce the dimensionality of F while retaining the most relevant features, resulting in the PC_1 and PC_2 principal components subspace. This facilitates the separation of data in clusters corresponding to different conditions or classes. For testing (stage iii), a new matrix $\boldsymbol{A'}$ undergoes similar processing as that of the signal acquisition stage. The corresponding foregrounds matrix $\boldsymbol{F'}$ is projected onto the reduced-dimensional PC_1 and PC_2 subspace obtained during training. Based on their proximity to the established clusters, we can classify the new signals into the defined classes or categories.

4 Acoustic Non-stationary Signals

The so-called guided waves are a special type of acoustic ultrasonic signals that are highly nonstationary (Fig. 4a). They propagate in bounded media (mechanical guide) such as cables, tubes, or plate structures. In addition to the non-stationary phenomena (called dispersion in acoustics), various vibration modes are generated. For guided wave propagating in a plate structure, these modes can be classified into symmetric (S) and antisymmetric vibration modes (A). In this work, we identify the lowest vibration modes: $A0$ and $S0$. Solving the wave equation for an isotropic plate free of traction gives the theoretical curves showing as solid and dashed lines in Fig. 4b. These curves typically can help to identify specific vibration modes traveling in the plate when the signal is represented in an STFT map [13].

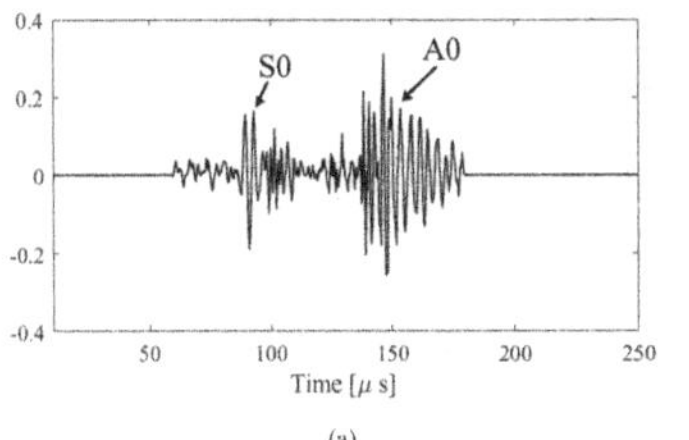

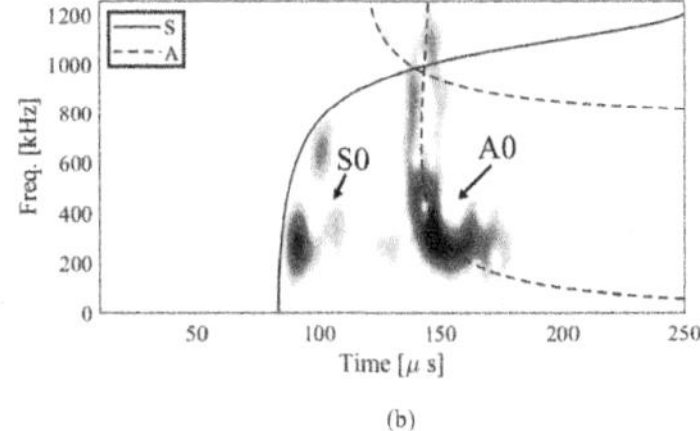

Fig. 4. a) Signal in the time domain and b) STFT map of signal showing the coincidence with the theoretical curves of fundamental vibration modes symmetric (S0) and antisymmetric (A0).

4.1 Signals Acquisition

The experimental setup for the tests is shown in Fig. 5 as a section view of a plate. guided waves were excited by the transmitter in an Aluminum thin plate with a thickness of 2 mm. The experiments were performed with two commercial 1 MHz longitudinal contact transducers in a pitch-catch arrangement separated by a distance of 40 cm (see Fig. 5). A set of signals (#1) was taken with a fixed location of the disturbance x = 20 cm, and a set #2 was taken varying the relative distance x of the disturbance, considering three positions x = 15, 20, 25 cm. The excitation pulse was generated by a pulser/receiver, and the signals were digitized and processed in a computer running MATLAB®.

To test the classifier, three experimental conditions were considered (Fig. 5): free of disturbances (Class 1); with a small through-hole (Class 2); with a contact pressure applied, as indicated in the figure. For the through-transmission test, the time-domain signals from the three classes show almost identical signal signatures (see Fig. 6). Since the considered experimental conditions have similar structural dimensions, the signal differences in the time domain are expected to be minimal. For these experiments, tests are affected by noise and test conditions. Thus, for each test, at least 4 repeated measurements were taken to assure repeatability. Following the methodology described in Fig. 3, two sets of signals were acquired, a set of 12 signals (set #1) with four measurements of each condition (Class 1, Class 2, Class 3), the experimental configuration has the same location of sensors and disturbance condition. To assess the influence of the disturbance location on the class discriminator, a second set of signals (set #2) was acquired. In this set #2, the distance between transducers was fixed at 40 cm with the relative position of the disturbance from the transmitter varying. Three positions were used: P1 = 15 cm; P2 = 20 cm; and P3 = 25 cm. Five repetition tests were taken for each measurement. Thus, 15 tests for each disturbance condition to total 45 signals were obtained.

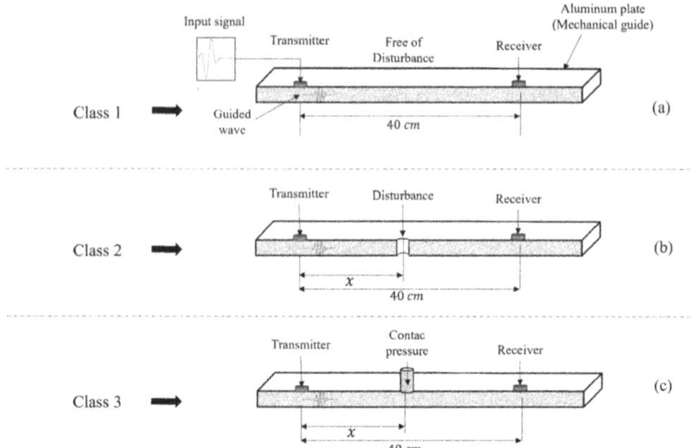

Fig. 5. Experimental conditions scheme, a) free of disturbance (class 1), b) Trough hole (Class2), and contact pressure (class 3).

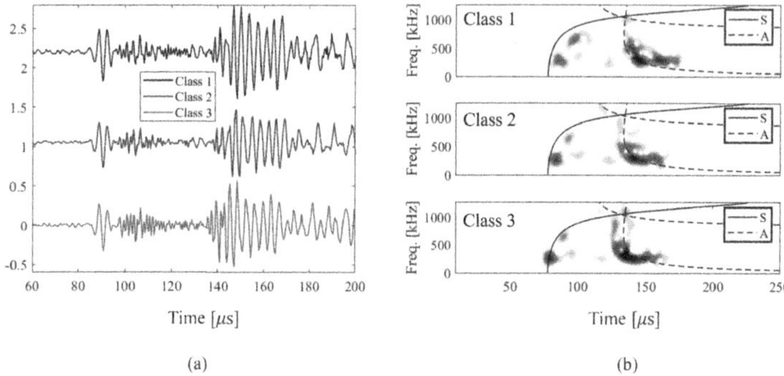

Fig. 6. a) Comparison of signals of the different classes, b) comparison of STFT maps of signals.

5 Classifier Results

5.1 Training and Classification

The background (B) was obtained from the SVD spectral decomposition of the matrix A as given by Eq. 6 considering only the first component of the matrix U. Figure 7 shows the results of background subtraction performed for each STFT map of the Class 1, Class 2, and Class 3 of set #1. The background (B) can be reconstructed using only a few principal components, and it resembles the observed STFT for the Class 1 condition (see Fig. 6). Some slight differences in the STFT maps for both modes A_0 and S_0 between maps can be observed, but are not enough for class classification.

Principal component analysis (PCA) is performed on the transpose of the vectorized foregrounds matrix (F). Thus, the columns in F^T represent the coordinates in the foreground maps, and the rows are the test conditions (Class 1,

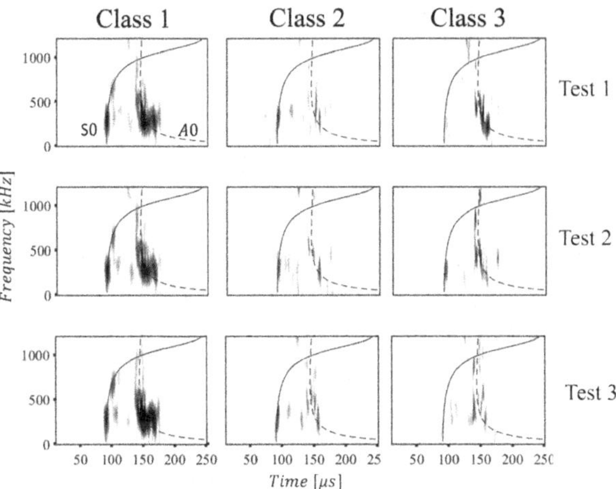

Fig. 7. Example of background subtraction on STFT maps, background, and foreground for Class 2 and Class 3 conditions for different tests

Class 2, and Class 3). This matrix operation allows higher sensitivity to details between coordinates in the foreground maps with the drawback that the size of the matrix increases. However, the computational cost in our study did not increase noticeably. Estimations for our database structure showed typically only an increase of about 3% when applying PCA on C^T instead of C of F.

In Fig. 8 the results of cumulative variance and plot of the first two principal components for the set #1 are given. From the cumulative variance results, we can see that most of the variance is explained by only a few principal components. Dimensionality reduction with only two principal components classifies the data into three clearly identified clusters for the test conditions (Fig. 8b).

In the second set (#2) of 45 tests, 36 tests (12 from each condition) were used to determine the background and 9 test samples (one for each position of every condition) were picked for the classifier testing. The explained variance analysis (Fig. 9a) showed that the first three components explain about 70% of the variance. Even with just two principal components (Fig. 9b), it is possible to achieve separation between classes.

To determine decision boundaries, the Bayesian classification technique can be utilized, which generates decision contours. For the testing stage of a new data matrix A', we employed signals that were not used during the calculation of the background subspace and the subsequent Principal Component Analysis (PCA). The foregrounds were derived by applying the precalculated background subspace to form a matrix F', containing the newly obtained foregrounds. To project the foregrounds onto the principal directions, we performed a matrix multiplication between F' and the matrix V from SVD that represents the principal directions derived from PCA. The projection onto the three first principal components shows class separation. Finally, 9 additional data samples were used

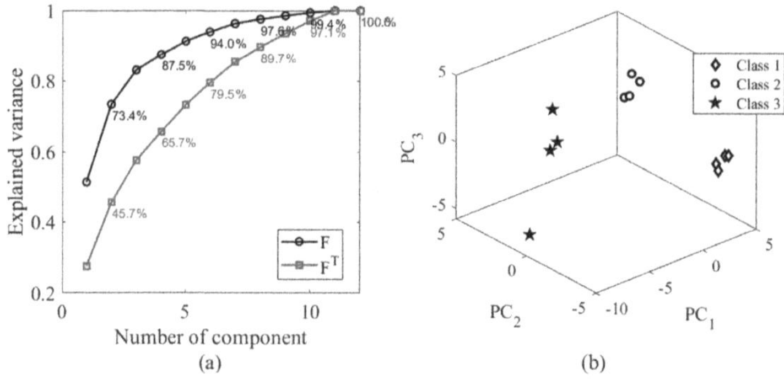

Fig. 8. Results of PCA on foregrounds for tests on set #1, having fixed relative distance between transducers and disturbance; a) Explained variance; b) Plot with the first three principal components.

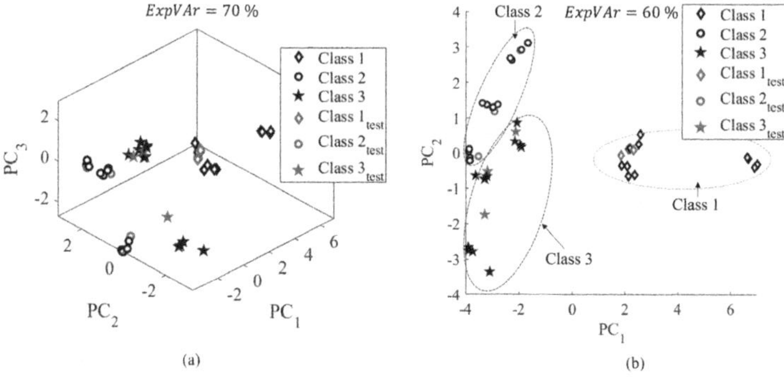

Fig. 9. Algorithm results for the test set #2, with varying relative positions between disturbance and transmitter transducer; dimensionality reduction plot with the first: a) three and b) two principal components.

to test the classifier. The new data was projected onto the principal components, as shown in Fig. 9a and b by the red markers. The markers positioned themselves within the corresponding clusters based on their class. The separation of the red markers into the corresponding clusters demonstrates the successful classification achieved by the proposed method.

Since the proposed method is based on surveillance cameras with a fixed view, the implementation of background subtraction requires maintaining a fixed sensor positioning as well as consistent contact conditions throughout the data acquisition process. In our experiments, even minor deviations in sensor test conditions can influence the outcomes of the generation of clusters. As a future work, we propose the integration of classification algorithms, such as the Support Vector Machine (SVM), into our methodology. Additionally, we plan to explore more complex classification scenarios, including the differentiation of patterns on bonded areas from various projection directions.

6 Conclusion

This work developed a signal classification method using unfiltered information from the STFT maps of guided wave signals taken from different wave propagation conditions by combining background subtraction and PCA. To test the method, signals taken from acoustic-guided waves propagating in a plate having three classes of structural conditions were considered. A careful analysis of the signals exhibits only subtle changes. These variations are difficult to set apart by only using direct observation in the STFT or time-domain but were enough for classification using the proposed method. We found that unsupervised signal clustering and class classification were achieved with the two-dimensional space reduction of the foreground matrices. The method performs well even for small variations in experimental conditions of the nonstationary signals. The computational cost of our proposed algorithm did not substantially increase.

Declarations

- Ethics approval and consent to participate 'Not applicable'
- Consent for publication 'Not applicable'
- Competing interests 'All authors certify that they have no affiliations with or involvement in any organization or entity with any financial interest or non-financial interest in the subject matter or materials discussed in this manuscript.'
- Funding 'Not applicable'
- Authors' contributions:
  Baltazar A. and Guerra-Bravo A. wrote main manuscript. Balvantin A., review guided wave related sections. All authors reviewed the manuscript
- Acknowledgments:

References

1. Tian, Z., Yu, L.: Lamb wave frequency-wavenumber analysis and decomposition. J. Intell. Mater. Syst. Struct. **25**(9), 1107–1123 (2014). https://doi.org/10.1177/1045389X14521875
2. Aryan, P., Kotousov, A., Ng, C.-T., Cazzolato, B.: A model-based method for damage detection with guided waves. Struct. Control. Health Monit. **24**(3), 1884 (2017)
3. Cantero-Chinchilla, S., Chiachío, J., Chiachío, M., Chronopoulos, D., Jones, A.: A robust Bayesian methodology for damage localization in plate-like structures using ultrasonic guided-waves. Mech. Syst. Signal Process. **122**, 192–205 (2019)
4. Chen, R.-C., Dewi, C., Huang, S.-W., Caraka, R.E.: Selecting critical features for data classification based on machine learning methods. J. Big Data **7**(1), 1–26 (2020)
5. Fernandez, K., Rojas, E., Baltazar, A., Mijarez, R.: Detection of torsional guided wave generation using macro-fiber composite transducers and basis pursuit denoising. Arch. Appl. Mech. **91**(5), 1945–1958 (2021)

6. Ramadhani, A.L., Musa, P., Wibowo, E.P.: Human face recognition application using pca and eigenface approach. In: 2017 Second International Conference on Informatics and Computing (ICIC), pp. 1–5 (2017). IEEE
7. Mohammed, A.A., Minhas, R., Wu, Q.J., Sid-Ahmed, M.A.: Human face recognition based on multidimensional PCA and extreme learning machine. Pattern Recogn. **44**(10–11), 2588–2597 (2011)
8. Uddin, M.P., Mamun, M.A., Hossain, M.A.: PCA-based feature reduction for hyperspectral remote sensing image classification. IETE Tech. Rev. **38**(4), 377–396 (2021)
9. Strang, G.: Computational science and engineering. Optimization **551**(563), 571–586 (2007)
10. Brunton, S.L., Kutz, J.N.: Data-driven science and engineering: Machine learning, dynamical systems, and control. Cambridge University Press (2022)
11. Garcia-Garcia, B., Bouwmans, T., Silva, A.J.R.: Background subtraction in real applications: challenges, current models and future directions. Comput. Sci. Rev. **35**, 100204 (2020)
12. Reitberger, G., Sauer, T.: Background subtraction using adaptive singular value decomposition. J. Math. Imag. Vision **62**(8), 1159–1172 (2020)
13. Rose, J.L.: Ultrasonic waves in solid media. Acoustical Society of America (2000)

Predict Email Success Based on Text Content

Edmundo Bernardo, Kaiulani Lorenzo(✉), Guillermo Reyes, and Hiram Ponce

Universidad Panamericana, Facultad de Ingeniería,
Augusto Rodin 498, Ciudad de México 03920, Mexico
{0154925,0218603,0266493,hponce}@up.edu.mx

Abstract. Email marketing works as a top channel to generate leads for many businesses. The marketing automation platforms are part of this strategy and can improve the success of email campaigns. Many of these platforms use subject line tools to predict if an email will be opened or not, as a success metric. However, the text content is unused. Thus, this work proposes to predict the likelihood of a user clicking the Call to Action button of an email based on the content. We implement our proposal in a real-case scenario of corporate communication emails from a private university in Mexico. After building a machine learning model, the results were promising and validated our proof-of-concept. We consider the results relevant for further investigation around other ways to improve the success of an email using the text content, and this model could be reliable in most campaigns and could be used to determine which words influence the click rate metric the most.

Keywords: Email Marketing · Automation · Call to action · Content Marketing

1 Introduction

Email marketing is an effective way to promote businesses and directly communicate with all customers and contacts. For 89% of companies, it is the primary channel for lead generation, and by 2024, daily email send are expected to have a 4.1% increase, totaling 361.6 billion daily sends [2]. With these numbers, it is easy to understand the importance of these tactics for the business.

Platforms like MailChimp help launch the content and automate the process, returning metrics based on the contact's behavior. These metrics guide the decision-making process improving the content and communication structure [5]. Therefore, content is a fundamental part of email marketing because it allows customers to know and adopt certain products or services, directly impacting sales.

Many studies and tools can help improve the metrics, such as subject line checkers, calendar reports for the best sending day, and global trends that make content more attractive [1,5]. While these are great solutions for improving the open rate, no direct tool on the market can help enhance the click-to-rate based on the content.

H. Calvo et al. (Eds.): MICAI 2023, LNAI 14391, pp. 77–83, 2024.
https://doi.org/10.1007/978-3-031-47765-2_6

This work aims to predict the success a user clicks the Call to Action (CTA) button of an email based on the content and the metrics of previous emails. We implement our proposal in a real case scenario of corporate communication emails from a private university in Mexico.

The rest of the paper is organized as follows. Section 2 describes some related works. Section 3 presents the methodology of the proposal. Section 4 shows the results and discussion. Lastly, Sect. 5 concludes the paper.

2 Related Work

The premise is that the human attention span is limited to a certain amount of time. Email marketing rises to the challenge of competing for a user's attention in a hyper-connected world in the palm of their hand. Many studies have been based on direct data on what influences a recipient's decision to open an email. According to Paulo M. [5], curiosity, the perceived utility of the message, and the email design characteristics affect an email's opening. Additionally, if the email is personalized to the recipient on the subject line, it has been tested that it increases the opening rate by 20%.

The literature reports some examples of related works proposing models based on the subject, specifically to predict the performance of the emails. Balakrishnan [1], worked on detecting the keywords included on the subject line with a random forest regressor that would result in a final score of the subject line. Miller [4] takes a more psychological approach to the quest. This work focused on inferring the recipient's profile and their emotional reaction to the subject line. Emotions were categorized as successful and less successful with a pondered value. An overall sentiment could be calculated when a subject line evokes various feelings. This study used a Support Vector Machine (SVM) model. A word and character count-based analysis also identified words that might not be as appealing and suggested alternatives.

A similar approach was found. Miller's work on email marketing [5] focused on the structure of the subject line. The variables considered in this study were the size of the subject line, count of words and characters, use of upper or lower case, punctuation, special characters, numbers, emojis, and whether the message was personalized. The preprocessing included dropping stop words and extracting the roots of the variants. The model had a performance of 62% by measuring the past performance of the stems. The following work doesn't necessarily aim to increase the open rate of a sent email. However, the methodology is of interest to this research. Junnarkar [3] studied the classification of email spam using machine learning and natural language processing. This model aims to prevent phishing cybersecurity incidents that extract information posing as attractive or catchy emails. The revised models are Naïve Bayes, k Nearest Neighbors, decision trees, random forest, and SVM.

As noted, the related work mainly reports a prediction of the successful of an email based on the subject line, but no at the content as we are proposing next.

3 Methodology

We propose the methodology shown in Fig. 1. We first collect the dataset of emails, and then we preprocess the data to accommodate the relevant information of content. After that, we build and train a machine learning model with optimized hyperparameters. Lastly, we validate the model. Details are described below.

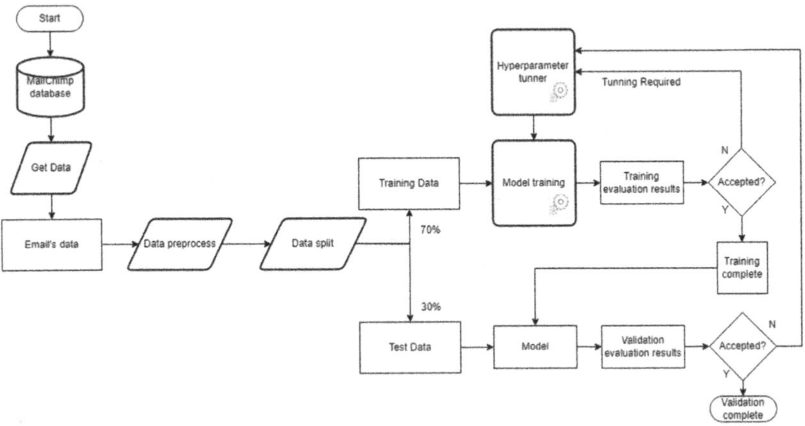

Fig. 1. Machine Learning Model Flow.

3.1 Description of the Dataset

The database was extracted from the marketing platform for corporate communication of a private university in Mexico City, Mexico. The database was downloaded from 2017 to 2023. It contains information about campaign titles, email subjects, audience, and metrics regarding the interaction of email recipients with them. All emails in the database were manually reviewed, and the subject, preheader, greetings, and call to action were added due to their relevance to the email content.

The database was optimized by removing empty values, and to reduce the dimensionality, the following columns were selected: subject, preheader, greetings, call to action, and click rate. Due to the nature of the database using text as a categorical value for success, the model uses the following preprocess: the four columns were concatenated into one column called "Texto", this new column was tokenized, stop words were deleted for more accurate results, and finally, our target value (click rate) was categorized. The latter measures the ratio of clicks on the CTA button.

For a better estimate of success, the click rate was divided into three categories, considering the database's whole population of click rates. These were split as:

- `df['Click Rate']` ≤ 0.02425 — Malo (Bad)
- $0.02425 <$ `df['Click Rate']` < 0.053625 — Regular (Regular)
- `df['Click Rate']` ≥ 0.053625 — Bueno (Good)

With the text processed and concatenated, we use the column "Texto" as the input feature and the click rate value as the target. The later was encoded, converting the text into numbers: Good – 0, Bad – 1, and Regular – 2.

3.2 Building and Training the Model

To make the model efficient, a pipeline was created. This pipeline has 3 steps:

- Tf-idf-vectorizer (Term Frequency - Inverse Document Frequency) was used to normalize the word count matrix. It calculates the frequency of each term and then assigns them a value. The higher the value, the more relevant the term is.
- TruncatedSVD (Truncated Singular Value Decomposition) was used to predict results more accurately and extract meaningful words from the text. It reduces the dimensionality to retain the first terms which capture the major variance.
- Support Vector Machine (SVD) was used because it fits perfectly with the main goals, such as flexibly classifying click rate into 3 classes, finding the maximum marginal hyperplane, and being able to accurately predict whether an email contains certain key terms that will result in a higher click-through rate

The data set was split into two, 70% of the dataset was used as the training set, and the remaining 30% was used for the testing. Then, the grid search was implemented for finding optimal hyperparameters. Five hyperparameters were optimized: the maximum document frequency, the ngram range, the number of components in the SVD, the SVM kernel, and the regularization value of the SVM. Figure 2 summarizes the hyperparameter settings. The stratified 5-fold cross-validation technique [7] was implemented to find the hyperparameters. The final result shown 64% of accuracy, and the optimal hyperparameters are depicted in Fig. 3.

```
params = {
    'tfidf__max_df': (0.5, 0.75, 1.0),
    'tfidf__ngram_range': ((1,1), (1,2)),
    'svd__n_components': (50, 100, 150, 200),
    'model__kernel': ['linear','rbf'],
    'model__C': [0.1,0.5,1.0]
}
```

Fig. 2. Initial hyperparameters

```
Best score: 0.638
Best parameters set:
        model__C: 1.0
        model__kernel: 'linear'
        svd__n_components: 150
        tfidf__max_df: 0.75
        tfidf__ngram_range: (1, 1)
```

Fig. 3. Best score and hyperparameters after grid search with 5 folds.

3.3 Model Evaluation

We use four metrics [6] to evaluate the performance of the model: *accuracy*, *precision*, *recall*, and F_1-*score*, as expressed in (1)–(4); where TP and TN are the true positives and true negatives, and FP and FN are the false positives and false negatives.

$$accuracy = \frac{TP + TN}{TP + TN + FP + FN} \tag{1}$$

$$precision = \frac{TP}{TP + FP} \tag{2}$$

$$recall = \frac{TP}{TP + FN} \tag{3}$$

$$F_1\text{-}score = 2 \cdot \frac{precision \times recall}{precision + recall} \tag{4}$$

4 Results and Discussion

In this section, we provide the results of the proposed model for predicting the click rate on the CTA button using the content of the emails. Figure 4 summarizes the performance of the model. As shown, the model obtained 60% of accuracy, 60% average precision, 57% of average recall, and 56% of F_1-score.

The confusion matrix presented in Fig. 5 shows that Regular (Regular) and Malo (Bad) can be confused by the model, 40% and 57% of precision, respectively. However, Bueno (Good) class is well predicted with 83% of precision. The latter results might be due to the small difference threshold between the classes.

On one hand, the current work validates that text content might be a relevant feature for predicting the click rate on the CTA button in emails. This can be seen as a proof-of-concept on how to use SVM for this classification problem. On the other hand, the work presents some weaknesses as the limited number of emails in the dataset. Also, the threshold in the click rate value was manually set, and more proper threshold procedure needs to be chosen.

	precision	recall	f1-score	support
0	0.83	0.68	0.75	28
1	0.57	0.86	0.68	44
2	0.40	0.18	0.25	33
accuracy			0.60	105
macro avg	0.60	0.57	0.56	105
weighted avg	0.58	0.60	0.56	105

Fig. 4. Summary results. Labels: Good – 0, Bad – 1, and Regular – 2.

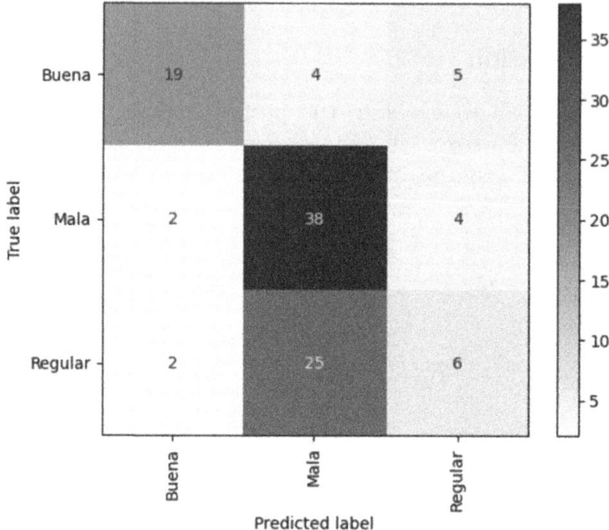

Fig. 5. Confusion Matrix Display

This work opens the opportunity to build a more robust machine learning model for predicting the click rate on CTA button in emails, so that the corporate communication department at the private university can test the email contents performance before sending them. This could improved the success of email campaigns.

5 Conclusions

This study successfully achieved its purpose, the model predicts the click rate classification based on the content. This model is beneficial and valuable for the private university because now they can analyze which words/terms positively impact the email metrics and perform better on each campaign.

Until now, the proof-of-concept validates the ability of text content to predict the success of emails in a campaign with 60% of accuracy. Also, the analysis showed that Good and Bad/Regular emails can be classified.

Future work considers to provide an improved model based on the other building model procedures. Another valuable task that needs to be done is to test whether the "open rate" and the sending email day variable should be used in the model, this is because they could also seriously affect how the user reacts to the campaign.

References

1. Balakrishnan, R., Parekh, R.: Learning to predict subject-line opens for large-scale email marketing. In: 2014 IEEE International Conference on Big Data (Big Data), pp. 579–584 (2014). https://doi.org/10.1109/BigData.2014.7004277
2. Holovach, H.: 105 email marketing statistics you should know in 2023. https://snov.io/blog/email-marketing-statistics/
3. Junnarkar, A., Adhikari, S., Fagania, J., Chimurkar, P., Karia, D.: E-mail spam classification via machine learning and natural language processing. In: 2021 Third International Conference on Intelligent Communication Technologies and Virtual Mobile Networks (ICICV), pp. 693–699 (2021). https://doi.org/10.1109/ICICV50876.2021.9388530
4. Miller, R., Charles, E.: A psychological based analysis of marketing email subject lines. In: 2016 Sixteenth International Conference on Advances in ICT for Emerging Regions (ICTer), pp. 58–65 (Sep 2016). https://doi.org/10.1109/ICTER.2016.7829899
5. Paulo, M., Miguéis, V.L., Pereira, I.: Leveraging email marketing: Using the subject line to anticipate the open rate. Expert Syst. Appl. **207**, 117974 (2022). https://doi.org/10.1016/j.eswa.2022.117974, https://www.sciencedirect.com/science/article/pii/S0957417422012040
6. Sokolova, M., Lapalme, G.: A systematic analysis of performance measures for classification tasks. Inform. Process. Manage. **45**(4), 427–437 (2009)
7. Wang, Z.: Working with, preparing bag-of-word data for regression (2016). https://stackoverflow.com/questions/37510014/working-with-preparing-bag-of-word-data-for-regression Accessed 4 June 2023

Neural Drone Racer Mentored by Classical Controllers

L. Oyuki Rojas-Perez, Alejandro Gutierrez-Giles, and Jose Martinez-Carranza(✉)

Computer Science Department of the Instituto Nacional de Astrofisica, Optica y Electronica, Puebla, Mexico
carranza@inaoep.mx

Abstract. The autonomous drone race has driven the development of various approaches to agile flight involving perception, planning and control. The latter is most effective when using external information such as high-frequency drone position. On the other hand, deep learning-based methods propose to train an artificial pilot to learn to associate sensory data with flight commands using only visual information. In this paper, we propose an approach for developing a neural drone racer based on the mentoring of three classical flight controllers combined with visual information. We performed a comparison of the three trained models. Our results demonstrated an improvement in navigation behaviour and increased the speed to complete a racetrack by a factor of 7 compared to that reported in the state of the art.

Keywords: Deep Learning · Neural Drone Racer · Exemplary Racetracks · Classical Controllers · Learning-based Methods

1 Introduction

Autonomous Drone Racing (ADR) presents the challenge of developing an artificial pilot capable of autonomously flying on a racetrack [9,22,25]. This research area has led to improvements in high-speed control algorithms and autonomous indoor drone navigation, even achieving speeds comparable to those of human pilots. However, agile flight solutions depend on positioning systems like VICON and optimisation methods based on time and trajectory [10]. In contrast, human pilots guide the drone towards the next gates and can identify areas on the track that allow them to increase or decrease speed, as well as position the drone for the next manoeuvre [28,29]. Additionally, human pilots do not necessarily seek optimal flight but instead familiarise themselves with the track to enhance overall performance.

Therefore, in this work, we propose a methodology based on imitation using Convolutional Neural Networks (CNN) and classical control techniques. We start with a neural drone racer called DeepPilot [35], which is a CNN that processes images from the drone's camera and generates real-time flight control commands

H. Calvo et al. (Eds.): MICAI 2023, LNAI 14391, pp. 84–98, 2024.
https://doi.org/10.1007/978-3-031-47765-2_7

to enable autonomous navigation of the drone on an unfamiliar racetrack. The flight commands provided by DeepPilot align the drone with the centre of the gate to cross it. However, the flight is performed at a low speed, as the model has learned to cross the gate until it is centred at the gate.

This work presents a methodology to train a neural drone racer using flight commands generated by classical control algorithms. For this purpose, we use the waypoint discovery method [37] to find points of interest that serve as references for classical control algorithms to follow a trajectory. Additionally, we design basic sections, such as straight lines, zig-zags, and climbs, to generalise the network's learning to navigate unknown racetracks without needing global positioning. We have evaluated our method in the RotorS simulator implemented for Gazebo [11]. The results show that our approach improves the performance of the neural drone racer and enables it to complete a racetrack without prior information such as track dimensions, number of gates, or global drone positioning.

We have organised this article as follows to describe our approach: Sect. 2 discusses related work; Sect. 3 describes our approach in more detail; Sect. 4 presents our experimental framework; and finally, Sect. 5 summarises our conclusions and future work.

2 Related Work

Most ADR strategies involve perception, localisation, trajectory tracking, and control processes executed simultaneously. In [33], the authors analyse ADR competition methods and highlight data processing's critical role in environment interpretation. Machine learning techniques such as deep and reinforcement learning, have been used to improve the drones' ability in different situations. For example, CNNs have been used for gate detection [2,14,15], drone's movement classification [25], CNN and Multilayer perceptron to estimate direction and velocity [16,17], the relative position [17], relative position respect to the gate [4,5], CNN to identify the blind spot [3,37] and CNN to flight commands [30–32,35].

Concerning the vehicle position and orientation estimation, common vision-based localisation systems in robotics include Simultaneous Localisation and Mapping (SLAM) [27] and Visual Odometry (VO) [6,7]. Nevertheless, these systems are computationally expensive, limiting the position estimate to less than 15 Hz in embedded systems [10,23,27]. In addition, they suffer from error accumulation and are unsuitable for agile flight requiring higher frequency pose estimation. An alternative solution to obtain a higher frequency position is using neural networks combined with the Extended Kalman Filter as shown in [34], that associates a 2D image with a 3D pose to relocate in an environment achieving a drone's position frequency of 65 Hz.

The trajectory planner module is crucial for ADR, requiring the drone's current state (position and orientation), start and destination points (GPS or 3D), and movement constraints like maximum speed, acceleration, and turning limits. Trajectory planning methods in ADR include optimisation-based trajectory methods like time-optimal planning, time-optimal flight [38], and minimum-time trajectory [40]. They generate smooth and controllable trajectories for dynamic environments with curves and obstacles. However, they require pre-processing and are computationally expensive since these methods seek to find an optimal trajectory that satisfies certain constraints, such as distance travelled, flight time [10], maximum speed, and maximum accelerations [24,26].

Finally, the control module must be able to drive the drone in real time. In ADR, the controllers implemented are feedback-based, observer-based and state estimation-based. Feedback-based controllers like Proportional Integral Derivative (PI) [3,5,25,36] and visual servoing [13–15,25] use visual or position feedback to adjust the drone's behaviour. Observer-based controllers, such as Kalman Filter, estimate the drone's position and velocity from sensor data like Inertial Measurement Units (IMU) [18–20,25]. Finally, state-estimation-based controllers, like Model Predictive Controller (MPC) [10,38], use a dynamic system model to compute control commands, enabling agile manoeuvres and future state prediction for the drone.

3 Methodology

In this section, we will describe the characteristics and architecture of the neural drone racer used in this work, as well as the classical control algorithms. These control algorithms act as mentors, providing guidance and direction in the navigation of the neural drone racer. Additionally, we will outline the training process of the neural drone racer, which involves using the flight commands generated by the classical control algorithms.

3.1 Neural Pilot

DeepPilot [35] is a neural drone racer based on a convolutional neural network (CNN). DeepPilot processes a set of images from a drone's camera and generates flight control commands in real time to navigate an unknown racetrack. The DeepPilot model learns seven basic movements: right, left, up, down, right rotation, left rotation, and forward displacement with respect to a gate. To achieve this, the authors utilised a dataset composed of mosaic images associated with manual flight values as labels.

The architecture of DeepPilot comprises four branches, working in parallel to obtain the four flight signals (roll, pitch, yaw, and altitude), see Fig. 1. Each branch comprises four convolutional layers, three inception modules that extract feature characteristics, and one fully connected layer with one regressor to obtain the flight signal values. This network identifies patterns in the images to associate the position of the gate with the appropriate control commands. As a result, these commands adjust the drone's speed, direction, and orientation, enabling autonomous navigation of the racetrack. Figure 1(b) illustrates the angular position of the drone's body frame. In this context, both pitch and roll angles contribute to translation motion, while roll specifically generates rotational speed, and changes in altitude result in vertical speed.

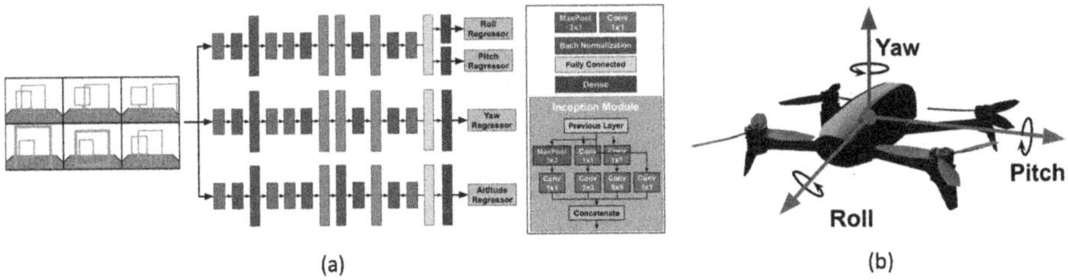

(a) (b)

Fig. 1. DeepPilot CNN-based network for generating flight commands (roll, pitch, yaw, and altitude). (a) Network architecture is composed of convolutional layers. (b) the angular position of the drone's body frame.

3.2 Proportional-Integral Controller

In the autonomous drone race (ADR) context, the Proportional-Integral (PI) controller allows the drone to respond quickly to real-time signals and adjust to its environment. Since the goal of the race is to complete the track as fast as possible, we have used the drone's position and a set of waypoints.

In this work, we implemented a PI controller for roll and height control and a proportional controller for yaw. We also set the pitch to maximum value (1) to move the drone forward as fast as possible. To reduce the inertia of the drone movement, we implemented a proportional pitch controller, which decreases the speed from 1 to 0.5 when the distance between the drone and the entry point is less than 3 m. This strategy allows the drone to turn towards the exit point. This is especially useful in curved sections of the circuit, where turning involves a significant change in yaw angle.

We assumed that the drone flies on a horizontal plane, so we operate with vectors obtained from the translation $\mathbf{t}$ and rotation matrix $\mathbf{R}$ obtained with the Gazebo simulator at 1000 Hz. We defined a unit vector as $\mathbf{v} = [1, 0, 0]$ and a heading vector as $\mathbf{h} = \mathbf{R}\mathbf{v}$. A departing waypoint $\mathbf{w}_s$ and the next waypoint $\mathbf{w}_g$ are used to define the direction vector $\mathbf{d} = \mathbf{w}_g - \mathbf{w}_s$, with its corresponding rotation matrix representation $\mathbf{R}_d = Rot(\mathbf{d})$, where $Rot(\cdot)$ is a function that calculates such matrix. Finally, we compute the drone's position relative to $\mathbf{w}_s$:

$$\mathbf{r} = \mathbf{R}_d^\top (\mathbf{t} - \mathbf{w}_s) \tag{1}$$

The control signals are calculated as follows:

$$s_\theta = \begin{cases} 1 : (\|\mathbf{d}\| - r_x) > 3 \\ 0.5 + 0.5\frac{(\|\mathbf{d}\| - r_x)}{3} : (\|\mathbf{d}\| - r_x) \leq 3 \end{cases} \tag{2}$$

$$s_\phi = K_{p_\phi}(-r_y) + K_{i_\phi} \int (-r_y)dt \tag{3}$$

$$\mathbf{n} = \mathbf{d} \times \mathbf{h} \tag{4}$$

$$s_{\psi} = K_{p_{\psi}} \text{sign}(\mathbf{n}) \text{acos}\left(\frac{\mathbf{d} \cdot \mathbf{h}}{\|\mathbf{d}\|\|\mathbf{h}\|}\right) \tag{5}$$

$$s_h = K_{p_h}(w_{gz} - r_z) + K_{i_h} \int (w_{gz} - r_z) dt \tag{6}$$

where sign$(\cdot)$ is defined as:

$$\text{sign}(\mathbf{n}) = \begin{cases} 1 : n_z \geq 0 \\ -1 : n_z < 0 \end{cases} \tag{7}$$

and $\mathbf{w}_g = [w_{gx}, w_{gy}, w_{gz}]$, $\mathbf{r} = [r_x, r_y, r_z]$, $\mathbf{n} = [n_x, n_y, n_z]$.

Finally, the gains $K_{p_\phi}, K_{i_\phi}, K_{p_\psi}, K_{p_h}, K_{i_h}$ were tuned empirically aiming to avoid oscillations or excessive flight speed that would make the drone hit a gate.

3.3 Model Predictive Controller

Model Predictive Control (MPC) has its roots in optimal control theory. An MPC optimises over a finite horizon at a given time step. At the next step, the horizon is moved forward in time, and the optimisation is carried out again with the aid of the new-step feedback information. Since the optimisation horizon is of a fixed length but moving along the time axis, it is commonly called *receding horizon.*

The main difference between MPC and the standard Linear Quadratic Regulator (LQR) is having a receding horizon instead of a fixed or infinite one, though there are some other differences. MPC can explicitly handle input and state constraints, both *hard* and *soft* ones. These constraints can be incorporated into an Optimisation Control Problem (OCP). The MPC can also handle nonlinear dynamic models and more general cost functions in contrast with the LQR controller that only handles linear systems and quadratic cost functions.

A dynamic model is required to implement the MPC. Since the goal is to obtain the least processing time required to solve the MPC problem, we consider a very simplified model of the quadrotor employed, i.e. a linear and decoupled one. The inputs of this model are the roll, pitch, yaw angles and the vertical thrust. The outputs are defined as the linear positions in all three Cartesian directions and the rotation around the vertical axis. Since the rotation around the vertical axis, i.e. the yaw coordinate is not critical for the ADR problem, it can be left out of the online optimisation carried out in the MPC framework. Instead, this coordinate will be controlled by a simple PI. In addition, time delays can be neglected to obtain a linear time-invariant model of the form.

$$\dot{\mathbf{x}} = \mathbf{A}\mathbf{x} + \mathbf{B}\mathbf{u} \tag{8}$$

$$\mathbf{y} = \mathbf{C}\mathbf{x}, \tag{9}$$

where $\mathbf{x} \in \mathrm{R}^6$ is the state vector containing both the Cartesian positions and velocities of the drone with respect to a fixed coordinate frame, $\mathbf{u} \in \mathrm{R}^3$ is the vector of inputs, which are the roll and pitch angles, and the thrust. Notice that these inputs are normalised, i.e. $|u_i| \leq 1, i = 1, 2, 3$, $\mathbf{y} \in \mathrm{R}^3$ is the vector of outputs, which are the Cartesian positions, and $\mathbf{A}, \mathbf{B}, \mathbf{C}$ are matrices of appropriate dimensions. This model is used both for the MPC implementation and for a Kalman filter, which is employed to obtain the unmeasured states, i.e. the drone velocities.

A third-order polynomial is proposed to generate the desired trajectory for each pair of gates in each Cartesian coordinate. The coefficients of such polynomials can be uniquely determined by defining the initial and final positions and velocities. The positions are given simply by the blind spot zone described in Sect. 3.5. In turn, the velocities are defined as vectors in the Cartesian space, whose magnitude is equal to the desired speeds at the start and the end of the trajectory, and its direction is computed as the normal vector from the entrance blind spot zone to the exit blind spot zone. The resulting trajectories are functions of the desired time t_{f} between waypoints. If in addition one imposes the constraint $\|\mathbf{v}(t_0)\| = \|\mathbf{v}(t_{\mathrm{f}})\| = \|\mathbf{v}((t_f - t_0)/2)\| = v_{\max}$, where $v_{\max}$ is the maximum attainable speed of the drone, then one obtains a minimum-time trajectory. Notice that this minimum-time trajectory is theoretical and it would be reachable only if all the dynamic forces are neglected. In practice, we can tune this value to have a percentage of the maximum speed, e.g. $0.8\,v_{\max}$.

To implement the MPC, the following OCP is defined:

$$\min_{\mathbf{u}} \int_{t_0}^{t_0+t_{\mathrm{h}}} \mathbf{x}^{\mathrm{T}}\mathbf{Q}\mathbf{x} + \mathbf{u}^{\mathrm{T}}\mathbf{R}\mathbf{u}\,dt + \mathbf{x}(t_{\mathrm{h}})^{\mathrm{T}}\mathbf{Q}_{\mathrm{h}}\mathbf{x}(t_{\mathrm{h}})$$

subject to

$$\dot{\mathbf{x}} = \mathbf{A}\mathbf{x} + \mathbf{B}\mathbf{u}$$

$$-1 \leq u_i \leq 1\,,\; i = 1,2,3\,,$$

where t_{h} is the *receding horizon* time, $\mathbf{Q} \in \mathrm{R}^{6\times6}$ and $\mathbf{R} \in \mathrm{R}^{3\times3}$ are weighting matrices accounting for the costs of the states and the inputs, respectively, and $\mathbf{Q}_{\mathrm{h}} \in \mathrm{R}^{6\times6}$ is the weighting matrix of the state at the end of the receding horizon.

The above OCP can be solved with the aid of the ACADO Toolkit libraries in C++[1] along with the qpOASES library. The employed method was *single shooting* with Gauss-Newton approximation of the Hessian matrix and a fourth-order Runge-Kutta numerical integrator.

3.4 Active Disturbance Rejection Control

Active Disturbance Rejection Control (ADRC) is a control technique developed during the last years by incorporating the ideas presented in the seminal works of Fliess [8], Han [12] and Sira-Ramirez [39]. The basic idea is to make a dynamic extension of the space-state model by incorporating a prototypical model with uncertain parameters as an internal model for some unknown additive perturbations, which can be external and/or internal sources. The dynamic extension allows an online estimate of the unknown parameters of the proposed dynamics for the unmodelled disturbances using a state observer. The estimated signals are then employed for online cancellation of the disturbances and therefore, by the principle of certain equivalence, performing a feedback linearisation of the dynamic system.

In this work, a modification of the classical ADRC algorithm [12] is employed by exploiting the passivity properties of the Lagrangian representation of the drone dynamic model [21]. For this controller, we consider only the linear motion in all three Cartesian axes, defined by the vector $\mathbf{x} = \begin{bmatrix} x\ y\ z \end{bmatrix}^{\mathrm{T}}$, whereas a PI controls the yaw.

[1] Available online: https://acado.github.io/,.

The basic idea is taken from [1], with a modification to include the gain $\gamma \in \mathbb{R}$, as follows. First, define the tracking error in the inertial frame as ${}^{\mathrm{w}}\mathbf{e} \triangleq \mathbf{x} - \mathbf{x}_{\mathrm{d}}$. This error can be converted to the drone coordinate frame using the rotation matrix, i.e. $\mathbf{e} \triangleq {}^{\mathrm{d}}\mathbf{e} = {}^{\mathrm{w}}\mathbf{R}_{\mathrm{d}}^{T}{}^{\mathrm{w}}\mathbf{e}$, where ${}^{\mathrm{w}}\mathbf{R}_{\mathrm{d}} \in SO(3)$ is the rotation matrix of the drone frame with respect to the inertial frame. Next, define the estimation error $\tilde{\mathbf{e}} = \mathbf{e} - \hat{\mathbf{e}}_1$. Now, the following controller-observer is proposed

$$\begin{aligned}
\dot{\hat{\mathbf{e}}}_1 &= \hat{\mathbf{e}}_2 - \boldsymbol{\Lambda}\hat{\mathbf{e}}_1 + (\lambda_3 - \boldsymbol{\Lambda})\tilde{\mathbf{e}} \\
\dot{\hat{\mathbf{e}}}_2 &= \lambda_2\tilde{\mathbf{e}} \\
\dot{\hat{\mathbf{z}}}_1 &= \hat{\mathbf{z}}_2 + \lambda_1\tilde{\mathbf{e}} \\
\dot{\hat{\mathbf{z}}}_2 &= \lambda_0\tilde{\mathbf{e}} \\
\mathbf{u} &= -\mathbf{K}_{\mathrm{v}}(\dot{\hat{\mathbf{e}}}_1 + \boldsymbol{\Lambda}\mathbf{e}) - \gamma\hat{\mathbf{z}}_1 \,,
\end{aligned}$$

where $\mathbf{K}_{\mathrm{v}}, \boldsymbol{\Lambda} \in \mathbb{R}^{3\times 3}$ are matrices of constant gains, and $\lambda_0, \ldots, \lambda_p \in \mathbb{R}^{n\times n}$ are the constant diagonal gain matrices of the matrix polynomial in the Laplace variable s

$$\lambda_p s^p + \lambda_{p-1}s^{p-1} + \ldots \lambda_1 s + \lambda_0 = \mathbf{O}\,. \tag{10}$$

Notice also that the polynomial order in (10) was chosen as $p = 3$ for this particular case.

Ultimately, the boundedness of both the tracking and the estimation error was proven for the original algorithm, i.e. $\gamma = 1$ in [1]. It also showed improved stability and performance with respect to the classic ADRC in the experimental part of the mentioned article.

The inclusion of the term γ improves further the performance of the algorithm when the inertia matrix is far from the identity, i.e. γ can be seen as a *grosso modo* scalar approximation of the inertia matrix. Due to the well-known properties of the inertia matrix, γ can be chosen as the inertia matrix eigenvalue that is farthest to 1. We are aware that this would mean that we have at least the model of the inertia matrix, which is not necessary for the algorithm of [1]. Still, since only an approximation is sufficient to improve the performance, it can be estimated by performing an open-loop step experiment in each Cartesian direction to identify a first-order response. Then, the inverse of the transfer function gains is a rough approximation of the inertia matrix eigenvalues. Finally, $\mathbf{K}_{\mathrm{v}}$ and $\boldsymbol{\Lambda}$ can be tuned as a PD controller by temporarily making $\gamma = 0$ and setting $\mathbf{K}_{\mathrm{v}} = \mathbf{K}_{\mathrm{d}}$ and $\boldsymbol{\Lambda} = \mathbf{K}_{\mathrm{d}}^{-1}\mathbf{K}_{\mathrm{p}}$, where $\mathbf{K}_{\mathrm{p}}$ and $\mathbf{K}_{\mathrm{d}}$ are the proportional and the derivative gains of the PD controller, respectively.

3.5 Training Process

1) Exemplary Racetracks. We propose to use key sections on a drone race track, which we will call "exemplary racetracks". This teaches the network how to act in the presence of the three nearest gates, not just the nearest gate. In Fig. 2, we show the eight exemplary racetracks used to generate the new training sets, where figure (b) to (e) have all gates placed at a height of 2 m, while figure (f) to (h) has height changes to obtain a variety of data. The sections cover an area of 40 m × 6 m and comprise the following shapes: (a) is a straight line; (b) zig-zag to the right; (c) zig-zag to the left; (d) half circle to the right; (e) half circle to the left; (f) straight line gate 1 at the height of 2m, gate 2 at the height of 2. 5 m and gate 3 at the height of 2 m; (g) straight line gate 1 at the height of 2.5 m, gate 2 at the height of 2m and gate 3 at the height of 2.5 m; (h) straight line gate 1 at the height of 2 m, gate 2 at the height of 2.5 m and gate 3 at the height of 3m. For each exemplary racetrack, we used the waypoints discovery method described in Sect. 3.5 to determine the entry and exit points of the blind zone. Figure 2 shows the entry points in blue and the exit points in red.

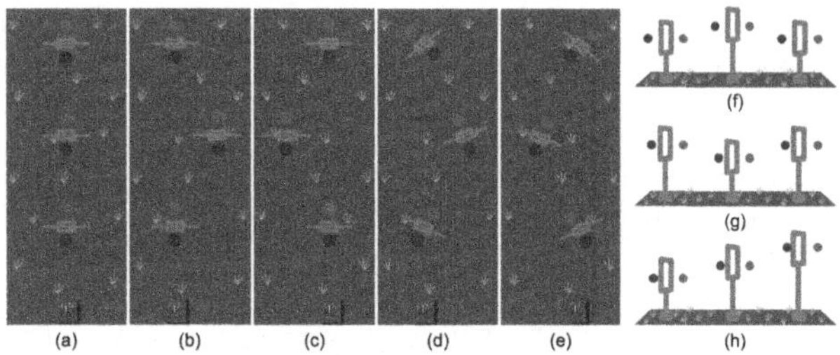

Fig. 2. Exemplary racetrack used to training a neural drone racer: (a) straight segments with gates at 2, 2.5, and 3 m; (b) right zig-zag segments; (c) left zig-zag segments; (d) right curve segments; (e) left curve segments; (f-h) straight segments with elevation change. The points in blue and red represent the entrance and exit of the blind spot zone. These points were found with the Waypoints Discovery method [37] (Color figure online).

2) Discovery Waypoints. Since the target position is an essential element in the control algorithms presented here, we adopt the strategy proposed in "Where are the gates" [37], based on how human pilots familiarise themselves with unfamiliar race tracks. This approach is useful for waypoint discovery as it does not require prior knowledge of the position, orientation, height or number of gates, or any details about the racetrack's dimensions. "Where are the gates" [37] allows us to obtain a set of waypoints corresponding to the entrance and exit (blind spot zone) of each gate of the racetrack. For this purpose, the authors use the neural drone racer "DeepPilot" to navigate the racetrack autonomously and a Single Shot Detector 7 (SSD7) (object detection network) to identify an orange gate.

The strategy for obtaining the set of track waypoints involves four key stages. First, the system identifies when the drone loses direct view of the gate, entering the "blind spot zone." Then, it avoids adding waypoints while the drone moves through the gate. A navigation point is added after a predetermined time interval to indicate the exit from the blind spot zone. Finally, the system ensures no duplicate or unnecessary navigation points in the list, ensuring safe and accurate drone navigation around the racetrack.

3) Dataset Generation. The generation of the dataset is divided into two stages. The first stage consists of finding the entry and exit points of the blind zone using the waypoints discovery method. We use the average waypoints found in ten runs to avoid drone collisions. Then, the average of the waypoints is used to generate a trajectory. Once the trajectory is defined, it serves as a reference for the classical controllers.

The next step is to associate the flight commands generated by the classical control algorithms with the images obtained from the drone at a frequency of 30 Hz while navigating the exemplary racetracks. In total, we collected three new datasets. The first dataset comprises 4,516 images associated with the flight commands generated by PI control. The second dataset comprises 5,885 images associated with the flight commands generated by the MPC. The third dataset comprises 5,894 images associated with the flight commands generated by the ADRC. In Table 1, we summarise the number of images captured in each dataset and the maximum and minimum values of each flight command recorded during navigation using classical control algorithms.

Table 1. Distribution of ground truth flight command (Flight CMD) values associated as labels to the images in the original dataset used in [35] to train DeepPilot and the three new datasets (PI, MPC and ADRC) recorded during navigation.

Dataset	Total of Mosaic Images	Flight CMD	Roll (S_ϕ)	Pitch (S_θ)	Yaw (S_ψ)	Altitude (S_h)
Original	10,334	**max**	± 0.9	+ 1	± 0.1	± 0.1
		min	± 0.1	± 0.1	± 0.05	± 0.05
PI	4,516	**max**	± 0.2	+ 1	± 0.99	± 0.3
		min	0.0	0.0	0.0	0.0
MPC	5,885	**max**	± 1	+ 1	± 1	± 1
		min	0.0	0.0002	0.0	± 0.00008
ADRC	5,894	**max**	± 0.7295	+ 1	± 0.09982	± 0.69443
		min	0.0	0.0	0.0	0.0

Finally, we used the PI, MPC and ADRC datasets to obtain three new models using the following parameters: 100 epochs, a batch size of 60, Adam optimiser, learning rate of 0.001, epsilon of 1e-08, and clip value of 1.5. Finally, the loss function used for each branch is shown in Eq. 11, where S_ϕ, S_θ, S_ψ *and* S_h corresponds to the flight command values for each image (I) recorded when piloting the drone using the PI controller and MPC, and $\hat{S_\phi}, \hat{S_\theta}, \hat{S_\psi}$ *and* $\hat{S_h}$ are the flight command predicted by the model. The loss function is evaluated four times, once for each control command: $S_\phi, S_\theta, S_\psi,$ *and* S_h. Thus, DeepPilot predicts values for $S_\phi, S_\theta, S_\psi, S_h$, and each variable falls within the $[-1, 1]$ range.

$$loss(I) = \alpha||\hat{S_\phi} - S_\phi||_2 + \alpha||\hat{S_\theta} - S_\theta||_2 + \alpha||\hat{S_\psi} - S_\psi||_2 + \alpha||\hat{S_h} - S_h||_2 \qquad (11)$$

We also multiply α by each term of the loss function to control the influence of each variable on the total loss function. Assigning a value of 0.3 to each term of the loss function indicates that each variable similarly influences the total loss function.

4 Experimental Framework

Our experimental framework runs on an Alienware R5 laptop with a Core i7 processor, 32 GB of RAM, and an NVIDIA GTX 1070 graphics card. The system operates on Ubuntu 20.04 LTS and uses the Robot Operating System (ROS) Noetic Ninjemys version. For communication, we leverage the Robot Operating System (ROS) as a channel

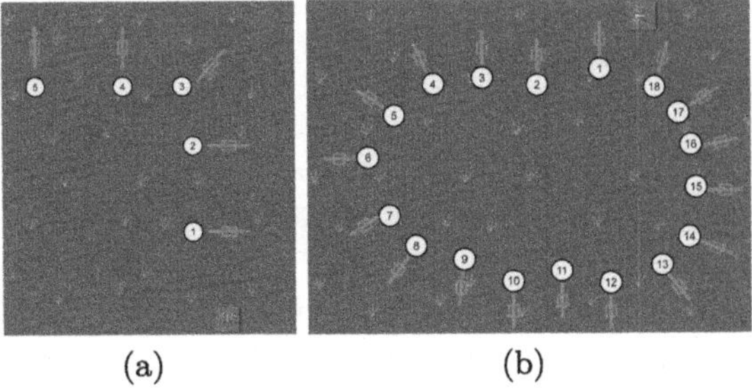

(a) (b)

Fig. 3. Test racetracks. (a) The first is composed of five gates placed at two meters, varying orientations. (b) The second test racetrack was composed of 18 gates at different heights and orientations in the RotorS simulator.

to obtain and transmit drone data. The simulation environment for the Parrot Bebop2 Drone is achieved using RotorS [11] in Gazebo 11. To run the DeepPilot network, we employed CUDA 11.6 and Cudnn 8.1 libraries, along with TensorFlow and Keras 2.8.0 frameworks.

We have used two racetracks to evaluate our approach. The first racetrack consists of five gates, each measuring two metres in height and positioned at varying angles to form a curved shape, as depicted in Fig. 3(a), within an area of 30 m $\times$ 20 m. The second racetrack has a reduced crossing space, increasing the difficulty of racing, with spacing between gates ranging from 6 to 15 m. The racetrack features 18 gates positioned at different heights and angles, as shown in Fig. 3(b), within an area of 68 m $\times$ 49 m. In addition, Gates 1, 2, 3, 5, 9, 12 and 14 have a height of 2 m, Gates 4, 7, 8, 11, 13, 15, 16 and 18 have a height of 2.5 m, and Gates 6, 10 and 17 are 3 m high. Note that this track involves significant turns for the drone, making it challenging to maintain a constant speed, as in real racetracks.

We compare the performance of seven pilots: 1) a human pilot (magenta); 2) a PI controller (green); 3) DeepPilot PI (light green); 4) an MPC (blue); 5) DeepPilot MPC (cyan blue); 6) an ADRC (red); and 7) DeepPilot ADRC (black). For this, we conducted ten runs for each pilot on the curved and ellipse racetracks. The DeepPilot models used only visual information, while classical controllers utilised feedback on drone position at 1000 Hz and a set of waypoints to follow a flight path. These waypoints were obtained using the Waypoint Discovery method [37]. We used the average waypoints discovered in ten runs to avoid collisions.

Figure 4 shows a top and side view of the best trajectories obtained during autonomous flight. MPC, ADRC, and DeepPilot ADRC exhibit oscillations between gates 2–4 in these trajectories. This behaviour is attributed to the vehicle's inertia, causing it to deviate from the reference path. However, this behaviour allows the network to learn to steer the drone more aggressively toward the gate when the gate is at a close distance, similar to how human pilots operate. On the other hand, the trajectories of PI and DeepPilot PI pilots tend to follow a more conservative path at lower speeds. While this approach allows the drone to navigate safely through the gates, it may limit its ability to respond when the drone is not centred on the gate and the gate is close.

Regarding speed performance, our results record a maximum speed of 2.81 m/s performed by the PI controller, followed by the human pilot with 2.65 m/s. Concerning

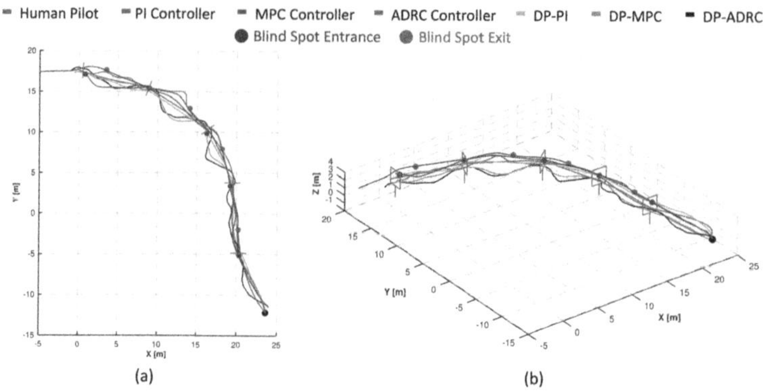

Fig. 4. Comparison of trajectories in the first test race tracks by human pilots, PI controller, DeepPilot PI (DP-PI), MPC, DeepPilot MPC (DP-MPC), ADRC, and DeepPilot ADRC (DP-ADRC). The left figure displays a top view, while the right figure shows a side view. The blind spot zone, obtained through the Waypoint Discovery method [37], is included. Classical controllers exclusively employ these points.

Table 2. Comparison of control signals generated in the second test track between classical controllers (mentors) and DeepPilot models that learned from the mentors.

	Flight CMD	Classic Controllers				DeepPilot Models			
		Roll (S_ϕ)	**Pitch** (S_θ)	**Yaw** (S_ψ)	**Altitude** (S_h)	**Roll** (S_ϕ)	**Pitch** (S_θ)	**Yaw** (S_ψ)	**Altitude** (S_h)
PI	**max**	± 0.29	+ 1	± 1	± 0.32	± 0.23	+ 0.57	± 1	± 0.17
	min	0.0	0.0	0.0	0.02	0.0	0.0	0.0	0.0
MPC	**max**	± 1	+ 1	± 0.78	± 1	± 0.53	+ 0.53	± 1	± 0.35
	min	0.0	0.01	0.0	0.0	0.0	0.0	0.0	0.0
ADRC	**max**	± 1	+ 1	± 0.24	± 0.2	± 1	+ 0.49	± 0.21	0.16
	min	0.01	0.0	0.0	0.0	0.0	0.01	0.0	0.008

the neural drone racer, DeepPilot MPC achieves a maximum speed of 0.90 m/s, followed by DeepPilot PI with a speed of 0.61 m/s.

To evaluate the performance of the DeepPilot models, we chose a more challenging track with gates at varying orientations and heights. Figure 5 shows that the human pilot performs a more stable trajectory than the other pilots. However, the PI controller and MPC exhibit stable movements like the human pilot. On the other hand, DeepPilot MPC and DeepPilot PI show some oscillations between gates, in contrast to the ADRC controller and DeepPilot ADRC, which do not oscillate as widely. Although this track shows more oscillatory behaviour in lateral movements, it is important to mention that this only happens when the gates have a separation distance of more than 5 m because the training set uses track segments with a separation distance of 4 m.

Regarding speed performance, our results record a maximum speed of 3 m/s performed by the human pilot, 2.6 m/s performed by the PI controller, and the MPC Controller with 2.39 m/s. Concerning the neural drone racer, DeepPilot MPC achieves a maximum speed of 1.0 m/s, followed by DeepPilot ADRC with a speed of 0.74 m/s.

In Table 2 we compare the maximum speeds recorded during a flight on the ellipse-shaped race track of the classical controllers and the DeepPilot models that learned from the flight signals obtained from classical control algorithms. It can be seen that

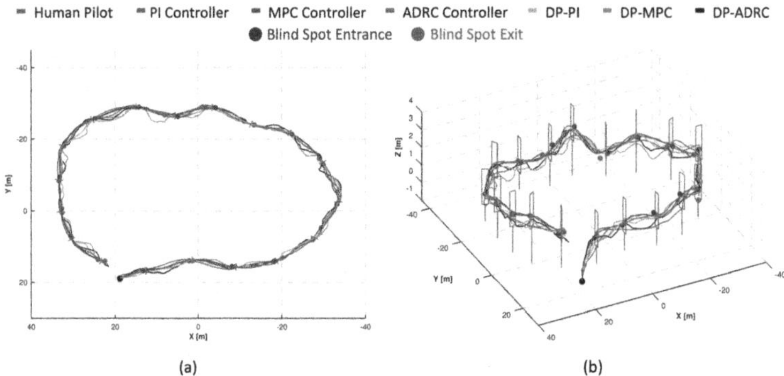

Fig. 5. Comparison of trajectories in the second test race tracks by human pilots, PI controller, DeepPilot PI (DP-PI), MPC, DeepPilot MPC (DP-MPC), ADRC, and DeepPilot ADRC (DP-ADRC). The left figure displays a top view, while the right figure shows a side view. The blind spot zone, obtained through the Waypoint Discovery method [37], is included. Classical controllers exclusively employ these points.

the predominant flight commands are roll and pitch for both the classical controllers and the new DeepPilot models. Note that flight controllers achieve better results, and this is because the controllers receive position feedback at a frequency of 1000 Hz and position references, allowing them to correct the drone's direction and velocity.

5 Conclusions

A learning-based methodology for the problem of Autonomous Drone Racing (ADR) using exemplary racetracks has been presented. With this approach, we propose a strategy to learn from track sections (straight line, zig-zag, semi-circle) instead of learning a single trajectory. Learning these key sections allows the drone to navigate any track as long as the gate is in view.

Our approach combines visual information with control techniques, enabling the drone to fly autonomously without human intervention. To achieve this, we utilise a Waypoint Discovery method to automatically identify the entry and exit positions of the blind spot zone (where the gate is no longer visible during the crossing) in each exemplary racetrack. After obtaining the set of waypoints, we conduct experiments using three classical control algorithms, PI, MPC, and ADRC, to follow a trajectory built with curves calculated from the waypoints. Subsequently, we generate a new dataset that associates temporal images captured in a mosaic image with flight commands provided by the controllers.

To evaluate the effectiveness of each controller in combination with the visual data, we train three new DeepPilot models: one model for each dataset. Each of the models is tested on two different tracks. The first track consists of two straight sections and one curve, while the second one contains all the exemplary racetrack elements. Our results demonstrate that our approach significantly improves the performance of the neural drone racer compared to the model that only learns basic movements. Furthermore, the neural drone racer does not rely on global positioning, unlike classical control methods. Although the DeepPilot models do not surpass the 3 m/s achieved by human pilots, with our approach, the neural drone racer navigates the track at a speed of 1 m/s using only visual information, just like human pilots do. As a future work, we will implement this methodology on high-speed cameras, as the flight controllers receive the drone's position at a frequency of 1000 Hz. In contrast, DeepPilot receives images at 30 Hz.

References

1. Arteaga-Pérez, M.A., Gutiérrez-Giles, A.: On the GPI approach with unknown inertia matrix in robot manipulators. Int. J. Control **87**(4), 844–860 (2014)
2. Cabrera-Ponce, A.A., Rojas-Perez, L.O., Carrasco-Ochoa, J.A., Martinez-Trinidad, J.F., Martinez-Carranza, J.: Gate detection for micro aerial vehicles using a single shot detector. IEEE Lat. Am. Trans. **17**(12), 2045–2052 (2019)
3. Cocoma-Ortega, J.A., Rojas-Perez, L.O., Cabrera-Ponce, A.A., Martinez-Carranza, J.: Overcoming the blind spot in CNN-based gate detection for autonomous drone racing. In: 2019 Workshop on Research, Education and Development of Unmanned Aerial Systems (RED UAS), pp. 253–259. IEEE (2019)
4. Cocoma-Ortega, J.A., Martinez-Carranza, J.: A CNN based drone localisation approach for autonomous drone racing. In: 11th International Micro Air Vehicle Competition and Conference (2019)
5. Cocoma-Ortega, J.A., Martínez-Carranza, J.: Towards high-speed localisation for autonomous drone racing. In: Martínez-Villaseñor, L., Batyrshin, I., Marín-Hernández, A. (eds.) Advances in Soft Computing: 18th Mexican International Conference on Artificial Intelligence, MICAI 2019, Xalapa, Mexico, October 27 – November 2, 2019, Proceedings, pp. 740–751. Springer, Cham (2019). https://doi.org/10.1007/978-3-030-33749-0_59
6. Davison, A.J., Reid, I.D., Molton, N.D., Stasse, O.: Monoslam: real-time single camera slam. IEEE Trans. Pattern Anal. Mach. Intell. **29**(6), 1052–1067 (2007)
7. Delmerico, J.A., Scaramuzza, D.: A benchmark comparison of monocular visual-inertial odometry algorithms for flying robots. null (2018). https://doi.org/10.1109/icra.2018.8460664
8. Fliess, M., Marquez, R., Delaleau, E., Sira-Ramírez, H.: Correcteurs proportionnels-intégraux généralisés. ESAIM: Control. Optim. Calculus Variations **7**, 23–41 (2002)
9. Foehn, P., et al.: Alphapilot: autonomous drone racing. arXiv preprint arXiv:2005.12813 (2020)
10. Foehn, P., Romero, A., Scaramuzza, D.: Time-optimal planning for quadrotor waypoint flight. Sci. Robot. **6**(56), eabh1221 (2021)
11. Furrer, F., Burri, M., Achtelik, M., Siegwart, R.: RotorS—a modular gazebo MAV simulator framework. In: Koubaa, A. (ed.) Robot Operating System (ROS). SCI, vol. 625, pp. 595–625. Springer, Cham (2016). https://doi.org/10.1007/978-3-319-26054-9_23
12. Han, J.: From PID to active disturbance rejection control. IEEE Trans. Industr. Electron. **56**(3), 900–906 (2009)
13. Jung, S., Cho, S., Lee, D., Lee, H., Shim, D.H., et al.: A direct visual servoing-based framework for the 2016 IROS autonomous drone racing challenge. J. Field Robot. **35**(1), 146–166 (2018)
14. Jung, S., Hwang, S., Shin, H., Shim, D.H., et al.: Perception, guidance, and navigation for indoor autonomous drone racing using deep learning. IEEE Robot. Autom. Lett. **3**(3), 2539–2544 (2018)

15. Jung, S., Lee, H., Hwang, S., Shim, D.H.: Real time embedded system framework for autonomous drone racing using deep learning techniques. In: 2018 AIAA Information Systems-AIAA Infotech@ Aerospace, p. 2138. Aerospace Research Central (2018)
16. Kaufmann, E., et al.: Beauty and the beast: Optimal methods meet learning for drone racing. In: 2019 International Conference on Robotics and Automation (ICRA), pp. 690–696. IEEE (2019)
17. Kaufmann, E., Loquercio, A., Ranftl, R., Dosovitskiy, A., Koltun, V., Scaramuzza, D., et al.: Deep drone racing: Learning agile flight in dynamic environments. In: Conference on Robot Learning, pp. 133–145. PMLR (2018)
18. Li, S., De Wagter, C., de Visser, C., Chu, Q., de Croon, G., et al.: In-flight model parameter and state estimation using gradient descent for high-speed flight. Int. J. Micro Air Veh. **11**, 1756829319833685 (2019)
19. Li, S., van der Horst, E., Duernay, P., De Wagter, C., de Croon, G.C., et al.: Visual model-predictive localization for computationally efficient autonomous racing of a 72-g drone. J. Field Robot. **37**(4), 667–692 (2020)
20. Li, S., Ozo, M.M., De Wagter, C., de Croon, G.C., et al.: Autonomous drone race: a computationally efficient vision-based navigation and control strategy. Robot. Auton. Syst. **133**, 103621 (2020)
21. Luukkonen, T.: Modelling and control of quadcopter. Independent Res. Project Appl. Math. Espoo **22**(22) (2011)
22. Madaan, R., et al.: Airsim drone racing lab. In: NeurIPS 2019 Competition and Demonstration Track, pp. 177–191. PMLR (2020)
23. Martinez-Carranza, J., Rojas-Perez, L.O.: Warehouse inspection with an autonomous micro air vehicle. Unmanned Syst. **10**(4), 329–342 (2022)
24. Mellinger, D., Kumar, V.: Minimum snap trajectory generation and control for quadrotors. In: 2011 IEEE International Conference on Robotics and Automation, pp. 2520–2525. IEEE (2011)
25. Moon, H., et al.: Challenges and implemented technologies used in autonomous drone racing. Intel. Serv. Robot. **12**(2), 137–148 (2019)
26. Mueller, M.W., Hehn, M., D'Andrea, R.: A computationally efficient motion primitive for quadrocopter trajectory generation. IEEE Trans. Rob. **31**(6), 1294–1310 (2015)
27. Mur-Artal, R., Tardós, J.D.: Orb-slam2: an open-source slam system for monocular, stereo and RGB-D cameras. IEEE Trans. Rob. (2017). https://doi.org/10.1109/tro.2017.2705103
28. Pfeiffer, C., Scaramuzza, D.: Expertise affects drone racing performance. arXiv preprint arXiv:2109.07307 (2021)
29. Pfeiffer, C., Scaramuzza, D.: Human-piloted drone racing: visual processing and control. IEEE Robot. Autom. Lett. **6**(2), 3467–3474 (2021)
30. Pham, H.X., Ugurlu, H.I., Le Fevre, J., Bardakci, D., Kayacan, E.: Deep learning for vision-based navigation in autonomous drone racing. In: Deep learning for robot perception and cognition, pp. 371–406. Elsevier (2022)
31. Rojas-Perez, L.O., Martinez-Carranza, J.: A temporal CNN-based approach for autonomous drone racing. In: 2019 Workshop on Research, Education and Development of Unmanned Aerial Systems (RED UAS), pp. 70–77. IEEE (2019)
32. Rojas-Perez, L.O., Martinez-Carranza, J.: Leveraging a neural pilot via automatic gain tuning using gate detection for autonomous drone racing. In: 13th International Micro Air Vehicle Conference at Delft, the Netherlands, pp. 110–118 (2022)
33. Rojas-Perez, L.O., Martínez-Carranza, J.: On-board processing for autonomous drone racing: an overview. Integration **80**, 46–59 (2021)

34. Rojas-Perez, L.O., Martinez-Carranza, J.: Deeppilot4pose: a fast pose localisation for MAV indoor flight using the oak-d camera. J. Real-Time Image Proc. **20**(1), 8 (2023)
35. Rojas-Perez, L.O., Martinez-Carranza, J.: Deeppilot: A CNN for autonomous drone racing. Sensors **20**(16), 4524 (2020)
36. Rojas-Perez, L.O., Martinez-Carranza, J.: Towards autonomous drone racing without GPU using an oak-d smart camera. Sensors **21**(22), 7436 (2021)
37. Rojas-Perez, L.O., Martinez-Carranza, J.: Where are the gates: discovering effective waypoints for autonomous drone racing. In: Advances in Artificial Intelligence-IBERAMIA 2022: 17th Ibero-American Conference on AI, Cartagena de Indias, Colombia, November 23–25, 2022, Proceedings, pp. 353–365. Springer (2023)
38. Romero, A., Penicka, R., Scaramuzza, D.: Time-optimal online replanning for agile quadrotor flight. IEEE Robot. Autom. Lett. **7**(3), 7730–7737 (2022)
39. Sira-Ramírez, H., Ramírez-Neria, M., Rodríguez-Angeles, A.: On the linear control of nonlinear mechanical systems. In: 49th IEEE Conference on Decision and Control (CDC), pp. 1999–2004. IEEE (2010)
40. Spedicato, S., Notarstefano, G.: Minimum-time trajectory generation for quadrotors in constrained environments. IEEE Trans. Control Syst. Technol. **26**(4), 1335–1344 (2017)

Eye Control and Motion with Deep Reinforcement Learning: In Virtual and Physical Environments

Sergio Arizmendi(✉), Asdrubal Paz, Javier González, and Hiram Ponce

Universidad Panamericana, Facultad de Ingeniería, Augusto Rodin 498, 03920 Ciudad de México, Mexico
{0213354,0264447,0215241,hponce}@up.edu.mx

Abstract. Attention mechanism in computer vision refers to scan, detect, and track a target object. This paper aims to develop and virtually train a machine learning model for object attention mechanism, combining object detection and mechanical automation. For this, we use Unity 3D Engine to model a simple scene in which two virtual cameras align together to realize a monocular attention in specific objects. Deep reinforcement learning, via ML-agent's library, was used to train a model that aligns the virtual cameras. Moreover, the model was transferred to a physical camera to replicate the performance of attention mechanism.

Keywords: Machine learning · Deep reinforcement learning · M.L. Agent · Unity · Learning environment. · Neural Network

1 Introduction

In the last ten years there has been an explosion in artificial intelligence (AI) development in mechanical task automation. Though there are many mechanical tasks already in the process of being automated by AI, the most popular example being self-driving cars [2], the primary required skill tying most mechanical task automatons is computer vision. Particularly in very precise tasks, like the potentially life changing AI aided surgery [5], AI vision helps us deal with complex visual inputs to identify and choose the best possible course of action.

Whilst a large amount of visual inputs can be inefficient to interpret manually for humans, the advancements in Convolutional Neural Networks (CNN) for image processing have allowed the development of large convolutional networks capable of learning from millions of images [9]. In particular, in the realm of object detection, there have been continuous improvements in the speed and in the number of distinct discernible categories. One of the most recognised and most recent of these models being YOLOv7 [8], a real time object detection AI well recognized for its speed and accuracy balance.

One of the main advantages of training AI on computer vision is the development of simultaneous localization and mapping (SLAM) [4]. Utilizing computer

H. Calvo et al. (Eds.): MICAI 2023, LNAI 14391, pp. 99–109, 2024.
https://doi.org/10.1007/978-3-031-47765-2_8

vision for an AI to form a visual understanding of its surroundings is fundamental to mechanical task automation, for example in self driving cars [2]. The key aspect of this being the capacity to train these models entirely from previously gather data, in a single word: virtually [10,11].

Although mapping the entirety of an agent's surroundings with computer vision is beyond the scope of this paper, we can use computer vision to develop an agent's capacity to focus on the relevant parts of its environment. In other words, with object detection an agent could recognise the relevant objects in its environment, and with mechanical automation of its eyes' motion it could also focus its vision on the relevant objects.

This paper aims to develop and virtually train a machine learning model for object attention mechanism, combining object detection and mechanical automation. For this, we use Unity 3D Engine to model a simple scene in which two virtual cameras align together to realize a monocular attention in specific objects. Deep reinforcement learning, via ML-agent's library, was used to train a model that aligns the virtual cameras. Moreover, the model was transferred to a physical camera to replicate the performance of attention mechanism.

The rest of the paper is organized as follows. Section 2 presents the proposal. Section 3 describes the experiments. Section 4 shows the results and discussion of the work. Lastly, Sect. 5 concludes the paper.

2 Proposed Solution

To fully train a functional AI model within a virtual environment there are two prerequisites: one is the virtual environment within which we'll be performing the training and the testing, and second is an AI model capable of visual learning and mechanical task automation.

For designing and testing within a virtual environment, we require the environment to be easily adaptable and fast when rendering our tests, as any AI model we decide to train will require a lot of trial and error before becoming fully viable. On the other hand, for the AI model, we require an easily adaptable model with zero to no input required from the user and that can learn from a simple but randomized scenario.

The options we came up with are as follows:

- The Unreal Engine with the Kythera AI plugin.
- The Unity Engine with the ml-agents library.
- A custom engineered engine with a Tensorflow or Pytorch based model.

Considering the requirements previously mentioned, we'll be utilizing Unity with the ml-agents library, as we'll be working with a physics engine we are familiar with. In addition, the ml-agents library already includes a comprehensive deep learning model used by the OpenAI team to design many mechanical task training scenarios [3]. Although the Unreal Engine posed an even more efficient and adaptable develop environment, the complexity of working with a fully C++ based engine was beyond the time scope of this paper.

Whilst there are limitations to the capabilities of the Unity Engine when simulating real world scenarios, for example: in Fig. 1 we can clearly see how cameras in the Unity Engine have a limited field of view (FoV) delimited by six planes; we can overcome those limitations by designing our training scenarios around them, in the Fig. 1 example: we could design our test scenarios to fit entirely within the FoV of the camera.

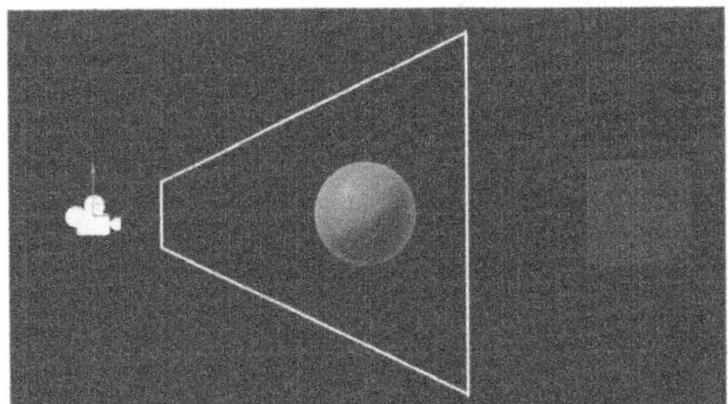

(a) Orthographic view of a camera's FoV with two objects in front.

(b) Camera's perspective with one of the objects not inside the FoV.

Fig. 1. Restrictions on the field of view (FoV) of a Unity Engine's camera.

2.1 Deep Reinforcement Learning and the NN's Structure

The ml-agent's library makes use of Deep Reinforcement Learning to calibrate an agent's response (resulting actions) from a given set of observations, using Proximal Policy Optimization (PPO) to maximise the amount of reward the agent receives [6] (for a visualized example see Fig. 2a). Thus, a set of steps must take place before and after every action taken by the agent (Fig. 2b):

1. Observation: Before any actions are taken by the agent, a set of observations must be passed to the agent via the CollectObservations method, called once per Fixed Update [7], or directly throw a Sensor component.
2. Decision: After this, the ml-agents' library runs inference on the deep neural network to determine the set of actions to be taken.
3. Action: A set of actions is passed via the OnActionReceived method, also called once per Fixed Update [7], where the agent must perform the relevant actions.
4. Rewards: Finally, in the OnActionReceived method as well, we must set the rewards for the agent's state, by calling either the SetReward or the AddReward methods. *Note: rewards can also be negative (as punishments).*

The resulting NN is shaped with a set of parameter provided before training (Fig. 3), the most important in regards to the NN's shape are:

- A goal condition type, which separates the hidden layer in two parts: one dedicated to the "goal observations" and another dedicated to every other observation.
- The number of layers, setting the total amount of hidden layers.
- The number of hidden units, setting the number of neurons per hidden layer.
- The memory sequence length / memory size, setting the number of layers and number of neurons per layer inside of the NN's memory.

By adjusting these parameters, we can also control the effectiveness and speed of training, reducing / increasing the focus on certain parameters and reducing / increasing the amount of neurons the agent has to train with.

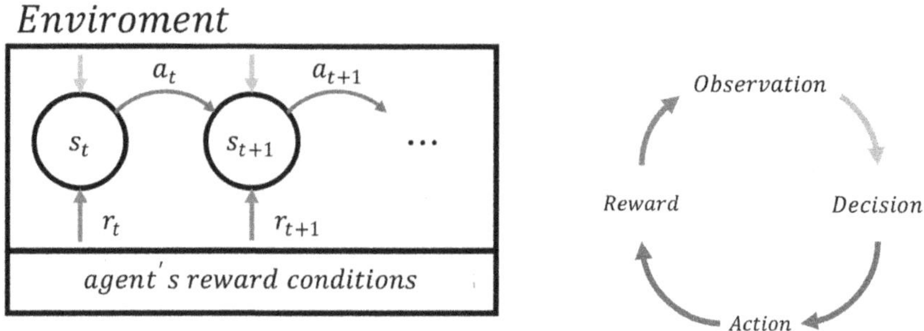

(a) Abstract model of reinforcement learning as a state transition.

(b) Reinforcement learning's 4 main steps.

Fig. 2. Reinforcement learning visualized.

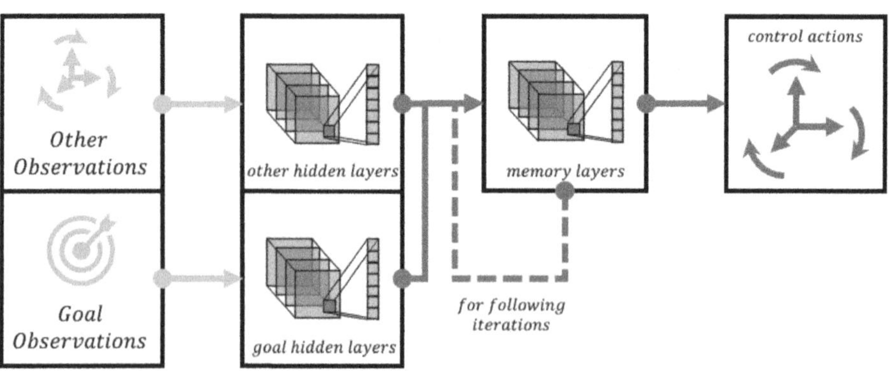

Fig. 3. Neural Network Model.

2.2 Optimising the Learning Process

One of the key disadvantages of utilizing the Unity Engine is the heavy use of processing resources (GPU and CPU), on running Unity itself. The main performance outlier being Unity's graphics engine, which is designed for very broad use cases. Whilst we might be able to design a graphically realistic training environment within Unity, training the ml-agents on such an environment would require more processing resources and time than we have currently available.

This is a serious issue for more realistic training with the ml-agents' library and for the purposes of this paper, as the main method of training is supposed to be virtual. The alternative we propose is training the agent's image processing outside of Unity using an image processing AI to handle the graphical aspects of training and Unity to handle the physics and motion control of the agent (Fig. 4). This alternative should vastly optimise training times and processing power, as the Unity's Graphics Engine won't be required.

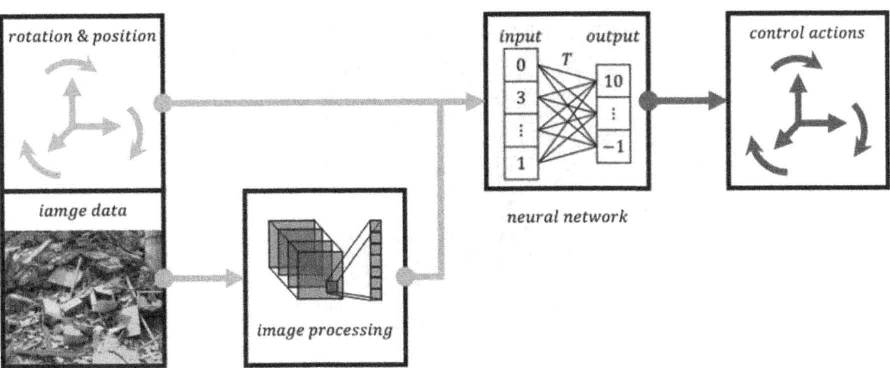

Fig. 4. Optimized model with image processing.

The selected image processing model was YOLO [8]. The advantages of this model are it's accessibility and efficiency, as it can be readily trained for in real-time object detection. Furthermore, the outputs of this image processing model are in the form of coordinates relative to the camera's view that can normalized and passed directly into the ml-agents NN's as observations.

3 The Experiment

The training scenario will consist of the agent (with only its two cameras as eyes) and a back wall with a target to aim at (Fig. 5). The specifics on the scenarios training can be found in the following table (Table 1).

The resulting scenario (Fig. 5) doesn't need to mimic a full 360° agent rotation to look at the target, as the intent is for the agent to also learn how to turn towards the target.

Table 1. Eye motion and target focusing scenario conditions.

Observations	Actions	Rewards/Punishments
Cameras' angles (4)	Camera rotations relative to each rotation plane, either positive or negative at a maximum speed of 30° per second (4)	Punish agent slightly every frame
Cameras' angle limits (4)		Reward agent on seeing the target partially
Target in view flag (2)		Reward agent on fully seeing the target
Cameras' compressed view ports as 256×256 pixel arrays		Reward agent for holding sight on target for five seconds

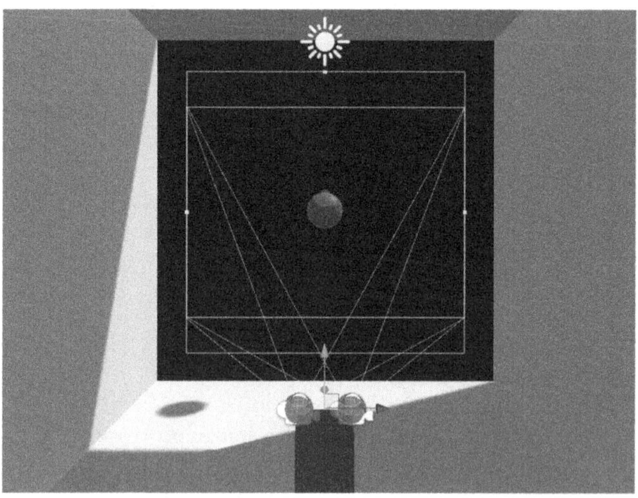

Fig. 5. Optimized model with image processing.

To pass the camera's view to the ml-agent, we'll be taking advantage of Unity's camera objects paired with the ml-agents library's CameraSensor component [1]. The camera object in the Unity Engine has multiple adaptable attributes like field of view, resolution, or even the ability to simulate a real camera's parameters. And, the ml-agents library's CameraSensor component can pre-process any cameras' input, compressing it into the desired pixel width and height.

3.1 Optimizing Training with Image Detection

Rather than using the cameras' as sensors, we can assume the image processing algorithm passes the target's relative position on each camera's view as a total of four observations. This would practically reduce observations from a 256×256 array for each camera to three observations per camera, with one added observation for when there is no object on the camera's view.

For this further learning process optimization, we'll be taking advantage of the VectorSensor component [1], as it will allow us to pass into the agent's brain model the relative positions of the desired object on the camera's view.

3.2 Testing with a Real Camera

To test the overall model's results, the model was adapted to move a security camera parsing the ml-agent's outputs as controls for the rotation of each axis (positive, negative or still). After combining each axis' movements, the camera can move in the desired directions (up, down, left, right, up-left, up-right, down-left and down-right).

To process the camera's results the following procedure was used:

1. First the camera will capture a single frame, passing the image via the ONVIF protocol to a computer.
2. Then, the YOLO algorithm will process the image, detecting the relative position of the desired object on the camera's view, in this case a "keyboard".
3. Finally the ml-agent would receive the relative position data and return to the camera the expected direction of motion.

3.3 Performance Metrics

Based on the rewards and punishments setup for the agent to train on, we'll be measuring the agent's performance relative to two metrics listed below:

- The reward obtained by the agent.
- The time the agent takes to complete each episode.

One consideration with these metrics is that the reward obtained will increase relative to how fast the agent finds its target. Although, not always, as some punishment was assigned for moving the camera away from the target (Table 1).

Another consideration is that the upper limit on episode length is 24 s, so the first agent's failing to find the target within those 24 s, will all be grouped around that maximum episode length.

On the other hand, to measure the overall model results with the real camera, well be looking at how the camera focuses on a "keyboard". The relative effectiveness of the model we'll focus on how fast the camera can place the keyboard into focus, and how well it can center on the keyboard.

4 Training Results and Discussion

Although the ml-agents package comes with a flexible set of training process's configurations that can be modified in order to improve the final training results [1], we carried out multiple tests with different parameters and the result presented here are the best obtained from all tested configurations for each scenario.

In the case of the first scenario with a CameraSensor component, the parameters modified over the default where:

- max_steps to 5,000,000
- batch_size to 128
- extrinsic → gamma to 0.8
- curiosity → strength to 0.1
- curiosity → gamma to 0.8
- network_settings → hidden_units to 32
- network_settings → num_layers to 2
- network_settings → memory → memory_size to 32
- network_settings → memory → sequence_length to 32

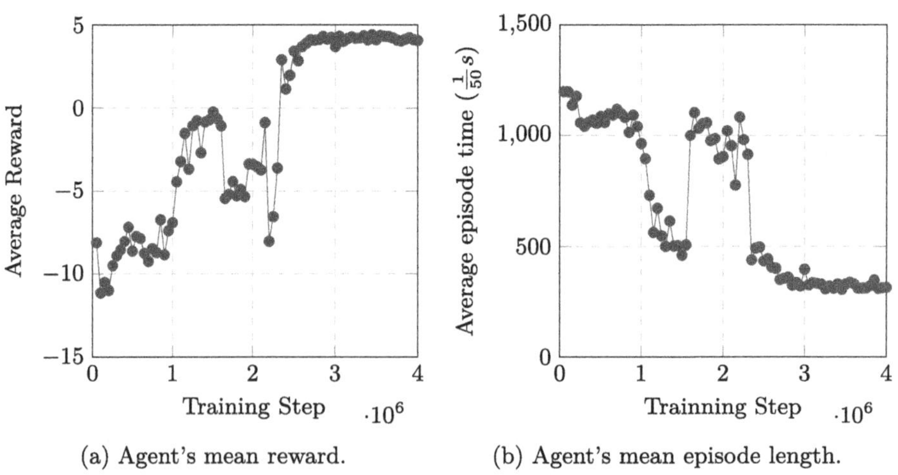

(a) Agent's mean reward. (b) Agent's mean episode length.

Fig. 6. CameraSensor based agent's training results by training step.

As can be seen in the previous graphs (Fig. 6), training peaked at around step 3,000,000 with a minimum episode length of around 5 s. This means the agents are capable of almost instantly finding the target, since 5 s is the minimum time the agent must hold the target in view for the episode to complete.

Whilst the final goal was achieved, it is clear from the agent's mean reward that training wasn't as smooth as expected, since around steps 1,500,000 to 2,500,000 the agent's completion times drastically increased before falling of again. This behaviour can be explained by the size of the resulting neural network. Because of the large amount of neurons required to process the 256×256 pixel arrays for each camera, the agents must learn to ignore most of the pixel signals. A process that could be leading to over-fitting in the early stages of training, thus under-performing after more rigorous training.

Overall training took about 12 h, which would also prove not ideal for more complex training tasks. To help reduce this issues, we trained a NN with the same learning settings but with the optimizations mentioned in Sect. 3.1.

In the case of the second scenario with the Optimized agent's training, the parameters modified over the default where:

- max_steps to 5,000,000
- batch_size to 32
- extrinsic → gamma to 0.8
- curiosity → strength to 0.1
- curiosity → gamma to 0.8
- network_settings → hidden_units to 64
- network_settings → num_layers to 1
- network_settings → memory → memory_size to 32

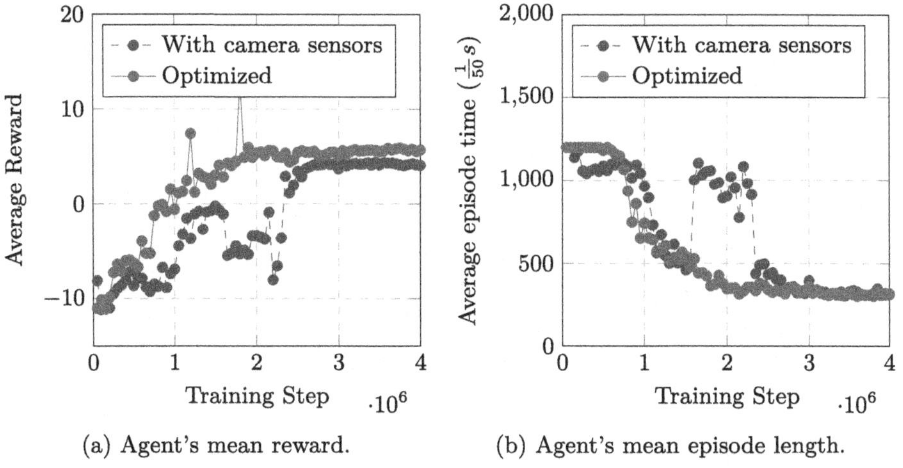

(a) Agent's mean reward.

(b) Agent's mean episode length.

Fig. 7. Optimized agent's training results by training step.

When compared to the previous model's results (Fig. 6), the optimized model is a clear improvement (Fig. 7); displaying a more controlled and constant improvement, with final episode length averaging around the same 5 s per episode.

With this new model, training times were reduced significantly, with training peaking at 2,000,000 steps, and overall training taking less than 2 h.

4.1 Testing with a Real Camera

Whilst the camera information processing procedure worked properly on a single frame basis (Fig. 8), the large delay from the ONVIF protocol (300 ms) and the inability to precompress the images coming from the camera slowed down the model significantly. Running the YOLO object detection model on the uncompressed images (1920 × 1080 pixels), took around (7000 ms) per frame.

Fig. 8. Single frame from camera test with a keyboard as object.

After attempting to compress the images before passing them into YOLO and increasing the overall delay, we decided to test just the focusing aspect of the agent with a virtually set target. In this case, we set the target on the center of a lamp (Fig. 9).

Fig. 9. Camera test with lamp and without object detection.

When tested on a virtually set target with no reference point, the NN was no consistently capable of finding the desired target point, without the object detection algorithm. But, although the image processing wasn't efficient enough to run in real time as expected, the trained NN did seem to couple well with the camera's motion.

5 Conclusions

Training ml-agents in virtual environments proved to be a very effective technique when tested on a very basic task. Throughout the tests, the ml-agents performed as expected, and with basic adjustments to the overall NN design the end results was a very efficient NN at finding its target within the expected amount of time.

Although when tested with the camera, the object detection algorithm didn't perform as expected, the NN coupled well with the camera. But, a very lacking aspect of the NN's results was its inability to find the virtually set target consistently if the latter one was set outside of the camera's field of view. A possible method, to be tested in a different paper, of optimizing the random search that the agent must do to find its target could be to directly process some of the image information within the NN, leaving the object detection to the rest of the model.

On the other hand, the object detection algorithm worked as expected on a frame by frame basis, but a more efficient approach is required for the complete model to run on real cameras with our currently available hardware. For future work we intend to dedicate more time optimising this aspect of the model, as it was the primary outlier in our results.

References

1. ml agents@unity3d.com: unity ml-agents toolkit (2022). https://github.com/Unity-Technologies/ml-agents/tree/develop/docs
2. Badue, C., et al.: Self-driving cars: a survey. Expert Syst. Appl. **165**, 113816 (2021)
3. Baker, B., et al.: Emergent tool use from multi-agent autocurricula. arXiv preprint arXiv:1909.07528 (2019)
4. Grisetti, G., Kümmerle, R., Stachniss, C., Burgard, W.: A tutorial on graph-based slam. IEEE Intell. Transp. Syst. Mag. **2**(4), 31–43 (2010)
5. Praeger, M., Xie, Y., Grant-Jacob, J.A., Eason, R.W., Mills, B.: Playing optical tweezers with deep reinforcement learning: in virtual, physical and augmented environments. Mach. Learn. Sci. Technol. **2**(3), 035024 (2021)
6. Schulman, J., Wolski, F., Dhariwal, P., Radford, A., Klimov, O.: Proximal policy optimization algorithms. arXiv preprint arXiv:1707.06347 (2017)
7. Technologies, U.: Monobehaviour.fixedupdate(). unity documentation (2021)
8. Wang, C.Y., Bochkovskiy, A., Liao, H.Y.M.: YOLOv7: trainable bag-of-freebies sets new state-of-the-art for real-time object detectors. In: Proceedings of the IEEE/CVF Conference on Computer Vision and Pattern Recognition (CVPR), pp. 7464–7475 (2023)
9. Ward, T.M., et al.: Computer vision in surgery. Surgery **169**(5), 1253–1256 (2021)
10. Won, J., Gopinath, D., Hodgins, J.: Control strategies for physically simulated characters performing two-player competitive sports. ACM Trans. Graph. (TOG) **40**(4), 1–11 (2021)
11. Zakka, K., Zeng, A., Lee, J., Song, S.: Form2Fit: learning shape priors for generalizable assembly from disassembly. In: Proceedings of the IEEE International Conference on Robotics and Automation (2020)

Fingerspelling Recognition in Mexican Sign Language (LSM) Using Machine Learning

Ricardo Fernando Morfín-Chávez[1], Jesús Javier Gortarez-Pelayo[2], and Irvin Hussein Lopez-Nava[1(✉)]

[1] Computer Science Department, Centro de Investigación Científica y de Educación Superior de Ensenada, 22860 Ensenada, BC, Mexico
{morfinrf,hussein}@cicese.edu.mx

[2] Faculty of Sciences, Universidad Autónoma de Baja California, 22860 Ensenada, BC, Mexico
jesus.gortarez@uabc.edu.mx

Abstract. Sign languages allow deaf people to express their thoughts, emotions, and opinions in a complex and complete way, just like oral languages. Each sign language is unique and has its own grammar, syntax, and vocabulary. Mexican Sign Language (LSM) is characterized by rich gestural and facial expression that gives it a great communicative and linguistic capacity. In the study of LSM, two main components have been identified: (i) fingerspelling, and (ii) ideograms. The first is similar to spelling in oral languages, and is used to communicate proper names, technical terms or words for which there are no specific signs or which are little known to the deaf community. In this paper, we propose a method for recognizing the LSM alphabet by using machine learning-based techniques capable of classifying the signs made by 10 test subjects. 21-keypoints of the hands were extracted from the MediaPipe library, in order to have a better representation to feed the classification models. The results when classifying the 21 letters exceeded an F1-score of 0.98 with 3 of the 4 trained classifiers, and scoring values below 0.95 for less than 3 letters. Tools such as those proposed in this work can facilitate seamless communication by translating Spanish into LSM and vice versa, allowing both communities to engage effectively in various settings.

Keywords: LSM · Sign language recognition · Sign language classification · Mexican Sign Language · Fingerspelling · Dactylology

1 Introduction

The importance of sign languages lies in their fundamental role in communication and access to information for the deaf community [9]. Through gestures, movements and facial expressions, sign languages allow deaf people to express

Supported by Consejo Nacional de Ciencia y Tecnología.

H. Calvo et al. (Eds.): MICAI 2023, LNAI 14391, pp. 110–120, 2024.
https://doi.org/10.1007/978-3-031-47765-2_9

their thoughts, emotions and opinions in as complex and complete a way as oral languages do, since this is the deaf person's native language and their natural form of communication [5].

It is essential to understand that each sign language is unique and has its own grammar, syntax and vocabulary, just like any oral language [14]. There is no universal sign language that all deaf people use around the world. Instead, each country or region has its own sign language, adapted to its culture and linguistic context. Even within a country, variations and regionalisms may exist, as well as in oral languages.

In the specific case of Mexico, the Mexican Sign Language, or *Lengua de Señas Mexicana* (LSM) in Spanish, has been officially recognized and is protected by the law for the inclusion of people with disabilities. This language serves as the primary language for the deaf community in urban regions of Mexico. Derived from the French Sign Language family [7], LSM boasts an estimated number of 250,000 speakers[1].

LSM is characterized by rich gestural and facial expression that gives it a great communicative and linguistic capacity. LSM is the mother tongue of many deaf people in Mexico and forms an essential part of their cultural identity. According to the general law for the inclusion of people with disabilities[2], LSM is defined as "A series of gestural signs articulated with the hands and accompanied by facial expressions, intentional gaze and body movement, endowed with linguistic function".

The importance of new technologies, including artificial intelligence (AI) models, for bridging the communication gap between the deaf and Spanish-speaking communities in Mexico is significant. AI-powered sign language interpretation tools can facilitate seamless communication by translating Spanish into LSM and vice versa, allowing both communities to engage effectively in various settings. These technologies empower the deaf community to access critical information and services while fostering greater inclusion and understanding among Spanish speakers.

In the study of LSM, two main components have been identified: (i) dactylology or fingerspelling, and (ii) ideograms. Dactylology is similar to spelling in oral languages, and is used to communicate proper names, technical terms or words for which there are no specific signs or which are little known to the deaf community. On the other hand, ideograms are gestural representations that can express a word or a complete idea, using specific hand configurations, facial expressions, and body movements [13].

The present work aims to develop a novel method to detect in real-time the static letters of the LSM alphabet from images captured by a webcam. This involves the application of computer vision technologies and the use of machine learning algorithms for the classification stage. The rest of the paper is organized

---

1 Boletín No. 5854: "El objetivo es impulsar la alfabetización", Cámara de Diputados, México, XLV Legislatura.

2 Ley general para la inclusión de las personas con discapacidad: https://www.diputados.gob.mx/LeyesBiblio/pdf/LGIPD.pdf (Accessed: Jul/23).

as follows. Section 2 details related work that has addressed the recognition of the LSM alphabet; in Sect. 3 the proposed methodology including data capture, processing and classification techniques, is described; Sect. 4 presents the results obtained in fingerspelling recognition; finally, Sect. 5 summarizes the findings, limitations of the study, and future work.

2 Related Work

In recent years, scientific research has been carried out, along with the development and implementation of systems, for the automatic recognition of static and dynamic LSM signs. Two approaches based on different types of sensing technologies have been identified: (i) from sensors that people can wear, such as inertial sensors or gloves, and (ii) from 2D and 3D cameras. The latter approach has the advantage of being non-intrusive and allows the capture of multiple users. However, it suffers from the challenges of vision systems, such as illumination and occlusion. Despite this, most work in the area has focused on this approach, due to the low cost of cameras and the development of models that allow human motion tracking.

In [6] the authors present a system for recognizing five signs that represent the vowels (A, E, I, O, U) and two consonants (B, L) of the LSM. This system uses one movement sensor for capturing depth images and obtaining information from the skeleton of the hands. Random forests, Decision trees and artificial neural networks were used for building the classifiers. The proposed system achieves an accuracy of 76.19% for recognizing the seven LSM signs.

In [8] the authors present a new method for LSM alphanumerical sign recognition based on 3D Haar-like features extracted from depth images captured by the Microsoft Kinect sensor. Features were processed with a boosting algorithm. The method is capable of recognizing a set of signs from the five vowels (A, E, I, O, U) and five numbers (1, 2, 3, 4, 5). Also, they compared the results with the use of traditional 2D Haar-like features. The system reached an overall 95% of accuracy.

In [10] the authors introduce a software capable of facilitating the data acquisition with the Intel Realsense camera. This software digitizes 22 keypoints from the hand of the user in coordinates (x, y, z). In addition, the software was evaluated with 19 users recording the 27 letters of the LSM alphabet. The dataset was comprised of 90,305 records after eliminating null records and was used for training an artificial neural network obtaining 80% of correctly classified instances.

In [11] the authors introduce an automatic sign language recognition system based on multiple gestures, including hands, body, and face. They used a depth camera to obtain the 3D coordinates of the motions and recurrent neural networks for classification. For this work, the authors collected 30 different signs of the LSM: alphabet (static: A, B, C, D; dynamic: J, K, Q, X), questions, days of the week, and frequent words. The best model obtained an accuracy of 97% on clean test data, and 90% on highly noisy data.

In [12] the authors present the methodology for recognizing objects in an image. The techniques used were: segmentation, feature extraction and classification of objects. The fuzzy c-means algorithm was used for segmentation, whilst for feature extraction Hu moments as geometrical descriptors. Finally, the geometric features that provide the seven moments were used as input to a classifier, recognizing static signs (21 letters) in the LSM correctly at a rate of 91%.

The studies mentioned above demonstrate various approaches, each employing distinct algorithms and technologies, contributing to the advancement of automatic LSM recognition and facilitating communication for the deaf community in Mexico.

3 Methods

This section will describe the methods used for automatic recognition of the LSM alphabet based on machine learning, which is illustrated in Fig. 1.

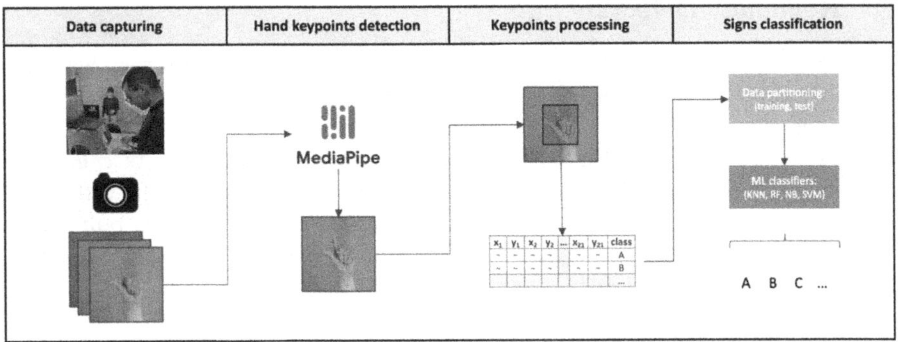

Fig. 1. Proposed steps for fingerspelling recognition of LSM alphabet.

3.1 Data Capturing

Data were captured with the help of 10 participants. Each participant captured 21 distinct signs, representing the alphabet of the Mexican Sign Language, with the exception of dynamic signs such as J, K, Ñ, Q, X, and Z. All signs were based on the LSM dictionary "Manos con Voz" [13].

Participants were instructed to perform each sign using their right hand in front of a green screen. For each sign, two videos of three seconds each were recorded: one with subtle wrist movements and another with pronounced movements. This approach aimed to capture signs in various variations and viewing angles, thereby assessing the models' robustness in recognizing different sign representations.

After recording the videos, frames were extracted and subjected to Mediapipe[3] processing for hand segmentation, producing images of hands against a green background. The dataset examples shown in Figs. 2b, c and d illustrate varying levels of variation, ranging from low to high.

[3] https://developers.google.com/mediapipe.

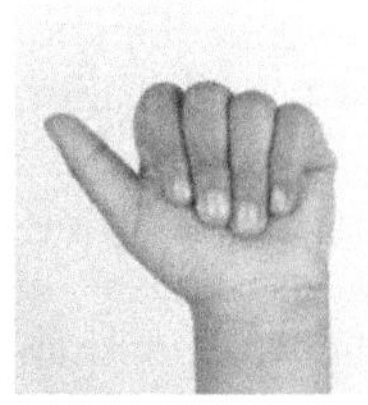

(a) Guide for letter A [13].

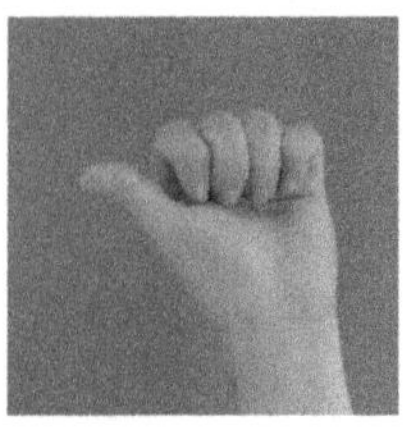

(b) Palm with little variation.

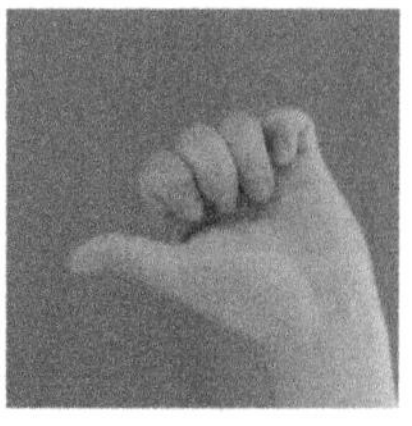

(c) Palm facing the front.

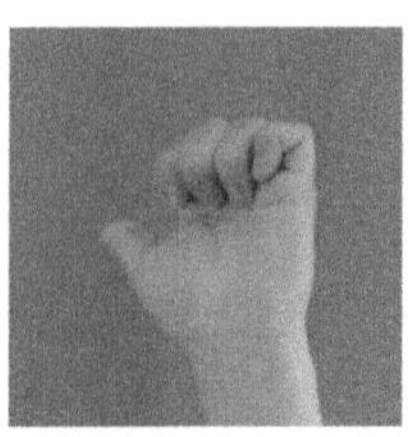

(d) Palm rotating inwards.

Fig. 2. Examples of the letter A sign: guide (a), with little variation (b), and with major variations (c)–(d).

3.2 Keypoints Detection

In addition to being used to segment the hand, the MediaPipe library was also used to extract landmarks, also called keypoints, of the hands found in the images segmented. For each detected hand, it is possible to extract a collection of 21 reference points (see Fig. 3), and each point is represented by its x, y, and z components. The x and y components are normalized according to the width and height of the image, respectively, while z represents the depth of the point from the wrist as the origin. In addition, it is possible to determine if the detected hand is right-handed or left-handed.

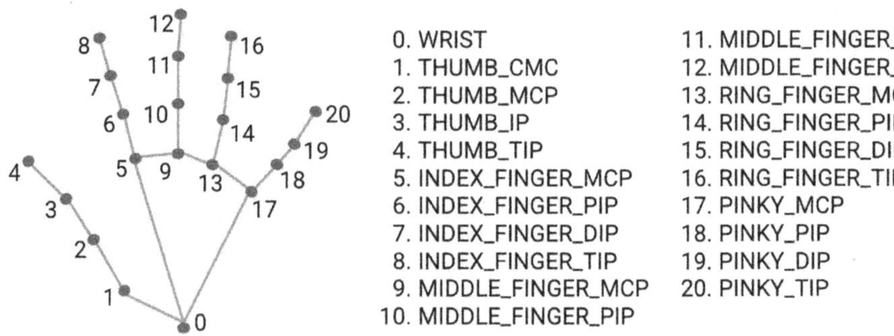

Fig. 3. Keypoints of the hand detected by MediaPipe

3.3 Keypoints Processing

The first step in data processing was to determine whether the hand being detected was a right hand or a left hand. In this work, only the right hands were used for sign recognition. After the 21 hand keypoints were extracted, for each keypoint, the depth component z was discarded, whilst the x and y components were normalized using Min-max normalization. This method transforms the data to a common scale by mapping each component to a value between 0 and 1.

The normalization procedure involved calculating the minimum and maximum values of both the x and y components instance-wise. Subsequently, each data point (x, y) was scaled using the following formula:

$$x_{scaled} = \frac{y - x_{min}}{x_{max} - x_{min}} \qquad y_{scaled} = \frac{y - y_{min}}{y_{max} - y_{min}} \tag{1}$$

As a result, the normalized keypoints can be seen graphically in Fig. 4. After normalizing each of the 21 keypoints, the new components are flattened into a single vector of the form $\chi = [x_1, y_1, x_2, y_2, ..., x_{21}, y_{21}]$, which will be used as a feature vector.

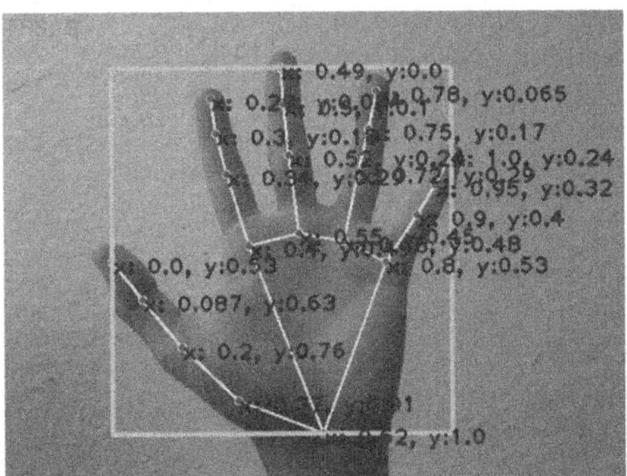

Fig. 4. Normalized keypoints of the hand.

3.4 Classification

Four inference algorithms were used for building the sign classifiers, which represent different families. First, k-nearest neighbors (k-NN) is a non-parametric and supervised learning method. It classifies a new data point (keypoint of the hand) by selecting the majority class among its k nearest neighbors in the feature space [3]. Random forest (RF) algorithm is an ensemble learning method that builds multiple decision trees and combines their predictions to make more accurate and robust classifications or regressions. It uses random subsets of features (keypoints) and data samples to reduce overfitting and improve generalization [1]. The Naive Bayes (NB) algorithm is a probabilistic classification method based on Bayes' theorem, assuming feature (keypoints) independence. It calculates the probability of a data point belonging to a specific class and selects the class with the highest probability [4]. Finally, Support Vector Machines (SVM) seek to find the optimal hyperplane that best separates data points into different classes, maximizing the margin between them. SVM is widely used for its ability to handle high-dimensional data and nonlinear decision boundaries [2].

4 Results

The total number of instances (set of keypoints that represent a sign from an image) was 91 326, with an average of 4 341 images per class and a standard deviation of 113. This dataset is considered fairly balanced due to the similar distribution of instances across classes. The model was offline validated using k-fold cross-validation, with $k = 10$; it means, the dataset is divided into 10 subsets, training on 9 and testing on the remaining one in a repeated and averaged process, providing a robust estimate of model performance.

For each of the classes (letters in LSM alphabet), the values of precision, recall, and F1-score were calculated. Precision (P) measures the accuracy of positive predictions, recall (R) assesses the classifier's ability to detect positive instances, and the F1-score (F1) combines both metrics to provide a balanced evaluation. These metrics were calculated as follows:

$$\text{Precision} = \frac{\text{True Positives}}{\text{True Positives} + \text{False Positives}} \tag{2}$$

$$\text{Recall} = \frac{\text{True Positives}}{\text{True Positives} + \text{False Negatives}} \tag{3}$$

$$\text{F1-score} = 2 \times \frac{\text{Precision} \times \text{Recall}}{\text{Precision} + \text{Recall}} \tag{4}$$

where True Positives refers to the number of correctly predicted positive instances by the classifier; False Positives refers to the number of instances that were incorrectly predicted as positive by the classifier, in fact, negative; False Negatives refers to the number of instances that were incorrectly predicted as negative by the classifier but are, in fact, positive.

In Table 1 the results of the models built from hand keypoints data in order to recognize the 21 static signs of the LSM alphabet are shown. The individual results by class (letter) and the weighted average (wt. avg.) by classifier are presented. Three of the classifiers score very good results based on F1-score, RF 0.98 ($\sigma = 0.015$), SVM 0.98 ($\sigma = 0.016$), and kNN 0.98 ($\sigma = 0.017$). Analyzing the letters individually and considering the average of the four classifiers, five of the letters recorded an F1-score higher than 0.98: G, H, I, L, Y, while three of the letters recorded an F1-score lower than 0.90: R, U, V.

These results by letter are consistent with the individual results by classifiers. The classifier kNN recorded F1-score values lower than 0.95 for the letters N, S, U; while for the letters I and L, it had a classification of 1. The classifier RF recorded F1-score values lower than 0.95 for the letters M, N, U. The classifier SVM recorded F1-score values

Table 1. Classification results for LSM alphabet. **Metrics**, P: Precision (Eq. 2), R: Recall (Eq. 3), F1: f1-score (Eq. 4). **Algorithms**, kNN: k-Nearest Neighbors, RF: Random Forest, NB: Naive Bayes, SVM: Support Vector Machines.

Letter	kNN			RF			NB			SVM		
	P	R	F1	P	R	F1	P	R	F1	P	R	F1
A	0.99	0.98	0.98	0.98	0.98	0.98	0.92	0.84	0.88	0.99	0.99	0.99
B	0.98	0.98	0.98	0.98	0.98	0.98	0.89	0.90	0.89	0.98	0.99	0.99
C	0.99	1.00	0.99	0.99	1.00	0.99	0.85	0.98	0.91	0.99	1.00	1.00
D	0.99	0.99	0.99	0.98	0.99	0.99	0.80	0.87	0.83	0.99	1.00	0.99
E	0.97	0.96	0.97	0.96	0.97	0.96	0.69	0.85	0.77	0.98	0.98	0.98
F	0.99	0.98	0.99	0.99	0.98	0.98	0.94	0.83	0.88	0.99	0.99	0.99
G	0.99	0.99	0.99	0.99	0.99	0.99	0.99	0.96	0.98	0.99	0.99	0.99
H	0.99	0.99	0.99	0.99	0.99	0.99	0.97	0.97	0.97	0.99	0.99	0.99
I	1.00	0.99	0.99	1.00	0.99	0.99	0.99	0.90	0.94	1.00	1.00	1.00
L	1.00	0.99	0.99	1.00	0.99	0.99	1.00	0.89	0.94	1.00	0.99	1.00
M	0.95	0.97	0.96	0.96	0.95	0.95	0.87	0.89	0.88	0.95	0.95	0.95
N	0.96	0.95	0.95	0.95	0.95	0.95	0.87	0.85	0.86	0.94	0.95	0.94
O	0.96	0.99	0.97	0.96	0.97	0.97	0.72	0.68	0.70	0.99	0.99	0.99
P	0.99	0.99	0.99	0.99	0.99	0.99	0.83	0.79	0.81	1.00	1.00	1.00
R	0.97	0.96	0.96	0.96	0.96	0.96	0.54	0.65	0.59	0.97	0.97	0.97
S	0.97	0.98	0.97	0.95	0.98	0.96	0.72	0.82	0.77	0.98	0.99	0.98
T	0.98	0.99	0.98	0.98	0.98	0.98	0.77	0.77	0.77	0.99	0.98	0.99
U	0.94	0.96	0.95	0.95	0.95	0.95	0.48	0.48	0.48	0.95	0.97	0.96
V	0.97	0.96	0.97	0.97	0.96	0.96	0.79	0.57	0.66	0.98	0.96	0.97
W	0.99	0.97	0.98	0.99	0.97	0.98	0.88	0.84	0.86	1.00	0.98	0.99
Y	0.99	0.99	0.99	0.99	0.99	0.99	0.91	0.99	0.95	1.00	0.99	0.99
wt. avg.	0.98	0.98	**0.98**	0.98	0.98	**0.98**	0.83	0.82	0.83	0.98	0.98	**0.98**

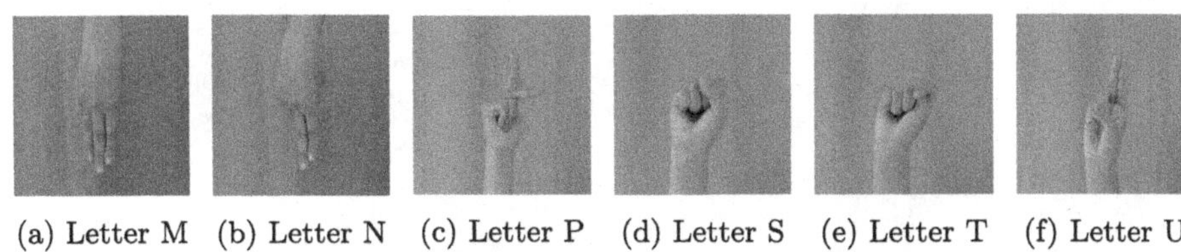

(a) Letter M (b) Letter N (c) Letter P (d) Letter S (e) Letter T (f) Letter U

Fig. 5. Examples of the letters in which the classifiers presented lower results.

lower than 0.95 for two letters: M, N; while for 4 letters it had perfect classification: C, I, L, P. Finally, the NB classifier, which had the lowest overall performance, recorded 19/21 letters below 0.95, including three of them with an F1-score below 0.6: R, U, V. Figure 5 shows some instances of the letters whose lowest performance values were obtained. As can be seen, there are some similarities between some of them, e.g., the letters M and N vary in a single-finger configuration, and even the letter U is the same configuration as the letter N but rotated 180°. The most difficult case, even to the human eye, are the letters S and T whose position of the index and ring fingers are opposed, but being flexed makes their identification difficult.

Finally, in the confusion matrix in Fig. 6, we present in detail the result of the classification of the letters of the LSM alphabet from the SVM classifier, which had the highest number of letters with classification close to 1. As can be noticed, a very low percentage of instances were misclassified, except for particular cases in which there was confusion between pair of letters, e.g., letters M and N, whose images were already analyzed from Subfigs. 5a and b, and the letters U and V, whose configuration also shares the same extension of the index and middle fingers (see Subfigs. 5f), but for the letter V they are separated.

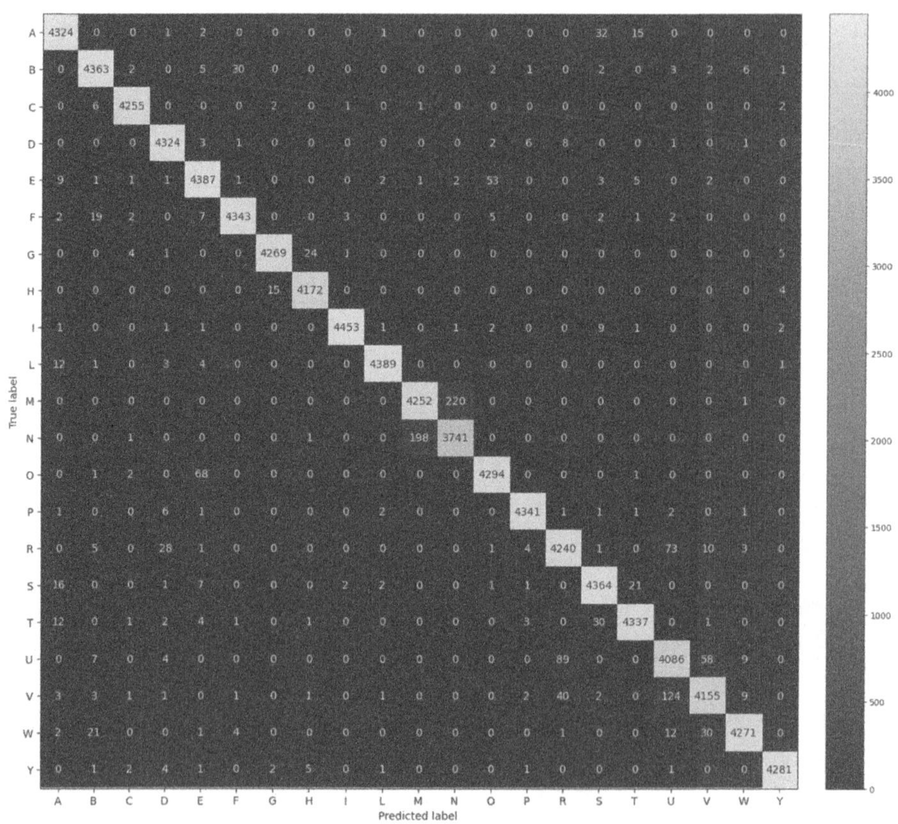

Fig. 6. Confusion matrix.

5 Conclusions

In the present work, a method for the recognition and classification of the LSM manual alphabet was proposed and evaluated, based on the use of images captured by a 2D camera and using machine learning techniques. This approach allows the processing of images from similar capture sources, such as smartphones or laptop cameras, which provides a wide application spectrum.

Most of the proposed classifiers were able to adequately identify all the addressed signs, except the classifier built with the Naive Bayes algorithm. It is important to highlight that the classifiers built with the kNN, Random Forest and SVM algorithms, obtained a performance higher than 0.95 of F1-score, emphasizing that the captured images were not in ideal configurations, since the participants were explicitly instructed to perform variations in the orientation of the hand with respect to the camera. The only aspect that was prioritized was capturing on a uniform background, to assist the MediaPipe library in extracting keypoints from the hands.

On the other hand, it is important to note that the work was limited to classifying static signs, however, the complete LSM also requires the movement of hands, arms and the use of facial expressions. It is suggested to use the method proposed in this work as a form of feature extraction that can be used in more complex models that allow classifying a larger number of signs in LSM, static and dynamic. Another limitation, which all computer vision-based systems have, is occlusion and illumination which in our case must be faced by the MediaPipe library, i.e., our models are fully dependent on advances in hand-tracking systems.

Another aspect we are working on is the continuous recognition of LSM signs, for both dactylology and ideograms. Since at the moment, our methods have been focused on the classification of previously segmented images, which limits their use in real-time applications.

By embracing these new technologies, Mexico can create an inclusive society where the communication barrier between the deaf and Spanish-speaking individuals is dissolved, enabling meaningful interactions and shared experiences for all.

References

1. Breiman, L.: Random forests. Mach. Learn. **45**, 5–32 (2001)
2. Cortes, C., Vapnik, V.: Support-vector networks. Mach. Learn. **20**, 273–297 (1995)
3. Cover, T., Hart, P.: Nearest neighbor pattern classification. IEEE Trans. Inf. Theor. **13**(1), 21–27 (1967)
4. Duda, R.O., Hart, P.E., et al.: Pattern Classification. Wiley (2006)
5. Escobedo, C.: Diccionario de lengua de señas mexicana de la ciudad de méxico. Instituto para las Personas con Discapacidad de la Ciudad de México (INDEPEDI CDMX). Ciudad de México, México (2017)
6. Galicia, R., Carranza, O., Jiménez, E., Rivera, G.: Mexican sign language recognition using movement sensor. In: 2015 IEEE 24th International Symposium on Industrial Electronics (ISIE), pp. 573–578. IEEE (2015)
7. Hendriks, B., Dufoe, S.: Non-native or native vocabulary in Mexican sign language. Sign Lang. Linguist. **17**(1), 20–55 (2014)
8. Jimenez, J., Martin, A., Uc, V., Espinosa, A.: Mexican sign language alphanumerical gestures recognition using 3D Haar-like features. IEEE Lat. Am. Trans. **15**(10), 2000–2005 (2017)

9. Kyle, J.G., Kyle, J., Woll, B.: Sign Language: The Study of Deaf People and Their Language. Cambridge University Press (1988)
10. Martínez-Gutiérrez, M.E., Rojano-Cáceres, J.R., Benítez-Guerrero, E., Sánchez-Barrera, H.E.: Data acquisition software for sign language recognition. Res. Comput. Sci. **148**(3), 205–211 (2019)
11. Mejía-Peréz, K., Córdova-Esparza, D.M., Terven, J., Herrera-Navarro, A.M., García-Ramírez, T., Ramírez-Pedraza, A.: Automatic recognition of Mexican sign language using a depth camera and recurrent neural networks. Appl. Sci. **12**(11), 5523 (2022)
12. Pérez, L.M., Rosales, A.J., Gallegos, F.J., Barba, A.V.: LSM static signs recognition using image processing. In: 2017 14th International Conference on Electrical Engineering, Computing Science and Automatic Control (CCE), pp. 1–5. IEEE (2017)
13. Serafín De Fleischmann, M., González Pérez, R.: Manos con voz diccionario de lengua de señas mexicana. Una herramienta indispensable para conocer el lenguaje de señas. Consejo Nacional para Prevenir la Discriminación (CONAPRED) México. Retrieved on April 24, 2019 (2011)
14. Stokoe, W.C.: Sign language structure. Annu. Rev. Anthropol. **9**(1), 365–390 (1980)

Load Demand Forecasting Using a Long-Short Term Memory Neural Network

Arturo Ortega[1], Monica Borunda[2(✉)], Luis Conde[3], and Carlos Garcia-Beltran[4]

[1] Facultad de Ciencias, Universidad Nacional Autónoma de México, Mexico, Mexico
arturoov12@ciencias.unam.mx

[2] Consejo Nacional de Ciencia y Tecnología Tecnológico Nacional de México Centro Nacional de Investigación y Desarrollo Tecnológico, Mexico, Mexico
monica.bp@cenidet.tecnm.mx

[3] Centro Nacional de Control de Energía Gerencia de Control Regional Oriental, Mexico, Mexico
luis.conde@cenace.gob.mx

[4] Tecnológico Nacional de México Centro Nacional de Investigación y Desarrollo Tecnológico, Mexico, Mexico
carlos.gb@cenidet.tecnm.mx

Abstract. Electric power load forecasting is very important for the operation and the planning of a utility company. Decisions of the electric market, electric power generation, load switching, and infrastructure development depend on load forecasting. There are many methods for load forecasting using statistical models, machine learning models and hybrid models. In this work, a Long-Short Term Memory Neural Network (LSTM NN) is used for short-term load forecasting, ranging from 1 h to 2 h ahead. Electric power demand time series provided by the National Center of Energy Control (CENACE) is used to train and validate the network. Results are compared with reported values from CENACE and Mean Absolute Percentage Errors (MAPEs) are calculated.

Keywords: Energy demand · LSTM model · hourly energy demand forecasting · short term forecasting · TensorFlow · RNN

1 Introduction

Since the Industrial Revolution, energy consumption, in its various configurations, has become essential for countless activities. Fossil fuels account for 80% of global energy consumption [1]. The absence of energy would lead to the collapse of all industries, consequently putting the entire economic system at risk. Therefore, managing energy demand is an important issue as environmental and economic sustainability is threatened by the way resources are being administered and distributed. The rate of resource consumption endangers the well-being of future generations, making political involvement necessary. It is predicted that if the current consumption pattern continues, global energy consumption will increase by over 50% before 2030 [1], leading greenhouse

H. Calvo et al. (Eds.): MICAI 2023, LNAI 14391, pp. 121–137, 2024.
https://doi.org/10.1007/978-3-031-47765-2_10

effect gases to increase in the atmosphere, causing irreversible damage to the biosphere and possibly triggering the most significant ecological crisis in human history. Thus, it is necessary to switch to renewable energy resources that have been established as sustainable, non-polluting, and renewable. Moreover, the actual rates of consumption are not sustainable even with the usage of green energies, governments are compelled to moderate the energy demand to achieve a long-term viability. Energy demand forecasting plays an important role in energy generation and transactions, security analysis, fuel scheduling, economic dispatch, and unit operation and maintenance [2]. Its forecasting can help us understand what needs to be modified to meet energy demand caring for the planet's sustainability. Managing energy demand should aid in identifying conservation measures and developing strategies to reduce consumption and emissions.

To achieve this, we must initially forecast electrical energy demand in the short, medium, or long term. There are multiple energy prediction models that can be classified into different categories based on the method and parameters being considered. In this work, a type of Neural Network (NN) is used for short-term load forecasting. Training and validation data consists of the time series of hourly energy consumption from the Eastern Control Area of Mexico provided by the National Center of Energy Control.

1.1 Artificial Neural Networks

Since 1988, there has been a growing trend of academic activities, research institutions, and other scholarly journals publishing a substantial volume of research articles centered around Artificial Neural Networks (ANN) [3]. It has been proved that deep learning has the potential to improve predictive performance in traditional applications, such as time series analysis. This paper will introduce a LSTM NN, a type of RNN (Recurrent Neural Network), which are both excellent predictors of time series data.

1.1.1 Recurrent Neural Networks

Recurrent Neural Networks (RNN) main characteristic is the connection between the current output of a sequence and its previous output, as seen in Fig. 2(a). This mechanism involves the network retaining prior information and integrating it into the computation of the present output. Consequently, the nodes within the hidden layers exhibit connectivity, and the input to the hidden layer encompasses not only the input layer's output but also the previous hidden layer's output.

In theory, RNNs possess the capability to handle sequences of varying lengths. Nevertheless, practical considerations often lead to the assumption that the current state is primarily influenced by a limited number of preceding states, aiming to mitigate complexity. Traditional RNNs commonly employ the Back Propagation Through Time (BPTT) algorithm. However, this approach suffers from drawbacks as time progresses and the number of network layers increases, potentially resulting in issues such as vanishing or exploding gradients. Consequently, traditional RNNs encounter challenges when dealing with long-term dependencies in real-world applications [4]. In this work, we use the Long-Short Term Memory RNN for load forecasting.

1.1.2 Long-Short Term Memory

The primary purpose behind the creation of Long-Short Term Memory LSTM neural network is to address the issue of long-term dependencies within neural networks and to naturally retain extended information, in contrast to necessitating extensive learning efforts. The LSTM architecture falls under the category of recurrent neural networks (RNNs), initially conceived to tackle these challenges. The key innovation of LSTM NN lies in its ability to selectively remember or forget information over time, thus enabling the network to retain relevant context and dependencies over long sequences. The architecture incorporates specialized memory cells, allowing it to maintain information for extended periods and process sequences with time lags between significant events more efficiently. Given their promising capabilities, LSTM NNs have become an indispensable tool in numerous fields. In particular, they have demonstrated remarkable performance in time series forecasting, making them well-suited for tasks like stock market prediction, weather forecasting, and energy consumption projections.

Traditional forecasting approaches, while useful in some contexts, often struggle to handle long-term dependencies and intricate patterns present in energy consumption time series data. The vanishing gradient problem, which inhibits RNNs from learning and retaining information over extended periods, poses a significant obstacle to accurate long-term forecasting. The LSTM NN, on the other hand, has shown promising capabilities in overcoming this limitation by incorporating specialized memory cells.

The implications of accurate short-term energy consumption forecasting are far-reaching, impacting various stakeholders in the energy sector, including power grid operators, utility companies, and policymakers. By developing a robust forecasting model, we seek to allow a clear analysis of the energy demand to policymakers that could enhance energy management strategies, optimize resource allocation, and foster sustainable energy practices. Additionally, our research contributes to the advancement of time-dependent data analysis techniques, ultimately contributing to the broader field of energy forecasting and sustainable energy management.

In this paper, we aim to present a comprehensive study of the LSTM NN architecture and its suitability for short-term energy consumption forecasting. Numerous correlated research studies have demonstrated that the collaboration of various methods leads to improved efficacy in prediction models. Hence, a LSTM neural network and a similar days approach will also be examined. By utilizing historical energy consumption data, we assess the LSTM NN's performance in forecasting energy demand for short time horizons, ranging from one hour to several hours ahead. In Sect. 2 we present the methodology of our approach. The source and description of our data set is presented in Sect. 2.1. The construction of the LSTM NN is described in Sect. 2.2. Data processing is outlined in Sect. 2.3. The extensions to 2 and 3 inputs LSTM are shown in Sects. 2.4 and 2.5 respectively. The metric to measure the accuracy of the forecasted results is shown in Sect. 2.6. Results are presented in Sect. 3. Double and triple input LSTM results are described in Subsects. 3.1 and 3.2. Finally, discussions and conclusions are outlined in Sect. 4.

2 Methodology

As mentioned before, this work aims to forecast energy demand by using a LSTM NN and a simple similar-days approach. In this section, we show the methodology employed to accomplish this goal. Initially, it is imperative to ensure the cleanliness and organization of our data set, as this step enables us to eliminate any systematic errors that may be present. Subsequently, we incorporate Machine Learning tools, specifically LSTM neural networks, and a rudimentary similar-days approach, to forecast energy demand of a specific region of Mexico. Next Subsection describes the data gathering and processing to train and validate the ANN.

2.1 Data Provided by CENACE

The National Electric System (SEN) in Mexico is divided in 8 regions to enhance energy management and conduct a regional-level analysis of the energy resource as shown in Fig. 1. In the following, we work with energy demand data from the Eastern Control Area of the SEN, which is formed by the states of Puebla, Morelos, Veracruz, Guerrero, Oaxaca, and Chiapas as shown in Fig. 1.

Fig. 1. Map of the National Interconnected System. Highlighted area represents the Eastern Control Area's geographical limitations [5].

CENACE counts with a free access site with available hourly data on electricity demand for each of the 8 Control Areas of the SEN from 2016 to 2023 [6]. In our experiments we use hourly energy demand data for the Eastern Control Area from 2016 to 2022.

2.2 LSTM Neural Network

An open-source library, TensorFlow [7], is used to build the desired NN. It is a flexible and adaptable framework designed to facilitate the creation, training, and deployment of machine learning models. Its underlying architecture is based on data flow graphs, where nodes represent mathematical operations, and edges signify data arrays (tensors) that flow between these operations. TensorFlow counts with tools, pre-built models, and libraries to use Machine Learning in a friendly way.

LSTM models, like the example shown in Fig. 2(b), implement a three-gate system which are called input-gate, forget-gate, and output gate presented in Figs. 2(c), 2(d) and 2(e), respectively [8, 9]. The forget gate takes as input the previous hidden state h_{t-1} and the current input x_t. It decides whether the information should be retained or forgotten from the previous cell state C_{t-1}. This gate's purpose is crucial for the network to remember important past information and discard irrelevant details. The gate produces a "forget factor" f_t that scales the previous cell state (Fig. 2(c)). The input gate, similarly, using the previous hidden state h_{t-1} and the current input x_t, determines what new information should be stored in the cell state C_t (Fig. 2(d)). This includes identifying elements that are relevant to the study using activation functions. A candidate cell state C_t is calculated and then integrated into the existing cell state C_{t-1} through the output of this gate. The output gate, Fig. 2(e), considers the modified cell state C_t and the current input x_t to decide what the next hidden state h_t should be. This gate's function is to control how much of the cell state C_t should be revealed to the last cell state of the LSTM network [10].

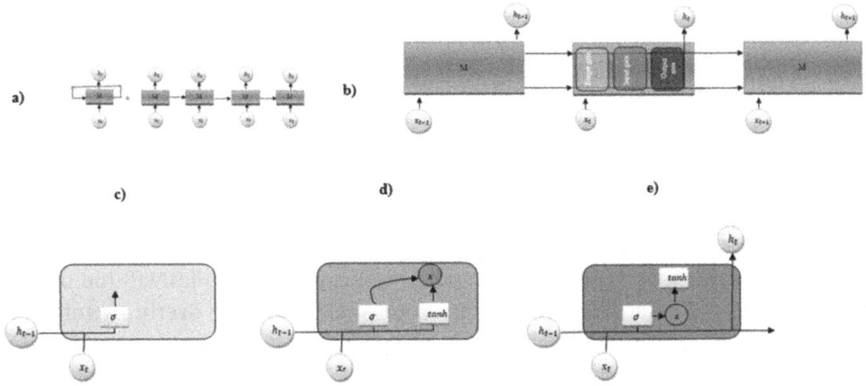

Fig. 2. (a) an unrolled RNN, (b) LSTM chain, (c) forget gate, (d) input-gate, and (e) output layer.

The LSTM processes are described by the following equations:

$$f_t = \sigma\left(W_f * \left[h_{t-1}, x_t\right] + b_f\right) \tag{1}$$

$$i_t = \sigma\left(W_i * \left[h_{t-1}, x_t\right] + b_i\right) \tag{2}$$

$$C_t = \tanh\left(W_i * \left[h_{t-1}, x_t\right]\right) + b_c \tag{3}$$

$$o_t = \sigma\left(W_o * \left[h_{t-1}, x_t\right] + b_o\right) \tag{4}$$

$$h_t = o_t * tanh(C_t) \tag{5}$$

The symbols and model parameters are described in Table 1.

Table 1. LSTM list of symbols and model parameters.

Symbol	Remark	Symbol	Remark
f_t	Forget gate	i_t	Input gate
o_t	Output gate	W_f	Weight for forget gate neurons
σ	Sigmoid function	W_i	Weight for input gate neurons
tanh	Hyperbolic tangent function	W_o	Weight for output gate neurons
h_{t-1}	Output for the previous LSTM	x_t	Input at current time step
b_f	Biases for forget gate	b_i	Biases for input gate
b_o	Biases for output gate	C_t	Candidate for cell state at time t

In Table 1, terminology used in the equations is thoroughly clarified. Since it is an automated process, we do not have to worry about computing these formulas in our Python script. In Table 2, the LSTM architecture parameters are depicted for the studied period. All parameters chosen were the same for the corresponding models to maintain consistency in our results. The learning rate established for all proposed models in this paper is 0.001, it was found that this learning rate suited better for our purposes, and it regulates how much the model changes when weights variate in response to the predicted error [11]. The batch size, number of sub-samples provided before updating parameters, picked was 14, i.e., we want our model to predict the following hour of consumption based on the information given by the previous 14 h. This number was empirically found, it allowed a superior performance of the prediction model. The epoch count serves as a hyperparameter dictating how many iterations the learning algorithm will run over the complete training dataset [10]. Ensure that your model does not overfit by refraining from assigning an excessively high number of epochs. It was observed that 15 epochs proved sufficient in our specific scenario.

2.3 Processing Data

To properly train our neural network, it is imperative to ensure the cleanliness of our data. This involves maintaining consistent data formatting and excluding columns from the CSV file that are not relevant as inputs for the neural network. Furthermore, it is crucial that all training data is presented in a numerical format. Therefore, if a date time input is employed it must be converted into its numerical counterpart through the utilization of a Python function. The chosen dataset for network training necessitates standardization to optimize its performance. In this instance, it was opted to employ the *StandardScaler* function for this purpose, as opposed to data normalization. Such function standardizes features by removing the mean and scaling to unit variance and it does not bound the data to a specific range. This choice was influenced by the activation function applied in the neural network, specifically *tanh*. Furthermore, empirical evidence has demonstrated the superior performance of the proposed LSTM neural network when utilizing *tanh* as opposed to a *sigmoid* function.

Table 2. Architecture of LSTM models.

Models	Hidden layer 1 Neurons	Hidden layer 2 Neurons	Activation Function	Recurrent Activation Function
LSTM-1	64	32	Hyperbolic Tangent	Linear
LSTM-1.1	64	32	Hyperbolic Tangent	Linear
LSTM-2	64	32	Hyperbolic Tangent	Linear
LSTM-2.1	64	32	Hyperbolic Tangent	Linear
LSTM-3	64	32	Hyperbolic Tangent	Linear
LSTM-3.1	64	32	Hyperbolic Tangent	Linear

2.4 Double-Input Long Short-Term Memory Neural Network

In this scenario, actual energy demand (measured in MWh) and hourly timestamps are utilized as inputs. Two different NNs were presented, LSTM-1and LSTM-1.1, all exclusively utilized data gathered solely during the month of January from the years 2016 to 2022. The initial network was trained with everyday data from the previous time span, while the second network exclusively learns with data from Thursdays within the same time frame. This day was chosen due to its stability, on average, it represents the day with a higher consumption rate of energy in the Eastern Control Area.

2.5 Triple-Input Long Short-Term Memory Neural Network

In this case, energy demand, hourly timestamps and date time values are utilized as inputs. The identical methodology employed in the preceding neural network was utilized. This ensures a dependable basis for comparing the performance of the two proposed networks.

2.6 4-input Long Short-Term Memory Neural Network

In this methodology, energy demand, hourly timestamps, date time values and temperature are utilized as training inputs. To train LSTM-3, we utilized historical data collected on every Thursday between the years 2016 and 2022. On the other hand, LSTM-3.1 was trained using a more detailed approach, specifically focusing on data from Thursdays in January from the same time period. The historical temperature data was retrieved from the NSRD [15].

2.7 Forecasting Errors

To quantify the accuracy prediction, we use forecasting errors, such as MAPE. It is a widely utilized metric in assessing the accuracy of predictive models. MAPE quantifies the extent of discrepancy between predicted values and actual observations in terms of percentage. This measurement is particularly effective in evaluating the performance of forecasting models, making it a valuable tool in our study's methodology.

MAPE is calculated by taking the absolute difference between predicted and actual values, dividing it by the actual value, and then multiplying the result by 100 to express it as a percentage [12]. The formula for MAPE is as follows:

$$MAPE = \frac{1}{n}\sum_{i=1}^{n}\left|\frac{Y_i - \widehat{Y_i}}{Y_i}\right| \times 100 \tag{6}$$

where n is the number of observations, Y_i represents the actual observed value for the ith observation, $\widehat{Y_i}$ denotes the predicted value for the ith observation. The resulting MAPE value indicates the average percentage error across all observations. A lower MAPE value signifies higher prediction accuracy, while a higher value suggests a greater level of deviation between predicted and actual values.

3 Results

The focus of our study was directed towards the month of January because of its unsteady nature. We could have extended this study for the rest of the months but observing the model´s success with a complex month, we inferred that the approach would be applicable to the remaining months of the year. As seen in Fig. 4, energy consumption has been growing throughout the years. The selected day for our combined LSTM/similar days approach exhibits a fluctuating consumption pattern, characterized by both decreasing and increasing energy demand, like any typical day (Fig. 3). As depicted in the figure below, the minimum consumption level is recorded at 5 a.m., whereas the peak demand occurs at 8 p.m.

The observed trend in Fig. 4 clearly indicates a consistent rise in load demand over the years, which is a common and expected pattern in the energy sector. However, it's important to note that this typical upward trajectory experienced an unusual deviation during the COVID-19 pandemic.

Typically, as economies grow and populations increase, the demand for electricity tends to follow suit, leading to a continuous upward trend. However, the emergence of the COVID-19 pandemic disrupted this conventional pattern. As depicted in Fig. 4, during the period between 2020 and 2021, a significant departure from the expected trend occurred, resulting in an all-time low in load demand.

This sudden decline can be attributed to the far-reaching impacts of the pandemic, which led to widespread lockdowns, business closures, and altered work patterns. These measures aimed at mitigating the spread of the virus had the effect of reducing overall economic activity, which, in turn, translated into reduced energy consumption. This anomaly serves as a stark reminder of how external factors, such as a global health crisis, can disrupt even well-established trends in the energy sector.

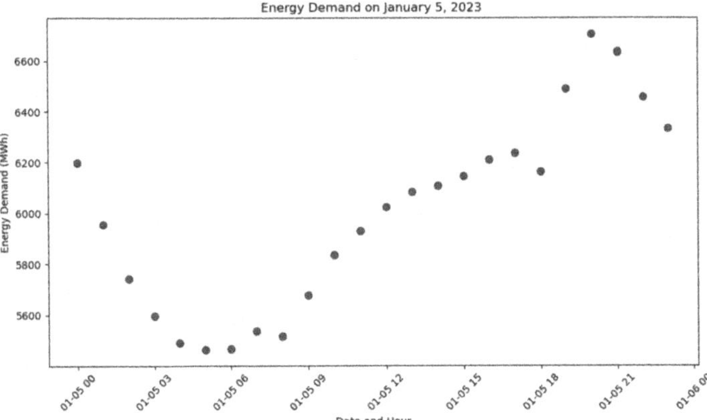

Fig. 3. Typical energy consumption pattern during a Thursday. Actual energy consumption of forecasting day.

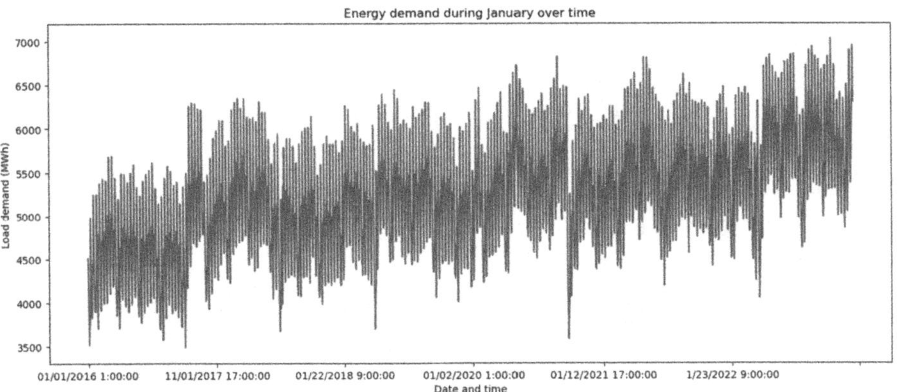

Fig. 4. Time series of hourly electrical energy consumption during January 2016–2022.

3.1 Double-Input LSTM

In the dual-input LSTM model, referred to as LSTM-1, the input array had a shape of (5194, 2). This is because we exclusively utilized energy demand and time as inputs, sourced from all January data spanning from 2016 to 2022. Despite achieving successful training for our network, the forecast accuracy of the first two hours was significantly lower. On the contrary, its accuracy sees a substantial improvement during the later hours, see Table 3.

On the other hand, the coarser similar days method applied in conjunction with LSTM yielded a slightly greater degree of accuracy in our prediction, this approach is referred to as LSTM-1.1, as seen in Table 4. Note that forecast precision follows the same pattern as in LSTM-1, it improves as it reaches a major consumption rate.

When we compare the outcomes of LSTM-1 and 1.1 with an alternative machine learning approach, the Random Forest Regressor (RFR) [13], commonly employed for

Table 3. Comparison between forecasted values and real values using LSTM method only. The training dataset encompassed data exclusively from the month of January.

LSTM-1			
Date	Energy demand (MWh)	Forecast (MWh)	MAPE %
01/05/2023 1:00:00	5955	5122	13.99
01/05/2023 2:00:00	5743	4923	14.28
01/05/2023 12:00:00	6024	5545	7.95
01/05/2023 13:00:00	6085	5614	7.74
01/05/2023 19:00:00	6488	6156	5.12
01/05/2023 20:00:00	6703	6446	3.83

Table 4. Comparison between two-hour ahead forecasted values and real values using LSTM and similar days approach. The training dataset encompassed data exclusively from the month of January.

LSTM-1.1			
Date	Energy demand (MWh)	Forecast (MWh)	MAPE %
01/05/2023 1:00:00	5955	5156	13.42
01/05/2023 2:00:00	5743	5078	11.57
01/05/2023 12:00:00	6024	5753	4.50
01/05/2023 13:00:00	6085	5811	4.50
01/05/2023 19:00:00	6488	6417	1.09
01/05/2023 20:00:00	6703	6320	5.71

tasks such as house price prediction, product demand estimation, and various numerical forecasting tasks, a noteworthy observation emerges. Table 5 clearly demonstrates that even the most basic form of our LSTM methodologies surpasses RFR by a significant margin.

3.2 Triple-Input LSTM

In this scenario, one would naturally anticipate an enhancement in energy demand forecasting. Surprisingly, our findings yielded a prediction that is notably less accurate for most of the forecasted hours when compared to LSTM-1. Delving into the details presented in Table 6, it is determined that the MAPE value falls considerably short of the established prediction standards. This variant of the model, encompassing three input variables, is referred to as LSTM-2.

Employing the LSTM-2.1 methodology, which exclusively incorporates days akin to our forecast day—wherein the neural network is trained exclusively with data from Thursdays, as in the case of LSTM-1.1, we achieved improved forecasting outcomes.

Table 5. Comparison between forecasted values and real values using Random Forest Regressor method. The training dataset encompassed annual data inputs from the month of January.

RFR			
Date	Energy demand (MWh)	Forecast (MWh)	MAPE %
01/05/2023 1:00:00	5955	4557	23.48
01/05/2023 2:00:00	5743	5449	5.12
01/05/2023 12:00:00	6024	4898	18.69
01/05/2023 13:00:00	6085	5745	5.59
01/05/2023 19:00:00	6488	5638	13.10
01/05/2023 20:00:00	6703	6564	2.07

Table 6. Comparison between forecasted values and real values using LSTM method only with a horizon of 2 h ahead. The training dataset encompassed annual data inputs.

LSTM-2			
Date	Energy demand (MWh)	Forecast (MWh)	MAPE %
01/05/2023 1:00:00	5955	5137	13.74
01/05/2023 2:00:00	5743	4874	15.13
01/05/2023 12:00:00	6024	5584	7.30
01/05/2023 13:00:00	6085	5641	7.30
01/05/2023 19:00:00	6488	5851	9.82
01/05/2023 20:00:00	6703	6416	4.28

As demonstrated in Table 7, there is a notable and significant reduction in MAPE values. This reduction is particularly substantial when compared to the values obtained from LSTM 1.1. Nevertheless, it's worth noting that these results do not align with the desired outcome or expectations. We expect forecasts to fall under the 5% error threshold.

3.3 Four-Input LSTM

It is evident that the forecasts have seen a substantial improvement (see Table 8), underscoring the significance of incorporating meteorological data into load demand forecasting models, particularly temperature data. Note that the aforementioned models tend to struggle during the first morning hours, meanwhile LSTM-3 shows an outstanding performance not only in the morning but consistently throughout the entire day. Observe that all MAPE measurements fall within the desired limits, with three of the forecasts having errors below 1%.

LSTM-3.1 was anticipated to outperform LSTM-3 due to its more refined approach using similar days. However, this expectation did not materialize as expected. While

Table 7. Comparison between real values and forecasted values using LSTM and similar days approach. The training dataset encompassed data exclusively from the month of January.

LSTM-2.1			
Date	Energy demand (MWh)	Forecast (MWh)	MAPE %
01/05/2023 1:00:00	5955	5265	11.56
01/05/2023 2:00:00	5743	5267	8.29
01/05/2023 12:00:00	6024	5729	5.14
01/05/2023 13:00:00	6085	5747	5.56
01/05/2023 19:00:00	6488	6259	3.53
01/05/2023 20:00:00	6703	6484	3.27

Table 8. Comparison between actual values and forecasted values generated using a LSTM model trained with meteorological factors and a similar-days approach. The training dataset encompassed annual data inputs.

LSTM-3			
Date	Energy demand (MWh)	Forecast (MWh)	MAPE %
01/05/2023 1:00:00	5955	5908	0.79
01/05/2023 2:00:00	5743	5898	2.70
01/05/2023 12:00:00	6024	6077	0.88
01/05/2023 13:00:00	6085	6158	1.20
01/05/2023 19:00:00	6488	6465	0.36
01/05/2023 20:00:00	6703	6943	3.58

Table 9. Comparison between actual values and forecasted values generated using a LSTM trained with a meteorological factor and similar days approach. The training dataset encompassed data exclusively from the month of January.

LSTM-3.1			
Date	Energy demand (MWh)	Forecast (MWh)	MAPE %
01/05/2023 1:00:00	5955	5975	0.34
01/05/2023 2:00:00	5743	5739	0.07
01/05/2023 12:00:00	6024	5513	8.48
01/05/2023 13:00:00	6085	5632	7.45
01/05/2023 19:00:00	6488	5938	8.48
01/05/2023 20:00:00	6703	6070	9.44

LSTM-3.1 did produce improved results during the early hours, particularly at 1 and 2 a.m., the quality of forecasts gradually deteriorated as the day progressed.

4 Discussion and Conclusion

Within the guidelines of CENACE´s forecasting manual, there are four methodologies for the demand forecasting model. Each of the CENACE Regional Control Areas employs a different method. In the Eastern Control Area, specifically in the city of Puebla, they employ the similar days methodology. This paper aims to establish a comparison between the proposed forecasting approach and the method currently employed in Puebla. This comparison serves to validate the credibility of the suggested approach, as it is being benchmarked against a well-established forecasting procedure. To achieve a thorough comparison, the dataset employed for training the neural network utilizes information sourced from CENACE´s database.

While the performances of LSTM-1, 1.1, 2, 2.1 and 3.1 are not remarkable, it is worth noting that we have successfully achieved satisfactory forecasting results through the methodology employed in LSTM-3. The results obtained with this methodology prove to be on par with CENACE's results [5], see Table 10.

Note that in some cases, the similar days approach by CENACE still exhibits a slightly superior performance compared to the predictions generated using the methodologies outlined in this paper. However, some outcomes of LSTM-3, refer to Table 10, display a smaller disparity from the actual demand when compared to CENACE´s results. Furthermore, the simplified similar days methodology adopted in this study pales in comparison to the intricate approach employed by the Eastern Control Area. Their approach employs factors to identify patterns resembling the forecasting day. It incorporates climatological variables, day type, and month to compute a coefficient of similarity between the target day and historical days [2]. Weighted factors are assigned to each variable, subsequently guiding the selection of 'n' days with the highest similarity to the forecast day, along with the two preceding days. Even though LSTM-3 used a simpler similar days approach, it performed just as well. Despite using a coarser method in LSTM.3–1 did not yield better forecasting results, it is believed that the set of similar days selected did not favor the architecture of the neural network and, therefore, its performance. Exploring a more comprehensive application of the similar days concept within the framework of the proposed LSTM neural network could yield even more intriguing results.

As we have mentioned previously, the data frame used to train the neural network spans from 2016 to 2022, which includes data recollected during the COVID-19 pandemic. During this period, energy demand was affected, the restrictions during the pandemic caused developed, developing, and underdeveloped economies to have a negative impact on their energy sectors [14]. Given that energy demand is intricately linked to various socio-economic elements, including population, urbanization, industrialization, net capital income, and technological advancements, any alteration in these factors will inevitably exert a direct influence on the electric grid. Historically, load demand trend has been growing consistently since it is directly linked to population growth. Nonetheless, Fig. 5 illustrates that this has not been the scenario during the period under investigation. Between 2016 and 2019, the average annual growth rate of total electricity consumption

Table 10. Forecasted values and its corresponding MAPE using LSTM-3 and CENACE´s similar days method.

Model	Date	Energy demand (MWh)	Forecasting (MWh)	MAPE %
CENACE	01/05/2023 1:00:00	5955	6046	1.53
LSTM-3	01/05/2023 1:00:00	5955	5908	0.79
CENACE	01/05/2023 2:00:00	5743	5787	0.77
LSTM-3	01/05/2023 2:00:00	5743	5898	2.70
CENACE	01/05/2023 12:00:00	6024	6183	2.64
LSTM-3	01/05/2023 12:00:00	6024	6077	0.88
CENACE	01/06/2022 13:00:00	6085	6266	2.98
LSTM-3	01/05/2023 13:00:00	6085	6158	1.20
CENACE	01/05/2023 19:00:00	6488	6771	4.36
LSTM-3	01/05/2023 19:00:00	6488	6465	0.36
CENACE	01/05/2023 20:00:00	6703	6857	2.30
LSTM-3	01/05/2023 20:00:00	6703	6943	3.58

was 2.2%. In 2020, due to the pandemic, the total load demand experienced a decline of 1.09% compared to the preceding year. This is logical, considering that global economic activities came to a complete halt during most of that time. In Mexico, the GDP experienced a significant decrease of 8.6% in 2020, as indicated in Table 11. Note that several other socioeconomic factors were also adversely affected during this period, including population growth, the construction index, and the global innovation index. The construction index of a nation provides insights into the performance and activity within the construction sector of that country. It typically reflects the level of construction and infrastructure development taking place. Economic slowdowns associated with declining construction activity, as witnessed in 2020, can lead to reduced electricity demand from industrial and commercial sectors. On the other hand, the Global Innovation Index (GII) of a nation was introduced by the World Intellectual Property Organization and it ranks the innovation performance of a country. As Table 11 shows, Mexico´s GII was increasing over the years until 2020 which presented a remarkable drop. In the subsequent years, we observed the typical growth pattern as activities returned to normalcy, total load demand increased 5.5% during 2021 when compared to 2020.

The observed decrease in the socioeconomic factors mentioned earlier, especially the significant decline in GDP and the unique challenges of the year 2020, may have raised questions about the robustness of our neural network models. This particular year marked an unusual phenomenon, and one might wonder how such economic turbulence could impact the performance of machine learning models.

However, it’s important to highlight the remarkable characteristics of LSTM (Long Short-Term Memory) models that contributed to the continued relevance and accuracy of our methodology despite these adversities. LSTM models are known for their ability to store and forget information selectively, making them adept at handling sequences of

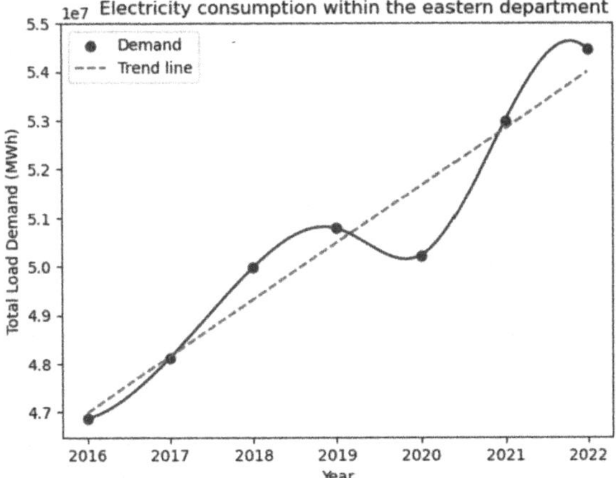

Fig. 5. Electricity total consumption spanning from 2016 to 2022, with a dotted line depicting the load demand trend over this period.

Table 11. Rate of Socioeconomic Factor Growth in Mexico. The population growth percentage is determined by comparing the annual rate of change to that of the previous year [16]. The GDP percentage variation is calculated in a similar manner, but it takes into account the quarterly measurement averages [17]. INEGI uses a reference index (100) to establish construction's growth rate in the country [18]. The Global Innovation Index (GII) is typically obtained through a comprehensive assessment of various factors related to innovation within countries [19]. Total Load demand rate of change was obtained comparing yearly results to its previous year [5].

Year	Population Growth %	GDP %	Construction index %	Global innovation index	Total Load Demand %
2016	1.1	1.8	8	34.56	0.6
2017	1.1	1.9	7	35.79	2.7
2018	1	2.0	0	35.34	3.9
2019	0.9	–0.3	–6	36.06	1.6
2020	0.7	–8.6	–23	33.60	-1.1
2021	0.6	6.6	–25	34.5	5.5
2022	0.6	3.9	–22	31	2.8

data, such as time-series data, with long-term dependencies. This capability allowed our models to adapt and provide valuable predictions even in challenging circumstances.

In summary, the LSTM-3 model demonstrated a commendable level of prediction accuracy, considering the absence of certain factors in our analysis. One key factor contributing to this success is the predominant use of electrical energy for domestic purposes within the studied region. Domestic energy consumption tends to exhibit more stable patterns compared to industrial or commercial sectors, making predictions more reliable. However, it's worth noting that in more industrialized regions or sectors with different consumption patterns, the forecasting outcomes might show a greater degree of variability. This underscores the importance of tailoring forecasting methodologies to the specific characteristics of the region or sector under consideration.

Conducting a comparative analysis between LSTM models and alternative machine learning methods, such as the Random Forest Regressor (RFR), significantly enhances the credibility of this study. LSTMs exhibit notable advantages, including their ability to seamlessly manage sequences of varying lengths without the need for fixed-length input data. In contrast, RFR primarily operates with fixed-size feature vectors.

Furthermore, an important strength of LSTMs lies in their capacity to handle missing data with finesse by intelligently imputing values based on available context. Conversely, RFR models often encounter challenges when confronted with missing data, necessitating special handling procedures.

It is worth noting that despite meticulous data treatment and training with identical inputs as LSTM-3, the RFR model fell notably short in performance compared to any of the methodologies employed in this paper.

In conclusion, our study showcases the resilience and adaptability of LSTM models in load demand forecasting, even when faced with unexpected challenges. While the results are promising, it's crucial to recognize the context in which these models are applied and consider potential variations in forecasting accuracy across different regions and industries.

Acknowledgments. A.O. wants to express its sincere appreciation to M.B. for her invaluable assistance and guidance throughout the entire process of crafting this article. M.B.´s expertise, insights, and unwavering support have been instrumental in shaping the content and direction of this work. A.O. is truly thankful for the time and effort she dedicated to providing her valuable input, which undoubtedly contributed to the article's depth and credibility. M.B. thanks CONAHCYT for her "Investigadora por México Research Position" with ID 71557. M.B. thanks TECNM-CENIDET for being her host institution.

References

1. CSIRO & The Natural Edge Project. Energy transformed: sustainable energy solutions for climate change mitigation p. 6. (2007). https://eprints.qut.edu.au/85180/1/85180.pdf
2. Mandal, P., Senjyu, T., Urasaki, N., Funabashi, T.: A neural network based several-hour-ahead electric load forecasting using similar days approach. Int. J. Electr. Power Energy Syst. **28**(6), 367–373 (2006). https://doi.org/10.1016/j.ijepes.2005.12.007
3. Okelola, M.O., Ayanlade, S.O., Ogunwole, E., I. An artificial neural network approach to short-term load forecasting for nigerian electrical power network. Int. J. Innov. Eng. Res. Technol. **8**(08), 168–177 (2021)
4. Heaton, J. B., Polson, N. G., Witte, J. H.: Deep Learning in Finance. http://arxiv.org/abs/1602.06561. (2016)
5. Métricas de Errores de Pronóstico. Gob.mx. Recovered from https://www.cenace.gob.mx/Paginas/SIM/MetricasErroresPron.aspx
6. Demanda Regional. (s/f). Gob.mx. Recovered from https://www.cenace.gob.mx/paginas/publicas/info/demandaregional.aspx
7. TensorFlow. TensorFlow. Recovered from https://www.tensorflow.org/?hl=es-419

8. Alam, S.: Recurrent neural networks in electricity load forecasting (2018). https://www.diva-portal.org/smash/get/diva2:1238889/FULLTEXT01.pdf
9. Lysfjord., M.J.W.: Modeling and forecasting the nord pool day-ahead power market throughdeep-learning (2017)
10. Brownlee, J.: Difference between a batch and an epoch in a neural network (2019). https://machinelearningmastery.com/difference-between-a-batch-and-an-epoch/
11. Brownlee, J.: Understand the impact of learning rate on neural network performance. machine learning mastery (2020). https://machinelearningmastery.com/ understand-the-dynamics-of-learning-rate-on-deep-learning-neural-networks/
12. Bozlak, Ç.B., Yaşar, C.F.: Studies on day-ahead electricity price forecasting: Sarimax, Lstm and Cnn-Lstm with the electrical consumption as an exogenous input. SSRN Electron. J. (2022). https://doi.org/10.2139/ssrn.4116243
13. Random Forest Algorithm. Javapoint.com. Recovered from. https://www.javatpoint.com/machine-learning-random-forest-algorithm
14. Mu, Q., Wu, Y., Pan, X., Huang, L., Li, X.: Short-term load forecas- ting using improved similar days method. In: Asia-Pacific Power and Energy Engineering Conference (2010)
15. National Solar Radiation Database. Nrel.gov. Recovered from. https://nsrdb.nrel.gov/data-viewer
16. Crecimiento de la poblaci6n (% anual) - Mexico. World Bank Open Data. Recovered from. https://datos.bancomundial.org/indicador/sp.pop.grow?locations=MX
17. Instituto Nacional de Estadística y Geografía (INEGI). Por actividad econ6mica. Org.mx. Recovered from. https://www.inegi.org.mx/temas/pib/
18. Instituto Nacional de Estadística y Geografía (INEGI). Construcci6n. Org.mx. Recovered from. https://www.inegi.org.mx/temas/construccion/
19. Global innvoation index. Wipo.int. Recovered from. https://www.wipo.int/publications/es/series/index.jsp?id=129

Computer Vision and Image Processing

Benchmark Analysis for Backbone Optimization in a Facial Reconstruction Model

Victor Hernández-Manrique[1(✉)], Miguel González-Mendoza[1], Carlos Vilchis[1], Mauricio Méndez-Ruiz[2], and Carmina Pérez-Guerrero[2]

[1] Tecnologico de Monterrey, Escuela de Ingeniería y Ciencias, Monterrey, Nuevo León, Mexico
{A01731594,mgonza,carlos.vilchis}@tec.mx

[2] Eugenia Virtual Humans S.A. de C.V., Laboratorio de Investigación, Naucalpan de Juárez, Estado de México, Mexico
{mauricio,carmina}@eugenia.tech

Abstract. Lightweight model development has emerged as an important study subject in computer vision in response to the need for resource-efficient solutions. These models attempt to strike a balance between model size, computing requirements, and accuracy. They give benefits such as efficient resource use, faster inference times, and improved accessibility. For 3D facial reconstruction models, lightweight architectures present an opportunity for implementation in less demanding hardware, since these algorithms usually rely on powerful processors such as NVIDIA graphic cards. The following research paper provides a benchmark comparison between diverse state-of-the-art lightweight models in a facial reconstruction model, with the aim to reduce its computational complexity so that it can be tested on a mobile device.

Keywords: 3DDFA-V1 · Lightweight Models · Facial Reconstruction Model · EfficientNet · MobileNetV1 · GhostNet · MobileFormer · MobileOne · Benchmark · Backbone Optimization

1 Introduction

In recent years, computer vision has transformed a wide range of industries, including driver-less vehicles, surveillance systems, medical imaging, and augmented reality [6,11,16,17]. The models rely on intricate design, deep neural networks, and vast computational capability [18]. While these models are extremely accurate, their resource requirements make real-time processing and deployment on limited-resource devices difficult [9].

Lightweight models are a novel field of computer vision research [27]. These models strive for a delicate balance of computational efficiency and visual interpretation accuracy. Because of revolutionary strategies such as model compression, parameter reduction, and network optimization, lightweight models outperform their heavyweight counterparts while substantially reducing processing requirements [2,15,25].

H. Calvo et al. (Eds.): MICAI 2023, LNAI 14391, pp. 141–151, 2024.
https://doi.org/10.1007/978-3-031-47765-2_11

The use of lightweight models in computer vision has various advantages. For example, they enable more effective resource utilization [23]. This makes it possible for real-time processing on devices with limited computing capabilities, such as smartphones, embedded systems, and IoT devices, by minimizing computational requirements. This efficiency increases the accessibility and application of computer vision in a wide variety of applications.

Developing lightweight computer vision models has a distinct set of challenges that must be overcome before they can be successfully integrated into real-world applications [5]. While these models promise benefits such as increased resource utilization and faster inference times, they face a variety of problems. Obtaining a proper balance between model size and precision is one of the most challenging issues. Because lightweight models strive to reduce computation requirements, there is a trade-off between efficiency and performance [4]. An adequate balance must be achieved to ensure that the model remains small enough to run on resource-constrained devices while retaining acceptable levels of accuracy. Extensive testing, architecture design, and optimization techniques are often required to establish this equilibrium.

Concerns about the loss of fine-grained features and complex representations have also been expressed. Because lightweight models have fewer parameters and a shorter network, they have a restricted ability to capture specific qualities and small data oscillations [24]. This constraint can have an effect on model accuracy and robustness, particularly in complicated real-world scenarios that necessitate sophisticated information. To guarantee lightweight models work consistently across different conditions and data sets, model simplicity must be matched with the capacity to capture crucial properties.

3D facial reconstruction has always been a computationally intensive procedure requiring complex methodologies and significant computing resources [13]. However, using lightweight models can dramatically cut computing costs while still giving excellent results. With the help of these lightweight models, 3D facial reconstruction may now be conducted more efficiently on a broader range of devices, such as smartphones and tablets, enabling real-time or near-real-time applications. This enhancement not only improves the accessibility and convenience of facial reconstruction but also opens the door to new applications in a variety of industries.

2 Related Work

2.1 Face Reconstruction Models

Facial reconstruction models are advanced computer algorithms that rebuild or generate realistic facial images from incomplete or inaccurate data [30]. Deep learning methods, a subset of machine learning, are used in these models to evaluate and interpret complicated patterns in massive volumes of facial data. These models learn to recognize the various characteristics, forms, and textures that constitute the human face by training on enormous databases of facial photos [7]. While diverse architectures have been developed over the years, one of the state-of-the-art algorithms in this area is the *3D Dense Face Alignment* [29].

3DDFA-V1 presents a comprehensive method for face alignment that addresses the difficult challenge of consistently computing facial landmarks over a large variety of positions. This 2018 study introduces a ground-breaking 3D complete approach that combines 3D face modeling, position estimation, and landmark recognition methodologies to achieve robust and exact facial alignment.

The proposed approach is made up of three main steps: 3D face modeling, pose estimation, and 2D landmark detection. The first stage is to create a 3D morphable face model from a 3D facial image database. This approach incorporates geometric distinctions between diverse facial forms and emotions, enabling more exact alignment in challenging settings.

The authors present a pose estimation method that accurately calculates the 3D rotation and translation of a face. By analyzing the relationship between facial landmarks and their corresponding 3D model, the system can predict the position with exceptional precision, even under extreme perspectives or rotations. By combining the 3D face model with location estimation, the authors significantly enhance the accuracy of 2D facial landmark localization. Overall, this comprehensive method enables precise alignment in various configurations, including profile views and slanted orientations.

2.2 Lightweight Backbone Architectures for Facial Reconstruction

The backbone architecture is the computational base of face reconstruction models and is responsible for obtaining important facial information [1]. By exploiting convolutional neural networks and their ability to form hierarchical representations, these models can capture precise facial features, landmarks, and expressions, allowing them to produce realistic and accurate facial reconstructions [19]. The backbone design, when combined with other modules, can improve the overall performance and capability of the facial reconstruction models [26].

MobileNet-V1. MobileNet V1 is a convolutional neural network (CNN) architecture tailored to mobile and embedded vision applications [12]. Google published MobileNet V1 in 2017, with the goal of striking a balance between model size and accuracy, making it suitable for deployment on resource-constrained devices. The primary innovation of MobileNet V1 is its depthwise separable convolutions, which significantly reduce computational complexity while maintaining performance.

MobileNet V1 uses depthwise separable convolutions instead of standard CNN convolutional layers. Depthwise separable convolutions are composed of two operations that are performed sequentially: depthwise and pointwise convolutions. Depthwise convolutions, as opposed to standard convolutions, apply a single filter to each input channel independently, decreasing the computational cost. To facilitate efficient information aggregation, the output channels are blended using a 1×1 convolution. By separating spatial and channel-wise filtering, the number of parameters and processes is reduced, resulting in a lower model size and faster inference times. Despite its lightweight architecture, MobileNet V1 delivers competitive accuracy on a wide variety of visual recognition tasks and is gaining popularity as a platform for mobile and embedded vision applications.

EfficientNetLite. EfficientNetLite is a model family for convolutional neural networks (CNNs) that offers an outstanding mix of model size, computational efficiency, and performance [22]. It is an evolution of Google's EfficientNet concept, which was introduced in 2019 [20]. EfficientNetLite models are designed for devices with little memory and computing power, such as mobile phones and edge devices.

EfficientNetLite achieves its efficiency by employing a compound scaling strategy that simultaneously optimizes the model's depth, width, and resolution. This method guarantees that the model is both concise and effective. EfficientNetLite improves the trade-off between accuracy and processing requirements by carefully adjusting these parameters. Advanced methods such as mobile-friendly architecture, squeeze-and-excitation (SE) blocks, and depthwise separable convolutions are integrated into the models to reduce the number of parameters and improve processing efficiency. The EfficientNetLite models have grown in favor of on-device inference in mobile applications and other scenarios.

GhostNet. GhostNet is a lightweight convolutional neural network (CNN) architecture developed in 2020 [10]. It features a new ghost module for balancing model size and accuracy. The ghost module is designed to reduce the computation and memory expenses associated with typical convolutional layers while maintaining performance. This is accomplished by the use of a split-transform-merge technique, which generates a low-cost "ghost" branch in order to learn additional properties that augment the original branch.

GhostNet employs two types of blocks: ghost bottleneck and ghost group blocks. In the ghost bottleneck blocks, a lightweight depthwise separable convolution is followed by a ghost module. To capture additional spatial information, the ghost group blocks employ grouped convolutions and ghost modules. By combining these modules, GhostNet reduces model size and processing needs while maintaining competitive accuracy on a variety of picture classification tasks. Because of GhostNet's efficiency, it may be installed on low-resource devices, enabling real-time picture processing and categorization in mobile and embedded systems.

MobileFormer. MobileFormer is a unique architecture that blends the efficiency of mobile-friendly CNNs with the expressive potential of Transformers for mobile vision challenges. Introduced in 2021, MobileFormer intends to address the issues of embedding large-scale Transformer models onto resource-constrained smartphones [3]. It provides an appropriate balance of accuracy and computing performance by leveraging depthwise separable convolutions and attention methods.

The MobileFormer concept employs a hybrid technique that combines CNNs and Transformers. It effectively captures spatial information with depthwise separable convolutions while minimizing processing costs and preserving performance. Furthermore, it employs Transformer-like self-attention processes with incoming data to give global context awareness and long-term reliance recording. This combination enables MobileFormer to adequately analyze visual input while remaining lightweight enough for deployment on mobile devices. The architecture has demonstrated its capacity to provide advanced visual recognition skills on resource-constrained devices in a number of mobile vision applications, yielding positive results.

MobileOne. MobileOne is an innovative deep-learning architecture designed to fulfill the growing demand for real-time item detection and identification on mobile and edge devices [21]. MobileOne builds on the success of the MobileNet and EfficientNet designs to provide a reliable yet lightweight solution for a wide range of computer vision tasks. This design enhances model size and computational efficiency by using efficient depthwise separable convolutions and innovative feature fusion techniques.

One of MobileOne's most remarkable characteristics is its high accuracy and efficiency in object detection operations. By combining the benefits of feature pyramids and progressive upsampling, the model successfully captures multi-scale contextual information. This enables it to thrive in scenarios where item size and context change, making it ideal for image categorization, object placement, and semantic segmentation on mobile platforms. MobileOne is a big step forward in the hunt for lightweight models capable of performing complicated vision tasks.

3 Methodology

There are three trainable parameters in the 3DDFA-V1: *PDC, VDC and WPDC.* The pixel-to-shape mapping is determined by PDC, the vertex displacements for facial variations are depicted by VDC, and the WPDC combines PDC and VDC with weights to properly match the 2D image to the 3D face model. These parameters are crucial in the 3DDFA-V1 model for obtaining precise and detailed 3D facial reconstruction and alignment. The model was trained on a NVIDIA-A6000 with the respective default configuration. The differences are found on the starting learning rate shown in the Table 1. The training dataset is *300W-LP*, which expands on the 300W dataset by including photos of faces in large postures spanning from 90° to 180°. It is a great resource for developing and testing face alignment algorithms in difficult circumstances [28]. The parameters chosen for comparison were determined by the results presented in the 3DDFA-V1 investigation, such as the inference speed or losses in the training or validation process.

Table 1. Learning rate for each parameter.

Starting Learning Rate	PDC	VDC	WPDC
MobileNetV1	2×10^{-5}	1×10^{-5}	4×10^{-3}
EfficientNetLite	2×10^{-5}	1×10^{-5}	4×10^{-3}
GhostNet	2×10^{-6}	1×10^{-6}	4×10^{-4}
MobileFormer	2×10^{-6}	1×10^{-6}	4×10^{-3}
MobileOne	2×10^{-6}	1×10^{-5}	8×10^{-6}

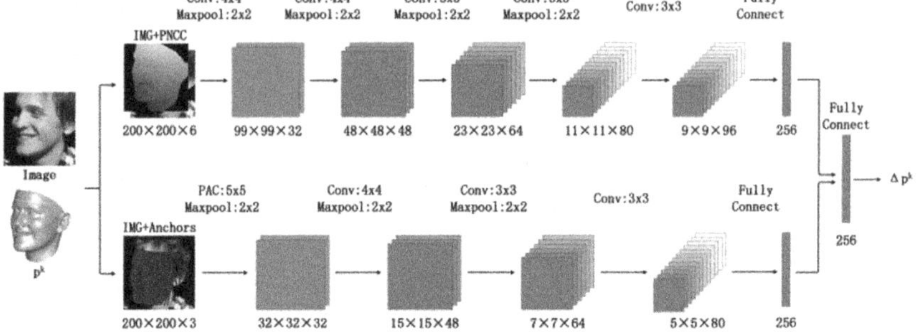

Fig. 1. Architecture of 3DDFA-V1 [29].

The Fig. 1 represents the architecture used for the 3DDFA-V1 model. The PDC parameters establish detailed correspondences between a 2D image and a 3D face model, while the VDC parameters capture facial variations. Weighted averaging (WPDC) combines these properties for the final 3D shape. The 3DMM provides a prior face shape model, constraining shape parameters for realistic results. The backbone used in this architecture is MobileNetV1 and it is found on the first layers of the network.

4 Results and Discussion

MobileNetV1 is the default backbone found on the 3DDFA-V1. During the training process, MobileFormer presented the minor loss in comparison with other models, as it was shown in the Figs. 2a and b. The difference is found for the *Weighted Parameter Distance Cost*, in which the MobileNetV1 returned the best results among the others (Fig. 3). In the validation process, MobileFormer had satisfactory results in PDC and WPDC, but EfficientNetLite provided a favorable outcome in VDC (Table 2). These scores lead us to conclude that MobileFormer is the most balanced backbone from all of the tested models. It is worth to mention that the runtime for each variable was 12 h, approximately. In the case of MobileFormer, it was around 20 h, presenting the longest time to train and validate from the tested backbones. The best inference speed is for the MobileNetV1, according to the Table 3. The number of FLOPs and Parameters,

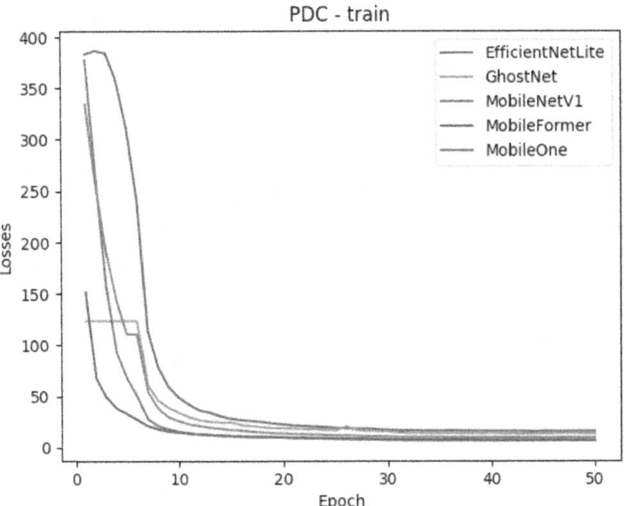

(a) Parameter Distance Cost (PDC).

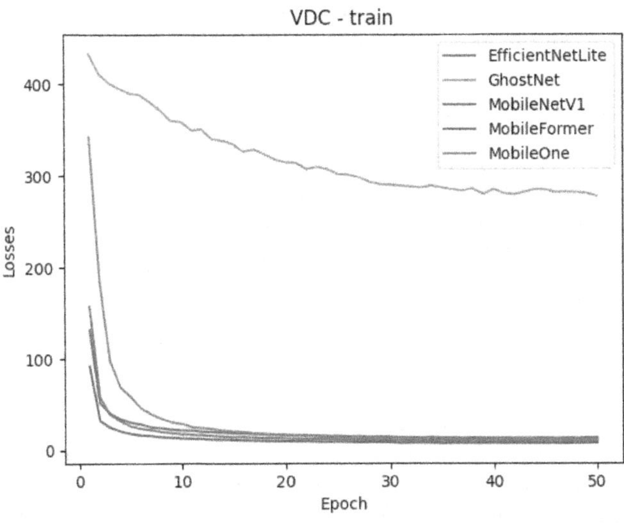

(b) Vertex Distance Cost (VDC).

Fig. 2. Losses of the cost functions with different backbones.

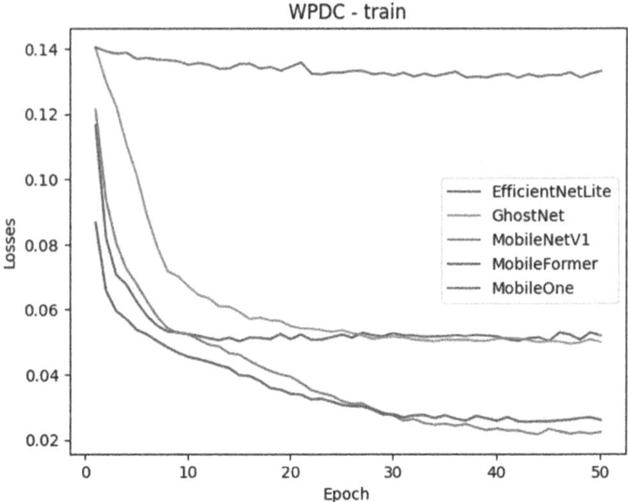

Fig. 3. Weighted Parameter Distance Cost (WPDC).

in unit of millions, is presented in the Table 4. GhostNet has the less FLOPs used from all the models and MobileNetV1 uses fewer parameters than the rest. From the results obtained above, we can conclude that the selection of a backbone for a facial reconstruction model depends on the characteristics that someone is looking for. MobileFormer provides a minor loss but with the highest number of FLOPs and inference speed. MobileNetV1 has the lowest inference speed and number of Parameters.

The backbone of a facial reconstruction model is critical to its performance and accuracy [1]. It is the foundation of the model, determining the model's capacity to extract useful properties from input data. The backbone should be capable of capturing the rich complexity and delicate details of the human face in the context of facial reconstruction. Facial landmarks, expressions, texture, and overall facial anatomy are examples of these details [19].

Furthermore, in order to enable real-time or near-real-time facial reconstruction applications, the backbone must be computationally efficient [8]. This is especially important when the model is used on low-resource devices or in circumstances requiring rapid inference, such as facial recognition systems.

Finally, the backbone architecture must be appropriate for both the provided dataset and the task at hand. Different backbone designs excel at different tasks. It is crucial to select a backbone that has been demonstrated to be effective for facial reconstruction or related tasks, as well as one that suits the dataset's features (e.g., size, diversity).

Table 2. Validation loss comparison between backbones.

Loss	PDC	VDC	WPDC
MobileNetV1	11.3394708	13.5553849	0.0569771
EfficientNetLite	12.4421664	**11.539531**	0.0521992
GhostNet	14.8614187	284.1875620	0.0563281
MobileFormer	**10.760656**	12.0656659	**0.050441**
MobileOne	11.9105363	15.9995884	0.1297856

Table 3. Inference speed of the models.

Model	Inference speed (ms)
MobileNetV1	**9.45 ± 1.11**
EfficientNetLite	16.36 ± 0.52
GhostNet	26.44 ± 0.81
MobileFormer	55.47 ± 1.80
MobileOne	29.44 ± 0.68

Table 4. FLOPs and Parameters of each model. The FLOPs and Params from Mobile-Former were obtained from the original paper [3].

Model	FLOPs (M)	Params (M)
MobileNetV1	581	**3.27**
EfficientNetLite	400	3.45
GhostNet	**150**	3.98
MobileFormer	508	14
MobileOne	1344	5.96

5 Conclusion

This research presented a benchmark comparison between multiple lightweight models for a facial reconstruction model, such as the 3DDFA-V1 [29]. The best scores for loss, inference speed, or number of FLOPs and Parameters were highlighted in each table. It was possible to obtain better results than the original architecture through modern backbones. The implementation of the results in a mobile device is now for the near future. The main challenges in this matter are still related to the hardware used for testing, as well as the trade-off between accuracy and velocity that has to be accomplished in order to provide a fully operational application without compromising its usability.

AI has been democratized by the use of lightweight models on common hardware, making it more accessible and helpful in a wide range of applications [14]. It has reduced the need for complex servers or cloud computing resources, allowing

AI algorithms to run directly on smartphones. This not only improves efficiency by removing the need for frequent data transfer, but it also enhances privacy and security by keeping critical data local.

We should expect significant breakthroughs in lightweight models and their implementation on common hardware in the future. As technology advances, it is possible that hardware manufacturers will create specialized processors and architectures tailored only for efficiently running AI algorithms. This boosts the speed and capability of lightweight models, enabling them to do increasingly complex AI tasks on devices with limited resources.

Acknowledgment. The authors would like to acknowledge the financial support of Tecnologico de Monterrey through the program "Challenge-Based Research Funding Program 2022". Project ID # E120 - EIC-GI06 - B-T3 - D.

References

1. Basak, S., Corcoran, P., McDonnell, R., Schukat, M.: 3D face-model reconstruction from a single image: a feature aggregation approach using hierarchical transformer with weak supervision. Neural Netw. **156**, 108–122 (2022)
2. Chang, X., Li, Y., Oymak, S., Thrampoulidis, C.: Provable benefits of overparameterization in model compression: from double descent to pruning neural networks. In: Proceedings of the AAAI Conference on Artificial Intelligence, vol. 35, pp. 6974–6983 (2021)
3. Chen, Y., et al.: Mobile-former: bridging MobileNet and transformer. arXiv arXiv:2108.05895 (2021)
4. Chen, Z., Sun, Y., Bi, X., Yue, J.: Lightweight image de-snowing: a better trade-off between network capacity and performance. Neural Netw. **165**, 896–908 (2023)
5. Deng, J., Guo, J., Zhang, D., Deng, Y., Lu, X., Shi, S.: Lightweight face recognition challenge. In: Proceedings of the IEEE/CVF International Conference on Computer Vision Workshops (2019)
6. Esteva, A., et al.: Deep learning-enabled medical computer vision. npj Digit. Med. **4**(1), 5 (2021)
7. Feng, M., Gilani, S.Z., Wang, Y., Mian, A.: 3D face reconstruction from light field images: a model-free approach. In: Ferrari, V., Hebert, M., Sminchisescu, C., Weiss, Y. (eds.) ECCV 2018. LNCS, vol. 11214, pp. 508–526. Springer, Cham (2018). https://doi.org/10.1007/978-3-030-01249-6_31
8. Gao, S.H., Cheng, M.M., Zhao, K., Zhang, X.Y., Yang, M.H., Torr, P.: Res2Net: a new multi-scale backbone architecture. IEEE Trans. Pattern Anal. Mach. Intell. **43**(2), 652–662 (2019)
9. Goel, A., Tung, C., Lu, Y.H., Thiruvathukal, G.K.: A survey of methods for low-power deep learning and computer vision. In: 2020 IEEE 6th World Forum on Internet of Things (WF-IoT), pp. 1–6. IEEE (2020)
10. Han, K., Wang, Y., Tian, Q., Guo, J., Xu, C., Xu, C.: GhostNet: more features from cheap operations. In: CVPR (2020)
11. Hodges, C., An, S., Rahmani, H., Bennamoun, M.: Deep learning for driverless vehicles. In: Balas, V.E., Roy, S.S., Sharma, D., Samui, P. (eds.) Handbook of Deep Learning Applications. SIST, vol. 136, pp. 83–99. Springer, Cham (2019). https://doi.org/10.1007/978-3-030-11479-4_4

12. Howard, A.G., et al.: MobileNets: efficient convolutional neural networks for mobile vision applications. arXiv preprint arXiv:1704.04861 (2017)
13. Lee, Y.J., Lee, S.J., Park, K.R., Jo, J., Kim, J.: Single view-based 3D face reconstruction robust to self-occlusion. EURASIP J. Adv. Sig. Process. **2012**, 1–20 (2012)
14. Li, Y., Liu, J., Wang, L.: Lightweight network research based on deep learning: a review. In: 2018 37th Chinese Control Conference (CCC), pp. 9021–9026. IEEE (2018)
15. Luo, X., Xie, Y., Zhang, Y., Qu, Y., Li, C., Fu, Y.: LatticeNet: towards lightweight image super-resolution with lattice block. In: Vedaldi, A., Bischof, H., Brox, T., Frahm, J.-M. (eds.) ECCV 2020. LNCS, vol. 12367, pp. 272–289. Springer, Cham (2020). https://doi.org/10.1007/978-3-030-58542-6_17
16. Mhalla, A., Chateau, T., Gazzah, S., Amara, N.E.B.: An embedded computer-vision system for multi-object detection in traffic surveillance. IEEE Trans. Intell. Transp. Syst. **20**(11), 4006–4018 (2018)
17. Nalbant, K.G., Uyanik, Ş: Computer vision in the metaverse. J. Metaverse **1**(1), 9–12 (2021)
18. O'Mahony, N., et al.: Deep learning vs. traditional computer vision. In: Arai, K., Kapoor, S. (eds.) CVC 2019. AISC, vol. 943, pp. 128–144. Springer, Cham (2020). https://doi.org/10.1007/978-3-030-17795-9_10
19. Shang, J., Chen, Y.: 3D-FERNet: a facial expression recognition network utilizing 3D information. In: 2022 26th International Conference on Pattern Recognition (ICPR), pp. 3265–3272. IEEE (2022)
20. Tan, M., Le, Q.: EfficientNet: rethinking model scaling for convolutional neural networks. In: International Conference on Machine Learning, pp. 6105–6114. PMLR (2019)
21. Vasu, P.K.A., Gabriel, J., Zhu, J., Tuzel, O., Ranjan, A.: MobileOne: an improved one millisecond mobile backbone. In: Proceedings of the IEEE/CVF Conference on Computer Vision and Pattern Recognition, pp. 7907–7917 (2023)
22. Wang, C.C., Chiu, C.T., Chang, J.Y.: EfficientNet-eLite: extremely lightweight and efficient CNN models for edge devices by network candidate search. J. Sig. Process. Syst. **95**, 657–669 (2022). https://doi.org/10.1007/s11265-022-01808-w
23. Xia, M., Huang, Z., Tian, L., Wang, H., Chang, V., Zhu, Y., Feng, S.: SparkNoC: an energy-efficiency FPGA-based accelerator using optimized lightweight CNN for edge computing. J. Syst. Architect. **115**, 101991 (2021)
24. Yao, D., Liu, H., Yang, J., Li, X.: A lightweight neural network with strong robustness for bearing fault diagnosis. Measurement **159**, 107756 (2020)
25. Zhang, X., et al.: A lightweight feature optimizing network for ship detection in SAR image. IEEE Access **7**, 141662–141678 (2019)
26. Zhou, J., Li, Y.: Detection-by-simulation: exposing DeepFake via simulating forgery using face reconstruction. In: 2022 IEEE 5th International Conference on Multimedia Information Processing and Retrieval (MIPR), pp. 210–215. IEEE (2022)
27. Zhou, Y., Chen, S., Wang, Y., Huan, W.: Review of research on lightweight convolutional neural networks. In: 2020 IEEE 5th Information Technology and Mechatronics Engineering Conference (ITOEC), pp. 1713–1720. IEEE (2020)
28. Zhu, X., Lei, Z., Liu, X., Shi, H., Li, S.Z.: Face alignment across large poses: a 3D solution. CoRR abs/1511.07212 (2015). http://arxiv.org/abs/1511.07212
29. Zhu, X., Liu, X., Lei, Z., Li, S.Z.: Face alignment in full pose range: a 3D total solution. IEEE Trans. Pattern Anal. Mach. Intell. **41**(1), 78–92 (2017)
30. Zollhöfer, M., et al.: State of the art on monocular 3D face reconstruction, tracking, and applications. Comput. Graph. Forum **37**, 523–550 (2018)

T(G)V-NeRF: A Strong Baseline in Regularized Neural Radiance Fields with Few Training Views

Erick Zúniga(✉), Thomas Batard(✉), and Jean-Bernard Hayet(✉)

Centro de Investigación en Matemáticas, A.C., Callejón Jalisco S/N, Guanajuato, GTO, Mexico
{erick.zuniga,thomas.batard,jbhayet}@cimat.mx

Abstract. Implicit representations such as Neural Radiance Fields (NeRFs) have become a *de facto* standard in the field of novel view synthesis for 3D scenes. However, their stunning results typically imply the use of dozens of training images, with their corresponding cameras well localized in the scene. This paper studies new, total variation-based regularization approaches to train NeRFs in the context of very few (less than 10) training images. It leverages the NeRF back-propagation algorithm to evaluate first-order and second-order derivatives terms on the inferred depth map to enforce smoothness on the scene underlying surfaces. Through state-of-the-art performance on standard real-images benchmarks, we show that the proposed methods, coined as TV-NeRF and TGV-NeRF, make strong baselines in novel view synthesis with few training views.

Keywords: 3D view synthesis · Neural Radiance Fields · Regularization

1 Introduction

In just a bit more than a couple of years, Neural Radiance Fields (NeRFs) have brought a major overhaul to the area of novel view synthesis of 3D scenes [9], i.e. the rendering of new images of a 3D scene, for user-specified viewpoints, given a collection of previously acquired images of this scene. Their appeal stems mainly from the use of machine learning to avoid both the explicit geometric and radiometric modelling of 3D surfaces, as done in traditional view synthesis pipelines [15]. Instead, NeRFs use a set of training views to learn to approximate the directional radiance function (the "radiance field") for any possible position and direction within a given volume. This 5D continuous function (3 dimensions for points positions, 2 dimensions for viewing angles) is implemented as a neural network and, once trained, it allows to synthesize novel views by integrating this radiance field along the rays induced by the desired novel view image pixels.

With their stunning results, NeRFs have received a lot of attention and many technical improvements have already been proposed to the initial proposal [9]

This work received financial support from Conahcyt under grant #319584.

H. Calvo et al. (Eds.): MICAI 2023, LNAI 14391, pp. 152–167, 2024.
https://doi.org/10.1007/978-3-031-47765-2_12

for obtaining more versatile view synthesis systems: Better handling of aliasing effects due to scale and depth variations between training and novel views [1]; Dealing with unbounded scenes [2]; Coping with heterogeneous datasets of images, taken in different conditions, with different cameras [7], to name a few.

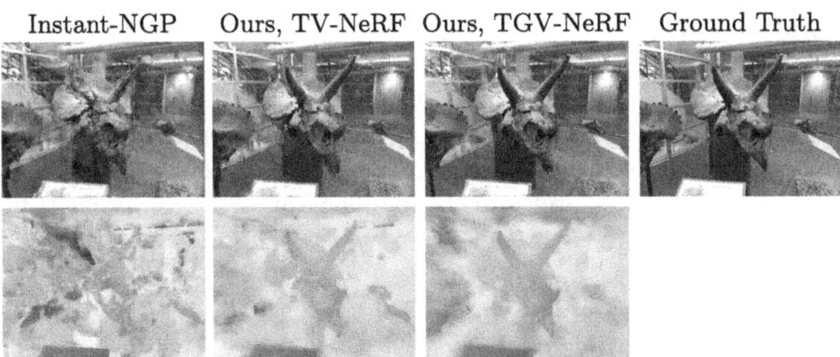

Fig. 1. Comparison of NeRF outputs on an unseen view from our first-order method TV-NeRF (2nd column) and second-order method TGV-NeRF (3rd column) for the HORNS scene of the LLFF dataset [8], with only 3 training views. The first column depicts the output from the state-of-the-art Instant-NGP [10] while the fourth column gives the ground truth. The second row depicts the depth maps evaluated as in Eq. 5.

In this work, we focus on one particular limitation of NeRFs: To produce high quality novel views, the amount of training images must be *large*, i.e. in the order of dozens of images, and the cameras corresponding to these images need to be localized in a common coordinate systems, which may be a burden. Hence, a natural question is: Can we produce faithful novel views with a much reduced number of training views, typically under 10? Intuitively, by reducing drastically the number of training views, the problem becomes ill-posed, without enough data to extract from the training views to constrain the radiance field parameters. A solution to this inverse problem [5] is *regularization*, i.e. recasting the optimization problem on the radiance field to leverage some prior on the potential solutions, by adding a soft constraint in the objective function. The work presented here explores first order and second order geometric regularizers operating on the depth map and brings a strong baseline coined T(G)V-NeRF. In Fig. 1, we depict generated views and depth maps for our two variants, altogether with the state-of-the-art Instant-NGP [10] and the ground truth, showing clear qualitative improvements in terms of reduction of holes and surface smoothness. In summary, we propose contributions in several directions:

- For mitigating the ill-posed problem occurring with very few views, we propose a combination of first and second order geometric regularizers that leverages the backprogagation over the NeRF neural network;
- Our regularization scheme is lightweight and uses only geometric terms. Yet, it gives better results than those of state of the art methods which also include appearance regularizers;

- As opposed to other regularization approaches such as [11], our approach does *not* have to fine-tune our regularizers on specific scenes;
- Our framework is computationally efficient, inheriting efficiency properties from the recently introduced hash grid encoding-based algorithms [10].

2 Related Work

As Neural Radiance Fields, and more generally implicit scene representations, form an extremely active burgeoning area, here we will only focus on the most important papers related to our regularization approach. For a more exhaustive overview on the area, please refer to the excellent survey by Sahariar [13].

2.1 Neural Radiance Fields

In the seminal work of Mildenhall et al. [9], the authors have proposed to represent the radiance field within a bounded, normalized volume as a continuous mapping F_θ, represented through a neural network with trainable parameters θ:

$$\begin{aligned} [-1,1]\times[-1,1]\times[-1,1]\times\mathbb{S}^2 \rightarrow &\quad [0,1]\times[0,1]\times[0,1]\times\mathbb{R}^+ \\ (\mathbf{x},\mathbf{v}) \mapsto &\quad F_\theta(\mathbf{x},\mathbf{v}) \triangleq (\mathbf{c}_\theta(\mathbf{x},\mathbf{v}),\sigma_\theta(\mathbf{x})), \end{aligned} \tag{1}$$

where $\mathbf{x}$ refers to a 3D position, $\mathbf{v}$ to a 3D direction, $\sigma_\theta(\mathbf{x})$ to the density/opacity value at position $\mathbf{x}$ and $\mathbf{c}_\theta(\mathbf{x},\mathbf{v})$ to the radiance emitted at $\mathbf{x}$ along direction $\mathbf{v}$ (and normalized in $[0,1]^3$). Actually, they use a rather classical Multiple Layer Perceptron (MLP) neural network for this task. Its inputs are positional encodings (through a sequence of Fourier coefficients) corresponding to the positions $\mathbf{x}$ and directions $\mathbf{v}$. Relating pixel values in an image to this radiance field is done by performing a *ray casting* operation within the field. This leads to apply the following equation of the ray $\mathbf{r}$ starting from a given camera origin $\mathbf{o}$ and with direction $\mathbf{v}$ (corresponding to the selected pixel),

$$\mathbf{r} \triangleq \{\mathbf{x}(t) = \mathbf{o} + t\mathbf{v},\ \text{for } t \in [t_n, t_f]\}, \tag{2}$$

and accessing the density/opacity value $\sigma_\theta(\mathbf{x}(t))$ and the radiance $\mathbf{c}_\theta(\mathbf{x}(t),\mathbf{v})$ at these points. Note that the ray is not taken along the full half-straight line, but along a line segment ($t \in [t_n, t_f]$), defining a limited frustum. At each of these points, along this ray, we can estimate an accumulated transmittance $T_\theta(t) \triangleq \exp(-\int_{t_n}^{t}\sigma_\theta(\mathbf{x}(\tau))d\tau)$, that corresponds to occlusion from the matter between the camera and the emission at point $\mathbf{x}(t)$. Finally, the color $\mathbf{C}_\theta(\mathbf{r}) \in \mathbb{R}^3$ associated to this ray (written at some pixel of the camera) is given by

$$\mathbf{C}_\theta(\mathbf{r}) = \int_{t_n}^{t_f} T_\theta(t)\sigma_\theta(\mathbf{x}(t))\mathbf{c}_\theta(\mathbf{x}(t),\mathbf{v})dt. \tag{3}$$

This integral is approximated as a discrete sum by sampling S points t_i along the ray $\mathbf{r}$, for $i = 1, ..., S$. In [9], stratified sampling is used, which implies using two identical networks, a coarse one and a refined one. The photogrammetric loss function $\mathcal{L}_{\text{photo}}(\theta)$ used to train the two networks is a mean squared error between N predicted colors $\mathbf{C}_\theta(\mathbf{r})$ and ground-truth colors $\mathbf{C}^*(\mathbf{r})$ corresponding to the pixels in the training images, each pixel being associated to a ray $\mathbf{r}$,

$$\mathcal{L}_{\text{photo}}(\theta) \triangleq \frac{1}{N} \sum_{\mathbf{r}} \|\mathbf{C}_\theta(\mathbf{r}) - \mathbf{C}^*(\mathbf{r})\|^2. \tag{4}$$

Among the most notable improvements to the original NeRF idea, [1] have proposed an elegant solution to handle better the potential aliasing effects due to scale and depth discrepancies between training and novel views; they propose to sum the radiance along conical *volumes* and implement this idea by revisiting the definition of positional encodings and integrating these encodings on ellipsoids that fit the conical volume. In [2], an extension of the aforementioned work deals with unbounded scenes by introducing a non-linear scene parametrization, and proposes a novel distorsion regularizer. In [7], a solution is proposed to cope with heterogeneous images, taken in different conditions, with different cameras, based on latent variables which allow to explain out this kind of variability.

The work of [10] has been a game changer of its kind, due to the introduction of a much faster encoding strategy based on hashing. Computational times required for training the radiance network have decreased dramatically, passing from several hours to the order of 30 minutes. In [6], more efficient sampling strategies are proposed, making of NeRF a very attractive option for the representation of 3D scenes. Implicit representations are now burgeoning in areas such as mobile robotics [12], providing alternatives to SLAM techniques.

2.2 Training a NeRF with (very) Few Images

In the works cited above, a large number of training images, typically dozens, are necessary to guarantee high-quality rendered images for new viewpoints. This may be a problem when acquiring these images is difficult or expensive. On the other hand, when using very few training images (typically, less than 10), the NeRF learning process from Eq. 4 becomes an ill-posed inverse problem: There are not enough observations through the pixels values to lead to an unambiguous model, and the optimization may get stuck to local minima. In this case, regularization approaches typically enforce priors on the potential solutions.

In [11], which is the most comparable work to ours, regularization is introduced at two levels. At the geometric level, a smoothness term is added to the loss function to penalize differences of depths between neighboring pixels. At the appearance level, a color likelihood term is added to favor likely patches. To emulate a probability density function on "natural" patches, a normalizing flow model is trained apart. Finally, an annealed sampling process is introduced to favor solutions concentrating the material density at the center of the scene, at least in the first steps of the training procedure.

In [4], a different regularization approach leverages the outputs of the Structure from Motion algorithm (e.g., Colmap [14]), which are necessary for NeRF to localize the cameras in the first place. The sparse 3D reconstructed points are used as anchors for the density $\sigma_\theta(\mathbf{x})$, with an optimization term enforcing the presence of these points on the surface implicitly associated to the NeRF.

3 Proposed Regularization Framework

Since dealing with few training images implies the use of regularization techniques, we propose to combine three regularization terms; the first one uses the first order derivatives of the depth image; the second one uses the second order derivatives of this same depth image; the last one avoids the formation of density blobs close to the camera. In the first two cases, the intuition is to introduce a prior enforcing a smoother depth map, which in turns should produce a smoother RGB image. In the following, we describe each of these terms.

3.1 Depth Map Regularization

Based on Eq. 3, one can render a *depth image*, instead of a color image, by integrating t instead of the directional radiance, which gives the following expression

$$d_\theta(\mathbf{o}, \mathbf{v}) = \int_{t_n}^{t_f} T_\theta(t)\sigma_\theta(\mathbf{o} + t\mathbf{v})t dt, \tag{5}$$

for $\mathbf{o} \in \mathbb{R}^3$ a position of the camera and $\mathbf{v} \in \mathbb{S}^2$ a viewing direction. We are interested in expressing the gradient of this depth map with respect to the image coordinates u, v. Given a camera-to-world rotation $\mathbf{R}$ and translation $\mathbf{o}$, and the intrinsic parameters matrix $\mathbf{K}$ of the camera, the ray originating at the camera origin $\mathbf{o}$ and passing through a pixel $\mathbf{p} = (u, v)$ in the image is described by

$$\mathbf{x}(t) = t\mathbf{R}\mathbf{K}^{-1} \begin{bmatrix} u \\ v \\ 1 \end{bmatrix} + \mathbf{o}. \tag{6}$$

For a depth map $d_\theta(u, v)$ built as in Eq. 5, the authors of RegNeRF [11] have introduced the following depth map regularization loss

$$\mathcal{L}_{\text{depth}} = \sum_{u,v} (d_\theta(u+1, v) - d_\theta(u, v))^2 + (d_\theta(u, v+1) - d_\theta(u, v))^2,$$

which can be viewed as a finite-difference approximation of $\int_\Omega \|\nabla d_\theta(u, v)\|^2 d\Omega$, the squared L_2 norm of $\nabla d_\theta(u, v)$, and which will make the main baseline method to compare our model to. Note an important general characteristic of this kind of loss: Because it does not depend on ground-truth values from the training images, it can also be applied to *unseen* views.

In the following, we show how we can form a better approximation of this integral over the gradients norms. Note that gradients are needed with respect to image coordinates $\mathbf{p} = (u, v)^T$ but that we only have direct access (through automatic differentiation) to the gradients with respect to the inputs to the network $(\mathbf{o}, \mathbf{v})$. We can relate them through a Jacobian matrix $\mathbf{J}$ such that

$$\nabla_{\mathbf{o},\mathbf{p}} d_\theta(\mathbf{o}, \mathbf{p}) = \mathbf{J}^T \nabla_{\mathbf{o},\mathbf{v}} d_\theta(\mathbf{o}, \mathbf{v}(\mathbf{p})).$$

with $\mathbf{J} = \begin{bmatrix} \frac{\partial \mathbf{o}}{\partial \mathbf{o}} & \frac{\partial \mathbf{o}}{\partial \mathbf{p}} \\ \frac{\partial \mathbf{v}}{\partial \mathbf{o}} & \frac{\partial \mathbf{v}}{\partial \mathbf{p}} \end{bmatrix} = \begin{bmatrix} \mathbf{J}_\mathbf{o} & \mathbf{0}_{3\times 2} \\ \mathbf{0}_{3\times 3} & \mathbf{J}_\mathbf{v} \end{bmatrix}$. By writing $\mathbf{v}(\mathbf{p}) = \mathbf{R}\mathbf{K}^{-1} \begin{bmatrix} \mathbf{p} \\ 1 \end{bmatrix}$, where $\mathbf{R} \triangleq [\mathbf{r}_1, \mathbf{r}_2, \mathbf{r}_3]$ is a rotation matrix and $\mathbf{K}$ is the camera's intrinsic parameters which we assume has the form $\begin{bmatrix} f & 0 & 0 \\ 0 & f & 0 \\ 0 & 0 & 1 \end{bmatrix}$, with f the camera focal length, it follows that

$$\mathbf{J}_\mathbf{v} = \frac{1}{f}\mathbf{R} \begin{bmatrix} 1 & 0 \\ 0 & 1 \\ 0 & 0 \end{bmatrix} = \frac{1}{f}\mathbf{R}\mathbf{I}_{3\times 2}.$$

Therefore $\nabla_{\mathbf{o},\mathbf{p}} d_\theta(\mathbf{o}, \mathbf{p}) = \begin{bmatrix} \mathbf{I}_{3\times 3} & \mathbf{0}_{3\times 3} \\ \mathbf{0}_{2\times 3} & \mathbf{J}_\mathbf{v}^T \end{bmatrix} \begin{bmatrix} \nabla_\mathbf{o} d_\theta(\mathbf{o}, \mathbf{v}) \\ \nabla_\mathbf{v} d_\theta(\mathbf{o}, \mathbf{v}) \end{bmatrix} = \begin{bmatrix} \nabla_\mathbf{o} d_\theta(\mathbf{o}, \mathbf{v}) \\ \mathbf{J}_\mathbf{v}^T \nabla_\mathbf{v} d_\theta(\mathbf{o}, \mathbf{v}) \end{bmatrix}$, and from this, we deduce that the squared norm of the gradient of the depth image, with respect to image coordinates, can be written as

$$\|\nabla_{\mathbf{o},\mathbf{p}} d_\theta(\mathbf{o}, \mathbf{p})\|^2 = \|\nabla_\mathbf{o} d_\theta(\mathbf{o}, \mathbf{v})\|^2 + \|\mathbf{J}_\mathbf{v}^T \nabla_\mathbf{v} d_\theta(\mathbf{o}, \mathbf{v})\|^2.$$

Focusing only on the second term,

$$\begin{aligned}
\|\mathbf{J}_\mathbf{v}^T \nabla_\mathbf{v} d_\theta(\mathbf{o}, \mathbf{v})\|^2 &= \frac{1}{f^2} \|\mathbf{I}_{2\times 3}\mathbf{R}^T \nabla_\mathbf{v} d_\theta(\mathbf{o}, \mathbf{v})\|^2 \\
&= \frac{1}{f^2} \|(\mathbf{e}_1\mathbf{e}_1^T + \mathbf{e}_2\mathbf{e}_2^T)\mathbf{R}^T \nabla_\mathbf{v} d_\theta(\mathbf{o}, \mathbf{v})\|^2 \\
&= \frac{1}{f^2} \|\mathbf{R}\mathbf{R}_{\mathbf{e}_3}(\pi/2)(\mathbf{e}_1\mathbf{e}_1^T + \mathbf{e}_2\mathbf{e}_2^T)\mathbf{R}^T \nabla_\mathbf{v} d_\theta(\mathbf{o}, \mathbf{v})\|^2 \\
&= \frac{1}{f^2} \|\mathbf{R}(\mathbf{e}_2\mathbf{e}_1^T - \mathbf{e}_1\mathbf{e}_2^T)\mathbf{R}^T \nabla_\mathbf{v} d_\theta(\mathbf{o}, \mathbf{v})\|^2 \\
&= \frac{1}{f^2} \|(\mathbf{r}_2\mathbf{r}_1^T - \mathbf{r}_1\mathbf{r}_2^T) \nabla_\mathbf{v} d_\theta(\mathbf{o}, \mathbf{v})\|^2 \\
&= \frac{1}{f^2} \|[\mathbf{r}_3]_\times \nabla_\mathbf{v} d_\theta(\mathbf{o}, \mathbf{v})\|^2 \\
&= \frac{\sin^2 \phi}{f^2} \|\nabla_\mathbf{v} d_\theta(\mathbf{o}, \mathbf{v})\|^2.
\end{aligned}$$

Finally, $\|\nabla_{\mathbf{o},\mathbf{p}} d_\theta(\mathbf{o}, \mathbf{p})\|^2 = \|\nabla_\mathbf{o} d_\theta(\mathbf{o}, \mathbf{v})\|^2 + \frac{\sin^2 \phi}{f^2} \|\nabla_\mathbf{v} d_\theta(\mathbf{o}, \mathbf{v}))\|^2$ with ϕ the angle between the optical axis $\mathbf{r}_3$ and the gradient $\nabla_\mathbf{v} d_\theta(\mathbf{o}, \mathbf{v})$. As a more general form for this expression, we have considered a variant with a hyperparameter μ weighting the contributions of the two squared gradients norms

$$\|\nabla_\mathbf{o} d_\theta(\mathbf{o}, \mathbf{v})\|^2 + \mu \|\nabla_\mathbf{v} d_\theta(\mathbf{o}, \mathbf{v}))\|^2. \tag{7}$$

Finally, regularization using the squared L_2 norm tends to produce over-smoothed results and to lose sharp edges [5]. Hence, the total variation (TV) norm is used instead, since it tends to preserves discontinuities better. The final regularization term we end up with is

$$\mathcal{L}_{\text{depth\_first}}(\theta) = \int_{\Omega} \sqrt{\|\nabla_{\mathbf{o}} d_\theta(\mathbf{o}, \mathbf{v})\|^2 + \mu \|\nabla_{\mathbf{v}} d_\theta(\mathbf{o}, \mathbf{v}))\|^2} d\Omega.$$

Since we only have samples of rays, the loss is implemented as the discrete sum

$$\mathcal{L}_{\text{depth\_first}}(\theta) = \frac{1}{N} \sum_{(\mathbf{o},\mathbf{v})} \sqrt{\|\nabla_{\mathbf{o}} d_\theta(\mathbf{o}, \mathbf{v})\|^2 + \mu \|\nabla_{\mathbf{v}} d_\theta(\mathbf{o}, \mathbf{v}))\|^2 + \eta}, \tag{8}$$

with N the number of rays we use with this regularizer and η a constant used for allowing differentiation even for small norm values. Now, as already commented, the two gradients in Eq. 8 can be evaluated from the backpropagation algorithm (once the forward passes to evaluate d are done), and the differentiation of $\mathcal{L}_{\text{depth\_first}}$ needs the gradients of d to be themselves differentiable. This has some consequences on the network design that we will expose in Sect. 4.1.

3.2 Second-Order Regularization

The regularizer from Eq. 8 can be improved by penalizing high values of higher-order derivatives, in what is called Total Generalized Variation [3] (TGV). To do so, we introduce the following objective function with second-order derivatives

$$\mathcal{L}_{\text{depth\_second}} = \int_{\Omega} \|\mathbf{H}_{\mathbf{v}}(d_\theta(\mathbf{o}, \mathbf{v}))\|_F d\Omega,$$

where $\mathbf{H}_{\mathbf{v}}(d(\mathbf{o}, \mathbf{v}))$ is the Hessian matrix of the depth with respect to the directions $\mathbf{v}$ and $\|\|_F$ is the Frobenius norm. Only the directions are considered to reduce calculations and also because we saw empirically that regularization over directions produces better results than with positions. Again, because we rely on a discrete set of rays, the term above is approximated as the discrete sum

$$\mathcal{L}_{\text{depth\_second}}(\theta) = \frac{1}{N} \sum_{(\mathbf{o},\mathbf{v})} \|\mathbf{H}_{\mathbf{v}}(d_\theta(\mathbf{o}, \mathbf{v}))\|_F. \tag{9}$$

3.3 Occlusion Regularization

With sparse inputs, NeRF tends to accumulate density near the camera. Depth regularization through derivatives, as described above, is in general not enough to solve this problem completely. Hence, we add a third type of regularization term, similar to the one introduced in [16], to prevent this accumulation:

$$\mathcal{L}_{\text{occ}}(\theta) = \frac{1}{N} \sum_{(\mathbf{o},\mathbf{v})} \sum_{i=1}^{S} \sigma_\theta(\mathbf{x}(t_i)) \exp(-\beta t_i), \tag{10}$$

where the sum is taken over rays $\mathbf{o}, \mathbf{v}$ in the training images and over the samples t_i along rays. Since t_i is the z-coordinate of the point $\mathbf{x}(t_i)$ in the camera frame (see Eq. 6), the factor $\exp(-\beta t_i)$ penalizes densities according to their depth to the camera, giving more weight to densities near the camera. The parameter β is such that $\frac{1}{\beta}$ acts as a cutting distance above which the penalization vanishes.

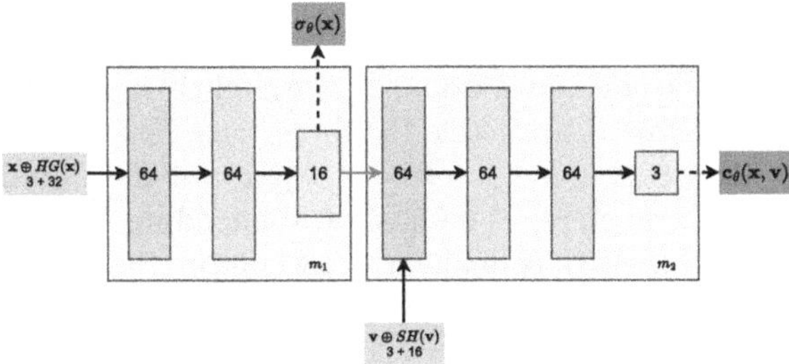

Fig. 2. Network architecture: Input values appear in green, input layers in orange, hidden layers in blue, output layers in yellow and output values in red. Black arrows between layers mean softplus activation, orange arrows mean no activation, and dashed ones are output activation (exp or sigmoid). The symbol $\oplus$ means concatenation. (Color figure online)

4 Experimental Results

In the following, we report our evaluations of the previously described regularization schemes and perform comparisons with other baselines.

4.1 Implementation Details

Architecture. Our model follows the InstantNGP [10] architecture and is depicted in Fig. 2. It consists of two small MLPs, one to generate the densities $\sigma_\theta(\mathbf{x})$ and the other one for the directional radiance $\mathbf{c}_\theta(\mathbf{x}, \mathbf{v})$

$$\mathbf{f}_\theta(\mathbf{x}) = m_1(\mathbf{x} \oplus HG(\mathbf{x})), \tag{11}$$

$$\sigma_\theta(\mathbf{x}) = \exp((\mathbf{f}_\theta(\mathbf{x}))_0), \tag{12}$$

$$\mathbf{c}_\theta(\mathbf{x}, \mathbf{v}) = m_2(\mathbf{v} \oplus SH(\mathbf{v}), \mathbf{f}_\theta(\mathbf{x})), \tag{13}$$

where $\oplus$ means concatenation. The first MLP m_1 takes as inputs (in green in Fig. 2) the 3D points $\mathbf{x}$ and their hash grid encoding $HG(\mathbf{x})$. It uses one hidden layer of width 64 and outputs a feature vector $\mathbf{f}_\theta(\mathbf{x})$ of size 16, through Eq. 11, where the first component is used to produce the density $\sigma_\theta(\mathbf{x})$, through Eq. 12 (in red in Fig. 2). The second MLP m_2 takes as inputs the feature vectors generated by m_1 and the view directions $\mathbf{v}$ with their spherical harmonics encoding

$SH(\mathbf{v})$. It uses two hidden layers of size 64 and a three-neuron output layer with sigmoid activations to produce the RGB color $\mathbf{c}_\theta(\mathbf{x}, \mathbf{v})$, through Eq. 13.

Our main modification is the substitution of some layers for differentiating Eq. 8 and Eq. 9 through the computational graph. To make these high-order derivatives available, the ReLU activation layers were modified into

$$\text{softplus}(x) = \frac{1}{\mu}\log(1 + \exp(\mu x)).$$

For the same reason, the encodings from [10] are slightly modified. Fourth-degree spherical harmonics are used to encode the directions. For positions, a hash grid with $L = 16$, $F = 2$, $T = 2^{19}$, $N_{\text{min}} = 16$ and $N_{\text{max}} = 4096$ is used (see [10] for a description of these parameters). The hash grid encoding used with a standard linear interpolation is only $\mathcal{C}^0$. To make it $\mathcal{C}^1$, we apply the smoothstep function $s(x) = x^2(3 - 2x)$ to produce the trilinear interpolation weights.

Training Process. The final loss used to train the network results from a weighted sum of the photogrammetric loss $\mathcal{L}_{\text{photo}}(\theta)$ from Eq. 4 and the regularizers proposed in Sect. 3. We propose two versions of our model. The first one (referred to as TV-NeRF) uses the first-order total variation regularizer $\mathcal{L}_{\text{depth}}\_\text{first}(\theta)$ of Eq. 8 and the occlusion term $\mathcal{L}_{\text{occ}}(\theta)$ of Eq. 10, producing the total loss:

$$\mathcal{L}_{\text{TV-NeRF}}(\theta) = \mathcal{L}_{\text{photo}}(\theta) + \lambda_1 \mathcal{L}_{\text{depth}}\_\text{first}(\theta) + \lambda_{occ}\mathcal{L}_{\text{occ}}(\theta). \tag{14}$$

The TGV-NeRF regularizer combines $\mathcal{L}_{\text{depth}}\_\text{first}(\theta)$ with the second order term $\mathcal{L}_{\text{depth}}\_\text{second}(\theta)$ of Eq. 9, in a total generalized variation regularizer [3]

$$\mathcal{L}_{\text{TGV-NeRF}}(\theta) = \mathcal{L}_{\text{photo}}(\theta) + \lambda_1(\mathcal{L}_{\text{depth}}\_\text{first}(\theta) + \lambda_2\mathcal{L}_{\text{depth}}\_\text{second}(\theta)). \tag{15}$$

The hyperparameters $\lambda_1, \lambda_2, \lambda_{occ}$ control the influence of each regularizer.

In both cases, Adam is used as the optimizer with a $\epsilon = 1 \times 10^{-15}$ (guard against division by zero) and a weight decay of 2×10^{-6}. As for the learning rate, we implement the scheduling scheme proposed in [1]

$$\eta_k = [\lambda_w + (1 - \lambda_w)\sin((\pi/2)\text{clip}(k/n_w, 0, 1))]\exp((1 - k/n)\log(\eta_0) + (k/n)\log(\eta_n))$$

where n is the total number of iterations, η_k is the learning rate for the k-th iteration which is an exponential interpolation between the initial learning rate $\eta_0 = 5 \times 10^{-3}$ and final learning rate $\eta_n = 5 \times 10^{-4}$. For the first $n_w = 512$ iterations, the learning rate is scaled by a weight that is smoothly annealed between $\lambda_w = 0.01$ and 1, and this serves as a warmup which stabilizes training.

The weight for the depth regularization λ_1 is scheduled to drop exponentially beginning in 2×10^{-4} and ending in 1×10^{-7}. In the case of the occlusion regularizer, the weight λ_{occ} is fixed at 0.1. The parameter β varies logarithmically from 10 at the start of training to 30 at the end. For the second order model TGV-NeRF, λ_1 is kept the same as in the first order one, and λ_2 is fixed at 0.1. If not said otherwise, all the experiments are done with 20000 iterations.

Evaluation Metrics and Dataset. In the experiments, we report three popular metrics for evaluating the similarity between the generated images (through Eq. 3) and the ground truth images. These metrics are the results of a double averaging process: over different testing viewpoints for each scene, and over 8 scenes of the LLFF dataset [8]. The Peak Signal-to-Noise Ratio (PSNR) (the larger, the better) is the most classical metric to quantify the degradation in image quality. Structural Similarity Index (SSIM) (again, the larger, the better) serves a similar purpose, with a stronger perceptual focus. LPIPS (the lower, the better) is a recently proposed perceptual approach [17], which has been shown to correlate better with human perception. We also report a geometric mean of the metrics, namely of the three quantities: $10^{-\text{PSNR}/10}$, $\sqrt{1-\text{SSIM}}$ and LPIPS.

4.2 Ablation Results

For these experiments, with only 3 training views, we have used TV-NeRF (Eq. 14) to evaluate which choice of μ leads to the best performance. The metrics results are presented in Table 1. The choice $\mu = 1$ brings the best results overall, hence for the rest of the experiments in this Section, we have taken this value $\mu = 1$.

Table 1. Image quality metrics on LLFF for different values of μ in Eq. 8.

Case	PSNR↑	SSIM↑	LPIPS↓	Average↓
$\mu = \frac{\sin^2 \phi}{f^2}$	19.38	0.7183	0.2326	0.1138
$\mu = 0$	19.41	0.7244	0.2282	0.1121
$\mu = 1$ w/o $\|\|\nabla_o d\|\|$	**19.70**	0.7296	0.2261	0.1084
μ=1	19.69	**0.7305**	**0.2213**	**0.1079**

Table 2. Ablation study for 3 views on TV-NeRF.

	PSNR↑	SSIM↑	LPIPS↓	Average↓
no regularizer	18.15	0.6855	0.2670	0.1329
only occlusion regularizer ($\mathcal{L}_{\text{occ}}$)	18.30	0.6808	0.2653	0.1314
only depth TV regularizer ($\mathcal{L}_{\text{depth\_first}}$)	18.84	0.7101	0.2314	0.1187
both regularizers	**19.40**	**0.7244**	**0.2278**	**0.1117**

Then, in Table 2, we compare the performance of TV-NeRF for three training views, again, under different regularization schemes: Without regularizer, with the occlusion regularizer $\mathcal{L}_{\text{occ}}$ only, with the TV regularizer only $\mathcal{L}_{\text{depth\_first}}$ and with both regularizers. We see that with any of the regularization cases, we get a significant improvement in performance compared to the non-regularized case. In particular, introducing the TV term (third line) leads to the strongest improvement (around 10%), and using both regularizers leads to the best performance.

4.3 Quantitative Results

In this Section, we compare the performance of our two models TV-NeRF and TGV-NeRF with variants of two baselines of the literature, namely, Instant-NGP [10], which does not include regularization at all and which we expect should struggle to cope with few training views, and Reg-NeRF [11], that combines a geometric and an appearance regularizer. RegNeRF is evaluated under two schemes: with and without the appearance regularizer. In Table 3, we report these comparisons under three scenarios: 3 (an "extreme" scenario), 6, and 9 training views. For 6 and 9 views, TGV-NeRF obtains the best results, but note that TV-NeRF is very close. The improvement with respect to Reg-NeRF, in particular, is significant and the small difference in performance between TV-NeRF and TGV-NeRF suggests that the main contribution comes from the first order regularization term, with the Hessian one allowing only marginal gains.

Table 3. Image quality metrics on LLFF for different methods and different scenarios (3, 6, 9 training views). The asterisk indicates results from [11], which have been obtained with many more training iterations than in our setup.

	Views	PSNR↑	SSIM↑	LPIPS↓	Average↓	Time
Instant-NGP	3	18.15	0.685	0.267	0.133	~18 min
Reg-NeRF w/o appearance loss		18.75	0.665	0.282	0.131	~2 h
Reg-NeRF w/o appearance loss*		18.90	0.677	0.262	0.126	~7 h
Reg-NeRF*		18.89	**0.745**	**0.190**	0.112	>7 h
TV-NeRF w/ over-smoothing		**19.69**	0.730	0.221	0.108	~27 min
TGV-NeRF		19.67	0.734	0.220	**0.107**	~1 h
Instant-NGP	6	22.69	0.830	0.143	0.071	~18 min
Reg-NeRF w/o appearance loss		22.79	0.797	0.177	0.079	~2 h
Reg-NeRF*		22.20	0.841	0.117	0.071	>14 h
TV-NeRF		23.84	0.855	0.117	0.059	~27 min
TGV-NeRF		**23.95**	**0.857**	**0.114**	**0.058**	~1 h
Instant-NGP	9	24.61	0.871	0.109	0.054	~18 min
Reg-NeRF w/o appearance loss		24.30	0.845	0.146	0.063	~2 h
Reg-NeRF*		24.86	0.820	0.161	0.067	>21 h
TV-NeRF		24.96	0.879	0.105	0.051	~27 min
TGV-NeRF		**25.10**	**0.880**	**0.104**	**0.050**	~1 h

The case of 3 views is interesting, as the most extreme case of data scarcity. Overall, under the averaged metrics, TV-NeRF and TGV-NeRF give the best results, but Reg-NeRF stands out in the LPIPS and SSIM metrics. Note that the rows with an asterisk, with relatively good performance, correspond to the results

Table 4. Effect of initial oversmoothing for TV-NeRF training with 3 views.

	PSNR↑	SSIM↑	LPIPS↓	Average↓
w/o oversmoothing	19.40	0.724	0.228	0.112
w/ oversmoothing	**19.69**	**0.730**	**0.221**	**0.108**

reported in the Reg-NeRF paper and have been run with *many more iterations than the other models* reported here[1]. Hence, to be fair, we have included a third Reg-NeRF version, which runs without the appearance regularizer and is trained for 20000 iterations only. The results for this version are quite degraded. Also, the appearance regularizer, in this case, seems to bring a notable improvement.

The training times appear in the last column of Table 3. Even in its 20000 iterations scheme, Reg-NeRF is about four times slower than our models. This is due to the simpler network inherited from [10], altogether with the hashing-based encodings. Because of the evaluation of the Hessians, TGV-NeRF takes twice the training time of TV-NeRF. Since its gains for 3 views w.r.t. TV-NeRF are marginal, but its computational times quite larger, one could prefer TV-NeRF in this case, depending on which of performance and time is more important.

Finally, in the case of 3 views, we have obtained a stabler convergence of the training process by starting this training process with an initial oversmoothing period. During this period, $\lambda_{\text{occ}} = 0.5$ is used instead of 0.1 and λ_1 is scaled by a factor of 100 during the first 256 iterations. In Table 4, the positive effect of this oversmoothing period is made clear for TV-NeRF in the 3-training views case. All the reported metrics are improved by approximately 4% on average.

4.4 Qualitative Results

In Table 5, we give qualitative examples of results obtained with 3 training views, providing the generated images and the depth images corresponding to Eq. 5, which are the object of regularization. As it can be seen, the rendering from our methods gives more spatial coherence, while Reg-NeRF (trained here with 20000 iteration as ours, and without the appearance regularizer) tends to struggle quite a bit in producing smooth surfaces. The third example illustrates that, given the data scarcity, our system has limits: Even though the dinosaur structure is rather well recovered, all the methods struggle with the roof and walls (in particular with the close roof section in the upper part of the image).

[1] This number of iterations varies with the scenario, please refer to [11] for details.

Table 5. Generated views: comparisons between methods, for 3 training views.

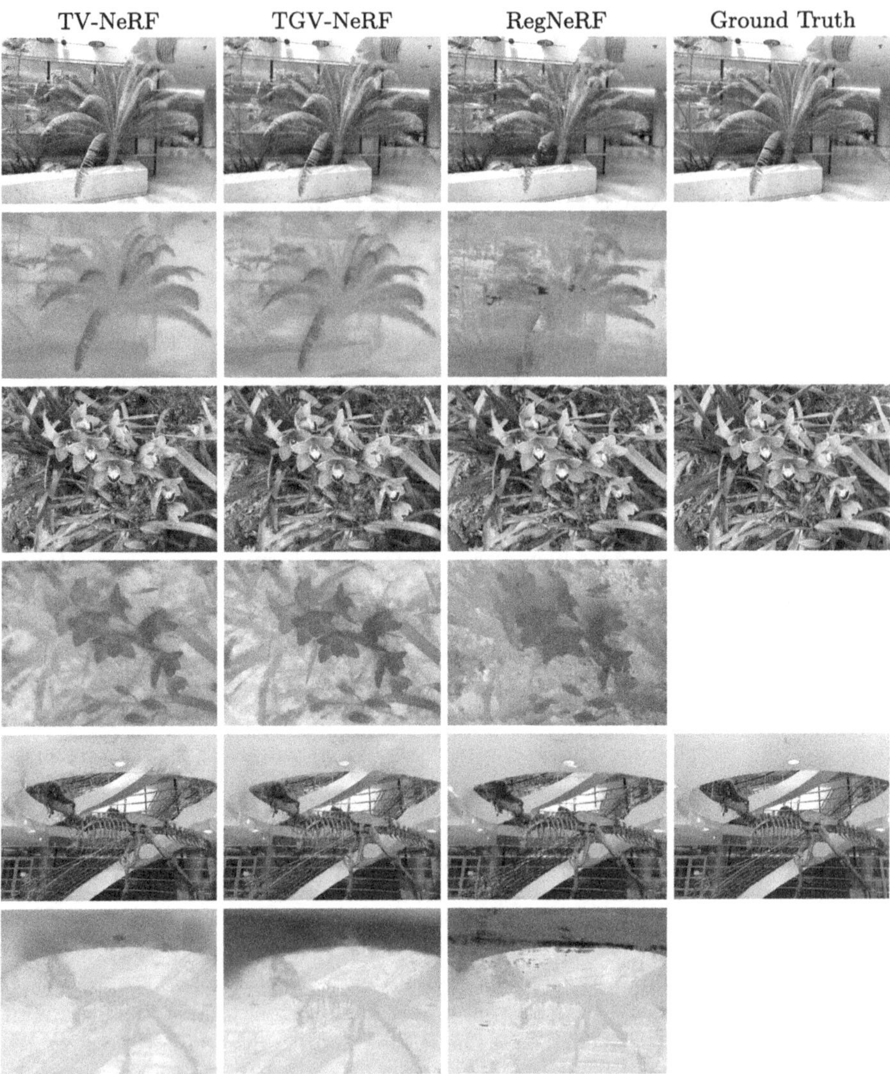

Similarly, in Table 6, we see that, overall, our methods give smoother surfaces with less holes than with Reg-NeRF, while preserving detailed structure, e.g. in the second example, where the tower has a lot of micro-structures. In the last example (office scenario), we see again some limits, for example with the textureless areas such as the table and the floor.

Table 6. Generated views: comparisons between methods, for 6 training views.

5 Conclusions

In this paper, we have proposed TV-NeRF and TGV-NeRF, two novel total variation-based regularization schemes for neural radiance fields optimized with (very) few training images. Using a modified Instant-NGP as a backbone, we have shown that these first-order and second-order geometric regularizers (operating on the depth map induced from the radiance field) allow to reach state-of-the-art results on the LLFF dataset, outperforming methods such as Reg-NeRF, even though the former uses appearance regularization in addition to geometric regularization, and with much more competitive training times.

As a future work, we will explore the use of this kind of regularization schemes for other implicit representations (e.g. signed distance fields) and will explore the introduction of regularizers to ensure consistency among several generated views.

References

1. Barron, J.T., Mildenhall, B., Tancik, M., Hedman, P., Martin-Brualla, R., Srinivasan, P.P.: MIP-NERF: a multiscale representation for anti-aliasing neural radiance fields. In: Proceedings of the International Conference on Computer Vision (ICCV) (2021)
2. Barron, J.T., Mildenhall, B., Verbin, D., Srinivasan, P.P., Hedman, P.: MIP-NERF 360: unbounded anti-aliased neural radiance fields. In: Proceedings of the IEEE Conference on Computer Vision and Pattern Recognition (CVPR) (2022)
3. Bredies, K., Kunisch, K., Pock, T.: Total generalized variation. SIAM J. Imag. Sci. **3**(3), 492–526 (2010)
4. Deng, K., Liu, A., Zhu, J.Y., Ramanan, D.: Depth-supervised nerf: fewer views and faster training for free. arXiv preprint arXiv:2107.02791 (2021)
5. Kirsch, A.: An Introduction to the Mathematical Theory of Inverse Problems, vol. 120. Springer, Cham (2011). https://doi.org/10.1007/978-1-4419-8474-6
6. Li, R., Gao, H., Tancik, M., Kanazawa, A.: NERFACC: efficient sampling accelerates nerfs. arXiv preprint arXiv:2305.04966 (2023)
7. Martin-Brualla, R., Radwan, N., Sajjadi, M.S.M., Barron, J., Dosovitskiy, A., Duckworth, D.: Nerf in the wild: Neural radiance fields for unconstrained photo collections. In: Proceedings of the IEEE Conference on Computer Vision and Pattern Recognition (CVPR) (2021). https://nerf-w.github.io/
8. Mildenhall, B., et al.: Local light field fusion: practical view synthesis with prescriptive sampling guidelines. ACM Trans. Graphics (TOG) **38**, 1–14 (2019)
9. Mildenhall, B., Srinivasan, P.P., Tancik, M., Barron, J.T., Ramamoorthi, R., Ng, R.: NERF: representing scenes as neural radiance fields for view synthesis. In: Proceedings of the European Conference on Computer Vision (ECCV) (2020)
10. Müller, T., Evans, A., Schied, C., Keller, A.: Instant neural graphics primitives with a multiresolution hash encoding. ACM Trans. Graph. **41**(4), 102:1-102:15 (2022)
11. Niemeyer, M., Barron, J.T., Mildenhall, B., Sajjadi, M.S.M., Geiger, A., Radwan, N.: Regnerf: regularizing neural radiance fields for view synthesis from sparse inputs. In: Proceedings of the IEEE Conference on Computer Vision and Pattern Recognition (CVPR) (2022)
12. Ortiz, J., et al.: ISDF: real-time neural signed distance fields for robot perception. In: Robotics: Science and Systems (2022)
13. Rabby, A.S.A., Zhang, C.: Beyondpixels: a comprehensive review of the evolution of neural radiance fields. arXiv e-prints pp. arXiv-2306 (2023). https://arxiv.org/abs/2306.03000
14. Schönberger, J.L., Frahm, J.M.: Structure-from-motion revisited. In: Proceedings of the IEEE Conference on Computer Vision and Pattern Recognition (CVPR) (2016)
15. Schönberger, J.L., Zheng, E., Pollefeys, M., Frahm, J.M.: Pixelwise view selection for unstructured multi-view stereo. In: European Conference on Computer Vision (ECCV) (2016)

16. Yang, J., Pavone, M., Wang, Y.: FREENERF: improving few-shot neural rendering with free frequency regularization. In: Proceedings of the IEEE Conference on Computer Vision and Pattern Recognition (CVPR) (2023)
17. Zhang, R., Isola, P., Efros, A.A., Shechtman, E., Wang, O.: The unreasonable effectiveness of deep features as a perceptual metric. In: Proceedings of the IEEE Conference on Computer Vision and Pattern Recognition (CVPR) (2018)

Nonlinear DIP-DiracVTV Model for Color Image Restoration

Natalia Huitzil Santamaría[1], Thomas Batard[1(✉)], and Carlos Brito-Loeza[2]

[1] Centro de Investigación en Matemáticas, A.C., Guanajuato, Mexico
{natalia.huitzil,thomas.batard}@cimat.mx

[2] Facultad de Matemáticas, Universidad Autónoma de Yucatán, Mérida, Mexico
carlos.brito@correo.uady.mx

Abstract. Variational models for inverse problems are mainly based on the choice of the regularizer, whose goal is to give the solutions some desirable property. Total Variation, one of the most popular regularizer for image restoration, is induced by the Euclidean gradient operator and promotes piece-wise constant solutions. In this paper, we present a new regularizer for color image restoration, which is induced by a generalization of the Dirac operator. This new regularizer also encourages the gradients of the three color components of the solutions to be aligned, which is actually a property of natural images. This property is also encoded when the regularizer is induced by a Riemannian gradient, for a well-chosen Riemannian metric, but with a different mathematical formulation. Then, we compare the different regularizers by combining them with the Deep Image Prior model, this latter assuming that the restored image is the output of a neural network. Experiments on denoising and deblurring show that the proposed Dirac operator provides better results than the Euclidean and Riemannian gradient operators.

Keywords: Color image restoration · Variational model · Total Variation · Dirac operator · Riemannian geometry · Deep Image Prior

1 Introduction

Over the last 30 years, variational methods have demonstrated their efficiency to solve different tasks in image restoration, e.g. denoising, deblurring, super-resolution, inpainting, segmentation [17]. The key idea in the seminal variational model of Rudin et al. [14] for grey-level image denoising is to take the Total Variation (TV) as a regularization term, which promotes piece-wise constant solutions. Since then, this model has been adapted to other image restoration tasks and improved in several ways. For instance, the Total Generalized Variation (TGV) [5] promotes piece-wise linear solutions, which reduces the undesirable stair-casing effect produced by the TV regularizer.

Extensions of TV-based models to color images mainly rely on the generalization of TV to vector-valued functions. The seminal extensions do not take into

H. Calvo et al. (Eds.): MICAI 2023, LNAI 14391, pp. 168–181, 2024.
https://doi.org/10.1007/978-3-031-47765-2_13

account any specific properties of color images [4,6]. In particular, the Vectorial Total Variation (VTV) [6] replaces the Euclidean operator of a grey-level image by the Jacobian operator of a color image. However, it is well-known that coupling color channels can provide better results by avoiding color smearing and edge distortion [8]. In particular, the Polyakov energy [7,13,15], which replaces the Euclidean gradient by an approximation of a Riemannian gradient in the regularization term, performs the coupling of the color channels of a given image $u = (u_1, u_2, u_3)$ by considering the square of the cross product between their gradients $(\nabla u_i \times \nabla u_j)^2$ for $i, j = 1, 2, 3$. The relevance of such a coupling is based on the fact that in natural images the directions of the gradients of their components are very similar, i.e. the angle between ∇u_i and ∇u_j is close to zero for $i \neq j$ (see [9] for details).

In recent years, the success of artificial neural networks (ANNs) in solving computer vision tasks has drastically modified the way these problems are approached, including the formulation of variational models for image restoration. In particular, Deep Image Prior (**DIP**) [16] takes advantage of the generative power of ANNs, by assuming that the clean image can be generated by a neural network. DIP achieves remarkable results on various image restoration tasks. However, since DIP generates noise, it was proposed to add a TV term to overcome this issue, yielding the **DIP-TV** model [12]. More recently, DIP-TV has been improved by the use of regularizers which are degradation dependent. The corresponding models, called **DIP-VBTV** [3] and **DIP-VBTV**$^{\alpha^*}$ [1], are used for denoising and deblurring color images.

In this paper, we introduce a new regularizer for color image restoration based on a generalization of the Euclidean Dirac operator, called Nonlinear Dirac Vectorial Total Variation (DiracVTV^{NL}). Like the Euclidean gradient operator, the Euclidean Dirac operator is a first order differential operator deeply related to the Laplace operator. Indeed, it is well-known that the Laplace operator is obtained by applying the divergence to the gradient operator, but it turns out that it can also be obtained by applying the Dirac operator to itself. The Euclidean Dirac operator and its generalizations have a fundamental role in the description of laws of quantum mechanics. On the other hand, Dirac operators have been very few employed in computer vision (see [10,11] for applications to 3D shape analysis and [2] for an application to grey-level image analysis). Because the Euclidean Dirac operator can not be applied directly to color images, we introduce in this paper some extensions of this operator to color images (Sect. 3). In particular, we present a nonlinear extension of the Dirac operator. We show that, as the Polyakov energy aforementioned, DiracVTV^{NL} encodes the cross products of the gradients of the image components, the difference being that the square $(\nabla u_i \times \nabla u_j)^2$ is now replaced by the absolute value $|\nabla u_i \times \nabla u_j|$. Then, we combine DiracVTV^{NL} with DIP, yielding the **DIP-DiracVTV**$^{\mathbf{NL}}$ model for color image restoration. Experiments on denoising and deblurring in Sect. 4 show that DIP-DiracVTV^{NL} gives better results than other models that combine DIP with a regularizer, including VTV and its Riemannian counterpart RiemannVTV, and described in Sect. 2.

2 DIP-Reg Models for Color Image Restoration

2.1 DIP-Reg Models

Let us consider the following degradation model

$$u_0 = Au^* + n$$

where u_0 is the degraded observed image, A is a degradation operator applied to the clean image u^*, and n some noise.

DIP assumes that u^* can be approximated by the output $\underline{u}$ of a well-chosen neural network [16]. More precisely, DIP is expressed as the following variational model

$$\begin{cases} \underline{\theta} = \arg\min_{\theta} \frac{1}{2} \|AT_\theta(z) - u_0\|_{L^2}^2 \\ \underline{u} = T_{\underline{\theta}} z \end{cases} \tag{1}$$

where T_θ is an ANN (a U-Net with skip connections between the encoder and decoder parts) whose input z is a random image. We refer the reader to [16] for more details on the architecture of the network. In practice, the model is solved by a gradient descent stopped after a well-chosen number of iterations (see Sect. 4 for details). Indeed, it is crucial to stop the gradient descent at the right moment, since DIP generates noise after a certain number of iterations.

In order to reduce this undesirable effect, a regularizer Reg can be added to the model, resulting in a DIP-Reg model

$$\begin{cases} \underline{\theta} = \arg\min_{\theta} \frac{1}{2} \|AT_\theta(z) - u_0\|_{L^2}^2 + \lambda\, Reg(T_\theta(z)) \\ \underline{u} = T_{\underline{\theta}} z \end{cases} \tag{2}$$

for $\lambda > 0$.

2.2 Euclidean Models: DIP-TV and DIP-VTV

The seminal article suggesting the use of a regularizer is [12], where the authors consider the anisotropic TV for grey-level images and its vectorial extension for color images, leading to the so-called DIP-TV model. In [3], the authors take the Vectorial Total Variation (VTV) as regularizer, which corresponds to the integral of the Frobenius norm of the Jacobian:

$$VTV(u) = \int_{\Omega} \sqrt{\sum_{k=1}^{3} \left(\frac{\partial u_k}{\partial x}\right)^2 + \left(\frac{\partial u_k}{\partial y}\right)^2}\, d\Omega \tag{3}$$

for $u = (u_1, u_2, u_3)\colon \Omega \subset \mathbb{R}^2 \longrightarrow \mathbb{R}^3$. They call this model **DIP-VTV**.

Experiments have shown that both DIP-TV and DIP-VTV outperform DIP in denoising and deblurring tasks.

2.3 Riemannian Model: DIP-RiemannVTV

Polyakov Action. In the Beltrami framework introduced by Sochen et al. [15], a color image is seen as a function $u = (u_1, u_2, u_3) \in C^1(\Omega; \mathbb{R}^3)$ where the domain Ω is equipped with the following Riemannian metric

$$g = \begin{pmatrix} 1 + \beta \sum_{k=1}^{3} \left(\frac{\partial u_k}{\partial x}\right)^2 & \beta \sum_{k=1}^{3} \frac{\partial u_k}{\partial x}\frac{\partial u_k}{\partial y} \\ \beta \sum_{k=1}^{3} \frac{\partial u_k}{\partial x}\frac{\partial u_k}{\partial y} & 1 + \beta \sum_{k=1}^{3} \left(\frac{\partial u_k}{\partial y}\right)^2 \end{pmatrix}. \tag{4}$$

The metric g corresponds to the metric induced by the embedding of the graph φ of u

$$\varphi\colon (x, y) \longmapsto (x, y, u_1(x, y), u_2(x, y), u_3(x, y))$$

into $\mathbb{R}^5$ equipped with the metric $diag(1, 1, \beta, \beta, \beta)$, $\beta > 0$.

The Polyakov energy of u is the quantity

$$\begin{aligned} S(u) &= \int_\Omega dg = \int_\Omega \sqrt{\det g}\, d\Omega \\ &= \int_\Omega 1 + \beta^2 \sum_{k=1}^{3} \|\nabla u_k\|^2 + \frac{\beta^4}{2} \sum_{1 \le i < j \le 3} (\nabla u_i \times \nabla u_j)^2\, d\Omega, \end{aligned} \tag{5}$$

where the cross product $\times$ is defined by

$$\nabla u_i \times \nabla u_j = \frac{\partial u_i}{\partial x}\frac{\partial u_j}{\partial y} - \frac{\partial u_i}{\partial y}\frac{\partial u_j}{\partial x}. \tag{6}$$

In particular, we have

$$(\nabla u_i \times \nabla u_j)^2 = \|\nabla u_i\|^2 \|\nabla u_j\|^2 \sin(\theta_{ij})^2$$

where θ_{ij} is the angle between ∇u_i and ∇u_j.

Minimizing the energy (5) produces an image with:

1. Small gradients norms due to the term $\sum_{k=1}^{3} \|\nabla u_k\|^2$. It encourages the solution to be noise-free.
2. Aligned gradients due to the term $\sum_{1 \le i < j \le 3} (\nabla u_i \times \nabla u_j)^2$. This term reduces the possibility that the solution possesses color artifacts.

Modified Beltrami Framework. Rosman et al. [13] modified the Beltrami framework by considering the following energy to minimize:

$$\frac{1}{2}\|Au - u_0\|_{L^2}^2 + \lambda R(u), \qquad \lambda > 0 \tag{7}$$

where

$$R(u) = \int_{\Omega} \sqrt{\beta_1 + \beta_2 \sum_{k=1}^{3} \|\nabla u_k\|^2 + \beta_3 \sum_{1\leq i<j\leq 3} (\nabla u_i \times \nabla u_j)^2}\, d\Omega \tag{8}$$

for $\beta_1, \beta_2, \beta_3 > 0$.

Minimizing the energy (7) has several advantages over the Beltrami framework:

1. By adding the data term $\frac{1}{2}\|Au - u_0\|_{L^2}^2$, the model removes not only the noise in u_0 but also the degradation modeled by A. Moreover, the parameter λ controls the level of regularization.
2. The weights β_2, β_3 enable a control of the relative weight between gradients norms and the crossed products of the gradients.
3. Minimizing the Polyakov energy can produce oversmoothed images. The square root in (8) reduces this undesirable effect.

DIP-RiemannVTV. More recently, Batard et al. [3] replaced the Polyakov action associated to the metric (4) by the Riemannian Vectorial Total Variation (RiemannVTV), which corresponds to the Riemannian L^1 norm of the differential of u

$$\begin{aligned} \text{RiemannVTV}(u) &= \|du\|_{L^1(g^{-1})} = \int_{\Omega} \|du\|_{g^{-1}} dg = \int_{\Omega} \|du\|_{g^{-1}} \sqrt{\det g}\, d\Omega \\ &= \int_{\Omega} \sqrt{\sum_{k=1}^{3} \|\nabla u_k\|^2 + 2\beta \sum_{1\leq i<j\leq 3} (\nabla u_i \times \nabla u_j)^2}\, d\Omega. \end{aligned} \tag{9}$$

Then, they considered the **DIP-RiemannVTV** model by combining DIP with the regularizer RiemannVTV. Experiments showed that DIP-RiemannVTV outperforms DIP and DIP-VTV in color image denoising.

3 Dirac Vectorial Total Variations of a Color Image

3.1 The Euclidean Dirac Operator and Its Main Properties

Let $(e_1, \cdots, e_n)$ be an orthonormal basis of $\mathbb{R}^n$, and $\mathbb{R}_{n,0}$ be the Clifford algebra of $\mathbb{R}^n$ induced by $(e_1, \cdots, e_n)$. As a vector space, $\mathbb{R}_{n,0}$ is of dimension 2^n and a basis is given by

$$\{1, e_1, \cdots, e_n, e_1e_2, \cdots, e_1e_2\cdots e_n\},$$

with

$$e_ie_j + e_je_i = 2\delta_{ij} \qquad i, j = 1, \cdots, n$$

and 1 is the neutral element. In particular, we have $\mathbb{R}^n \subset \mathbb{R}_{n,0}$. We denote by $\mathbb{R}^0_{n,0}$ resp. $\mathbb{R}^1_{n,0}$ the subspace of $\mathbb{R}_{n,0}$ of elements of even resp. odd degree.

Let $(x_1, \cdots, x_n)$ be a coordinate system on $\Omega \subset \mathbb{R}^n$. We denote by $C^l(\Omega; \mathbb{R}_{n,0})$ the set of l-differentiable functions from Ω to $\mathbb{R}_{n,0}$.

The Euclidean Dirac operator D is the linear differential operator of order 1 defined by

$$D: \begin{array}{ccc} C^l(\Omega; \mathbb{R}_{n,0}) & \longrightarrow & C^{l-1}(\Omega; \mathbb{R}_{n,0}) \\ u & \longmapsto & \sum_{k=1}^n e_k \dfrac{\partial u}{\partial x_k} \end{array} \tag{10}$$

The main properties of the Euclidean Dirac operator are:

1. It satisfies that
$$D^2 := D \circ D = \Delta,$$
where Δ is the component-wise Laplace operator.
2. It is self-adjoint: We have
$$\langle D\eta, u \rangle = -\langle \eta, Du \rangle$$
provided that η has compact support.

In particular, for $n = 2$ and $u = u_1 e_1 + u_2 e_2$, we have

$$Du = \left(\frac{\partial u_1}{\partial x} + \frac{\partial u_2}{\partial y} \right) 1 + \left(\frac{\partial u_2}{\partial x} - \frac{\partial u_1}{\partial y} \right) e_1 e_2. \tag{11}$$

A straightforward computation gives

$$\|Du\| = \sqrt{\|\nabla u_1\|^2 + \|\nabla u_2\|^2 + 2\,\nabla u_1 \times \nabla u_2} \tag{12}$$

Finally, let us mention that, by the identification between $\mathbb{R}^2$ and $\mathbb{R}^0_{2,0}$, the Dirac operator can be defined as the operator

$$D: \begin{array}{ccc} C^l(\Omega; \mathbb{R}^2) & \longrightarrow & C^{l-1}(\Omega; \mathbb{R}^2) \\ u & \longmapsto & \left(\dfrac{\partial u_1}{\partial x} + \dfrac{\partial u_2}{\partial y}, \dfrac{\partial u_2}{\partial x} - \dfrac{\partial u_1}{\partial y} \right). \end{array} \tag{13}$$

In particular, the Euclidean norm of Du in (13) leads to expression (12).

3.2 Dirac Operators for Color Images

Motivation. We observe a strong connection between the norm of the Dirac operator (12) and the norm of the Riemannian gradient (9) in the sense that both encode the norms of the gradients of the image components and the cross products between the gradients. The main differences between the two expressions are:

1. The expression (12) only considers images of 2 components, while the expression (9) considers images of three components.

2. The expression (9) contains a parameter that controls the relative weight between the gradients norms and the cross products, which can be desirable. On the other hand, the smaller the number of parameters in a model the better.
3. The term encoding the cross product in (12) can be negative, which can produce undesirable effects when minimizing the energy.

In what follows we develop two extensions of the operator (13) in order to encode the properties 1. and 3.

Linear Vectorial Dirac Operator for Color Images. There is not an unique way to extend D to functions $u = (u_1, u_2, u_3) \in C^l(\Omega; \mathbb{R}^3)$. We propose the following extension.

Definition 1. *The linear vectorial Dirac operator* $\overline{D}$ *is the operator*

$$\begin{array}{rccl} & C^l(\Omega;\mathbb{R}^3) & \longrightarrow & C^{l-1}(\Omega;\mathbb{R}^6) \\ \overline{D}: & u & \longmapsto & (Du_{1,2}, Du_{2,3}, Du_{3,1}). \end{array} \tag{14}$$

where we denote by $u_{i,j}$ the function (u_i, u_j).

In particular, we have

$$\|\overline{D}u\| = \sqrt{\sum_{k=1}^{3} 2\|\nabla u_k\|^2 + 2(\nabla u_1 \times \nabla u_2 + \nabla u_2 \times \nabla u_3 + \nabla u_3 \times \nabla u_1)}. \tag{15}$$

Nonlinear Vectorial Dirac Operator for Color Images. We first define a nonlinear Dirac operator for $u = (u_i, u_j)$.

Definition 2. *The nonlinear Dirac operator* D^{NL} *is the operator*

$$\begin{array}{rccl} & C^l(\Omega;\mathbb{R}^2) & \longrightarrow & C^{l-1}(\Omega;\mathbb{R}^2) \\ D^{NL}: & u & \longmapsto & \left(\dfrac{\partial u_i}{\partial x} + \dfrac{\nabla u_i \times \nabla u_j}{|\nabla u_i \times \nabla u_j|}\dfrac{\partial u_j}{\partial y}, \dfrac{\nabla u_i \times \nabla u_j}{|\nabla u_i \times \nabla u_j|}\dfrac{\partial u_j}{\partial x} - \dfrac{\partial u_i}{\partial y}\right) \end{array} \tag{16}$$

Combining the nonlinear Dirac operator with the linear vectorial Dirac operator, we define the nonlinear vectorial Dirac operator $\overline{D^{NL}}$.

Definition 3. *The nonlinear vectorial Dirac operator* $\overline{D^{NL}}$ *is the operator*

$$\begin{array}{rccl} & C^l(\Omega;\mathbb{R}^3) & \longrightarrow & C^{l-1}(\Omega;\mathbb{R}^6) \\ \overline{D^{NL}}: & u & \longmapsto & (D^{NL}u_{1,2}, D^{NL}u_{2,3}, D^{NL}u_{3,1}) \end{array} \tag{17}$$

In particular, we have

$$\|\overline{D^{NL}u}\| = \sqrt{\sum_{k=1}^{3} 2\|\nabla u_k\|^2 + 2\sum_{1\le i<j\le 3} |\nabla u_i \times \nabla u_j|}. \tag{18}$$

Definition 4. *The Linear and Nonlinear Dirac Vectorial Total Variation of* $u = (u_1, u_2, u_3) \in C^1(\Omega; \mathbb{R}^3)$ *are respectively defined by*

$$DiracVTV(u) = \int_\Omega \sqrt{\sum_{k=1}^{3} 2\|\nabla u_k\|^2 + 2(\nabla u_1 \times \nabla u_2 + \nabla u_2 \times \nabla u_3 + \nabla u_3 \times \nabla u_1)}\; d\Omega \tag{19}$$

$$DiracVTV^{NL}(u) = \int_\Omega \sqrt{2\sum_{k=1}^{3} \|\nabla u_k\|^2 + 2 \sum_{1\leq i<j\leq 3} |\nabla u_i \times \nabla u_j|}\; d\Omega. \tag{20}$$

4 Experiments

We test and compare different DIP-Reg models (2) on denoising and deblurring: DIP, DIP-VTV, DIP-RiemannVTV, DIP-DiracVTV^{NL}. We decided to fix the parameter value β of RiemannVTV (9) in order to make the corresponding DIP-RiemannVTV model depend only on the trade-off parameter λ, as the DIP-VTV and DIP-DiracVTV^{NL} models do. In the experiments conducted in this Section, the value of β is set to 1.

We test the models on the Kodak dataset, which contains 24 natural images (http://r0k.us/graphics/kodak/). For denoising, we consider the images at their original sizes (768×512 or 512×768) corrupted with additive white Gaussian noise of variance 25. For deblurring, we reduce the image size (384×256 or 256×384) and corrupt the images first with uniform blur of size 9×9 and then with additive white Gaussian noise of variance $\sqrt{2}$. Note that the aim of reducing the image size is to limit the number of iterations required for the DIP-Reg models to reach their maximum Peak Signal-to-Noise Ratio (PSNR). Indeed, this optimal number of iterations greatly depends on the image itself but also on the degradation. In particular, deblurring requires more iterations than denoising.

4.1 Numerical Scheme

We use the same network T_θ in all experiments conducted in this Section. It is an encoder-decoder with skip connections between the down and up layers. It corresponds to the default network in [16], to which we refer for details on the architecture. In particular, for an input image u_0 of size $M \times N \times 3$ (where 3 represents the number of color channels), the input z of the network is a random image of size $M \times N \times 32$, i.e. it contains 32 channels.

Following the approach in [16], and denoting by $E(\theta; z)$ the energy in (2), we consider the following numerical scheme to approximate the solutions of the DIP-Reg models

$$\begin{cases} n_{k+1} \sim \mathcal{N}(0, \sigma) \\ z_{k+1} = z_0 + n_{k+1} \\ \theta_{k+1} = \theta_k - lr\nabla E(\theta_k; z_{k+1}) \\ u_{k+1} = \gamma\, u_k + (1-\gamma)\, T_{\theta_{k+1}}(z_{k+1}), \end{cases} \tag{21}$$

where z_0 is a fixed random image, lr denotes the learning rate, $\nabla E(\theta_k; z_{k+1})$ stands for the gradient of E with respect to θ_k, and $0 < \gamma < 1$. The iterative scheme is stopped after a certain number of iterations $\underline{k}$ and the output image is $\underline{u} = u_{\underline{k}}$.
We can observe from (21) that the input z_k of the network is different at each iteration by perturbing the initial random image z_0 with additive white Gaussian noise of variance σ. This technique is called noise-based regularization, and experiments have shown that the restoration benefits from this type of regularization.

The last line in (21) reveals another boosting technique employed in the numerical scheme, which consists of using an exponential sliding window for some weight γ.

4.2 Application to Denoising

On the Choice of the Color Space. A good strategy to remove noise in a color image is to work in an opponent space OPP (instead of the RGB color space) and to denoise the achromatic component of the image in a smaller extent than its chromatic components. Indeed, since standard denoising methods assimilate noise to details and the latter are mainly in the achromatic component of the image, we conclude that details can be better preserved if the noise of the achromatic component is removed is a small extent. Moreover, from a perceptual viewpoint, it can even be desirable that a small amount of achromatic noise is present in an image as it can be assimilated to the notion of grain in photography, which gives an aesthetic and realistic aspect to images. On the other hand, chromatic noise is undesirable because it is not present in natural images and is perceptually unpleasant.

In [3], it has been proposed to formulate these two ideas by means of the following base change

$$\underbrace{\begin{pmatrix} 5/3\sqrt{3} & 1/\sqrt{2} & 1/\sqrt{6} \\ 5/3\sqrt{3} & -1/\sqrt{2} & 1/\sqrt{6} \\ 5/3\sqrt{3} & 0 & -2/\sqrt{6} \end{pmatrix}}_{\text{basis change}} = \underbrace{\begin{pmatrix} 5/3 & 0 & 0 \\ 5/3 & 0 & 0 \\ 5/3 & 0 & 0 \end{pmatrix}}_{\text{weight}} \underbrace{\begin{pmatrix} 1/\sqrt{3} & 1/\sqrt{2} & 1/\sqrt{6} \\ 1/\sqrt{3} & -1/\sqrt{2} & 1/\sqrt{6} \\ 1/\sqrt{3} & 0 & -2/\sqrt{6} \end{pmatrix}}_{\text{from RGB to OPP}} \tag{22}$$

We follow this strategy in the experiments conducted in this Section, i.e. we express the DIP-Reg models in the basis (22).

Results. We tested the different DIP-Reg models on the entire dataset for different values of λ. For each model and λ value, the numerical scheme (21) was stopped after 8000 iterations. Then, for each image of the dataset, we computed the highest PSNR value reached and the iteration at which it was reached. Table 1 reports, for each model, the value of λ providing the best average highest PSNR over the dataset, as well as this PSNR value and the average number

Table 1. Mean results of different DIP-Reg models on denoising over the Kodak dataset. For each model, we report the maximum PSNR reached by the numerical scheme (21) which was stopped after 8K iterations, the number of iterations at which the maximum PSNR is reached, and the λ value providing the maximum PSNR.

Results	Model			
	DIP	DIP-VTV	DIP-RiemannVTV	DIP-DiracVTV^{NL}
Optimal λ value	–	0.01	0.02	0.03
Max PSNR	30.76	30.85	30.86	30.96
Number of iterations	4818	5125	5869	6834

Table 2. Mean results of different DIP-Reg models on denoising over the Kodak dataset tested with the corresponding optimal λ value. For each model, we report the mean PSNR over the dataset obtained at the corresponding stopping criteria.

Results	Model			
	DIP	DIP-VTV	DIP-RiemannVTV	DIP-DiracVTV^{NL}
Stopping criterion (Number of iterations)	4800	5000	6000	6750
PSNR	30.56	30.66	30.69	30.83

of iterations at which it is reached. We can deduce the importance of the regularization term from Table 1, as we observe that the models DIP-VTV, DIP-RiemannVTV and DIP-DiracVTV^{NL} outperform DIP. The model providing the best results is DIP-DiracVTV^{NL}, while DIP-VTV and DIP-RiemannVTV give similar results. We observe a correlation between the regularization parameter and the number of iterations: the higher λ, the higher the number of iterations. Based on the "optimal" number of iterations reported in Table 1, we determine an automatic stopping criterion for each model. Table 2 shows the automatic stopping criterion and the corresponding average PSNR for each model. We observe that the chosen automatic stopping criteria do not change the order of the models, as DIP-DiracVTV^{NL} still gives the best result, DIP the worse, while DIP-VTV and DIP-RiemannVTV are similar.

Figure 1 compares the results of the DIP-Reg models tested on the image "kodim17" of the dataset, where the parameters (λ, stopping criterion) are those given in Table 2. For each method, we report the PSNR of the denoised image with respect to the clean one and we show the directions of the gradients of the RGB components at 3 different points in the image domain. We observe that, as expected according to [9], the gradients are aligned in the original image and this property is lost when noise is added to the image. The results show that DIP-DiracVTV^{NL} is the model that best restores the alignment of the gradients and gives the highest PSNR value. The improvement of DIP-DiracVTV^{NL} over DIP-RiemannVTV can be explained by the use of the absolute values of the cross products $|\nabla u_i \times \nabla u_j|$ instead of their squares $(\nabla u_i \times \nabla u_j)^2$. In fact, it is known that minimizing the absolute value promotes sparse solutions as opposed to minimizing the square, which is desirable in our case.

Fig. 1. Results of DIP-Reg models on "kodim17". For each image, the directions of the gradients of the RGB components are indicated at different points, and the PSNR with respect to the original image is indicated below.

4.3 Application to Deblurring

On the Choice of the Color Space. Unlike denoising, it is not so clear which color space performs the best for deblurring. For the sake of shortness, we will only test the models in RGB in this paper, and leave experiments in Opponent spaces for future work.

Results. The experimental setting is similar to the one in the denoising case. Indeed, we tested the different models on the whole dataset for different values of λ. For each model and λ value, the numerical scheme (21) was stopped after 30000 iterations. Then, for each image of the dataset, we computed the highest PSNR value reached and the iteration at which it was reached. Table 3 reports, for each model, the value of λ providing the best average highest PSNR

Table 3. Mean results of different DIP-Reg models for deblurring on the Kodak dataset. For each model, we report the maximum PSNR reached by the numerical scheme (21) which was stopped after 30K iterations, and the number of iterations at which the maximum PSNR is reached.

	Model			
	DIP	DIP-VTV	DIP-RiemannVTV	DIP-DiracVTV^{NL}
Optimal λ value	–	10^{-4}	10^{-4}	10^{-4}
Max PSNR	28.66	29.14	29.17	**29.30**
Number of iterations	10795	17766	19785	23356

Table 4. Mean results of different DIP-Reg models for deblurring on the Kodak dataset. For each model, we report the mean PSNR over the dataset obtained after the corresponding number of iterations.

Results	Model			
	DIP	DIP-VTV	DIP-RiemannVTV	DIP-DiracVTV^{NL}
Stopping criterion (Number of iterations)	10000	18000	20000	23000
PSNR	28.6	29.08	29.10	**29.22**

over the dataset as well as this PSNR value and the average number of iterations at which it is reached. As in the case of denoising, the models DIP-VTV, DIP-RiemannVTV and DIP-DiracVTV^{NL} outperform DIP. Moreover, the model providing the best result is still DIP-DiracVTV^{NL}, while DIP-VTV and DIP-RiemannVTV give similar results. Based on the "optimal" number of iterations reported in Table 3, we determine an automatic stopping criterion for each model. Table 4 shows the automatic stopping criterion and the corresponding average PSNR for each model. We observe that the chosen automatic stopping criteria do not change the order of the models, as DIP-DiracVTV^{NL} still gives the best result, DIP the worse, while DIP-VTV and DIP-RiemannVTV are similar.

Figure 2 compares the results of the DIP-Reg models tested on the image "kodim19" of the dataset, where the parameters (λ, stopping criterion) are those given in Table 4. For each method, we report the PSNR of the deblurred image with respect to the clean one and we show the directions of the gradients of the RGB components at 4 different points in the image domain. We can see that reducing the image size dealign the gradients of the original image. The results also show that DIP-DiracVTV^{NL} is again the model that provides the best recovery of the alignment of the gradients. Because the image to be recovered (the downsampled image) has its gradients misaligned, one could think that a model that promotes aligned gradients would be inefficient. However, the PSNR values indicate that DIP-DiracVTV^{NL} gives the best result despite its gradient alignment property.

Fig. 2. Results of DIP-Reg models on "kodim19". For each image, the directions of the gradients of the RGB components are indicated at different points, and the PSNR with respect to the original image is indicated below.

5 Conclusion

In this paper, we introduced a new Dirac operator from which we derived a regularizer for color image restoration that generalizes the vectorial total variation. The main property of this regularizer is to promote, through its minimization, images in which the gradients of their components are aligned, which turns out to be a property of natural images. This alignment property is also present in a regularizer derived from a Riemannian gradient, albeit with a different mathematical formulation.

Experiments on denoising and deblurring show that the regularizer induced by the proposed Dirac operator produces superior results (higher PSNR) than the ones induced by the Euclidean and Riemannian gradient operators.

Further work will be devoted to apply the proposed framework to other restoration tasks such as super-resolution and inpainting, and to compare the proposed regularizer to other existing extensions of the vectorial total variation.

References

1. Batard, T.: A class of priors for color image restoration parametrized by lie groups acting on pixel values. SIAM J. Imag. Sci. **16**(3), 1235–1280 (2023)
2. Batard, T., Berthier, M.: Clifford-fourier transform and spinor representation of images. In: Hitzer, E., Sangwine, S.J. (eds.) Quaternion and Clifford Fourier Transforms and Wavelets, pp. 177–195. Springer, Basel (2013)
3. Batard, T., Haro, G., Ballester, C.: DIP-VBTV: a color image restoration model combining a deep image prior and a vector bundle total variation. SIAM J. Imag. Sci. **14**(4), 1816–1847 (2021)
4. Blomgren, P., Chan, T.F.: Color tv: total variation methods for restoration of vector-valued images. IEEE Trans. Image Process. **7**(3), 304–309 (1998)
5. Bredies, K., Kunisch, K., Pock, T.: Total generalized variation. SIAM J. Imag. Sci. **3**(3), 492–526 (2010)
6. Bresson, X., Chan, T.F.: Fast dual minimization of the vectorial total variation norm and applications to color image processing. Inverse Probl. Imaging **2**(4), 455–484 (2008)
7. Duan, Y., Zhong, Q., Tai, X.-C., Glowinski, R.: A fast operator-splitting method for beltrami color image denoising. J. Sci. Comput. **92**(89), 1–28 (2022)
8. Duran, J., Moeller, M., Sbert, C., Cremers, D.: Collaborative total variation: A general framework for vectorial tv models. SIAM J. Imag. Sci. **9**(1), 116–151 (2016)
9. Kimmel, R., Malladi, R., Sochen, N.: Images as embedding maps and minimal surfaces: Movies, color, texture, and volumetric medical images. Int. J. Comput. Vision **39**(2), 111–129 (2000)
10. Kostrikov, I., Jiang, Z., Panozzo, D., Zorin, D., Bruna, J.: Surface networks. In: Proceedings of the IEEE Conference on Computer Vision and Pattern Recognition (CVPR), pp. 2540–2548 (2018)
11. Liu, H.-T.D., Jacobson, A., Crane, K.: A DIRAC operator for extrinsic shape analysis. In: Baerentzen, J.A., Hildebrandt, K. (eds.) Eurographics Symposium on Geometry Processing 2017, vol. 36, pp. 139–149 (2017)
12. Liu, J., Xu, X., Kamilov, U.S.: Image restoration using total variation regularized deep image prior. In: 2019 IEEE International Conference on Acoustics, Speech and Signal Processing (ICASSP), pp. 7715–7719 (2019)
13. Rosman, G., Tai, X.-C., Dascal, L., Kimmel, R.: Polyakov action minimization for efficient color image processing. In: Kutulakos, K.N. (ed.) ECCV 2010 Workshops. Part II, LNCS 6554, pp. 50–61. Springer, Heidelberg (2012)
14. Rudin, L.I., Osher, S., Fatemi, E.: Nonlinear total variation based noise removal algorithms. Physica D **60**(1–4), 259–268 (1992)
15. Sochen, N., Kimmel, R., Malladi, R.: A general framework for low-level vision. IEEE Trans. Image Process. **7**(3), 310–318 (1998)
16. Ulyanov, D., Vedaldi, A., Lempitsky, V.: Deep image prior. Int. J. Comput. Vision **128**(7), 1867–1888 (2020)
17. Vese, L., Le Guyader, C.: Variational Methods in Image Processing. Chapman and Hall/CRC (2015)

An Efficient Facial Verification System for Surveillance that Automatically Selects a Lightweight CNN Method and Utilizes Super-Resolution Images

Filiberto Perez-Montes(✉), Jesus Olivares-Mercado, and Gabriel Sanchez-Perez

Instituto Politecnico Nacional, ESIME Culhuacan, Mexico City 04440, Mexico
fperezm1704@alumno.ipn.mx, {jolivares,gasanchezp}@ipn.mx

Abstract. In the last decade, facial recognition and verification methods have been extensively used for surveillance and security purposes. However, most of the time, recognizing and/or verifying faces is challenging due to the low facial resolution of the obtained or captured images. Likewise, low-resolution facial images contain different facial features, such as variations in pose, lighting, resolution, and camera-to-subject distance. Moreover, the methods commonly used for facial verification in images are based on deep architectures, which rely on complex deep learning models with promising verification results but come with high computational costs. On the other hand, real-world requirements for facial verification demand lightweight methods that are inspired by their counterparts but are also compact and efficient enough to be used in unrestricted scenarios, such as video surveillance or security cameras. This paper proposes a lightweight facial verification system (LFVS) that automatically selects a lightweight facial verification method based on images characteristics, such as facial rotation variations and low resolutions. Additionally, a dynamic scaling approach is proposed to upscale images to the required size. The system uses this scaling to enhance the image resolution and succeeded in improving facial verification performance. Experimental results demonstrated that the lightweight facial verification system achieved better results when using super-resolution images in low-resolution reference points, with minimal memory usage and computational complexity.

Keywords: lightweight face verification · surveillance · super-resolution · facial rotation · low-resolution

1 Introduction

In biometrics, facial recognition and verification are among the most widely used methods [1,2]. Facial recognition is responsible for identifying the identity of a face in an image within a dataset, while verification examines facial features in an image to determine if the identity of that person matches their claim. In

H. Calvo et al. (Eds.): MICAI 2023, LNAI 14391, pp. 182–197, 2024.
https://doi.org/10.1007/978-3-031-47765-2_14

recent years, both facial recognition and verification have been present in surveillance or security applications, where it is often challenging to recognize and/or verify faces due to various issues such as pose variations, lighting changes, resolution differences, and camera-to-subject distance [3]. These issues are typically addressed through the use of deep Convolutional Neural Networks (CNNs) [4], which require a large number of parameters or memory, making their implementation challenging in real-world applications and resource-constrained devices [5,6]. Consequently, lightweight CNN methods have emerged to fulfill the mentioned requirements for a lightweight facial verification system [7], and some of the existing methods include MobileFaceNet [8], EfficientNet-B0 [9], and GhostNet [10]. However, these lightweight methods can be enhanced by incorporating a super-resolution technique (based on CNN or Vision Transformers) to improve facial verification performance in low-resolution images. Some super-resolution methods that could be employed in the system are FSRCNN [11], ESPCN [12], EDSR [13], and RestoreForme [14]. Both facial verification and super-resolution methods are used in existing facial verification systems based on resolution or facial rotation variations, but not both.

This paper proposes a Lightweight Facial Verification System (LFVS), which utilizes images features such as resolution and facial rotation variations to perform automatic selection of one of the lightweight facial verification methods (MobileFaceNet [8], EfficientNet-B0 [9], and GhostNet [10]). Additionally, to enhance facial verification performance, a super-resolution method is employed to improve image details for better facial verification. Therefore, several methods (FSRCNN [11], ESPCN [12], EDSR [13], and RestoreForme [14]) capable of dynamically scaling resolution and facilitating implementation on resource-constrained devices are selected. A dynamic scaling approach is proposed with the chosen methods to determine the best super-resolution method for low-resolution images. The LFVS will be evaluated using the QMUL-SurvFace [15] dataset and a custom dataset [16], comprising 3,000 images with different facial rotations, derived from the CPLFW [17] and CFPW [18] datasets, where low-resolution images are obtained by modifying their dimensions. Additionally, a PC and two embedded systems (Jetson Nano and TX2) will be used to assess verification performance, inference times for each method, and execution times. Based on the experimental results, the system demonstrated superior facial verification performance with the QMUL-SurvFace dataset and the custom dataset when combined with the super-resolution method compared to the baseline lightweight facial verification methods. The main contributions of this work are as follows:

- A dynamic scaling that helps obtain different scales from the base models (Scale $\times 2$, $\times 3$, and $\times 4$) of super-resolution to scale the images to the required dimensions.
- A lightweight facial verification system based on images features, such as resolution and facial rotation variations, that can select the best lightweight CNN methods.

- An automatic selection that chooses one of the lightweight facial verification methods (MobileFaceNet [8], EfficientNet-B0 [9], and GhostNet [10]) based on images features.
- To use the best super-resolution method to enhance low-resolution images and achieve improved facial verification performance in the system.

2 Related Work

In early 2023, the article [16] was presented, focusing on the analysis of resolution and facial rotation variations, addressing challenges in surveillance and security applications. In this work, three state-of-the-art lightweight real-time facial verification CNN methods were compared. These (MobileFaceNet [8], EfficientNet-B0 [9], and GhostNet [10]) methods are capable of real-time implementation and can run on resource-constrained devices. To evaluate facial verification performance, the Cross-Pose LFW (CPLFW) [17] and QMUL-SurvFace [15] datasets were used, containing images with varying facial rotations and low resolution. Additionally, the authors examined the effects of facial rotations and low-resolution issues by proposing a custom dataset comprising 3,000 facial images, combining samples from the CPLFW dataset [17] and Celebrities in Frontal-Profile in the Wild (CFPW) [18].

There is a work [19] that utilizes lightweight CNN methods to assess the verification performance with low-resolution datasets. The methods they employ and compare in the analysis are MobileFaceNet [8] and ShuffleFaceNet [20]. Additionally, they analyze the effect of synthetic data on the images used during the training of these methods, as well as the combination of the methods. They found that combining methods with different degradations enhances the performance on surveillance images.

On the other hand, there are works in the literature that integrate different methods to create a facial recognition system. Here are some works with the same approach. In [21], the authors designed a real-time facial recognition system using a conventional CNN and evaluated it with the AT&T dataset, proposing a systematic approach to fine-tune parameters to improve system performance. In this work [22], the focus is on facial mask detection, where they used the facial detection method called Single Shot Multibox Detector and for classification, they utilized MobileNetV2. The evaluation was performed using a combination of two datasets (Mikolaj Witkowski's Kaggle's Medical Mask Dataset and Prajna Bhandary's dataset, along with an artificial dataset created by Prajna Bhandary). Lastly, there is a real-time system [7] that employed the Yolo V5 object detector to detect the face and evaluated it with the Winder-Face dataset. For facial verification, they utilized five CNN methods, ranging from deep to lightweight architectures, including FaceNet, VGG-Face, Light CNN-29, ShuffleFaceNet, and MobileFaceNet, and evaluated their performance with the LFW dataset. However, these systems do not address the challenges present in surveillance and security applications.

3 Super-Resolution Methods

Fast SRCNN (FSRCNN) [11] (FSRCNN-large 12.4M & FSRCNN-small 8.8M parameters) is based on Super-Resolution with CNN (SRCNN), where the authors propose using an hourglass structure with compact CNNs. The original SRCNN structure was redesigned in three stages. Firstly, a deconvolution layer is introduced at the end of the network to obtain high-resolution images directly from the original low-resolution images. Secondly, the mapping layer is modified by reducing the dimension of the input image before mapping and then expanding it. Thirdly, smaller filter sizes but more mapping layers are used. The model they proposed achieves faster acceleration with better restoration quality.

Efficient sub-pixel CNN (ESPCN) [12] ($\approx$8M parameters) proposes a CNN architecture where feature maps extract features from low resolutions. They introduce a convolutional sub-pixel layer to learn from a series of staggered filters that scale the final low-resolution feature maps into the high-resolution output. The proposed model manages to be used in both images and video, in an order of magnitude faster.

Enhanced deep super-resolution network (EDSR) [13] (43M parameters) uses DCNN, but its improvement lies in optimizing by eliminating unnecessary blocks in the conventional ResNet (removing the batch normalization). This is because the batch normalization layer limits the range flexibility of the networks when normalizing the functions; therefore, it is better to eliminate it. The model showed that this modification increases performance.

RestoreFormer [14] (72.3M parameters) is based on Vision Transformers (VTs). This method explores fully spatial attentions to model contextual information. One of the first enhancements lies in the incorporation of a multi-headed cross-attention layer to learn fully spatial interactions between corrupted queries and high-resolution key-value pairs. Second, key-value pairs are sampled from a high-quality reconstruction-oriented dictionary, rich in high-resolution facial features specifically designed for facial reconstruction. Third, they produce images with improved resolution.

These four selected methods are open-source based on deep learning (CNNs and VTs) and are chosen as follows: the first three (FSRCNN, ESPCN, and EDSR) are selected because they can be used for quick and efficient inferences. These three algorithms contain pre-trained models with a magnification ratio of 2, 3, and 4 times the image size and are suitable for general use (applications in medical imaging, surveillance, security, etc.). The fourth method (RestoreFormer) is chosen because it produces images with better resolution and is specifically designed for facial restoration. It can be implemented in the real world and has a pre-trained model that can scale images at different sizes. Moreover, it is a method presented in 2022. The focus is on architectures that can dynamically scale images as close as possible to the required or needed dimensions while being implementable in systems with limited resources.

4 Light Facial Verification Methods

This work employs three lightweight CNN-based facial recognition and verification methods as references. The first one is MobileFaceNet [8] (1.2M parameters & 228M MACs). Its primary contribution is replacing the Global Average Pooling (GAPool) layer with the global depth convolutional (GDConv) layer to obtain a more discriminative facial representation. This method is based on the lightweight MobileNetV2 architecture, which uses bottleneck residual blocks with a lower expansion factor than MobileNetV2 and employs the non-linear activation function PReLU to enhance verification performance. The second method is EfficientNet [9] (33M parameters & 78M MACs), which utilizes neural architecture search (NAS) in combination with a compound scaling method to optimize both training speed and efficiency. The goal is to uniformly scale the width, depth, and resolution of the grid using a single variable. EfficientNet-B0 is obtained by calculating the α, β, and γ coefficients through a small grid search when $\phi = 1$, and the more complex versions of EfficientNet are achieved by scaling the reference network. Lastly, GhostNet [10] (27M parameters & 194M MACs) is mainly composed of Ghost modules. Its key contribution is replacing a representative portion of convolutional filters with a set of economical linear transformations, generating Ghost feature maps.

These three methods were selected considering the number of parameters and multiply-accumulate operations (MACs) for lightweight facial verification systems. Specifically, the search was limited to architectures with approximately 30M parameters and 200M MACs, with the possibility of implementation in systems with limited resources.

5 Proposed Dynamic Scaling with Super-Resolution Methods

The dynamic image scaling with super-resolution methods was designed to scale images to the required dimensions using pre-trained models of FSRCNN (large and small), ESPCN, and EDSR, which have scaling factors of 2, 3, and 4 times their dimensions, respectively. The basic idea is to generate different scales using these three base factors, as shown in Fig. 1.

As observed in the Fig. 1, the base models $\times 2$, $\times 3$ and $\times 4$ scale) of each super-resolution method can generate other scaling factors ($\times 6$, $\times 8$, $\times 9$, $\times 12$, $\times 16$, $\times 18$ and $\times 24$), which come close to the required needs. The Fig. 2 depicts the block diagram of how an image is generated using dynamic scaling with the super-resolution method.

The following is a description of the block diagram in the Fig. 2. The input is an image of $m \times n \times c$ dimensions, from which its size will be obtained as $W \times H$ dimensions (width and height). To determine the scale, it is necessary to divide the dimension to be scaled by the image's height. The result is the scale factor (integer variable) to which the image should be scaled. Only scaling factors generated by the base models can be used. Therefore, the image is scaled

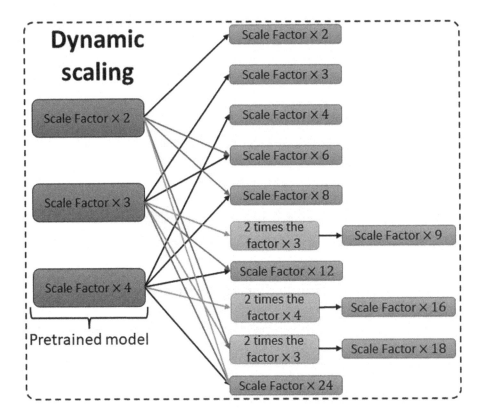

Fig. 1. Dynamic scaling composition.

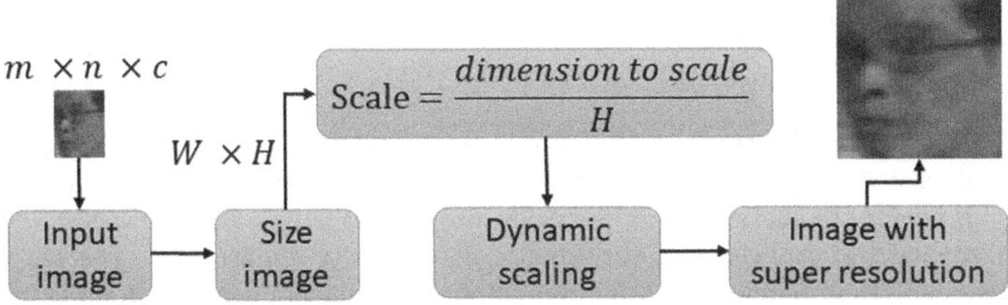

Fig. 2. Block diagram of the dynamic scaling implementation.

to the next consecutive factor, provided that the scaling factor is not already generated. Once the scaling factor is obtained, the super-resolution image is generated.

RestoreFormer is not part of the dynamic scaling process since its pre-trained model allows for dynamically scaling images to different scales. The only change in the Fig. 2 is replacing the dynamic scaling block with RestoreFormer to obtain the super-resolution image. The Table 1 shows the average inference times for each method without dynamic scaling (applying the base scale) and with dynamic scaling (applying the generated scales) for 100 images from QMUL-SurvFace on a PC using an Intel Core i7 seventh-generation processor.

Table 1. Verification performance with QMUL-SurvFace [12] dataset.

Model	EDSR	ESPCN	FSRCNN -large	FSRCNN -small	RestoreFormer
Time (no dynamic scaling)	886.68 ms	5.11 ms	6.98 ms	6.64 ms	106.49 ms
Time (dynamic scaling)	1.51 s	20.59 ms	25.19 ms	21.99 ms	1.4 s

6 Proposed Lightweight Facial Verification System

Table 2. The Best Lightweight CNN methods for each interval and resolution level, based in [16]. MobileFaceNet (MFN), EfficientNet-B0 (EN-B0) and GhostNet (GN).

Intervals	14^2 pixels	28^2 pixels	42^2 pixels	84^2 pixels	112^2 pixels
$[0°; 20°]$	EN-B0	GN	EN-B0	MFN	MFN
$(20°; 40°]$	EN-B0	EN-B0	EN-B0	MFN	MFN
$(40°; 60°]$	EN-B0	MFN	EN-B0	GN	EN-B0
$(60°; 80°]$	EN-B0	EN-B0	EN-B0	EN-B0	EN-B0
$(80°; 180°]$	GN	MFN	MFN	MFN	MFN

The lightweight facial verification system (LFVS) was designed based on facial resolution and rotation variations in images to perform automatic selection using one of the methods like MobileFaceNet, EfficientNet-B0, and GhostNet, addressing the challenges in surveillance and security applications. The automatic selection of one of the lightweight facial verification methods relies on the results presented in the article [16] and the image characteristics (resolution and facial rotation variations) to determine the best method. To achieve better facial verification results, the best super-resolution method that meets the required needs (low-resolution images and real-world application) will be utilized. The LFVS is described as follows:

In the first stage, the size of the image pair is acquired. In the second stage, facial rotation is estimated in the image pair using 6DRepNet (6DRN) [23], and the difference in facial rotation angle between the images in the pair is obtained. Once these two images characteristics are acquired, the automatic selection of the facial verification method is performed based on the image size (very small,

small, medium, medium-large, and large) falling within a specific size range and one of the five angle intervals (facial rotation). Then, the super-resolution method is applied to the images as mentioned in the previous section. Finally, facial verification is performed with the selected method. Table 2 displays the methods in terms of five angle intervals and five resolution levels, as described in the results of the article [16]. Figure 3 illustrates the configuration of the lightweight facial verification system.

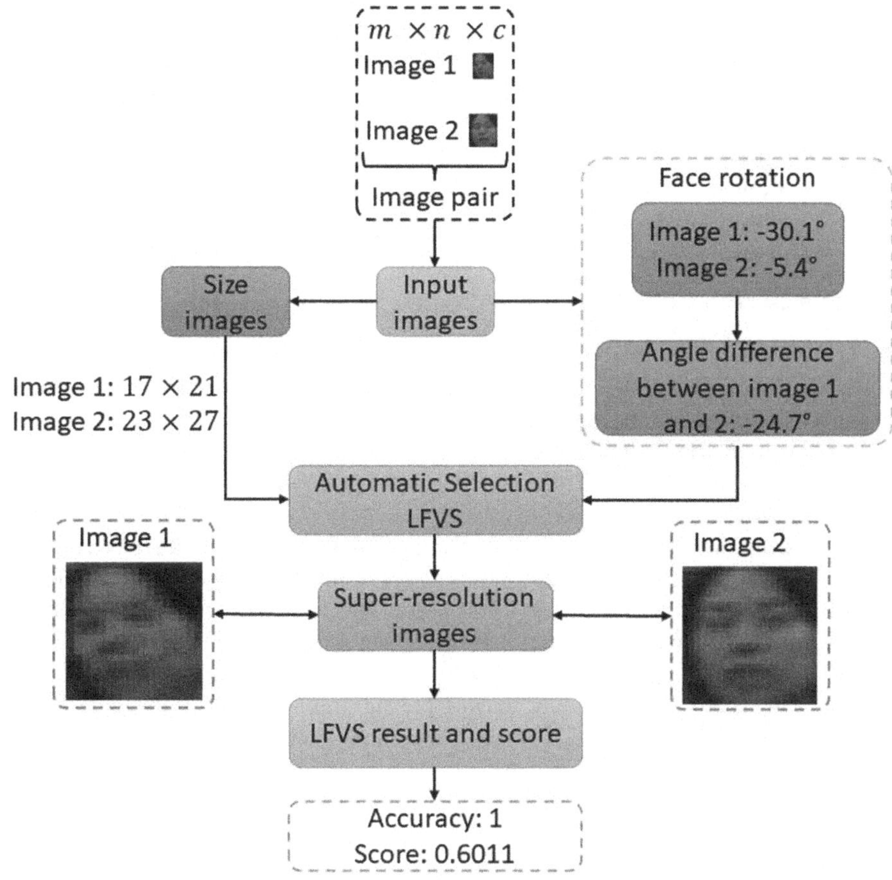

Fig. 3. Proposed LFVS.

7 Experiments

7.1 Implementation Details

All experiments were conducted on a PC and two Jetson embedded systems (Nano and TX2). The PC has an Intel Core i7 seventh-generation processor,

32 GB of RAM, and a single NVIDIA GTX 1060 GPU. The Jetson Nano features an ARM Cortex-A57 MPCore processor, 4GB of RAM, and a single NVIDIA MAXWELL GPU. The Jetson TX2 is equipped with a NVIDIA Denver and ARM Cortex-A57 MPCore processor, 8GB of RAM, and a single NVIDIA PASCAL GPU. Python 3.10, Torch 1.12.0, and Torchvision 0.13.0 with CUDA 11.3 were used for implementation. The pretrained $6DRepNet\_300W\_LP\_AFLW2000$ model was utilized to obtain the rotation angle, which was obtained from the 6DRepNet repository [23], and the same configurations were applied. To obtain the verification accuracy, the pretrained models MobileFaceNet [8], EfficientNet-B0 [9], and GhostNet [10] were used, which were obtained from the FaceX-Zoo repository [24]. These models were trained on the MS-Celeb1M-v1c dataset [25] with a Stochastic Gradient Descent (SGD) optimizer, a momentum of 0.9, and the MV-Softmax loss function [26]. The training batch size was set to 512 with a total of 18 epochs, an initial learning rate of 0.1, and a learning rate decay by a factor of 10 at epochs 10, 13, and 16. The same configurations as [24] were used for dataset utilization.

7.2 Datasets

The QMUL-SurvFace dataset [15] contains 463,507 facial images collected from surveillance cameras with 15,573 identities. It is divided into 220,890 training images with 5,319 identities and 242,617 test images with 10,254 identities. Among the identities, 10,638 have two or more images with resolutions ranging from 6×5 to 124×106 pixels. The average resolution is 24×20 pixels, making it suitable for facial verification.

The custom dataset [16] is a combination of images from the CPLFW [17] and CFPW [18] datasets, containing 1,526 and 1,474 images, respectively, resulting in a total of 3,000 images forming 1,500 pairs (750 positives and 750 negatives). Each pair consists of one image in a frontal view and another in one of the five defined intervals: $[0°; 20°]$, $(20°; 40°]$, $(40°; 60°]$, $(60°; 80°]$, and $(80°; 180°]$. For each interval, there are 200 pairs, except for the interval $(80°; 180°]$, which has 700 pairs. This dataset emulates surveillance and security applications and can be used to address challenges related to the distance between the subject and the camera by resizing the resolution of the custom dataset. It was specifically designed for facial verification.

7.3 Selection of Super-Resolution Method

To determine the best super-resolution method among the four selected methods (FSRCNN [11], ESPCN [12], EDSR [13], and RestoreForme [14]) and utilize the best one in the LVFS, the QMUL-SurvFace [15] dataset is used. This dataset contains images from unconstrained scenarios, similar to surveillance camera images with low resolution. Using this dataset allows us to enhance the resolution of the images and seek improved facial verification to determine the best super-resolution method.

Fig. 4. Examples of super-resolution with the four methods with QMUL-SurvFace [15] dataset.

For this initial experiment, the QMUL-SurvFace training set with super-resolution is used for Fine-tuning with each facial verification method. Subsequently, facial verification is performed with the Fine-tuned model on the QMUL-SurvFace test set with super-resolution. This process is repeated for each of the super-resolution methods. Figure 4 shows examples of images for the different super-resolution methods with QMUL-SurvFace. Table 3 displays the results for each facial verification method with super-resolution.

As shown in Table 3, the best super-resolution method is FSRCNN in both its large and small versions. It achieves the highest facial verification performance, and its inference time (Table 1) allows for real-world implementation. For the FSRCNN-large version, MobileFaceNet was the best method, and for the FSRCNN-small version, EfficientNet-B0 and GhostNet were the best methods.

Table 3. Verification performance with QMUL-SurvFace [15] dataset.

Model	EDSR [%]	ESPCN [%]	FSRCNN -large [%]	FSRCNN -small [%]	RestoreForme [%]
MobileFaceNet	84.06	84.23	**84.93**	84.47	82.96
EfficientNet-B0	84.05	84.57	84.51	**84.58**	83.31
GhostNet	84.65	84.36	84.47	**84.76**	83.76

7.4 Evaluation with the Custom Dataset

For this second experiment, the custom dataset [16] is evaluated using the three facial verification methods and the selected super-resolution method (FSRCNN) in its two versions (Large and Small). The process involves applying super-resolution to the custom dataset, followed by facial verification. This process is repeated for both versions of the super-resolution method. Table 4 and Table 5 present the results for each facial verification method for the two versions of the super-resolution method.

7.5 Evaluation of the LFVS with the Datasets

For this third experiment, the LFVS was used to evaluate the facial verification performance with QMUL-SurvFace [15] and the custom dataset [16], using the FSRCNN method in its two versions. Table 6 presents the results of the facial verification performance with QMUL-SurvFace and the comparison with the state-of-the-art lightweight CNN methods.

Table 4. Verification performance with custom dataset [16] and FSRCNN-large [11].

Model/Large	14^2 pixels [%]	28^2 pixels [%]	42^2 pixels [%]	84^2 pixels [%]
MobileFaceNet	63.86	72.46	**75.40**	**77.00**
EfficientNet-B0	65.40	72.86	74.93	75.73
GhostNet	**66.00**	**73.00**	74.73	76.46

Table 5. Verification performance with custom dataset [16] and FSRCNN-small [11].

Model/Small	14^2 pixels [%]	28^2 pixels [%]	42^2 pixels [%]	84^2 pixels [%]
MobileFaceNet	63.53	**73.06**	75.06	**76.93**
EfficientNet-B0	66.53	72.00	74.93	75.60
GhostNet	**66.73**	72.86	**75.26**	76.20

As observed in Table 6, the LFVS achieved an improvement in facial verification performance. This is attributed to the selected super-resolution method in its two versions, which enhances the images, providing better details. These improvements assist the method chosen by LFVS's automatic selection in conducting a more accurate facial verification on low-resolution images typically encountered in surveillance or security applications. Consequently, LFVS achieves better facial verification performance compared to the state-of-the-art methods.Table 7 presents the results of the facial verification performance with the custom dataset and the comparison with lightweight CNN methods.

As shown in Table 7, LFVS utilizes the selected FSRCNN method in its two versions and achieves an improvement in facial verification performance compared to the article [16]. Once again, a similar trend to that observed with the QMUL-SurvFace dataset is observed. Table 8 also displays the inference time of LFVS for 100 pairs of images. The Fig. 5 presents the results of the LFVS implementation.

8 Discussion

The three facial verification methods and the selected super-resolution method used in the system improve the results. This improvement can be attributed to FSRCNN in its two versions, which utilizes an hourglass-like architecture with compact CNNs that learn directly from the original low-resolution images. It aims to map the images into lower dimensions and then expand them, preserving the information for high-resolution images through additional mapping layers. Consequently, using these super-resolution images in the three facial verification methods could lead to better results. For MobileFaceNet, the improvement might be due to its global depthwise convolutional modules that acquire enriched facial feature maps in specific facial areas. In EfficientNet-B0, it could be attributed to the inverted mobile bottlenecks that generate discriminative feature maps, generalizing facial features like mouth, nose, eyes, eyebrows, etc. In GhostNet, this might be caused by the Ghost modules using economical operations (linear transformations instead of standard convolutional operations), aiding in the acquisition of facial features and better representation of the face. Therefore, LFVS is built upon these methods to address issues in surveillance and security applications. Overfitting in lightweight facial verification models could be avoided by focusing on a careful selection of training data that reflects real-world scenarios and conditions. Additionally, simplifying the model architecture

Table 6. Verification performance with QMUL-SurvFace [15] dataset.

Model	Pretrain	Fine-Tuning	Acc. [%]
MobileFaceNet [19]	MS1M [27]	QMUL-SurvFace Train [15]	83.2
ShuffleFaceNet [19]	MS1M [27]	QMUL-SurvFace Train [15]	82.3
LFVS (FSRCNN-large)	MS1M-v1c [25]	QMUL-SurvFace Train [15]	**85.52**
LFVS (FSRCNN-small)	MS1M-v1c [25]	QMUL-SurvFace Train [15]	85.05

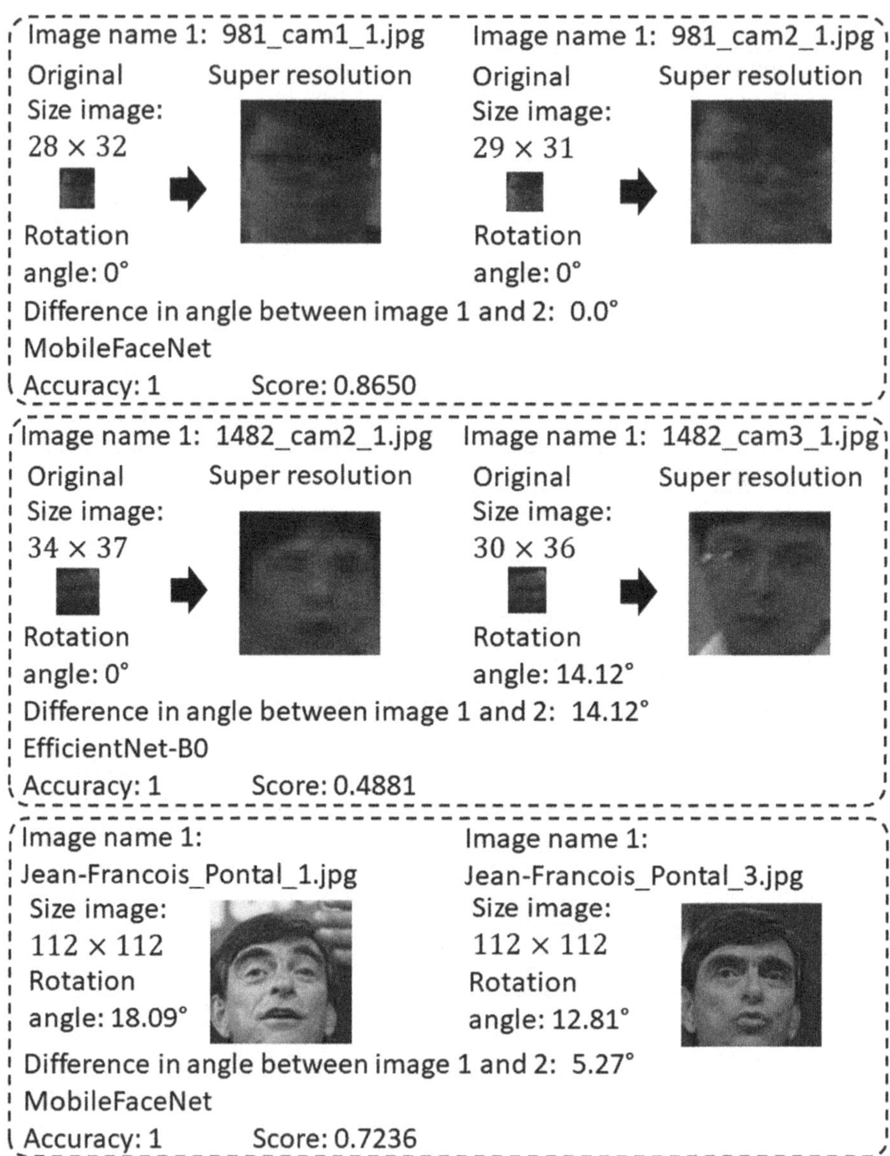

Fig. 5. Result LFVS with QMUL-SurvFace [15] and Custom dataset [16].

and constraining its complexity, along with the implementation of regularization techniques and ongoing evaluation on validation sets, could help ensure that the model fits efficiently without memorizing specific data, likely resulting in improved performance across a wide range of facial verification scenarios.

Table 7. Verification performance with custom dataset [16].

Model	14^2 pixels [%]	28^2 pixels [%]	42^2 pixels [%]	84^2 pixels [%]	112^2 pixels [%]
MobileFaceNet [16]	59.06	72.26	75.33	77.80	76.93
EfficientNet-B0 [16]	61.96	71.26	73.80	75.00	75.06
GhostNet [16]	61.40	71.86	74.73	75.46	75.86
SLVF (FSRCNN-large)	64.93	72.60	**76.33**	**77.60**	**77.00**
SLVF (FSRCNN-small)	**67.06**	**73.06**	75.66	77.46	**77.00**

Table 8. Inference time.

LFVS	PC with GPU 1060	Jetson TX2	Jetson Nano
Image load	0.55 ms	63.67 ms	76.10 ms
Image size	0.002 ms	0.01 ms	0.01 ms
6DRepNet	552.22 ms	2.16 s	4.27 s
Automatic selec	0.008 ms	0.0001 ms	0.0001 ms
FSRCNN	4.38 ms	44.79 ms	125.22 ms
FV Method	245.67 ms	1.11 s	2.32 s
Total time	803.98 ms	3.39 s	6.80 s

9 Conclusion

In this work, it was observed that the methods used in LFVS improved the results by increasing image resolution through super-resolution in different experiments, effectively dealing with resolution and facial rotation variations. LFVS improved the verification performance by approximately more than 2% with QMUL-SurvFace compared to the state-of-the-art; for the custom dataset, the verification performance improved by approximately up to 5% for small images and up to 1% for large images, mainly due to its focus on low resolutions and facial rotations, enabling better selection. The results obtained in LFVS demonstrate that the methods utilized can achieve better performance when super-resolution is applied, as the images contain more details. LFVS can be executed on both PCs and resource-limited devices.

Acknowledgements. The authors thank the Instituto Politecnico Nacional (IPN) as well as the Consejo Nacional de Humanidades Ciencia y Tecnologia de Mexico (CONAHCYT) for the support provided during the realization of this research.

References

1. Haji, S., Varol, A.: Real time face recognition system (RTFRS). In: 2016 4th International Symposium on Digital Forensic and Security (ISDFS), pp. 107–111, Little Rock, AR, USA. IEEE (2016)
2. Kortli, Y., Jridi, M., Al Falou, A., Atri, M.: Face recognition systems: a survey. Sensors **20**(2), 342 (2020)

3. de Freitas Pereira, T., Schmidli, D., Linghu, Y., Zhang, X., Marcel, S., Günther, M.: Eight Years of Face Recognition Research: Reproducibility, Achievements and Open Issues. arXiv, no. 2208.04040 (2022)
4. Guo, G., Zhang, N.: A survey on deep learning based face recognition. Comput. Vis. Image Underst. **189**, 102805 (2019)
5. Boutros, F., Siebke, P., Klemt, M., Damer, N., Kirchbuchner, F., Kuijper, A.: Pocketnet: extreme lightweight face recognition network using neural architecture search and multistep knowledge distillation. IEEE Access **10**, 46823–46833 (2022)
6. Boutros, F., Damer, N., Kuijper, A.: QuantFace: towards lightweight face recognition by synthetic data low-bit quantization. In: 2022 26th International Conference on Pattern Recognition (ICPR), pp. 855-862, Montreal, QC, Canada. IEEE (2022)
7. Ghimire, A., Werghi, N., Javed, S., Dias, J.: Real-Time Face Recognition System. arXiv, no. 2204.08978 (2022)
8. Chen, S., Liu, Y., Gao, X., Han, Z.: MobileFaceNets: efficient CNNs for accurate real-time face verification on mobile devices. In: Zhou, J., et al. (eds.) CCBR 2018. LNCS, vol. 10996, pp. 428–438. Springer, Cham (2018). https://doi.org/10.1007/978-3-319-97909-0_46
9. Tan, M., Le, Q.: Efficientnet: rethinking model scaling for convolutional neural networks. In: Proceedings of the 36th International Conference on Machine Learning: Proceedings of Machine Learning Research (PMLR), vol. 97, pp. 6105–6114 (2019)
10. Han, K., Wang, Y., Tian, Q., Guo, J., Xu, C., Xu, C.: Ghostnet: more features from cheap operations. In: Proceedings of the IEEE/CVF Conference on Computer Vision and Pattern Recognition (CVPR), pp. 1580–1589 (2020)
11. Dong, C., Loy, C.C., Tang, X.: Accelerating the super-resolution convolutional neural network. In: Leibe, B., Matas, J., Sebe, N., Welling, M. (eds.) ECCV 2016. LNCS, vol. 9906, pp. 391–407. Springer, Cham (2016). https://doi.org/10.1007/978-3-319-46475-6_25
12. Shi, W., et al.: Real-time single image and video super-resolution using an efficient sub-pixel convolutional neural network. In: Proceedings of the IEEE Conference on Computer Vision and Pattern Recognition (CVPR), pp. 1874–1883 (2016)
13. Lim, B., Son, S., Kim, H., Nah, S., Mu Lee, K.: Enhanced deep residual networks for single image super-resolution. In: Proceedings of the IEEE Conference on Computer Vision and Pattern Recognition Workshops (CVPR), pp. 136–144 (2017)
14. Wang, Z., Zhang, J., Chen, R., Wang, W., Luo, P.: Restoreformer: high-quality blind face restoration from undegraded key-value pairs. In: Proceedings of the IEEE/CVF Conference on Computer Vision and Pattern Recognition (CVPR), pp. 17512–17521 (2022)
15. Cheng, Z., Zhu, X., Gong, S.: Surveillance face recognition challenge. arXiv, no. 1804.09691 (2022)
16. Perez-Montes, F., Olivares-Mercado, J., Sanchez-Perez, G., Benitez-Garcia, G., Prudente-Tixteco, L., Lopez-Garcia, O.: Analysis of real-time face-verification methods for surveillance applications. J. Imaging **9**(2), 21 (2023)
17. Zheng, T., Deng, W.: Cross-pose lfw: a database for studying cross-pose face recognition in unconstrained environments. Beijing University of Posts and Telecommunications, vol. 5, no. 7, China (2018)
18. Sengupta, S., Chen, J.C., Castillo, C., Patel, V.M., Chellappa, R., Jacobs, D.W.: Frontal to profile face verification in the wild. In: 2016 IEEE Winter Conference on Applications of Computer Vision (WACV), pp. 1-9, Lake Placid, NY, USA. IEEE (2016)

19. Martínez-Díaz, Y., Méndez-Vázquez, H., Luevano, L.S., Chang, L., Gonzalez-Mendoza, M.: Lightweight low-resolution face recognition for surveillance applications. In: 2020 25th International Conference on Pattern Recognition (ICPR), Milan, Italy, pp. 5421–5428. IEEE (2021)
20. Martindez-Diaz, Y., et al.: Shufflefacenet: a lightweight face architecture for efficient and highly-accurate face recognition. In: Proceedings of the IEEE/CVF International Conference on Computer Vision (ICCV) Workshops (2019)
21. Pranav, K.B., Manikandan, J.: Design and evaluation of a real-time face recognition system using convolutional neural networks. Procedia Comput. Sci. **171**, 1651–1659 (2020)
22. Nagrath, P., Jain, R., Madan, A., Arora, R., Kataria, P., Hemanth, J.: SSDMNV2: a real time DNN-based face mask detection system using single shot multibox detector and MobileNetV2. Sustain. Urban Areas **66**, 102692 (2021)
23. Hempel, T., Abdelrahman, A. A., Al-Hamadi, A.: 6d rotation representation for unconstrained head pose estimation. In: 2022 IEEE International Conference on Image Processing (ICIP), pp. 2496–2500, Bordeaux, France. IEEE (2022)
24. Wang, J., Liu, Y., Hu, Y., Shi, H., Mei, T.: Facex-zoo: a pytorch toolbox for face recognition. In: Proceedings of the 29th ACM International Conference on Multimedia, New York, NY, USA, pp. 3779–3782 (2021)
25. DeepGlint: Trillion Pairs Testing Faceset. DeepGlint, Beijing, China (2019)
26. Wang, X., Zhang, S., Wang, S., Fu, T., Shi, H., Mei, T.: Mis-classified vector guided softmax loss for face recognition. In: Proceedings of the AAAI Conference on Artificial Intelligence, vol. 34, no. 07, pp. 12241–12248, USA (2020)
27. Guo, Y., Zhang, L., Hu, Y., He, X., Gao, J.: MS-Celeb-1M: a dataset and benchmark for large-scale face recognition. In: Leibe, B., Matas, J., Sebe, N., Welling, M. (eds.) ECCV 2016. LNCS, vol. 9907, pp. 87–102. Springer, Cham (2016). https://doi.org/10.1007/978-3-319-46487-9_6

Nonlinear L^2-DiracVTV Model for Color Image Restoration

Keny Chin and Thomas Batard(✉)

Centro de Investigación en Matemáticas, A.C., Guanajuato, Mexico
{keny.chin,thomas.batard}@cimat.mx

Abstract. Variational models for inverse problems are mainly based on the choice of the regularizer, whose goal is to give the solutions some desirable property. Vectorial Total Variation, one of the most popular regularizer for color image restoration, is induced by the Euclidean gradient operator. In this paper, we introduce a new regularizer for color image restoration, induced by a nonlinear extension of the Dirac operator to color images. Whereas the Vectorial Total Variation only promotes piece-wise constant solutions, the regularizer induced by the proposed Dirac operator also promotes solutions having the gradients of their color components aligned, which turns out to be a property of natural images. Then, we insert this regularizer into a variational model for image restoration, and we approximate its numerical solution by adapting the primal-dual algorithm of convex optimization. Experiments on denoising and deblurring show that the proposed Dirac operator provides a better regularizer than the Euclidean operator.

Keywords: Color image restoration · Variational model · Total Variation · Dirac operator · Convex optimization · Primal-dual algorithm

1 Introduction

Over the last 30 years, variational methods have demonstrated their efficiency to solve different tasks in image restoration, e.g. denoising, deblurring, super-resolution, inpainting, segmentation [15]. The key idea of the Rudin-Osher-Fatemi (ROF) model for grey-level image denoising is to take the Total Variation (TV) as a regularization term, which promotes piece-wise constant solutions [12]. Since then, this model has been improved and extended in several ways.

Improvements of the model include improvement of both the regularizer and the numerical scheme. For instance, the Total Generalized Variation [2], a regularizer promoting piece-wise linear solutions, reduces the stair-casing effect inherent to TV. The numerical solution in the original paper [12] is obtained through the gradient descent of a differentiable approximation of the energy to minimize. Since then, more efficient algorithms like dual methods, augmented Lagrangian, split Bregman and primal-dual methods [6,16] have been developed in order to obtain better approximations of the solution. We refer to [5] for a detailed analysis of the model.

H. Calvo et al. (Eds.): MICAI 2023, LNAI 14391, pp. 198–212, 2024.
https://doi.org/10.1007/978-3-031-47765-2_15

The ROF model has also been extended to other image restoration tasks and to color images (see [8] and references therein for an overview on color extensions of TV). The standard extensions of TV to color images $u = (u_1, u_2, u_3)$ are straightforward generalizations of TV to vector-valued functions, meaning that they do not take into account any specific properties of color images. For instance, the Vectorial Total Variation (VTV) [4] corresponds to the integral of the Frobenius norm of the Jacobian. To the best of our knowledge, the first model of color image restoration describing properties of natural images is the Polyakov energy [7,11,13] which encodes the property of natural images of having the gradients of their color components aligned [10]. More precisely, the regularizer contains terms of the form $(\nabla u_i \times \nabla u_j)^2, i,j = 1,2,3$, and minimizing these cross products promotes solutions with aligned gradients.

In a recent paper [9], an alternative formulation of this property has been proposed, replacing the square of the cross products by their absolute value $|\nabla u_i \times \nabla u_j|$, and from which the authors derived a new regularizer for color image restoration. This regularizer arises as the L^1 norm of a generalized Dirac operator $\overline{D^{NL}}$, which they call DiracVTV^{NL}. Then, they combined this regularizer to the Deep Image Prior (DIP) [14], which assumes that the clean image can be generated from a neural network, yielding the DIP-DiracVTV^{NL} for color image restoration. Experiments on denoising and deblurring showed that DIP-DiracVTV^{NL} outperforms DIP-VTV, while combining DIP to the Polyakov energy gives similar results to DIP-VTV.

The aim of this paper is to corroborate the results obtained in [9] by showing that Dirac operators can also provide better regularizers than the gradient operator in the context of color extension of the ROF model. In Sect. 3, we introduce a weighted extension $\overline{D^{NL}_{\alpha,\beta}}$ of the operator $\overline{D^{NL}}$ proposed in [9], from which we derive the DiracVTV$^{\text{NL}}_{\alpha,\beta}$ regularizer and the subsequent L^2-DiracVTV$^{\text{NL}}_{\alpha,\beta}$ model for color image restoration. The aim of the parameters α, β is to control the relative weights of the cross products in the regularizer. In Sect. 4, we compare the model L^2-DiracVTV$^{\text{NL}}_{\alpha,\beta}$ to the model L^2-VTV described in Sect. 2. Both models are implemented using a primal-dual algorithm. Results on denoising and deblurring show that, for well-chosen values of α and β, the improvement of L^2-DiracVTV$^{\text{NL}}_{\alpha,\beta}$ over L^2-VTV is similar to the one of DIP-DiracVTV^{NL} over DIP-VTV observed in [9].

2 The L²-VTV Model for Color Image Restoration

2.1 Variational Models for Image Restoration

Let us consider the following degradation model

$$u^0 = Au^* + n, \tag{1}$$

where u^0 is the degraded observed image, A the degradation operator applied to the clean image u^*, and n some noise.

The aim of inverse problems is to recover u^*, or at least obtain a good approximation of it, from u^0 and some information about A and n. Assuming that A is known, standard variational models to solve this inverse problem are of the form

$$\underset{u \in X}{\arg\min} \frac{1}{2}\|Au - u^0\|_{L^2}^2 + \gamma R(u) \tag{2}$$

where:

- the term $\frac{1}{2}\|Au - u^0\|_{L^2}^2$ is called fidelity term or data term. Its aim is to encourage the solution $\underline{u}$ of (2) to satisfy that $A\underline{u}$ is close to u^0.
- the term R is called regularizer or penalty term. Its aim is to impose some properties on $\underline{u}$, and X is a function space modeling these properties.
- the parameter $\gamma > 0$ serves as a trade-off between the fidelity and penalty terms.

2.2 The L²-VTV Model and Its Solutions

VTV is a straightforward extension of TV to color images, and is given for $u = (u_1, u_2, u_3) \colon \Omega \subset \mathbb{R}^2 \longrightarrow \mathbb{R}^3$ differentiable by

$$\mathrm{VTV}(u) = \|\nabla u\|_{L^1} = \int_\Omega \sqrt{\sum_{k=1}^{3} \left(\frac{\partial u_k}{\partial x}\right)^2 + \left(\frac{\partial u_k}{\partial y}\right)^2} \; d\Omega, \tag{3}$$

where ∇ stands for the Jacobian operator, and (x, y) is the cartesian coordinate system on Ω.

Because model (2) with $R(u)$ of the form (3) does not have solution, a generalization of VTV is considered, as described in what follows.

Let $u \in L^1(\Omega; \mathbb{R}^3)$. The Vectorial Total Variation of u is defined as

$$\mathrm{VTV}(u) = \sup\left(\int_\Omega \langle u, \nabla^* \eta\rangle \, d\Omega;\ \eta \in C_c^1(\Omega; \mathbb{R}^{3\times 2}), \|\eta(x,y)\|_F \leq 1 \ \forall (x,y) \in \Omega\right), \tag{4}$$

where $C_c^1(\Omega; \mathbb{R}^{3\times 2})$ denotes the space of 3×2 matrix fields on Ω whose elements are differentiable and of compact support, and $\| \ \|_F$ denotes the Frobenius norm. Moreover, the operator ∇^* is the adjoint of ∇ and $\langle \ , \ \rangle$ denotes the Euclidean scalar product in $\mathbb{R}^3$.

Note that both definitions of VTV are compatible as formula (4) leads to (3) if u is L^1 integrable and differentiable.

Then, the space $\mathrm{VBV}(\Omega; \mathbb{R}^3)$ is defined by

$$\mathrm{VBV}(\Omega; \mathbb{R}^3) := \{u \in L^1(\Omega; \mathbb{R}^3), \mathrm{VTV}(u) < \infty\}.$$

Finally, let us consider the L²-VTV model

$$\underset{u \in X}{\arg\min} \ \frac{1}{2}\|Au - u^0\|_{L^2}^2 + \gamma\, VTV(u), \tag{5}$$

where $X = L^2(\Omega;\mathbb{R}^3) \cap VBV(\Omega;\mathbb{R}^3)$.

Assuming that A is injective, model (5) possesses an unique solution. We refer to ([3], Theorem 6.115) for the proof of this result.

2.3 Primal-Dual Algorithm

We refer to [5] for more details about this Section. Assuming that $\Omega = M \times N$ is a discrete grid, the L^2-VTV model reads

$$\underset{u\in\mathbb{R}^{M\times N\times 3}}{\arg\min} \sum_{\Omega} \frac{1}{2}\|Au - u^0\|_2^2 + \gamma\|\nabla u\|_2 \tag{6}$$

where the discrete Jacobian operator is defined in the interior of Ω by

$$\nabla u(i,j) = \begin{pmatrix} u_1(i+1,j) - u_1(i,j) & u_1(i,j+1) - u_1(i,j) \\ u_2(i+1,j) - u_2(i,j) & u_2(i,j+1) - u_2(i,j) \\ u_3(i+1,j) - u_3(i,j) & u_3(i,j+1) - u_3(i,j) \end{pmatrix}. \tag{7}$$

Model (6) is of the form

$$\min_{u\in X} G(u) + F(Ku), \tag{8}$$

where $X = \mathbb{R}^{M\times N\times 3}$ is a finite-dimensional real vector space equipped with an inner product, the maps $G\colon u \longmapsto \frac{1}{2}\sum \|Au - u^0\|_2^2$ and $F = \sum \|\ \|$ are proper, convex, lower semi-continuous. Moreover, the operator $K = \nabla : X \longrightarrow Y = \mathbb{R}^{M\times N\times 3\times 2}$ is a continuous linear operator possessing an adjoint $K^* = \nabla^* : Y \longrightarrow X$ defined in the interior of Ω by

$$\begin{aligned} \nabla^*\eta(i,j) =& (\eta_{11}(i,j) - \eta_{11}(i-1,j) + \eta_{12}(i,j) - \eta_{12}(i-1,j), \\ & \eta_{21}(i,j) - \eta_{21}(i-1,j) + \eta_{22}(i,j) - \eta_{22}(i-1,j), \\ & \eta_{31}(i,j) - \eta_{31}(i-1,j) + \eta_{32}(i,j) - \eta_{32}(i-1,j)). \end{aligned} \tag{9}$$

Then, using Legendre-Fenchel's duality, model (8) can also be expressed as a primal-dual problem

$$\min_{u\in X}\max_{\eta\in Y} G(u) + \langle Ku, \eta\rangle - F^*(\eta), \tag{10}$$

where $\langle\ ,\ \rangle$ is the Euclidean scalar product in Y, and F^* is the convex conjugate of F. Finally, a solution $\underline{u}$ of the primal problem (6) corresponds to the first argument of a saddle-point $(\underline{u}, \underline{\eta})$ of the primal-dual problem (10). This can be numerically solved through the primal-dual algorithm described in Algorithm 1, where *prox* denotes the proximal operator.

The convex conjugate of $F = \|\ \|_Y$ is the indicator function δ_P of the convex set

$$P\colon = \left\{\zeta \in \mathbb{R}^{M\times N\times 3\times 2}, \|\zeta(i,j)\|_2 \le 1\ \forall i,j \in \Omega\right\}.$$

Algorithm 1. Primal-Dual Algorithm

1: **Initialization:** Choose $\tau, \sigma > 0$ with $\sigma\tau \leq 1/\|K\|_2^2$ and $(u^0, \eta^0) \in X \times Y, \theta \in (0, 1]$
2: **Iterations:** For $n = 0, 1, \ldots$ until a stopping criterion is reached

$$\begin{aligned} u^{n+1} &= prox_{\tau G}(u^n - \tau K^* \eta^n) \\ \overline{u}^n &= u^{n+1} + \theta(u^{n+1} - u^n) \\ \eta^{n+1} &= prox_{\sigma F^*}(\eta^n + \sigma K \overline{u}^n) \end{aligned}$$

It follows that the proximal operator of σF^* is given by

$$prox_{\sigma F^*}(\zeta) = \frac{\zeta}{\max(1, \|\zeta\|_2)}. \tag{11}$$

Under the assumption that $A = H*$, a convolution with a kernel H, the proximal operator of τG is given by

$$prox_{\tau G}(f) = \mathcal{F}^{-1}\left(\frac{\mathcal{F}(u^0)\mathcal{F}(H)^* + \frac{\gamma}{\tau}\mathcal{F}(f)}{\frac{\gamma}{\tau} + \mathcal{F}(H)^2}\right) \tag{12}$$

where $\mathcal{F}, \mathcal{F}^{-1}$ are the Fourier transform and its inverse, and $\mathcal{F}(H)^*$ is the complex conjugate of $\mathcal{F}(H)$.

Finally, Algorithm 1 in the context of model (6) with $A = H*$ reads

$$\begin{aligned} u^{n+1} &= \mathcal{F}^{-1}\left(\frac{\mathcal{F}(u^0)\mathcal{F}(H)^* + \frac{\gamma}{\tau}\mathcal{F}(u^n - \tau\nabla^*\eta^n)}{\frac{\gamma}{\tau} + \mathcal{F}(H)^2}\right), \\ \overline{u}^n &= u^{n+1} + \theta(u^{n+1} - u^n), \\ \eta^{n+1} &= \frac{\eta^n + \sigma\nabla\,\overline{u}^n}{\max\left(1, \|\eta^n + \sigma\nabla\,\overline{u}^n\|_2\right)}. \end{aligned} \tag{13}$$

3 Non Linear L²-DiracVTV Model for Color Image Restoration

3.1 Dirac Operators for Color Images

Let us denote by $C^k(\Omega; \mathbb{R}^n)$ the set of k-differentiable functions from Ω to $\mathbb{R}^n$. Let (x, y) be the cartesian coordinate system on Ω. Starting from the following Dirac operator defined, for $u = (u_1, u_2)$, by

$$\begin{aligned} & C^k(\Omega; \mathbb{R}^2) \longrightarrow \quad C^{k-1}(\Omega; \mathbb{R}^2) \\ D\colon \quad & u \quad \longmapsto \left(\frac{\partial u_1}{\partial x} + \frac{\partial u_2}{\partial y}, \frac{\partial u_2}{\partial x} - \frac{\partial u_1}{\partial y}\right), \end{aligned} \tag{14}$$

it has been introduced in [9] a nonlinear extension D^{NL} of the form

$$D^{NL}: \begin{array}{ccc} C^k(\Omega;\mathbb{R}^2) & \longrightarrow & C^{k-1}(\Omega;\mathbb{R}^2) \\ u & \longmapsto & \left(\frac{\partial u_1}{\partial x} + \frac{\nabla u_1 \times \nabla u_2}{|\nabla u_1 \times \nabla u_2|}\frac{\partial u_2}{\partial y}, \frac{\nabla u_1 \times \nabla u_2}{|\nabla u_1 \times \nabla u_2|}\frac{\partial u_2}{\partial x} - \frac{\partial u_1}{\partial y}\right). \end{array} \tag{15}$$

Then, the authors extended these two operators to color images $u = (u_1, u_2, u_3)$, yielding the so-called **Linear vectorial Dirac operator** $\overline{D}$ and **Nonlinear vectorial Dirac operator** $\overline{D^{NL}}$, and defined as follows:

$$\overline{D}: \begin{array}{ccc} C^k(\Omega;\mathbb{R}^3) & \longrightarrow & C^{k-1}(\Omega;\mathbb{R}^6) \\ u & \longmapsto & (Du_{1,2}, Du_{2,3}, Du_{3,1}), \end{array} \tag{16}$$

$$\overline{D^{NL}}: \begin{array}{ccc} C^k(\Omega;\mathbb{R}^3) & \longrightarrow & C^{k-1}(\Omega;\mathbb{R}^6) \\ u & \longmapsto & (D^{NL}u_{1,2}, D^{NL}u_{2,3}, D^{NL}u_{3,1}) \end{array} \tag{17}$$

where we denote by $u_{i,j}$ the function (u_i, u_j).

3.2 Weighted Dirac Operators for Color Images

Adding weights to D, $\overline{D}$ and $\overline{D^{NL}}$, we obtain the following operators.

Definition 1. *The* ***Weighted Dirac operator*** *is the operator*

$$D_{\alpha,\beta}: \begin{array}{ccc} C^k(\Omega;\mathbb{R}^2) & \longrightarrow & C^{k-1}(\Omega;\mathbb{R}^2) \\ u & \longmapsto & \left(\alpha\frac{\partial u_1}{\partial x} + \beta\frac{\nabla u_1 \times \nabla u_2}{|\nabla u_1 \times \nabla u_2|}\frac{\partial u_2}{\partial y}, \beta\frac{\nabla u_1 \times \nabla u_2}{|\nabla u_1 \times \nabla u_2|}\frac{\partial u_2}{\partial x} - \alpha\frac{\partial u_1}{\partial y}\right) \end{array} \tag{18}$$

where $\alpha, \beta \in C^0(\Omega)$.

Definition 2. *The* ***Linear weighted vectorial Dirac operator*** *is the operator*

$$\overline{D_{\boldsymbol{\alpha},\boldsymbol{\beta}}}: \begin{array}{ccc} C^k(\Omega;\mathbb{R}^3) & \longrightarrow & C^{k-1}(\Omega;\mathbb{R}^6) \\ u & \longmapsto & (D_{\alpha_{1,2},\beta_{1,2}}u_{1,2}, D_{\alpha_{2,3},\beta_{2,3}}u_{2,3}, D_{\alpha_{3,1},\beta_{3,1}}u_{3,1}) \end{array} \tag{19}$$

where $\boldsymbol{\alpha} = (\alpha_{1,2}, \alpha_{2,3}, \alpha_{3,1}), \boldsymbol{\beta} = (\beta_{1,2}, \beta_{2,3}, \beta_{3,1}) \in C^0(\Omega;\mathbb{R}^3)$.

Definition 3. *The* ***Nonlinear weighted vectorial Dirac operator*** *is the operator*

$$\overline{D^{NL}_{\boldsymbol{\alpha},\boldsymbol{\beta}}}: \begin{array}{ccc} C^k(\Omega;\mathbb{R}^3) & \longrightarrow & C^{k-1}(\Omega;\mathbb{R}^6) \\ u & \longmapsto & (D^{NL}_{\alpha_{1,2},\beta_{1,2}}u_{1,2}, D^{NL}_{\alpha_{2,3},\beta_{2,3}}u_{2,3}, D^{NL}_{\alpha_{3,1},\beta_{3,1}}u_{3,1}) \end{array} \tag{20}$$

where $\boldsymbol{\alpha} = (\alpha_{1,2}, \alpha_{2,3}, \alpha_{3,1}), \boldsymbol{\beta} = (\beta_{1,2}, \beta_{2,3}, \beta_{3,1}) \in C^0(\Omega;\mathbb{R}^3)$.

3.3 Linear Weighted Dirac Vectorial Total Variation and Its Dual Formulation

The Differentiable Case. Let $u = (u_1, u_2, u_3) \in C^1(\Omega; \mathbb{R}^3)$, and $\boldsymbol{\alpha}, \boldsymbol{\beta} \in C^0(\Omega; \mathbb{R}^3)$.

Definition 4. *The* ***Linear weighted Dirac Vectorial Total Variation*** *of u is the quantity*

$$DiracVTV_{\boldsymbol{\alpha},\boldsymbol{\beta}}(u) := \|\overline{D_{\boldsymbol{\alpha},\boldsymbol{\beta}}}u\|_{L^1}. \tag{21}$$

In particular, for $\alpha_{1,2} = \alpha_{2,3} = \alpha_{3,1} = \alpha, \beta_{1,2} = \beta_{2,3} = \beta_{3,1} = \beta$, we have $DiracVTV_{\boldsymbol{\alpha},\boldsymbol{\beta}}(u) =$

$$\int_\Omega \sqrt{(\alpha^2+\beta^2)\sum_{k=1}^{3}\|\nabla u_k\|^2 + 2\alpha\beta\,(\nabla u_1 \times \nabla u_2 + \nabla u_2 \times \nabla u_3 + \nabla u_3 \times \nabla u_1)}\; d\Omega.$$

Definition 5. *The* ***Nonlinear weighted Dirac Vectorial Total Variation*** *of u is the quantity*

$$DiracVTV^{NL}_{\boldsymbol{\alpha},\boldsymbol{\beta}}(u) := \|\overline{D^{NL}_{\boldsymbol{\alpha},\boldsymbol{\beta}}}u\|_{L^1}. \tag{22}$$

In particular, for $\alpha_{1,2} = \alpha_{2,3} = \alpha_{3,1} = \alpha, \beta_{1,2} = \beta_{2,3} = \beta_{3,1} = \beta$, we have

$$\mathrm{DiracVTV}^{\mathrm{NL}}_{\boldsymbol{\alpha},\boldsymbol{\beta}}(u) = \int_\Omega \sqrt{(\alpha^2+\beta^2)\sum_{k=1}^{3}\|\nabla u_k\|^2 + 2\alpha\beta \sum_{1\leq i<j\leq 3} |\nabla u_i \times \nabla u_j|}\; d\Omega.$$

The Non Differentiable Case. The Linear weighted Dirac Vectorial Total Variation can be extended to non differentiable functions. As in the case of VTV, it involves the notion of adjoint operator.

Proposition 1. *Assuming that* $\boldsymbol{\alpha}, \boldsymbol{\beta}$ *are constant, the adjoint of* $\overline{D_{\boldsymbol{\alpha},\boldsymbol{\beta}}}$ *is the operator*

$$\begin{aligned}
\overline{D_{\boldsymbol{\alpha},\boldsymbol{\beta}}}^{*}: \quad C^k(\Omega;\mathbb{R}^6) &\longrightarrow C^{k-1}(\Omega;\mathbb{R}^3) \\
\eta &\longmapsto \Big(\alpha_{1,2}\frac{\partial \eta_1}{\partial x} - \alpha_{1,2}\frac{\partial \eta_2}{\partial y} + \beta_{3,1}\frac{\partial \eta_5}{\partial y} + \beta_{3,1}\frac{\partial \eta_6}{\partial x}, \\
&\qquad \beta_{1,2}\frac{\partial \eta_1}{\partial y} + \beta_{1,2}\frac{\partial \eta_2}{\partial x} + \alpha_{2,3}\frac{\partial \eta_3}{\partial x} - \alpha_{2,3}\frac{\partial \eta_4}{\partial y}, \\
&\qquad \beta_{2,3}\frac{\partial \eta_3}{\partial y} + \beta_{2,3}\frac{\partial \eta_4}{\partial x} + \alpha_{3,1}\frac{\partial \eta_5}{\partial x} - \alpha_{3,1}\frac{\partial \eta_6}{\partial y}\Big)
\end{aligned} \tag{23}$$

for $\eta = (\eta_1, \eta_2, \eta_3, \eta_4, \eta_5, \eta_6)$.

Proof.

$$\begin{aligned}\langle\overline{D_{\alpha,\beta}}u,\eta\rangle =& \eta_1\left(\alpha_{1,2}\frac{\partial u_1}{\partial x}+\beta_{1,2}\frac{\partial u_2}{\partial y}\right)+\eta_2\left(\beta_{1,2}\frac{\partial u_2}{\partial x}-\alpha_{1,2}\frac{\partial u_1}{\partial y}\right)\\ &+\eta_3\left(\alpha_{2,3}\frac{\partial u_2}{\partial x}+\beta_{2,3}\frac{\partial u_3}{\partial y}\right)+\eta_4\left(\beta_{2,3}\frac{\partial u_3}{\partial x}-\alpha_{2,3}\frac{\partial u_2}{\partial y}\right)\\ &+\eta_5\left(\alpha_{3,1}\frac{\partial u_3}{\partial x}+\beta_{3,1}\frac{\partial u_1}{\partial y}\right)+\eta_6\left(\beta_{3,1}\frac{\partial u_1}{\partial x}-\alpha_{3,1}\frac{\partial u_3}{\partial y}\right).\end{aligned}$$

Assuming η has a compact support, integration by parts gives

$$\begin{aligned}\langle\overline{D_{\alpha,\beta}}u,\eta\rangle =& -u_1\left(\alpha_{1,2}\frac{\partial\eta_1}{\partial x}-\alpha_{1,2}\frac{\partial\eta_2}{\partial y}+\beta_{3,1}\frac{\partial\eta_5}{\partial y}+\beta_{3,1}\frac{\partial\eta_6}{\partial x}\right)\\ &-u_2\left(\beta_{1,2}\frac{\partial\eta_1}{\partial y}+\beta_{1,2}\frac{\partial\eta_2}{\partial x}+\alpha_{2,3}\frac{\partial\eta_3}{\partial x}-\alpha_{2,3}\frac{\partial\eta_4}{\partial y}\right)\\ &-u_3\left(\beta_{2,3}\frac{\partial\eta_3}{\partial y}+\beta_{2,3}\frac{\partial\eta_4}{\partial x}+\alpha_{3,1}\frac{\partial\eta_5}{\partial x}-\alpha_{3,1}\frac{\partial\eta_6}{\partial y}\right)\end{aligned}$$

from which we deduce the expression of the operator $\overline{D_{\alpha,\beta}}^*$.

Definition 6. *Let $u \in L^1(\Omega;\mathbb{R}^3)$ and $\boldsymbol{\alpha},\boldsymbol{\beta}$ constant. The* ***Linear weighted Dirac Total Variation*** *of u is the quantity*

$$DiracVTV_{\alpha,\beta}(u)=\sup\left(\int_\Omega\langle u,\overline{D_{\alpha,\beta}}^*\eta\rangle;\eta\in C_c^1(\Omega;\mathbb{R}^6),\|\eta(x,y)\|_2\le 1\ \ \forall(x,y)\in\Omega\right) \tag{24}$$

It can be shown that, if u is L^1 integrable and differentiable, then both definitions (21) and (24) coincide. The proof is similar to the VTV case mentioned in Sect. 2.

Then, we define the space DiracVBV$(\Omega;\mathbb{R}^3)$ as

$$DiracVBV(\Omega;\mathbb{R}^3):=\{u\in L^1(\Omega;\mathbb{R}^3), DiracVTV_{\alpha,\beta}(u)<\infty\}.$$

3.4 Variational Models for Color Image Restoration

Linear Model. Let $\boldsymbol{\alpha},\boldsymbol{\beta}$ be constant. We consider the L^2-DiracVTV$_{\alpha,\beta}$ model defined by

$$\arg\min_{u\in X}\frac{1}{2}\|Au-u^0\|_{L^2}^2+\gamma\, DiracVTV_{\alpha,\beta}(u) \qquad \gamma>0 \tag{25}$$

where $X = L^2(\Omega;\mathbb{R}^3)\cap$ DiracVBV$(\Omega;\mathbb{R}^3)$. Model (25) has an unique solution provided that A is injective. The proof is similar to the VTV case mentioned in Sect. 2.

Let Ω be a 2D grid of size $M \times N$. The discretization of model (25) is

$$\underset{u \in \mathbb{R}^{M \times N \times 3}}{\arg\min} \sum_{\Omega} \frac{1}{2} \|Au - u^0\|_2^2 + \gamma \|\overline{D_{\alpha,\beta}} u\|_2 \tag{26}$$

where the Dirac operator $\overline{D_{\alpha,\beta}}$ is discretized using forward derivatives as in (7).

It can easily be shown that model (26) satisfies the same properties as the discrete L2-VTV model (6). As a consequence, the primal-dual algorithm described in Algorithm 1 can also be applied to solve model (26). In the particular case where A is a convolution with some kernel H, the algorithm reads

$$\begin{aligned} u^{n+1} &= \mathcal{F}^{-1}\left(\frac{\mathcal{F}(u^0)\mathcal{F}(H)^* + \frac{\gamma}{\tau}\mathcal{F}(u^n - \tau \overline{D_{\alpha,\beta}}^* \eta^n)}{\frac{\gamma}{\tau} + \mathcal{F}(H)^2}\right), \\ \overline{u}^n &= u^{n+1} + \theta(u^{n+1} - u^n), \\ \eta^{n+1} &= \frac{\eta^n + \sigma \overline{D_{\alpha,\beta}}\, \overline{u}^n}{\max(1, \|\eta^n + \sigma \overline{D_{\alpha,\beta}}\, \overline{u}^n\|_2)}. \end{aligned} \tag{27}$$

where the adjoint $\overline{D_{\alpha,\beta}}^*$ is discretized using backward differences.

Nonlinear Model. We consider the L^2-DiracVTV$^{\mathrm{NL}}_{\alpha,\beta}$ model defined by

$$\arg\min_u \frac{1}{2} \|Au - u^0\|_{L^2}^2 + \gamma\, DiracVTV^{NL}_{\alpha,\beta}(u), \qquad \gamma > 0 \tag{28}$$

where $\alpha_{ij} \equiv 1$ and $\beta_{ij} = \beta > 0$.

Model (28) can be reformulated as the following constrained variational model

$$\arg\min_u \; \frac{1}{2} \|Au - u^0\|_{L^2}^2 + \gamma\, DiracVTV_{\alpha,\widetilde{\beta}}(u), \qquad \text{such that} \qquad \widetilde{\beta_{ij}} = \beta \frac{\nabla u_i \times \nabla u_j}{|\nabla u_i \times \nabla u_j|}. \tag{29}$$

We propose the following adaptation of algorithm (27) to solve the (discretization of) model (29)

$$\begin{aligned} \widetilde{\beta_{i,j}}^n &= \beta \frac{\nabla u_i^n \times \nabla u_j^n}{|\nabla u_i^n \times \nabla u_j^n|} \\ u^{n+1} &= \mathcal{F}^{-1}\left(\frac{\mathcal{F}(u^0)\mathcal{F}(H)^* + \frac{\gamma}{\tau}(\mathcal{F}(u^n - \tau \overline{D_{\alpha,\widetilde{\beta}^n}}^* \eta^n))}{\frac{\gamma}{\tau} + \mathcal{F}(H)^2}\right), \\ \overline{u}^n &= u^{n+1} + \theta(u^{n+1} - u^n), \\ \eta^{n+1} &= \frac{\eta^n + \sigma \overline{D_{\alpha,\widetilde{\beta}^n}}\, \overline{u}^n}{\max(1, \|\eta^n + \sigma \overline{D_{\alpha,\widetilde{\beta}^n}}\, \overline{u}^n\|_2)}. \end{aligned} \tag{30}$$

Note that even if convergence of algorithm (30) is not proved, experiments on denoising and deblurring show convergence provided that the value of β is not too high.

4 Experiments

In this section, we compare the models L^2-VTV (5) and L^2-DiracVTV$^{NL}_{\alpha,\beta}$ (28) on denoising and deblurring. Model (5) is implemented with the primal-dual algorithm (13) while model (28) is implemented with the modified primal-dual algorithm (30). The stopping criterion is $\mathrm{MSE}(u^{n+1}, u^n) < 0.001$, and $\theta = 1$. The parameters τ, σ have been manually tuned in order to give the best average PSNR values among the datasets tested. When different parameters values give similar results, we select the highest ones as they make the models reach faster the stopping criterion.

4.1 On the Choice of the Color Space

A good strategy to remove noise in a color image is to work in an opponent space OPP (instead of the RGB color space) and to denoise the achromatic component of the image in a smaller extent than its chromatic components. Indeed, since standard denoising methods assimilate noise to details and these latter are mainly in the achromatic component of the image, we conclude that details can be better preserved if the noise of the achromatic component is removed is a small extent. Moreover, from a perceptual viewpoint, it can even be desirable that a small amount of achromatic noise is present in an image as it can be assimilated to the notion of grain in photography, which gives an aesthetic and realistic aspect to images. On the other hand, chromatic noise is undesirable because it is perceptually unpleasant.

In [1], it has been proposed to formulate these two ideas by means of the following basis change

$$\underbrace{\begin{pmatrix} 5/3\sqrt{3} & 1/\sqrt{2} & 1/\sqrt{6} \\ 5/3\sqrt{3} & -1/\sqrt{2} & 1/\sqrt{6} \\ 5/3\sqrt{3} & 0 & -2/\sqrt{6} \end{pmatrix}}_{\text{basis change}} = \underbrace{\begin{pmatrix} 5/3 & 0 & 0 \\ 5/3 & 0 & 0 \\ 5/3 & 0 & 0 \end{pmatrix}}_{\text{weight}} \underbrace{\begin{pmatrix} 1/\sqrt{3} & 1/\sqrt{2} & 1/\sqrt{6} \\ 1/\sqrt{3} & -1/\sqrt{2} & 1/\sqrt{6} \\ 1/\sqrt{3} & 0 & -2/\sqrt{6} \end{pmatrix}}_{\text{from RGB to OPP}} \tag{31}$$

We follow this strategy in the experiments conducted in this Section, i.e. we express the models in the basis (31). Then, we compare the results to the ones obtained in the RGB color space to determine whether the models benefit from the use of an opponent space or not.

4.2 Denoising

We assume a degradation model (1) of the form

$$u^0 = u^* + n$$

where n is white Gaussian noise of standard deviation 25. In this case, the kernel H in (13) and (30) is the Dirac delta function. We test the models on the Kodak dataset which contains 24 natural images of size 768×512 or 512×768

Table 1. Denoising. Average PSNR over the Kodim dataset of the two models tested with parameters γ, β optimized for each image. In parenthesis, the color space in which each model has been tested.

Model	
Results	Average optimal PSNR
L^2-VTV (RGB)	28.87
L^2-DiracVTV$^{NL}_{\alpha,\beta}$ (RGB)	28.94
L^2-VTV (OPP)	29.20
L^2-DiracVTV$^{NL}_{\alpha,\beta}$ (OPP)	**29.33**

Table 2. Denoising. Average PSNR over the Kodim dataset of the two models tested with the average values of the parameters γ, β optimized for each image. In parenthesis, the color space in which each model has been tested.

Model			
Results	Average optimal γ	Average optimal β	Average PSNR
L^2-VTV (RGB)	27.5	–	28.78
L^2-DiracVTV$^{NL}_{\alpha,\beta}$ (RGB)	30.5	0.25	28.84
L^2-VTV (OPP)	37.5	–	29.14
L^2-DiracVTV$^{NL}_{\alpha,\beta}$ (OPP)	41	0.23	**29.24**

(http://r0k.us/graphics/kodak/). We found that, among all the parameters values tested, $\tau = \sigma = 0.1$ and $\tau = \sigma = 0.01$ are the best values for (13) and (30) respectively.

For each model and each image of the dataset, we manually tune the parameters γ, β and determine the values giving the best PSNR. Table 1 reports, for each model and color space, the average PSNR obtained with this strategy. We observe that the opponent space OPP gives much better results than RGB. Moreover, L^2- DiracVTV$^{NL}_{\alpha,\beta}$ outperforms L^2-VTV, with an increase of +0.07 dB in RGB and +0.13 dB in OPP.

In order to automatize the tuning of the parameters, we compute the average of the optimal values γ, β, test again the models on each image with these average values, and report the average PSNR in Table 2. As expected, the average PSNR of each model has slightly decreased (from −0.06 dB for L^2-VTV (OPP) to −0.1 dB for L^2-DiracVTV$^{NL}_{\alpha,\beta}$ (RGB)). The fact that the largest decreases occur for L^2-DiracVTV$^{NL}_{\alpha,\beta}$ models is coherent since this model has two parameters to tune. Finally, the automatization of the parameters does not modify the order of the models.

Figure 1 (right) shows the result of L^2-DiracVTV$^{NL}_{\alpha,\beta}$ (OPP) applied to a degraded version (center) of the image "kodim23" (left) of the dataset. The optimal values of the parameters are $\gamma = 53$, $\beta = 0.2$, and the PSNR is 32.45 dB.

Let us mention that the optimal parameter value for the model L^2-VTV (OPP) on this image is $\gamma = 44$ and the PSNR is 32.3 dB.

4.3 Deblurring

We assume a degradation model (1) of the form

$$u^0 = H * u^* + n$$

where H is a 25×25 normalized Gaussian kernel of standard deviation 1.6 and n is white Gaussian noise of standard deviation $\sqrt{2}$. We test the models on a small dataset of 4 natural images of size 256×256 (see Fig. 2). We found that, among all the parameters values tested, $\tau = \sigma = 0.01$ and $\tau = \sigma = 0.0075$ are the best values for (13) and (30) respectively.

Fig. 1. From left to right: original image "kodim23", degraded image, solution of L^2-DiracVTV$^{\mathrm{NL}}_{\alpha,\beta}$ (OPP) with optimal parameters γ, β.

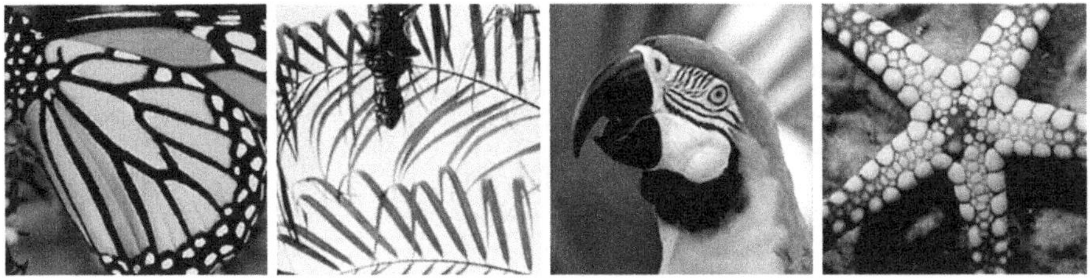

Fig. 2. Dataset used for experiments on deblurring

As in the denoising case, we manually tune the parameters γ, β and determine the values giving the best PSNR for each model and each image of the dataset. Table 3 reports, for each model and color space, the average PSNR obtained with this strategy. We observe that the opponent space OPP gives slightly better results than RGB. Unlike denoising, the models do not benefit much from the use of an opponent space. The results also show that L^2- DiracVTV$^{\mathrm{NL}}_{\alpha,\beta}$ outperforms L^2-VTV, with an increase of +0.18 dB in the OPP color space.

In order to automatize the tuning of the parameters, we compute the average of the optimal values γ, β, test again the models on each image with these average values, and report the average PSNR in Table 4. The average PSNR of each model has slightly decreased (from −0.01 dB for L^2-VTV (RGB-OPP) to −0.06 dB for L^2-DiracVTV$^{\mathrm{NL}}_{\alpha,\beta}$ (OPP)). We observe that the automatization of the parameters does not modify the order of the models.

Figure 3 (right) shows the result of L^2-DiracVTV$^{\mathrm{NL}}_{\alpha,\beta}$ (OPP) applied to a degraded version (center) of the image "butterfly" (left) of the dataset. The optimal values of the parameters are $\gamma = 0.12$, $\beta = 0.3$, and the PSNR is 33.49 dB. Let us mention that the optimal parameter value for the model L^2-VTV (OPP) on this image is $\gamma = 0.14$ and the PSNR is 33.35 dB.

Fig. 3. From left to right: original image "butterfly", degraded image, solution of L^2-DiracVTV$^{\mathrm{NL}}_{\alpha,\beta}$ (OPP) with optimal parameters γ, β.

Table 3. Deblurring. Average PSNR over the dataset of the two models tested with parameters γ, β optimized for each image. In parenthesis, the color space in which each model has been tested.

Model Results	Average optimal PSNR
L^2-VTV (RGB)	33.49
L^2-DiracVTV$^{\mathrm{NL}}_{\alpha,\beta}$ (RGB)	33.63
L^2-VTV (OPP)	33.49
L^2-DiracVTV$^{\mathrm{NL}}_{\alpha,\beta}$ (OPP)	**33.67**

Table 4. Deblurring. Average PSNR over the dataset of the two models tested with the average values of the parameters γ, β optimized for each image. In parenthesis, the color space in which each model has been tested.

Model Results	Average optimal γ	Average optimal β	Average PSNR
L^2-VTV (RGB)	0.08	–	33.48
L^2-DiracVTV$^{\mathrm{NL}}_{\alpha,\beta}$ (RGB)	0.07	0.3	33.58
L^2-VTV (OPP)	0.12	–	33.48
L^2-DiracVTV$^{\mathrm{NL}}_{\alpha,\beta}$ (OPP)	0.11	0.27	**33.61**

5 Conclusion

In this paper, we introduced a new regularizer for color image restoration, called Nonlinear weighted Dirac Vectorial Total Variation and denoted by $\text{DiracVTV}^{\text{NL}}_{\alpha,\beta}$. This regularizer encodes the property of natural images of having the gradients of their color components aligned. Then, we derived from this regularizer the L^2-$\text{DiracVTV}^{\text{NL}}_{\alpha,\beta}$ variational model which generalizes the L^2-VTV model. We solved numerically our model by adapting the primal-dual algorithm of Chambolle and Pock. Experiments on denoising and deblurring showed that our model outperforms the L^2-VTV model by an amount of +0.13 dB on denoising and +0.18 dB on deblurring. Further work will be devoted to perform a detailed analysis of the model L^2-$\text{DiracVTV}^{\text{NL}}_{\alpha,\beta}$ and to construct a more efficient algorithm to solve it numerically. Moreover, we intend to test the model on other image restoration tasks and compare it to other color extensions of the ROF model.

References

1. Batard, T., Haro, G., Ballester, C.: DIP-VBTV: a color image restoration model combining a deep image prior and a vector bundle total variation. SIAM J. Imag. Sci. **14**(4), 1816–1847 (2021)
2. Bredies, K., Kunisch, K., Pock, T.: Total generalized variation. SIAM J. Imag. Sci. **3**(3), 492–526 (2010)
3. Bredies, K., Lorenz, D.: Mathematical Image Processing. Springer, Cham (2018). https://doi.org/10.1007/978-3-030-01458-2
4. Bresson, X., Chan, T.F.: Fast dual minimization of the vectorial total variation norm and applications to color image processing. Inverse Probl. Imaging **2**(4), 455–484 (2008)
5. Chambolle, A., Caselles, V., Cremers, D., Novaga, M., Pock, T.: Theoretical foundations and numerical methods for sparse recovery. In: An Introduction to Total Variation for Image Analysis. De Gruyter (2010)
6. Chambolle, A., Pock, T.: A first-order primal-dual algorithm for convex problems with applications to imaging. J. Math. Imaging Vision **40**(1), 120–145 (2011)
7. Duan, Y., Zhong, Q., Tai, X.-C., Glowinski, R.: A fast operator-splitting method for Beltrami color image denoising. J. Sci. Comput. **92**(89), 1–28 (2022)
8. Duran, J., Moeller, M., Sbert, C., Cremers, D.: Collaborative total variation: A general framework for vectorial tv models. SIAM J. Imag. Sci. **9**(1), 116–151 (2016)
9. Huitzil Santamaría, N., Batard, T., Brito-Loeza, C.: Nonlinear dip-diracvtv model for color image restoration. In: Proceedings of the 22nd Mexican International Conference on Artificial Intelligence MICAI (2023)
10. Kimmel, R., Malladi, R., Sochen, N.: Images as embedding maps and minimal surfaces: movies, color, texture, and volumetric medical images. Int. J. Comput. Vision **39**(2), 111–129 (2000)
11. Rosman, G., Tai, X.-C., Dascal, L., Kimmel, R.: Polyakov action minimization for efficient color image processing. In: Kutulakos, K.N. (ed.) ECCV 2010 Workshops. Part II, LNCS 6554, pp. 50–61. Springer, Berlin (2012). https://doi.org/10.1007/978-3-642-35740-4_5

12. Rudin, L.I., Osher, S., Fatemi, E.: Nonlinear total variation based noise removal algorithms. Physica D **60**(1–4), 259–268 (1992)
13. Sochen, N., Kimmel, R., Malladi, R.: A general framework for low-level vision. IEEE Trans. Image Process. **7**(3), 310–318 (1998)
14. Ulyanov, D., Vedaldi, A., Lempitsky, V.: Deep image prior. Int. J. Comput. Vision **128**(7), 1867–1888 (2020)
15. Vese, L., Le Guyader, C.: Variational Methods in Image Processing. Chapman and Hall/CRC, Boca Raton (2015)
16. Wu, C., Tai, X.-C.: Augmented lagrangian method, dual methods, and split Bregman iteration for ROF, vectorial tv, and high order models. SIAM J. Imag. Sci. **3**(3), 300–339 (2010)

An FPGA Smart Camera Implementation of Segmentation Models for Drone Wildfire Imagery

Eduardo Guarduño[1], Jorge Francisco Ciprian-Sanchez[2], Valente Vazquez-Garcia[3], Miguel Gonzalez-Mendoza[1], Gerardo Rodriguez-Hernandez[1], Adriana Palacios[4], Lucile Rossi-Tisson[5(✉)], and Gilberto Ochoa-Ruiz[1(✉)]

[1] School of Engineering and Sciences, Tecnologico de Monterrey, Monterrey, Mexico
gilberto.ochoa@tec.mx

[2] Digital Engineering Faculty, Hasso Plattner Institute, Potsdam, Germany

[3] Maestria en Cs. Computacionales, Universidad Autonoma de Guadalajara, Zapopan, Mexico

[4] Department of Chemical, Food and Environmental Engineering, Universidad de las Americas Puebla, Puebla, Mexico

[5] Università di Corsica, Laboratoire Sciences Pour lEnvironnement, Campus Grimaldi - BP, Corti, France
rossi_l@univ-corse.fr

Abstract. Wildfires represent one of the most relevant natural disasters worldwide, due to their impact on various societal and environmental levels. Thus, a significant amount of research has been carried out to investigate and apply computer vision techniques to address this problem. One of the most promising approaches for wildfire fighting is the use of drones equipped with visible and infrared cameras for the detection, monitoring, and fire spread assessment in a remote manner but in close proximity to the affected areas. However, implementing effective computer vision algorithms on board is often prohibitive since deploying full-precision deep learning models running on GPU is not a viable option, due to their high power consumption and the limited payload a drone can handle. Thus, in this work, we posit that smart cameras, based on low-power consumption field-programmable gate arrays (FPGAs), in tandem with binarized neural networks (BNNs), represent a cost-effective alternative for implementing onboard computing on the edge. Herein we present the implementation of a segmentation model applied to the Corsican Fire Database. We optimized an existing U-Net model for such a task and ported the model to an edge device (a Xilinx Ultra96-v2 FPGA). By pruning and quantizing the original model, we reduce the number of parameters by 90%. Furthermore, additional optimizations enabled us to increase the throughput of the original model from 8 frames per second (FPS) to 33.63 FPS without loss in the segmentation performance: our model obtained 0.912 in Matthews correlation coefficient (MCC), 0.915 in F1 score and 0.870 in Hafiane quality index (HAF), and comparable qualitative segmentation results when contrasted to the original full-precision model. The final model was integrated into a low-cost FPGA, which was used to implement a neural network accelerator.

H. Calvo et al. (Eds.): MICAI 2023, LNAI 14391, pp. 213–226, 2024.
https://doi.org/10.1007/978-3-031-47765-2_16

Keywords: SoC FPGA · Computer vision · Segmentation · Binarized neural networks · Artificial intelligence · Infrared imaging · Pruning

1 Introduction

A wildfire is an exceptional or extraordinary free-burning vegetation fire that may have been started maliciously, accidentally, or through natural means that could significantly affect the global carbon cycle by releasing large amounts of C02 into the atmosphere. It has profound economic effects on people, communities, and countries, produces smoke that is harmful to health, devastates wildlife, and negatively impacts bodies of water [26]. The three main categories of remote sensing for wildfire monitoring and detection systems are ground-based systems, manned aerial vehicle-based systems, and satellite-based systems. However, they present the following technological and practical problems: ground-based have limited surveillance ranges. Satellite-based have problems when planning routes, their spatial resolution may be low, and the information transmission may be delayed. Manned aerial vehicle-based systems are expensive and potentially dangerous due to hazardous environments and human error. Unmanned aerial vehicles (UAVs) provide a mobile and low-cost solution using computer vision-based remote sensing systems that can perform long-time, monotonous, and repetitive tasks [31]. Drones, in particular, represent an excellent opportunity due to their easy deployment. However, the ability to implement these fire detection systems, based on deep learning (DL), is limited by the maximum payload of the drone and the high power consumption.

In this paper, we posit that a convolutional neural network (CNN) can be implemented on a hardware accelerator that can be embedded as part of a smart camera and installed on a drone for the detection of wildfires. A review of the literature on hardware implementation for various artificial intelligence (AI) algorithms was published by Talib et al. [22] reviewing 169 different research reports published between 2009 and 2019, which focus on the implementation of hardware accelerators by using application-specific integrated circuits (ASICs), FPGAs, or GPUs. They found that most implementations were based on FPGAs, focusing mainly on the acceleration of CNNs for object detection, letting the GPU-based implementations in second place.

Due to the diversity of applications, AI models such as CNNs need to meet various performance requirements for drones and autonomous vehicles, with the essential demands of low latency, low weight overhead, long-term battery autonomy, and low power consumption being the most pressing requirements. The complexity of the tasks that CNNs must perform continues to increase as models evolve. As a result, deeper networks are designed in exchange for higher computational and memory demands. In this context, the reconfiguration capabilities of FPGAs enable the creation of CNN hardware implementations that are high-performance, low-power, and configurable to fit system demands [27]. A smart camera is an embedded system for computer vision applications that has attracted great interest in various application domains, as it offers image capture and image processing capabilities in a compact system [20]. This paper describes the methodology, implementation, design cycle, and experimental protocol of porting a modified U-Net model into a Xilinx Ultra96-V2 FPGA for the wildfire semantic segmentation task for the smart camera system.

The rest of the paper is organized as follows: Sect. 2 discusses recent works applying computer vision models for wildfire segmentation, highlighting their strengths and limitations; the second part of the section discusses related works regarding smart camera implementations in order to better contextualize our work. Section 3 details our contribution, discussing in detail the proposed model, the dataset used for evaluating our models, and the design flow followed for optimizing the model and testing it in the target embedded FPGA board. Section 4 discusses the results of our optimization process and provides a quantitative and qualitative comparison between full precision and the BNN model. Finally, Sect. 5 concludes the paper and discusses future areas of research.

2 State-of-the-Art

2.1 Segmentation Models for Wildfire Detection and Characterization

Detecting a wildfire by categorizing each pixel in an infrared image is a semantic segmentation problem; therefore, for this task, AI models have been used, such as fully convolutional networks as well as the U-Net model proposed by Ronnenberger et al. in 2015 [19], which allow precise segmentation with few training images. For the specific task of fire segmentation, artificial intelligence models have already been implemented to solve this problem with visible images of fire [2], the fusion of visible and infrared images of fire [8], and visible images of fire and smoke [18]. For instance, Akhloufi et al. [2] proposed Deep-Fire, a semantic segmentation model based on the U-Net architecture. The authors trained and evaluated their model using the Corsican Fire Database [25]. With an F1 score ranging from 64.2% to 99% on the test set, Akhloufi et al. claimed successful results using the Dice similarity coefficient as the loss function for the model.

Ciprián-Sánchez et al. [8] evaluated thirty-six different DL combinations of the U-Net-based Akhloufi architecture [2], the FusionNet-based Choi architecture [6], and the VGG16-based Frizzi architecture [9], the Dice [16], Focal Tversky [1], Unified Focal [30] losses, and the visible and near-infrared (NIR) images of the Corsican Fire Database [25] and fused visible-NIR images produced by the methods by Li et al. [15] and Ciprián-Sánchez et al. [7]. After evaluating these models, the combination with the best results was Akhloufi + Dice + visible with a 0.9323 F1 score, also known as the Dice coefficient.

Although these works have highlighted the potential of using AI in this domain, many of these algorithms are incapable of operating in real-time, as they inherently suffer from very high inference times and are prohibitive as they require many computing resources, which impedes their usability on drone missions and thus we posit that new paradigms are needed for their successful deployment, particularly in terms of inference time (FPS) and power consumption.

2.2 Smart Camera Implementations for Computer Vision

Smart cameras are devices that process, analyze, and extract data from the images they capture. Different video processing algorithms are used for the extraction. Smart cameras have been employed in a variety of applications, including human gesture recognition [29], surveillance [4], smart traffic signal optimization systems [23], and a fire detection system based on conventional image processing methods [10]. We propose a DL implementation capable of performing a precise segmentation that can be used as a first step in wildfire characterization and risk assessment systems.

FPGAs are excellent choices for creating smart cameras because they offer significant processing capabilities while maintaining a low power consumption, which makes them good candidates for particular edge tasks creating efficient hardware accelerators capable of high throughput [27], and maintaining a high degree of flexibility and reconfigurability. The disadvantage of FPGAs is that developers need to be skilled in hardware design to accomplish these goals. The design process frequently takes longer with FPGAs than with CPU and GPU systems. To address such issues, FPGA vendors and other academic and industrial tool developers have introduced several (CAD) tools for training and optimizing DL models and mapping such models into the reconfigurable fabric.

Convolutional neural networks provide high-accuracy results for computer vision tasks, and their applications could be benefited from being implemented in edge devices such as FPGAs. Still, for applications such as smart cameras, limited use of hardware resources and power requirements are of the utmost importance. Therefore, to implement models that generally require a large number of computational resources, large storage capabilities for the model parameters, and the use of high-energy-consuming hardware [27,28], such as GPUs, it is necessary to use model optimization techniques such as pruning and quantization [3] for the compression of the model, to implement it in devices such as an FPGA while achieving high inference speed.

3 Proposed Method

The implementation of a BNN for the segmentation of wildfire images was done using the Xilinx tool Vitis AI because each operation of the model is mapped into a hardware-accelerated microinstruction, in which a series of sequential microinstructions can represent the whole DL model, while a scheduler is in charge of managing the hardware calls and data flow. This enables the customization of the HW accelerator while considering the resources of the FPGA. In the particular context of our application, Vitis AI is indeed the best choice as we target a small FPGA device (Xilinx Ultra96-V2) for deep embedded image processing.

3.1 General Overview of the Optimization Approach

Figure 1 depicts the Vitis AI Pytorch flow followed in this paper. The design process begins by training a segmentation with NIR images from the Corsican

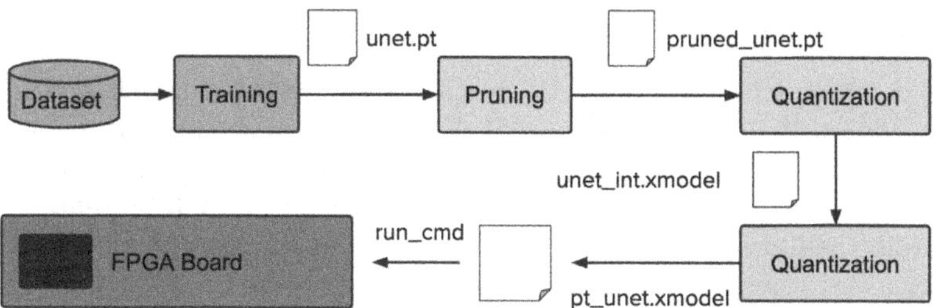

Fig. 1. General overview of the Pytorch flow for Vitis AI. This flow allows us to optimize a given full precision model and target an embedded device such as an FPGA, consuming less power while attaining a higher throughput in terms of processed FPS.

Fire Database [25] and their corresponding ground truths for fire region segmentation. Subsequently, a pruning process to reduce the number of filters in the convolution layers using the Pytorch framework is performed. Then, both the original and the pruned models are saved in pt files. The next module is in charge of changing the numerical representation of the DL model by performing an 8-bit quantization using the Vitis AI quantizer module, producing an xmodel file. Finally, the quantized model is compiled, producing an xmodel file containing all the instructions needed by the DPU to execute the model. After the model has been compiled, it can be loaded on the target FPGA board and tested. In our work, this model is a U-Net model modified to accommodate the needs of our application. The rest of this section will detail the implementation of such an optimized segmentation model.

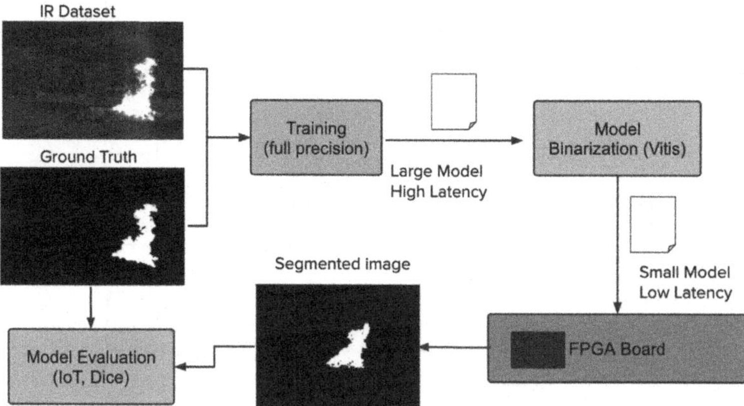

Fig. 2. Overall implementation flow for FPGA-based systems based on Vitis AI.

3.2 Dataset: Corsican Fire Database

In this paper, we employ the NIR images from the Corsican Fire Database, first introduced by Toulouse et al. [25]. For fire region segmentation tasks, this dataset includes 640 pairs of visible and NIR fire images along with the matching ground truths created manually by experts in the field. A representative NIR image from the Corsican Fire Database is shown in the top left corner of Fig. 2, along with its corresponding ground truth.

3.3 Segmentation Model Training

The proposed architecture for this paper is a modified version of a U-Net model [19] with the number of filters from the deepest layers reduced to reduce training and inference times. Furthermore, we add batch normalization layers [12] after every convolutional layer. The final architecture is shown in Fig. 3; the numbers in black are the number of filters before pruning, and the numbers in blue are the number of filters after pruning.

As depicted in Fig. 2, every image in the training set was resized to a width of 320 and a height of 240 pixels for training. For the training of the proposed model, the dataset was divided into 80% for training and 20% for testing. The model was trained with a learning rate of 0.0001 for 350 epochs with a batch size of 5 using cross-entropy loss and Adam optimizer.

3.4 Optimization

Pruning. The pruning method (contained in the binarization block of Fig. 2) employed in the present paper is based on the work of [14] in which, as shown in Fig. 4, when a filter is pruned, the corresponding feature map is removed and the kernels of the input feature maps for the next convolution that correspond to the output feature maps of the pruned filters are also removed. Figure 5 briefly

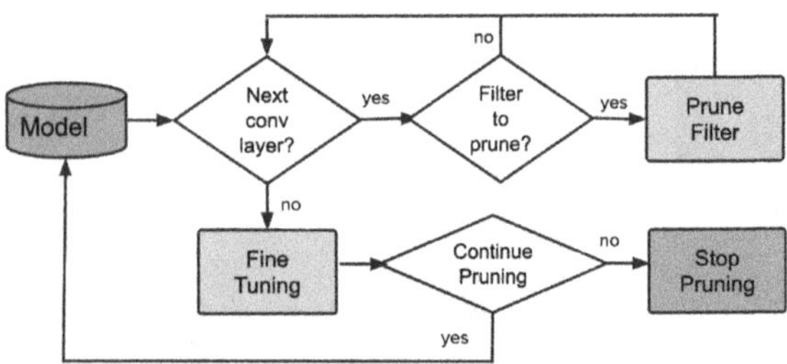

Fig. 3. Proposed architecture. The original U-Net architecture has been extended by introducing batch normalization layers and fewer filters in the deepest layers to reduce training and inference times. The numbers on black on the top of the blocks represent the original filter sizes, whereas the blue one (below) represents the filter size after the optimization process. (Color figure online).

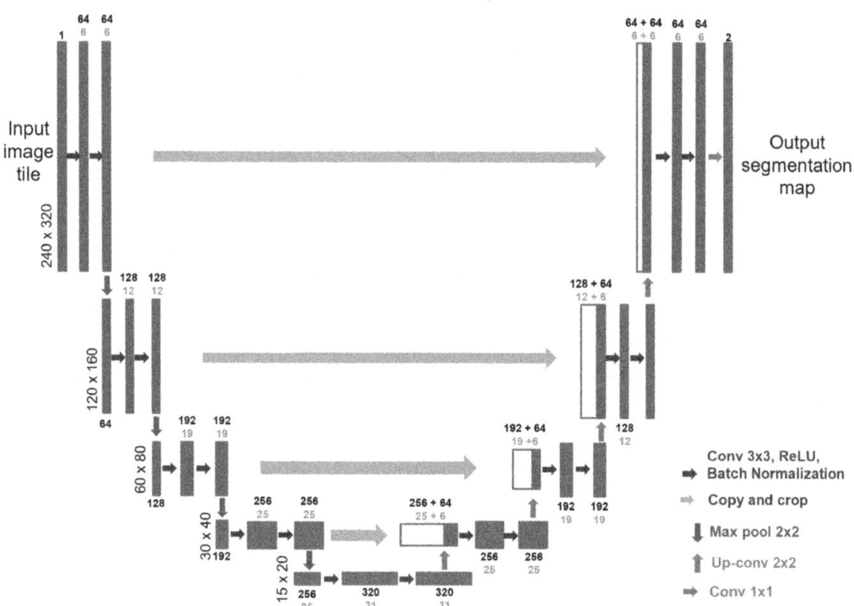

Fig. 4. When a filter is pruned, the matching feature map and associated kernels in the following layer are removed. Retrieved from: Hao Li et al. [14].

explains the pruning process used for this paper, with which it was possible to reduce the number of filters in each convolutional layer by approximately 90%. In Fig. 3, we can see the final architecture of the model, the numbers in blue being the number of filters after the pruning process.

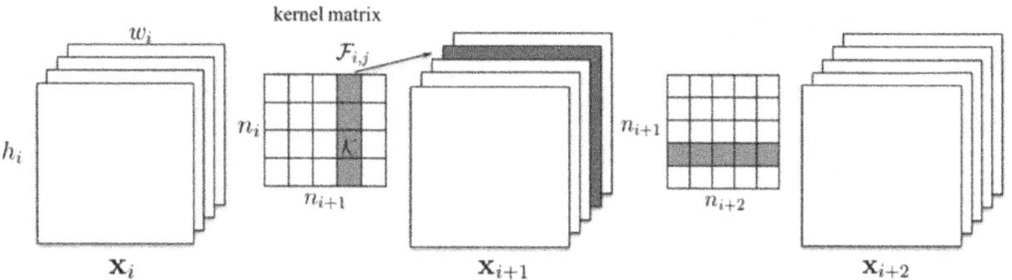

Fig. 5. Schematic flow for optimizing a model in Vitis AI.

Quantization. The model was quantized using the Vitis AI quantizer module; resulting in a CNN model with all its values represented with only 8 bits. That is, the floating-point checkpoint model in converted into a fixed-point integer checkpoint. After confirming there was no significant degradation in the model's performance, the quantized model was compiled with the Vitis compiler, which creates a *xmodel file* with all the instructions required by the DPU to execute the model.

3.5 Proposed FPGA-Based Smart Camera System

Figure 6 shows the system implementation for the smart camera solution of wildfire detection. The processing system (PS) controls every step of the application's life cycle, including retrieving images from the camera, feeding them to the programmable logic (PL) section of the SoC (hardware accelerator implementing the proposed model), and processing the segmented image.

An infrared (IR) camera is attached to the Ultra96 board using a USB port in the SoC. The PS block (an ARM processor) block (an ARM processor) processes the input picture before feeding it to the PL section, which runs the binarized U-Net model mapped into the reconfigurable fabric. The image is processed and then passed back into the PS block for feature extraction. If a complete IIoT solution is implemented, these features may be used for viewing on a TFT screen or communicated via a communication protocol (i.e., LORA) to a cloud. These capabilities are not yet implemented here and are left for future work. In order to make the picture more straightforward, the AXI connection, which is not illustrated here, is used for all communication between the PS, PL, and peripherals.

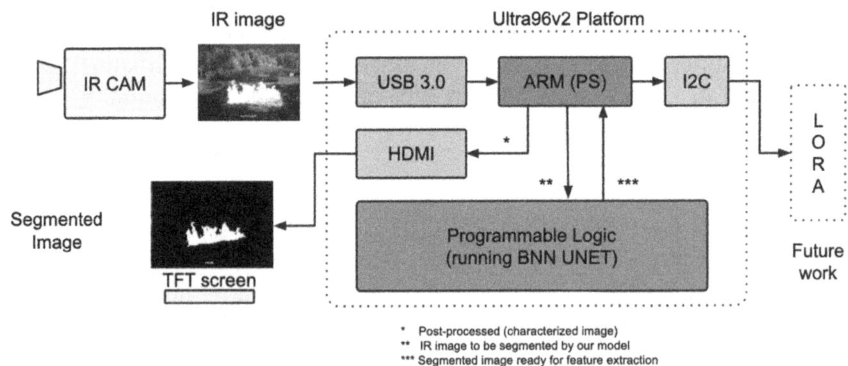

Fig. 6. Proposed solution model for implementing a smart camera for wildfire detection. Our current implementation processes images from external memory or an IR camera; communication capabilities have not yet been implemented.

In our experiments, the overall performance of the model implemented using single-thread execution was not satisfactory, as we obtained only a throughput of 15.77 FPS, even after the pruning and quantization of the model. Therefore, we explored the use of a multi-thread approach supported by the Ultra89-v2 board. The use of this functionality enabled us to attain a higher performance. The main limitation of the single-threaded approach is the bottleneck introduced by the DPU when performing inference in the FPFA, as it introduces a significant latency. This problem arises from the use of queues for exchanging information among the different threads. In Fig. 7, we provide a flow chart comparing both software implementations.

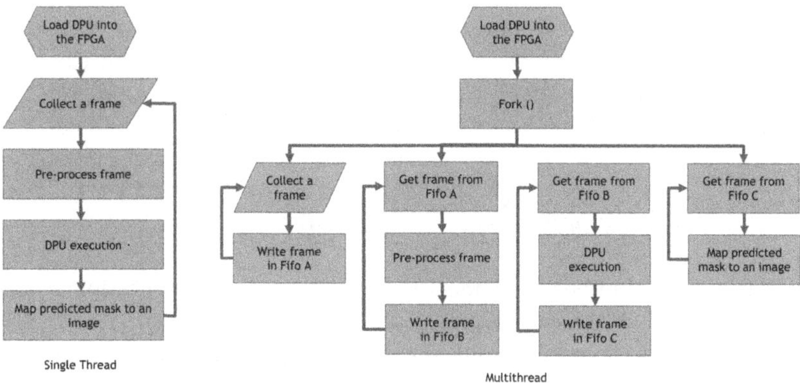

Fig. 7. Flow chart for single and multi-threading inference approaches.

4 Results and Discussion

In the subsequent section, we will discuss the results obtained from implementing the U-Net model for segmenting images of the Corsican Fire Database, comparing both the original full-precision model and the optimized model running on the FPGA platform. We will also compare our results with previous works in the state-of-the-art based on a number of metrics used in the literature, which will be described in the next subsection. Then, quantitative and qualitative results will be provided, based on these metrics, followed by a discussion of the obtained results.

4.1 Comparison Metrics

Matthews Correlation Coefficient. First proposed by Matthews [17], it measures the correlation of the true classes with their predicted labels [5]. The MCC represents the geometric mean of the regression coefficient and its dual, and is defined as follows [24]:

$$MCC = \frac{(TP * TN) - (FP * FN)}{\sqrt{(TN + FN)(TN + FP)(TP + FN)(TP + FP)}}, \tag{1}$$

where TP is the number of true positives, TN the number of true negatives, FP the number of false positives, and FN the number of false negatives.

F1 Score. Also known as the Dice coefficient or overlap index [21], the F1 score is the harmonic mean of the precision Pr and recall Re. The F1 score is defined as the harmonic mean of Pr and Re as follows:

$$F1 = 2 * \frac{Pr * Re}{Pr + Re}, \tag{2}$$

Hafiane Quality Index. Proposed by Hafiane et al. [11] for fire segmentation evaluation, it measures the overlap between the ground truth and the segmentation results, penalizing as well the over- and under-segmentation [11].

First, the authors define a matching index M as follows [24]:

$$M = \frac{1}{Card(I^S)} \sum_{j=1}^{NR^S} \frac{Card(R_{i*}^{GT} \cap R_j^S) \times Card(R_j^S)}{Card(R_{i*}^{GT} \cup R_j^S)}, \tag{3}$$

where NR^S is the number of connected regions in the segmentation result I^S. R_j^S represents one of the said regions, and R_{i*}^{GT} is the region in the reference image I^{GT} that has the most significant overlapping surface with the R_j^S region.

Next, Hafiane et al. define an additional index η to take into account the over- and under-segmentation as follows [24]:

$$\eta = \begin{cases} NR^{GT}/NR^S & \text{if } NR^S \geq NR^{GT} \\ log(1 + NR^S/NR^{GT}) & \text{otherwise} \end{cases}. \tag{4}$$

Finally, the Hafiane quality index is defined as follows:

$$HAF = \frac{M + m \times \eta}{1 + m}, \tag{5}$$

where m is a weighting factor set to 0.5.

4.2 Quantitative Results

Table 1 shows the results obtained by the final implementation of the optimized model in the FPGA using MCC, HAF, and F1 score. It can be observed the pruned model presented a slight drop in performance (3% in MCC) whereas the FPGA model presented a slightly higher drop (of about 5% both in MCC and F1 score) of performance for all metrics.

This slight degradation is expected given the heavy optimization undergone by the model when passing from 64-bit to 8-bit data representation. However, the gain in throughput (and thus inference time) is significant: the full precision model runs at 8 FPS in a GPU, consuming a large amount of power, whereas our model can attain up to 33.64 FPS in the selected FPGA when running in multi-threaded mode (15.77 FPS for the single-threaded mode), for a fraction of the power consumption.

Table 2 provides a comparison with other models in the literature. A recent and thorough comparison of the state-of-the-art carried out by Ciprián-Sánchez

Table 1. Segmentation comparison for the different model implementations.

Model	MCC	F1 score	Hafiane
Proposed Model Original (Validation)	**0.964**	0.964	**0.946**
Proposed Model Original (Test)	0.933	0.934	0.902
Proposed Model Pruned (Validation)	0.964	**0.965**	0.941
Proposed Model Pruned (Test)	0.924	0.926	0.877
Proposed Model FPGA (Validation)	0.932	0.933	0.899
Proposed Model FPGA (Test)	0.912	0.915	0.870

Table 2. Comparison of the proposed model (full-precision and FPGA implementation) with other models in the state-of-the-art.

Model	MCC	F1 score	Hafiane
Akhloufi + Dice + NIR	0.910	0.915	0.890
Akhloufi + Focal Tversky + NIR	0.914	0.916	0.889
Akhloufi + Mixed focal + NIR	0.828	0.843	0.802
Proposed Model Original (Test)	**0.933**	**0.934**	**0.902**
Proposed Model FPGA (Test)	0.912	0.915	0.870

et al. [8] compared different architectures, image types, and loss functions on the Corsican Fire Database. Here, we compared the bests model from this study (by Akhloufi et al. [2] with various losses) using the base metrics (i.e., MCC, HAF, and F1 score). From the table, it can be observed that the original model outperforms this previous work by about 2% (0.933 MCC), whereas the FPGA implemented model attains a similar performance to the best configuration obtained by Akhloufi (0.912 vs 0.910 MCC), using a much smaller footprint.

4.3 Qualitative Results

Table 3 provides a qualitative comparison of the different models compared in Table 1. It shows the original images of the Corsican Fire Database and the segmentation results using the original model before the optimization process, after the pruning method, and finally, the final model used in the FPGA. It can be observed that for the 3 examples provided, both the pruned model and the FPGA implementation yielded practically the same results as the full-precision model, albeit at a much higher frame rate (33 FPS vs the 8 the U-Net running on a V100 GPU). Such results can be used in the smart camera for higher image processing tasks in real-time, such as fire spread prediction by using the processing section (ARM processor) of the Ultra96-v2 platform.

Table 3. Qualitative visual comparison of the segmented images produced by three model configurations: original (full-precision), pruned and quantized (FPGA implementation).

Image	Example 1	Example 2	Example 3
Ground truth			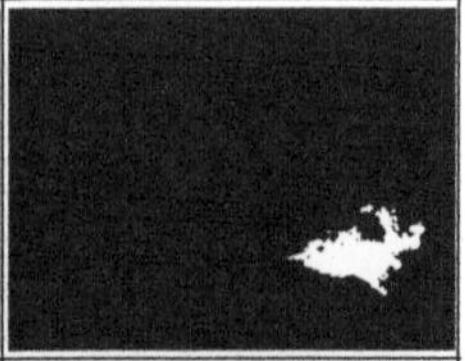
Original model		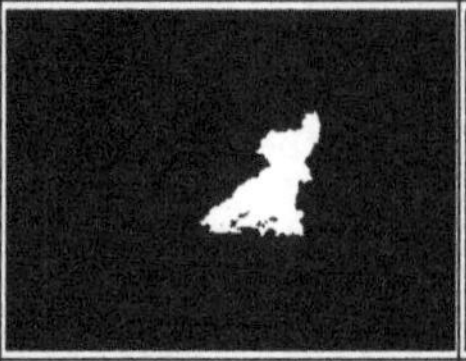	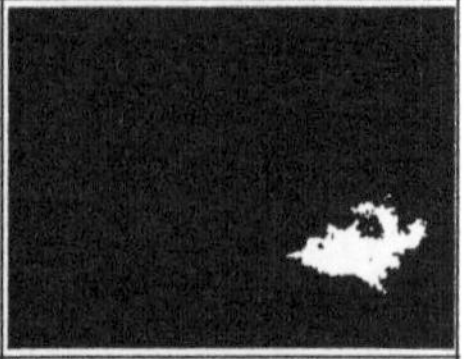
Pruned model		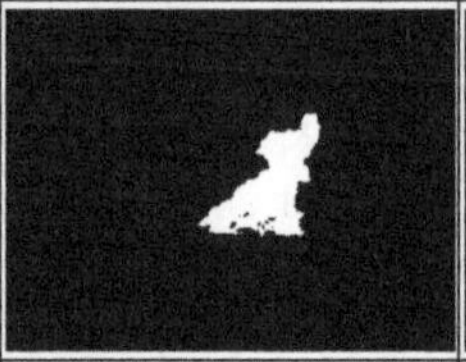	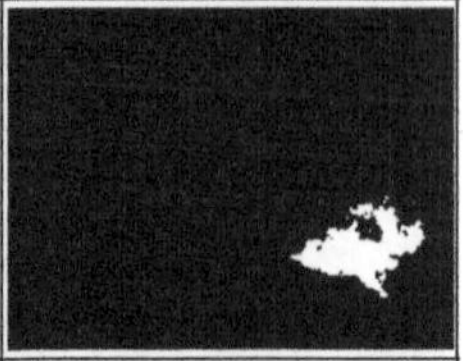
FPGA model		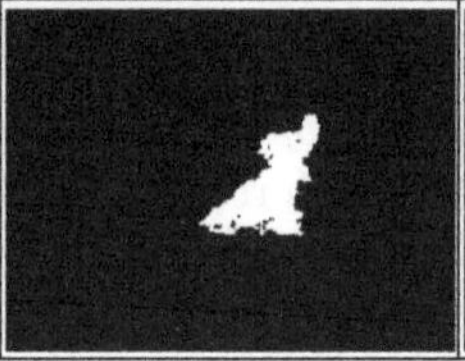	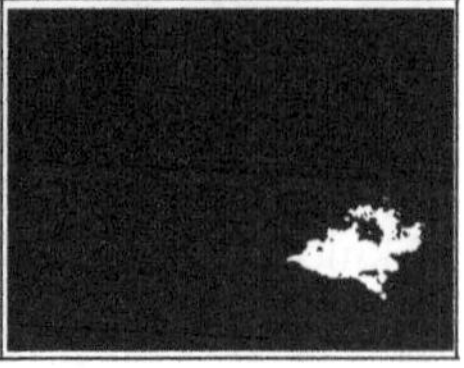

5 Conclusions

In the present paper, we implement and analyze the performance of a smart camera system based on an FPGA accelerator. A modified version of the U-Net architecture was used, to which optimization methods such as quantization and pruning were applied, effectively reducing the inference time and, at the same time, obtaining good results in the wildfire segmentation task. The frame rate obtained in the segmentation task was 33.63 FPS. It is believed that there is still some potential to improve the speed of inference by using other strategies, such as the conversion of CNN models to spiking neural networks (SNN), whose conversion has been shown to reduce inference times by reducing the number of operations performed [13]. Finally, given the results obtained, heavy computational tasks are believed to benefit from the accelerators implemented in FPGAs for their use in real-time applications such as wildfire surveillance using drones.

Acknowledgments. The authors wish to acknowledge the Mexican Council for Science and Technology (CONACYT) for the support in terms of postgraduate scholarships in this project, and the Data Science Hub at Tecnologico de Monterrey for their support on this project. This work was supported in part by the SEP CONACYT ANUIES ECOS NORD project 315597.

References

1. Abraham, N., Khan, N.M.: A novel focal Tversky loss function with improved attention U-Net for lesion segmentation. In: 2019 IEEE 16th International Symposium on Biomedical Imaging (ISBI 2019), pp. 683–687 (2019)
2. Akhloufi, M.A., Tokime, R.B., Elassady, H.: Wildland fires detection and segmentation using deep learning. In: Alam, M.S. (ed.) Pattern Recognition and Tracking XXIX, vol. 10649, p. 106490B. International Society for Optics and Photonics, SPIE (2018)
3. Berthelier, A., Chateau, T., Duffner, S., Garcia, C., Blanc, C.: Deep model compression and architecture optimization for embedded systems: a survey. J. Signal Process. Syst. **93**(8), 863–878 (2021)
4. Bramberger, M., Doblander, A., Maier, A., Rinner, B., Schwabach, H.: Distributed embedded smart cameras for surveillance applications. Computer **39**(2), 68–75 (2006)
5. Chicco, D., Tötsch, N., Jurman, G.: The Matthews Correlation Coefficient (MCC) is more reliable than balanced accuracy, bookmaker informedness, and markedness in two-class confusion matrix evaluation. BioData Mining **14**(1), 13 (2021)
6. Choi, H.-S., Jeon, M., Song, K., Kang, M.: Semantic fire segmentation model based on convolutional neural network for outdoor image. Fire Technol. **57**, 3005–3019 (2021)
7. Ciprián-Sánchez, J.F., Ochoa-Ruiz, G., Gonzalez-Mendoza, M., Rossi, L.: Fire-GAN: a novel deep learning-based infrared-visible fusion method for wildfire imagery. Neural Comput. Appl. **35**, 18201–18213 (2021)
8. Ciprián-Sánchez, J.F., Ochoa-Ruiz, G., Rossi, L., Morandini, F.: Assessing the impact of the loss function, architecture and image type for deep learning-based wildfire segmentation. Appl. Sci. **11**(15), 7046 (2021)
9. Frizzi, S., Bouchouicha, M., Ginoux, J.-M., Moreau, E., Sayadi, M.: Convolutional neural network for smoke and fire semantic segmentation. IET Image Process. **15**, 634–647 (2021)
10. Gomes, P., Santana, P., Barata, J.: A vision-based approach to fire detection. Int. J. Adv. Rob. Syst. **11**(9), 149 (2014)
11. Hafiane, A., Chabrier, S., Rosenberger, C., Laurent, H.: A new supervised evaluation criterion for region based segmentation methods. In: Blanc-Talon, J., Philips, W., Popescu, D., Scheunders, P. (eds.) ACIVS 2007. LNCS, vol. 4678, pp. 439–448. Springer, Heidelberg (2007). https://doi.org/10.1007/978-3-540-74607-2_40
12. Ioffe, S., Szegedy, C.: Batch normalization: accelerating deep network training by reducing internal covariate shift, February 2015
13. Xiping, J., Fang, B., Yan, R., Xiaoliang, X., Tang, H.: An FPGA implementation of deep spiking neural networks for low-power and fast classification. Neural Comput. **32**, 182–204 (2020)
14. Li, H., Kadav, A., Durdanovic, I., Samet, H., Graf, H.P.: Pruning filters for efficient convnets, August 2016

15. Li, H., Wu, X.-J., Kittler, J.: Infrared and visible image fusion using a deep learning framework. In: 2018 24th International Conference on Pattern Recognition (ICPR), pp. 2705–2710 (2018)
16. Ma, J.: Segmentation loss odyssey, May 2020
17. Matthews, B.W.: Comparison of the predicted and observed secondary structure of T4 phage lysozyme. Biochimica et Biophysica Acta (BBA) - Protein Struct. **405**(2), 442–451 (1975)
18. Perrolas, G., Niknejad, M., Ribeiro, R., Bernardino, A.: Scalable fire and smoke segmentation from aerial images using convolutional neural networks and quad-tree search. Sensors **22**(5), 1701 (2022)
19. Ronneberger, O., Fischer, P., Brox, T.: U-Net: convolutional networks for biomedical image segmentation. In: Navab, N., Hornegger, J., Wells, W.M., Frangi, A.F. (eds.) MICCAI 2015. LNCS, vol. 9351, pp. 234–241. Springer, Cham (2015). https://doi.org/10.1007/978-3-319-24574-4_28
20. Shi, Y., Real, F.D.: Smart cameras: fundamentals and classification. In: Navab, N., Hornegger, J., Wells, W., Frangi, A. (eds.) Smart Cameras, pp. 19–34. Springer, New York (2009). https://doi.org/10.1007/978-1-4419-0953-4_2
21. Taha, A.A., Hanbury, A.: Metrics for evaluating 3D medical image segmentation: analysis, selection, and tool. BMC Med. Imaging **15**(1), 29 (2015)
22. Talib, M.A., Majzoub, S., Nasir, Q., Jamal, D.: A systematic literature review on hardware implementation of artificial intelligence algorithms. J. Supercomputing **77**, 1897–1938 (2021)
23. Tchuitcheu, W.C., Bobda, C., Pantho, M.J.H.: Internet of smart-cameras for traffic lights optimization in smart cities. Internet Things **11**, 100207 (2020)
24. Toulouse, T., Rossi, L., Akhloufi, M., Celik, T., Maldague, X.: Benchmarking of wildland fire colour segmentation algorithms. IET Image Proc. **9**(12), 1064–1072 (2015)
25. Toulouse, T., Rossi, L., Campana, A., Celik, T., Akhloufi, M.A.: Computer vision for wildfire research: an evolving image dataset for processing and analysis. Fire Saf. J. **92**, 188–194 (2017)
26. United Nations Environment Programme. Spreading like wildfire the rising threat of extraordinary landscape fires, pp. 8, 10, 11 (2022)
27. Venieris, S.I., Kouris, A., Bouganis, C.-S.: Toolflows for mapping convolutional neural networks on FPGAs: a survey and future directions. ACM Comput. Surv. **51**(3) (2018)
28. Véstias, M.P.: A survey of convolutional neural networks on edge with reconfigurable computing. Algorithms **12**(8), 154 (2019)
29. Wolf, W., Ozer, B., Lv, T.: Smart cameras as embedded systems. Computer **35**(9), 48–53 (2002)
30. Yeung, M., Sala, E., Schönlieb, C.-B., Rundo, L.: Unified focal loss: generalising dice and cross entropy-based losses to handle class imbalanced medical image segmentation, February 2021
31. Yuan, C., Zhang, Y., Liu, Z.: A survey on technologies for automatic forest fire monitoring, detection and fighting using UAVs and remote sensing techniques. Can. J. For. Res. **45**, 150312143318009 (2015)

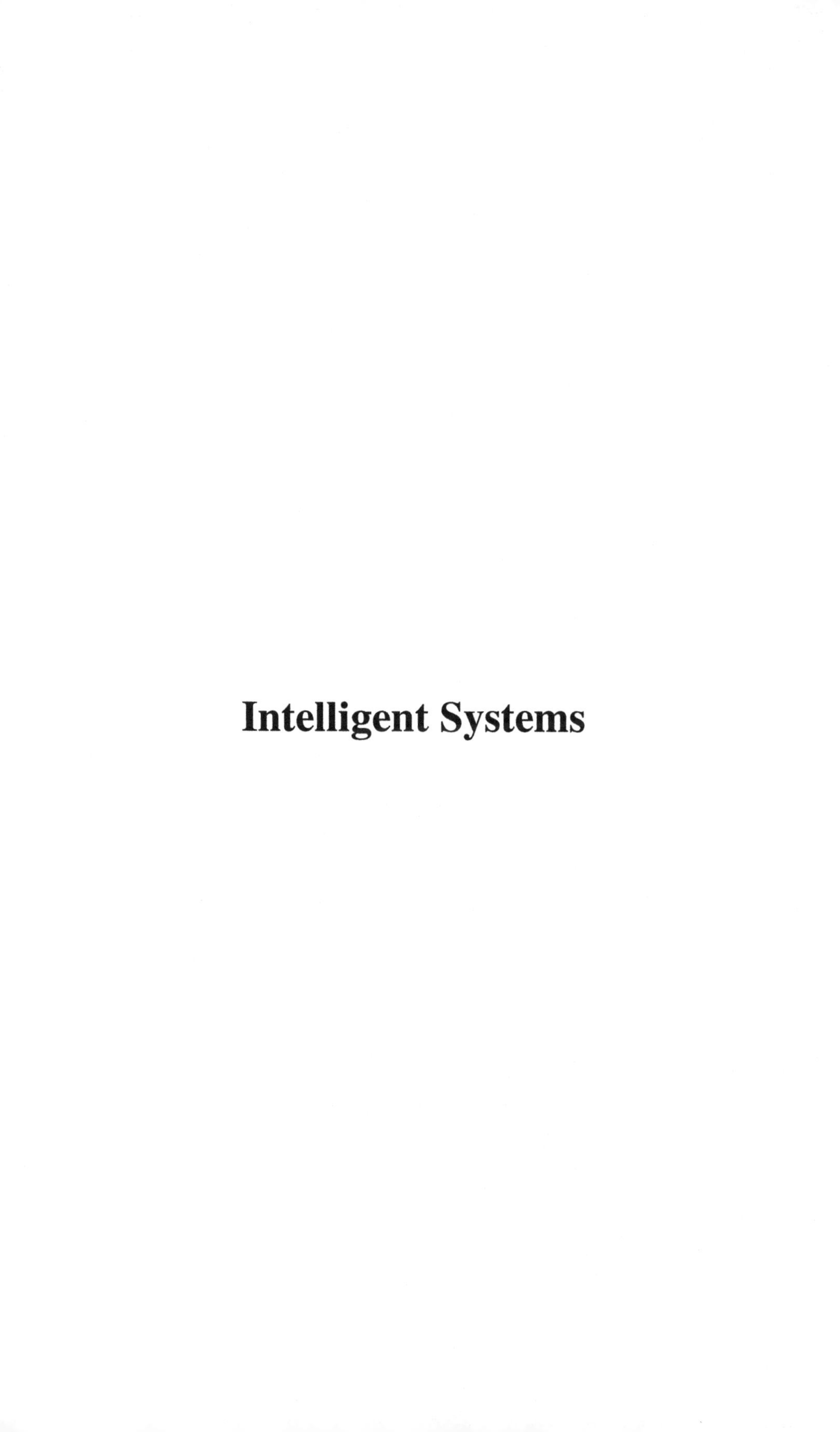

Intelligent Systems

An Argumentation-Based Approach for Generating Explanations in Activity Reasoning

Mariela Morveli-Espinoza[1(✉)], Juan Carlos Nieves[2], and Cesar Augusto Tacla[1]

[1] Graduate Program in Electrical and Computer Engineering (CPGEI), Federal University of Technology of Parana (UTFPR), Curitiba, Brazil
morveli.espinoza@gmail.com

[2] Department of Computing Science, Umeå University, Umeå, Sweden

Abstract. Human-aware Artificial Intelligent systems are goal-directed autonomous systems that are capable of interacting, collaborating, and teaming with humans. Some relevant tasks of these systems are recognizing human's desires and intentions and exhibiting explicable behavior, giving cogent explanations on demand and engendering trust. This article tackles the problems of reasoning about activities a human is performing and generating explanations about the recognized activities. For the activity reasoning, our approach is divided in two steps: a local selection and a global selection. The former aims to distinguish possible performed activities and the latter aims to determine the status of the recognized activities. For local selection, from a set of observations, a model of the world and the human is constructed in form of hypothetical fragments of activities, which are goal-oriented actions and may be conflicting. Such conflicts indicate that they belongto different activities. In order to deal with conflicts, we base on formal argumentation; thus, we use argumentation semantics for identifying possible different activities from conflicting hypothetical fragments. The result will be consistent sets of hypothetical fragments that are part of an activity or are part of a set of non-conflicting activities. For global selection, we base on the consistent sets of hypothetical fragments to determine if an activity is achieved, partially achieved, or not achieved at all. Besides, we determine the degrees of fulfillment of the recognized activities. Regarding the explanations generation, we generate two types of explanations based on the outputs of the global selection. We apply our proposal to a scenario where a man performs different activities. Finally, we make a theoretical evaluation of the explanation generation.

Keywords: Activity reasoning · Explainability · Formal argumentation

Supported by organization CAPES/Brazil and CNPq Proc. 409523/2021-6.

H. Calvo et al. (Eds.): MICAI 2023, LNAI 14391, pp. 229–240, 2024.
https://doi.org/10.1007/978-3-031-47765-2_17

1 Introduction

In the last years, some Artificial Intelligence (AI) researchers have focused their efforts on human-centric applications such as intelligent tutoring systems (read [1] for a survey about this topic) or social robotics (e.g., [2] [10] [3]). Thus, as human-AI interaction increases, there is a need for developing human-aware AI systems. The idea behind these systems is to develop approximate models about the goals or capabilities of the human in order to better interact with him/her. In [9], Kambhampati discusses some challenges about human-aware AI systems. Such challenges include recognizing the human's desires and intentions, providing proactive support, exhibiting explicable behavior, giving cogent explanations on demand, and engendering trust. In this sense, activity reasoning (AR) includes (i) recognizing activities – such as walking, running, sitting, sleeping, standing, showering, cooking, driving, etc.– which can be done by considering the recognized human's goals and (ii) reasoning about them in order to distinguish them, for example. The data for the recognition can be collected from wearable sensors or through video frames or images. AR can be used in medical diagnosis for keeping track of elderly people and in smart home environments or in driving context for providing proactive support. On the other hand, exhibiting explicable behavior or endowing systems with explainability abilities is necessary for ethical principles that must be respected to reach the trustworthiness of AI systems [8] [11]. Indeed, explainability is the main part of transparency, which can be considered the most prevalent principle in the current literature [8].

For a better illustration of the problem, let us present the following scenario. This is a scenario where a person (let us call him `Mike`) is performing some activities such as preparing the dinner, watching the tv, and talking with his mom. A supporter robot (let us call it `BOB`) observes the different actions `Mike` performs in order to recognize what dish `Mike` is preparing and what other activities he is performing. `BOB` may employ the observations about the actions and the environment for distinguishing and recognizing the activities. Thus, he can determine the status of the observed activities, that is, if they were finished or not. After the activities are recognized, `BOB` can be interrogated about the reasons that determined a given status or a degree of fulfillment of a certain activity or activities. Thus, the AR executed by `BOB` can be showed by means of explanations, which gives more transparency and trust to its results.

Endowing with explainable abilities to activity recognition systems is not a novelty. Cengiz et al. [4] provide human-level explanations for smart sensor data by means of charts, that is, image-based explanations. Das et al. [5] generate explanations in natural language for end-users about a smart home's activity recognition. That is, the explanations answer the question: why did the house do a given action?. Hayes and Shah [7] present an approach that generates explanations in natural language in the context of anomaly detection during collaborative robotics tasks. We can notice that explanations take different forms and answer different questions. Unlike these approaches, we aim to provide a proposal based on reasoning techniques, which can enrich the returned explanations.

Against this background, we can now present the research questions that are addressed in this paper: *(i) how to distinguish different activities from a set of observations?* and *(ii) how to generate explanations in AR?*

In order to address the first question, we consider that an activity is the sum of parts, which we call hypothetical fragments. These hypothetical fragments include observations about the environment, an observed action, and a goal that is achieved. For distinguishing activities, we will take into account the conflicts that may emerge between hypothetical fragments; thus, conflicting hypothetical fragments may indicate that they belong to different activities, which means that different activities were performed. We will use formal argumentation, which is an adequate technique for dealing with conflicts (also known as inconsistencies or attacks). Let us recall that an AF is basically a set of arguments and an attack relation between them; a function called argumentation semantics is applied over the AF for returning sets – known as extensions – of non-conflicting arguments. In our approach such arguments represent hypothetical fragments. Thus, we will define an argumentation framework (AF) for AR and apply an argumentation semantics for determining sets of non-conflicting hypothetical fragments. We call this part of our approach of *local selection.* The output of this part are sets of hypothetical fragments that may belong to the same activity or to activities that can be performed together. These sets are the input to the second part of our approach, called *global selection.* This part concerns about determining the status of the activities, that is, if they were achieved (completely recognized and finished), partially- achieved, or none achieved at all. Besides, it also returns how many parts of an activity were recognized.

Regarding the second question, we generate two types of explanation related to the outputs of the global selection. The first type answers the question *why is x the status of activity*`act`*?* and the second one answers the question *why is x the degree of fulfillment of activity* `act`? where `act` represents the name or the activity and x the status or the degree of fulfillment, which will be defined in Sect. 3. For generating these explanations, we will take into account the extensions returned by local selection and the definitions of activities. Figure 1 shows an schema of our proposal.

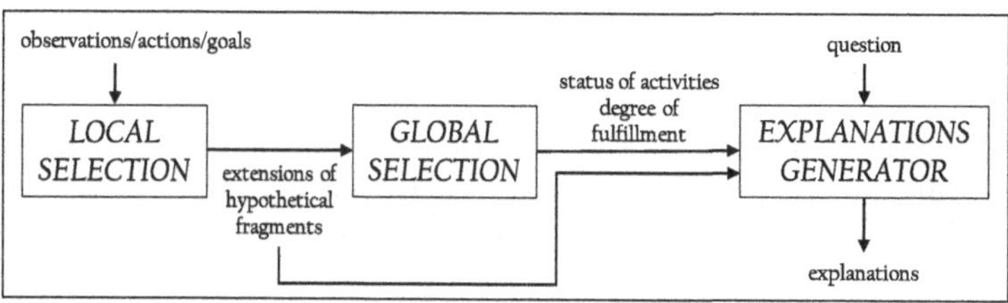

Fig. 1. Schema of our proposed approach.

Next Section presents main definitions about formal argumentation. Section 3 presents the concepts of human activity framework and hypothetical fragment of activity. Besides local and global selections are studied. In Sect. 4, we present the explanations that are generated for AR. Section 5 is devoted to the theoretical evaluation. Finally, Sect. 6 summarizes this article and outlines future research.

2 Background

In this section, we will recall basic concepts related to the Abstract AF defined by Dung [6], including the notion of acceptability and the main semantics.

Definition 1. ***(Abstract AF)*** *An Abstract AF is a tuple* $\mathtt{AF} = \langle \mathtt{ARG}, \mathcal{R} \rangle$ *where* $\mathtt{ARG}$ *is a finite set of arguments and* $\mathcal{R}$ *is a binary relation* $\mathcal{R} \subseteq \mathtt{ARG} \times \mathtt{ARG}$ *that represents the attack relation between two arguments of* $\mathtt{ARG}$*, so that* $(A, B) \in \mathcal{R}$ *denotes that the argument* A *attacks the argument* B *or* B *is attacked by* A*.*

Next, we introduce the concepts of conflict-freeness, defense, admissibility and the semantics proposed in [6].

Definition 2. ***(Argumentation Semantics)*** *Given an Abstract AF* $\mathtt{AF} = \langle \mathtt{ARG}, \mathcal{R} \rangle$ *and a set* $\mathcal{E} \subseteq \mathtt{ARG}$*:*

- $\mathcal{E}$ *is conflict-free if* $\forall A, B \in \mathcal{E}$, $(A, B) \notin \mathcal{R}$.
- $\mathcal{E}$ *defends an argument* A *iff for each argument* $B \in \mathtt{ARG}$*, if* $(B, A) \in \mathcal{R}$*, then there exist an argument* $C \in \mathcal{E}$ *such that* $(C, B) \in \mathcal{R}$.
- $\mathcal{E}$ *is admissible iff it is conflict-free and defends all its elements.*
- *A conflict-free* $\mathcal{E}$ *is a complete extension iff we have* $\mathcal{E} = \{A | \mathcal{E}\ defends\ A\}$.
- $\mathcal{E}$ *is a preferred extension iff it is a maximal (w.r.t set inclusion) complete extension.*
- $\mathcal{E}$ *is a grounded extension iff it is the smallest (w.r.t set inclusion) complete extension.*

3 Proposal

In this section, we introduce the human activity framework and the local and global selections. We study arguments in the sense of the hypothetical fragments of activities and the attack relation that may emerge between them.

3.1 Human Activity Framework and Local Selection

We start by presenting the logical language that will be used. Let $\mathcal{L}$ be a first order logic language used to represent the mental states of the agent, $\vdash$ stands for the inference of classical logic, $\top$ and $\bot$ denote truth and falsum respectively, and $\equiv$ denotes classical equivalence. We use lowercase roman characters to denote atoms and uppercase Greek characters to denote formulae, such that an atomic proposition b is a formula. If b is a formula, then so is $\neg b$. If b and c are formulae, then so are $b \wedge c, b \vee c$, and $b \rightarrow c$.

Definition 3. ***(Human Activity Framework)*** *A human activity framework is a tuple of the form* $\mathtt{ActF} = \langle \mathcal{T}, \mathcal{H}_A, \mathcal{G}, \mathcal{O}, \mathtt{ACTS}, \mathcal{C} \rangle$ *in which:*

- $\mathcal{T} \subseteq \mathcal{L}$ *is a theory.* $\mathcal{T}_A$ *denotes the set of atoms that appears in* $\mathcal{T}$*;*
- $\mathcal{H}_A = \{a_1, ..., a_n\}$ *denotes the set of hypothetical actions that a human can perform in a world. It holds that* $\mathcal{H}_A \subseteq \mathcal{T}_A$*;*
- $\mathcal{G} = \{g_1, ..., g_n\}$ *denotes a set of goals of the human. It holds that* $\mathcal{G} \subseteq \mathcal{T}_A$*;*
- $\mathcal{O} = \{o_1, ..., o_n\}$ *denotes a set of observation from a world. It holds that* $\mathcal{O} \subseteq \mathcal{T}_A$*;*
- $\mathtt{ACTS} \subset 2^{\mathcal{G}}$ *denotes a set of activities. We assume that a set of goals defines an activity;*
- $\mathcal{C} = \{(x, y) | x, y \in \mathcal{H}_A,\ x, y \in \mathcal{G},\ or\ x, y \in \mathcal{O}\ and\ x \equiv \neg y\}$.

Besides, it holds that $\mathcal{H}_A, \mathcal{G}$*, and* $\mathcal{O}$ *are pairwise disjoint.*

Example 1. Let us apply our proposal to the scenario presented in the introduction section. First let us present the theory $\mathcal{T}$ and the set of atoms $\mathcal{T}_A$ that are part of the human activity framework $\mathtt{ActF}_{mike}$. The set os rules constitute the theory: $\mathcal{T} = \{r_1, r_2, r_3, r_4, r_5, r_6, r_7, r_8, r_9, r_{10}\}$ and the set of atoms includes actions, observations, and goals: $\mathcal{T}_A = \{a_1, a_2, a_3, a_4, a_5, a_6, a_7, a_8, a_9, a_{10}, a_{11}, a_{12}, o_1, o_2, o_3, o_4, o_5, o_6, o_7, o_8, o_9, o_{10}, g_1, g_2, g_3, g_4, g_5, g_6, g_7, g_8, g_9, g_{10}, g_{11}, g_{12}, g_{13}, g_{14}, g_{15}, g_{16}\}$. The detail is presented below. The set of rules is the following:

$r_1 = in\_kitchen(x) \wedge ingredient(y) \wedge use(x, knife, y) \rightarrow have(cut, y)$
$r_2 = in\_kitchen(x) \wedge ingredient(y) \wedge peel(x, y) \rightarrow have(ready, y)$
$r_3 = in\_kitchen(x) \wedge ingredient(y) \wedge use(x, grater, y) \rightarrow have(grated, y)$
$r_4 = in\_kitchen(x) \wedge ingredient(y) \wedge use(x, frying\_pan, y) \rightarrow have(fried, y)$
$r_5 = in\_kitchen(x) \wedge fry(tomates, onion, salt) \rightarrow have(ready, seasoning)$
$r_6 = in\_living(x) \wedge take(x, rem\_control) \rightarrow turn\_on(x, tv)$
$r_7 = in\_living(x) \wedge search(x, film) \rightarrow find(x, good\_film)$
$r_8 = in\_living(x) \wedge turned\_on(tv) \wedge lie(x, sofa) \rightarrow watch(x, film)$
$r_9 = in\_living(x) \wedge muted(tv) \wedge take(x, mobile) \rightarrow make(x, call)$
$r_{10} = in\_living(x) \wedge muted(tv) \wedge speak\_with(x, y, mobile) \rightarrow have\_conversation(x, y)$

The observations and the actions perceived by $\mathtt{BOB}$ are:

$a_1 = use(mike, knife, potatoes)$, $a_2 = use(mike, knife, beef)$
$a_3 = use(mike, knife, chicken)$, $a_4 = use(mike, knife, onion)$,
$a_5 = use(mike, knife, tomatoes)$, $a_6 = use(mike, grater, carrots)$
$a_7 = use(mike, knife, carrots)$, $a_8 = peel(chickpeas)$,
$a_9 = fry(tomatoes, onion, salt)$, $a_{10} = search(mike, film)$
$a_{11} = take(mike, mobile)$, $a_{12} = take(mike, rem\_control)$
$o_1 = in\_kitchen(mike)$, $o_2 = heat(oven)$, $o_3 = ingredient(potatoes)$,
$o_4 = ingredient(tomatoes)$, $o_5 = ingredient(onion)$, $o_6 = ingredient(carrots)$
$o_7 = ingredient(chickpeas)$, $o_8 = ingredient(chicken)$,
$o_9 = in\_living(mike)$, $o_{10} = muted(tv)$

The goals associated to activities are the following:

$g_1 = have(cut, potatoes)$, $g_2 = have(cut, carrots)$, $g_3 = have(cut, onion)$,
$g_4 = have(cut, tomatoes)$, $g_5 = have(cut, chicken)$, $g_6 = have(cut, beef)$
$g_7 = have(ready, chickpeas)$ $g_8 = have(ready, seasoning)$,

$g_9 = have(fried, potatoes)$, $g_{10} = have(fried, beef)$
$g_{11} = have(grated, carrots)$, $g_{12} = turn\_on(mike, tv)$
$g_{13} = find(mike, good\_film)$, $g_{14} = watch(mike, film)$
$g_{15} = make(mike, call)$, $g_{16} = have\_conversation(mike, mom)$

Let us now define the human activity framework for the scenario. We will define three possible dinners in form of activities, activity *watching tv*, and activity *talking with mom*. The possible dinners are chicken stew, beef stew, and beef with fries potatoes. Thus, we have $\mathtt{ActF}_{mike} = \langle \mathcal{T}, \mathcal{H}_A, \mathcal{G}, \mathcal{O}, \mathtt{ACTS}, \mathcal{C} \rangle$ where:
$\mathcal{H}_A = \{a_1, a_2, a_3, a_4, a_5, a_6, a_7, a_8, a_9, a_{10}, a_{11}, a_{12}\}$
$\mathcal{G} = \{g_1, g_2, g_3, g_4, g_5, g_6, g_7, g_8, g_9, g_{10}, g_{11}, g_{12}, g_{13}, g_{14}, g_{15}, g_{16}\}$
$\mathcal{O} = \{o_1, o_2, o_3, o_4, o_5, o_6, o_7, o_8, o_9, o_{10}\}$
$\mathtt{ACTS} = \{\mathtt{act}_{chi\_stew}, \mathtt{act}_{be\_stew}, \mathtt{act}_{be\_pot}, \mathtt{act}_{tv}, \mathtt{act}_{talk}\}$ where
$\mathtt{act}_{chi\_stew} = \{g_1, g_2, g_3, g_4, g_5, g_7, g_8\}$, $\mathtt{act}_{be\_stew} = \{g_1, g_2, g_3, g_4, g_6, g_7, g_8\}$,
$\mathtt{act}_{be\_pot} = \{g_1, g_6, g_9, g_{10}, g_{11}\}$, $\mathtt{act}_{tv} = \{g_{12}, g_{13}, g_{14}\}$, and $\mathtt{act}_{talk} = \{g_{15}, g_{16}\}$
$\mathcal{C} = \{(o_1, o_9), (a_6, a_7), (a_1, a_{10}), (a_1, a_{12}), (a_2, a_{10}), (a_2, a_{12}), (a_3, a_{10}), (a_3, a_{12}),$
$(a_4, a_{10}), (a_4, a_{12}), (a_5, a_{10}), (a_5, a_{12}), (a_6, a_{10}), (a_6, a_{12}), (a_7, a_{10}), (a_7, a_{12}),$
$(a_8, a_{10}), (a_8, a_{12}), (a_9, a_{10}), (a_9, a_{12}), (g_2, g_{11})\}$

For the contraries, regarding observations, we consider that if Mike is in the kitchen he cannot be in the living at the same time. Regarding actions, we consider that activities for cooking cannot be performed at the same time with actions such as *searching a film* and *taking the remote control*; however, *taking the mobile* is an action that can be performed in any place of the house. Finally, regarding goals, we consider that only one action can be performed over an element. In this case, Mike either slices carrots or grates them. Indeed, some of these contraries can be dismissed and others considered.

Given a human activity framework, one can build small pieces of knowledge that give hypothetical evidence of the fulfilment of an activity. These pieces are made up of a hypothetical action and a set of observations of the world. These small pieces of knowledge will be called *hypothetical fragments of activities*:

Definition 4. ***(Hypothetical Fragment of an Activity)*** *Let* $\mathtt{ActF} = \langle \mathcal{T}, \mathcal{H}_A, \mathcal{G}, \mathcal{O}, \mathtt{ACTS}, \mathcal{C} \rangle$ *be a human activity framework. A hypothetical fragment of an activity (henceforth, hypothetical fragment) is represented by* $A = \langle \mathcal{S}, \mathcal{O}', a, g \rangle$ *such that: (i)* $\mathcal{S} \subseteq \mathcal{T}$ *,* $\mathcal{O}' \subseteq \mathcal{O}$*,* $a \in \mathcal{H}_A$ *and* $g \in \mathcal{G}$*, (ii)* $\mathcal{S} \cup \mathcal{O}' \cup \{a\}$ *is consistent, (iii)* $\mathcal{S} \cup \mathcal{O}' \cup \{a\} \vdash g$*, and* $\mathcal{S}$ *and* $\mathcal{O}'$ *are minimal w.r.t. set inclusion.*
$\mathtt{HF}_{\mathtt{ActF}}$ *denotes the set of hypothetical fragments that we can construct from* $\mathtt{ActF}$.

Example 2. (Cont. Example 1) From the activity framework $\mathtt{ActF}_{mike}$, a set of hypothetical fragments can be constructed, these are: $\mathtt{HF}_{\mathtt{ActF}_{mike}} = \{A, B, C, D, E, F, G, H\}$. Table 1 shows the details about these hypothetical fragments.

Observe that a hypothetical fragment is basically *a goal-oriented action* which takes as input observations of the world. From an intuitive point of view, the construction of hypothetical fragments represents the process of building *hypotheses* about the fulfillment of some possible activities. Since the hypothetical fragments are based on *hypothetical actions*, the hypothetical fragments are *defeasible*, which means that the fragments may be weakened or overturned in light of new evidence. In order to deal with the defeasible information which is present in the hypothetical fragments, we will follow a *defeasible reasoning process* based on *attack relations* between hypothetical fragments and argumentation semantics. Thus, the construction of an Activity AF that includes hypothetical fragments and their attacks along with the application of an argumentation semantics over it constitute the *local selection* of hypothetical fragments.

Table 1. Hypothetical Fragments constructed from $\texttt{ActF}_{mike}$.

ID	$\mathcal{S}$	$\mathcal{O}'$	a	g	ID	$\mathcal{S}$	$\mathcal{O}'$	a	g
A	$\{r_1\}$	$\{o_1, o_3\}$	a_1	g_1	G	$\{r_3\}$	$\{o_1, o_6\}$	a_6	g_{11}
B	$\{r_1\}$	$\{o_1, o_4\}$	a_5	g_4	H	$\{r_5\}$	$\{o_1\}$	a_9	g_8
C	$\{r_1\}$	$\{o_1, o_5\}$	a_4	g_3	I	$\{r_6\}$	$\{o_9\}$	a_{12}	g_{12}
D	$\{r_1\}$	$\{o_1, o_6\}$	a_7	g_2	J	$\{r_7\}$	$\{o_9\}$	a_{10}	g_{13}
E	$\{r_1\}$	$\{o_1, o_8\}$	a_3	g_5	K	$\{r_9\}$	$\{o_9, o_{10}\}$	a_{11}	g_{15}
F	$\{r_2\}$	$\{o_1, o_7\}$	a_8	g_7					

Attacks between hypothetical fragments lead to the identification of conflicts among activities, which determines different activities. These attacks between hypothetical fragments are defined over $\texttt{HF}_{\texttt{ActF}}$ and are captured by the binary relation $\mathcal{R} \subseteq \texttt{HF}_{\texttt{ActF}} \times \texttt{HF}_{\texttt{ActF}}$. We denote with (A, B) the attack relation between two hypothetical fragments A and B. In other words, if $(A, B) \in \mathcal{R}$, it means that the hypothetical fragment A attacks the hypothetical fragment B. For determining attacks; beliefs, actions, and goals are taken into account. Thus, a hypothetical fragment A attacks a hypothetical fragment B when (i) an observation of A is inconsistent with an observation of B, (ii) the action of A is inconsistent with the action of B, and (iii) the goal of A is inconsistent with the goal of B.

Definition 5. ***(Attacks)*** *Let* $\texttt{ActF} = \langle \mathcal{T}, \mathcal{H}_A, \mathcal{G}, \mathcal{O}, \text{ACTS}, \mathcal{C} \rangle$ *be a human activity framework,* $\texttt{HF}_{\texttt{ActF}}$ *the set of fragments constructed from* $\texttt{ActF}$*, and* $A, B \in \texttt{HF}_{\texttt{ActF}}$ *such that* $A = \langle \mathcal{S}_A, \mathcal{O}'_A, a_A, g_A \rangle$ *and* $B = \langle \mathcal{S}_B, \mathcal{O}'_B, a_B, g_B \rangle$*.* $(A, B) \in \mathcal{R}$ *if one of the following conditions hold: (i)* $\exists o \in \mathcal{O}'_A$ *and* $\exists o' \in \mathcal{O}'_B$ *such that* $o \equiv \neg o'$*, (ii)* $a_B \equiv \neg a_A$*, or (iii)* $g_B \equiv \neg g_A$*.*

So far, we have defined hypothetical fragments, which can be seen as *arguments* and an attack relation between them. We can now define an Activity AF, over which an argumentation semantics can be applied for selecting sets of consistent hypothetical fragments, that is, fragments that do not attack each other. The idea is that each set is related to an activity or a set of consistent activities, that is, activities that can be performed together.

Definition 6. ***(Activity AF)*** *Given a human activity framework* $\texttt{ActF} = \langle \mathcal{T}, \mathcal{H}_A, \mathcal{G}, \mathcal{O}, \texttt{ACTS}, \mathcal{C} \rangle$*, let* $\texttt{HF}_{\texttt{ActF}}$ *be the set of hypothetical fragments that can be built from* $\texttt{ActF}$ *and* $\mathcal{R}$ *the attack relation between them. An Activity AF is defined as a tuple* $\texttt{AAF} = \langle \texttt{HF}_{\texttt{ActF}}, \mathcal{R} \rangle$.

Before presenting the example, let us notice that a hypothetical fragment is always associated with a goal; thus, a set of hypothetical fragments can be regarded as a set of goals. To this end, let us define the following notation: Given a set of hypothetical fragments $\mathcal{E}$, $\mathcal{E}^{\mathcal{G}}$ is defined as follows: $\mathcal{E}^{\mathcal{G}} = \{g | \langle \mathcal{S}, \mathcal{O}', a, g \rangle \in \mathcal{E}\}$, this means that $\mathcal{E}^{\mathcal{G}}$ is a set of goals associated to extension $\mathcal{E}$.

Example 3. (Cont. Example 2) Let us recall that we have $\texttt{HF}_{\texttt{ActF}_{mike}} = \{A, B, C, D, E, F, G, H, I, J, K\}$. Let us now identify the emerging attacks: $\mathcal{R}_{mike}= \{(A, I), (I, A), (A, J), (J, A), (A, K), (K, A), (B, I), (I, B), (B, J), (J, B), (B, K), (K, B), (C, I), (I, C), (C, J), (J, C), (C, K), (K, C), (D, I), (I, D), (D, J), (J, D), (D, K), (K, D), (E, I), (I, E), (E, J), (J, E), (E, K), (K, E), (F, I), (I, F), (F, J), (J, F), (F, K), (K, F), (G, I), (I, G), (G, J), (J, G), (G, K), (K, G), (H, I), (I, H), (H, J), (J, H), (H, K), (K, H), (D, G), (G.D)\}$. We can now define the Activity AF: $\texttt{AAF}_{mike} = \langle \texttt{HF}_{\texttt{ActF}_{mike}}, \mathcal{R}_{mike} \rangle$.

Let us recall that the first step of activity recognition is local selection. So, let us now apply a semantics in order to obtain consistent sets of hypothetical fragments. We will apply the preferred semantics to the Activity AF $\texttt{AAF}_{mike}$. The result are four preferred extensions. Next, we present the extensions and their respective set of goals:
$\mathcal{E}_1 = \{J, K\}, \mathcal{E}_1^{\mathcal{G}} = \{g_{13}, g_{15}\}, \mathcal{E}_2 = \{I, J\}, \mathcal{E}_2^{\mathcal{G}} = \{g_{12}, g_{13}\}$
$\mathcal{E}_3 = \{A, B, C, D, E, F, H\}, \mathcal{E}_3^{\mathcal{G}} = \{g_1, g_4, g_3, g_2, g_5, g_7, g_8\}$
$\mathcal{E}_4 = \{A, B, C, E, F, G, H\}, \mathcal{E}_4^{\mathcal{G}} = \{g_1, g_4, g_3, g_5, g_7, g_{11}, g_8\}$

3.2 Global Selection

Selecting hypothetical fragments by considering argumentation semantics is only one of the steps of AR. An argumentation semantics can only suggest *multiple competing* sets of hypothetical fragments which could suggest the fulfillment of some activities. Therefore, we require *a global selection* of hypothetical fragments. By global selection, we mean a selection able to suggest:

- the status of activities, that is, if an activity was completely recognized, partially recognized, or if it was recognized at all, and
- degrees of both fulfillment and non-fulfillment of activities

Considering that a set of hypothetical fragments can be regarded as a set of goals, the status of an activity is defined as follows.

Definition 7. ***(Status of Activities)*** *Let* $\texttt{ActF} = \langle \mathcal{T}, \mathcal{H}_A, \mathcal{G}, \mathcal{O}, \texttt{ACTS}, \mathcal{C} \rangle$ *be a human activity framework,* $\texttt{AAF} = \langle \texttt{HF}_{\texttt{ActF}}, \mathcal{R} \rangle$ *be an Activity AF with respect to* $\texttt{ActF}$*, and* $\texttt{SEM}$ *be an argumentation semantics. An activity* $\texttt{act} \in \texttt{ACTS}$ *is:*

- *achieved if* $\forall \mathcal{E} \in \texttt{SEM}(\texttt{AAF})$, $\texttt{act} \subseteq \mathcal{E}^{\mathcal{G}}$

- *partially-achieved if* $\exists \mathcal{E} \in \mathtt{SEM(AAF)}$ *such that* $\mathtt{act} \subseteq \mathcal{E}^{\mathcal{G}}$ *and* $\exists \mathcal{E}' \in \mathtt{SEM(AAF)}$ *such that* $\mathtt{act} \not\subseteq \mathcal{E}'^{\mathcal{G}}$
- *null-achieved if* $\forall \mathcal{E} \in \mathtt{SEM(AAF)}$, $\mathtt{act} \not\subseteq \mathcal{E}^{\mathcal{G}}$

It is important to observe that an extension $\mathcal{E} \in \mathtt{SEM(AAF)}$ represents hypothetical fragments that argue why a particular activity is fulfilled. Thus, considering the number of goals of each activity, we can define different degrees of achievement *w.r.t.* each activity. Indeed, we can define a degree of achievement and a degree of non-achievement.

Definition 8. *Let* $\mathtt{ActF} = \langle \mathcal{T}, \mathcal{H}_A, \mathcal{G}, \mathcal{O}, \mathtt{ACTS}, \mathcal{C} \rangle$ *be a human activity framework,* $\mathtt{AAF} = \langle \mathtt{HF_{ActF}}, \mathcal{R} \rangle$ *be an Activity AF w.r.t.* ActF, SEM *be an argumentation semantics, and* $\mathtt{act} \in \mathtt{ACTS}$ *such that* $\mathtt{goals\_act} \subseteq \mathtt{act}$*:*

- act *is* (i/n)*-achieved if* goals_act *is achieved w.r.t.* SEM(AAF)*,* $i = |\mathtt{goals\_act}|$ *and* $n = |\mathtt{act}|$.
- act *is* $(1 - i/n)$*-null-achieved if* goals_act *is achieved w.r.t.* SEM(AAF)*,* $i = |\mathtt{goals\_act}|$ *and* $n = |\mathtt{act}|$.

Example 4. (Cont. Example 3*)* The second step of our approach is the global selection. Regarding the status of activities:

- $\mathtt{act}_{chi\_stew}$ is partially-achieved, all their goals are part of only $\mathcal{E}_3$
- $\mathtt{act}_{be\_stew}$ is null-achieved because only some of their goals are part of $\mathcal{E}_3$ and $\mathcal{E}_4$
- $\mathtt{act}_{be\_pot}$ is null-achieved because only some of their goals are part of $\mathcal{E}_3$ and $\mathcal{E}_4$
- $\mathtt{act}_{tv}$ is null-achieved since only some of their goals are part of $\mathcal{E}_2$
- $\mathtt{act}_{talk}$ is null-achieved since only some of their goals are part of $\mathcal{E}_1$

Regarding the degrees of fulfillment of the activities:

- $\mathtt{act}_{chi\_stew}$ is $7/7$ achieved with respect to extension $\mathcal{E}_3$ and $6/7$ achieved with respect to extension $\mathcal{E}_4$
- $\mathtt{act}_{be\_stew}$ is $6/7$ achieved with respect to extension $\mathcal{E}_3$ and $5/7$ achieved with respect to extension $\mathcal{E}_4$
- $\mathtt{act}_{be\_pot}$ is $1/7$ achieved with respect to extensions $\mathcal{E}_3$ and $\mathcal{E}_4$
- $\mathtt{act}_{tv}$ is $2/3$ achieved with respect to extension $\mathcal{E}_2$
- $\mathtt{act}_{talk}$ is $1/2$ achieved with respect to extension $\mathcal{E}_1$

4 Generating Explanations

In this section we introduce the possible explanations that can generated based on the approach presented in previous section.

In this work, the generated explanations have two parts: (i)*a core*, which includes formal parts of the AR approach and (ii) *a cover*, which includes natural language that complements the core. Thus, an explanation is a result of putting together the core and its cover for delivering a friendly answer to the user.

Let us recall that after the global selection, activities have an status and a degree of achievement. Our two explanations have to do with this information. The first question aims to answer*why does a given activity have a certain status?*. For the achieved and the partially-achieved statuses, the core of the explanation is a set of extensions, which contain all of the goals associated to the questioned activity. For the null-achieved status, the core is empty.

Definition 9. ***(Explanation for activity status)*** *Let* $\mathtt{ActF} = \langle \mathcal{T}, \mathcal{H}_A, \mathcal{G}, \mathcal{O}, \mathtt{ACTS}, \mathcal{C} \rangle$ *be a human activity framework,* $\mathtt{act} \in \mathtt{ACTS}$ *an activity,* $\mathtt{sta} \in \{\mathtt{achieved}, \mathtt{partially\_achieved}, \mathtt{null\_achieved}\}$ *an activity status, and* $\mathtt{SEM}$ *an argumentation semantics. An explanation* $\mathtt{EXP}^{\mathtt{act}}_{\mathtt{sta}}$ *for the question* $\mathtt{WHY}(\mathtt{act}, \mathtt{sta})$ *is the following:*

- ***For*** $\mathtt{WHY}(\mathtt{act}, \mathtt{achieved})$*:* $\mathtt{EXP\_CORE} = \mathtt{SEM}(\mathtt{AAF})$.
  The explanation is: $\mathtt{EXP}^{\mathtt{act}}_{\mathtt{sta}}$ = *\$*act*\$*[1] *is achieved because all of their hypothetical fragments are part of all the extensions returned by semantics \$SEM\$. These extension are: \$EXP_CORE\$.*
- *For* $\mathtt{WHY}(\mathtt{act}, \mathtt{partially\_achieved})$*:* $\mathtt{EXP\_CORE} = \{\mathcal{E} \mid \mathcal{E} \in \mathtt{SEM}(\mathtt{AAF})$ *and* $\mathtt{act} \subseteq \mathcal{E}^{\mathcal{G}}\}$.
  The explanation is: $\mathtt{EXP}^{\mathtt{act}}_{\mathtt{sta}}$ = *\$*act*\$ is partially-achieved because all of their hypothetical fragments are part of some the extensions returned by semantics \$SEM\$. These extensions are: \$EXP_CORE\$.*
- *For* $\mathtt{WHY}(\mathtt{act}, \mathtt{null\_achieved})$*:* $\mathtt{EXP\_CORE} = \emptyset$.
  The explanation is: $\mathtt{EXP}^{\mathtt{act}}_{\mathtt{sta}}$ =*\$*act*\$ is null-achieved because none of their hypothetical fragments are part of any of the extensions returned by semantics \$SEM\$.*

The next question has to do with the degree of achievement of a given activity. The explanation answers the following question: *why is an activity* act *i/n achieved w.r.t. a certain extension?*. The answer to this question provides the goals that were achieved and the goals that were not achieved. Those that were achieved are part of the extension while the non-achieved ones are not.

Definition 10. ***(Explanation for degree of fulfillment)*** *Let* $\mathtt{ActF} = \langle \mathcal{T}, \mathcal{H}_A, \mathcal{G}, \mathcal{O}, \mathtt{ACTS}, \mathcal{C} \rangle$ *be a human activity framework,* $\mathtt{act} \in \mathtt{ACTS}$ *an activity,* $n = |\mathtt{act}|$ *the amount of goals of activity* act*,* SEM *an argumentation semantics,* $\mathcal{E} \in \mathtt{SEM}$ *an extension,* $\mathtt{goals\_act} = \mathtt{act} \cap \mathcal{E}$ *a set of achieved goals for activity* act*, and* $i = |\mathtt{goals\_act}|$*. The core of the explanation for the question* $\mathtt{WHY}(\mathtt{act}, \mathtt{i/n\_achieved}, \mathcal{E})$ *is:* $\mathtt{EXP\_CORE} = \mathtt{act} \cap \mathcal{E}$ *and* $\mathtt{EXP\_CORE}^{-} = \mathtt{act} - \mathtt{EXP\_CORE}$*. The returned explanation is the following:*

- ***When*** $i = n$*:* $\mathtt{EXP}^{\mathtt{act}}_{\mathtt{degree}}$ =*\$*act*\$ is '\$i/n\$_achieved w.r.t. \$$\mathcal{E}$\$ because all their associated goals were achieved, these goals are \$EXP_CORE\$.*

[1] Text between \$\$ represent variables.

- ***When*** $i < n$: $\texttt{EXP}^{\texttt{act}}_{\texttt{degree}}$ =\$act\$ *is \$i/n\$_achieved w.r.t. \$$\mathcal{E}$\$ because it has \$i\$ associated goals achieved, these goals are \$EXP_CORE\$. Besides, its non-achieved goals are \$EXP_CORE$^-$\$.*

Example 5. (Cont. Example 4) Now, let us present some explanations for the activities status and degree of fulfillment in our scenario:

- WHY($\texttt{act}_{\texttt{chi\_stew}}$, partially_achieved): $\texttt{EXP}^{\texttt{act}_{\texttt{chi\_stew}}}_{\texttt{sta}}$= $\texttt{act}_{\texttt{chi\_stew}}$ *is partially-achieved because all of their hypothetical fragments are part of some the extensions returned by semantics* preferred. *These extensions are:* $\mathcal{E}_3$.
- WHY($\texttt{act}_{\texttt{tv}}$, null_achieved): $\texttt{EXP}^{\texttt{act}_{\texttt{tv}}}_{\texttt{sta}}$= $\texttt{act}_{\texttt{tv}}$ *is null-achieved because none of their hypothetical fragments are part of any of the extensions returned by semantics* preferred.
- WHY($\texttt{act}_{\texttt{chi\_stew}}$, 7/7_achieved, $\mathcal{E}_3$): $\texttt{EXP}^{\texttt{act}_{\texttt{chi\_stew}}}_{\texttt{degree}}$ = act_{chi_stew} *is 7/7_achieved w.r.t.* $\mathcal{E}_3$ *because all their associated goals were achieved, these goals are* $\{g_1, g_2, g_3, g_4, g_5, g_7, g_8\}$.
- WHY($\texttt{act}_{\texttt{tv}}$, 2/3_achieved, $\mathcal{E}_2$): $\texttt{EXP}^{\texttt{act}_{\texttt{tv}}}_{\texttt{degree}}$ = $\texttt{act}_{\texttt{tv}}$ *is 2/3_achieved w.r.t.* $\mathcal{E}_2$ *because it has 2 associated goals achieved, these goals are* $\{g_{12}, g_{13}\}$. *Besides, its non-achieved goals are* $\{g_{14}\}$.

5 Theoretical Evaluation

This section presents a theoretical evaluation of the explanation generator method presented in previous section. The first theorem concerns with the soundness of the explanations generator method and the second one with its completeness. Both theorems aim to demonstrate that whenever the global selection has an output about a given activity, an explanation can be generated and when an explanation about an activity exists, there is a output from the global selection.

Theorem 1. ***(Soundness)*** *Let* ActF $= \langle \mathcal{T}, \mathcal{H}_A, \mathcal{G}, \mathcal{O}, \texttt{ACTS}, \mathcal{C}\rangle$ *be a human activity framework.*

- *If* $\exists\texttt{EXP}^{\texttt{act}}_{\texttt{sta}}$*, then* $\exists\texttt{act} \in \texttt{ACTS}$ *such that* act *has a status* sta*, where* sta $\in$ {achieved,partially_achieved, null_achieved}*;*

- *If* $\exists\texttt{EXP}^{\texttt{act}}_{\texttt{degree}}$*, then* $\exists\texttt{act} \in \texttt{ACTS}$ *such that* act *has a degree of fulfillment* (i/n)*-achieved.*

Proof. By reduction *ab absurbo*. Assume that $\nexists\texttt{act} \in \texttt{ACTS}$. This means that the global selection did not have an output about its status or degree of fulfillment. This in turn means that any explanation for act could be generated, that is, $\nexists\texttt{EXP}^{\texttt{act}}_{\texttt{sta}}$ and $\nexists\texttt{EXP}^{\texttt{act}}_{\texttt{degree}}$. This contradicts the premise of the theorem.

Theorem 2. ***(Completeness)*** *Let* ActF $= \langle \mathcal{T}, \mathcal{H}_A, \mathcal{G}, \mathcal{O}, \texttt{ACTS}, \mathcal{C}\rangle$ *be a human activity framework:*

- *If* $\exists\texttt{act} \in \texttt{ACTS}$ *such that* act *has a status* sta*, where* sta $\in$ {achieved,partially_achieved, null_achieved}*, then* $\exists\texttt{EXP}^{\texttt{act}}_{\texttt{sta}}$.

- *If* $\exists\texttt{act} \in \texttt{ACTS}$ *such that* act *has a degree of fulfillment* (i/n)*-achieved, then* $\exists\texttt{EXP}^{\texttt{act}}_{\texttt{degree}}$.

Proof. By reduction *ab absurbo*. Assume that $\nexists \mathtt{EXP}^{\mathtt{act}}_{\mathtt{sta}}$ (or $\nexists \mathtt{EXP}^{\mathtt{act}}_{\mathtt{degree}}$). This means that the global selection did not have an output about its status or degree of fulfillment about act, which means that act does not exist, that is, $\nexists \mathtt{act} \in \mathtt{ACTS}$. This contradicts the premise of the theorem.

6 Conclusions and Future Work

This paper tackled the problem of activity reasoning and explanation generation. We based on formal argumentation techniques for activity reasoning and using the output of the reasoning we generate two types of explanations. We demonstrated that the explanation generation is sound and complete with respect to the reasoning.

As future research, we aim to improve the explanation generation by including new types of explanation. We have dealt with one kind of conflict; however, we want to deal with other conflicts like one relate with resources. Finally, we would like to take into account the time for reasoning with activities that occur in different time lapses.

References

1. Akkila, A.N., et al.: Survey of intelligent tutoring systems up to the end of 2017. In: IJARW (2019)
2. Belpaeme, T., Kennedy, J., Ramachandran, A., Scassellati, B., Tanaka, F.: Social robots for education: a review. Sci. Robot. **3**(21) (2018)
3. Cabibihan, J.J., Javed, H., Ang, M., Aljunied, S.M.: Why robots? A survey on the roles and benefits of social robots in the therapy of children with autism. Int. J. Soc. Robot. **5**(4), 593–618 (2013)
4. Cengiz, A.B., Birant, K.U., Cengiz, M., Birant, D., Baysari, K.: Improving the performance and explainability of indoor human activity recognition in the internet of things environment. Symmetry **14**(10), 2022 (2022)
5. Das, D., et al.: Explainable activity recognition for smart home systems. ACM Trans. Interact. Intell. Syst. **13**(2), 1–39 (2023)
6. Dung, P.M.: On the acceptability of arguments and its fundamental role in nonmonotonic reasoning, logic programming and n-person games. Artif. Intell. **77**(2), 321–357 (1995)
7. Hayes, B., Shah, J.A.: Interpretable models for fast activity recognition and anomaly explanation during collaborative robotics tasks. In: 2017 IEEE International Conference on Robotics and Automation (ICRA), pp. 6586–6593. IEEE (2017)
8. Jobin, A., Ienca, M., Vayena, E.: Artificial intelligence: the global landscape of ethics guidelines, 7 (2019)
9. Kambhampati, S.: Challenges of human-aware AI systems. arXiv preprint arXiv:1910.07089 (2019)
10. Leite, I., Martinho, C., Paiva, A.: Social robots for long-term interaction: a survey. Int. J. Soc. Robot. **5**(2), 291–308 (2013)
11. Smuha, N.A.: The EU approach to ethics guidelines for trustworthy artificial intelligence. Comput. Law Rev. Int. **20**(4), 97–106 (2019)

A Decision Tree Induction Algorithm for Efficient Rule Evaluation Using Shannon's Expansion

Vitali Herrera-Semenets[1], Lázaro Bustio-Martínez[2(✉)], Raudel Hernández-León[1], and Jan van den Berg[3]

[1] Advanced Technologies Application Center (CENATAV), La Habana, Cuba
{vherrera,rleon}@cenatav.co.cu

[2] Department of Engineering Studies for Innovation, Iberoamerican University, Mexico City, Mexico
lazaro.bustio@ibero.mx

[3] Intelligent Systems Department, Delft University of Technology, Delft, The Netherlands
j.vandenberg@tudelft.nl

Abstract. Decision trees are one of the most popular structures for decision-making and the representation of a set of rules. However, when a rule set is represented as a decision tree, some quirks in its structure may negatively affect its performance. For example, duplicate sub-trees and rule filters, that need to be evaluated more than once, could negatively affect the efficiency. This paper presents a novel algorithm based on Shannon's expansion, which guarantees that the same rule filter is not evaluated more than once, even if repeated in other rules. This fact increases efficiency during the evaluation process using the induced decision tree. Experiments demonstrated the viability of the proposed algorithm in processing-intensive scenarios, such as in intrusion detection and data stream analysis.

Keywords: Decision Tree · Rule-Based Systems · Data Processing

1 Introduction

Rules are principles or regulations defined to guide actions or behaviors. An advantage of using rules is that it is possible to represent human knowledge naturally. This advantage could be why rule-based systems share roots with cognitive science and artificial intelligence (AI) [14]. Rule-based applications are extensively used in firewall systems [7], clinical decision support systems [10], and intrusion detection systems [6]. In these situations, immediate action is usually required after the reception of new data or, in other words, these systems require (near) real-time data processing [5].

A rule consists of two parts: the premise α and the conclusion β. The premise can be composed of some so-called *filters* and the conclusion can be represented

H. Calvo et al. (Eds.): MICAI 2023, LNAI 14391, pp. 241–252, 2024.
https://doi.org/10.1007/978-3-031-47765-2_18

by a label [8]. A single filter X_i can be represented as $f_i \oplus v$, where f_i is a conditional feature, v is a value from the domain of f_i, and $\oplus$ is a relational operator from the set of relations $\{<, \leq, =, \neq, >, \geq, \in\}$. A premise can be formed from one or more filters by joining them with logical operators. A rule like that is usually denoted as $\alpha \rightarrow \beta$, and it is applicable if its premise is satisfied.

Efficiently evaluating multiple rules on a real-time data stream could be solved using a parallel or sequential approach, replicating the data flow or not. This could be more or less efficient depending on the hardware resources available for the task. However, the rule set may contain overlapping rules [12], or simply rules that share the same filters, which means that the same filter must be evaluated several times.

Having a data structure that allows evaluating all the rules simultaneously while evaluating each filter only once would be very useful and can be applied in many common-life situations. For example, decision trees are one of the most popular data structures for decision-making and representing a set of rules. However, when a rule set is represented as a decision tree, duplicate sub-trees are usually kept in the obtained structure, which could affect spatial efficiency and evaluation time [8].

The main goal of this research paper is to propose a new decision tree induction algorithm for rules evaluation without omitting any filters. The proposed algorithm follows the theoretical principles of Shannon's expansion [13], which allows to obtain a more concise rule representation, and avoids duplicate subtrees while the same filter is evaluated only once. This is very valuable in such cases where evaluating rules in (near) real-time is required, for example in intrusion detection and data streams processing tasks.

The remainder of this paper is structured as follows. First, the background about the motivation underlying this research, decision tree induction, and Shannon's expansion is described in Sect. 2. Second, the proposed strategy is presented in Sect. 3. Third, in Sect. 4, the experimental results using different settings are presented and discussed. Finally, the conclusions and future work are outlined in Sect. 5.

2 Background

When a decision tree is induced from a predefined rules set (which is not modified frequently), the temporary cost is not essential. However, in scenarios where data stream processing in (near) real-time is required, or where the time taken to add a new rule may have negative implications from a financial or business point of view, the temporary cost of inducing the decision tree acquires greater importance [2]. In addition, once the data used to create the decision tree changes significantly, restructuring the decision tree becomes a necessary task. However, it is difficult to manipulate or restructure decision trees. This is because a decision tree is a representation of procedural knowledge, which imposes an order of evaluation on the attributes [1]. One way to deal with this situation is to induce the decision tree again. This process could be performed on-demand without any noticeable delay if the amount of rules is small [1].

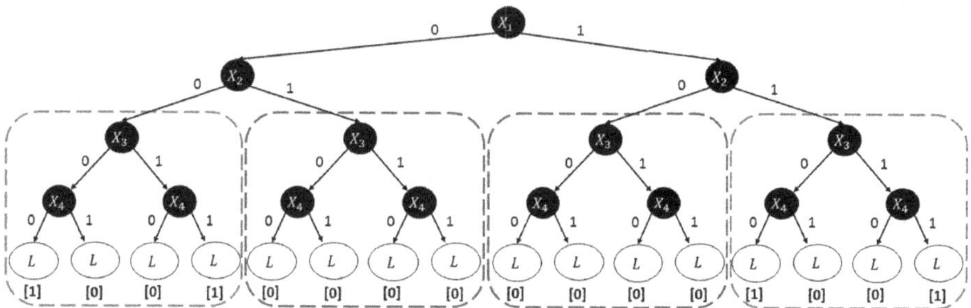

Fig. 1. Example of an induced decision tree.

There are two approaches widely addressed in the literature for decision tree induction [4]. In the most commonly used approach, the decision tree is induced from a data set [11]. In the other approach, the decision tree is induced from a rule set [1].

The primary goal of this paper differs from the latter approach. The intention here is to induce a decision tree that allows evaluating the same rules used for its induction without omitting any of the filters that make up each rule. In such a way, all rules of the rule set are applied when an instance is processed.

A decision tree is used to specify a decision procedure, where the proper sequence of filters can be evaluated [8]. The tree is traversed top-down, *i.e.*, from the root node to a leaf node, evaluating the appropriate filter at each node. Depending on the result (which can be true "1" or false "0"), the corresponding branch is selected, and the next filter to which the branch leads is evaluated. The final decision is determined after reaching a leaf node. This idea has been described in several works [8]. Figure 1 shows the induced decision tree to determine the truth-value of the following premise: $(X_1 \Leftrightarrow X_2) \wedge (X_3 \Leftrightarrow X_4)$.

As it can be seen in Fig. 1, two paths lead to two neighboring leaves labeled with 0. The paths leading to them are identical, regardless of the last edges; in fact, one is labeled with 0 and the other with 1. However, regardless of the value taken by X_4, the decision is the same $\beta = 0$. Therefore, it makes no sense to keep two separate branches leading to the same conclusion (see both sub-trees framed in red), so they can be merged and removed. This allows the final decision label to move up and the tree to be simplified. From a logical point of view, the process that allows a reduction is based on the application of backward dual resolution [8]. Such a process is applied recursively, from bottom to top, until no further reduction is possible. It is valid to highlight that only neighboring nodes can be merged and reduced, and only if they have the same decision value. Although the backward dual resolution is applied, two equal sub-trees are still present (see both sub-trees framed in blue in Fig. 1). This means that the tree obtained can be reduced even more. The literature describes a process to break down a Boolean function by Shannon's expansion [13], which can be helpful for handling the previous situation.

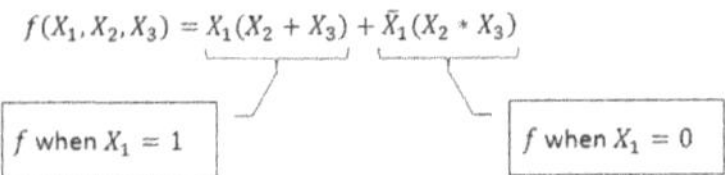

Fig. 2. Example of Shannon's expansion.

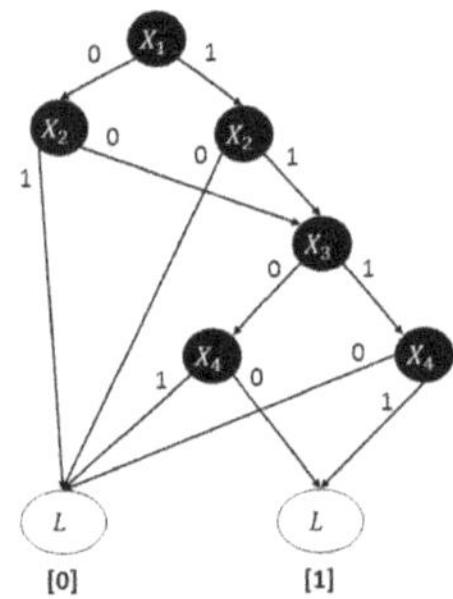

Fig. 3. Representation of the premise $(X_1 \Leftrightarrow X_2) \wedge (X_3 \Leftrightarrow X_4)$ applying the Shannon's expansion.

Shannon's expansion theorem states that every Boolean function of many variables $f(X_1, X_2, ..., X_i, X_n)$ can be decomposed as the sum of two terms, one with a particular variable X_i set to 0, and one with it set to 1. This can be seen in Eq. 1, where for $X_i = 1$ takes place $X_i f$ and for $X_i = 0$ takes place $\overline{X}_i f$.

$$f(X_1, X_2, ..., X_n) = \overline{X}_i f(X_i, ..., X_{i-1}, 0, X_{i+1}, ..., X_n) + X_i f(X_i, ..., X_{i-1}, 1, X_{i+1}, ..., X_n) \quad (1)$$

For example, given a function $f(X_1, X_2, X_3) = X_1 \times X_2 + X_1 \times X_3 + X_2 \times X_3$, its expansion in terms of X_1 is shown in Fig. 2.

If the example depicted in Fig. 2 is used for a decision tree induction, a rule could represent a Boolean function, where each variable X_j is a filter. In this sense, the operators $\times$ and $+$ are represented by the logical operators $\wedge$ and $\vee$ respectively. Therefore, once X_i is evaluated, there are two paths to follow: one path for the case where it is met ($X_i = 1$) or the other path for when it is not met ($X_i = 0$). Whatever the way forward, X_i is no longer evaluated. In theory, using Shannon's expansion allows inducing a decision tree where all the filters of the rules are evaluated optimally. This means that for every possible path that can be traversed from the root node to the leaf nodes, it is guaranteed that the filters are evaluated only once, even if the same filter is present several times. Also, Shannon's expansion allows each subtree to be explicitly displayed only once since the repeated occurrences are merged. As shown in Fig. 3, it is possible to obtain a more concise representation of the premise $(X_1 \Leftrightarrow X_2) \wedge (X_3 \Leftrightarrow X_4)$.

As can be seen in Fig. 3, the number of leaf nodes (highlighted with the label L) and filter evaluation nodes (highlighted with the label X_i) is considerably reduced regarding the representations obtained in Fig. 1. The following section

Algorithm 1: Shannon's expansion-based decision tree induction

```
   Input: R: Rule list
   Output: DT: Decision tree
1  DT ← New_Decision_Tree()
2  currentNode ← 0
3  foreach r in R do
4  |  tmpRule.Disjunction_List ← Create_Disjunction_List(r)
5  |  DT[currentNode].Rules.Add(tmpRule)
6  end
7  Set_Root_Node(DT[currentNode])
8  while DT.amountNodes != currentNode do
9  |  if DT[currentNode].Rules != empty then
10 |  |  result_0 ← Shannon(DT[currentNode].Rules, 0, DT[currentNode].Filter)
11 |  |  next_0 ← Search(DT, result_0, 0, currentNode)
12 |  |  DT[currentNode].next_by_zero ← next_0
13 |  |  result_1 ← Shannon(DT[currentNode].Rules, 1, DT[currentNode].Filter)
14 |  |  next_1 ← Search(DT, result_1, 1, currentNode)
15 |  |  DT[currentNode].next_by_one ← next_1
16 |  |  DT[currentNode].Rules ← empty
17 |  end
18 |  else
19 |  |  DT[currentNode].next_by_zero ← 0
20 |  |  DT[currentNode].next_by_one ← 0
21 |  end
22 |  currentNode + +
23 end
24 return DT
```

describes the decision tree induction algorithm proposed in this work based on Shannon's expansion principle.

3 Proposal

This paper proposed a novel algorithm based on Shannon's expansion theorem. The proposed algorithm receives a list of rules R, which is used to induce the decision tree DT. As shown in lines 1–2 of Algorithm 1, the first step is to initialize DT and place the $currentNode$ position in the root node. Then each premise is represented as a list of disjunctions, where each disjunction will contain the filters that compose it (see lines 3–6 of Algorithm 1) [8]. For example, the premise $\alpha = (X_1 \vee X_2) \wedge X_3$ is represented by a list of two disjunctions: (1) X_1, X_2 and (2) X_3. In this context, the variable X_i is called *filter*.

Each node in DT stores a list of rules with their respective disjunctions that need to be evaluated. Also, each node has a list with the rule(s) IDs that are satisfied and those IDs that are no longer satisfied at that moment. Note that this is a different feature regarding the examples analyzed in the previous section, where the final decision is determined after reaching a leaf node. In line 7 of Algorithm 1, the position of the current node is declared as the root node. Moreover, in this step, the first filter of the first rule is selected to be evaluated at the root.

Then, the loop that recursively builds the decision tree begins (see lines 8–23 of Algorithm 1). In this loop, if there are rules to be inserted in the current node,

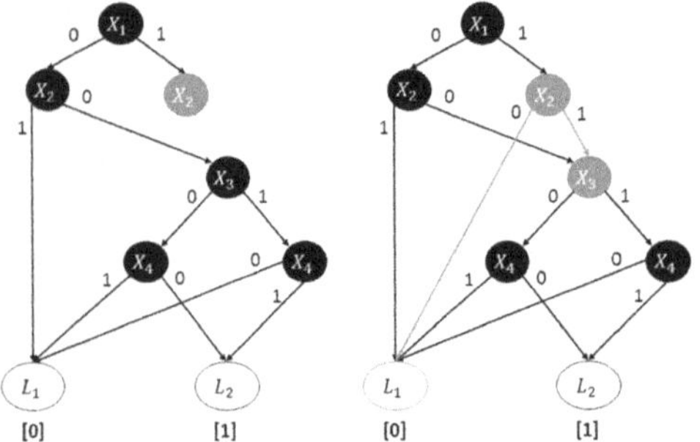

(a) Tree induced by edge 0 of the root node

(b) Leaf node L_1 and node X_3 meet the search criteria

Fig. 4. Decision tree induction using Shannon's expansion.

the Shannon's expansion is applied (see lines 9–17 of Algorithm 1). The lines 10–12 of Algorithm 1 are performed for the case where the filter evaluated in the current node is equal to zero. In line 10, the Shannon's expansion is carried out, and in line 11 of Algorithm 1 it is searched if there is any node that evaluates the same rules resulting from the expansion. The search result is set as the next node to scroll through zero (see line 12 of Algorithm 1). In the next three lines, the same three previous steps are executed, but this time for the case where the filter evaluated in the current node is equal to one (see lines 13–15 of Algorithm 1).

Let us further illuminate this step by giving an example using an example: the premise $(X_1 \Leftrightarrow X_2) \wedge (X_3 \Leftrightarrow X_4)$, introduced in the previous section, is used here. After having the tree induced by edge 0 of the root node, it is ready to perform its induction by edge 1 of the root node (see Fig. 4(a)). After applying the Shannon's expansion for the case in which the filter X_2 is fulfilled, a structure is obtained that stores the filters that remain to be evaluated (X_3 and X_4) and the rule (s) IDs that are met and those that are not met. Then, it is sought if there is any node in the decision tree that meets the result of the Shannon's expansion. As it can be seen in Fig. 4(b), the subtree with root node X_3 meets the search criteria; therefore, a new node is not created, but edge 1 of node X_2 is redirected towards the found node X_3. The same happens with edge 0 of X_2, which is redirected to the leaf node L_1.

In line 16 of Algorithm 1, after expanding the tree by 0 and by 1, the list of rules of the current node is emptied. If the current node is a leaf node, the next positions to move through 0 and 1 are defined as zero (see lines 18–21 of Algorithm 1). Line 22 increases the *currentNode* pointer to the next node in the list. Once all nodes are visited, a decision tree is returned (see line 24 of Algorithm 1).

Algorithm 2 describes how Shannon's expansion performs. For this, each rule is checked (see lines 2–13 of Algorithm 2); verifying whether its disjunctions are

Algorithm 2: Shannon

```
Input: R: Rule list, result_Type: Expanded by 1 or 0, currentFilter: Filter evaluated on
       the current node
Output: result: Shannon's expansion result
1  result ← New_Result()
2  foreach r in R do
3  |   tmpRule ← New_Rule()
4  |   foreach disj in r.Disj_List do
5  |   |   tmpDisj ← New_Disjunction()
6  |   |   Searching_Filter(tmpDisj, currentFilter, disj.Filter_List, result_Type)
7  |   |   if len(tmpDisj.Filter_List > 0) then tmpRule.Disj_List.Add(tmpDisj)
8  |   |   else if result_Type == 0 then tmpRule.Disj_List ← empty, break
9  |   end
10 |   if len(tmpRule.Disj_List > 0) then result.Rules.Add(tmpRule)
11 |   else if result_Type == 1 then result.rules_in_one.Add(r.ID)
12 |   else result.rules_in_zero.Add(r.ID)
13 end
14 return result
```

checked (see lines 4–9 of Algorithm 2); and verifying for each disjunction whether the filters are checked (see line 6 of Algorithm 2).

If the expansion is performed for the scenario in which the current node's filter is satisfied ($result\_Type = 1$), and if any of the filters within a disjunction matches the current node's filter ($currentFilter$), the disjunction is replaced by a new one devoid of filters, and the execution exits the Searching_Filter function. This occurs because, with a single filter match, the entire disjunction is satisfied. In cases where the filters are not identical or the current node's filter is not met ($result\_Type = 0$), the examined filter is added to the temporary disjunction ($tmpDisj$).

After checking all filters, if at least one filter was added to $tmpDisj$, then $tmpDisj$ is added to the list of disjunctions $tmpRule.Disj\_List$ that holds the temporary rule $tmpRule$ (see line 7 of Algorithm 2). If no filter was added to $tmpDisj$ and it is expanded for the case in which the current node filter is not satisfied, the list $tmpRule.Disj\_List$ is emptied, and the disjunctions are no longer checked (see line 8 of Algorithm 2). In line 10 of Algorithm 2, if at least one disjunction was added to $tmpRule.Disj\_List$, then, $tmpRule$ is added to the list of rules $result.Rules$ of the expansion result. If no disjunction was added to $tmpRule.Disj\_List$ and it is expanded for the case in which the current node filter is satisfied, then, the identifier of the checked rule is added to the list of rules $result.rules\_in\_one$ that are satisfied (see line 11 of Algorithm 2). If no disjunction was added, but it is expanded for the case in which the current node filter is not met, then the identifier of the checked rule is added to the list of rules $result.rules\_in\_zero$ that are not satisfied (see line 12 of Algorithm 2). In line 14, after checking all the rules, the result of the Shannon's expansion containing the rules to be evaluated, the identifiers of the rules that were satisfied and those that were not, is returned.

Algorithm 3 describes how to search for a node that meets the result of the Shannon's expansion. The search is performed in a range from the position of the

Algorithm 3: Search

Input: *DT*: Decision tree, *result*: Shannon's expansion result, *result_Type*: Expanded by 1 or 0, *currentNode*: Current node position
Output: *N*: Node

```
1  N ← 0
2  foreach N in range(currentNode, DT.amountNodes) do
3  |   if result.Rules == DT[N].Rules then
4  |   |   if result_Type == 1 then
5  |   |   |   if result.rules_in_one == DT[N].rules_in_one then return N
6  |   |   end
7  |   |   else if result.rules_in_zero == DT[N].rules_in_zero then return N
8  |   end
9  end
10 DT.Append(New_Node())
11 filter ← result.Rules[0].Disjunction_List[0].GetFilter(0)
12 DT[DT.amountNodes].Filter ← filter
13 DT[DT.amountNodes].Rules ← result.Rules
14 if result_Type == 1 then DT[DT.amountNodes].rules_in_one ← result.rules_in_one
15 else DT[DT.amountNodes].rules_in_zero ← result.rules_in_zero
16 DT.amountNodes + +
17 return N + 1
```

current node to the last node in the list. This decision avoids finding a previously created node that could create a contradiction during the decision tree induction.

For example, Fig. 5(a) shows the decision tree induced by the zero edge of the root node using two rules: (1) $X_1 \vee (X_2 \wedge X_3) \rightarrow 1$ and (2) $X_1 \wedge X_4 \wedge X_3 \rightarrow 2$. The six nodes depicted in Fig. 5(a) occupy the first six positions in the list of nodes that make up the decision tree (see Fig 5(c)). When the edge one of the root begins to be built, a node is generated with the filter X_4, in which the rule 1 is already satisfied, therefore after this node, it would only be necessary to evaluate the filter X_3 of rule 2 (see Fig. 5(b)). If the search for X_3 is performed from the beginning of the list of nodes, in position 3, there is a node that fulfills the search (see Fig. 5(c)). Therefore, an edge from X_4 to X_3 is created, which generates a contradiction in the decision tree, since the rule 1 is satisfied in the node that evaluates the filter X_4, and if it continues along the created edge, it can reach the leaf node L_2 where rule 1 is not satisfied.

To avoid the contradictions described in Fig. 5(b), the search is carried out from the current position of the node forward (see lines 2–9 of Algorithm 3). If the rules of the Shannon's expansion result are equal to those of the node being compared, then it is checked if the node contains the same rules identifiers as the Shannon result, taking into account whether the expansion was performed for the case in which the filter is met or not (see lines 3–8 of Algorithm 3). If a node that satisfies these conditions is found, it is returned (see lines 5 and 7 of Algorithm 3).

If no node was found in the search process described before, then a new node is created, and the filter to be evaluated is assigned (see lines 10–12 of Algorithm 3). In line 13, the rules that remain to be evaluated from Shannon's expansion result are added to the new node. If the rules were expanded by 1 (this is the case in which the node filter is satisfied), the rules' identifiers that

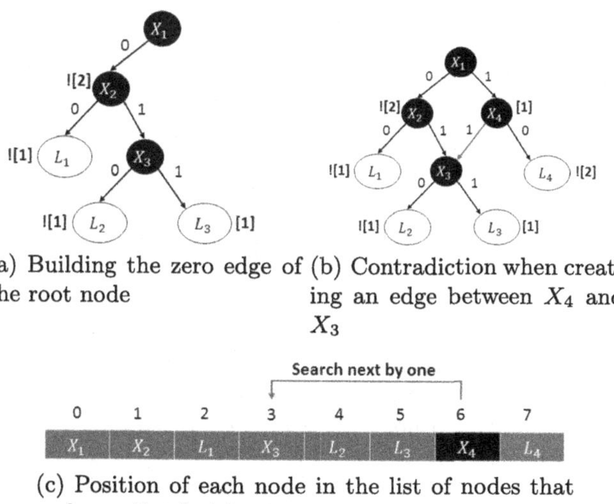

(a) Building the zero edge of the root node

(b) Contradiction when creating an edge between X_4 and X_3

(c) Position of each node in the list of nodes that make up the decision tree.

Fig. 5. Example of contradiction in a decision tree.

were satisfied in the Shannon's expansion result are added to the new node (see line 14 of Algorithm 3). If the rules were expanded by 0 (this is the case in which the node filter is not satisfied), the rules' identifiers that were not satisfied in the Shannon's expansion result are added to the new node (see line 15 of Algorithm 3). Then, the number of nodes in the decision tree is increased, and the position of the new node is returned (see lines 16 and 17 of Algorithm 3).

4 Experimental Results

The experimental results are focused on evaluating the spatial and time efficiency of the proposed algorithm, given by the number of resulting nodes in the decision tree and the estimated time to build it respectively. Considering the example presented in Sect. 2, where it is shown that the use of the Shannon expansion allows the construction of more compact decision trees than the double-backward resolution method, it is evident that the proposed algorithm offers greater efficiency in this regard. Taking this into account, it would not be fair to make comparisons with the double-backward resolution method, which is why it was not included in the experiments.

The experiments were performed on a PC equipped with an Intel Quad-Core at 2.5 GHz CPU and 4 GB of RAM. The performance of the proposed algorithm was evaluated using 25 different rules.

As can be seen in Table 1, while the number of rules and filters increases, the spatial and time efficiency of the algorithm is negatively affected. Notice that every possible path from the root node to any leaf node must evaluate all the filters of the processed rules. Therefore, if the number of rules and filters grows,

Table 1. Efficiency achieved by the proposed algorithm using different amounts of rules.

Number of rules	Number of filters	Number of nodes	Time (s)
5	10	21	0.001
10	29	597	0.01
15	39	1 562	2
20	58	17 892	143
25	68	33 225	370

then also grows the number of paths needed for evaluating all the rules. This directly affects the number of nodes that are generated and the time needed for inducing the decision tree. However, this process can be conducted offline, so once it is finished, the decision tree can be replaced.

The following experiment consists of evaluating the advantage offered, in terms of time efficiency, by using the decision tree induced by the proposed algorithm over the rules set used to induce it. In this sense, we proceed to identify a data set composed by a high number of instances that allows us to highlight the differences in processing times.

The KDD'99 data set was used for this experiment [3]. Such data set provides connection records (instances) generated by a simulation of a military network. The training collection contains 4 898 431 instances and was used to evaluate the rule sets and the induced decision trees.

As it can be seen in Table 2, five sets of rules were created for this experiment. Note in Table 2 that some rules share equal filters, and the more rules there are in the set, the greater the number of equal filters. This fact can affect the performance when the rules are evaluated individually since the same filters must be processed more than once.

The results achieved show that the induced decision tree turns out to be more efficient concerning the processing time expressed in Table 2 than the rules set. Therefore, there is a fundamental advantage of representing rules set as a decision tree using the proposed algorithm. When a rules set is evaluated, if there are equal filters in different rules, they are evaluated several times (for each rule). In contrast, when any path is traversed from the root to a leaf node of the decision tree, all the rules are evaluated without repeating a single filter, which makes the evaluation process more efficient. This fact is very appreciated in situations where processing data in (near) real-time is required.

The improvement achieved in terms of time efficiency, at first glance, it may seem insignificant. However, in some scenarios (such as intrusion detection or data stream evaluation) the volume of information generated in one second can be considerably large. For example, a 1 Gb/s Ethernet interface can deliver anywhere between 81 274 and 1 488 096 packets/s. In perspective, a 10 Gb/s Ethernet interface can deliver 10 times more packets, that is, between 812 740 and 14 880 960 packets/s [9]. Therefore, the improvement in efficiency offered

Table 2. Time taken to process the KDD'99 training collection with different rule sets and decision trees.

Number of rules	Number of equal filters	Evaluation strategy	Time (s)
5	1	Decision tree	72
		Rules set	73
10	6	Decision tree	108
		Rules set	115
15	9	Decision tree	129
		Rules set	143
20	15	Decision tree	148
		Rules set	166
25	21	Decision tree	163
		Rules set	189

by the induced decision tree could be fundamental in scenarios that require data processing in (near) real-time.

For processing high-speed data streams, a parallel or distributed approach to evaluating the decision tree could be considered. Note that even if the decision tree is parallelized, it would still be more efficient than parallelizing the rules set, since for each process there would be a decision tree that evaluates all the rules optimally. While when parallelizing the rules set, each process would have a rule, therefore to classify an instance it would have to iterate over each process until all the rules were evaluated.

It is valid to notice that no experiments were conducted to estimate the classification accuracy since the decision tree evaluates exactly the same rules used to induce it. Therefore, the results in terms of classification accuracy are the same using the decision tree or the rules set.

5 Conclusions

The algorithm proposed in this research allows inducing a decision tree from rules set where all the filters of the rules are evaluated optimally. In other words, the induced decision tree allows that by any path traveled from the root node to some leaf node, each rule filter is evaluated only once, even if it is repeated in more than one rule. This aspect allows for improving the efficiency of the evaluation process, which makes it feasible to use it in scenarios that require data stream processing in real-time or very close to it.

The experiments conducted show that when the number of nodes and filters increases, the spatial and time efficiency of the decision tree building process is negatively affected. As future work, it is intended to address this issue with an incremental proposal. Another aspect to address in future work is the use of multiple decision trees to boost up the speed of the evaluation process by applying parallel or distributed programming paradigms.

Acknowledgement. This research was supported by the Universidad Iberoamericana (Ibero) and the Institute of Applied Research and Technology (InIAT) by the project "Detection of phishing attacks in electronic messages using Artificial Intelligence techniques."

References

1. Abdelhalim, A., Traore, I., Nakkabi, Y.: Creating decision trees from rules using rbdt-1. Comput. Intell. **32**(2), 216–239 (2016)
2. Ahmim, A., Maglaras, L., Ferrag, M.A., Derdour, M., Janicke, H.: A novel hierarchical intrusion detection system based on decision tree and rules-based models. In: 2019 15th International Conference on Distributed Computing in Sensor Systems (DCOSS), pp. 228–233. IEEE (2019)
3. Al-Daweri, M.S., et al.: An analysis of the kdd99 and unsw-nb15 datasets for the intrusion detection system. Symmetry **12**(10), 1666 (2020)
4. Charbuty, B., Abdulazeez, A.: Classification based on decision tree algorithm for machine learning. J. Appl. Sci. Technol. Trends **2**(01), 20–28 (2021)
5. Herrera-Semenets, V., Pérez-García, O.A., Gago-Alonso, A., Hernández-León, R.: Classification rule-based models for malicious activity detection. Intell. Data Anal. **21**(5), 1141–1154 (2017)
6. Herrera-Semenets, V., Pérez-García, O.A., Hernández-León, R., van den Berg, J., Doerr, C.: A data reduction strategy and its application on scan and backscatter detection using rule-based classifiers. Exp. Syst. Appl. **95**, 272–279 (2018)
7. Jaïdi, F.: A novel concept of firewall-filtering service based on rules trust-risk assessment. In: Madureira, A.M., Abraham, A., Gandhi, N., Silva, C., Antunes, M. (eds.) Proceedings of the Tenth International Conference on Soft Computing and Pattern Recognition (SoCPaR 2018), pp. 298–307. Springer, Cham (2020). https://doi.org/10.1007/978-3-030-17065-3_30
8. Ligêza, A.: Logical Foundations for Rule-Based Systems. Springer, Heidelberg (2006)
9. Schudel, G.: Bandwidth, packets per second, and other network performance metrics. Abgerufen am **10**, 2010 (2010)
10. Soufi, M.D., Samad-Soltani, T., Vahdati, S.S., Rezaei-Hachesu, P.: Decision support system for triage management: a hybrid approach using rule-based reasoning and fuzzy logic. Int. J. Med. Informatics **114**, 35–44 (2018)
11. Yates, D., Islam, M.Z., Gao, J.: SPAARC: a fast decision tree algorithm. In: Islam, R., et al. (eds.) AusDM 2018. CCIS, vol. 996, pp. 43–55. Springer, Singapore (2019). https://doi.org/10.1007/978-981-13-6661-1_4
12. Zhang, G., Gionis, A.: Diverse rule sets. In: Proceedings of the 26th ACM SIGKDD International Conference on Knowledge Discovery and Data Mining (KDD20), pp. 1532–1541. Association for Computing Machinery, New York (2020)
13. Zhang, J., Yang, G., Hung, W.N., Zhang, Y., Wu, J.: An efficient NPN Boolean matching algorithm based on structural signature and Shannon expansion. Clust. Comput. **22**(3), 7491–7506 (2019)
14. Zhao, J., Wu, M., Zhou, L., Wang, X., Jia, J.: Cognitive psychology-based artificial intelligence review. Front. Neurosci. **16**, 1024316 (2022)

Reasoning in $DL\text{-}Lite_R$ Based Knowledge Base Under Category Semantics

Rodrigo Albarrán[1,2(✉)] and Chan Le Duc[2(✉)]

[1] Consejo Nacional de Humanidades, Ciencias y Tecnologías, Mexico City, Mexico
[2] Université Sorbonne Paris Nord, LIMICS, Bobigny, France
rodrigo.rodrigoalbarran@edu.univ-paris13.fr,
chan.leduc@univ-paris13.fr

Abstract. We propose in this paper a rewriting of the usual set-theoretical semantics of the Description Logic $DL\text{-}Lite_{\mathcal{R}}$ by using categorical language based on objects and arrows which are the two fundamental elements of category theory. This Description Logic is showed to be useful for extending a relational database (ABox) with an ontology (TBox) for answering conjunctive queries over such an extended database. Based on this rewriting, we define category-theoretical satisfiability of a $DL\text{-}Lite_{\mathcal{R}}$ knowledge base and show that a $DL\text{-}Lite_{\mathcal{R}}$ knowledge base is set-theoreticallly satisfiable iff it is category-theoretically satisfiable. We also introduce a tractable algorithm for checking category-theoretical satisfiability. The simplicity of the construction of such an algorithm shows the power of categorical language in comparison with existing algorithms based on the construction of a model.

1 Introduction

An advantage of using Description Logics (DLs) [1] as modeling languages lies in their ability to structure the domain of interest by grouping classes (or concepts) with properties. These properties establish connections between concepts using binary relations (or roles) to other concepts. DLs allow to represent constraints that resemble those found in conceptual modeling formalisms, enabling information structuring through features such as is-a hierarchies (inclusions), disjointness for concepts and roles, domain and range constraints for roles, mandatory participation in roles [1–3]. Within a DL knowledge base (KB), these constraints are combined to form a TBox, which contains intentional knowledge. Simultaneously, an ABox contains extensional knowledge about individuals (elements), such as whether an individual is an instance of a concept or if a pair of individuals are connected by a role [1,4]. DLs have been employed to facilitate access to extensive datasets via an intuitive high-level conceptual interface, which holds significance for both data integration and ontology-based data access. In this context, the TBox represents the conceptual and high-level depiction of the information managed by the system, while the ABox is physically stored in a relational database and accessed using standard relational database technology [2,5,6].

The primary objective of this paper is to use categorical language to rewrite the usual set-theoretical semantics of $DL\text{-}Lite_{\mathcal{R}}$ which allows for unqualified existential restrictions, inverse roles, negation of *basic* concepts and roles, and inclusion axioms of

H. Calvo et al. (Eds.): MICAI 2023, LNAI 14391, pp. 253–270, 2024.
https://doi.org/10.1007/978-3-031-47765-2_19

concepts and roles. Such a rewriting has been introduced in [7] for the Description Logic $\mathcal{ALC}$ where an object and an arrow of a concept category represent respectively a concept and a subsumption relationship between two concepts. To achieve this, we start by translating semantic constraints associated with each $DL\text{-}Lite_{\mathcal{R}}$ constructor into *properties* referring to objects and arrows of a concept category and a role category. These categories are connected with two *functors*, namely π_L and π_R, that can be viewed as projections of the domain and codomain of a role. From this, category-theoretical satisfiability of a $DL\text{-}Lite_{\mathcal{R}}$ knowledge base can be defined as the absence of arrows such as $\top \rightarrow \bot$ and $\{a\} \rightarrow \bot$ from *saturated* categories, i.e. those to which no property mentioned above is applicable, where a is an individual occurring in the ABox. The first key result of this stage consists of the equivalence of the two semantics, i.e. a $DL\text{-}Lite_{\mathcal{R}}$ knowledge base is set-theoretically satisfiable iff is it is category-theoretically satisfiable. To illustrate the simplicity and homogeneity of categorical language with respect to existing approaches based on set-theoretical semantics, we consider the following example.

Example 1. Given a $DL\text{-}Lite_{\mathcal{R}}$ knowledge base with a TBox including the following three axioms:

$$\begin{aligned} \top &\sqsubseteq A \\ A &\sqsubseteq \exists P^- \\ \exists P &\sqsubseteq \bot \end{aligned}$$

To checking satisfiability of this TBox, a set-based algorithm has to build an interpretation $\mathcal{I}$ with two individuals x, y such that $y \in A^{\mathcal{I}}$, $y \in (\exists P^-)^{\mathcal{I}}$, $x \in (\exists P)^{\mathcal{I}}$ and $(x, y) \in P^{\mathcal{I}}$. However, the third axiom forces $(\exists P)^{\mathcal{I}} = \varnothing$. Hence, the TBox is not set-theoretically satisfiable. Instead of generating individuals, a category-based algorithm creates a concept category including arrows $\top \rightarrow A$, $A \rightarrow \pi_R(P)$, $\pi_L(P) \rightarrow \bot$. By transitivity of arrows via functors π_L, π_R, we get a saturated concept category that contains an arrow $\top \rightarrow \bot$, which makes the TBox category-theoretically unsatisfiable. A key result in Sect. 3 shows that set-theoretical and category-theoretical satisfiabilities are equivalent. □

From the definition of saturated categories, we can directly design an algorithm for checking satisfiability of a $DL\text{-}Lite_{\mathcal{R}}$ knowledge base by using a set of rules devised from the properties introduced in this definition. One of the most significant advantages of this novel approach consists of considering all semantic constraints as arrows of categories without referring to set membership. This enables us to handle the ABox and TBox in a unified manner, and thus facilitate dealing with conjunctive queries.

An early application of category theory to logic consists in an appropriate axiomatization of set theory that involves extending the description of algebraic theories in category-theoretic terms to first-order theories by introducing quantification as a specific type of adjunction [8]. Goldblatt [9] and Saunders et al. [10] turned out a possibility to use categorical structures such as product, coproduct and adjunction to represent conjunction, disjunction and quantifications. Despite being relatively scarce in the literature, there have been connections between category theory and Description Logics (DLs). Notably, Spivak et al. [11] employed category theory to define a high-level graphical language, akin to OWL (which is based on DLs), for knowledge representation, rather than using it as a foundational formalism for reasoning. Recently, a novel reformulation of the description logic $\mathcal{ALC}$ with general TBoxes has been developed by utilizing categorical language [7]. In this paper we propose category-theoretical semantics of ABoxes and some constructors such as inverse roles and role subsumptions which are not allowed in $\mathcal{ALC}$.

The paper is organized as follows. Section 2 presents the essential of $DL\text{-}Lite_{\mathcal{R}}$ with its usual set-theoretical semantics. Section 3 introduces category-theoretical semantics of $DL\text{-}Lite_{\mathcal{R}}$ and shows that it is equivalent to the usual set-theoretical one in terms of satisfiability. In Sect. 4, we propose a tractable algorithm for checking category-theoretical satisfiability of a $DL\text{-}Lite_{\mathcal{R}}$ knowledge base and illustrate our algorithm with an example. In Sect. 5, we discuss the results and future work.

2 Set-Theoretical Semantics of $DL\text{-}Lite_{\mathcal{R}}$

We start by introducing the syntax and semantics of $DL\text{-}Lite_{\mathcal{R}}$ [1]. Let **I**, **C** and **R** be non-empty sets of individual, concept and role names respectively. In $DL\text{-}Lite_{\mathcal{R}}$, a concept or role can be atomic, basic or general which is defined as follows.

Definition 1 (Syntax). *We use A, B, C to denote atomic, basic and general concepts, and P, R, E to denote atomic, basic and general roles respectively such that:*

- *a concept or role name is an atomic concept or role.*
- *a basic concept B is either A or $\exists R$*
- *a general concept C is either B or $\neg B$*
- *a basic role R is either P or P^-*
- *a general role E is either R or $\neg R$*

An ABox is a finite set of assertions of the following forms
$A(a)$ $\quad$ $P(a, b)$
A TBox is a finite set of axioms of the following forms
$B \sqsubseteq C$ $\quad$ $R \sqsubseteq E$
A $DL\text{-}Lite_{\mathcal{R}}$ knowledge base $\mathcal{K}$ consists of a TBox $\mathcal{T}$ and an ABox $\mathcal{T}$, written $\mathcal{K} = \langle \mathcal{T}, \mathcal{A} \rangle$.

Definition 2 (Set-theoretical semantics). *The semantics of concept descriptions is defined by using an interpretation $\mathcal{I} = (\Delta^{\mathcal{I}}, \cdot^{\mathcal{I}})$ where the interpretation domain $\Delta^{\mathcal{I}}$ is a non-empty set, and the interpretation function $\cdot^{\mathcal{I}}$ maps each concept name $C \in$ **C** to a set $C^{\mathcal{I}} \subseteq \Delta^{\mathcal{I}}$ and each role name $P \in$ **R** to a binary relation $P^{\mathcal{I}} \subseteq \Delta^{\mathcal{I}} \times \Delta^{\mathcal{I}}$. The mapping $\cdot^{\mathcal{I}}$ is extended to $\top, \bot$, basic and general concepts as follows:*

$$\bot^{\mathcal{I}} = \varnothing,\ \top^{\mathcal{I}} = \Delta^{\mathcal{I}}$$
$$(P^-)^{\mathcal{I}} = \{(b, a) \in \Delta^{\mathcal{I}} \times \Delta^{\mathcal{I}} | (a, b) \in P^{\mathcal{I}}\}$$
$$(\exists P)^{\mathcal{I}} = \{a \in \Delta^{\mathcal{I}} | \exists b : (a, b) \in P^{\mathcal{I}}\}$$
$$(\neg B)^{\mathcal{I}} = \Delta^{\mathcal{I}} \backslash B^{\mathcal{I}},\ (\neg R)^{\mathcal{I}} = \Delta^{\mathcal{I}} \times \Delta^{\mathcal{I}} \backslash P^{\mathcal{I}}$$

An interpretation $\mathcal{I}$ assigns each individual name $a \in \boldsymbol{I}$ to an element $a^{\mathcal{I}} \in \Delta^{\mathcal{I}}$ such that $a^{\mathcal{I}} \in A^{\mathcal{I}}$ for each concept assertion $A(a)$, and $(a^{\mathcal{I}}, b^{\mathcal{I}}) \in P^{\mathcal{I}}$ for each role assertion $P(a, b)$. If $\mathcal{I}$ satisfies all the concept assertions and role assertions from an ABox, then we say that $\mathcal{I}$ is a model of the ABox, written $\mathcal{I} \models \mathcal{A}$.

An interpretation $\mathcal{I}$ satisfies an axiom or GCI (general concept inclusion) $B \sqsubseteq C$ if $B^{\mathcal{I}} \subseteq C^{\mathcal{I}}$. If $\mathcal{I}$ satisfies all axioms from a TBox, then we say that $\mathcal{I}$ is a model of the TBox, written $\mathcal{I} \models \mathcal{T}$.

A knowledge base $\mathcal{K} = \langle \mathcal{T}, \mathcal{A} \rangle$ is set-theoretically satisfiable if there is an interpretation $\mathcal{I}$ such that $\mathcal{I} \models \mathcal{A}$ and $\mathcal{I} \models \mathcal{T}$, written $\mathcal{I} \models \mathcal{K}$. In this case, we say that $\mathcal{I}$ is a model of $\mathcal{K}$. A concept C is set-theoretically satisfiable with respect to a knowledge base $\mathcal{K}$ if there is a model $\mathcal{I}$ of $\mathcal{K}$ such that $C \neq \varnothing$.

3 Category-Theoretical Semantics of $DL\text{-}Lite_{\mathcal{R}}$

In order to characterize the semantics of $DL\text{-}Lite_{\mathcal{R}}$ in terms of category theory without set membership, we use objects and arrows of categories to represent concepts/roles and subsumption relationships respectively. We use ideas from [7] to introduce the following definitions.

Definition 3. *Let **C** and **R** be non-empty sets of concept names and role names respectively. We define a concept category $\mathscr{C}_C$ and a role category $\mathscr{C}_R$ such that the following properties are fulfilled:*

- *Each concept name from **C** is an object in the category $\mathscr{C}_C$. In particular $\bot$ and $\top$ are respectively initial and terminal objects in $\mathscr{C}_C$.*
- *Each role name from **R** is an object in the category $\mathscr{C}_R$. In particular $R_\bot$ and $R_\top$ are respectively initial and terminal objects in $\mathscr{C}_R$.*
- *There is an identity arrow $Id : C \to C$ for each object C from $\mathscr{C}_C$ and $Id : R \to R$ for each object R from $\mathscr{C}_R$.*
- *If there are two arrows f, g such that $f : E \to F$ and $g : F \to G$ from $\mathscr{C}_C$ (resp. $\mathscr{C}_R$), then the arrow $g \circ f : E \to G$ is in $\mathscr{C}_C$ (resp. $\mathscr{C}_R$).*

According to Definition 3, for any arrow $C \to D$, C and D are called the *domain* and *codomain* of the arrow. We use $Ob(\mathscr{C})$, $Hom(\mathscr{C})$ to denote the collections of objects and arrows of a category $\mathscr{C}$. Thereafter, we assume that these collections do not have duplicates. Hence, we can deal with these collections as sets.

Definition 4. *For concept and role categories $\mathscr{C}_C$ and $\mathscr{C}_R$, we define two functors $\pi_L : \mathscr{C}_R \to \mathscr{C}_C$ and $\pi_R : \mathscr{C}_R \to \mathscr{C}_C$ that associate objects $\pi_L(R)$, $\pi_R(R)$ of $\mathscr{C}_C$ to each object R of $\mathscr{C}_R$ such that the following properties hold.*

4.1 The functors preserve the initial and terminal objects, i.e. $\pi_L(R_\bot) = \bot$, $\pi_R(R_\bot) = \bot$, $\pi_L(R_\top) = \top$ and $\pi_R(R_\top) = \top$.
4.2 The functors preserve arrows, i.e. $\pi_L(f) : \pi_L(R_1) \to \pi_L(R_2)$ and $\pi_R(f) : \pi_R(R_1) \to \pi_R(R_2)$ for each arrow $f : R_1 \to R_2$ of $\mathscr{C}_R$.

The two last definitions allow us to equip $\mathscr{C}_C$ and $\mathscr{C}_R$ with categorical basis from category theory. We need to instantiate it to obtain categories which capture semantic constraints coming from TBox and ABox. The following definition extends $\mathscr{C}_C$ and $\mathscr{C}_R$ in such a way that they express the axioms of a TBox and assertions of an ABox as arrows. In particular, we use individual objects $\{a\}$ in $\mathscr{C}_C$ or $\{(a, b)\}$ in $\mathscr{C}_R$ to represent individuals a, b occurring in an ABox.

Definition 5 (Category-theoretical semantics of TBox and ABox). *Let $\mathcal{K} = \langle \mathcal{T}, \mathcal{A} \rangle$ be a $DL\text{-}Lite_{\mathcal{R}}$ knowledge base, and $\mathscr{C}_C$, $\mathscr{C}_R$ are concept and role categories. We say that $\mathscr{C}_C$ and $\mathscr{C}_R$ are concept and role categories for $\mathcal{K}$ if the following conditions are fulfilled.*

1. *If $B \sqsubseteq C \in \mathcal{T}$ then $B, C \in Ob(\mathscr{C}_C)$ and $B \to C \in Hom(\mathscr{C}_C)$.*
2. *If $R \sqsubseteq E \in \mathcal{T}$ then $R, E \in Ob(\mathscr{C}_R)$ and $R \to E \in Hom(\mathscr{C}_R)$.*
3. *If $A(a) \in \mathcal{A}$ then $\{a\}, A \in Ob(\mathscr{C}_C)$ and $\{a\} \to A \in Hom(\mathscr{C}_C)$.*
4. *If $P(a, b) \in \mathcal{A}$ then $\{a\}, \{b\} \in Ob(\mathscr{C}_C)$, $\{(a, b)\}, P \in Ob(\mathscr{C}_R)$ and $\{(a, b)\} \to P \in Hom(\mathscr{C}_R)$.*

It is straightforward to prove that if the arrows in categories $\mathscr{C}_C$ and $\mathscr{C}_R$ are viewed as usual subsumption relationships, then set-theoretical and category-theoretical semantics are equivalent. For instance, (i) if $B \sqsubseteq C \in \mathcal{T}$ then, by Definition 5, we have $B \to C \in Hom(\mathscr{C}_C)$, and $B^{\mathcal{I}} \subseteq C^{\mathcal{I}}$ for all model $\mathcal{I}$ of $\mathcal{T}$; (ii) if $P(a, b) \in \mathcal{A}$ then, by Definition 5, we have $\{(a, b)\} \to P \in Hom(\mathscr{C}_R)$, and $(a, b)^{\mathcal{I}} \in P^{\mathcal{I}}$ for all model $\mathcal{I}$ of $\mathcal{A}$.

4 Category-Theoretical Satisfiability for $DL\text{-}Lite_{\mathcal{R}}$

In order to put together all semantic constrains defined in terms of categorical language, we introduce the following definition that captures the category semantics for $DL\text{-}Lite_{\mathcal{R}}$ in terms of rules.

Definition 6. *Let $\mathcal{K} = \langle \mathcal{T}, \mathcal{A} \rangle$ be a $DL\text{-}Lite_{\mathcal{R}}$ knowledge base. Let $\mathscr{C}_C$ and $\mathscr{C}_R$ be a concept and role categories for $\mathcal{K}$. We say that $\mathscr{C}_C$ and $\mathscr{C}_R$ are saturated if the following properties are satisfied.*

Categorical basis:

6.1 *If $E \in Ob(\mathscr{C}_R)$, then $\pi_L(E), \pi_R(E) \in Ob(\mathscr{C}_C)$*
6.2 *If $C \in Ob(\mathscr{C}_C)$, then $C \to C$, $C \to \top$ and $\bot \to C \in Hom(\mathscr{C}_C)$*
6.3 *If $E \in Ob(\mathscr{C}_R)$, then $E \to E$, $E \to R_\top$ and $R_\bot \to E \in Hom(\mathscr{C}_R)$*
6.4 *$\pi_L(E) \to \bot \in Hom(\mathscr{C}_C)$ or $\pi_R(E) \to \bot \in Hom(\mathscr{C}_C)$ iff $E \to R_\bot \in Hom(\mathscr{C}_R)$*
6.5 *If $C_1, C_2, C_3 \in Ob(\mathscr{C}_C)$ and $C_1 \to C_2$, $C_2 \to C_3 \in Hom(\mathscr{C}_C)$ then $C_1 \to C_3 \in Hom(\mathscr{C}_C)$*
6.6 *If $E_1, E_2, E_3 \in Ob(\mathscr{C}_R)$ and $E_1 \to E_2$, $E_2 \to E_3 \in Hom(\mathscr{C}_R)$ then $E_1 \to E_3 \in Hom(\mathscr{C}_R)$*

TBox:

6.7 *If $B \sqsubseteq C \in \mathcal{T}$ then $B, C \in Ob(\mathscr{C}_C)$ and $B \to C \in Hom(\mathscr{C}_C)$*

6.8 *If* $R \sqsubseteq E \in \mathcal{T}$ *then* $R, E \in Ob(\mathscr{C}_R)$ *and* $R \to E$, $\pi_L(R) \to \pi_L(E)$, $\pi_R(R) \to \pi_R(E) \in Hom(\mathscr{C}_R)$

ABox:

6.9 *If* $A(a) \in \mathcal{A}$ *then* $A, \{a\} \in Ob(\mathscr{C}_C)$, $\{a\} \to A \in Hom(\mathscr{C}_C)$

6.10 *If* $P(a,b) \in \mathcal{A}$ *then* $\{a\}, \{b\} \in Ob(\mathscr{C}_C)$, $P, P^-, \{(a,b)\} \in Ob(\mathscr{C}_R)$, $\{a\} \to \pi_L(P)$, $\{b\} \to \pi_R(P) \in Hom(\mathscr{C}_C)$ *and* $\{(a,b)\} \to P \in Hom(\mathscr{C}_R)$

Existential restriction:

6.11 *If* $\exists P \in Ob(\mathscr{C}_C)$, *then* $P \in Ob(\mathscr{C}_R)$, $\pi_L(P) \leftrightarrows \exists P \in Hom(\mathscr{C}_C)$

6.12 *If* $\exists P^- \in Ob(\mathscr{C}_C)$, *then* $P, P^- \in Ob(\mathscr{C}_R)$, $\pi_R(P) \leftrightarrows \exists P^- \in Hom(\mathscr{C}_C)$

Inverse role:

6.13 *If* $P^- \in Ob(\mathscr{C}_R)$ *then* $\pi_L(P) \leftrightarrows \pi_R(P^-), \pi_R(P) \leftrightarrows \pi_L(P^-) \in Hom(\mathscr{C}_C)$

6.14 $P_1 \to P_2 \in Hom(\mathscr{C}_R)$ *iff* $P_1^- \to P_2^- \in Hom(\mathscr{C}_R)$; *and* $P_1 \to P_2^- \in Hom(\mathscr{C}_R)$ *iff* $P_1^- \to P_2 \in Hom(\mathscr{C}_R)$

6.15 $\{(a,b)\} \to P \in Hom(\mathscr{C}_R)$ *and* $P^- \in Ob(\mathscr{C}_R)$ *iff* $\{(b,a)\} \to P^- \in Hom(\mathscr{C}_R)$

Negation:

6.16 *If* $R \to R_1 \in Hom(\mathscr{C}_R)$ *and* $R \to \neg R_1 \in Hom(\mathscr{C}_R)$, *then* $R \to R_\perp \in Hom(\mathscr{C}_R)$

6.17 *If* $B \to B_1 \in Hom(\mathscr{C}_C)$ *and* $B \to \neg B_1 \in Hom(\mathscr{C}_C)$, *then* $B \to \perp \in Hom(\mathscr{C}_C)$

Note that Definition 6 tells us just objects and arrows that should be contained in a saturated category. It never prevents any object or an arrow from occurring in such a category. For this reason, we need the following definition.

Definition 7. *A saturated category (either concept or role)* $\mathscr{C}$ *is minimal if it satisfies the following conditions:*

7.1 *There is no other saturated category* $\mathscr{C}'$ *such that* $Hom(\mathscr{C}') \subsetneq Hom(\mathscr{C})$,
7.2 $C \in Ob(\mathscr{C})$ *iff there is some* $C \to D \in Hom(\mathscr{C})$ *or* $D \to C \in Hom(\mathscr{C})$.

In Definition 7, the first condition ensures that $Hom(\mathscr{C})$ contains only arrows added by applying a property in Definition 6, i.e. $X \to Y \in Hom(\mathscr{C})$ iff $X \to Y$ occurs in the conclusion of a property in Definition 6. The second condition ensures that $Ob(\mathscr{C})$ contains only objects coming from arrows in $Hom(\mathscr{C})$. Moreover, Definition 7 guarantees that there always exists a minimal saturated category.

Lemma 1. *Let* $\mathcal{K} = \langle \mathcal{T}, \mathcal{A} \rangle$ *be a DL-Lite*$_\mathcal{R}$ *knowledge base. Let* $\mathscr{C}_C$ *and* $\mathscr{C}_R$ *be minimal saturated concept and role categories for* $\mathcal{K}$. *For every model* $\mathcal{I}$ *of* $\mathcal{K}$, *if* $C \to D \in Hom(\mathscr{C}_C) \cup Hom(\mathscr{C}_R)$, *i.e. for each arrow added by the Definition 6, then* $C^\mathcal{I} \subseteq D^\mathcal{I}$.

Proof. We prove the lemma for each arrow added to $Hom(\mathscr{C}_C)$ or $Hom(\mathscr{C}_R)$ by applying properties in the Definition 6.

- Property 6.2 adds arrows $C \to C$, $C \to \top$, $\perp \to C$ to $Hom(\mathscr{C}_C)$. By the definition of $\mathcal{I}$, we have $C^\mathcal{I} \subseteq C^\mathcal{I}$, $C^\mathcal{I} \subseteq \top^\mathcal{I}$, $\perp^\mathcal{I} \subseteq C^\mathcal{I}$ for all concept object C.
- Property 6.3 adds arrows $R \to R$, $R \to R_\top$, $R_\perp \to R$ to $Hom(\mathscr{C}_R)$. By the definition of $\mathcal{I}$, we have $R^\mathcal{I} \subseteq R^\mathcal{I}$, $R^\mathcal{I} \subseteq (R_\top)^\mathcal{I}$, $(R_\perp)^\mathcal{I} \subseteq R^\mathcal{I}$ for all role object R.

- Assume that $\pi_L(E) \rightarrow \perp \in Hom(\mathscr{C}_C)$ or $\pi_R(E) \rightarrow \perp \in Hom(\mathscr{C}_C)$. By Property 4.1, we have $E \rightarrow R_\perp \in Hom(\mathscr{C}_R)$ since π_L and π_R are functors. In this case, Property 6.4 adds to $Hom(\mathscr{C}_R)$ an arrow $E \rightarrow R_\perp$. By the definition of $\mathcal{I}$, we have $E^\mathcal{I} \subseteq (R_\perp)^\mathcal{I}$. Conversely, assume that $E \rightarrow R_\perp \in Hom(\mathscr{C}_R)$. Since π_L and π_R are functors, we have $\pi_L(E) \rightarrow \perp \in Hom(\mathscr{C}_C)$ and $\pi_R(E) \rightarrow \perp \in Hom(\mathscr{C}_C)$. In this case, Property 6.4 adds to $Hom(\mathscr{C}_C)$ arrows $\pi_L(E) \rightarrow \perp$ and $\pi_R(E) \rightarrow \perp$. By the definition of $\mathcal{I}$ and $E^\mathcal{I} \rightarrow (R_\perp)^\mathcal{I}$, we have $\pi_L(E)^\mathcal{I} \rightarrow \perp^\mathcal{I}$ and $\pi_R(E)^\mathcal{I} \rightarrow \perp^\mathcal{I}$.
- Property 6.5 adds an arrow $C_1 \rightarrow C_3$ to $Hom(\mathscr{C}_C)$ if $C_1 \rightarrow C_2$, $C_2 \rightarrow C_3 \in Hom(\mathscr{C}_C)$. By the hypothesis, we have $C_1^\mathcal{I} \subseteq C_2^\mathcal{I}$, $C_2^\mathcal{I} \subseteq C_3^\mathcal{I}$. This implies that $C_1^\mathcal{I} \subseteq C_3^\mathcal{I}$.
- Property 6.6 adds an arrow $E_1 \rightarrow E_3$ to $Hom(\mathscr{C}_R)$ if $E_1 \rightarrow E_2$, $E_2 \rightarrow E_3 \in Hom(\mathscr{C}_R)$. By the hypothesis, we have $E_1^\mathcal{I} \subseteq E_2^\mathcal{I}$, $E_2^\mathcal{I} \subseteq E_3^\mathcal{I}$. This implies that $E_1^\mathcal{I} \subseteq E_3^\mathcal{I}$.
- Property 6.7 adds arrow $B \rightarrow C$ to $Hom(\mathscr{C}_C)$ with $B \sqsubseteq C \in \mathcal{T}$. Since $\mathcal{I}$ is a model of $\mathcal{K}$, we have $B^\mathcal{I} \subseteq C^\mathcal{I}$.
- Property 6.8 adds arrows $R \rightarrow E$, $\pi_L(R) \rightarrow \pi_L(E)$ and $\pi_R(R) \rightarrow \pi_R(E)$ to $Hom(\mathscr{C}_R)$ if $R \sqsubseteq E \in \mathcal{T}$. Since $\mathcal{I}$ is a model of $\mathcal{K}$, we have $R^\mathcal{I} \subseteq E^\mathcal{I}$. By Property 4.2 we have π_L, π_R are functors. Since $\mathcal{I}$ is a model of $\mathcal{K}$, we have $\pi_L(R)^\mathcal{I} \subseteq \pi_L(E)^\mathcal{I}$, $\pi_R(R)^\mathcal{I} \subseteq \pi_R(E)^\mathcal{I}$ for all roles R and E.
- Property 6.9 adds arrow $\{a\} \rightarrow A$ to $Hom(\mathscr{C}_C)$. By the definition of $\mathcal{I}$ and by the Definition 5 we have $\{a\}^\mathcal{I} \subseteq A^\mathcal{I}$ for individual $\{a\}$ and concept A.
- Property 6.10 adds arrows $\{a\} \rightarrow \pi_L(P), \{b\} \rightarrow \pi_R(P)$ to $Hom(\mathscr{C}_C)$ and $\{(a,b)\} \rightarrow P$ to $Hom(\mathscr{C}_R)$ if $P(a,b) \in \mathcal{A}$. By the definition of $\mathcal{I}$ and Definition 5, we have $(a,b) \in P^\mathcal{I}$, $\{a\}^\mathcal{I} \subseteq (\pi_L(P))^\mathcal{I}$ and $\{b\}^\mathcal{I} \subseteq (\pi_R(P))^\mathcal{I}$. Therefore by the definition of $\mathcal{I}$, we have $\{(a,b)\}^\mathcal{I} \subseteq P^\mathcal{I}$.
- Property 6.11 adds arrows $\pi_L(R) \leftrightarrows \exists R$ to $Hom(\mathscr{C}_C)$ if $\exists P \in Ob(\mathscr{C}_C)$. π_L is a functor that represents the left projection of the role R. By the definition of $\mathcal{I}$, we have $(\pi_L(R))^\mathcal{I} \subseteq (\exists R)^\mathcal{I}$ and $(\exists R)^\mathcal{I} \subseteq (\pi_L(R))^\mathcal{I}$ for all role R.
- Property 6.12 adds arrows $\pi_R(R) \leftrightarrows \exists R^-$ to $Hom(\mathscr{C}_R)$ if $\exists P^- \in Ob(\mathscr{C}_C)$ π_R is a functor that represents the right projection of the role R. By the definition of $\mathcal{I}$, we have $(\pi_R(R))^\mathcal{I} \subseteq (\exists R^-)^\mathcal{I}$ and $(\exists R^-)^\mathcal{I} \subseteq (\pi_R(R))^\mathcal{I}$.
- Assume that $\{(a,b)\} \rightarrow R \in Hom(\mathscr{C}_R)$. Property 6.15 adds arrow $\{(b,a)\} \rightarrow R^-$ to $Hom(\mathscr{C}_R)$. By the definition of $\mathcal{I}$, we have $\{(b,a)\}^\mathcal{I} \subseteq (R^-)^\mathcal{I}$. Conversely, assume that $\{(b,a)\} \rightarrow R^- \in Hom(\mathscr{C}_R)$. Property 6.15 adds arrow $\{(a,b)\} \rightarrow R$ to $Hom(\mathscr{C}_R)$. By the definition of $\mathcal{I}$, we have $\{(a,b)\}^\mathcal{I} \subseteq R^\mathcal{I}$.
- Assume that $R \rightarrow R_1, R \rightarrow \neg R_1 \in Hom(\mathscr{C}_R)$. Property 6.16 adds an arrow $R \rightarrow R_\perp$ to $Hom(\mathscr{C}_R)$. By the hypothesis, we have $R^\mathcal{I} \subseteq R_1^\mathcal{I}, R^\mathcal{I} \subseteq \neg R_1^\mathcal{I}$. This implies that $R^\mathcal{I} \subseteq R_1^\mathcal{I} \cap (\neg R_1^\mathcal{I}) = R_\perp^\mathcal{I}$.
- Assume that $C \rightarrow C_1, C \rightarrow \neg C_1 \in Hom(\mathscr{C}_C)$. Property 6.17 adds an arrow $C \rightarrow \perp$ to $Hom(\mathscr{C}_C)$. By the hypothesis, we have $C^\mathcal{I} \subseteq C_1^\mathcal{I}, C^\mathcal{I} \subseteq \neg C_1^\mathcal{I}$. This implies that $C^\mathcal{I} \subseteq C_1^\mathcal{I} \cap (\neg C_1^\mathcal{I}) = \perp^\mathcal{I}$. This completes the proof of the lemma.

Definition 8. *Let $\mathcal{K}$ be an $DL\text{-}Lite_\mathcal{R}$ knowledge base. $\mathcal{K}$ is category-theoretically satisfiable if there are minimal and saturated concept and role categories $\mathscr{C}_C$ and $\mathscr{C}_R$ for $\mathcal{K}$ such that $\top \longrightarrow \perp \notin \mathsf{Hom}(\mathscr{C}_C)$, and $\{a\} \rightarrow \perp \notin Hom(\mathscr{C}_C)$ for all individual object $\{a\} \in Ob(\mathscr{C}_C)$.*

We now state and prove the key result of the current section.

Theorem 1. *Let $\mathcal{K}$ be an $DL\text{-}Lite_{\mathcal{R}}$ knowledge base. $\mathcal{K}$ is category-theoretically satisfiable iff $\mathcal{K}$ is set-theoretically satisfiable.*

Proof. We need to prove the following two directions.

1. Assume that $\mathcal{K}$ is set-theoretically satisfiable. This implies that there is a model $\langle \Delta^{\mathcal{I}}, \cdot^{\mathcal{I}} \rangle$ of $\mathcal{K} = \langle \mathcal{T}, \mathcal{A} \rangle$ such that $\top^{\mathcal{I}} \neq \varnothing$. We have to prove that there is a minimal and saturated concept category $\mathscr{C}_C$ for $\mathcal{K}$ such that $\top \rightarrow \bot \notin Hom(\mathscr{C}_C)$ and $\{a\} \rightarrow \bot \notin Hom(\mathscr{C}_C)$ fora all individual a occurring in $\mathcal{A}$.
First, we procedurally define concept and role categories $\mathscr{C}_C$ and $\mathscr{C}_R$ as follows:
   (a) Initialize $Ob(\mathscr{C}_C)$, $Ob(\mathscr{C}_R)$, $Hom(\mathscr{C}_C)$ and $Hom(\mathscr{C}_R)$ to an empty set.
   (b) For each property in Definition 6, if its condition holds, then we add necessary objects or arrows to $\mathscr{C}_C$ and $\mathscr{C}_R$ such that the property is satisfied.

   Hence, the obtained $\mathscr{C}_C$ and $\mathscr{C}_R$ are saturated. We have to prove that they are minimal. Let $S = \langle r_1, \cdots, r_n \rangle$ be the sequence of applications of properties to build $\mathscr{C}_C$ and $\mathscr{C}_R$. It holds that n is finite since the number of objects added to the categories is finite. Assume that $\mathscr{C}'_C$ and $\mathscr{C}'_R$ be saturated categories We prove minimality of $\mathscr{C}_C$ by induction on the length n of S. We use $\mathscr{C}^i_C$ and $\mathscr{C}^i_R$ to denote categories after applying r_i. Thus, $Ob(\mathscr{C}^0_C) = \varnothing$, $Ob(\mathscr{C}^0_R) = \varnothing$, $Hom(\mathscr{C}^0_C) = \varnothing$ and $Hom(\mathscr{C}^0_R) = \varnothing$.

   Base Case $n = 1$. It is obvious that if the condition of r_1 holds, then it holds also for $\mathscr{C}'_C$ and $\mathscr{C}'_R$ since r_1 adds first objects and arrows to categories. Hence, $Ob(\mathscr{C}^1_C) \subseteq Ob(\mathscr{C}'_C)$, $Hom(\mathscr{C}^1_C) \subseteq Hom(\mathscr{C}'_C)$, $Ob(\mathscr{C}^1_R) \subseteq Ob(\mathscr{C}'_R)$, and $Hom(\mathscr{C}^1_R) \subseteq Hom(\mathscr{C}'_R)$.

   Inductive Case n. The inductive hypothesis assumes that $Ob(\mathscr{C}^i_C) \subseteq Ob(\mathscr{C}'_C)$, $Hom(\mathscr{C}^i_C) \subseteq Hom(\mathscr{C}'_C)$, $Ob(\mathscr{C}^i_R) \subseteq Ob(\mathscr{C}'_R)$, and $Hom(\mathscr{C}^i_R) \subseteq Hom(\mathscr{C}'_R)$ for all $i \leqslant n-1$. We have to show that $Ob(\mathscr{C}^n_C) \subseteq Ob(\mathscr{C}'_C)$, $Hom(\mathscr{C}^n_C) \subseteq Hom(\mathscr{C}'_C)$, $Ob(\mathscr{C}^n_R) \subseteq Ob(\mathscr{C}'_R)$, and $Hom(\mathscr{C}^n_R) \subseteq Hom(\mathscr{C}'_R)$ (†).

   Since r_n is applicable in $\mathscr{C}^{n-1}_C$ and $\mathscr{C}^{n-1}_R$, it must be applicable in $\mathscr{C}'_C$ and $\mathscr{C}'_R$ due to the inductive hypothesis. Hence, what is added to $\mathscr{C}^{n-1}_C$ and $\mathscr{C}^{n-1}_R$ by applying r_n belongs also to $\mathscr{C}'_C$ and $\mathscr{C}'_R$. Hence, (†) is proved. Therefore, we showed that $Hom(\mathscr{C}_C) \subseteq Hom(\mathscr{C}'_C)$, $Ob(\mathscr{C}_R) \subseteq Ob(\mathscr{C}'_R)$ for all saturated concept and role categories $\mathscr{C}'_C$ and $\mathscr{C}'_R$. In addition, each object X added to $Ob(\mathscr{C}_C)$ and $Ob(\mathscr{C}_R)$ has an identity arrow $X \rightarrow X$. This implies that both conditions in Definition 7 are satisfied, and thus $\mathscr{C}_C$ and $\mathscr{C}_R$ are minimal.

   It remains to show that $\{a\} \rightarrow \bot \notin Hom(\mathscr{C}_C)$ for all individual object $\{a\} \in Ob(\mathscr{C}_C)$, and $\top \rightarrow \bot \notin Hom(\mathscr{C}_C)$.
By contradiction, assume that a property in Definition 6 adds an arrow $\{a\} \rightarrow \bot$ or $\top \rightarrow \bot$. This implies that $a^{\mathcal{I}} \subseteq \varnothing$ or $\top^{\mathcal{I}} \subseteq \varnothing$ according to Lemma 1, which contradicts the fact that $\mathcal{I}$ is a model of $\mathcal{K}$.

2. Assume that $\mathcal{K}$ is category-theoretically satisfiable. This implies that there is a minimal and saturated concept category $\mathscr{C}_C$ and $\mathscr{C}_R$ for $\mathcal{K}$ such that $\top \to \bot \notin Hom(\mathscr{C}_C)$. We have to show that $\mathcal{K} = \langle \mathcal{T}, \mathcal{A} \rangle$ is satisfiable, i.e. there is a model $\langle \Delta^{\mathcal{I}}, \cdot^{\mathcal{I}} \rangle$ of $\mathcal{K} = \langle \mathcal{T}, \mathcal{A} \rangle$ such that $\top^{\mathcal{I}} \neq \varnothing$. For this, we define inductively $\mathcal{I}$ from $\mathscr{C}_C$ and $\mathscr{C}_R$ as follows:
   (a) If $\mathcal{A} = \varnothing$ then add a new individual a_0 to $\Delta^{\mathcal{I}}$.
   (b) For each individual object $\{a\} \in Ob(\mathscr{C}_C)$, we add to $\Delta^{\mathcal{I}}$ an individual a.
   (c) For each individual object $\{(a, b)\} \in Ob(\mathscr{C}_R)$, we add to $\Delta^{\mathcal{I}}$ two individuals a, b.
   (d) If there is some arrow $\{a\} \to \pi_L(R) \in Hom(\mathscr{C}_C)$, we add a fresh individual $x(a, P)$ (resp. $x(P, a)$) to $\Delta^{\mathcal{I}}$ if $R = P$ (resp. $R = P^-$)
   (e) For each $z \in \Delta^{\mathcal{I}}$
      i. If $z = x(a, P_1)$ and $\pi_L(P_1) \to \pi_L(P) \in Hom(\mathscr{C}_C)$, then we add to $\Delta^{\mathcal{I}}$ a fresh individual $x(a, P)$.
      ii. If $z = x(a, P_1)$ and $\pi_L(P_1) \to \pi_R(P) \in Hom(\mathscr{C}_C)$, then we add to $\Delta^{\mathcal{I}}$ a fresh individual $x(P, a)$.
      iii. If $z = x(P_1, a)$ and $\pi_R(P_1) \to \pi_L(P) \in Hom(\mathscr{C}_C)$, then we add to $\Delta^{\mathcal{I}}$ a fresh individual $x(a, P)$.
      iv. If $z = x(P_1, a)$ and $\pi_R(P_1) \to \pi_R(P) \in Hom(\mathscr{C}_C)$, then we add to $\Delta^{\mathcal{I}}$ a fresh individual $x(P, a)$.
   (f) $A^{\mathcal{I}} = \{a \in \Delta^{\mathcal{I}} \mid \{a\} \to A \in Hom(\mathscr{C}_C) \vee (a = x(P, b) \wedge \pi_L(P) \to A \in Hom(\mathscr{C}_C)) \vee (a = x(b, P) \wedge \pi_R(P) \to A \in Hom(\mathscr{C}_C))\}$
   (g) $P^{\mathcal{I}} = \{(a, b) \in (\Delta^{\mathcal{I}})^2 \mid \{(a, b)\} \to P \in Hom(\mathscr{C}_R) \vee \{(b, a)\} \to P^- \in Hom(\mathscr{C}_R) \vee (b = x(a, P_1) \wedge P_1 \to P \in Hom(\mathscr{C}_R)) \vee (a = x(b, P_1) \wedge P_1 \to P^- \in Hom(\mathscr{C}_R))\}$

Note that each individual in $\Delta^{\mathcal{I}}$ has a unique name. Indeed, the name of an individual that does not occur in $\mathcal{A}$ is uniquely written as $x(\cdots(x(P_1, a), P_2)\cdots)$ where P_i is atomic and a occurs in $\mathcal{A}$. For instance, $x(P_1, (x(a, P_2))$.

We can write $x(a, R)$ or $x(R, a)$ where R is a basic role. In this case, $x(a, R) = x(a, P)$ if $R = P$ and $x(a, R) = x(P, a)$ if $R = P^-$. Furthermore, we can use relative name such as $b = x(P, a)$ where a does not occur in $\mathcal{A}$.

We have to show that $\mathcal{I}$ defined as above is a model of $\mathcal{K}$, i.e. $\mathcal{I}$ is an interpretation of $\mathcal{K}$ and it satisfies all ABox assertions, all TBox axioms, and $\Delta^{\mathcal{I}} \neq \varnothing$. We have $\Delta^{\mathcal{I}} \neq \varnothing$ since $a_0 \in \Delta^{\mathcal{I}}$ according to Step 2a of the construction of $\mathcal{I}$. We show the following two claims.

Claim 1. 1.1 $\{a\} \to B \in Hom(\mathscr{C}_C)$ iff $a \in B^{\mathcal{I}}$ where a occurs in $\mathcal{A}$.
1.2 For $a \in \Delta^{\mathcal{I}}$, there is some $b = x(a, R) \in \Delta^{\mathcal{I}}$ iff $a \in (\exists R)^{\mathcal{I}}$.
1.3 $x(a, R) \in \Delta^{\mathcal{I}}$ implies $\pi_L(R) \to \bot \notin Hom(\mathscr{C}_C)$ and $\pi_R(R) \to \bot \notin Hom(\mathscr{C}_C)$.

We prove each item of the claim.

(a) We consider each possible structure of the basic concept B.
   - $B = A$. Item 1.1 is a consequence of Step 2f of the construction of $\mathcal{I}$ since a occurs in $\mathcal{A}$.

- $B = \exists R$. Assume $\{a\} \rightarrow \exists R \leftrightarrows \pi_L(R) \in Hom(\mathscr{C}_C)$. By Step 2d of the construction of $\mathcal{I}$, we have $b = x(a, R) \in \Delta^{\mathcal{I}}$. By Step 2g of the construction of $\mathcal{I}$ with $b = x(a, P)$ and $P \rightarrow P \in Hom(\mathscr{C}_C)$, we have $(a, b) \in P^{\mathcal{I}}$ if $R = P$. Thus, $a \in (\exists P)^{\mathcal{I}}$ .By Step 2g of the construction of $\mathcal{I}$ with $a = x(b, P)$ and $P \rightarrow P \in Hom(\mathscr{C}_C)$, we have $(b, a) \in P^{\mathcal{I}}$ if $R = P^-$ Hence, $a \in (\exists P^-)^{\mathcal{I}}$.
Conversely, assume $a \in (\exists P)^{\mathcal{I}}$. By the definition of interpretation, there is some $b \in \Delta^{\mathcal{I}}$ such that $(a, b) \in P^{\mathcal{I}}$. According to Step 2g of the construction of $\mathcal{I}$ where a occurs in $\mathcal{A}$, there are 2 possibilities:

  (i) $\{(a, b)\} \rightarrow P \in Hom(\mathscr{C}_R)$. By the construction of $\mathscr{C}_R$, this happens only if there is some $P_1(a, b) \in \mathcal{A}$ such that $P_1 \rightarrow P \in Hom(\mathscr{C}_R)$. Due to Properties 6.10, 6.11 and 6.8 in Definition 6, we have $\{a\} \rightarrow \pi_L(P_1) \rightarrow \pi_L(P) \leftrightarrows \exists P$.

  (ii) $b = x(a, R_1) \in \Delta^{\mathcal{I}}$ and $R_1 \rightarrow P \in Hom(\mathscr{C}_R)$. In this case, we can use Property 6.14 to convert arrows according to different possibilities: $P_1^- \rightarrow P$ is equivalent to $P_1 \rightarrow P^-$; and $P_1^- \rightarrow P^-$ is equivalent to $P_1 \rightarrow P$ where $R_1 = P_1$ or $R_1 = P_1^-$. By Step 2d of the construction of $\mathcal{I}$ with $\{a\} \rightarrow \pi_L(R_1) \rightarrow \pi_L(P) \in Hom(\mathscr{C}_C)$, we have $\{a\} \rightarrow \exists P \in Hom(\mathscr{C}_C)$.
  Assume $a \in (\exists P^-)^{\mathcal{I}}$. By the definition of interpretation, there is some $b \in \Delta^{\mathcal{I}}$ such that $(a, b) \in (P^-)^{\mathcal{I}}$. According to Step 2g of the construction of $\mathcal{I}$ where a occurs in $\mathcal{A}$, there are 2 possibilities:

  (i) $\{(a, b)\} \rightarrow P^- \in Hom(\mathscr{C}_R)$. By the construction of $\mathscr{C}_R$, this happens only if there is some $P_1(a, b) \in \mathcal{A}$ such that $P_1 \rightarrow P^- \in Hom(\mathscr{C}_R)$. Due to Properties 6.10, 6.11 and 6.8 in Definition 6, we have $\{a\} \rightarrow \pi_L(P_1) \rightarrow \pi_R(P) \leftrightarrows \exists P^-$.

  (ii) $a = x(b, R_1) \in \Delta^{\mathcal{I}}$ and $R_1 \rightarrow P \in Hom(\mathscr{C}_R)$. Since a occurs in $\mathcal{A}$, we have $\{a\} \rightarrow \pi_R(P_1) \rightarrow \pi_R(P) \leftrightarrows \exists P^- \in Hom(\mathscr{C}_C)$ by the construction of $\mathcal{I}$ with $R_1 = P_1$.

(b) Assume there is some $b = x(a, R) \in \Delta^{\mathcal{I}}$. Assume $R = P$. By Step 2g of the construction of $\mathcal{I}$ with $b = x(a, P)$ and $P \rightarrow P$, we have $(a, b) \in P^{\mathcal{I}}$, and thus $a \in (\exists P)^{\mathcal{I}}$.

Conversely, assume $a \in (\exists P)^{\mathcal{I}}$. By the construction of $\mathcal{I}$, there is some $b \in \Delta^{\mathcal{I}}$ such that $(a, b) \in P^{\mathcal{I}}$. By Step 2g of the construction of $\mathcal{I}$, we have either $x(a, P_1) \in \Delta^{\mathcal{I}}$ and $P_1 \rightarrow P \in Hom(\mathscr{C}_R)$, or $\{(a, b)\} \rightarrow P \in Hom(\mathscr{C}_R)$ and thus $\{a\} \rightarrow \pi_L(P) \in Hom(\mathscr{C}_C)$. The latter implies $x(a, P) \in \Delta^{\mathcal{I}}$ by Step 2d of the construction of $\mathcal{I}$. For the former, we have $x(a, P) \in \Delta^{\mathcal{I}}$ due to Step 2e of the construction of $\mathcal{I}$ with $x(a, P_1) \in \Delta^{\mathcal{I}}$ and $\pi_L(P_1) \rightarrow \pi_L(P) \in Hom(\mathscr{C}_C)$.

Assume $R = P^-$. We have $a = x(b, P) \in \Delta^{\mathcal{I}}$ from $a = x(P^-, b) \in \Delta^{\mathcal{I}}$. By Step 2g of the construction of $\mathcal{I}$ with $a = x(b, P)$ and $P \rightarrow P$, we have $(b, a) \in P^{\mathcal{I}}$, and thus $(b, a) \in (\exists P)^{\mathcal{I}}$. This implies that $a \in (\exists P^-)^{\mathcal{I}}$.

Conversely, assume $a \in (\exists P^-)^{\mathcal{I}}$. By the construction of $\mathcal{I}$, there is some $b \in \Delta^{\mathcal{I}}$ such that $(b, a) \in P^{\mathcal{I}}$. By Step 2g of the construction of $\mathcal{I}$, we have either $a = x(b, P_1) \in \Delta^{\mathcal{I}}$ and $P_1 \to P \in Hom(\mathscr{C}_R)$, or $\{(b, a)\} \to P \in Hom(\mathscr{C}_R)$ and thus $\{a\} \to \pi_R(P) \in Hom(\mathscr{C}_C)$. The latter implies $x(P, a) \in \Delta^{\mathcal{I}}$ by Step 2d of the construction of $\mathcal{I}$. For the former, we can use the same argument above to obtain $x(P, a) \in \Delta^{\mathcal{I}}$.

(c) Assume $a_n = x(a_{n-1}, R_{n-1}) \in \Delta^{\mathcal{I}}$. This implies that $a_{i+1} = x(a_i, R_i)$ and $\{a_1\} \to \pi_L(R_1)$, $\pi_R(R_i) \to \pi_L(R_{i+1})$ for $1 \leqslant i \leqslant n-1$ according to the construction of $\mathcal{I}$ by Steps 2d and 2e. By contradiction, assume that $\pi_L(R_{n-1}) \to \bot \in Hom(\mathscr{C}_C)$. This implies that $\{a_1\} \to \pi_L(R_1)$, which contradicts category-theoretical satisfiability of $\mathcal{K}$.

We now use Claim 1 to show that $\mathcal{I}$ is a model of $\mathcal{A}$ and $\mathcal{T}$.

- $A(a) \in \mathcal{A}$ implies $a \in A^{\mathcal{I}}$. By Property 6.9 in Definition 6, we have $\{a\} \to A \in Hom(\mathscr{C}_C)$. By Step 2g of the construction of $\mathcal{I}$, we obtain $a \in A^{\mathcal{I}}$.
- $P(a, b) \in \mathcal{A}$ implies $(a, b) \in P^{\mathcal{I}}$. By Property 6.10 in Definition 6, we have $\{(a, b)\} \to P \in Hom(\mathscr{C}_R)$. By Step 2g of the construction of $\mathcal{I}$, we obtain $(a, b) \in P^{\mathcal{I}}$.
- $B \sqsubseteq C \in \mathcal{T}$ implies $B^{\mathcal{I}} \subseteq C^{\mathcal{I}}$. We have $B \to C \in Hom(\mathscr{C}_C)$ due to Property 6.7 in Definition 6. Assume $a \in B^{\mathcal{I}}$. We consider the following cases according to the structure of B.
  - $B = A$. According to Step 2f of the construction of $\mathcal{I}$, we consider different cases:

    (i) $\{a\} \to A \in Hom(\mathscr{C}_C)$ and a occurs in $\mathcal{A}$.
    Assume that $C = B_1$. By contradiction, assume that $a \notin (B_1)^{\mathcal{I}}$. Due to Claim 1.1 (Item 1), we have $\{a\} \to B_1 \notin Hom(\mathscr{C}_C)$, which contradicts $\{a\} \to B \to B_1 \in Hom(\mathscr{C}_C)$.

    Assume that $C = \neg B_1$. By contradiction assume that $a \notin (\neg B_1)^{\mathcal{I}}$, and thus $a \in B_1^{\mathcal{I}}$. Due to Claim 1.1, we have $\{a\} \to B_1 \in Hom(\mathscr{C}_C)$. Moreover, it holds that $\{a\} \to B \to \neg B_1 \in Hom(\mathscr{C}_C)$. Hence, $\{a\} \to \bot \in Hom(\mathscr{C}_C)$, which contradict category-theoretical satisfiability of $\mathcal{K}$.

    (ii) $a = x(R, b)$ and $\pi_L(R) \to A \in Hom(\mathscr{C}_C)$. This implies that $\pi_L(R) \to C \in Hom(\mathscr{C}_C)$.

    Assume $C = A_1$. By Step 2f of the construction of $\mathcal{I}$ with $\pi_L(R) \to A \to C = A_1 \in Hom(\mathscr{C}_C)$, we have $a \in (A_1)^{\mathcal{I}}$.

    Assume $C = \exists R_1$. By Step 2f of the construction of $\mathcal{I}$ with $\pi_L(R) \to A \to C = \exists R_1 \leftrightarrows \pi_L(R_1) \in Hom(\mathscr{C}_C)$ and $b = x(a, R)$, we have $x(a, R_1) \in \Delta^{\mathcal{I}}$. By 1.2, we have $a \in (\exists R_1)^{\mathcal{I}}$.

Assume $C = \neg\exists R_1$. By contradiction assume that $a \notin (\neg\exists R_1)^{\mathcal{I}}$, and thus $a \in (\exists R_1)^{\mathcal{I}}$. By Claim 1.2, we have $x(a, R_1) \in \Delta^{\mathcal{I}}$. By Step 2e of the construction of $\mathcal{I}$ there is a first creation of an individual $x(a, R_0) \in \Delta^{\mathcal{I}}$ such that $\pi_L(R_0) \rightarrow \pi_L(R) \in Hom(\mathscr{C}_C)$ and $\pi_L(R_0) \rightarrow \pi_L(R_1) \in Hom(\mathscr{C}_C)$ since $x(a, R), x(a, R_1) \in \Delta^{\mathcal{I}}$. This implies that $\pi_L(R_0) \rightarrow \pi_L(R) \rightarrow C = \neg\exists R_1 \in Hom(\mathscr{C}_C)$ and $\pi_L(R_0) \rightarrow \pi_L(R_1) \leftrightarrows \exists R_1 \in Hom(\mathscr{C}_C)$. Hence, $\pi_L(R_0) \rightarrow \bot$, which contradicts category-theoretical satisfiability of $\mathcal{K}$.

- $B = \exists R$. We have $a \in (\exists R)^{\mathcal{I}}$ and thus $a = x(R, b) \in \Delta^{\mathcal{I}}$ or $\{(a, b)\} \rightarrow R \in Hom(\mathscr{C}_R)$.

  Assume that $C = A$. By Step 2g of the construction of $\mathcal{I}$ with $\pi_L(R) \leftrightarrows \exists R = B \rightarrow C = A \in Hom(\mathscr{C}_C)$ and $a = x(R, b) \in \Delta^{\mathcal{I}}$, we have $a \in A^{\mathcal{I}}$.

  Assume that $C = \neg A$. By contradiction assume that $a \notin (\neg A)^{\mathcal{I}}$, and thus $a \in A^{\mathcal{I}}$. By Step 2g of the construction of $\mathcal{I}$, we have $\pi_L(R) \rightarrow A \in Hom(\mathscr{C}_C)$. This implies that $\pi_L(P_1) \rightarrow \bot \in Hom(\mathscr{C}_C)$ due to $\pi_L(R) = B \rightarrow C = \neg A \in Hom(\mathscr{C}_C)$, which contradicts Claim 1.3.

  Assume $C = \exists R_1$. From $B = \exists R \rightarrow C = \exists R_1$ and $b = x(a, R)$, we have $x(a, R_1) \in \Delta^{\mathcal{I}}$ by Step 2f of the construction of $\mathcal{I}$. Due to Claim 1.2 we obtain $a \in (\exists R_1)^{\mathcal{I}}$.

  Assume that $C = \neg\exists R_1$. By contradiction assume that $a \notin (\neg\exists R_1)^{\mathcal{I}}$, and thus $a \in (\exists R_1)^{\mathcal{I}}$. Due to Claim 1.2, we have $x(a, R_1) \in \Delta^{\mathcal{I}}$. By Step 2e of the construction of $\mathcal{I}$ there is a first creation of an individual $x(a, R_0) \in \Delta^{\mathcal{I}}$ such that $\pi_L(R_0) \rightarrow \pi_L(R) \in Hom(\mathscr{C}_C)$ and $\pi_L(R_0) \rightarrow \pi_L(R_1) \in Hom(\mathscr{C}_C)$ since $x(a, R), x(a, R_1) \in \Delta^{\mathcal{I}}$. This implies that $\pi_L(R_0) \rightarrow \pi_L(R) \rightarrow C = \neg\exists R_1 \in Hom(\mathscr{C}_C)$ and $\pi_L(R_0) \rightarrow \pi_L(R_1) \leftrightarrows \exists R_1 \in Hom(\mathscr{C}_C)$. Hence, $\pi_L(R_0) \rightarrow \bot$, which contradicts category-theoretical satisfiability of $\mathcal{K}$.

– $R \sqsubseteq E \in \mathcal{T}$ implies $R^{\mathcal{I}} \subseteq E^{\mathcal{I}}$. We have $R \rightarrow E \in Hom(\mathscr{C}_R)$ due to Property 6.8 in Definition 6. Assume $(a, b) \in R^{\mathcal{I}}$. According to Step 2g of the construction of $\mathcal{I}$, we consider the following cases:
  - $\{(a, b)\} \rightarrow R \in Hom(\mathscr{C}_R)$. This implies that $\{(a, b)\} \rightarrow E \in Hom(\mathscr{C}_R)$. Assume $E = P_1$. By Step 2g of the construction of $\mathcal{I}$, we have $(a, b) \in E^{\mathcal{I}}$.

    Assume $E = P_1^-$. By Property 6.15 in Definition 6, we have $\{(b, a)\} \rightarrow P_1 \in Hom(\mathscr{C}_R)$. By Step 2g of the construction of $\mathcal{I}$, we have $(b, a) \in (P_1)^{\mathcal{I}}$, and thus $(a, b) \in (P_1^-)^{\mathcal{I}} = E^{\mathcal{I}}$.

    Assume $E = \neg R_1$. By contradiction assume that $(a, b) \notin (\neg R_1)^{\mathcal{I}}$, and thus $(a, b) \in R_1^{\mathcal{I}}$. By Step 2g of the construction of $\mathcal{I}$, we have $\{(a, b)\} \rightarrow R_1 \in Hom(\mathscr{C}_R)$ since a, b occur in $\mathcal{A}$. With $\{(a, b)\} \rightarrow E = \neg R_1 \in Hom(\mathscr{C}_R)$, we obtain $\{(a, b)\} \rightarrow R_\bot \in Hom(\mathscr{C}_R)$, thus $\{a\} \rightarrow \pi_L(R_1) \rightarrow \bot \in Hom(\mathscr{C}_C)$, which contradicts categorical satisfiability of $\mathcal{K}$.

- $b = x(a, P_1)$ and $P_1 \rightarrow P$ with $R = P$.
Assume $E = P_2$. By Step 2g of the construction of $\mathcal{I}$ with $P_1 \rightarrow R = P \rightarrow P_2 \in Hom(\mathscr{C}_R)$, we have $(a, b) \in P_2^{\mathcal{I}}$.
Assume $E = P_2^-$. We obtain $P_1 \rightarrow P_2^- \in Hom(\mathscr{C}_R)$ from $P_1 \rightarrow R = P \rightarrow P_2^- \in Hom(\mathscr{C}_R)$. By Step 2g of the construction of $\mathcal{I}$ with $b = x(a, P_1)$ and $P_1 \rightarrow P_2^-$, we have $(b, a) \in (P_2)^{\mathcal{I}}$. Hence, $(a, b) \in (P_2^-)^{\mathcal{I}}$.

  Assume $E = \neg R_2$. By contradiction assume that $(a, b) \notin (\neg R_2)^{\mathcal{I}}$, and thus $(a, b) \in R_2^{\mathcal{I}}$.

  Assume $R_2 = P_2$. By Step 2g of the construction of $\mathcal{I}$, we have $P_1 \rightarrow P_2 \in Hom(\mathscr{C}_R)$. With $P_1 \rightarrow R \rightarrow E = \neg P_2 \in Hom(\mathscr{C}_R)$, we obtain $P_1 \rightarrow R_\perp \in Hom(\mathscr{C}_R)$ and thus $\pi_L(R_1) \rightarrow \perp \in Hom(\mathscr{C}_C)$, which contradicts Claim 1.3 (Item 4).
Assume $R_2 = P_2^-$. This implies $(b, a) \in (P_2)^{\mathcal{I}}$. By Step 2g of the construction of $\mathcal{I}$ with $b = x(a, P_1)$, we have $P_1 \rightarrow P_2^-$. With $P_1 \rightarrow R = P \rightarrow E = \neg P_2^-$, we obtain $R_1 \rightarrow R_\perp \in Hom(\mathscr{C}_R)$ and thus $\pi_L(R_1) \rightarrow \perp \in Hom(\mathscr{C}_C)$, which contradicts Claim 1.3 (Item 4).
- $a = x(b, P_1)$ and $P_1 \rightarrow P^-$ with $R = P$.
Assume $E = P_2$. By Step 2g of the construction of $\mathcal{I}$ with $P_1 \rightarrow P^- \rightarrow P_2^- \in Hom(\mathscr{C}_R)$ and Property 6.14, we have $(a, b) \in P_2^{\mathcal{I}}$.

  Assume $E = P_2^-$. We obtain $P_1 \rightarrow P_2 \in Hom(\mathscr{C}_R)$ from $P_1 \rightarrow P^- \in Hom(\mathscr{C}_R)$ and $P \rightarrow P_2^- \in Hom(\mathscr{C}_R)$ due to Property 6.14. By Step 2g of the construction of $\mathcal{I}$ with $a = x(b, P_1)$ and $P_1 \rightarrow P_2$, we have $(b, a) \in (P_2)^{\mathcal{I}}$. Hence, $(a, b) \in (P_2^-)^{\mathcal{I}}$.

  Assume $E = \neg R_2$. By contradiction assume that $(a, b) \notin (\neg R_2)^{\mathcal{I}}$, and thus $(a, b) \in R_2^{\mathcal{I}}$.

  Assume $R_2 = P_2$. By Step 2g of the construction of $\mathcal{I}$ with $(a, b) \in P_2^{\mathcal{I}}$ and $a = x(b, P_1)$, we have $P_1 \rightarrow P_2^- \in Hom(\mathscr{C}_R)$. Due to Property 6.14, we have $P_1^- \rightarrow P_2 \in Hom(\mathscr{C}_R)$. Moreover, we have $P_1 \rightarrow P^- \in Hom(\mathscr{C}_R)$ and $P \rightarrow \neg P_2 \in Hom(\mathscr{C}_R)$. Due to Property 6.14, we have $P_1^- \rightarrow \neg P_2 \in Hom(\mathscr{C}_R)$. Due to Property 6.16, we obtain $P_1^- \rightarrow R_\perp \in Hom(\mathscr{C}_R)$, which contradicts $a = x(b, P_1) \in \Delta^{\mathcal{I}}$ and Claim 1.3.

  Assume $R_2 = P_2^-$. This implies $(b, a) \in (P_2)^{\mathcal{I}}$. By Step 2g of the construction of $\mathcal{I}$ with $(b, a) \in P_2^{\mathcal{I}}$ and $a = x(b, P_1)$, we have $P_1 \rightarrow P_2 \in Hom(\mathscr{C}_R)$. Due to Property 6.14, we have $P_1^- \rightarrow P_2^- \in Hom(\mathscr{C}_R)$. Moreover, we have $P_1 \rightarrow P^- \in Hom(\mathscr{C}_R)$ and $P \rightarrow \neg P_2^- \in Hom(\mathscr{C}_R)$. Due to Property 6.14, we have $P_1^- \rightarrow \neg P_2^- \in Hom(\mathscr{C}_R)$. Due to Property 6.16, we obtain $P_1^- \rightarrow R_\perp \in Hom(\mathscr{C}_R)$, which contradicts $a = x(b, P_1) \in \Delta^{\mathcal{I}}$ and Claim 1.3. We can use the same argument above to prove the lemma for case $R = P^-$. This completes the proof. □

Based on Definition 8, we can propose an algorithm for build concept and role categories for a knowledge base $\mathcal{K} = \langle \mathcal{T}, \mathcal{A} \rangle$. Algorithm 1 starts by initializing two categories and applies rules in Table 1 for $\mathcal{K}$ until no rule is applicable. Rules in Table 1 are directly defined from the properties in Definition 8.

Input : Consistency of a $DL\text{-}Lite_{\mathcal{R}}$ knowledge base $\mathcal{K} = \langle \mathcal{T}, \mathcal{A} \rangle$
Output: true or false

$Ob(\mathscr{C}_c) \leftarrow \varnothing$, $Hom(\mathscr{C}_c) \leftarrow \varnothing$, $Ob(\mathscr{C}_r) \leftarrow \varnothing$ and $Hom(\mathscr{C}_r) \leftarrow \varnothing$;
changed $\leftarrow$ true;
while changed **do**
  changed $\leftarrow$ false;
  if *there is a saturation rule* **r** *from Table 1 that is applicable to* $\mathscr{C}_C$ *or* $\mathscr{C}_R$ **then**
    Apply **r** to $\mathscr{C}_C$ or $\mathscr{C}_R$;
    changed $\leftarrow$ true;
  end
end
if $\top \rightarrow \bot \in Hom(\mathscr{C}_C)$ *or* $\{a\} \rightarrow \bot \in Hom(\mathscr{C}_C)$ *for some individual a in* $\mathcal{A}$ **then**
  return false ;
end
else
  return true ;
end

Algorithm 1: isSatisfiable($\mathcal{K}$)

Note that Algorithm 1 provides a procedure to build a concept category that is a finite representation of all models of a $DL\text{-}Lite_{\mathcal{R}}$ KB. In fact, the proof of Theorem 1 shows how to devise a model from such a category by using "paths" whose nodes are objects, and edges are arrows or roles occurring in existential restrictions. Conversely, every model of a $DL\text{-}Lite_{\mathcal{R}}$ KB has to obey a such path in its concept category. To illustrate this observation we can use a very simple $KB = \langle \mathcal{T}, \mathcal{A} \rangle$ where $\mathcal{T} = \{\exists P^- \sqsubseteq \exists P\}$ and $\mathcal{A} = \{P(a, b)\}$ [2]. In the concept category of the KB, there is a loop composed of two objects $\pi_L(P)$ and $\pi_R(P)$, an arrow edge from $\pi_L(P)$ to $\pi_R(P)$, and a role edge P from $\pi_R(P)$ to $\pi_L(P)$. One can devise an infinite model or a finite one from this loop.

Example 2. Consider the following TBox in $DL\text{-}Lite_{\mathcal{R}}$, denoted $\mathcal{T}$, with atomic concepts $Patient$, $Doctor$, $Medication$, and atomic roles $MedicatedWith$, $PrescribedBy$.

$$Patient \sqsubseteq \exists MedicatedWith \quad (1)$$
$$\exists MedicatedWith^- \sqsubseteq Medication \quad (2)$$
$$Medication \sqsubseteq \exists PrescribedBy \quad (3)$$
$$\exists PrescribedBy^- \sqsubseteq Doctor \quad (4)$$
$$Doctor \sqsubseteq \neg Patient \quad (5)$$

Table 1. Saturation Rules

If $X \to Y \in Hom(\mathscr{C}_Z), \{X, Y\} \nsubseteq Ob(\mathscr{C}_Z), Z \in \{C, R\}$
then add X, Y to $Ob(\mathscr{C}_Z)$ (1)
If $E_1 \to E_2 \in Hom(\mathscr{C}_R), \{\pi_L(E_1) \to \pi_L(E_2), \pi_R(E_1) \to \pi_R(E_2)\} \nsubseteq Hom(\mathscr{C}_C)$ (2)
then add $\pi_L(E_1) \to \pi_L(E_1), \pi_R(E_1) \to \pi_R(E_1)$ to $Hom(\mathscr{C}_C)$ (3)
If $C \in Ob(\mathscr{C}_C)$ and $\{C \to C, C \to \top, \bot \to C\} \nsubseteq Hom(\mathscr{C}_C)$ (4)
then add $C \to C, C \to \top, \bot \to C$ to $Hom(\mathscr{C}_C)$
If $E \in Ob(\mathscr{C}_R)$ and $\{E \to E, E \to R_\top, R_\bot \to E\} \nsubseteq Hom(\mathscr{C}_R)$ (5)
then add $E \to E, E \to R_\top, R_\bot \to E$ to $Hom(\mathscr{C}_R)$
If $\{\pi_L(E) \to \bot, \pi_R(E) \to \bot\} \cap Hom(\mathscr{C}_C) \neq \varnothing$ and $E \to R_\bot \notin Hom(\mathscr{C}_R)$ (6)
then add $E \to R_\bot$ to $Hom(\mathscr{C}_R)$
If $E \to R_\bot \in Hom(\mathscr{C}_R)$ and $\{\pi_L(E) \to \bot, \pi_R(E) \to \bot\} \nsubseteq Hom(\mathscr{C}_C)$ (7)
then add $\pi_L(E) \to \bot, \pi_R(E) \to \bot$ to $Hom(\mathscr{C}_C)$
If $C_1 \to C_2, C_2 \to C_3 \in Hom(\mathscr{C}_C)$ and $C_1 \to C_3 \notin Hom(\mathscr{C}_C)$ (8)
then add $C_1 \to C_3$ to $Hom(\mathscr{C}_C)$
If $E_1 \to E_2, E_2 \to E_3 \in Hom(\mathscr{C}_R)$ and $E_1 \to E_3 \notin Hom(\mathscr{C}_R)$ (9)
then add $E_1 \to E_3$ to $Hom(\mathscr{C}_R)$
If $B \sqsubseteq C \in \mathcal{T}$ and $B \to C \notin Hom(\mathscr{C}_C)$ **then add** $B \to C$ to $Hom(\mathscr{C}_C)$ (10)
If $R \sqsubseteq E \in \mathcal{T}$ and $R \to E \notin Hom(\mathscr{C}_R)$ **then add** $R \to E$ to $Hom(\mathscr{C}_R)$, (11)
If $A(a) \in \mathcal{A}$ and $\{a\} \to A \notin Hom(\mathscr{C}_C)$ **then add** $\{a\} \to A$ to $Hom(\mathscr{C}_C)$ (12)
If $P(a, b) \in \mathcal{A}$ and $\{(a, b)\} \to P \notin Hom(\mathscr{C}_R)$ **then add** $\{(a, b)\} \to P$ to $Hom(\mathscr{C}_R)$ (13)
If $\exists P \in Ob(\mathscr{C}_C)$, and $\pi_L(P) \leftrightarrows \exists P \notin Hom(\mathscr{C}_C)$ (14)
then add P to $Ob(\mathscr{C}_R), \pi_L(P) \leftrightarrows \exists P$ to $Hom(\mathscr{C}_C)$
If $\exists P^- \in Ob(\mathscr{C}_C)$ and $\pi_R(P) \leftrightarrows \exists P^- \notin Hom(\mathscr{C}_C)$ (15)
then add P^- to $Ob(\mathscr{C}_R), \pi_R(P) \leftrightarrows \exists P^-$ to $Hom(\mathscr{C}_C)$
If $\{(a, b)\} \to P \in Hom(\mathscr{C}_R), \{(b, a)\} \to P^- \notin Hom(\mathscr{C}_R)$ (16)
then add $\{(b, a)\} \to P^-$ to $Hom(\mathscr{C}_R)$
If $P^- \in Ob(\mathscr{C}_R), \{\pi_L(P) \leftrightarrows \pi_R(P^-), \pi_L(P) \leftrightarrows \pi_R(P^-)\} \nsubseteq Hom(\mathscr{C}_C)$ (17)
then add $\pi_L(P) \leftrightarrows \pi_R(P^-), \pi_L(P) \leftrightarrows \pi_R(P^-)$ to $Hom(\mathscr{C}_C)$
If $P_1 \to P_2$ or $P_1^- \to P_2^- \in Hom(\mathscr{C}_R)$, and $P_1 \to P_2 \notin Hom(\mathscr{C}_R)$ or (18)
$P_1^- \to P_2^- \notin Hom(\mathscr{C}_R)$ **then add** $P_1 \to P_2, P_1^- \to P_2^-$ to $Hom(\mathscr{C}_R)$
If $P_1 \to P_2^-$ or $P_1^- \to P_2 \in Hom(\mathscr{C}_R)$, and $P_1 \to P_2^- \notin Hom(\mathscr{C}_R)$ or (19)
$P_1^- \to P_2 \notin Hom(\mathscr{C}_R)$ **then add** $P_1 \to P_2^-, P_1^- \to P_2$ to $Hom(\mathscr{C}_R)$
If $R \to R_1, R \to \neg R_1 \in Hom(\mathscr{C}_R), R \to R_\bot \notin Hom(\mathscr{C}_R)$ (20)
then add $R \to R_\bot$ to $Hom(\mathscr{C}_R)$
If $B \to B_1, B \to \neg B_1 \in Hom(\mathscr{C}_C), B \to \bot \notin Hom(\mathscr{C}_C)$ (21)
then add $B \to \bot$ to $Hom(\mathscr{C}_C)$

Axioms (1) and (2) in $\mathcal{T}$ state that a patient is medicated with some medication. Axiom (2) and (3) tell that medication is prescribed by a doctor. Axiom (5) ensures that no patient is a doctor. We also consider the following ABox $\mathcal{A}$:

$$Patient(\mathsf{Tiph}), MedicatedWith(\mathsf{Tiph}, \mathsf{Paracetamol}),$$
$$PrescribeBy(\mathsf{Paracetamol}, \mathsf{Hugo})$$

To illustrate the construction of saturated and minimal categories with Algorithm 1 by applying rules in Table 1, we use the following table in which we omit trivial arrows such as identity arrows, and those going out/in from the initial/terminal object. To simplify the description of the categories we use concept and role names P, M, D, Mw, Pb for $Patient, Medication, Doctor, MedicatedWith, PrescribedBy$. When we read a line in this table, it is supposed that all objects and arrows in the columns $Ob(\mathscr{C}_C)$, $Hom(\mathscr{C}_C)$, $Ob(\mathscr{C}_R)$ and $Hom(\mathscr{C}_R)$ in the previous lines are already added and thus available in the categories. This availability decides whether the rule mentioned the current line is applicable. For instance, Rule (10) is applicable in the first line of the table because Axiom (1) is available in the Tbox $\mathcal{T}$. The application of Rule 10 requires nothing in the categories in this case. However, the application of Rule (14) in the sixth line needs the object $\exists Mw$ to be available in $Ob(\mathscr{C}_C)$. The Rules 12 and 13 are applicable in the second section of the table because the concept and role assertions correspond to the ABox $\mathcal{A}$. The application of Rules 12 and 13 do not require the use of the categories in this case. However the application of the Rule 8 expands the table by increasing the number of arrows in $Hom(\mathscr{C}_C)$.

We can observe that $Hom(\mathscr{C}_C)$ generated by the algorithm does not contain an arrow $\top \rightarrow \perp$ or $\{a\} \rightarrow \perp$ for all individual $\{a\}$ occurring the ABox. We can conclude that $\mathcal{K}$ is category-theoretically satisfiable. □

Theorem 2 (Complexity, Soundness and Completeness). *Let $\mathcal{K} = \langle \mathcal{T}, \mathcal{A} \rangle$ be a DL-Lite$_{\mathcal{R}}$ knowledge base.*

1. *Algorithm 1 runs in polynomial time in the size of $\mathcal{K}$.*
2. *If Algorithm 1 returns* `true` *with the input $\mathcal{K}$, then $\mathcal{K}$ is category-theoretically satisfiable.*
3. *If $\mathcal{K}$ is category-theoretically satisfiable, then Algorithm 1 returns* `true` *with the input $\mathcal{K}$.*

Proof. Algorithm 1 adds just subconcept objects of concept objects occurring in $\mathcal{T}$ and $\mathcal{A}$. In addition, there are at most 2 arrows between two objects in $Ob(\mathscr{C}_C)$ and $Ob(\mathscr{C}_R)$. Hence, the cardinality of $Ob(\mathscr{C}_C)$, $Ob(\mathscr{C}_R)$, $Hom(\mathscr{C}_C)$ and $Hom(\mathscr{C}_R)$ is bounded by $2(m+p)$ where $m = 2\ell^2$, $p = m^2$ and ℓ is the size in byte of $\mathcal{K}$. It holds that each application of a rule in Table 1 adds at least one new object or arrow. Moreover, the loop in Algorithm 1 continues only if there is a rule that is applicable. This implies that the number of iterations of the loop is bounded by $2(m+p)$. Therefore, Algorithm 1 runs in polynomial time in ℓ. Assume that Algorithm 1 returns `true` with the input $\mathcal{K}$. This implies that there are saturated and minimal categories built by Algorithm 1 such that $\top \rightarrow \perp \notin Hom(\mathscr{C}_C)$ and $\{a\} \rightarrow \perp \notin Hom(\mathscr{C}_C)$ for all individual a in $\mathcal{A}$. Minimality of the categories can be obtained by using the same argument in the proof of Theorem 1. By Definition 8, $\mathcal{K}$ is category-theoretically satisfiable. Conversely, assume that $\mathcal{K}$ is category-theoretically satisfiable. By Definition 8, there are minimal and saturated categories $\mathscr{C}_C$ and $\mathscr{C}_R$ such that $\top \rightarrow \perp \notin Hom(\mathscr{C}_C)$ and $\{a\} \rightarrow \perp \notin Hom(\mathscr{C}_C)$ for all individual a. Moreover, Algorithm 1 initializes $\mathscr{C}'_C$ and $\mathscr{C}'_R$ to empty.

Applied Rule	$Ob(\mathscr{C}_C)$	$Hom(\mathscr{C}_C)$	$Ob(\mathscr{C}_R)$	$Hom(\mathscr{C}_R)$
(10)	$P, \exists Mw$	$P \to \exists Mw$		
(10)	$M, \exists Mw^-$	$\exists Mw^- \to M$		
(10)	$\exists Pb$	$M \to \exists Pb$		
(10)	$D, \exists Pb^-$	$\exists Pb^- \to D$		
(10)	$\neg P$	$D \to \neg P$		
(14)		$\pi_L(Mw) \leftrightarrows \exists Mw$	Mw	
(14)		$\pi_L(Pb) \leftrightarrows \exists Pb$	Pb	
(15)		$\pi_R(Mw) \leftrightarrows \exists Mw^-$	Mw^-	
(15)		$\pi_R(Pb) \leftrightarrows \exists Pb^-$	Pb^-	
(8)		$\exists Pb^- \to \neg P$		
(8)		$\exists Mw^- \to \exists Pb$		
(12)	$\{t\}$	$\{t\} \to P$		
(13)	$\{pa\}$	$\{t\} \to \pi_L(Mw)$, $\{pa\} \to \pi_R(Mw)$	$\{(t, pa)\}$	$\{(t, pa)\} \to Mw$
(13)	$\{h\}$	$\{pa\} \to \pi_L(Pb)$, $\{h\} \to \pi_R(Pb)$	$\{(pa, h)\}$	$\{(pa, h)\} \to Pb$
(8)		$\{t\} \to \exists Mw$		
(8)		$\{h\} \to \exists Pb^-$		
(8)		$\{h\} \to D$		
(8)		$\{pa\} \to \exists Mw^-$		
(8)		$\{pa\} \to M$		
(8)		$\{h\} \to \neg P$		
(8)		$\{pa\} \to \exists Pb$		

Each object added to $\mathscr{C}'_C$ and $\mathscr{C}'_R$ by applying a rule in Table 1 must be contained in $\mathscr{C}_C$ and $\mathscr{C}_R$ since $\mathscr{C}_C$ and $\mathscr{C}_R$ are saturated. Since there is no arrow $\top \to \bot$ and $\{a\} \to \bot$ in $\mathscr{C}_C$ and $\mathscr{C}_R$, it follows that there is no arrow $\top \to \bot$ and $\{a\} \to \bot$ in $\mathscr{C}'_C$ and $\mathscr{C}'_R$. Therefore, Algorithm 1 can build minimal and saturated categories without arrows $\top \to \bot$ and $\{a\} \to \bot$. This complete the proof of the theorem. □

5 Conclusion

We have presented a rewriting of the usual set-theoretical semantics of the $DL\text{-}Lite_\mathcal{R}$ by using categorical language without set membership. We also proposed a tractable algorithm for checking category-theoretical satisfiability in $DL\text{-}Lite_\mathcal{R}$. The main advantage of this categorical approach is that it allows us to design straightforwardly the satisfiability algorithm and implement it more easily because it consists in applying rules coming from the category semantics of the logical constructors. For future work, we plan to introduce a categorical formalization of conjunctive queries and propose an algorithm for query answering.

References

1. Baader, F., Horrocks, I., Lutz, C., Sattler, U.: Introduction to Description Logic. Cambridge University Press, Cambridge (2017)
2. Calvanese, D., De Giacomo, G., Lembo, D., Lenzerini, M., Rosati, R.: Tractable reasoning and efficient query answering in description logics: the DL-Lite family. J. Autom. Reason. **39**, 385–429 (2007)
3. Baader, F.: The Description Logic Handbook: Theory, Implementation and Applications. Cambridge University Press, Cambridge (2003)
4. Artale, A., Calvanese, D., Kontchakov, R., Zakharyaschev, M.: The DL-Lite family and relations. J. Artif. Intell. Res. **36**, 1–69 (2009)
5. Poggi, A., Lembo, D., Calvanese, D., De Giacomo, G., Lenzerini, M., Rosati, R.: Linking data to ontologies. In: Spaccapietra, S. (eds.) Journal on Data Semantics X. LNCS, vol. 4900, pp. 133–173. Springer, Heidelberg (2008). https://doi.org/10.1007/978-3-540-77688-8_5
6. Calvanese, D., Giacomo, G.D., Lenzerini, M.: Conjunctive query containment and answering under description logic constraints. ACM Trans. Comput. Logic (TOCL) **9**(3), 1–31 (2008)
7. Brieulle, L., Le Duc, C., Vaillant, P.: Reasoning in the description logic ALC under category semantics (extended abstract). In: Proceedings of the 35th International Workshop on Description Logics (DL2022), vol. 3263 of CEUR Workshop Proceedings, CEUR-WS.org (2022)
8. Lawvere, F.W.: An elementary theory of the category of sets. Proc. Natl. Acad. Sci. **52**(6), 1506–1511 (1964)
9. Goldblatt, R.: Topoi: The Categorial Analysis of Logic, Mathematics. Dover Publications, New York (2006)
10. Mac Lane, S., Moerdijk, I.: Sheaves in Geometry and Logic. Springer, New York (1992). https://doi.org/10.1007/978-1-4612-0927-0
11. Spivak, D.I., Kent, R.E.: Ologs: a categorical framework for knowledge representation. PLoS ONE **7**(1), e24274 (2012)

Applying Genetic Algorithms to Validate a Conjecture in Graph Theory: The Minimum Dominating Set Problem

Jorge Cervantes-Ojeda, María C. Gómez-Fuentes(✉), and Julian A. Fresán-Figueroa

Universidad Autónoma Metropolitana, Vasco de Quiroga 4871, 05348 México City, Mexico
{jcervantes,mgomez,jfresan}@cua.uam.mx

Abstract. This paper presents a case study where the interdisciplinary approach between artificial intelligence, specifically genetic algorithms, and discrete mathematics has been instrumental in verifying a conjecture in graph theory. The focus of our research lies in the Minimum Dominating Set (MDS) problem, which involves identifying a dominating set with the minimum cardinality for a given graph. While previous works have primarily aimed at utilizing genetic algorithms to efficiently find satisfactory solutions to the MDS problem, our study aims to discover the optimal solution. The Rank GA algorithm employed in our work possesses the ability to escape local optima while simultaneously conducting local search to refine the best available solution. Since the MDS problem is known to be NP-hard, the characteristics of Rank GA, coupled with the identification of regularities in one of the solutions, enabled us to verify the conjecture for graphs comprising 30, 80, 312, and 800 vertices. This research serves as a testament to the versatility of genetic algorithms, showcasing their utility not only in practical problem-solving but also in tackling theoretical challenges.

Keywords: GA for theoretical problems · Rank GA · Genetic algorithms · Minimum Dominating Set

1 Introduction

Genetic Algorithms (GAs) have gained significant popularity for solving practical problems; however, their application in pure mathematics remains relatively limited. In this study, we present a compelling case where the Rank Genetic Algorithm [1] has facilitated the verification of a conjecture within the realm of discrete mathematics, particularly in the field of graph theory.

The Minimum Dominating Set (MDS) problem holds great significance in algorithmic graph theory, finding applications in various domains and prompting extensive research endeavors [2]. A vast array of literature, encompassing articles, books, and surveys, has been dedicated to the MDS problem [3, 4]. Notably, the MDS problem and

H. Calvo et al. (Eds.): MICAI 2023, LNAI 14391, pp. 271–282, 2024.
https://doi.org/10.1007/978-3-031-47765-2_20

its variants find prominent applications in communication networks [5], and social networks [6–8]. For further exploration of the MDS problem's application areas, pertinent works can be referred to in [9].

The MDS problem is widely acknowledged to be NP-hard, prompting significant research efforts in developing heuristics to attain high-quality solutions within a reasonable timeframe. Noteworthy works in this domain can be found in [10] and [11]. Numerous studies have been undertaken to devise efficient algorithms for solving the MDS problem, with the aim of improving upon the trivial bound of $O(\frac{2n}{\sqrt{n}})$ [12]. Consequently, most works employing heuristic methods for MDS focus on finding good solutions as quickly as possible. In contrast, our objective is to uncover the best possible solution through the utilization of a genetic algorithm. Specifically, we seek real solutions that aid in verifying the validity of a theoretical conjecture. To accomplish this, we employed the Rank GA due to its reliability in escaping local optima while conducting a local search to refine the best solution obtained thus far. Through the utilization of Rank GA, we generated empirical data that aids in determining an upper bound for the cardinality of the minimal dominating set in incidence graphs of classical generalized quadrangles.

The paper follows the following structure: In Sect. 2, we provide an overview of previous works where Genetic Algorithms (GAs) have been successfully employed to solve mathematical problems. Section 3 presents a detailed explanation of the conjecture that is to be verified in our study. In Sect. 4, we describe the Rank GA and elaborate on its utilization in determining the minimal dominating set of a graph. The experimental results are presented in Sect. 5, while the conclusions drawn from our research are outlined in Sect. 6.

2 Background

Genetic Algorithms (GAs) are widely recognized for their utility in engineering problems, but it is important to highlight their applicability in advancing mathematical research as well [13]. For instance, Jong and Spears [14] demonstrated that GAs can be effectively employed to solve NP-Complete problems. Additionally, Jakobs [15] applied a GA to tackle a geometry problem, while Pourrajabian et al. [16] successfully utilized a GA to solve nonlinear algebraic equations. In more recent studies, Cervantes et al. [17] utilized a Rank GA to enhance an upper bound that governs the rainbow k-connectivity of $(k; 6)$-cages.

In traditional usage, Genetic Algorithms (GAs) are typically employed to optimize a given fitness function by exploring a solution space and aiming to find the optimal solution. However, in the study by García-Altamirano et al. [18], the Rank GA underwent a unique adaptation: it was designed to exclusively perform Hajós operators with the objective of finding a path to reach a predetermined resulting directed graph. This represents a notable departure from the conventional usage of GAs. The algorithm started from an initial state where each individual represented a starting digraph, while the goal digraph that the algorithm aimed to reach was known in advance. The intriguing aspect was to uncover the method by which the Rank GA traversed the solution space to achieve the final state. By closely analyzing the algorithm's steps in the specific case, a general approach applicable to all cases was discovered.

Indeed, showcasing the potential contributions of Genetic Algorithms (GAs) in the realm of mathematics is not only valuable but also inspiring. Demonstrating how GAs can be effectively employed in mathematical problems can serve as a catalyst for progress in other areas where scientific advancements are primarily theoretical. By highlighting the application of GAs in mathematics, researchers can explore new avenues and innovative approaches to solve complex theoretical problems. This interdisciplinary approach can lead to novel insights, methodologies, and solutions, bridging the gap between theoretical and practical domains. Thus, presenting such works can provide motivation and inspiration for researchers in various fields to explore the potential of GAs beyond their traditional applications.

3 The Conjecture to Be Verified

In this section, we introduce key concepts that provide the necessary context for the conjecture that was verified using the Rank GA.

3.1 Generalized Quadrangle

Let k and r be positive integers greater than 2. A Generalized Quadrangle $CG(k-1, r-1)$ refers to a system comprising lines and points, where an incidence relation is established based on the following axioms:

1. Two lines intersect at most in one point.
2. At most one line passes through any two points.
3. Exactly r lines pass through each point.
4. Each line contains exactly k points.
5. If a point p is not contained in a line l, there exists precisely one line that passes through p and intersects l.

These axioms define the fundamental properties of a Generalized Quadrangle, providing the framework for studying and analyzing their characteristics.

Figure 1 illustrates the classical Generalized Quadrangle $G(q, q)$ for the specific case of $q = 2$. In this case, the values of r and k are both equal to 3.

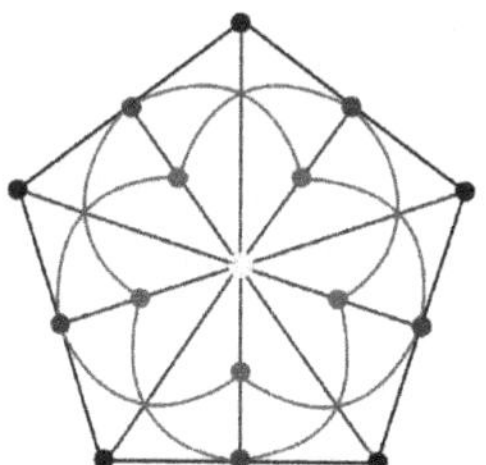

Fig. 1. Classical generalized quadrangle $CG(q, q)q = 2$

Considering a Generalized Quadrangle $G(q, q)$ with q as a prime number, the incidence relation between points and lines can be depicted as a bipartite graph, where the points and lines correspond to vertices of the graph and a point is adjacent to a line if they are incident. The number of vertices in each part of the bipartite graph can be determined using expression (1):

$$q^3 + q^2 + q + 1 \tag{1}$$

Figure 2 shows the incidence bipartite graph for the classical Generalized Quadrangle. $CG(q, q)q = 2$

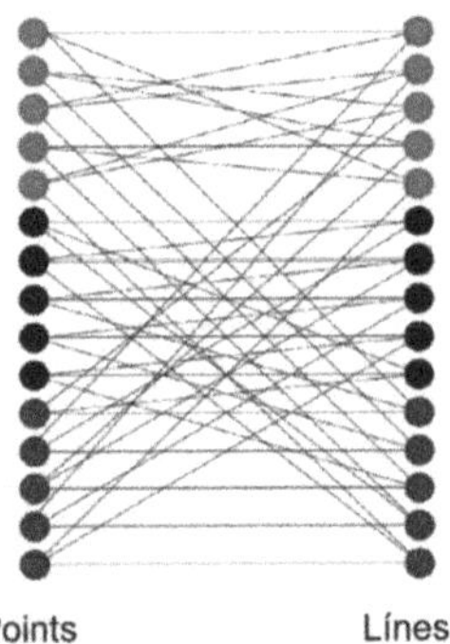

Fig. 2. Incidence graph of the classical generalized quadrangle $CG(q, q)q = 2$

3.2 The Minimum Dominating Set Problem

The Minimum Dominating Set (MDS) problem revolves around identifying a dominant set in a given graph G. A graph G is defined as a set of vertices V and a set of edges E, denoted as $G = (V, E)$. In the context of the MDS problem, a dominant set is a subset D of V, where every vertex that does not belong to D is connected to (at least) one vertex in D through an edge in E. To illustrate this concept, Fig. 3 showcases examples of various dominant sets for a given graph.

Dominating Set (Mathematical Definition): Given a simple undirected graph $G = (V, E)$, where V represents the set of vertices and E represents the set of edges, a subset D of vertices $D \subseteq V$ is a dominating set of G if, for every vertex u in $V \setminus D$, there exists a vertex x in D that is adjacent to u. In other words, every vertex not in D is adjacent to at least one vertex in D.

Vertex Domination: A vertex u is said to dominate a vertex v if either $u = v$ or u is adjacent to v. This concept signifies the relationship between vertices within the context of domination in the graph.

Minimal Dominating Set (Mathematical Definition): The minimal dominating set of a graph G is a dominating set D such that removing any element from D would render it non-dominant. In other words, for every element x in D, the set D - $\{x\}$ is not a dominating set.

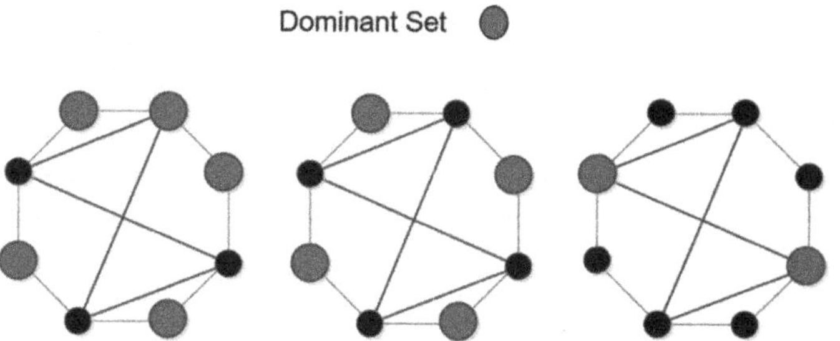

Fig. 3. Examples of Dominant Sets in a Graph

Domination Number: The domination number $\gamma(G)$, of a graph G is defined as the cardinality (size) of the smallest dominating set in G. It represents the minimum number of vertices required for a set in G to be a dominating set.

3.3 The Conjecture

The conjecture proposes that for a prime number q, the incidence bipartite graph associated with the classical generalized quadrangle $CG(q, q)$ possesses an upper bound on the domination number $\gamma(G)$. The domination number, denoted as $\gamma(G)$, represents the minimum number of vertices required to form a dominating set in the graph G.

According to the conjecture, the upper bound for the domination number $\gamma(G)$ in the incidence graph associated with $CG(q, q)$ can be determined using Eq. (2):

$$\gamma(G) = 2q^2 + 1 \tag{2}$$

Equation (2) provides an expression that bounds the value of the domination number in the incidence bipartite graph associated with the classical generalized quadrangle $CG(q, q)$, where q is a prime number. The conjecture suggests that the domination number does not exceed this upper bound. Further investigation and verification are required to confirm the validity of this conjecture.

4 Rank Genetic Algorithm for Finding Minimal Dominating Set

In the field of evolutionary computation, there is a fundamental trade-off between exploration and exploitation. If exploitation dominates, the population converges prematurely, restricting the search to a small subspace of the search space. This can lead to the algorithm getting stuck in a local optimum, resulting in suboptimal solutions. On the other hand, excessive exploration leads to searching in a large region, making it difficult for the algorithm to converge and obtain a solution.

The Rank Genetic Algorithm (Rank GA) [1] is a heuristic approach designed to strike a balance between exploration and exploitation. It achieves this by applying genetic operators that allow for both local and global search simultaneously. In the Rank GA, individuals within the population are evaluated and ranked from best to worst based on their fitness just before applying selection, recombination, and mutation operators to each individual. The operators are applied to individuals based on their current rank. The highly ranked individuals tend to remain unchanged and primarily recombine with better-performing individuals, promoting the exploitation of favorable genetic traits. On the other hand, lower-ranked individuals tend to recombine with worse-performing individuals, facilitating the exploration of distant genotypes in the search space, thus enabling the escape from local optima in the fitness landscape.

The probability of mutation assigned to each individual follows a monotonously increasing pattern according to their rank in the population, which is determined by their fitness. This means that individuals with higher ranks have a lower probability of mutation, while individuals with lower ranks have a higher probability.

In [19], it has been demonstrated that the Rank GA outperforms a simple GA in challenging fitness landscapes, especially those with binary string genotypes, where a good balance between exploration and exploitation is crucial. This balance is particularly necessary when the fitness landscape contains numerous local optima, and a modular solution can be constructed through evolution. In such cases, finding each module's solution may be challenging, requiring high exploration levels. Simultaneously, the integration of already found modules' solutions necessitates high exploitation levels within the algorithm.

By effectively balancing exploration and exploitation, the Rank GA offers superior performance in difficult fitness landscapes, providing a robust approach for problems that require a good trade-off between exploration and exploitation in evolutionary computation.

4.1 Solution Representation

The Rank GA adopts a binary representation for solutions in this case. Each solution X in the population is represented as an array of Booleans, where the size of the array corresponds to the number of vertices in the graph. The order of the array follows a fixed arrangement that aligns with the vertices of the graph.

In this representation, if the i-th vertex of the graph is included in the solution X, then the corresponding element x_i in the array is set to 1. Conversely, if the i-th vertex is not part of the solution, x_i is assigned a value of 0.

4.2 Fitness Function

To evaluate a solution X, we employ two metrics. Firstly, we use the metric k to evaluate the number of vertices in $V(G)$ that are dominated by X. In this context, a larger value of k is desirable. Secondly, we consider the cardinality c of X, which represents the number of elements in X. Here, a smaller value of c is preferred.

The fitness function to be maximized is defined by Eq. (3) as follows:

$$fitness(X) = k + c \tag{3}$$

The fitness function combines the metrics of the number of dominated vertices (k) and the cardinality of the solution (c) into a single value. By maximizing the fitness function, we want to achieve solutions that dominate a larger number of vertices while minimizing the cardinality of the solution. This allows for the identification of solutions that strike a balance between domination and the size of the minimal dominating set.

Note that with this fitness function, there is an element of neutrality that can be advantageous for the search process. For example, consider the scenario where the best individual has a fitness value of 50, with $k = 80$ and $c = 30$. In this case, another solution with $k = 81$ and $c = 31$ would be just as favorable for the algorithm. This implies that either solution could occupy the top position in the rank of solutions. At the top, they would be protected from being lost during the application of genetic operators, as per the Rank GA scheme, and the search would be "located" around that top solution.

This neutrality aspect in the fitness function allows for a broader exploration of the search space. Rather than being strictly limited to search from a single current best solution, the search can shift its "center" between different neutral solutions, thus expanding the exploration to encompass nearby solutions to any of them.

4.3 The Rank GA Operators

The Rank GA follows a specific procedure, beginning with the random initialization of the population. Individuals are then evaluated and sorted from best to worst based on their fitness. The rank of the i-th individual in the sorted population, denoted as r_i, is determined using Eq. (4):

$$r_i = \frac{i}{N - 1} \tag{4}$$

where i ranges from 0 to $N-1$, and N represents the number of individuals in the population.

The Rank GA then applies the following operations iteratively until a stopping criterion is met:

1. Rank Selection
2. Sort and rank
3. Rank Recombination
4. Evaluation, sort and rank
5. Rank Mutation
6. Evaluation, sort and rank

Rank Selection: Rank selection involves cloning individuals according to a two-step procedure.

First, the desired number of clones, *cloneNbr*, is calculated for each individual i using Eq. (5):

$$cloneNbr_i = S * (1 - r_i)^{S-1} \tag{5}$$

Here, r_i represents the rank of individual i, ranging from 0 to 1, and S corresponds to the selective pressure of the Rank Selection operator. The floor of $cloneNbr_i$ is taken, resulting in the number of clones to generate for each individual i.

Secondly, additional clones are produced as follows. The procedure initializes $i = 0$. While the total number of clones is less than the original number of individuals N, the fractional part of $cloneNbr_i$ is used as the probability of producing an extra clone of individual i. If a random number in the range [0,1) is lower than that probability, a clone of individual i is generated. The value of i is incremented modulo N to ensure it cycles through the individuals. The main idea in this step is to increase the likelihood of producing extra clones for individuals who lost a larger fractional part when the floor of $cloneNbr_i$ was taken in the first step.

The selective pressure (S) determines the intensity with which the selection operator concentrates the population towards a single dominant genotype. Lower selective pressure allows for more genetic diversity to be preserved in the population after each application of the selection operator.

By implementing Rank Selection, the Rank GA can effectively guide the cloning process, favoring individuals with higher ranks and promoting the retention and reproduction of genetic traits associated with higher fitness while maintaining some genetic diversity in the population. The adjustable selective pressure provides control over the concentration of individuals, influencing the balance between exploitation and exploration during the evolutionary process.

Rank Recombination: The Rank Recombination operator forces mating between individuals with indexes i and i+1 in the sorted population, where i increases by 2. This strategy ensures that individuals mate with others that are nearby in terms of rank. The purpose is to prevent individuals from mating with those that are significantly different in rank. By doing so, the best individuals are safeguarded from being recombined with poorly performing ones, as such combinations could disrupt the advantageous gene value combinations present in the best individuals. In contrast, recombination between two high-performing individuals can result in the fusion of their respective already found building blocks of the optimal solution, potentially leading to the creation of improved offspring.

Rank Recombination is done as uniform crossover with parent substitution. This means that all genes have an equal probability of being switched between parents, and the offspring always replaces the parents. The probability of switching genes, referred to as the switch probability (p_{switch}), is typically set to 0.5 as the recommended value.

In the selection operator, a selective pressure value of $S = 3$ is commonly used. With $S = 3$, three clones of the fittest individual are generated. This approach ensures that the best-ranked clone has the opportunity to recombine with a clone of itself (the second-best ranked), thereby preserving the advantageous genetic traits present in the best individual. The third-ranked clone would recombine with the second-best individual (ranked fourth), which is expected to possess different chromosomes, resulting in the production of diverse offspring. This way, the Rank GA not only preserves the best individual but also allows for recombination with another high-performing individual.

By employing Rank Recombination with a selective pressure value of $S = 3$, the Rank GA strikes a balance between preserving the advantageous genes of the best individual and introducing local search through recombination with other good individuals. This approach enhances the algorithm's ability to explore the search space effectively while retaining and propagating beneficial genetic traits.

Rank Mutation: The probability of mutation assigned to each individual, denoted as *pi* is determined by a monotonic increasing function of their rank. The function is de-fined as follows:

$$p_i = p_{max} * r_i^{\left(\frac{In(P\max *G)}{In(N-1)}\right)} \quad (6)$$

In this equation, p_{max} represents the maximum probability of mutation that can be assigned, r_i is the rank of individual i, G is the size of the genotype, and N is the population size.

The function assigns a mutation probability of 0 to the best individual, $1/G$ to the second-best individual, and p_{max} to the worst individual. As Rank Mutation is applied after Rank Recombination, it is highly likely that the first two individuals in the ranked list are identical. This means that the best individual remains unchanged (by mutation), while the second-best individual is likely to undergo exactly one mutation. This mechanism promotes exploration in the immediate vicinity of that second individual which is likely to be a clone of the best.

Conversely, poor-performing individuals undergo significant mutations to facilitate their escape from the basins of attraction of local optima. The larger mutations applied to these individuals ensure they can explore alternative regions in the search space and break free from suboptimal solutions.

By employing Rank Mutation with a probability assigned based on the rank, the Rank GA combines the preservation of advantageous traits in the best individual with exploratory mutations in the neighborhood of the second individual. Simultaneously, it encourages significant mutations in poorly performing individuals to facilitate their exploration of alternative regions in the search space. This approach enhances the algorithm's ability to strike a balance between exploitation and exploration, promoting the search for optimal solutions in complex fitness landscapes.

5 Results

To verify the conjecture presented in Eq. (2), we conducted experiments on four bipartite graphs of generalized quadrangles with 30, 80, 312, and 800 vertices. These cases come from the Incidence graph of the classical generalized quadrangle $CG(q, q)$ with $q = 2, 3, 5\, and\, 7$ respectively. Using the Rank GA algorithm, we searched for a minimal dominating set in each of these incidence bipartite graphs of Classical Generalized Quadrangles. By determining the cardinality of the minimal dominating set, we were able to verify the conjecture stated in Eq. (2).

For the graphs with 30 and 80 vertices, the Rank GA algorithm quickly obtained solutions with $\gamma(G)$ equal to the conjectured result. However, for the graph with 312 vertices, although the solutions found were very close to the conjectured result, they were not exactly equal to it. Upon analyzing the solutions for 30 and 80 vertices, we observed a particular pattern illustrated in Fig. 4. Specifically, on the left side of the bipartite graph, only the last bits were set to 1, while on the right side, only the first few bits were set to 1. This led us to consider the possibility of similar solutions existing in the case of 312 vertices. We tested a solution where the number of bits set to 1 on the left side was determined by Eq. (7):

$$\frac{(2q^2+1)}{2}+\frac{1}{2} \tag{7}$$

and the number of bits set to 1 on the right side was given by Eq. (8):

$$\frac{(2q^2+1)}{2}-\frac{1}{2} \tag{8}$$

This solution turned out to be a valid dominating set when applied to the graph with 312 vertices. Encouraged by these findings, we further tested the case of 800 vertices, which also yielded a dominating set. These results strongly support the conjecture presented in Eq. (2).

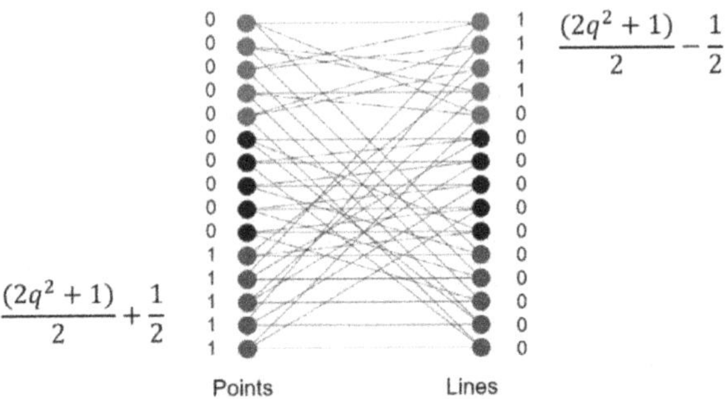

Fig. 4. Regularity in one of the solutions

As shown in Table 1, the domination number $\gamma(G)$ predicted by the conjecture was found to be equal to the $\gamma(G)$ obtained through the Rank GA algorithm.

Table 1. Comparison of $\gamma(G)$ predicted by the conjecture and $\gamma(G)$ obtained through Rank GA

q	# Vertices	$\gamma(G)$ Conjecture	$\gamma(G)$ Rank GA
2	30	9	9
3	80	19	19
5	312	51	51
7	800	99	99

6 Conclusions

In this research article, we explored the application of the Rank Genetic Algorithm (Rank GA) in verifying a conjecture in the field of graph theory. Specifically, we focused on the Minimum Dominating Set (MDS) problem and its relationship with incidence graphs of classical Generalized Quadrangles.

Through our investigation, we demonstrated that the Rank GA algorithm is capable of effectively searching for minimal dominating sets in some bipartite graphs. By evaluating the domination number $\gamma(G)$ of the obtained solutions, we were able to verify the validity of the conjecture proposed for the incidence graphs of generalized quadrangles. Moreover, we were able to construct specific sets attaining the conjectured bound. This is an important result because many conjectures in mathematics do not have explicit constructions.

Our results showed that the Rank GA algorithm performed very well in finding solutions that aligned with the conjectured domination numbers. For graphs with 30 and 80 vertices, the algorithm quickly identified solutions that matched the expected values. Although the solutions for the graph with 312 vertices were very close to the conjectured result, they were not exact. However, further analysis revealed that the pattern observed in the smaller graphs also held true for the larger graphs, supporting the conjecture.

The use of the Rank GA algorithm allowed us to strike a balance between exploration and exploitation, ensuring efficient search capabilities in the fitness landscapes of the MDS problem. The rank-based selection, recombination, and mutation operators employed in the Rank GA algorithm provided a robust framework for navigating the search space and escaping local optima.

The experimental results presented in this study, along with the consistent agreement between the conjectured domination numbers and those obtained through the Rank GA algorithm, validate the effectiveness of using genetic algorithms for theoretical problems in graph theory. The Rank GA algorithm demonstrated its ability to contribute not only to practical problem-solving but also to the exploration and verification of a mathematical conjecture and the construction of objects satisfying the conjecture.

Overall, this research highlights the potential of genetic algorithms, specifically the Rank GA, in the field of graph theory. The successful verification of the conjecture in the context of the Minimum Dominating Set problem for incidence graphs of classical Generalized Quadrangles emphasizes the potential of genetic algorithms to advance theoretical understanding in mathematics. Future studies could further explore the capabilities of genetic algorithms in other areas of theoretical research and extend their application to different problem domains.

By bridging the gap between artificial intelligence and discrete mathematics, this research opens up new possibilities for leveraging computational methods in solving complex theoretical problems and advancing scientific knowledge.

References

1. Cervantes, J., Stephens, C.R.: Rank based variation operators for genetic algorithms. In: Proceedings of the 10th annual conference on Genetic and evolutionary computation, pp. 905–912, ACM (2008)

2. Hedar, A.R., Ismail, R.: Hybrid genetic algorithm for minimum dominating set problem. In: Taniar, D., Gervasi, O., Murgante, B., Pardede, E., Apduhan, B.O. (eds.) International conference on computational science and its applications, vol. 6019, pp. 457–467. Springer, Heidelberg (2010). https://doi.org/10.1007/978-3-642-12189-0_40
3. Couturier, J.F., Heggernes, P., Van't Hof, P., Kratsch, D.: Minimal dominating sets in graph classes: combinatorial bounds and enumeration. Theoret. Comput. Sci. **487**, 82–94 (2013)
4. Liu, Z., Wang, B., Guo, L.: A survey on connected dominating set construction algorithm for. Inf. Technol. J. **9**(6), 1081–1092 (2010)
5. Bai, X., Zhao, D., Bai, S., Wang, Q., Li, W., Mu, D.: Minimum connected dominating sets in heterogeneous 3D wireless ad hoc networks. Ad Hoc Netw. **97**, 102023 (2020)
6. Bouamama, S., Blum, C.: An improved greedy heuristic for the minimum positive influence dominating set problem in social networks. Algorithms **14**(3), 79 (2021)
7. Chalupa, D.: An order-based algorithm for minimum dominating set with application in graph mining. Inf. Sci. **426**, 101–116 (2018)
8. Dinh, T.N., Shen, Y., Nguyen, D.T., Thai, M.T.: On the approximability of positive influence dominating set in social networks. J. Comb. Optim. **27**(3), 487–503 (2014)
9. Levin, M.S.: Note on dominating set problems. J. Commun. Technol. Electron. **66**(1), S8–S22 (2021). https://doi.org/10.1134/S1064226921130040
10. Li, B., Zhang, X., Cai, S., Lin, J., Wang, Y., Blum, C.: NuCDS: an efficient local search algorithm for minimum connected dominating set. In: Proceedings of the Twenty-Ninth International Conference on International Joint Conferences on Artificial Intelligence, pp. 1503–1510 (2021, January)
11. Pinacho-Davidson, P., Blum, C.: BARRAKUDA: A hybrid evolutionary algorithm for minimum capacitated dominating set problem. Mathematics **8**(11), 1858 (2020)
12. Fomin, F.V., Grandoni, F., Pyatkin, A.V., Stepanov, A.A.: Combinatorial bounds via measure and conquer: bounding minimal dominating sets and applications. ACM Trans. Algorithms (TALG) **5**(1), 1–17 (2008)
13. Mitchell, M.: Introduction to Genetic Algorithms. MIT Press (1996)
14. De Jong K.A., Spears W.M.: Using genetic algorithms to solve NP-complete problems. In: International Computer Games Association, pp. 124–132 (1989)
15. Jakobs, S.: On genetic algorithms for the packing of polygons. Eur. J. Oper. Res. **88**(1), 165–181 (1996)
16. Pourrajabian, A., Ebrahimi, R., Mirzaei, M., Shams, M.: Applying genetic algorithms for solving nonlinear algebraic equations. Appl. Math. Comput. **219**(24), 11483–11494 (2013)
17. Cervantes-Ojeda J., Gómez-Fuentes M.C., González-Moreno D., Olsen M.: Rainbow connectivity using a rank genetic algorithm. J. Appl. Math. **2019**(7), (2019) https://doi.org/10.1155/2019/4073905
18. García-Altamirano, J. C., Olsen, M., Cervantes-Ojeda, J.: How to construct the symmetric cycle of length 5 using Hajós construction with an adapted Rank Genetic Algorithm. Discrete Math. Theor. Comput. Sci., **25**(1), 1–11 (2023) https://doi.org/10.46298/dmtcs.10189
19. Cervantes, J., Stephens., C. R.: Limitations of existing mutation rate heuristics and how a rank GA overcomes them. IEEE Trans. Evol. Comput. **13**(2) 369–397 (2008)

Random Number Generator Based on Hopfield Neural Network with Xorshift and Genetic Algorithms

Cristobal Lecca, Armando Zegarra, and Julio Santisteban(✉)

Universidad Católica San Pablo, Arequipa, Peru
{cristobal.lecca,armando.zegarra,jsantisteban}@ucsp.edu.pe

Abstract. Generating random numbers plays a fundamental role in matters of computer security. New high-security standards for data encryption have emerged with the increasing demand for secure communication, storage, and management of sensitive data on public networks. Data encryption techniques have expanded rapidly. In this paper, we present two methods of pseudorandom number generation; the first method combines the existing architectures of Hopfield neural networks and the XORShift algorithm, an the second is based on genetic algorithms. Our approaches pass the NIST and Diehard tests, which give us numbers that satisfy the statistical requirements. Compared with other architectures, the results demonstrated a robust consistency in the quality of the generated random numbers, which shows that it is a reliable method.

Keywords: Random Number · XORShift · Genetic Algorithms

1 Introduction

Randomness emphasises well-defined statistical properties in statistics, such as lack of bias or correlation. When a variable is said to be random, the variable follows a given probability distribution. The term arbitrary implies that there is no such determinable probability distribution. A number sequence containing no patterns or regularities is known as a statistically random sequence. When a number is chosen arbitrarily from some specific distribution, it can be called a random number. Such numbers are expected to be independent and uncorrelated with successive numbers.

Algorithms or processes that generate random numbers must be capable of complying with the characteristics regarding those above. These are known as PRNs (Pseudo-Random Numbers).

There has been a growing interest in the search for more efficient and reliable methods to generate high-quality random numbers. Traditional methods, such as congruential linear generators (GLCs) or clock-based pseudorandom number generators, have limitations and weaknesses [3,8]. Also, asymmetry has been

H. Calvo et al. (Eds.): MICAI 2023, LNAI 14391, pp. 283–295, 2024.
https://doi.org/10.1007/978-3-031-47765-2_21

considered as a means of feature extraction for better pseudorandom number generators [16].

The creation of a new pseudorandom number generation method, which takes advantage of the complementary strengths and features of Hopfield neural networks and the XORShift algorithm, has a significant impact on the validity of statistical experiments to generate random numbers.

Hopfield networks were first introduced by John Hopfield [7]. These are recurrent neural networks, that is, networks with cycles in their structures. Hopfield neural networks have a multi-loop feedback system in their [6] structure. Each neuron in these networks is connected to all other neurons but has no feedback. All neurons are input and output neurons. Hopfield neural networks are placed in the category of associative memory.

Regarding the activation function of neurons in a neural network can be continuous or discrete, Hopfield neural networks are recognized and denoted as *Discrete Hopfield NN* and *Continuous Hopfield NN.*

The Xorshift algorithm is a pseudorandom number generator characterized by its simplicity and fast computational performance. George Marsaglia proposed it in 2003 [12] as an efficient alternative to congruential linear generators (GLC) and other more complex algorithms. The method relies on shift operations and bitwise XOR operations to generate sequences of apparently random numbers showing good statistical properties.

Another algorithm we use to generate pseudorandom numbers is the Genetic Algorithm (GA), a stochastic search algorithm inspired by the principles of biological evolution. GA is a robust and adaptable optimization strategy efficiently [9]. We show that GA is viable for the pseudorandom numbers generation.

The next section presents the state of the art, followed by our two proposals and their respective test and results. Lastly, we conclude.

2 NIST Testing Module

It has been used NIST SP 800-22 Rev. 1 statistical tests [15] and DieHarder which is described by Brown [4]. DieHarder reimplements and extends George Marsaglia's Diehard Battery of Tests of Randomness [13]. Due to its robust performance over various random number generators, it is suitable to test a random number generator. which are the most accepted in the state of the art. Statistical RNG tests analyze randomness as a probabilistic property and describe it in terms of probability used in the NIST testing module [2].

3 Related Works

3.1 Approaches Based on Chaotic Systems

- Generator based on Chen's system improved by Liu et al. (2018): Liu et al. propose an improvement to PRN based on Chen's system. Through careful

adjustments of the system parameters, they improved the quality and statistical properties of the generated sequence. However, a limitation was identified regarding the dependence on the system parameters [10].
- Generator based on the Ikeda system proposed by Yang et al. (2019): used the Ikeda system which is a nonlinear dynamical system in PRN. By mapping the orbits of the Ikeda system to numerical values. A limitation regarding the ability to resist cryptographic attacks was identified [17].
- Zhao et al.(2023) uses a compound chaotic system to PRN. The system shows a complex and promising dynamic behaviour regarding randomness and uniform distribution of the outputs. A limitation is the sensitivity to initial conditions and external disturbances [18].

Despite the limitations identified in some of the chaotic systems-based methods mentioned above, it is important to note that many of them still manage to get a very good pass rate (around 98–99%) [10,17,18] in standard pseudorandom number generation tests. These methods exhibit attractive properties, such as chaotic behaviour, high generation speed, and the potential to improve the distribution and uniformity of the generated sequences.

Limitations may affect the quality, randomness, and safety of the generated sequences. According to [11], chaotic systems do not guarantee the correct generation of pseudorandom numbers.

3.2 Hybrid Pseudo Random Number Generator (PRNG)

- Riera et al. (2021) uses linear methods, specifically the Lehmer generator. Although this generator may exhibit acceptable behaviour under certain parameter conditions, it exhibits undesirable characteristics that make it unsuitable for various stochastic simulations. A limitation in computational complexity is identified due to the calculation of the inverse module [14].
- Aydin et al. (2020) uses a lightweight devices with limited resources, such as smart cards and RFID tags. The generator has proven efficient in performance, resource usage, and randomness, outperforming other known PRNGs, holds a limitation in security and resistance to cryptographic attacks [1].
- Alnajim et al. (2023) uses one-dimensional (1D) map that addresses the limitations of traditional 1D chaotic maps. The new map combines different elements to expand the range of control parameters and generate more diverse chaotic behaviour. It require further study to identify its limitations.
- Hameed and Mohammed (2019) uses the *Hopfield Neural Network* (HNN) that has produced unpredictable outputs under specific circumstances. The numbers generated using HNN are evaluated through the NIST Statistical and ORL tests [5].

Hybrid methods outperforming the most straightforward methods in performance in particular tests and analyses such as Kolmogorov-Smirnov Test or Poker Test [3]. However, hybrid methods also have limitations on the implementation, parameter-tuning and computational resources.

3.3 Genetic Algorithms

Jhajharia and Mishra [5] propose a classical method for generating pseudorandom numbers using mutation and crossover techniques. First, a selection operator is applied, in which two parents are randomly selected from the initial population. The selected parents are used to produce the individuals for the next generation through crossbreeding. After the first generation of individuals, a selection is made based on comparing the population with each other using Shannon Entropy. To apply a crossover operator, the parents are matched using Ring crossover from one point to another. The two parents are combined in a ring shape, and a random cut point is generated. It is applied in each individual is randomly changed from what occurs in the previous cross.

Lehrer [4] presented the congruent linear technique to produce pseudorandom numbers where a new number (Xn + 1) obtained from the previous value Xn by:

$$(aX_n + c) \bmod m$$

Kumar and Banka [10] proposed a new scheme based on gap shift, full gap column remover and space fusion mutation operators to solve the problem. They have improved the quality of the first individuals using this method.

Soni and Agrawal [11] proposed a technique in which Genetic Algorithms is used for the key generation process. Genetic Algorithms's crossover and mutation operations cause the generators to produce very complex keys, and it uses the Advanced Encryption Standard algorithm to encrypt the image. In this case, ring crossover and ring mutation methods were used.

4 PRNG Based on Hopfield Neural Network and Xorshift

Our proposal combines a Hopfield Neural Network (HNN) with the Xorshift algorithm to generate PRNG. This proposal arises as a solution to the limitations found in traditional approaches. It aims to improve the quality and randomness of the generated numbers, especially in applications that require stochastic simulations and secure communications.

One of the main motivations for combining these two methods lies in the individual characteristics that each contributes. The Hopfield neural network has demonstrated its ability to pass statistical tests of randomness and its ability to generate high-quality pseudorandom sequences. On the other hand, the Xorshift algorithm is known for its computational simplicity and ability to generate fast and efficient sequences.

The following conditions are considered to guarantee non-convergence:

- The structure of the proposed HNN is fully connected; that is, there is self-feedback. The structure of these Hopfield networks is presented in the figure. Connecting each neuron to itself breaks one of the stability conditions of the Lyapunov energy function for Hopfield Neural Networks.

- A non-linear function (in this case, arctan) is used as the activation function of the neurons, where x is the sum of all the inputs of the neuron. The nonlinear activation function increases the complexity of the neural network output.
- The HNN weight matrix is asymmetric, where the upper triangle of the weight matrix contains positive numbers and the lower triangle of the matrix contains negative numbers. Selecting an asymmetric weight matrix breaks one of the stability conditions of the Lyapunov energy function for the Hopfield neural network.
- The weight matrix is strongly diagonally dominated. So the diagonal elements of the weight matrix contain large positive numbers compared to other elements of our weight matrix.
- We use a large number of neurons, 100.
- If, for neuron $i, Xi >= 1$, then in the next iteration, that neuron amplifies itself by the weight of the corresponding branch independently of other neuron inputs. This is also valid for output $Xi <= 1$ with decreasing impact on the neuron. In other words, this means that the neuron is always fired with its output $>= 1 or <= 1$ in all iterations and, consequently, amplifying or decreasing. To prevent this, Anderson put an upper bound and a lower bound on the output of each neuron.

Although there are simpler and less computationally expensive methods for pseudorandom number generation, the use of the HNN, together with the Xorshift algorithm, provides superior results regarding the quality of the generated numbers and the ability to pass statistical tests of randomness. This is because the combination of these two components makes it possible to eliminate possible patterns and correlations that can be detected in sequences of numbers generated by other methods with unpredictable of outputs and patterns.

It is important to note that implementing this architecture may require higher computational power and a more careful generation of the necessary seeds for the HNN.

5 PRNG Based on Genetic Algorithms

Our proposal is configured as follows:

- Selection function: The racing test.
- crossover: We use a variant of ring crossover.
- Mutation: Binflip and XOR.
- Coding: Full and binary.

The Full is the most optimal representation of these subsets since it gives us greater visibility of how random one is. We only migrate to a binary representation when doing a bitflip to execute a mutation.

First Population Generation. A population of 100 random subsets is generated; these are given by the native Python generator or any other configurable in the same declaration of the instance of our main class.

Crossbreeding. The crossover ring, proposed by Kaya et al. [15], combine pairs of parental chromosomes into rings by joining genes in head-to-head and tail-to-tail arrangements. The cut point is randomly selected at the position of each ring to separate it into halves. We use a variant of this method, which combines two pseudorandom subsets, cuts them in half, and then combines them together.

Mutation

- Bitflip: We loop through the entire selected subset of the population and execute a bit flip on each element. This will generate a randomly different number than the initial one. For this, we must first transform the element into a binary representation.
- XOR: Like the previous method, we convert its number to a binary representation and then XOR it with a randomly generated key for each subset element.

5.1 Selection

The run test is a statistical test used to verify the randomness in the data. It is a non-parametric test and uses data series to decide whether the data presented is random or tends to follow a pattern. A run is defined as a series of increasing or decreasing values. The number of increasing or decreasing values is the duration of the execution.

The first step in the run test is to count the number of runs in the data stream. There are several ways to define runs; however, in all cases, the formulation must produce a dichotomous sequence of values. In our case, values above the median are treated as positive and values below the median as negative. A run is defined as a series of consecutive positive or negative values.

In our case, to select the individuals, we run this test and determine a score for each one. Since this test does not contain parameters, it is one of the most objective since it does not depend on input.

5.2 Loop

The loop of the algorithm until reaching a score of 0.00037 in the test:

1. 100 random subsets are generated.
2. 50 extra sets are generated with crossover.
3. 25 sets with bitflip mutation are generated.
4. 25 sets with XOR mutation are generated.
5. Sort random subsets based on their selection score.
6. The best 100 are taken.
7. The loop is executed again.

6 Tests and Results: PRNG Based on Hopfield Neural Network and Xorshift

In this first approach, we evaluated with the randomness tests created by NIST [2], as well as the Diehard tests [13].

Combining these two techniques allows us to take advantage of the individual strengths of each. The Hopfield network gives us the ability to store and retrieve specific patterns, while XORShift provides us with a source of reliable pseudorandom numbers needed.

Unlike recent methods focusing on chaotic systems-based approaches, our hybrid approach takes advantage of the Hopfield network's ability to store and retrieve specific patterns. Our approach is hybrid Unlike the state of the art that have used the architecture of the Hopfield network by modifying the parameters or optimizing the network.

By combining the Hopfield network with the XORShift generator, our method seeks to take advantage of the simplicity and pseudorandom number generation capabilities of XORShift. The XORShift algorithm is an efficient and easy-to-implement that performs well. By integrating this generator with the Hopfield network, we can enrich our exploration capabilities and improve the diversity of generated patterns.

6.1 Results of the NIST Module

In the test module, the parameter α is set to 0.01 (i.e. the confidence level of the test is set to 99%) and the sequence length to 1,000,000. Based on the NIST PRNG test module, each statistical test's minimum ratio pass rate is 0.96015.

Table 1 shows us the results obtained after the respective tests in the NIST module with our proposed architecture. It should be noted that prop values with * mean that they failed to pass desirable features. We must define that prop is the proportion of the results for 100 sequences in these experiments, and the minimum accepted value is the one mentioned above.

Tables 2, 3 and 4 exhibit detailed outcomes of NIST statistical tests applied to various traditional pseudo-random number generators. It serves as a basis for comparing our proposed PRNG methods, enabling us to assess the performance of traditional and innovative approaches to pseudo-random number generation. Within these tables, "Ok" signifies that the method successfully passed the test, while "X" indicates that it did not meet the criteria. These results offer insights into the strengths and weaknesses of commonly used PRNG techniques, including linear congruential generators, Micali-Schnorr generators, and Blum-Blum-Shub generators. Our research utilizes these comparative findings to highlight the effectiveness and reliability of our novel PRNG methods.

It is observed that the proposed architecture based on a Hopfield neural network with the Xorshift algorithm has improved compared to other state-of-the-art methods. When performing statistical tests using the NIST PRNG module, a significant improvement in the average of the experiments has been found, indicating progress in the generation of pseudorandom numbers.

Table 1. Results of tests performed

PRNG Test	Experiment 1		Experiment 2		Experiment 3	
	P-Value	Prop	P-Value	Prop	P-Value	Prop
Frequency	0.6163	0.97	0.5141	0.96	0.7399	0.99
Block Frequency	0.3190	0.99	0.2622	0.99	0.2622	1.0
Cumulative Sums-Forward	0.0329	0.98	0.9463	0.97	0.9114	0.99
Cumulative Sums-Reverse	0.6976	0.96	0.0269	0.95*	0.4372	0.99
Runs	0.3152	0.96	0.3838	0.97	0.1022	0.94*
Longest Run	0.5544	0.99	0.2896	0.99	0.4011	0.99
Rank	0.5749	0.99	0.1537	1.0	0.1153	1.0
Non Overlapping Template	0.4142	0.99	0.4476	0.97	0.5004	0.99
Overlapping Template	0.5544	0.99	0.2757	0.99	0.9114	0.99
Universal	0.6579	1.0	0.1153	0.98	0.7197	0.96
Approximate Entropy	0.2372	0.96	0.4590	0.98	0.7791	0.96
Random Excursions	0.4682	0.99	0.3344	0.99	0.3656	0.99
Random Excursions Variant	0.2955	0.99	0.3274	0.95*	0.3912	0.98
Serial (m = 5)	0.4127	0.96	0.4404	0.97	0.7357	0.99
Linear Complexity	0.5341	0.99	0.8343	0.98	0.1453	0.99

Table 2. Results of different PRNs with the NIST module, Table 1 of 3

PRNG/NIST Test	Frequency	Block frequency	Cumulative Sums-Forward	Cumulative Sums-Reverse
Hopfield NN	Ok	Ok	Ok	Ok
Linear Congruential	Ok	Ok	Ok	Ok
Quadratic Congruential-1	X	Ok	X	X
Quadratic Congruential-2	X	Ok	X	X
Cubic Congruential	X	X	X	X
Micali Schnorr	Ok	Ok	Ok	Ok
Blum Blum Shub	Ok	Ok	Ok	Ok
Modular Exponentiation	X	Ok	X	X
G function SHA1	Ok	Ok	Ok	Ok

Table 3. Results of different PRNs with the NIST module, Table 2 of 3

PRNG/NIST Test	Runs	Longest Run	Rank	Non Overlapping Template	Overlapping Template	Universal
Hopfield NN	Ok	Ok	Ok	Ok	Ok	Ok
Linear Congruential	Ok	Ok	Ok	Ok	Ok	Ok
Quadratic Congruential-1	X	Ok	Ok	X	Ok	Ok
Quadratic Congruential-2	Ok	Ok	Ok	Ok	Ok	Ok
Cubic Congruential	X	Ok	Ok	Ok	Ok	Ok
Micali Schnorr	Ok	Ok	Ok	Ok	Ok	Ok
Blum Blum Shub	Ok	Ok	Ok	Ok	Ok	Ok
Modular Exponentiation	Ok	Ok	Ok	Ok	Ok	Ok
G function SHA1	Ok	Ok	Ok	Ok	Ok	Ok

Table 4. Results of different PRNs with the NIST module, Table 3 of 3

PRNG/NIST Test	Approximate Entropy	Random Excursions	Random Excursions Variant	Serial (m = 5)	Linear Complexity
Hopfield NN	Ok	Ok	Ok	Ok	Ok
Linear Congruential	Ok	Ok	Ok	Ok	Ok
Quadratic Congruential-1	Ok	X	Ok	X	Ok
Quadratic Congruential-2	Ok	X	X	X	Ok
Cubic Congruential	X	Ok	Ok	X	Ok
Micali Schnorr	Ok	Ok	Ok	Ok	Ok
Blum Blum Shub	Ok	Ok	Ok	Ok	Ok
Modular Exponentiation	Ok	Ok	Ok	X	Ok
G function SHA1	Ok	Ok	Ok	Ok	Ok

By examining the specific results of each statistical test, it can be highlighted that the proposed architecture shows favourable results in several tests. For example, in tests for frequency, block frequency, forward cumulative sums, longest run, range, non-overlapping templates, overlapping templates, universal randomness, and approximate entropy, the results show a high pass ratio, reaching prop values greater than 0.96, and in some cases as high as 1.0. These results indicate that the proposed architecture generates pseudorandom number sequences that exhibit suitable distribution and desirable characteristics according to these tests.

Notice that although the proposed architecture shows better results in several tests, it also has some weaknesses. For example, in the tests of backward cumulative sums, approximate entropy, random displacements, and linear complexity, lower prop values are obtained, and some cases with * indicate that they do not fully meet the desirable characteristics. These results can be attributed to the particular characteristics of the Xorshift algorithm and its influence on the statistical properties of the generated sequences.

6.2 Diehard Test Suite Results

Below are the results of three experiments in each test of the Diehard ensemble for the PRNG based on the Hopfield algorithm and XORShift. The tests carried out include 30 tests that have been evaluated (Table 5):

Some tests have low p-values, indicating that the numbers generated did not pass these tests for randomness. For example, the tests *Minimum Distance* and *Runs* have p-values that can be considered low in experiments, suggesting that the numbers generated do not meet certain patterns of randomness expected in those specific tests.

Despite this, we must consider the consistency of the generations, which suggests that for many cases and applications of random numbers, these would perform very well. Most of the tests show consistently high p values in the different experiments. This implies that the generated numbers passed these tests and exhibit a generally good quality of randomness. For example, tests such as *Overlapping 5-Permutation* and *Squeeze* have high p-values in all experiments, indicating that the numbers generated exhibit a fair degree of randomness by the criteria of those tests.

Table 5. Results of experiments on the Diehard test set, P values for each test

Test	Experiment 1	Experiment 2	Experiment 3
Birthday Spacings	0.211	**0.016***	0.352
Overlapping 5-Permutation	0.678	0.643	0.694
Ranks of 31 × 31 Matrices	0.512	0.578	0.481
Ranks of 6 × 8 Matrices	0.721	0.549	0.597
Monkey Tests	0.405	0.371	0.324
Count the Ones 1	0.456	0.387	0.401
Count the Ones 2	0.612	0.534	0.635
Parking Lot	0.701	0.559	0.533
Minimum Distance	0.165	0.522	**0.115***
3D Spheres	0.541	0.583	0.621
Squeeze	0.749	0.768	0.784
Overlapping Perm. 1	0.618	0.624	0.595
Overlapping Perm. 2	0.472	0.354	0.408
Runs	0.211	0.320	**0.098***
Craps Wins	0.693	0.625	0.751
Craps Throws	0.738	0.712	0.641
Minimum Distance (2D)	0.669	0.672	0.697
Permutation Test	0.505	0.564	0.488
Binary Rank 1	0.678	0.651	0.662
Binary Rank 2	0.602	0.678	0.585
Binary Rank 3	0.666	0.652	0.639
Binary Rank 4	0.602	0.634	0.663
Count the 1's (stream)	0.631	0.630	0.612
Parking Lot (max 8)	0.709	0.722	0.671
Count the 1's (byte)	0.598	0.668	0.645
Parking Lot (no 0)	0.612	0.679	0.655
Bits (stream)	0.658	0.624	0.637
Bits (bytes)	0.646	0.629	0.642
Craps Wins (x3)	0.721	0.692	0.748
Craps Throws (x3)	0.663	0.696	0.662

Values in black with * fail the test; the rest of the tests are passed. The p values represent the probability of obtaining the observed results if the generated sequence were truly random.

7 Tests and Results: PRNG Based on Genetic Algorithms

In this second approach, we carry out our proposal using a Monte Carlo simulation averaging the results of the 30 tests since we cannot ensure that with a single iteration, our results are favourable or not.

7.1 Models to Compare with Ours

- Jhajharia and Mishra random number generator.
- Python random number generator.
- Random number generator quantum random.

7.2 DieHarder Suite of Random Number Generator Tests

Table 6. Results DieHarder suite of Random Number Generator Tests

Test	PGA	Python	Jhajharia y Mishra	Quantum Random
Birthday spacings	0.000308	0.053712	0.004314	0.003911
Ranks of matrices	0.02661	0.47516	0.00717	0.09013
Count the 1 s	0.01093	0.51283	0.01811	0.32737
Minimum distance test	0.00450	0.23433	0.00091	0.09348
The squeeze test	0.00067	0.09682	0.00123	0.06422
The craps test	0.00069	0.28141	0.09252	0.05195
Overlapping permutations	0.00682	0.15067	0.00056	0.00399
Monkey tests	0.00072	0.01043	0.00821	0.00867
Parking lot test	0.00468	0.58211	0.00240	0.13283
Overlapping sums test	0.01276	0.82462	0.00937	0.54254
Run test	0.00026	0.02485	0.00982	0.01145

Table 7. Average Performance Results for Results DieHarder suite.

Model	Score
PGA	0.00824
Python	0.29990
Jhajharia and Mishra	0.01299
Quantum Random	0.12736

We can see in Tables 6 and 7, on average, our model obtained a lower p-value in each test, meaning we have greater randomness.

Our model performed better in the following tests: Birthday spacings, the Monkey test, Count the 1 s, The squeeze test, The craps test, and the Run test.

At the same time, we can see that we obtained a ten times better result in the Run test than the Jhajharia and Mishra genetic algorithms; this is because we execute the selection function using it and not a generic entropy equation.

Quantum and native Python algorithms do not perform well compared to models using genetic algorithms because they generate a single subset without considering any selection.

Applying the XOR algorithm on the mutation also decreases the number of mutations to reach a given p-value since the randomness increases instead of executing a bit flip.

8 Discussion

The ability to pass these statistical tests is crucial in applications where a high quality of randomness and resistance to security tests are required. For example, in encryption systems, gambling, and number simulations, having pseudorandom sequences pass these tests provides additional assurance of the randomness and unpredictability of the generated numbers.

In practical terms, The proposed architecture is based on a Hopfield neural network with the Xorshift; test results suggest that the proposed architecture may be suitable for applications that require uniform randomness, non-patterning, and unpredictable behaviour. This may include applications in cryptography, scientific simulations, and cryptographic key generation systems. On the other hand, the proposed architecture may not be the most suitable for applications that depend on precise random displacements or linear complexity.

The proposal using genetic algorithms for generating pseudo-random numbers is viable; we obtain better quality and stability in all the generated sets. Since at the moment of generating subsets with the tests that do not execute the crossing, mutation and selection techniques, they do not have a stable or good p-value in terms of quality compared to the genetic models.

It has been proven that the selection function, executing a random test such as the Run test, is beneficial for the quality of random numbers since a better selection of subsets is obtained compared to the entropy equations.

9 Conclusion

The results obtained in the experiments show that the proposed architecture based on a Hopfield neural network with the Xorshift algorithm significantly improves number generation. The proposal using genetic algorithms is suitable for low resources contexts. At the same time, the proposed base on a Hopfield neural network, with the Xorshift requiring more resources but with robust test validity.

Our proposals can be run efficiently on a standard computer without consuming much resources and obtain random numbers with a grade degree of confidence and randomness. We expect to continue working on including other algorithms and combining them to make the process faster and with higher reliability and use other measurement tools to guarantee effective randomness generation.

References

1. Aydin, Ö., Kösemen, C.: XorshiftUL+: a novel hybrid random number generator for Internet of Things and wireless sensor network applications. Pamukkale Üniversitesi Mühendislik Bilimleri Dergisi **26**(5), 953–958 (2020)
2. Bassham III, L.E., et al.: SP 800-22 Rev. 1a. A statistical test suite for random and pseudorandom number generators for cryptographic applications. National Institute of Standards & Technology (2010)
3. Bouteghrine, B., Tanougast, C., Sadoudi, S.: A survey on chaos-based cryptosystems: implementations and applications. In: Skiadas, C.H., Dimotikalis, Y. (eds.) 14th Chaotic Modeling and Simulation International Conference, pp. 65–80. Springer, Cham (2022). https://doi.org/10.1007/978-3-030-96964-6_6
4. Brown, R.G.: DieHarder: a GNU public licensed random number tester. Draft paper included as file manual/dieharder.tex in the dieharder sources. Last version dated 20 (2006)
5. Hameed, S.M., Ali, L.M.M.: Utilizing Hopfield neural network for pseudo-random number generator. In: 2018 IEEE/ACS 15th International Conference on Computer Systems and Applications (AICCSA), pp. 1–5. IEEE (2018)
6. Haykin, S.: Neural Networks and Learning Machines, 3/E. Pearson Education India (2009)
7. Hopfield, J.J.: Neural networks and physical systems with emergent collective computational abilities. Proc. Natl. Acad. Sci. **79**(8), 2554–2558 (1982)
8. Kietzmann, P., Schmidt, T.C., Wählisch, M.: A guideline on pseudorandom number generation (PRNG) in the IoT. ACM Comput. Surv. (CSUR) **54**(6), 1–38 (2021)
9. Liao, T.L., Wan, P.Y., Yan, J.J.: Design and synchronization of chaos-based true random number generators and its FPGA implementation. IEEE Access **10**, 8279–8286 (2022)
10. Liu, J., et al.: A hardware pseudo-random number generator using stochastic computing and logistic map. Micromachines **12**(1), 31 (2020)
11. Marroquin, W., Santisteban, J.: Generation of pseudo-random numbers based on network traffic. In: Martínez-Villaseñor, L., Herrera-Alcántara, O., Ponce, H., Castro-Espinoza, F.A. (eds.) MICAI 2020. LNCS (LNAI), vol. 12468, pp. 481–493. Springer, Cham (2020). https://doi.org/10.1007/978-3-030-60884-2_37
12. Marsaglia, G.: Xorshift RNGs. J. Stat. Softw. **8**, 1–6 (2003)
13. Marsaglia, G.: The Marsaglia random number CDROM including the diehard battery of tests of randomness (2008). http://www.stat.fsu.edu/pub/diehard/
14. Riera, C., Roy, T., Sarkar, S., Stanica, P.: A hybrid inversive congruential pseudorandom number generator with high period. Eur. J. Pure Appl. Math. **14**(1), 1–18 (2021)
15. Rukhin, A., et al.: NIST special publication 800-22 Revision 1a: a statistical test suite for random and pseudorandom number generators for cryptographic applications. NIST, US Department of Commerce, USA (2010)
16. Santisteban, J., Tejada-Cárcamo, J.: Unilateral Jaccard similarity coefficient. In: GSB@ SIGIR, pp. 23–27 (2015)
17. Wang, L., Cheng, H.: Pseudo-random number generator based on logistic chaotic system. Entropy **21**(10), 960 (2019)
18. Zhao, W., Chang, Z., Ma, C., Shen, Z.: A pseudorandom number generator based on the chaotic map and quantum random walks. Entropy **25**(1), 166 (2023)

Using Compiler Errors Messages to Feedback High School Students Through Machine Learning Methods

Víctor Gonzalo Rivero Martínez(✉), Maricela Quintana López, Asdrúbal López Chau, and Víctor Manuel Landassuri Moreno

Universidad Autónoma del Estado de México, Centro Universitario UAEM Valle de México, CP 54500 Ciudad López Mateos, Estado de México, Mexico
vriverom001@alumno.uaemex.mx, {mquintanal,alchau, vmlandassurim}@uaemex.mx

Abstract. Teaching programming is essential for science and technology development in any country. Studies indicate high failure rates in programming subjects, which often lead to frustration or discouragement among students when they encounter coding and compiler error message. This is due to the language and interpretation of such error messages. Several efforts have been made to improve this situation, using neural networks or machine learning techniques to either fix the compiler error or give a more understandable error message. In this work, error-based learning is considered, and instead of fixing errors in the code, compiler error messages are used to provide feedback on syntax errors to programming students. The feedback consists of four components: a translation of the message to Spanish, syntax information about the language item, the error's relation to possible causes and a reference to relevant topics for review. All the given information is intended to help students understand the error, allowing them to rewrite the code and compile it successfully. To achieve that goal, supervised learning was used to build a classifier using the compiler error messages. A set of documents was generated by injecting errors into model programs, thereafter, labelled according to the type of syntax error. The Machine Learning algorithms used were Decision Tree, Support Vector Machine, Random Forest, Multi-layer Perceptron and K-Nearest Neighbors. These classifiers were trained using 80% of the documents and evaluated with the remaining 20%, achieving an accuracy of over 90% for making new predictions and providing feedback.

Keywords: Compiler Error Messages · Machine Learning · Text Classifier

1 Introduction

Nowadays, programming courses are essential components of high school and early university studies because they enable students to apply, develop, or enhance their computational skills. Previous studies indicate high failure rates in programming subjects because students often struggle when given programming problems to solve, specifically when coding and compiler error messages appear, which often discourage them

H. Calvo et al. (Eds.): MICAI 2023, LNAI 14391, pp. 296–308, 2024.
https://doi.org/10.1007/978-3-031-47765-2_22

[1, 2, 3]. In [4] a survey is conducted among IT students and found that these difficulties are related to algorithmic thinking, programming logic, dividing the program into modules, creating and using functions or subprograms, error correction, identifying errors in programs, and programming language syntax. Particularly, a survey was conducted at UAEM Valle de Mexico University Center [5], and similar results were obtained (see Fig. 1). It is important to highlight that 39.4% of respondents have problem with algorithmic thinking, while 23.3% face difficulties with compiler errors.

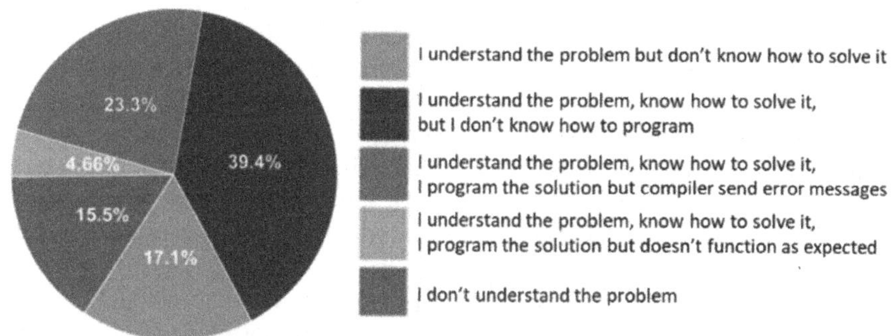

Fig. 1. Faced difficulties when solving problems [5].

As established by [6] one of the problems that have more influence in learning programming is the interpretation of the error messages delivered by compiler. For native Spanish speakers, the fact that these messages are in English adds a difficulty to overcome.

Several efforts have been made to address this problem. On one hand, there are tools that repair or correct the errors as TRACER: Targeted Repair of Compilation Errors [7], Dr Repair [8], MultiFix [9], Synshine [10] among others. These tools utilize artificial neural networks and deep learning to repair compilation errors in C, C + + or Java languages, using on error messages as input, except for Tfix [11], that directly uses which directly uses the program's source code to repair java programs.

On the other hand, there are tools that provide error-related feedback, such as Grammar Guru or Decaf. Grammar Guru is designed for learning programming in JavaScript and utilizes an artificial neural network to identify syntax errors, their locations, and provide suggestions to correct them [12]. Decaf is designed for Java programming, and its main contribution is enhancing the compiler error messages to make them more understandable and correctable by students [1]. Targeted Example Generation for Compilation Errors [13], and DeepDelta [14] are designed for C and Java programming, respectively. The main distinction from the previously mentioned tools is that, to suggest corrections, these tools compare the user's code with stored corrected code. This implies that both the error and its correction are retained.

Additionally, Learnskell [15] is a type error debugger for Haskell Language that diagnose errors at the expression level and generate high quality error messages using machine learning techniques. It focuses on programs with nonstructural errors such as parentheses and brackets, achieving a detection rate of 86% for all nonstructural errors and a maximum accuracy of 67% in identifying their causes. For the training set, 1604 programs with errors generated by students were used. Once the feature vector was constructed, the training set was manually labeled, and the unbalanced set was resampled. CLACER [16] (Classification of Compilation Errors) is a deep learning model based on the program token types to categorized error compilation, improving the error localization accuracy with a prediction performance over 98%. RING [17] is a multilingual repair engine powered by Codex in which Artificial Intelligence proposes corrections to the programmer's code on three stages of automate program repair: error localization, code transformation, and candidate ranking.

The primary distinction between the proposed work and the previously mentioned approaches is that the focus is on elucidating the causes of errors to students and providing suggestions for correction as well as related topics for further study. This approach is supported by [18], which suggests that students can learn from their errors when they comprehend the underlying causes and have alternatives for rectification. In this regard, the main purpose of this work is to contribute to learning programming by developing a tool that enables students to learn from their errors when programming in the C language. The focus is on syntax usage and error interpretation. To achieve this objective, a classifier is built, it takes an error message as input and produces feedback as output.

The feedback is composed of four components: a translation of the message to Spanish, possible causes for the error, information about the syntax of the grammatical rules related to the error, and the topics that students can review to improve their performance. The classifier is built using machine learning techniques, specifically, K-Nearest Neighbors, Decision Tree, Random Forest, Multi-layer Perceptron, Support Vector Machine and the voting of this algorithms.

The rest of the paper is structured as follows: Sect. 2 presents the methodology used to build the classifier, Sect. 3 describes the development and results of the classifier, Sect. 4 presents an example of use, and finally, Sect. 5 provides the conclusions and outlines future work.

2 Methodology

Text mining involves extracting, processing and analyzing text documents to identify patterns and trends. One task in text mining is classification, which refers to labeling papers written in natural language with predefined categories. This means that each document (a sequence of words) is assigned a category [19]. To automate this assignment, machine learning algorithms can be used.

Since text documents can often be considered unstructured data, text mining was employed for classification purposes to transform them into structured data using vectorization techniques [20]. Subsequently, a machine learning technique was utilized to construct the classifier.

The methodology employed in this paper is based on a process for constructing an automated classifier [21] and is shown in Fig. 2. This approach uses a supervised learning system to perform the predictive task. However, instead of the traditional data preparation steps involving data collection, selection, and transformation, this methodology includes corpus generation.

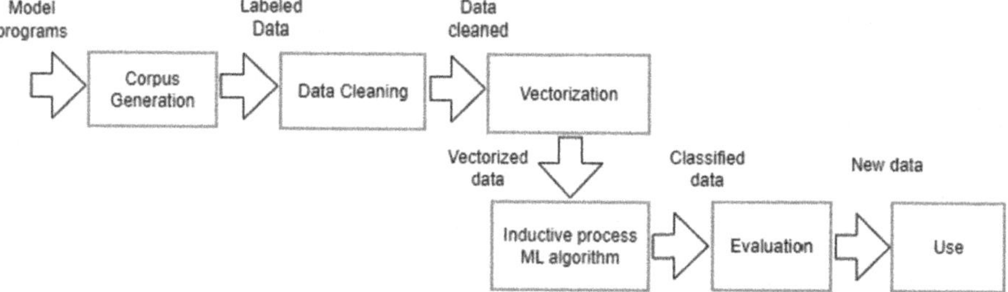

Fig. 2. Building process for automated classifier.

Corpus generation refers to the dataset used to train the predictive model responsible for classifying the type of syntax error and generating feedback thereafter. This process entails injecting errors into the model programs which consist in removing characters that generate errors, compiling them and saving the corresponding compiler error messages and their respective error types proposed. The data cleaning process removes text from the documents that do not contribute to the data categorization. Next, the vectorization step involves transforming the documents into vectors using the statistical TF-IDF (Term Frequency–Inverse Document Frequency). Afterwards, the inductive process involving machine learning is performed to build the classifiers. Finally, the evaluation and application stages are conducted to assess the performance of the classifiers. This evaluation is based on the percentage of correct predictions achieved on a test set. If the classifier's performance is unacceptable, it is possible to return to the early stages and consider different data, transformations, or algorithms. Conversely, if the classifier's performance is satisfactory, it can be used with new data to determine the type of error and provide appropriated feedback.

3 Classifier Development

This section describes the stages to build the classifier, using the methodology presented on Sect. 2.

3.1 Corpus Generation

For corpus generation, the data (compiler error messages) and its type of error (labels) were generated simultaneously using model programs through an error injection process (see Fig. 3). For this purpose, were created 35 model programs written in the C programming language considering the main topics of an introductory programming course which encompassed processor directives, main function, input/output functions, selective structures, variable declarations, and loops.

Taking into account the most frequent errors made by students [22], such as missing semicolons, colons, parentheses, variables, quotation marks among others, an error injection process is done, specifically deleting elements, that it is known to cause compilation errors, and simultaneously labeling data with a function name. For instance,

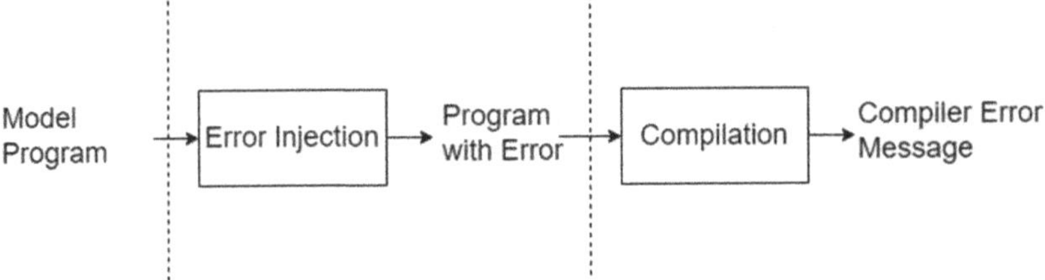

Fig. 3. Corpus Generation.

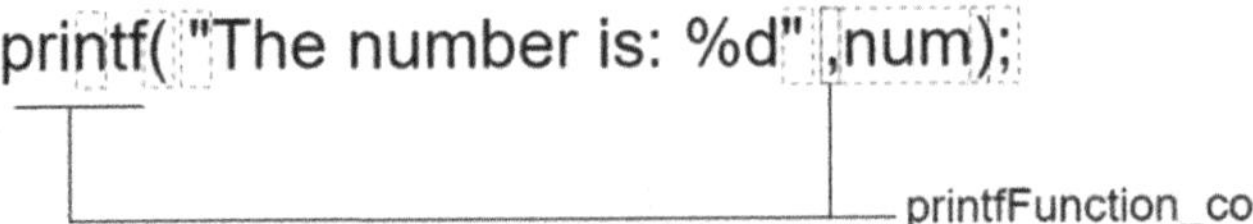

Fig. 4. Labeling data example.

if a comma is removed in the printf function, the class or label proposed for this error message is printfFunction_co (see Fig. 4).

Table 1 shows the items removed from the programs according with input/output functions, processor directives, select structures, etc., for instance, for the 'Printf Function' set, encompass five classes according to the item removed: comma, parenthesis (left or right), quotation marks, variable (va) and a letter which indicates removing a character from the keyword.

Table 1. Items removed from programs.

Class/Items	,	(	)	:	#	“	[	]	.	>	<	{	}	;	va	letter	Data
Loop for		•	•											•	•	•	107
Main		•	•													•	108
Printf	•	•	•			•									•	•	653
Scanf	•	•	•			•									•	•	357
Processor directives					•				•	•	•					•	228
Semicolon														•			300
Braces												•	•				316
Switch		•	•	•											•	•	197
Variable declaration						•	•	•									95
Logic expression		•	•												•		191
if structure		•	•												•		24
while cicle															•	•	42
Return sentence															•	•	35
Total																	**2653**

3.2 Data Cleaning

The compiler error messages may contain standard strings, words, or characters, such as ‘error’, ‘In function’, and ‘:’. Additionally, certain words from the specific context of each program, such as file names or output function text, which although are important for locating where the error is, they do not contribute to class differentiation, may be present. Therefore, in the cleaning step, such words were removed (refer to Fig. 5).

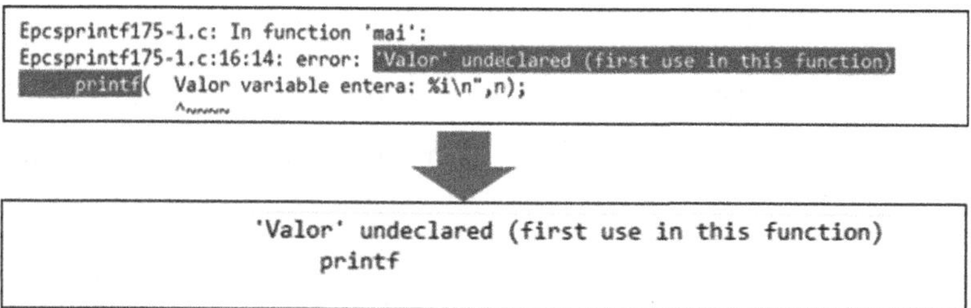

Fig. 5. Original and cleaned error message.

After the data cleaning step, the error messages were stored along with their corresponding class. An extract from this file is presented in Table 2. These cleaned messages serve as the input for the subsequent step: vectorization. The process of vectorization will be explained in the next section.

Table 2. Extract from class storage of compiler error messages.

Error Message	Class
expected declaration specifiers before 'printf'	curlyBracket_{_
expected '}' before 'else'	curlyBracket_}_
expected '(' before 'n' for	forCicle_pr
Id returned 1 exit status	mainFunction_ln
missing terminating "character printf	printfFunction_cs

3.3 Vectorization

Transforming documents into vectors is achieved using the TF-IDF statistic, which compares the number of occurrences of a term in a document to the number of documents in which the term appears, the higher the value of a term, the rarer it is in the document and the most it contributes to class separation. An example of this process is shown in Table 3.

Table 3. Extract of the vectorization through TF-IDF statistic.

Message	before	declaration	expected	identifier	initialized
expected declaration specifiers before 'printf'	0.27239	0.51345	0.25114	0.00000	0.00000
parameter 'n' is initialized	0.00000	0.00000	0.00000	0.00000	0.59148
expected identifier or '(' before 'while'	0.20624	0.00000	0.19015	0.68071	0.00000

3.4 Modelling the Classifier

To build the classifier, supervised learning is employed. The dataset was divided into two parts: 80% of the data is used to train the classifier, and the remaining 20% is used to evaluate its accuracy; the same train and test sets were used to build all the classifiers. The inductive process (see Fig. 6) in which the model learns to classify from a labeled set of data (train set), is carried out using the free software machine learning library for the Python programming language scikit-learn, specifically the algorithms: Decision Tree (DT), Support Vector Machine (SVM), K-Nearest Neighbors (KNN), Random Forest (RF), Multilayer Perceptron (MPL).

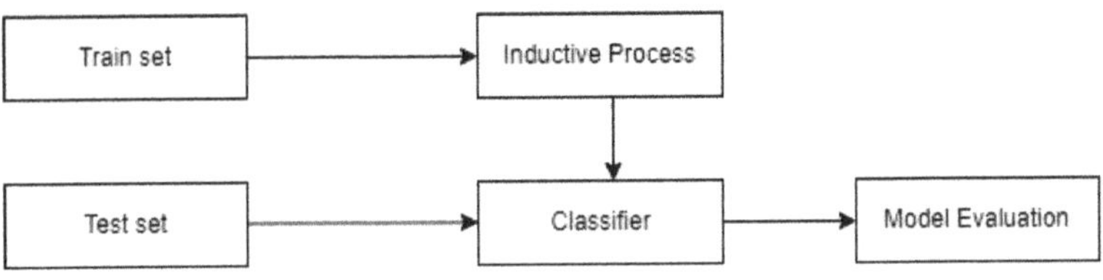

Fig. 6. Inductive process.

3.5 Model Evaluation

The metrics used to evaluate the model performance are following:

- Accuracy: percentage of correct predictions
- Precision: measures positive instances correctly predicted
- Recall: measures negative instances correctly predicted
- F1 Score: Harmonic between precision and recall

Hyperparameters are the external configuration variables to manage the training of a machine learning model and are tuned before the model is trained. The best hyperparameters found using the Random Search based on cross validation implementation of the scikit-learn library for each algorithm are shown in Table 4. For the Decision Tree algorithm, the optimal number of samples required at each node (min_samples_leaf) was determined to be two, the optimal maximum tree depth (max_depth) is 20, and *entropy* was found to be the best selection criterion. For the Support Vector Machine algorithm, the linear kernel was determined to be optimal, the parameter c that defines the margin size was determined to be 1000 and the gamma parameter that defines the decision margin between the observations to 1. The optimal number of neighbors found for the KNN algorithm was 15, and the weights of the points are determined based on the Euclidean distance with respect to a query point and the type of distance to perform the calculations is *euclidean.* The number of trees (n_estimators for the Random Forest algorithm is determined to be 150, the function that measures the quality of the division is *entropy*, the number of leaves(max_leaf_nodes) unlimited, the maximum number of features was determined by sqrt (max_features = sqrt (n_features)), the maximum depth of the tree until the leaves are pure, and the randomness of the bootstrapping of the samples used when building the tree (random_state) to 45. For the Multi-layer perceptron algorithm, the number of neurons in the layer hidden was set to 100, *lbfgs* as the optimization algorithm to learn the weights and bias, *adaptive* for the percentage of change with which the weights are updated at each iteration and the activation function was set to *logistic* i.e. f(x) = 1 / (1 + exp(-x)).

Table 4. Hyperparameters configuration.

Algorithms	Best Params
Decision Tree	min_samples_leaf=2, max_depth=20,criterion=entropy
Support Vector Machine	kernel=linear, gamma=1, C=1000
K-Nearest Neighbors	weights=distance, n_nighbors=15, metric=euclidean
Random Forest	n_estimators=150, max_leaf_nodes=None, max_features=sqrt, max_depth=None, criterion=entropy, random_state=45
Multi-layer Perceptron	activation=logistic, hidden_layer_sizes=100, learning_rate=adaptiva, solver=lbfgs

With the previous configuration, most of the algorithms demonstrated a high performance, achieving an accuracy of 90% on the test set (See Table 5).

Table 5. Evaluation Metrics Result.

	Precision	Recall	F1 Score	Accuracy
Decision Tree	0.94	0.90	0.90	0.90
Support Vector Machine	0.94	0.89	0.89	0.89
K-Nearest Neighbors	0.89	0.90	0.89	0.90
Random Forest	0.94	0.90	0.90	0.90
Multilayer Perceptron	0.94	0.90	0.90	0.90

A final experiment was performed by creating an ensemble with the classifiers using majority voting to determine the class. The results of individual and ensemble classifiers on test set are shown in Table 6. It is worth mentioning that for greater precision, two decimal places were considered, resulting the K-Nearest Neighbors and Random Forest algorithms achieving the best performance.

Table 6. Test set evaluation results.

Classifier	Test Set	
	# Fails	% Success
Decision Tree	53	90.01%
Support Vector Machine	57	89.26%
K-Nearest Neighbors	51	90.39%
Random Forest	51	90.39%
Multilayer Perceptron	54	89.83%
Voting	53	90.01%

For reasons of space, only the confusion matrix of the random forest algorithm on test set is shown in Fig. 7. On the diagonal of the matrix, all correctly classified instances are observed and in other cases incorrectly classified instances. For example, it can be noted that 10 instances of the mainFunction_pr class (Parenthesis from main function) are incorrectly classified as processorDirectives_li (Standar library). These occurrences could be attributed to the similarity of compiler error messages among these classes.

3.6 Use of the Classifier

The process for classifying new messages is as follows (see Fig. 8).

1. The system fetches the c file with error.
2. The program code is compiled; the error message is cleaned, and its characteristics are extracted using the TF-IDF (vectorization) statistic.
3. The new vectorized document is classify.

It is worth mentioning that, if the user generates an unconsidered error, such as a semantic error, the model will erroneously classify it in one of the existing classes.

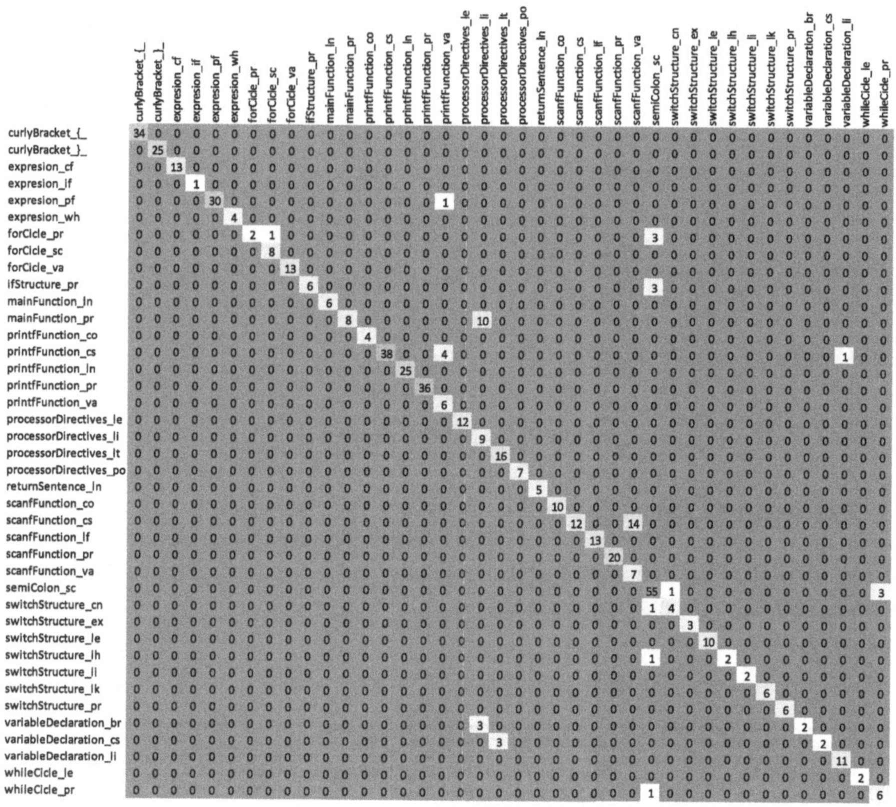

	curlyBracket_{_	curlyBracket_}_	expresion_cf	expresion_if	expresion_pf	expresion_wh	forCicle_pr	forCicle_sc	forCicle_va	ifStructure_pr	mainFunction_ln	mainFunction_pr	printfFunction_co	printfFunction_cs	printfFunction_ln	printfFunction_pr	printfFunction_va	processorDirectives_le	processorDirectives_li	processorDirectives_lt	processorDirectives_po	returnSentence_ln	scanfFunction_co	scanfFunction_cs	scanfFunction_lf	scanfFunction_pr	scanfFunction_va	semiColon_sc	switchStructure_cn	switchStructure_ex	switchStructure_le	switchStructure_lh	switchStructure_li	switchStructure_lk	switchStructure_pr	variableDeclaration_br	variableDeclaration_cs	variableDeclaration_li	whileCicle_le	whileCicle_pr
curlyBracket_{_	34	0	0	0	0	0	0	0	0	0	0	0	0	0	0	0	0	0	0	0	0	0	0	0	0	0	0	0	0	0	0	0	0	0	0	0	0	0	0	0
curlyBracket_}_	0	25	0	0	0	0	0	0	0	0	0	0	0	0	0	0	0	0	0	0	0	0	0	0	0	0	0	0	0	0	0	0	0	0	0	0	0	0	0	0
expresion_cf	0	0	13	0	0	0	0	0	0	0	0	0	0	0	0	0	0	0	0	0	0	0	0	0	0	0	0	0	0	0	0	0	0	0	0	0	0	0	0	0
expresion_if	0	0	0	1	0	0	0	0	0	0	0	0	0	0	0	0	0	0	0	0	0	0	0	0	0	0	0	0	0	0	0	0	0	0	0	0	0	0	0	0
expresion_pf	0	0	0	0	30	0	0	0	0	0	0	0	0	0	0	0	1	0	0	0	0	0	0	0	0	0	0	0	0	0	0	0	0	0	0	0	0	0	0	0
expresion_wh	0	0	0	0	0	4	0	0	0	0	0	0	0	0	0	0	0	0	0	0	0	0	0	0	0	0	0	0	0	0	0	0	0	0	0	0	0	0	0	0
forCicle_pr	0	0	0	0	0	0	2	1	0	0	0	0	0	0	0	0	0	0	0	0	0	0	0	0	0	0	0	3	0	0	0	0	0	0	0	0	0	0	0	0
forCicle_sc	0	0	0	0	0	0	0	8	0	0	0	0	0	0	0	0	0	0	0	0	0	0	0	0	0	0	0	0	0	0	0	0	0	0	0	0	0	0	0	0
forCicle_va	0	0	0	0	0	0	0	0	13	0	0	0	0	0	0	0	0	0	0	0	0	0	0	0	0	0	0	0	0	0	0	0	0	0	0	0	0	0	0	0
ifStructure_pr	0	0	0	0	0	0	0	0	0	6	0	0	0	0	0	0	0	0	0	0	0	0	0	0	0	0	0	3	0	0	0	0	0	0	0	0	0	0	0	0
mainFunction_ln	0	0	0	0	0	0	0	0	0	0	6	0	0	0	0	0	0	0	0	0	0	0	0	0	0	0	0	0	0	0	0	0	0	0	0	0	0	0	0	0
mainFunction_pr	0	0	0	0	0	0	0	0	0	0	0	8	0	0	0	0	0	0	10	0	0	0	0	0	0	0	0	0	0	0	0	0	0	0	0	0	0	0	0	0
printfFunction_co	0	0	0	0	0	0	0	0	0	0	0	0	4	0	0	0	0	0	0	0	0	0	0	0	0	0	0	0	0	0	0	0	0	0	0	0	0	0	0	0
printfFunction_cs	0	0	0	0	0	0	0	0	0	0	0	0	0	38	0	0	4	0	0	0	0	0	0	0	0	0	0	0	0	0	0	0	0	0	0	0	0	1	0	0
printfFunction_ln	0	0	0	0	0	0	0	0	0	0	0	0	0	0	25	0	0	0	0	0	0	0	0	0	0	0	0	0	0	0	0	0	0	0	0	0	0	0	0	0
printfFunction_pr	0	0	0	0	0	0	0	0	0	0	0	0	0	0	0	36	0	0	0	0	0	0	0	0	0	0	0	0	0	0	0	0	0	0	0	0	0	0	0	0
printfFunction_va	0	0	0	0	0	0	0	0	0	0	0	0	0	0	0	0	6	0	0	0	0	0	0	0	0	0	0	0	0	0	0	0	0	0	0	0	0	0	0	0
processorDirectives_le	0	0	0	0	0	0	0	0	0	0	0	0	0	0	0	0	0	12	0	0	0	0	0	0	0	0	0	0	0	0	0	0	0	0	0	0	0	0	0	0
processorDirectives_li	0	0	0	0	0	0	0	0	0	0	0	0	0	0	0	0	0	0	9	0	0	0	0	0	0	0	0	0	0	0	0	0	0	0	0	0	0	0	0	0
processorDirectives_lt	0	0	0	0	0	0	0	0	0	0	0	0	0	0	0	0	0	0	0	16	0	0	0	0	0	0	0	0	0	0	0	0	0	0	0	0	0	0	0	0
processorDirectives_po	0	0	0	0	0	0	0	0	0	0	0	0	0	0	0	0	0	0	0	0	7	0	0	0	0	0	0	0	0	0	0	0	0	0	0	0	0	0	0	0
returnSentence_ln	0	0	0	0	0	0	0	0	0	0	0	0	0	0	0	0	0	0	0	0	0	5	0	0	0	0	0	0	0	0	0	0	0	0	0	0	0	0	0	0
scanfFunction_co	0	0	0	0	0	0	0	0	0	0	0	0	0	0	0	0	0	0	0	0	0	0	10	0	0	0	0	0	0	0	0	0	0	0	0	0	0	0	0	0
scanfFunction_cs	0	0	0	0	0	0	0	0	0	0	0	0	0	0	0	0	0	0	0	0	0	0	0	12	0	0	14	0	0	0	0	0	0	0	0	0	0	0	0	0
scanfFunction_lf	0	0	0	0	0	0	0	0	0	0	0	0	0	0	0	0	0	0	0	0	0	0	0	0	13	0	0	0	0	0	0	0	0	0	0	0	0	0	0	0
scanfFunction_pr	0	0	0	0	0	0	0	0	0	0	0	0	0	0	0	0	0	0	0	0	0	0	0	0	0	20	0	0	0	0	0	0	0	0	0	0	0	0	0	0
scanfFunction_va	0	0	0	0	0	0	0	0	0	0	0	0	0	0	0	0	0	0	0	0	0	0	0	0	0	0	7	0	0	0	0	0	0	0	0	0	0	0	0	0
semiColon_sc	0	0	0	0	0	0	0	0	0	0	0	0	0	0	0	0	0	0	0	0	0	0	0	0	0	0	0	55	1	0	0	0	0	0	0	0	0	0	0	3
switchStructure_cn	0	0	0	0	0	0	0	0	0	0	0	0	0	0	0	0	0	0	0	0	0	0	0	0	0	0	0	1	4	0	0	0	0	0	0	0	0	0	0	0
switchStructure_ex	0	0	0	0	0	0	0	0	0	0	0	0	0	0	0	0	0	0	0	0	0	0	0	0	0	0	0	0	0	3	0	0	0	0	0	0	0	0	0	0
switchStructure_le	0	0	0	0	0	0	0	0	0	0	0	0	0	0	0	0	0	0	0	0	0	0	0	0	0	0	0	0	0	0	10	0	0	0	0	0	0	0	0	0
switchStructure_lh	0	0	0	0	0	0	0	0	0	0	0	0	0	0	0	0	0	0	0	0	0	0	0	0	0	0	0	1	0	0	0	2	0	0	0	0	0	0	0	0
switchStructure_li	0	0	0	0	0	0	0	0	0	0	0	0	0	0	0	0	0	0	0	0	0	0	0	0	0	0	0	0	0	0	0	0	2	0	0	0	0	0	0	0
switchStructure_lk	0	0	0	0	0	0	0	0	0	0	0	0	0	0	0	0	0	0	0	0	0	0	0	0	0	0	0	0	0	0	0	0	0	6	0	0	0	0	0	0
switchStructure_pr	0	0	0	0	0	0	0	0	0	0	0	0	0	0	0	0	0	0	0	0	0	0	0	0	0	0	0	0	0	0	0	0	0	0	6	0	0	0	0	0
variableDeclaration_br	0	0	0	0	0	0	0	0	0	0	0	0	0	0	0	0	0	0	3	0	0	0	0	0	0	0	0	0	0	0	0	0	0	0	0	2	0	0	0	0
variableDeclaration_cs	0	0	0	0	0	0	0	0	0	0	0	0	0	0	0	0	0	0	0	3	0	0	0	0	0	0	0	0	0	0	0	0	0	0	0	0	2	0	0	0
variableDeclaration_li	0	0	0	0	0	0	0	0	0	0	0	0	0	0	0	0	0	0	0	0	0	0	0	0	0	0	0	0	0	0	0	0	0	0	0	0	0	11	0	0
whileCicle_le	0	0	0	0	0	0	0	0	0	0	0	0	0	0	0	0	0	0	0	0	0	0	0	0	0	0	0	0	0	0	0	0	0	0	0	0	0	0	2	0
whileCicle_pr	0	0	0	0	0	0	0	0	0	0	0	0	0	0	0	0	0	0	0	0	0	0	0	0	0	0	0	1	0	0	0	0	0	0	0	0	0	0	0	6

Fig. 7. Confusion Matrix using Random Forest classifier.

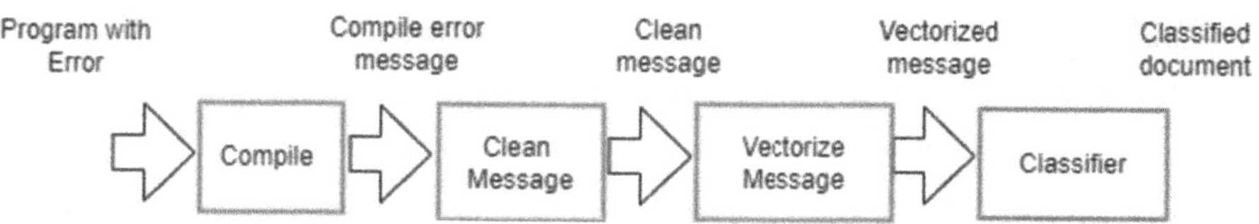

Fig. 8. Classifying new messages.

4 Giving Feedback

Once a new instance has been classified, the next step is to provide feedback about the error. For this purpose, each class has been previously associated through the knowledge module with recommendations that include message translation to Spanish, information about the syntax related with error, possible causes for error, and the topic to review (see Fig. 9).

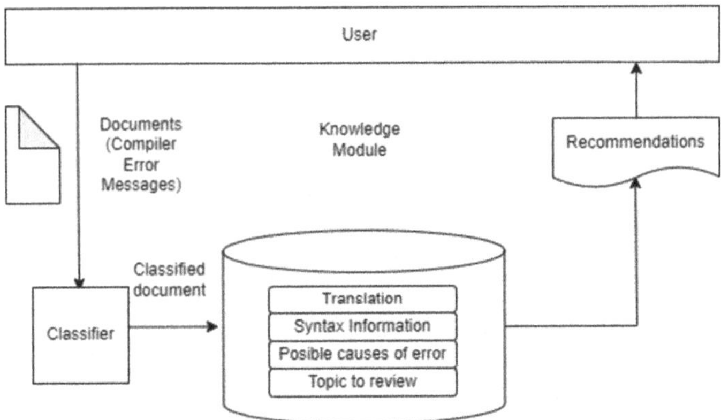

Fig. 9. Knowledge Module.

Therefore, for example, when classifying a new compiler error message, such as 'expected expression before ' = ' token for', which indicates an undeclared variable in a 'for' loop, the classifier identifies the 'forCicle_var' class providing feedback in the form of four components (see Table 7).

Table 7. Components of the given feedback.

Traslation of the message	expresion esperada antes del token '=' for
Syntax information	for(Initial expression; Conditional expression; Increment/Decrement expression) {instructions block}
Posible causes of error	It is possible that in the expressions of Loop for, the variable was not correctly declared. Verify the expressions initial, conditional and increment/decrement separated by a semicolon
Topic to review	Loop for

5 Conclusions and Future Work

In this work, the use of compiler error messages was proposed to provide feedback to high school students through supervised learning techniques. First, the corpus was generated using an error injection process, allowing the document labelling at the same time. After cleaning and vectorization, the documents were inputted into the Machine Learning algorithms using 80% for training and 20% for test. The algorithms used, individually and as an ensemble, were Decision Tree, Support Vector Machine, Random Forest, Multi-layer perceptron, K-Nearest Neighbors. After training and evaluating the model, the algorithms with the best performance were the Random Forest and K-Nearest Neighbors. The predictions serve as inputs to the knowledge module, which associates each class with feedback provided to the student. The feedback consists of four components: a translation of the message to Spanish, syntax information about language item, identification of possible causes related to the error, and topics to review.

For future work, the inclusion of semantic errors, particularly the related to type checking, are considered to extend. On the other hand, depending on the performance of the classifier, it may be considered to use the information given by the confusion matrix to give alternative feedback. it is also intended to extend this work by developing an interface to assess the classifier's performance in real conditions with a pilot group of students.

References

1. Becker. B.: An effective approach to enhancing compiler error messages. In: Proceedings of the 47th ACM Technical Symposium on Computing Science Education (2016)
2. Noriega, R., Mendoza, A., Robledo, I., Acosta, A., Esquivel. C.: Análisis de resultados del examen departamental: caso de estudio departamental de Fundamentos de Programación. Universidad Autónoma de Ciudad Juarez, p. 26 (2016)
3. Viveros, J.L., López. M. Villareal. Y.: Estrategias para Reducir el Indice de Reprobación en Fundamentos de Programación de Sistemas Computacionales del I.T. Mexicali. Revista de gestón empresarial y sustemtabilidad, 2(1), 25–41 (2016)
4. Santimateo, G.N., González, E.: Study of dificulties in teaching and learning in the basic courses in computer programming in panama. RITI J. **6**, 11 (2018)
5. Rivero, V. Quintana, M. López, A.: Analysis of the behavior of programming students during their learning process using decision trees. Res. Comput. Sci. 151(8), 75–86 (2022)
6. Kadar, R., Wahab, N.A., Othman, J.S.M., Mahlan, S.B.: A study of difficulties in teaching and learning programming. a systematic literature review, Int. J. Acad. Res. Progressive Educ. Dev. **10**(3), 591–605 (2021)
7. Ahmed, U., Kumar, P., Karkare, A. Kar. P., Gulwani. S.: Compilation Error Repair For the Student Programs. From the Programs, Gothenburg, Sweden (2018)
8. Yasunaga, M., Liang. P.: Graph-based, Self-Supervised Program Repair from Diagnostic Feedback. International Conference on Machine Learning (2020)
9. HyeonTae, S. Yo-Sub. H. Sang-Ki, K.: MultiFix.: Learning to Repair Multiple Errors by Optimal Alignment Learning. Association for Computational Linguistics, Findings of the Association for Computational Linguistics: EMNLP, p. 4850–4855 (2021)
10. Ahmed, T., Ledesma. N.R. Devanbu. P.: Synshine: improved fixing of syntax errors, IEEE Trans. Software Eng. 49(4), pp. 2169–2181 (2022)
11. Berabi, B., Jingxuan, H., Raychev, V., Vechev. M.,: TFix: Learning to Fix Coding Errors with a Text-to-Text Transformer. In: International Conference on Machine Learning, (2021)
12. Santos, E. Campbell, J., Hindle, A., Amaral., J.: Finding and correcting syntax errors using recurrent neural networks. PeerJ Preprints. **5**, e3123v1 (2017)
13. Ahmed, U. Sindhgatta, R. Srivastava, N., Karkare, A.: Targeted Example Generation for Compilation Errors. In 34th IEEE/ACM International Conference on Automated Software Engineering (ASE) (2019)
14. Mesbah, A., Rice, A., Aftandilian, E., Johnston, E. Glorioso, N.: DeepDelta.: Learning to Repair Compilation Errors. In Proceedings of the 2019 27th ACM Joint Meeting on European Software Engineering Conference and Symposium on the Foundations of Software Engineering (2019)
15. Wu, B., Campora III, J., Chen. S.: Learning User Friendly Type-Error Messages. Proc. ACM Program.Lang. **1**(OOPSLA), 1–29 (2017)
16. Wang, H., Henyuan, L., Li, Z., Liu, Y., Sun, F., Chen, X.: A Token-based Compilation Error Categorization and Its Applications. J. Soft. Evol. Process. 35(2), (2022)

17. Joshi, H., Cambronero, J., Gulwani, S., Le, V., Radicek. I., Verbruggen, G.: Repair Is Nearly Generation: Multilingual Program Repair with LLMs, in The Thirty-Seventh AAAI Conference on Artificial Intelligence (AAAI-23) (2023)
18. Álvarez. J.F.: El error como estrategia pedagógica para generar un aprendizaje eficaz. In Conference Proceedings CIVINEDU, España (2019)
19. Dasari, D.B., R. K., V.G.: Text categorization and machine learning methods: current state of the art, Global J. Comput. Sci. Technol. Soft. Data Eng. **12**(11), 36–40 (2012)
20. Maheswariy. M.U., J. G. R., S.: Text Mining: survey on techniques and applications. Int. J. Sci. Res. (IJSR). **6**(6), 1660–1664 (2017)
21. Mariñelarena, L. Errecalde, M., Castro. A.: Extracción de conocimiento con técnicas de minería de textos aplicadas a la psicología. Revista Argentina de Ciencias del Comportamiento, 9(2), 65–76 (2017)
22. Radaković, D. Steingartner, W.: High School Students Common Errors in Programing. In International Cientific Conference on Information Technology and data related research (2022)

Bayesian Network-Based Multi-objective Estimation of Distribution Algorithm for Feature Selection Tailored to Regression Problems

José A. López[1], Felipe Morales-Osorio[2], Maximiliano Lara[3], Jonás Velasco[1,4], and Claudia N. Sánchez[3](✉)

[1] Centro de Investigación en Matemáticas (CIMAT), A.C., 20200 Aguascalientes, Mexico
{jose.portillo,jvelasco}@cimat.mx
[2] Massachusetts Institute of Technology, Cambridge, MA 02139, USA
fmorales@mit.edu
[3] Facultad de Ingeniería, Universidad Panamericana, 20296 Aguascalientes, Mexico
{0218259,cnsanchez}@up.edu.mx
[4] Consejo Nacional de Humanidades Ciencias y Tecnologías (CONAHCYT), 03940 Ciudad de México, Mexico

Abstract. Feature selection is an essential pre-processing step in Machine Learning for improving the performance of models, reducing the time of predictions, and, more importantly, identifying the most significant features. Sometimes, this identification can reduce the time and cost of obtaining feature values because it could imply buying fewer sensors or spending less human time. This paper proposes an Estimation of Distribution Algorithm (EDA) for feature selection tailored to regression problems with a multi-objective approach. The objective is to maximize the performance of learning models and minimize the number of selected features. We use a Bayesian Network (BN) as the EDA distribution probability model. The main contribution of this work is the process used to create this BN structure. It aims to capture the redundancy and relevance among features. Also, the BN is used to create the initial EDA population. We test and compare the performance of our proposal with other multi-objective algorithms: an EDA with a Bernoulli distribution probability model, NSGA II, and AGEMOEA, using different datasets. The experimental results show that the proposed algorithm found solutions with a considerably fewer number of features. Additionally, the proposed algorithm achieves comparable results on models' performance compared with the other algorithms. Our proposal generally expended less time and had fewer objective function evaluations.

Keywords: Feature selection · estimation distribution algorithms · bayesian network · multi-objective optimization · regression problems

H. Calvo et al. (Eds.): MICAI 2023, LNAI 14391, pp. 309–326, 2024.
https://doi.org/10.1007/978-3-031-47765-2_23

1 Introduction

In Machine Learning, most real-world problems involve a large amount of data. Usually, this data has a high number of features, which makes the learning process difficult. However, not all features are essential since many of them are redundant or even irrelevant, which may reduce the performance of a learning algorithm. Feature Selection (FS) problems involve reducing the size of the original datasets by selecting a small subset of relevant features from the original dataset while maintaining model performance [1,23]. According to the mathematical definition presented on [1], an FS problem can be formulated as follows. Assume a dataset consists of a set of features $\mathcal{F}$ with exactly d number of features, $\mathcal{F} = \{\mathcal{F}_1, \mathcal{F}_2, \mathcal{F}_3, \ldots, \mathcal{F}_d\}$, the objective is to select the best subsets of features of size k from $\mathcal{F}$, where $k < d$. Feature selection becomes a difficult task as the number of features increases. For d features, there are 2^d subsets that can be selected to train a learning algorithm [6,9,23].

According to [8], there are three different approaches for solving the FS task: filter, wrapper, and embedded methods. Filter methods consist of finding the best subset of features according to the intrinsic characteristics of the data (e.g., correlation coefficient) that measure the relevance and redundancy of features. They are independent of the learning algorithms. Because of this, they are computationally faster than the other methods. Wrapper methods train a learning algorithm on a selected subset of features and use the algorithm's performance to evaluate the quality of the subset. They aim to find a subset of features that minimizes the learning algorithm's error. However, because they need to train on each subset of features, they are computationally more expensive than filter methods but generally offer better performance. Embedded methods incorporate feature selection into model training. For example, decision trees can be used in these models. After generating the prediction model, decision trees return a feature's importance, which can be used to create new solutions. As pointed out in [12], hybrid methods have been developed to exploit the benefits of different approaches (e.g., using a filter method to reduce computation time and a wrapper method to increase model performance).

Most of the documents tailored to feature selection have recently used a multi-objective approach [12]. Commonly, the first objective function is related to the performance of a learning model, and the second objective aims to reduce the number of features. These techniques return a set of feature subsets, and the end user can use the one better adapted to its application. Since FS is an optimization problem whose search space grows exponentially according to the number of features d, Evolutionary Algorithms (EAs) are techniques that can be used to solve this problem. Some of the EAs that have been applied for solving FS with a multi-objective approach are Genetic Algorithms [21], Particle Swarm Optimization (PSO) [22], and Differential Evolution (DE) [24]. The choice of the solution representation is highly related to the applied EA [23], but using continuous representations, such as the one used in PSO or DE, increases the search space. Genetic Algorithms and Estimation of Distribution Algorithms are techniques that can use binary representation. Specifically, NSGA

II (Nondominated Sorting Genetic Algorithm) [7] is a fast and powerful technique for solving multi-objective problems. It has been widely used for FS [10,19,21].

In this work, we explore the Estimation of Distribution Algorithms (EDAs) because they can combine filter metrics for measuring the redundancy and the relevance of features with the wrapper techniques evaluating the performance of learning models. Soliman and Rassem [20] proposed a filter technique that consisted of a quantum bio-inspired EDA for correlation-based feature selection to obtain optimal feature subsets. Maza and Touahria [16] proposed an EDA, a hybrid methodology, for FS in classification problems. Instead of randomly creating the initial population, they use the relevance between features and the class. In addition, they propose four probabilistic models for estimating the probability of each feature being selected. Those models use metrics of relevance and redundancy among features. However, they calculate the probability of features being selected separately. We propose using a Bayesian Network as the probabilistic model for sampling the selection values of features according to the selection values previously assigned to other features.

Some documents previously used Bayesian Networks for FS in EDAs. Their creation of the net is described as follows. Larrañaga *et al.* [11] used Estimation of Bayesian Networks Algorithm (EBNA) [14], which is a greedy search which starts with an arc-less structure and, at each step, adds the arc with the maximum improvement in the measure used. The algorithm stops when adding an arc would not increase the scoring measure. Castro and Von Zuben [3] begins with an initial network generated at random. Next, the probability distribution of each variable is estimated using the dataset, and the network score is computed. The search process generally proposes small changes to the structure to obtain a network with a higher score than the previous one. These small changes can be accomplished by adding or deleting an edge or reversing the edge direction. Every time a change is made, it is necessary to compute the probability distribution of the variables for the modified network. In contrast, our proposal creates the network structure as a tree, where each node represents an input feature and the arcs represent the redundancy among them. We use this graph structure because we are interested in establishing a unique dependence among the variables in order to create the simplest algorithm while keeping complexity as low as possible. The objective is to maximize a redundance metric among the connected features.

This paper proposes a Bayesian network-based multi-objective estimation of distribution algorithm for feature selection tailored to regression problems. The regression problems have numeric vectors from $\mathbb{R}^d$ as inputs, where d is the number of features, and numeric scalars from $\mathbb{R}$ as outputs. We focus on two criteria: maximizing the performance of the learning models and minimizing the number of selected features. The main contribution of our proposal is that the probabilistic model of the EDA is a Bayesian Network defined to capture the relevance and redundancy in the features. Mainly, the difference between our proposal and others using EDAs with Bayesian Networks is how the BN is created. In our case, it is a tree where the arcs represent the redundancy among features. In addition, the first generation is a filter method that creates solutions based on the BN structure, maximizing relevance and minimizing redundancy among features.

The rest of the paper is organized as follows. Section 2 presents the background concepts. Our proposal is described in the Methodology Sect. 3. The experiments and results are presented in Sect. 4. Finally, Sect. 5 concludes this document and describe the future work.

2 Background

In this section, we briefly review the fundamental concepts of this research. We started with Multi-objective Evolutionary Optimization, followed by Estimation of Distribution Algorithms (EDAs), and finalized with Bayesian Networks (BN).

2.1 Multi-objective Evolutionary Optimization

In multi-objective optimization [4], a variety of optimization problems are tackled, each involving one of the n distinct objective functions $f_1(s), \ldots, f_n(s)$. These functions operate on s, a vector of parameters from a specific domain. Consider $\mathcal{S}$ to be the potential solution space for such a multi-objective optimization problem. A solution set is classified as non-dominated (alternatively referred to as Pareto optimal) when there is no $t \in \mathcal{S}$ that, for any $s \in \mathcal{S}$, can satisfy the following:

- $\exists i$, where $i \in \{1, \ldots, n\}$, $f_i(t)$ enhances $f_i(s)$,
- $\forall j$, where $j \in \{1, \ldots, n\}$ and $j \neq i$, $f_j(s)$ cannot improve $f_j(t)$.

The main point is that one solution s is considered to dominate another t if s surpasses t on at least one objective and is not inferior on the remaining ones. We term s as non-dominated when no other solution outperforms it. The set of these non-dominated solutions within $\mathcal{S}$ is known as the Pareto front. The goals of multiobjective optimization is to find set of solutions as close as possible to Pareto-optimal front and to find a set of solutions as diverse as possible. When it comes to multi-objective optimization, multi-objective evolutionary algorithms are particularly beneficial as they concurrently pursue multiple best solutions. These algorithms can locate a collection of top solutions in the end population with just a single run, and once this set is ready, the most pleasing solution can be picked based on a preference criterion.

Feature selection consists of two main objectives: minimizing the cardinality of the subset of selected features and maximizing the model's performance. These objectives often conflict, giving space for multiobjective optimization techniques such as evolutionary multi-objective optimization. In these algorithms, more than one solution is returned, and each solution corresponds to a specific trade-off between the objectives. This way, of the reported solutions, some will represent a larger subset with better performance. In comparison, others will give a smaller subset but diminish the model's performance.

In this work, we use two algorithms: the Non-dominated Sorting Genetic Algorithm II (NSGA-II) [7] and Adaptive Geometry Estimation based Multi-Objective Evolutionary Algorithms (AGEMOEA) [18]. The NSGA-II and AGE-MOEA are examples of Evolutionary Algorithms designed for solving multi-objective optimization problems. The former finds a diverse set of solutions and covers near the true Pareto optimal set. The latter, AGEMOEA, modifies NSGA-II by replacing the fitness assigned to the solutions in each non-dominated front. In AGEMOEA, the crowding distance of NSGA-II is replaced by a survival score that combines both diversity and proximity of the solutions within the same non-dominated front.

2.2 Estimation of Distribution Algorithms (EDAs)

Introduced in [17], Estimation of Distribution Algorithms (EDAs) are based on Evolutionary Algorithms where a population of N individuals becomes better to their fitness value each iteration [14]. This algorithm replaces crossover and mutation operators of EAs by estimation of parameters of the M best individuals of the population. The probability distribution function is used to sample new N individuals who will become part of the next generation of the algorithm. This process is repeated until a stopping criterion is met. It could be the maximum number of iterations, convergence criterion based on stagnation, etc. The algorithm learns from the population and modifies the probability distribution in each generation. The overall fitness value of the population will be better in each iteration. It is important to see that exploitation and exploration in the search space are controlled by random sampling of new individuals.

Algorithm 1: The basic steps of an EDA.

Input : population size N, selection size M, where $M < N$
Output: the best solution(s) found S_{Best}

$P_0 \leftarrow$ Generate initial population with N random individuals
Evaluate each individual s in P_0 using the objective function
$S_{\text{Best}} \leftarrow$ Get the best solution(s) from P_0
$t \leftarrow 0$
while *termination criteria are not met* **do**
  $S_t \leftarrow$ Select M individuals from P_t according to a selection method
  $\bar{p}_t \leftarrow$ Estimate the probability density of solutions in S_t
  $P_{t+1} \leftarrow$ Sample N individuals from $\bar{p}_t$
  Evaluate P_{t+1} using the objective function
  Update S_{Best} according to the solutions in P_{t+1}
  $t \leftarrow t + 1$
end
return S_{Best}

Algorithm 1 shows the basic pseudo-code of a typical EDA. EDAs utilize several parameters, including the population size N, the number of generations (or iterations) G, and the number of individuals selected, M for estimate the probability density of solutions, $\bar{p}_t$. The set of selected solutions S_t serves as a training dataset to estimate the probabilistic model and leads the search towards regions with better fitness. The set of new solutions P_{t+1} is generated using the probabilities encoded in the probabilistic model in accordance with the statistics collected from the solutions in S_t.

Early EDAs were developed for discrete domains, as it is common in evolutionary algorithms to represent solutions with binary representations. Variations of EDAs are widely used for combinatorial optimization problems where more sophisticated distributions are used for sampling new individuals. For solving optimization problems in continuous domains, variations of the original EDAs approach also exist.

EDA algorithms are commonly grouped according to the degree of interaction among variables into univariate, bivariate, and multivariate EDAs. Univariate EDAs, such as Univariate Marginal Distribution Algorithm (UMDA), assume that all variables are independent and factorize the joint probability of the selected solutions as a product of univariate marginal probabilities. Multivariate EDAs do not necessarily limit the degree of interactions among variables and can be modelled with unrestricted Bayesian Networks. The choice of probabilistic model can have a major influence on the performance and efficiency of EDAs.

2.3 Bayesian Networks

A Bayesian Network (BN) [13] is a probabilistic graphical model which provides a robust general approach especially suited to modeling complex non-deterministic systems. A BN models the causal relationships between the features of a model. It consists of a Directed Acyclic Graph (DAG) $\mathcal{G}$ [13], and a set of parameters Θ, defining the strength and the shape of the relationships between features. To use a BN, one must define the graph $\mathcal{G}$ and then calculate its parameters Θ. Defining the graph $\mathcal{G}$ is a task that can be done by learning through data or by consulting human experts in a specific field [13].

$\mathcal{G}$ consists of a set of vertices $\mathcal{V}$ and a set of directed edges $\mathcal{E}$. The vertices in $\mathcal{V}$ represent the features whose relationship is modeled by the BN, and the edges in $\mathcal{E}$ represent the relationships between the features. A directed edge from V_i to V_j where $V_i, V_j \in \mathcal{V}$ is symbolically represented by the tuple $(V_i, V_j) \in \mathcal{E}$ or graphically represented as $V_i \rightarrow V_j$. The directed edge $(V_i, V_j) \in \mathcal{E}$ indicates that V_i is the parent of V_j and that V_j is the child of V_i. A BN models a parent-child relationship as the parent variable causing the child variable. Therefore, the directed edge (V_i, V_j) in a BN means that the parent variable V_i causes the child variable V_j. Additionally, every directed edge $(V_i, V_j) \in \mathcal{E}$ has a parameter $\theta_{i,j} \in \Theta$. The parameter $\theta_{i,j}$ associated with this edge is a matrix modeling $\Pr(V_j \mid V_i)$ (the conditional probability of V_j given V_i). If V_i, V_j can take on $|V_i|$, $|V_j|$ different values respectively, then this matrix $\theta_{i,j}$ will have $|V_i| \times |V_j|$ different entries.

Finally, a BN assumes that the joint probability distribution of the variables $P(V_1 = v_1, V_2 = v_2, \ldots, V_n = v_n)$, defined in Eq. (1), can be decomposed as the product of the conditional distribution of the variables given the value of their parents $P(V_i = v_i \mid \mathbf{Pa}(V_i))$.

$$P(V_1 = v_1, V_2 = v_2, \ldots, V_n = v_n) = \prod_{i=1}^{n} P(V_i = v_i \mid \mathbf{Pa}(V_i)) \tag{1}$$

3 Methodology

Our proposal is an Estimation of Distribution Algorithm for feature selection tailored to regression problems with a multi-objective approach. Our regression problems have numeric vectors from $\mathbb{R}^d$ as inputs, where d is the number of features, and numeric scalars from $\mathbb{R}$ as outputs. We focus on two criteria: maximizing the performance of the learning models and minimizing the number of selected features. Our main contribution is using a Bayesian Network (BN) as the sample distribution model. The BN aims to capture the redundancy among features. Additionally, the first generation can be seen as a filter method that creates solutions that maximize relevance and minimize redundancy among features.

We follow the Algorithm 1, explained in the previous section. In this section, we describe the details of the implementation. First, in Subsect. 3.1, we explain the individuals' representation and evaluation. The selection of the individuals used for calculating the distribution model, in this case, the BN, is described in Subsect. 3.2. The creation of the structure of the BN is described in Subsect. 3.3. Subsection 3.4 describes the initialization of the population. In this case, instead of being totally random, it is initialized using the BN. The BN's probabilities calculation is explained in Subsect. 3.5. Finally, Subsect. 3.6 describes how the individuals of the new population are sampled using the BN.

3.1 Representing and Evaluating Individuals

Our proposal aim to solve the feature selection in regression problems. Regression can be mathematically expressed as follows. We are given a set $\mathcal{D} = \{(\vec{x_1}, y_1), ..., (\vec{x_n}, y_n)\}$ of n input-output data pairs with d features in the inputs where $\vec{x_i} \in \mathbb{R}^d$ and $y_i \in \mathbb{R}$ for all $i \in \{1 \ldots n\}$. The regression model $\mathcal{M}$ aims to minimize $\sum_{(\vec{x},y)\in\mathcal{D}} E(\mathcal{M}(\vec{x}), y)$, where E is a function that measures the difference or error between $\mathcal{M}(\vec{x})$ and y. The ideal scenario would be $\mathcal{M}(\vec{x}) = y \ \forall(\vec{x}, y) \in \mathcal{D}$. The model predictions $\mathcal{M}(\vec{x})$ also are defined as $\widehat{y}$. Feature selection consists of selecting the best subsets of features of size k, where $k < d$. An individual representing a solution for the feature selection problem is a binary vector of size d, where the i-th element corresponds to the i-th feature in the dataset. A value of 1 means that the i-th feature is selected for fitting the model, while 0 indicates that the i-th feature is left out.

We define two criteria as objective functions. The first is related to the regression models' performance, and the other to the number of selected features. Regression involves finding a mathematical model that relates input features to an output feature to reduce an error. The determination of coefficient R^2 (Eq. 2) can be used for measuring the performance of a regression model. If its value is close to 1 indicates a good performance of the model, or in other words, that the regression model explains a large portion of the variability in the response. A number near 0 indicates that the regression does not explain much of the variability in the response, and it is almost equal to random guesses according to the output feature distribution. Finally, negative values indicate that the regression model gives worse results than random guesses. In our proposal, for having minimization objective functions, we define $\overline{R^2} \equiv 1 - R^2$. By doing this, we focus on minimizing the performance of the regression model trained with a subset of features.

$$R^2(y, \widehat{y}) = 1 - \frac{\sum_i (y_i - \widehat{y}_i)^2}{\sum_i (y_i - \overline{y}_i)^2} \tag{2}$$

The second objective function is designed to minimize the number of selected features. It is defined as $|\mathcal{F}|$ and corresponds to the number of selected features in the subset divided by the total number of features in the data set. A number near to 0 indicates that the subset has a few features selected. On the other hand, a number close to 1 indicates that most of the features have been selected.

3.2 Selection of Individuals for Estimating the Parameters of the Bayesian Network

Step 6 of Algorithm 1 consists of selecting the best M individuals from the population to calculate the parameters of the distribution model, in this case, the probabilities of the Bayesian Network. For sorting the individuals, we use the fast non-dominated sorting algorithm presented in [7] and the non-domination rank that corresponds to the non-dominated front an individual belongs to.

3.3 Creating Bayesian Network Graph

A BN must be a DAG by definition. However, our BN is more restrictive because it is a tree. Our Bayesian Network $\mathcal{G} = (\mathcal{V}, \mathcal{E})$ is a tree whose vertices $V_i \in \mathcal{V}$ represent the feature at index i and whose edges $(V_i, V_j) \in \mathcal{E}$ represent the causal relationship between feature i and feature j. The strength of the causal relationship between V_i, V_j is approximated by $|C_{i,j}|$, corresponding to the absolute value of the Pearson correlation coefficient between the two features i, j in a dataset. Our objective is to construct a tree capturing the redundancy between variables. In other words, we want to construct a tree with an edge set $\mathcal{E}$ that maximizes $R(\mathcal{E})$ as defined in Eq. (3).

$$R(\mathcal{E}) = \sum_{(V_i, V_j) \in \mathcal{E}} |C_{i,j}| \tag{3}$$

Maximizing $R(\mathcal{E})$ is equivalent to finding the maximum spanning tree of $\mathcal{H}$ where $\mathcal{H}$ is a fully connected graph containing the vertices in our problem and the weighted edges (V_i, V_j) are the values of $|C_{i,j}|$ between features. We use a modified version of Prim's Minimum Spanning Tree [5] algorithm to find the maximum spanning tree. In particular, we set the root vertex to the feature that has maximum relevance with the output feature in a dataset. We approximate relevance with $|C_i|$, the absolute value of the Pearson correlation coefficient between the feature i and the output feature in the dataset.

Figure 1 illustrates the Bayesian Network produced by our algorithm using the Concrete Compressive Strength dataset (See Table 5). The root vertex corresponds to the feature Fly Ash because this is the one with the highest relevance to the output feature. In other words, Fly Ash had the highest absolute value of the Pearson correlation coefficient with the output variable. Next, an edge from the root to the vertex Blast Furnace Slag is drawn because it has the greatest redundancy with the root. This means it has the highest absolute value of the Pearson correlation coefficient with the root. Then, each successive edge added to the tree must not produce a cycle while also being the edge with the highest possible redundancy.

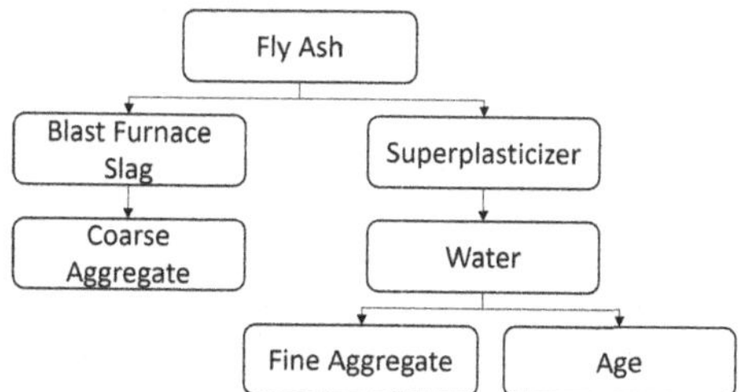

Fig. 1. Bayesian Network produced from concrete data.

3.4 Creating Initial Population

To create the initial population of individuals for the EDA, we use the parent-child structure of the BN and using the redundance and the relevance of features calculated with the Pearson correlation coefficient. Our proposal generates half of the individuals of the initial population via relevance and half via redundancy.

To generate individuals via redundancy, we want to avoid selecting two features that have a high redundancy with each other. To achieve this, we want every child variable to be more likely be the binary opposite of its parent variable if the parent-child redundancy metric is high. For example, if a parent $V_i = 1$, then the child $V_j = 0$ should have a high probability of occurring if the redundancy $|C_{i,j}|$ is high. Similarly, if a parent $V_i = 0$, then the child $V_j = 1$ should occur with high probability when $|C_{i,j}|$ is high. We model this expected probability distribution using a Bernoulli trial. `BERNOULLI`(p) runs a Bernoulli trial to generate a binary value. The single parameter p specifies the probability of a success. A success generates a 1 while a failure generates a 0. The desired outcome v_j for a child V_j given value v_i of its parent V_i is the result of the Bernoulli trial with the parameter $p = |v_i - |C_{i,j}||$ as $v_j = \texttt{BERNOULLI}\,(|v_i - |C_{i,j}||)$.

To generate individuals via relevance, we want the probability of feature i being selected to be proportional to its relevance $|C_i|$ with the output. If a feature has high relevance, then it should have a high probability of being selected. Again, we model this probability distribution using a Bernoulli trial. The binary value v_i of the variable V_i should be determined as $v_i = \texttt{BERNOULLI}(|C_i|)$.

3.5 Calculating Bayesian Network Parameters

The Bayesian Network parameters are related to probability distributions; each vertex has its values. The probabilities are calculated based on the best individuals selected for making the distribution model in each algorithm iteration. First, we estimate $P(V_r)$, which corresponds to the probability distribution of V_r, the root variable of the tree. Table 1 shows the equations for calculating the $P(V_r)$ values, where F represents the occurrence frequency of the feature values in the selected individuals. The rest of the vertices on the BN corresponds to conditional probabilities $P(V_j \mid V_i)$, where vertex V_i can be seen as the parent of vertex V_j. Table 2 shows the equations for calculating the $P(V_j \mid V_i)$ values.

Table 1. Probability distribution of the root vertex $P(V_r)$

V_r	$P(V_r)$
0	$F(V_r = 0)/(F(V_r = 0) + F(V_r = 1))$
1	$F(V_r = 1)/(F(V_r = 0) + F(V_r = 1))$

Table 2. Probability distribution $P(V_j \mid V_i)$

V_i	V_j	$P(V_j \mid V_i)$
0	0	$F(V_i = 0, V_j = 0)/F(V_i = 0)$
0	1	$F(V_i = 0, V_j = 1)/F(V_i = 0)$
1	0	$F(V_i = 1, V_j = 0)/F(V_i = 1)$
1	1	$F(V_i = 1, V_j = 1)/F(V_i = 1)$

3.6 Sampling from Bayesian Network

Once the structure of the Bayesian Network and its parameters are calculated, it can be used to generate a new population of individuals. To start, we generate the binary value v_r associated with the root V_r using the BERNOULLI function based on $P(V_r)$. Once we have generated the root's binary value, we generate the binary values associated with the remaining vertices from top to bottom. This is done so that the values of parent vertices are decided before the values of child vertices. To generate the binary value v_j associated with vertex V_j we must have a value v_i associated with the parent vertex V_i. We generate the binary value associated with V_j using the `BERNOULLI` function based on $P(V_j \mid V_i = v_i)$.

4 Experiments and Results

In this section, we present our proposal's experiments and results. We used Linear Regression as the regression model because it is simple and fast. To analyze the performance of our proposal, we compare it with Non-dominated Sorting Genetic Algorithm II (NSGA-II) and Adaptive Geometry Estimation based Multi-Objective Evolutionary Algorithms (AGEMOEA) previously mentioned in Sect. 2. We used the implementation of those algorithms provided by the library Pymoo [2]. The hyper-parameters of those algorithms, defined by default in Pymoo, are presented in Table 3.

In addition, we compare our results with an Estimation of Distribution Algorithm that uses a Bernoulli model as the probability distribution, defined as EDA Bernoulli. This implementation initializes the population P of individuals using Bernoulli trials. As mentioned in the previous section, an individual is a binary vector whose entry v_i associated with feature i is decided via a Bernoulli trial. In the initial population, the entry v_i is given by the Bernoulli trial $v_i = \texttt{BERNOULLI}(0.5)$. In the following generations of the algorithm, the population is sampled using the Bernoulli trial $v_i = \texttt{BERNOULLI}(\texttt{PROPORTION}(v_i))$ where $\texttt{PROPORTION}(v_i)$ is the proportion of times $v_i = 1$ in the selected population. The hyper-parameters of the EDA implementations are presented in Table 4.

Table 3. Hyper-parameters of NSGA II and AGEMOEA

Algorithm	Population size N	Max Iterations	Sampling	Crossover	Mutation
NSGA II	50	10	Binary random sampling	Two point crossover	Bitflip mutation
AGEMOEA	50	10	Binary random sampling	Two point crossover	Bitflip mutation

Our implementation was developed in the Python programming language, and we use the libraries Scikit-learn and numpy. Our computational experiments were run with an Intel Core i7-5500U Dual-Core Processor @ 2.40 GHz running the Windows 10 64-bit operating system based on an ×64 processor with 8.00 GB of RAM.

Table 4. Hyper-parameters of EDA Bernoulli and EDA Bayesian Network

Algorithm	Population size N	Max iterations	Individuals selected M	Probability distribution
EDA Bernoulli	50	5	25	Bernoulli
EDA Bayesian Network	50	5	25	Bayesian Network

4.1 Datasets

Five datasets are adopted from the UCI repository [15] (See Table 5). The datasets are of different dimensions, varying from 8 to 100, and the number of instances is 395 to 515345. Since we are solving a regression problem, we need the input features, and the output feature, to be of numerical type. For each dataset, the last column corresponds to the target feature. We had to preprocess this data because some of the features were categorical, or it contained missing values. The preprocess methodology is described as follows. First, columns with a high ratio of missing values were deleted. For example, the Communities and Crime dataset had many columns with around 84% missing values. Rows containing null values were removed from the datasets. Categorical variables with only two possible values were transformed into numerical variables by changing the value of one class to 0 and the other to 1. Those variables with three or more possible values were transformed into numerical variables by applying one-hot encoding. In the case the categorical variables had more than 30 categories, they were removed from the dataset. In the Forest Fires dataset, the values of the feature month were transformed from 'jan', 'feb', 'mar', ..., 'dec' to 1, 2, 3, ...,12. And for the feature day, values were transformed from 'mon', 'tue', 'wed', ..., 'sun' to 1, 2, 3, ...,7. We randomly divided the datasets into training (70%) and testing (30%) sets to validate the results.

Table 5. Datasets

Name	Before processing		After processing	
	# instances	# features	# instances	# features
Concrete Compressive Strength	1030	8	1030	8
Forest Fires	517	12	517	12
Student Performance Math	395	32	395	45
YearPredictionMSD	515345	90	515345	90
Communities and crime	1993	127	1993	100

4.2 Comparison of Our Proposal Against Other Techniques

To the best of our knowledge, no study has been conducted on feature selection for the datasets described in Table 5. Most of the documents related to feature selection are related to classification. However, we compare the results of our proposal, EDA Bayesian Network, with other multi-objective evolutionary algorithms: EDA Bernoulli, NSGA-II, and AGEMOEA. Each experiment was executed 100 times, except the experiment of the YearPredictionMSD dataset, which was executed only ten times for the expensive time required.

Figure 2, 3, 4, 5 and 6 show the non-dominated solutions found by the different algorithms. They contain the best solutions for different executions. In Fig. 2 and Fig. 3 can be observed that all the algorithms obtain similar results in the two smallest datasets, Concrete Compressive Strength and Forest Fires. On the medium dataset, Student Performance Math, EDA Bayesian Network found solutions with a less number of features (see Fig. 4). And in the two biggest datasets, YearPredictionMSD and Communities and crime, AGMOEA got better results in the regression model performance, but our proposal got considerably better results in the number of selected features (see Fig. 5 and Fig. 6).

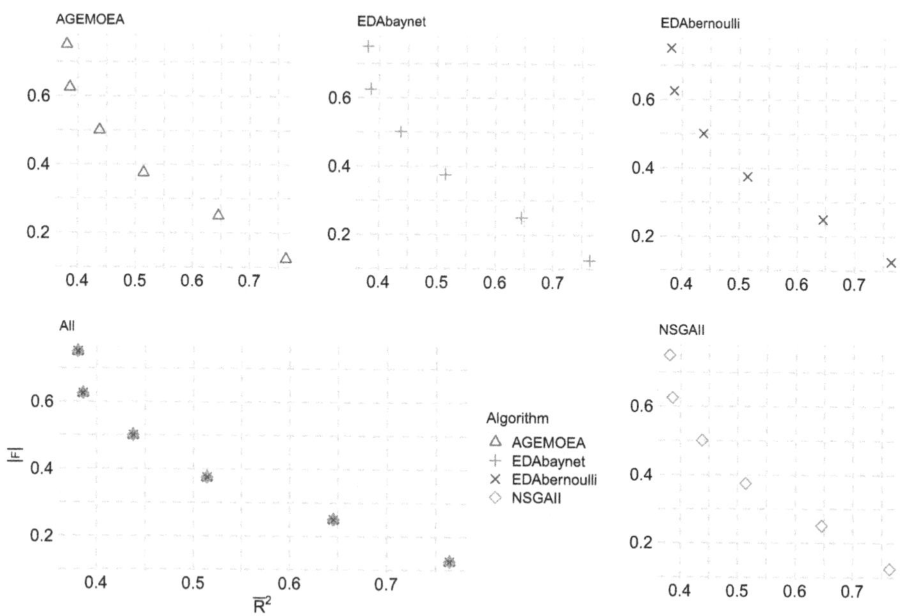

Fig. 2. Non-dominated solutions for the Concrete Compressive Strength dataset.

We also compare the algorithms based on the time (in seconds) and the number of evaluations of the regression model. For optimizing the execution time, we store the model's evaluation of different solutions aiming to evaluate only once time each different subset of features. Table 6 shows this comparison. It can be observed that in most cases, our implementation, EDA Bayesian Network, presented the best performance having less number of evaluations and the shortest time. In the case of the Communities Crime dataset, NSGA II was better in the

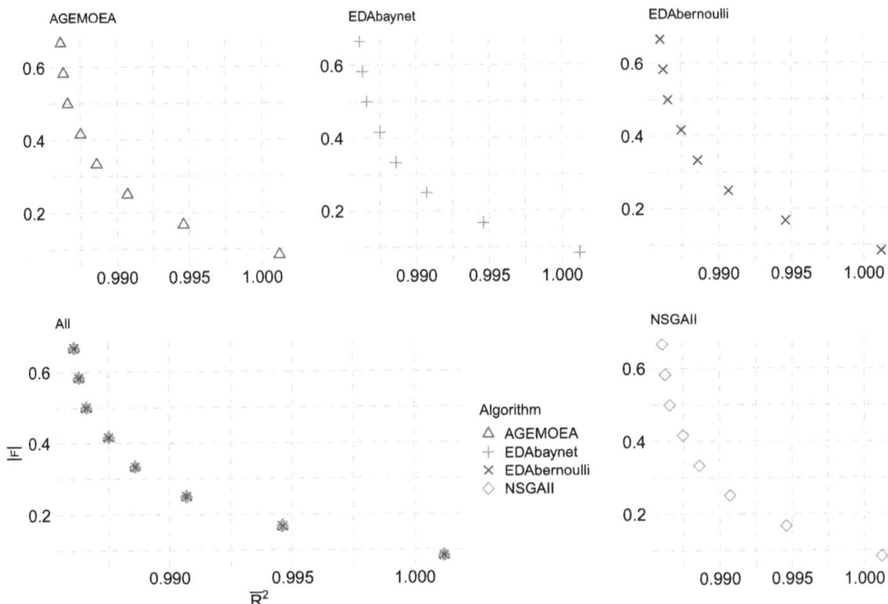

Fig. 3. Non-dominated solutions for the Forest Fires dataset.

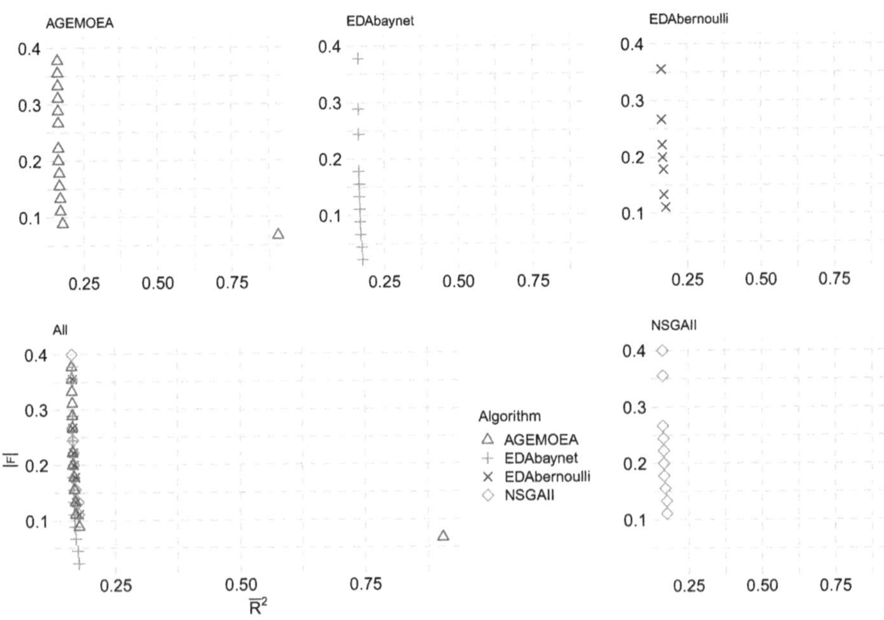

Fig. 4. Non-dominated solutions for the Student Performance Math dataset.

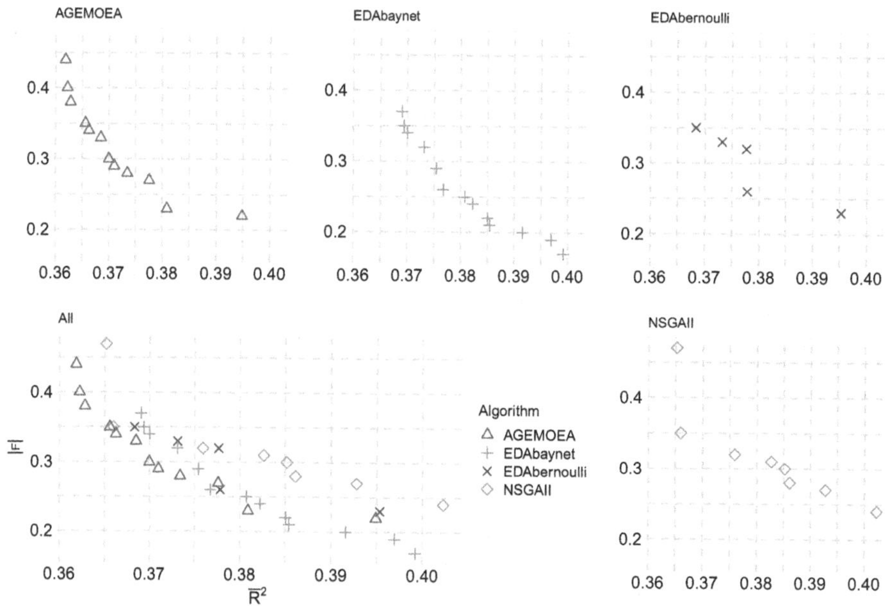

Fig. 5. Non-dominated solutions for the Communities and crime dataset.

number of evaluations, and EDA Bernoulli was better in time. In the case of the Student Performance dataset, EDA Bernoulli was better in time. The number of evaluations can be seen as how much the search space is explored because it is related to the different solutions found. In some cases, when the objective function is expensive, we wanted good results with a few evaluations. In this experiment, our proposal proportionate good results with the smallest number of evaluations. It indicates that we can improve the exploration in future work and maybe get better results.

Table 6. Comparison of time and number of evaluations between algorithms for all datasets. Bold numbers correspond to the smallest values in time or number of evaluations.

Algorithm	Concrete Compressive		Forest Fires		Student Performance		Year Prediction MSD		Communities Crime	
	Time	Eval	Time	Eval	Time	Eval	Time	Eval	Time	Eval
AGEMOEA	0.39	157.96	0.71	330.55	0.97	463.41	384.15	439.37	4.67	424.49
NSGA-II	0.47	172.35	0.73	366.89	0.91	431.24	211.57	312.50	1.52	**298.90**
EDA Bernoulli	0.28	122.79	0.42	241.60	**0.53**	299.99	211.28	300.00	**1.36**	300.00
EDA BayNet	**0.25**	**88.10**	**0.32**	**182.49**	0.57	**295.64**	**132.45**	**294.36**	1.50	299.97

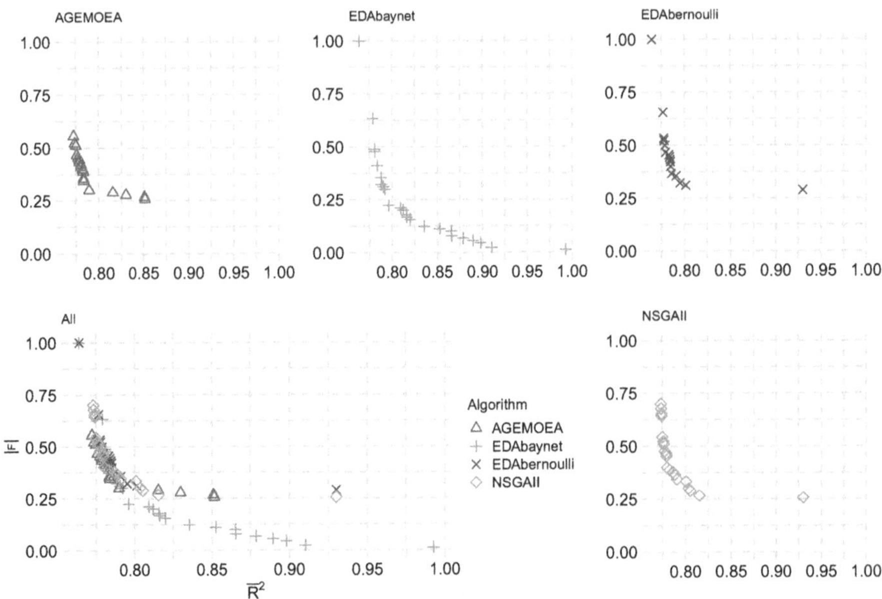

Fig. 6. Non-dominated solutions for the Year Predictions MSD dataset.

5 Conclusion

This paper proposes an Estimation of Distribution Algorithm for feature selection tailored to regression problems with a multi-objective approach. The main objective was maximizing the learning models' performance, calculated as the determination coefficient R^2, and minimizing the number of selected features. Our proposal used a Bayesian Network (BN) as the distribution model. The BN aims to capture the redundancy among features. The generation of the initial population can be seen as a filter method that randomly creates solutions maximizing the relevance and minimizing the redundancy among features. The relevance and the redundancy were measured using the Pearson correlation coefficient.

We compared our proposal with other multi-objective algorithms such as EDA Bernoulli, NSGA II, and AGEMOEA, and we used five different datasets. According to the performance of the regression and the number of features of the non-dominated solutions found, all the algorithms obtain similar results in the two smallest datasets. On the medium dataset, our proposal found solutions with a less number of features. Finally, in the two biggest datasets, AGMOEA got better results in the regression model performance, but our proposal got considerably better results in the number of selected features. However, our proposal generally expended less time and evaluated fewer times the objective function. The experimental results indicate that it could be improved for exploring more the search space.

In future work, we expect to improve the exploration of our proposed algorithm. It obtains good results in the number of features but can improve the model's performance. We plan to extend the experiments by trying different regression models, and we can optimize the hyper-parameters values of the evolutionary algorithms.

References

1. Agrawal, P., Abutarboush, H.F., Ganesh, T., Mohamed, A.W.: Metaheuristic algorithms on feature selection: a survey of one decade of research (2009–2019). IEEE Access **9**, 26766–26791 (2021). https://doi.org/10.1109/ACCESS.2021.3056407
2. Blank, J., Deb, K.: Pymoo: multi-objective optimization in Python. IEEE Access **8**, 89497–89509 (2020). https://doi.org/10.1109/ACCESS.2020.2990567
3. Castro, P.A., Von Zuben, F.J.: Multi-objective feature selection using a Bayesian artificial immune system. Int. J. Intell. Comput. Cybern. **3**(2), 235–256 (2010). https://doi.org/10.1108/17563781011049188
4. Collette, Y., Siarry, P.: Multiobjective Optimization. Principles and Case Studies. Springer, Heidelberg (2004). https://doi.org/10.1007/978-3-662-08883-8
5. Cormen, T.H., Leiserson, C.E., Rivest, R.L., Stein, C.: Introduction to Algorithms. MIT Press (2002)
6. Dash, M., Liu, H.: Feature selection for classification. Intell. Data Anal. **1**(1–4), 131–156 (1997). https://doi.org/10.1016/S1088-467X(97)00008-5. http://linkinghub.elsevier.com/retrieve/pii/S1088467X97000085
7. Deb, K., Pratap, A., Agarwal, S., Meyarivan, T.: A fast and elitist multiobjective genetic algorithm: NSGA-II. Technical report 2 (2002)
8. Dhal, P., Azad, C.: A comprehensive survey on feature selection in the various fields of machine learning. Appl. Intell. **52**(4), 4543–4581 (2022). https://doi.org/10.1007/s10489-021-02550-9
9. Guyon, I., De, A.M.: An introduction to variable and feature selection André Elisseeff. Technical report (2003)
10. Hamdani, T.M., Won, J.M., Alimi, A.M., Karray, F.: LNCS 4431 - multi-objective feature selection with NSGA II. Technical report (2007)
11. Inza, I., Larrañaga, P., Etxeberria, R., Sierra, B.: Feature subset selection by Bayesian network-based optimization. Technical report (2000)
12. Jiao, R., Nguyen, B.H., Xue, B., Zhang, M.: A survey on evolutionary multiobjective feature selection in classification: approaches, applications, and challenges. IEEE Trans. Evol. Comput. (2023). https://doi.org/10.1109/TEVC.2023.3292527. https://ieeexplore.ieee.org/document/10173647/
13. Kitson, N.K., Constantinou, A.C., Guo, Z., Liu, Y., Chobtham, K.: A survey of Bayesian Network structure learning. Artif. Intell. Rev. **56**, 8721–8814 (2023). https://doi.org/10.1007/s10462-022-10351-w
14. Larragaña, P., Lozano, J.: Genetic algorithms and evolutionary computation. In: OmeGA: A Competent Genetic Algorithm for Solving Permutation and Scheduling Problems (2002)
15. Markelle, K., Rachel, L., Kolby, N.: The UCI Machine Learning Repository. https://archive.ics.uci.edu
16. Maza, S., Touahria, M.: Feature selection for intrusion detection using new multi-objective estimation of distribution algorithms. Appl. Intell. **49**(12), 4237–4257 (2019). https://doi.org/10.1007/s10489-019-01503-7

17. Mühlenbein, H.: The equation for response to selection and its use for prediction. Evol. Comput. **5**(3), 303–346 (1997). https://doi.org/10.1162/EVCO.1997.5.3.303. https://pubmed.ncbi.nlm.nih.gov/10021762/
18. Panichella, A.: An adaptive evolutionary algorithm based on non-Euclidean geometry for many-objective optimization. In: Proceedings of the 2019 Genetic and Evolutionary Computation Conference, GECCO 2019, July 2019, pp. 595–603. Association for Computing Machinery, Inc. (2019). https://doi.org/10.1145/3321707.3321839
19. Rehman, A.U., Nadeem, A., Malik, M.Z.: Fair feature subset selection using multiobjective genetic algorithm. In: Proceedings of the 2022 Genetic and Evolutionary Computation Conference, GECCO 2022 Companion, July 2022, pp. 360–363. Association for Computing Machinery, Inc. (2022). https://doi.org/10.1145/3520304.3529061
20. Soliman, O.S., Rassem, A.: Correlation based feature selection using quantum bio inspired estimation of distribution algorithm. Technical report (2012)
21. Spolaôr, N., Lorena, A.C., Lee, H.D.: Multi-objective genetic algorithm evaluation in feature selection. In: Takahashi, R.H.C., Deb, K., Wanner, E.F., Greco, S. (eds.) EMO 2011. LNCS, vol. 6576, pp. 462–476. Springer, Heidelberg (2011). https://doi.org/10.1007/978-3-642-19893-9_32
22. Xue, B., Zhang, M., Browne, W.N.: Particle swarm optimization for feature selection in classification: a multi-objective approach. IEEE Trans. Cybern. **43**(6), 1656–1671 (2013). https://doi.org/10.1109/TSMCB.2012.2227469
23. Xue, B., Zhang, M., Browne, W.N., Yao, X.: A survey on evolutionary computation approaches to feature selection. IEEE Trans. Evol. Comput. **20**(4), 606–626 (2016). https://doi.org/10.1109/TEVC.2015.2504420
24. Zhang, Y., Gong, D., Gao, X., Tian, T., Sun, X.: Binary differential evolution with self-learning for multi-objective feature selection. Inf. Sci. **507**, 67–85 (2020). https://doi.org/10.1016/J.INS.2019.08.040

Implementation of Parallel Evolutionary Convolutional Neural Network for Classification in Human Activity and Image Recognition

Juan Villegas-Cortez[1(✉)], Graciela Román-Alonso[2], Francisco Fernandez De Vega[3], Yafte Aaron Flores-Morales[2], and Salomon Cordero-Sanchez[4]

[1] Departamento de Sistemas, Universidad Autónoma Metropolitana, Unidad Azcapotzalco, Azapotzalco. Av. Sn. Pablo 180, 02200 Col Reynosa Tamps., Mexico City, Mexico
juanvc@azc.uam.mx

[2] Departamento de Ingeniería Eléctrica, Universidad Autónoma Metropolitana, Unidad Iztapalapa, Iztapalapa, Mexico City, Mexico
grac@xanum.uam.mx

[3] Department of Computer Science, University of Extremadura, C/. Santa Teresa de Jornet, 38, 06800 Mérida, Spain
fcofdez@unex.es

[4] Department of Chemistry, Universidad Autónoma Metropolitana, Unidad Iztapalapa, Iztapalapa, Mexico City, Mexico
scs@xanum.uam.mx

Abstract. Pattern recognition has been evolving to include problems posed by new sceneries containing a high number of pattern components. Processing this volume of information allows a more exact classification in wider types of applications; however, some of the difficulties of this scheme is the maintenance of numerical precision and mainly the reduction of the execution time. During the last 15 years, several Machine Learning solutions have been implemented to reduce the number of pattern components to be analyzed, such as artificial neural networks. Deep learning is an appropriate tool to accomplish this task. In this paper, a convolutional neural network is implemented for recognition and classification of human activity signals and digital images. It is achieved by automatically adjusting the parameters of the neural network through genetic algorithms using a multiprocessor and GPU platform. The results obtained show the reduction of computational costs and the possibility of better understanding of the solutions provided by Deep Learning.

Keywords: Deep Learning · Pattern recognition · HAR · Image Recognition · Parallel Genetic Algorithms

1 Introduction

For the last few years, Artificial Neural Networks (ANN) have been proven to be very effective in addressing problems of recognition and classification of complex patterns. They have also been evolved to incorporate hybrid and profound architectures,

H. Calvo et al. (Eds.): MICAI 2023, LNAI 14391, pp. 327–345, 2024.
https://doi.org/10.1007/978-3-031-47765-2_24

which is the case of Convolutional Neural Networks (CNN). These new paradigms have reframed the interpretation of the complexity of images by treating the structure of new profound networks with multiple layers, seeking to reduce the dimensionality of the pattern under analysis in order to extract relevant features. Also, they operate in a new way that is not completely known, but manages to get relevant information for several applications such as human image recognition or Human Activity Recognition (HAR).

The importance of pattern recognition of images lies in its capability to formulate the recognition task, identification or classification of an image from numerical features associated with the digital images under study. This is made by assuming the idea that an image has a raster format, which is conceived as a big set of "image elements" or pixels. The digital image dimension $N \times M \times O$, such as O is the number of matrix layers, which for the condition $O = 1$ corresponds to the case of binary or gray level images, and for $O = 3$ to the case of more than one layer, i.e., images in different color spaces: RGB, HSI, HSV, CMYK, and so on; being each of these color spaces a numerical representation of a set of colors. This way, for the case of multispectral images, where there are more than three layers forming the image components, such as electromagnetic waveband frequencies, e.g., infrared (IR) and ultraviolet (UV) radiation, then the conditions are $O = \{3, ..., 15\}$; which results from the fact that these type of images measure the light on a discrete scale of layers typically from 3 to 15, that goes beyond the range of visible light.

The complexity of images as a pattern without processing can be addressed into two orders, the range of values or intensity of the pixel measured in its corresponding layer, and the number of pixels on the basis of dimension and size of the associated image.

The HAR signals capture the physical activity of the human body and it is worth to infer the kind of activity performed by the subject in a trustworthy manner and associate it to health issues. The latter concerns health professionals, however, from our engineering perspective we aim to process it in order to identify the activities with better accuracy. On the other hand, there is another problem posed by the recognition of human activity by means of discrete patterns obtained from mobile devices. These patterns conform to very complex interpretations of the human activity with different purposes, i.e. health and physical activity [23,37].

The fact of getting more than 90% of recognition or classification of patterns makes that these deep learning techniques require a lot of operations, which implies a high requirement of computing; either for the case of the recognition of images or the HAR signal, which are examples of complex signals with abstract information concerning interpretation of human perception, both problems have been solved satisfactorily by using the power of deep learning and Convolutional Neural Networks (CNN). Both AI techniques require high computing power and it is advisable to optimize algorithms and implement them through parallel and distributed computing, minimizing the executing time and keeping the level of recognition of patterns.

In this work, we present the implementation of a strategy composed of evolutionary and parallel computing that optimizes the parameters of Coarse-Fine Convolutional Neural Networks (CFCNN) [5]. It is applied to two types of complex patterns:*(i)* image recognition, and *(ii)* HAR. The initial CNN [5] conducts a parallel feeding of the input patterns through three different levels of granularity: coarse, medium and fine (CFCNN), in such a way that it conforms a robust characteristic pattern with these three representations of granularity (Coarse-to-fine), that is adequate to be applied to the recognition and classification of HAR and images. The parallelization of the CFCNN is presented in accordance with its design and it is put into effect with a huge amount of images.

The modification of the CFCNN is made by means of a Genetic Algorithm (GA) while the parallel evolutionary execution is set through a model of communicated islands that finds the best modified network by modified parameters in accordance with the patterns to be recognized. The parallel version was developed using MPI and CUDA to exploit the computational resources of multiple CPUs and GPUs architectures. The results obtained with this proposal show the feasibility of their use by the fact that our methodology was tested with data bases found in the literature improving in most cases the classification percentage.

In Sect. 2, state of the art of the problem is presented, additionally, we describe in detail the CFCNN that was utilized in our study. In Sect. 3 we present our proposed modification of the CFCNN through the construction and design of nine components of one individual that allows the implementation of the genetic algorithm and both its fitness and evolutionary parameters. Then in Sect. 4 we formulate the parallelization of the GA through the model of communicating islands. The results carried out are given in Sect. 5. Finally, conclusions and future work are discussed in Sect. 6

2 State of the Art

ANN have proven to be a very useful tool to classify patterns and predict answers of systems as long as their values of weights are optimized. Also, they have been used to address different problems; however the more complex and numerous the patters are, the less effective they become. This is why new ANN architectures were developed giving rise to Deep Learning (DL), which achieves noticeable improvements but at the expense of increased computational cost. Likewise, the issue of how to adjust the ANN under the framework of DL, considering parameters, connections and layers, constitutes a very recent subject of research.

There are several types of DL networks: Multilayer perceptrons (MLPs), Convolutional Neural Networks (CNNs), Recurrent neural networks (RNNs), Long short-term memory neural network (LSTMs), and autoencoders.

The learning characteristics of the ANN have been used in recent years to solve different problems of artificial intelligence, providing important advancements in several domains and leading to next generation results such as the recognition of images from their own content [33]. The CNN specifically shows the capacity to extract features from patterns under analysis. Their use in computer vision has involved different problems such as: $1D$ pattern classification of automatic speech recognition, electrocardiogram signal and biomedical time series classification; all the above constitutes examples of HAR signals [24].

HAR signal research field has received attention in the light of the increasing tendency of its applications in diverse areas such as health and sport signal monitoring, such that we have price reduction of integrated sensors of portable devices and their massive production [1,26]. Different papers conduct studies about the important characteristics of sensors such as finger print, oximeter, etc.; type, cost, capacity, amount. However, most papers employ smartphones, which have already integrated these type of sensors on account of both quality-price ratio and accessibility [45]. Basly [7] proposes a profound temporal residual system to recognize daily life of people through RGB images. On the one hand, it employs profound convolutional residual neural network (RCN) to keep the discriminatory visual characteristics that describe appearance, and on the other hand, it uses a short term/long term memory neural network to capture temporal evolution of human actions.

Abdelbaky [1] proposes a new method of human activity recognition by means of the temporal spatial characteristics learned from a simple unsupervised CNN, in combination with a bag of descriptor vectors locally added. Finally, a support vector machine is used for sport activities recognition. In [32] it is performed a human behavior analysis through images via the use of one convolutional two flow CNN. First, the images of the history of movement are extracted and then they are put into the VGG-16 convolutional neural network in order to initiate the training stage. Next, the RGB image is feeded to the R-CNN Faster algorithm to continue training by using annotation of data assisted by the Kalman filter. Finally, the results of the VMHI and FRGB flows are merged to achieve the classification of the action verified within the images. The algorithm is able to recognize not only the behavior of a single person but also the interaction of two people and additionally it improves the recognition precision of similar actions.

Martinez [35] utilizes computer vision and other HAR approaches, obtaining results higher than 90%. Another approach is based on the signals coming from sensors, such as gyroscope and accelerometer, placed on different parts of the body. However, the CNN topologies involve a lot of different parameters and, in most cases, the design is made manually, which implies considerable effort and significant amount of trial and error steps.

Baldominos [6] have examined the application of neural evolution for the automatic design of CNN topologies, bringing in a common framework for this task and developing two novel solutions based on genetic algorithms and grammatical evolution. This proposal was evaluated through the MNIST data set for the recognition of handwritten digits, getting competitive results and without any type of increase of either data or preprocessing when compared to the state of the art approaches.

Desell [18] presents improvements of a neuro evolutionary algorithm called explorative evolution of augmented convolutional topologies (EXACT), that is capable of evolving the structure of CNN. EXACT has been deployed on parallel and multiprocessing implementations. These improvements include the development of a new operator of mutation that increased in one order of magnitude the rate of evolution and they also demonstrated to be substantively more reliable than the traditional method for generating new CNN. In [16] the evolution of CNN parameters verified in the classification of breast cancer problem is employed and presented by means of a Genetic Algorithm (GA), while in [12], a parallel genetic algorithm is implemented in combination with the Support Vector Machine, that uses an island topology coupled with migration strategies.

Table 1. Proposed database.

Data set	Classes	Training	Test
UCI HAR [4]	6	7,352	2,947
UCI HAPT [40]	12	8,919	3,823
WISMD 1.1v [25]	6	12,010	5,148
WISMD 2.0v [25] [49] [34]	6	32,601	13,972
MNIST [27]	10	60,000	10,000

In this paper we focus on the approach of evolving a CFCNN with a GA oriented to different databases obtained from the state of the art. For the recognition of human activity we consider from the literature survey: UCI HAR [4], WISDM v1.1 [25], WISDM v2.0 [25] and HAPT [40], while MNIST [27] was considered for the recognition of images. Table 1 shows the data sets used to evaluate the proposed model.

Figure 1 depicts the initial CNN architecture [5] that comprises our CFCNN network. The main idea is founded on extracting different levels of characteristics so that the levels fine, medium and coarse, extract respectively subtle, robust and crude (lines, circles, colors and so on) characteristics of the data. In this way the CFCNN architecture is comprised of three levels:

1. **Fine:** It is composed of four convolutional layers. Each one of them is followed by one layer of maximum grouping. The maps of characteristics are reduced in each layer. The first two convolutional layers consist of 18 filters and the last two of them have 36 filters. Each convolutional layer has a filter size of (1×2). The maximum window for grouping is (1×2) with a step equal to 2.
2. **Medium:** It is made of two convolutional layers. Each one of them is followed by one layer of maximum grouping. The maps of characteristics are reduced in each layer. The first convolutional layer has 18 filters and the last one consists of 36 filters. Each convolutional layer has a filter size of (1×2). The maximum window for grouping is (1×4) with a step equal to 4.
3. **Coarse:** It is composed of one convolutional layer that is followed by a layer of maximum grouping. The convolutional layer has 36 filters of size (1×2). The maximum window for grouping is (1×16) with a step equal to 16.

The output of the three levels are grouped and flattened forming a vector that is conducted to the classification stage through a totally connected neural network. Lastly, the output of the totally connected neural network goes through a softmax layer that calculates the probability distribution of classes [19]. Table 2 lists the CFCNN parameters.

Adjustments made to the CFCNN architecture of our proposal are made up two parts: channels and the adjustment of levels of extraction of features, which are detailed as follows: **Channels:** Reduction of the number of channels for the processing of images, since the original proposal has six channels for the HAR data set, which are based on time stamps. However, in order to apply the CFCNN to images, a reduction necessary for either three channels for the data sets in the RGB space color or one channel for images in the gray scale. **Adjustment of levels of extraction of features:**

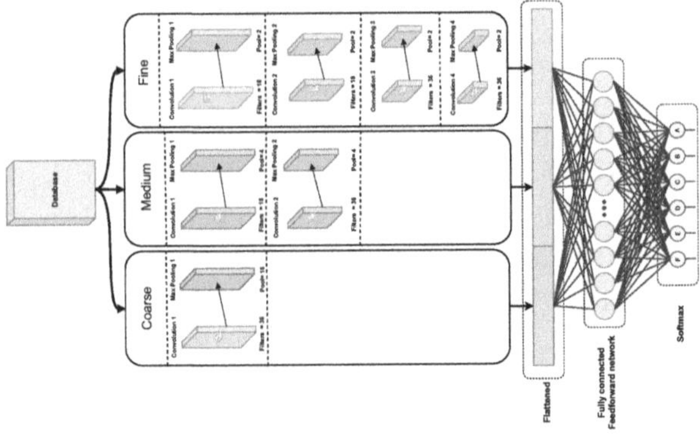

Fig. 1. Coarse to Fine Convolutional Neural Network model.

Table 2. Preset parameters of the CFCNN.

Parameters	Value	Type
Epoch numbers	500	Integer
Batch size	300	Integer
Dropout	0.8	Float
Activation function	ReLU	Function
Loss function	Cross Entropy	Function
Filter number	18,36	Integer
Filter dimension (row)	1	Integer
Filter dimension (column)	2	Integer
Dimensi6n maxpooling (row)	1	Integer
Dimensi6n maxpooling (column)	2,4,16	Integer
Maxpooling subsamplig	2,4,16	Integer
Optimizer	ADADELTA	Function

Number of levels of extraction of features relies upon data size. On the one hand, if data size is big, then the CFCNN raises both levels and convolution layers. On the other hand, if data size is small, then the CFCNN decreases level sizes since it is not required to retain further information to classify or recognize.

3 Evolving the Coarse-Fine CNN by Means of the Genetic Algorithm

One of the difficulties when training a CFCNN entails the calibration of the network initial parameters through trial and error. Some of the CFCNN key parameters are: learning rate, dropout, number and dimension of filters, and so on.

A GA is a search algorithm inspired of both natural selection and the transfer of learning to a new generation of individuals [17], such that it gets a balance between efficiency effectiveness to provide at least one solution to the raised problem, which in our case consists of reducing the complexity of the CFCNN parameters.

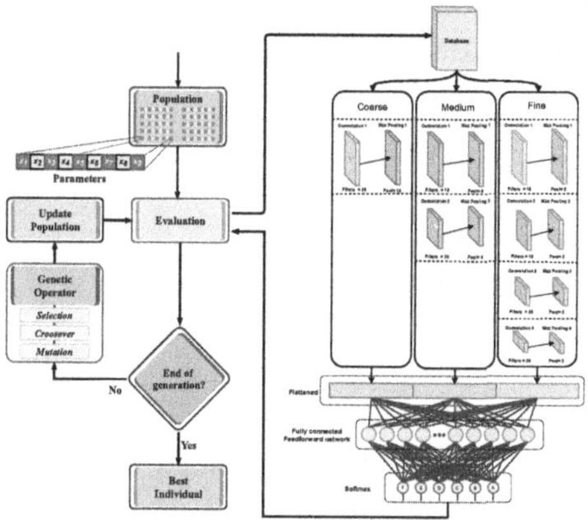

Fig. 2. GA methodology and its intervention in CFCNN model.

In this work a modification of the CFCNN from a GA has been raised, in such a way that the fitness function is considered as the percentage of recovery of the whole new CFCNN, which is proposed by the evolutionary process itself as a modified individual. This new CFCNN is such that if it has a population of $N-$individuals, then there are $N-$CFCNN modified proposals to be tested as solutions for classifying either HAR or image patterns, trying to minimize the complexity of the CNN and increasing its efficiency for any application that could arise.

Figure 2 shows the CFCNN architecture along with the proposed evolutionary modification. It comprises of a GA that modifies the CFCNN, such that it proposes the optimization of the network parameters.

3.1 Codification

The proposed individual resulting from the codification defined in our GA comprises of a collection of normalized integer numbers that represent the normalized values of the CFCNN parameters. Equation 1 defines the structure of each individual, I, as a tuple of n arranged elements.

$$I = \left(x_1, x_2, \ldots, x_n\right),\ such\ that\ \left\{x_i\right\}_{i=1}^{n} \in [1, \sigma] \tag{1}$$

where $\{x_1, x_2, \ldots, x_n\}$ stands for the structure of the individual, genotype, I, such that each x_i represents the normalized value of the corresponding CFCNN parameter, now called *gene*; σ is an integer constant that represents the normalization scale. In this proposal we consider only $n = 9$ parameters; in Table 3 the details of each component x_i are listed.

Table 3. Proposed GA individual structure.

Gene	Parameter	Values	Gene	Parameter	Values
x_1	Number of epochs	$[1, 50]$	x_5	Convolutions	$[1, 30]$
x_2	Batch size	$[100, 500]$	x_6	Filter dimension	$[1, 10]$
x_3	Dropout	$[0, 0.9]$	x_7	Maxpooling dimension	$[1, 10]$
x_4	Activation function	0: None	x_8	Optimizer	0: Adagrad
		1: Tanh			1: RMSprop
		2: ReLU			2: Adadelta
		3: Selu			3: Adamax
		4: Sigmoid			4: Nadam
		5: ReLU6			5: Adam
					6: SGD
			x_9	Learning rate	[0.5, 0.0005]

3.2 Fitness

In this proposal the fitness function is taken as the percentage of recovery, given in Eq. 2, such that the true positive (TP), true negative (TN), false positive (FP) and false negative (FN) values are comprised.

$$Fitness = \frac{TP + TN}{TP + FP + FN + TN} \tag{2}$$

The applied *genetic operators* are the selection by elitism of the best individual of each population. The operations of crossover and mutation with repetition are also considered in this proposal.

4 Parallel GA Strategies

The main problem that arises when implementing a genetic algorithm to optimize the parameters of a CNN, is the long execution time required when evaluating each individual; in our case, as shown in previous section, each individual fitness is represented by the accuracy obtained after a complete CFCNN classification process is performed. In order to speed up the GA execution time, three levels of parallelism were developed.

- CPU-GPU version: In this level the heavy part of the convolution calculation (including the 3 layers, fine, medium and coarse) was performed using a GPU. For this purpose, the special parallel libraries of the Tensorflow tool were used. As it is schematized in Fig. 3a, in this version there is a master node that executes the procedure shown on Fig. 2, excluding the Evaluation module, which runs on the GPU.
- Multi CPU version, MCPU: Here, in order to use the computing power of a computer cluster, the main GA procedure was parallelized following the synchronous Island-Model [9]. At this level, the processing of the population is distributed in a

set of processors or nodes that share information through message exchange communication. This system contains a master node and a set of slave nodes (as shown in Fig. 3b). The total population is evenly divided among the slave nodes which have the purpose of executing the sequential genetic algorithm, but now working with a smaller population (or subpopulation).

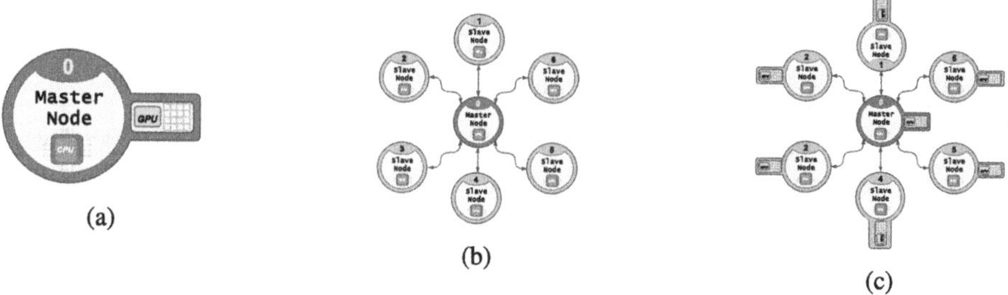

Fig. 3. (a) CPU-GPU version, (b) Multi-CPU version and (c) Multi CPU-GPU version respectively.

In the Island model each slave node is synchronized with the master for the correct operation of the algorithm. A migration strategy is performed and based on the gathering by the master node of a number, p, of the best local individuals obtained from each of the slave nodes when a certain number, q, of generations have elapsed. In this work, p is set to 2 and q to 3. Once the master node collects the best local individuals from each slave, it proceeds with the identification of the best global one. So that the characteristics of the best global individual have an influence on the distributed populations, it is sent to all slaves. Finally, before generating a new population, the slave nodes replace their worst local individual with the best global one received.

- Multi CPU-GPU version, MCPU-GPU: In this solution the level of parallelism integrates the previous two levels. Now we are working with a set of nodes where each one of them has access to a GPU (as represented in Fig. 3c). The Island-Model is executed in the same way as in the multi-CPU version; but also internally, each node behaves as in the CPU-GPU version, where a GPU is used for executing the convolution step on a GPU required to evaluate each individual of its subpopulation.

5 Experiments and Results

This section describes and shows the tests and results obtained through CFCNN employing each one of the five selected databases depicted in Table 1. Table 4 shows the parameters of the sequential and parallel GA versions that evolve the proposed individual codified to obtain the CFCNN parameters when using a specific data set.

The implementation was carried out in a Workstation with the following characteristics: Linux OS, 8 GB RAM, Intel Core i7 processor, and GPU NVIDIA GTX-1050.

5.1 CFCNN Performance and Classification Results

Table 5 shows the execution times and classification (the best individual fitness) results of the proposed sequential and parallel GA algorithms implementation, for each of the databases.

Table 4. Evolutionary parameters for the sequential and parallel GA implementations.

Evolutionary parameters	Sequential and parallel versions
Generations	15
Population size	60
Percentage of elitism	10%
Percentage of crossover	60%
Percentage of mutation	30%
Mutation factor	0.1

Table 5. Comparison of fitness and execution times obtained by the proposed AG versions described in Section 4: sequential (CPU), CPU-GPU, MCPU, and MCPU-GPU, working with five different data sets.

Data set		CPU	CPU-GPU	MCPU	MCPU-GPU
UCI HAR	Time (hr)	12.07	4.50	4.10	3.45
	Fitness (%)	99.40	99.40	100.00	100.00
UCI HAPT	Time (hr)	13.76	6.30	5.20	4.40
	Fitness (%)	95.27	95.27	95.80	95.80
WISDM v1.1	Time (hr)	17.65	9.51	9.20	8.48
	Fitness (%)	98.30	98.30	98.92	98.92
WISDM v2.0	Time (hr)	31.13	24.40	23.20	20.50
	Fitness (%)	95.10	95.10	95.40	95.40
MNIST	Time (hr)	35.30	21.80	11.23	10.26
	Fitness (%)	99.50	99.50	99.50	99.50

Table 6. Optimized CFCNN parameters found by the evolutionary GA models using the UCI HAR data set.

Parameters	CPU	CPU-GPU	MCPU	MCPU-GPU
Epoch number	540	530	502	570
Batch size	350	300	320	305
Dropout	0.92	0.95	0.94	0.97
Activation function	ReLU6	ReLU	ReLU6	ReLU6
Convolutions	{26, 52}	{26, 52}	{26, 52}	{26, 52}
Filter dimension	(1×2)	(1×2)	(8×8)	(1×2)
Maxpooling dimension	(1×2)	(1×2)	(2×2)	(2×2)
Optimizer	Adadelta	Adadelta	Adadelta	Adadelta
Learning rate	0.005	0.005	0.005	0.005

We can see that the execution of the sequential version, CPU, and that of CPU-GPU achieved the same accuracy of 99.4%, when working with the UCI HAR dataset; however the CPU execution time was 12.07 h, whereas the CPU-GPU execution spent only 4.50 h, involving a 63% of time reduction. On the other hand, the benefit obtained by increasing the diversity of individuals when working with several processors through the island model allowed MCPU and MCPU-GPU parallel versions to achieve the accuracy of 100% considering the UCI HAR dataset. Comparing with the CPU version run time, MCPU obtained a time reduction of 66% (4.10 h) while MCPU-GPU could decrease the time up to 71% (3.45 h).

Table 7. Optimized CFCNN parameters found by the evolutionary GA models applied to UCI HAPT data set.

Parameters	CPU	CPU-GPU	MCPU	MCPU-GPU
Epoch number	33	33	33	33
Batch size	209	209	210	220
Dropout	0.76	0.76	0.83	0.80
Activation function	ReLU6	ReLU	ReLU6	ReLU6
Convolutions	{26, 56}	{26, 52}	{26, 56}	{26, 56}
Filter dimension	(8×8)	(8×8)	(8×8)	(8×8)
Maxpooling dimension	(2×2)	(2×2)	(2×2)	(2×2)
Optimizer	Adadelta	Adadelta	Adadelta	Adadelta
Learning rate	0.005	0.005	0.005	0.005

From Table 5 we can also see that, in general, for all databases the CPU and CPU-GPU versions obtain the same classification percentage, since only one processor generates the initial population. For the UCI HAPT dataset the CPU and the CPU-GPU versions achieved an accuracy of 95.27%; with WISDM v1.1 they got 98.30%; the accuracy using WISDM v2.0 was 95.10%; and for MNIST database the classification accuracy was 99.50%.

On the other hand, something similar happens with the MCPU and MCPU-GPU versions that get equal accuracy; in all the cases, these parallel versions based on the island model obtain a better or equal classification percentage than the other versions, as we have mentioned before this is due to the diversity of the population that increases when using several processors. The obtained accuracy of MCPU and MCPU-GPU considering the UCI HAPT data set is 95.8%, they obtained 98.92% when using WISDM v1.1, 95.40% with WISDM v2.0, and 99.50% when working with MNIST database.

Even though the percentage of classification is the same for CPU and CPU-GPU version, the CPU-GPU execution time outperformed that of CPU. With UCI HAPT, CPU version spent 13.76 h and CPU-GPU 6.3 h, attaining 54% time reduction; using WISDM v1.1 the time decreased 46%, going from 17.65 to 9.51 h; with WISDM v2.2 CPU-GPU obtained 21% reduction (CPU got 31.13 h, and CPU-GPU 24.4 h), and 38% when using MNIST (CPU got 35.3 h, and CPU-GPU 21.8 h).

As mentioned before, there is no difference between the classification percentage values achieved by MCPU and MCPU-GPU; however, with these versions the execution time continued to decrease with respect to that obtained by CPU-GPU.

Considering the HAPT database, MCPU lowered the CPU-GPU runtime by 17% (getting 5.2 hrs) while MCPU-GPU reached a 30% reduction (with 4.4 h). For the

WISDM v1.1 database, MCPU got 9.2 h reducing the CPU-GPU execution time by 3%, yet the MCPU-GPU execution lasted 8.48 h which corresponds to a 10% reduction. The runtimes of MCPU (23.2 h) and MCPU-GPU (20.5 h) working with the WISDM v2.0 database were shorter than those of CPU-GPU, decreasing them by 4% and 15%, respectively. With the MNIST database, a more significant decrease in time is observed when using MCPU and MCPU-GPU, compared to CPU-GPU; MCPU (11.23 h) and MCPU-GPU (10.26 h) runtimes correspond to 48 % and 52 % reduction with respect to CPU-GPU runtime (21.8 h).

Note that, in all tests, the execution time decreases as the degree of parallelism increases. Figure 4a presents the speedup achieved by each parallel version working with the different databases. The sequential execution of the AG using the GPU (CPU-GPU) obtained an average speedup of 1.9 ; however, when using the 6 node cores with the MCPU version the average speedup increased to 2.4. The MCPU-GPU version got the best execution times; using the set of 6 cores and the GPU allowed to obtain an average speedup of 2.7. For now, this version was performed using the available single-GPU system; however, we believe that it could give even better results when working with a multi-GPU system.

We noticed that, in general, the versions presented to optimize the parameters of the coarse-fine network gave very close values; in Tables 6 and 7 we show two examples of the parameters found by the proposed evolutionary models when using the UCI HAR and UCI HAPT databases, respectively.

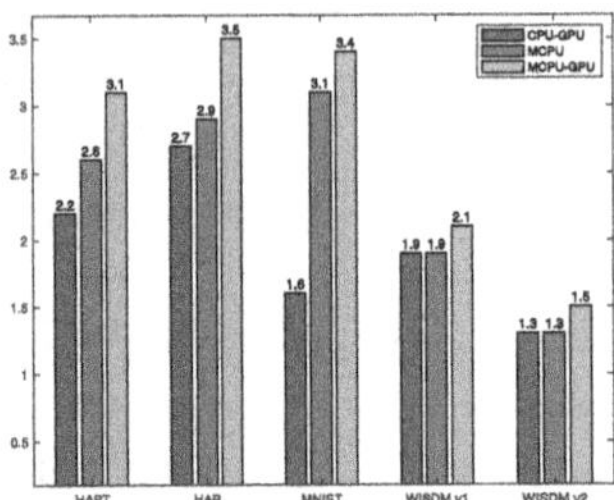

(a) Speedup obtained by the proposed parallel AG versions described in Section 4.

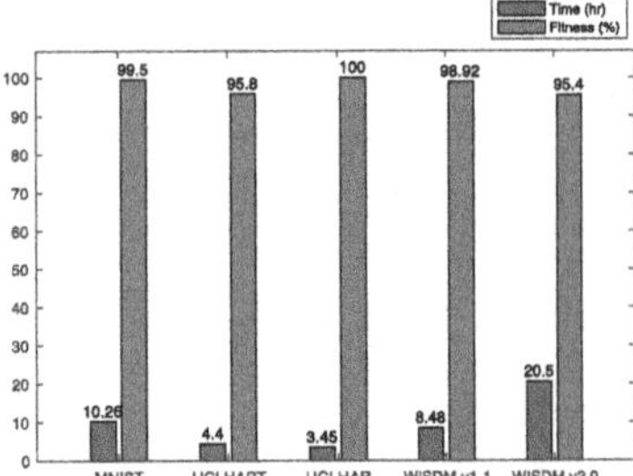

(b) Fitness and execution times obtained by the proposed MCPU-GPU AG version described in Section 4.

Fig. 4. Comparison between speedup, fitness and execution.

As described above, the MCPU-GPU version obtained the best results in time and classification. Figure 4b summarizes this behavior using the different databases. We selected this version to show how the fitness of the best individual evolved during each of the GA generations.

Figure 5a depicts the increase of accuracy in each generation using MCPU-GPU version while Fig. 5b shows the reduction of error also for each generation. These graphs illustrates the results obtained with the five data sets. Through the modifications found by the GA evolutionary process, the improvement of the accuracy was achieved automatically.

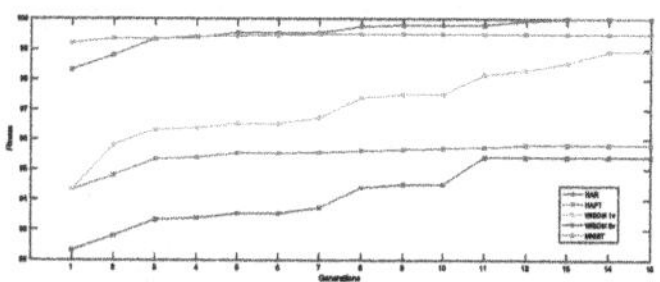

(a) Fitness evolution of ten tests performed with the datasets.

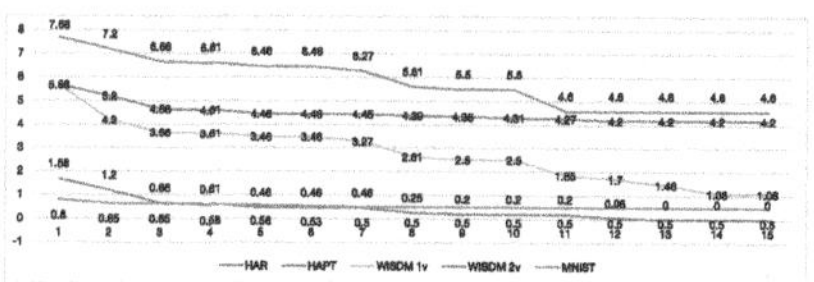

(b) Results of the error behavior in ten tests carried out with the datasets.

Fig. 5. Comparison between fitness and error using MCPU-GPU model.

5.2 State of the Art Comparison

This section provides the state of the art tables with the purpose to contrast the implemented models, presented in this paper, with ML and DL techniques. In order to simplify the analysis regarding the obtained classification accuracy, in this comparison we only refer to the proposed versions, CPU-GPU and MCPU-GPU, which obtained the same accuracy value as the other approaches (CPU and MCPU) respectively, but with better efficiency.

Table 8 shows the comparison of results provided by the UCI HAR database. From this table an improvement of the automatic learning techniques such as Márkov chains and support vector machines can be seen. It can also be seen that the existent CFCNN method [5] reached 100%, however, the calibration of parameters was not made automatically. Table 9 shows the comparison of results coming from the UCI HAPT database. The best result in this table corresponds to the Random Forest technique.

The comparison of results provided by the WISDM v1.1 database are depicted in Table 10. It can be seen that some results surpassed the CPU-GPU method. It can be noted that the approaches based on DL obtained best results. Table 11 shows the comparison of results given by the WISDM v2.0 database. Table 12 shows the comparison of the accuracy obtained with the MNIST database, where it can be seen that the best result is with CNN Dropconnect, not far from our proposal.

Table 8. Comparison of accuracy with UCI HAR [4] using our proposal (*).

Reference	Year	Fitness	Approach	Method
Avilés C [5]	2019	100.0	DL	CFCNN
MCPU-GPU	2020	100.0	DL	CFCNN+ parallel GA + GPU
CPU-GPU	2020	99.40	DL	CFCNN+ GA + GPU
Yong Z [52]	2018	98.40	DL	U-CNN
San-Segundo [42]	2016	98.00	ML	Markov chain
Andrey I [22]	2018	97.63	DL	CNN
Heeryon C [13]	2018	97.62	DL	CNN+Sharpen
Xiangbin Z [54]	2016	96.61	ML	Markov chain
Davide A [4]	2013	96.00	ML	SVM
Charissa A R [41]	2016	95.75	DL	CNN+Fourier
Charissa A R [41]	2016	94.79	DL	CNN

Table 9. Comparison of accuracy with UCI HAPT [40] with our proposal (*).

Reference	Year	Fitness	Approach	Method
Taufeeq [46]	2016	100.0	ML	Random Forrest
Zheng [53]	2018	96.26	ML	TASG+SVM
Bustoni [8]	2019	96.00	ML	Random Forrest
Zheng [53]	2018	95.83	ML	TASG+RNN
MCPU-GPU	2020	95.80	DL	CFCNN + parallel GA + GPU
CPU-GPU	2020	95.27	DL	CFCNN + GA + GPU
Yong Zhang [52]	2018	93.10	DL	U-CNN

Table 10. Comparison of accuracy with WISDM v1.1 [25].

Reference	Year	Fitness	Approach	Method
Avilés [5]	2019	100.0	DL	CFCNN
MCPU-GPU	2020	98.92	DL	CFCNN+parallel GA+GPU
Xinxin H [21]	2020	98.83	DL	CNN+FusionTrial
Yan X [50]	2017	98.80	ML	ECDF-PCA-MLCF
Daniele R [38]	2017	98.60	DL	CNN
CPU-GPU	2020	98.30	DL	CFCNN+ GA + GPU
Mohammad A [3]	2016	98.23	DL	CNN
Daniel R [39]	2016	98.20	DL	CNN
Kishor [47]	2016	98.09	ML	Random forest
Yong Z [52]	2018	97.00	DL	U-CNN
Haoxi Z [51]	2020	96.40	DL	CNN-multiHead
Jeniffer K [25]	2011	91.70	ML	Multi Perceptron
Cagatay C [10]	2015	91.60	ML	Ensemble learning
Jeniffer K [25]	2011	85.10	ML	J48
Jeniffer K [25]	2011	78.10	ML	Logistic Regression

Table 11. Comparison of accuracy with WISDM v2.0 [25] [49] [34].

Reference	Year	Fitness	Approach	Method
Girmaw Abebe [2]	2017	97.90	DL	CNN+LSTM+ Handcrafted
MCPU-GPU	2020	95.40	DL	CFCNN + parallel GA + GPU
CPU-GPU	2020	95.10	DL	CFCNN + GA + GPU
Majid A K Q [36]	2019	94.02	ML	GA
Andrey I [22]	2018	93.32	DL	CNN
Daniele R [38]	2017	92.70	DL	CNN
Sarbagya R S [44]	2018	92.22	DL	CNN

Table 12. Comparison of accuracy with MNIST [27].

References	Year	Fitness	Approach	Method
Li Wan [48]	2013	99.79	DL	CNN Dropconnect
Dan C C [14]	2012	99.77	DL	CNN Multi-Column
Ikuro S [43]	2015	99.77	DL	CNN APAC
Jian R C [11]	2015	99.76	DL	CNN Batch
Chen Y L [28]	2015	99.71	DL	CNN Pooling function
Ming L [29]	2015	99.69	DL	Recurrent CNN
Zhibin L [31]	2015	99.69	DL	Normalisation CNN
B Graham [20]	2014	99.68	DL	CNN Fractional
Zhibin L [30]	2015	99.67	DL	CNN Multi-scale
Dan C C [15]	2010	99.65	DL	Big Deep CNN
MCPU-GPU	2020	99.50	DL	CFCNN + parallel GA + GPU
CPU-GPU	2020	99.50	DL	CFCNN + GA + GPU

6 Conclusions

This paper presents a new implementation of a convolutional neural network proposal that was previously reported in the literature. The existent work was applied only for the recognition and classification of HAR patterns, in such a way that the strategy is based on the parallel retrieval carried out through three stages: fine, medium and coarse.

In our approach, the combination of evolutionary computing and the deep learning of neural networks has been beneficial. We developed a GA in order to automatically optimize the parameters of a neural network, looking for the improvement of classification quality. This solution avoids the expert intervention and the time needed setting the neural network parameters, since this calibration may require very fine adjustments.

We considered nine main parameters that control the convolutional neural network functioning, to be included in the codification of an individual in our GA approach: number of epochs, batch size, dropout, activation function, convolutions, filter dimension, maxpooling dimension, optimizer, and learning rate. This way, an individual could be managed as a tuple of nine normalized integer numbers representing the normalized values of the CFCNN parameters. The result of our approach obtained classification percentages very close to the best results reported in the literature.

Another contribution of this work is the implementation and analysis of three parallel versions of the proposed GA. These versions consider different levels of parallelism starting from the use of a single processor and a GPU, then a set of 6 processors without GPU were employed, and in the third version the inclusion of 6 processors together with the GPU was achieved; the last two versions worked under the parallel GA islands model. The version that used the highest level of parallelism allowed to achieve better levels of accuracy and obtain the shortest times, reaching an average speedup of 2.7.

Despite the good results that have been obtained through the proposed evolutionary computing, as future work it would be useful to incorporate a different kind of heuristic such as the simulating annealing, swarm search based or scatter search to focus in diversification or even studying the behavior through Monte Carlo Simulation. It could also be interesting to apply the optimization of parameters in more simple architectures to carry out a more detailed study of the effects of parameter values.

Acknowledgements. We acknowledge the support of Project PID2020-115570GB-C21 funded by MCIN/AIE/10.13039/501100011033/ and Junta de Extremadura, Consejería de Economía e Infraestructuras, of the European Regional Development Fund, "Una manera de hacer Europa", grant GR21108.

References

1. Abdelbaky, A., Aly, S.: Two-stream spatiotemporal feature fusion for human action recognition. Vis. Comput. **37**(7), 1821–1835 (2021). https://doi.org/10.1007/s00371-020-01940-3
2. Abebe, G., Cavallaro, A.: Inertial-vision: cross-domain knowledge transfer for wearable sensors. In: 2017 IEEE International Conference on Computer Vision Workshops (ICCVW), pp. 1392–1400 (2017). https://doi.org/10.1109/ICCVW.2017.165
3. Abu Alsheikh, M., Selim, A., Niyato, D., Doyle, L., Lin, S., Tan, H.: Deep activity recognition models with triaxial accelerometers. In: AAAI Conference on Artificial Intelligence. AAAI Workshop - Technical Report, vol. WS-16-01 - WS-16-15, pp. 8–13. AI Access Foundation, United States (2016)
4. Anguita, D., Ghio, A., Oneto, L., Parra, X., Reyes-Ortiz, J.L., et al.: A public domain dataset for human activity recognition using smartphones. In: Esann. vol. 3, p. 3 (2013)
5. Avilés-Cruz, C., Ramírez, A., Zúñiga López, A., Villegas Cortez, J.: Coarse-fine convolutional deep-learning strategy for human activity recognition. Sensors 2019 (2019). https://doi.org/10.3390/s19071556
6. Baldominos, A., Saez, Y., Isasi, P.: Evolutionary convolutional neural networks: An application to handwriting recognition. Neurocomputing **283**, 38–52 (2018). https://doi.org/10.1016/j.neucom.2017.12.049, https://www.sciencedirect.com/science/article/pii/S0925231217319112
7. Basly, H., Ouarda, W., Sayadi, F.E., Ouni, B., Alimi, A.M.: DTR-HAR: deep temporal residual representation for human activity recognition. Vis. Comput. 38, 993–1013 (2021). https://doi.org/10.1007/s00371-021-02064-y
8. Bustoni, I.A., Hidayatulloh, I., Ningtyas, A., Purwaningsih, A., Azhari, S.: Classification methods performance on human activity recognition. J. Phys.: Conf. Series **1456**, 012027 (01 2020). https://doi.org/10.1088/1742-6596/1456/1/012027
9. Cantú-Paz, E., Goldberg, D.E.: On the scalability of parallel genetic algorithms. Evol. Comput. **7**(4), 429–449 (1999). https://doi.org/10.1162/evco.1999.7.4.429
10. Catal, C., Tufekci, S., Pirmit, E., Kocabag, G.: On the use of ensemble of classifiers for accelerometer-based activity recognition. Appl. Soft Comput. **37**, 1018–1022 (2015). https://doi.org/10.1016/j.asoc.2015.01.025
11. Chang, J.R., Chen, Y.S.: Batch-normalized maxout network in network (2015)
12. Chen, Z., Lin, T., Tang, N., Xia, X.: A parallel genetic algorithm based feature selection and parameter optimization for support vector machine. Sci. Program. **2016**, 1–10 (2016). https://doi.org/10.1155/2016/2739621
13. Cho, H., Yoon, S.M.: Divide and conquer-based 1D CNN human activity recognition using test data sharpening. Sensors 18(4) (2018). https://doi.org/10.3390/s18041055, https://www.mdpi.com/1424-8220/18/4/1055

14. Cireşan, D., Meier, U., Schmidhuber, J.: Multi-column deep neural networks for image classification. In: Proceedings / CVPR, IEEE Computer Society Conference on Computer Vision and Pattern Recognition. IEEE Computer Society Conference on Computer Vision and Pattern Recognition (2012). https://doi.org/10.1109/CVPR.2012.6248110
15. Cireşan, D.C., Meier, U., Gambardella, L.M., Schmidhuber, J.: Deep, big, simple neural nets for handwritten digit recognition. Neural Comput. **22**(12), 3207–3220 (2010). https://doi.org/10.1162/NECO_a_00052, pMID: 20858131
16. Davoudi, K., Thulasiraman, P.: Evolving convolutional neural network parameters through the genetic algorithm for the breast cancer classification problem. Simulation 0(0), 0037549721996031 (0). https://doi.org/10.1177/0037549721996031
17. De Jong, K., Fogel, D., Schwefel, H.P.: A history of evolutionary computation, pp. A2.3:1–12 (1997)
18. Desell, T.: Developing a volunteer computing project to evolve convolutional neural networks and their hyperparameters. In: 13th IEEE International Conference on eScience (8109119), 19–28 (2017)
19. Goodfellow, I., Bengio, Y., Courville, A.: Deep Learning. MIT Press (2016). http://www.deeplearningbook.org
20. Graham, B.: Fractional max-pooling (2015)
21. Han, X., Ye, J., Luo, J., Zhou, H.: The effect of axis-wise triaxial acceleration data fusion in CNN-based human activity recognition. IEICE Trans. Inform. Syst. **E103.D**(4), 813–824 (2020). https://doi.org/10.1587/transinf.2018EDP7409
22. Ignatov, A.: Real-time human activity recognition from accelerometer data using convolutional neural networks. Appl. Soft Comput. **62**, 915–922 (9 2017). https://doi.org/10.1016/j.asoc.2017.09.027
23. Iqbal, A., et al.: Wearable internet-of-things platform for human activity recognition and health care. Int. J. Distrib. Sensor Netw. **16**(6), 1550147720911561 (2020). https://doi.org/10.1177/1550147720911561
24. Jiao, L., et al.: Golf swing classification with multiple deep convolutional neural networks. Int. J. Distrib. Sensor Netw. **14**(10), 1550147718802186 (2018). https://doi.org/10.1177/1550147718802186
25. Kwapisz, J., Weiss, G., Moore, S.: Activity recognition using cell phone accelerometers. SIGKDD Explor. **12**, 74–82 (2010). https://doi.org/10.1145/1964897.1964918
26. Lane, N., Miluzzo, E., lu, H., Peebles, D., Choudhury, T., Campbell, A.: A survey of mobile phone sensing. IEEE Commun Mag. Commun. Mag. IEEE **48**, 140–150 (10 2010). https://doi.org/10.1109/MCOM.2010.5560598
27. Lecun, Y., Bottou, L., Bengio, Y., Haffner, P.: Gradient-based learning applied to document recognition. Proc. IEEE **86**, 2278–2324 (1998). https://doi.org/10.1109/5.726791
28. Lee, C.Y., Gallagher, P.W., Tu, Z.: Generalizing pooling functions in convolutional neural networks: Mixed, gated, and tree. ArXiv:1509.08985 (2016)
29. Liang, M., Hu, X.: Recurrent convolutional neural network for object recognition, pp. 3367–3375 (2015). https://doi.org/10.1109/CVPR.2015.7298958
30. Liao, Z., Carneiro, G.: Competitive multi-scale convolution (2015)
31. Liao, Z., Carneiro, G.: On the importance of normalisation layers in deep learning with piecewise linear activation units, pp. 1–8 (2016). https://doi.org/10.1109/WACV.2016.7477624
32. Liu, C., Ying, J., Yang, H., Hu, X., Liu, J.: Improved human action recognition approach based on two-stream convolutional neural network model. Vis. Comput. **37**(6), 1327–1341 (2021). https://doi.org/10.1007/s00371-020-01868-8
33. Liu, Y., Tian, M., Xu, C., Zhao, L.: Neural network feature learning based on image self-encoding. Int. J. Adv. Robot. Syst. **17**(2), 1729881420921653 (2020). https://doi.org/10.1177/1729881420921653

34. Lockhart, J., Weiss, G., Xue, J., Gallagher, S., Grosner, A., Pulickal, T.: Design considerations for the WISDM smart phone-based sensor mining architecture. SensorKDD 11 (2011). https://doi.org/10.1145/2003653.2003656
35. Martinez, F., González-Fraga, J., Cuevas-Tello, J.C., Rodriguez, M.: Activity inference for ambient intelligence through handling artifacts in a healthcare environment. Sensors (Basel, Switzerland) **12**, 1072–1099 (2012). https://doi.org/10.3390/s120101072
36. Quaid, M.A., Jalal, A.: Wearable sensors based human behavioral pattern recognition using statistical features and reweighted genetic algorithm. Multimed. Tools Appl. **79**, 6061–6083 (2019). https://doi.org/10.1007/s11042-019-08463-7
37. Ranasinghe, S., Machot, F.A., Mayr, H.C.: A review on applications of activity recognition systems with regard to performance and evaluation. Int. J. Distrib. Sensor Netw. **12**(8), 1550147716665520 (2016). https://doi.org/10.1177/1550147716665520
38. Ravì, D., Wong, C., Lo, B., Yang, G.Z.: A deep learning approach to on-node sensor data analytics for mobile or wearable devices. IEEE J. Biomed. Health Inform. **21**(1), 56–64 (2016). https://doi.org/10.1109/JBHI.2016.2633287
39. Ravì, D., Wong, C., Lo, B., Yang, G.Z.: Deep learning for human activity recognition: A resource efficient implementation on low-power devices, pp. 71–76 (06 2016). https://doi.org/10.1109/BSN.2016.7516235
40. Reyes-Ortiz, J., Oneto, L., Ghio, A., Anguita, D., Parra, X.: Human activity recognition on smartphones with awareness of basic activities and postural transitions (2014)
41. Ronao, C., Cho, S.B.: Human activity recognition with smartphone sensors using deep learning neural networks. Expert Syst. Appl. **59**, 235–244 (2016). https://doi.org/10.1016/j.eswa.2016.04.032
42. San-Segundo, R., Lorenzo-Trueba, J., Martínez-González, B., Pardo, J.: Segmenting human activities based on HMMs using smartphone inertial sensors. Pervasive Mobile Comput. **30**, 84–96 (2016). https://doi.org/10.1016/j.pmcj.2016.01.004
43. Sato, I., Nishimura, H., Yokoi, K.: APAC: augmented pattern classification with neural networks (2015)
44. Shakya, S., Zhang, C., Zhou, Z.: Comparative study of machine learning and deep learning architecture for human activity recognition using accelerometer data. Int. J. Mach. Learn. Comput. **8** (2018). https://doi.org/10.18178/ijmlc.2018.8.6.748
45. Stisen, A., et al.: Smart devices are different: assessing and mitigatingmobile sensing heterogeneities for activity recognition, pp. 127–140 (2015)
46. Uddin, M.T., Billah, M.M., Hossain, M.F.: Random forests based recognition of human activities and postural transitions on smartphone. In: 2016 5th International Conference on Informatics, Electronics and Vision (ICIEV), pp. 250–255 (2016)
47. Walse, K., Dharaskar, R., Thakare, V.M.: Performance evaluation of classifiers on WISDM dataset for human activity recognition (2016). https://doi.org/10.1145/2905055.2905232
48. Wan, L., Zeiler, M., Zhang, S., Lecun, Y., Fergus, R.: Regularization of neural networks using dropconnect (2013)
49. Weiss, G., Lockhart, J.: The impact of personalization on smartphone-based activity recognition. In: AAAI Workshop - Technical Report (2012)
50. Xu, Y., et al.: Learning multi-level features for sensor-based human action recognition. Pervasive Mobile Comput. **40**, 324—338 (2016). https://doi.org/10.1016/j.pmcj.2017.07.001
51. Zhang, H., Xiao, Z., Wang, J., Li, F., Szczerbicki, E.: A novel IoT-perceptive human activity recognition (HAR) approach using multi-head convolutional attention. IEEE Int. Things J. **7**(2), 1072–1080 (2019). https://doi.org/10.1109/JIOT.2019.2949715
52. Zhang, Y., Zhang, Y., Zhang, Z., Bao, J., Song, Y.: Human activity recognition based on time series analysis using U-Net (2018)

53. Zheng, Z., Du, J., Sun, L., Huo, M., Chen, Y.: TASG: an augmented classification method for impersonal HAR. Mobile Inform. Syst. 1–10 (2018)
54. Zhu, X., Qiu, H.: High accuracy human activity recognition based on sparse locality preserving projections. PLOS ONE **11**(11), 1–18 (2016). https://doi.org/10.1371/journal.pone.0166567, https://doi.org/10.1371/journal.pone.0166567

Author Index

H. Calvo et al. (Eds.): MICAI 2023, LNAI 14391, pp. 347–349, 2024.
https://doi.org/10.1007/978-3-031-47765-2

Printed in the United States
by Baker & Taylor Publisher Services